Whales, Dolphins, and Other Marine Mammals of the World

Hadoram Shirihai
Illustrated by Brett Jarrett

Edited by Guy M. Kirwan
Editorial consultants: Graeme Cresswell, Merel Dalebout, Peter G. H. Evans, William F. Perrin, and Robert L. Pitman
Maps by Kelly Macleod, Dylan Walker, and Julie Dando

Princeton University Press
Princeton and Oxford

We dedicate this work to the marine mammals themselves, and to those humans who take an interest in, and seek to protect, these wonderful creatures and their threatened environments.

Princeton Field Guides

Rooted in field experience and scientific study, Princeton's guides to animals and plants are the authority for professional scientists and amateur naturalists alike. **Princeton Field Guides** present this information in a compact format carefully designed for easy use in the field. The guides illustrate every species in color and provide detailed information on identification, distribution, and biology.

Recent Titles

Nests, Eggs, and Nestlings of North American Birds, Second Edition, by Paul J. Baicich and Colin J. O. Harrison

Birds of Southeast Asia, by Craig Robson

Birds of the Dominican Republic and Haiti, by Steven Latta, Christopher Rimmer, Allan Keith, James Wiley, Herbert Raffaele, Kent McFarland, and Eladio Fernandez

Birds of East Africa: Kenya, Tanzania, Uganda, Rwanda, and Burundi, by Terry Stevenson and John Fanshawe

Raptors of the World, by James Ferguson-Lees and David A. Christie

We would like to thank the following who provided further help with the manuscript and/or checked the page proofs:
Chas Anderson, Regina A. Asmutis-Silvia, Robin W. Baird, Annalisa Berta, Richard Condit, Annie Douglas, Jennifer Green, Thomas A. Jefferson, Morten Jørgensen, Todd Pusser, Graham J. B. Ross, Brent S. Stewart, and Dylan Walker.

Published in 2006 in the United States, Canada, and the Philippine Islands by Princeton University Press, 41 William Street, Princeton, New Jersey 08540

In the United Kingdom and European Union, published in 2006 by A&C Black Publishers Ltd, 38 Soho Square, London W1D 3HB

Commissioning Editor: Nigel Redman
Project Editor: Julie Bailey
Designer: Julie Dando, Fluke Art, Cornwall

Library of Congress Control Number 2006925819
ISBN-13: 978-0-691-12756-9 (cloth)
ISBN-10: 0-691-12756-5 (cloth)
ISBN-13: 978-0-691-12757-6 (pbk.)
ISBN-10: 0-691-12757-3 (pbk.)

nathist.princeton.edu

Printed and bound in China by 1010 Printing International Limited

10 9 8 7 6 5 4 3 2 1

Contents

Preface

The relationship between man and marine mammals can be divided into several periods. These animals have been hunted for food since the Stone Age (and, indeed, such 'traditional' harvesting continues in some arctic communities), but especially after the 1600s whales were increasingly taken for commercial reasons and, with the advent of powered harpoons and factory ships (in the late 19th and early 20th centuries) such exploitation assumed near-industrial proportions. Populations of the great whales and fur seals were brought to critically low levels by ignorance that even the ocean's resources are not limitless. However, in recent decades there has been a huge change: man has, almost overnight, learned to love marine mammals, especially whales and dolphins, and virtually all species are now protected by law. Problems remain, of course, from pollution to overfishing and incidental bycatch, to vessel strikes and ongoing smaller-scale whaling by some countries, but overall the tide has very much turned.

Even former whalers have become whale-watchers in recent decades. Observing marine mammals, be it on an organised excursion or merely through a chance encounter with an animal at sea or from land, has nowadays attracted a huge public, a body of people who favour the protection of these animals and want to know more about them, but firstly seek information as to how to identify all those, at times baffling, fins and flukes. For many years, Brett Jarrett, the artist, and I had a vision to make, for the first time, a true field guide to the world's marine mammals. Our desire was to bring to the present subject the great advances that had been made in bird field guides in recent years, creating a book people could use in the 'field', which would show known variation, depict similar species together for easy comparison, and marshal text, photographs and plates solely for the purpose of identification.

Our principal hope is that this guide will encourage more people to watch marine mammals, and that research will lead to increased understanding of these amazing animals with which we are fortunate to share our planet, both for the sake of 'filling the gaps' in our knowledge but also to design better conservation measures to protect them.

Finally, in these few lines, I thank several close friends and colleagues for their assistance. Firstly, Guy Kirwan, the book's editor, put as much into this work as if it were his own; Brett Jarrett brought the greatest challenge – to illustrate all of the animals correctly – to a most successful completion, due in no small part to his wealth of first-hand field experience; Julie Bailey at A&C Black and Julie Dando of Fluke Art harnessed their considerable editorial, organisational and design skills to create a beautiful book, whilst Nigel Redman at A&C Black was the driving force behind this project; and last but not least the five principal editorial consultants – Graeme Cresswell, Merel Dalebout, Peter Evans, William Perrin and Robert Pitman – made many invaluable contributions which can be considered but a small reflection of their lifetimes of work devoted to the research and conservation of marine mammals.

Hadoram Shirihai, April 2006

Only when humans start to address the serious conservation issues associated with marine environments will their mammals, such as this Harbour Seal, enjoy a more assured future.

What is a marine mammal?

Marine mammal is a broad-brush term which is not even strictly true given that a number of taxa included here, and in other similar guides, are principally or entirely freshwater species. They are united in spending all, or most, of their lives in water, but their origins are diverse. For instance, seals form a relatively early radiation among carnivores, whilst Polar Bear represents a rather recent 'return' to the sea. Cetaceans evolved from the land-mammal group of even-toed ungulates, with hippos as perhaps their closest living relatives, but manatees are most closely related to elephants! Two otters are included in this book as they are essentially marine throughout their ranges, but other otters, which may occasionally venture into saltwater or be more-or-less marine in parts of their ranges (e.g. Eurasian Otter), are excluded, along with a number of other mammals, e.g. several bats, which sometimes use marine environments.

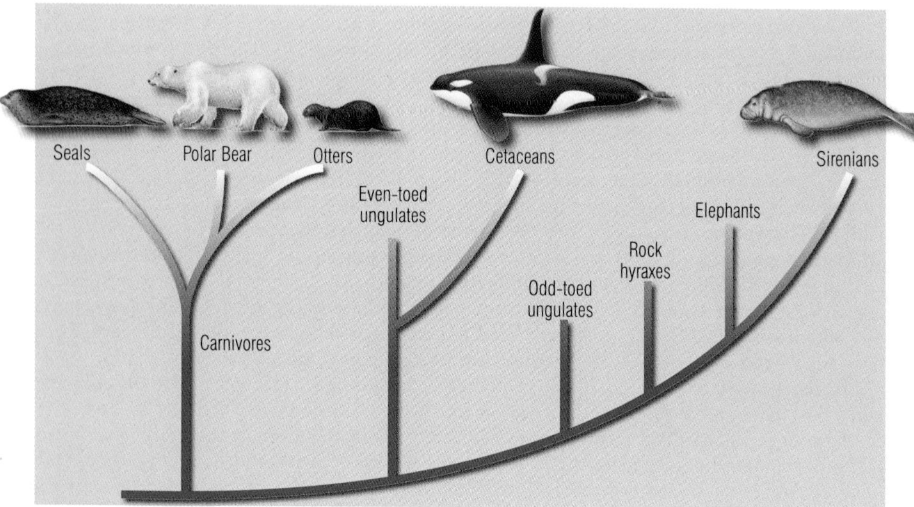

Fig. 1. One view of evolutionary relationships of marine mammals (genetic and morphological analyses to some extent do not agree).

Main groups of marine mammals

Most marine mammals belong to one of two major groups, the Cetacea (cetaceans) and Pinnipedia (seals). Of these, the latter retain a greater number of land-mammal characteristics, including four limbs, a covering of fur or a pelt, and some have external ears. The group comprises three families (the **eared seals**, comprising fur seals and sea lions, the ***eared seals***, the **walrus** and the ***true seals***) and has been variously treated as a suborder of the Carnivora or as a separate order. In contrast, the order Cetacea consists of three principal suborders, of which two have living representatives. The Mysticeti are the ***baleen whales*** (four families: the right whales, Pygmy Right Whale, Grey Whale and the ***rorquals*** – including the streamlined-bodied whales of the genus *Balaenoptera* and the Humpback Whale), which lack teeth but possess two external blowholes. In contrast, the Odontoceti possess teeth, a single blowhole and lack baleen, and are generally defined as the ***toothed whales*** and ***dolphins*** (ten families, the largest in terms of species being the ***oceanic dolphins*** and ***beaked whales***, whilst, for example, Sperm Whale forms its own family, and there are several families of ***river dolphins***). To understand the classification of the main groups better, Fig. 2 illustrates the evolutionary relationships of the main orders. Further information concerning family and subfamily relationships is located in the group introductions within the species accounts and in the checklist on pages 369–377.

Modern taxonomy of marine mammals

This guide follows a largely well-worn and principally conservative approach to taxonomy, relying in large part on the work of Rice (1998) for a list of current marine mammal taxa. The path is 'well worn' because readers will find few differences in taxonomy and nomenclature between the present work and the other guides mentioned in the bibliography, and 'conservative' because in many ways the study of geographic variation among still-living taxa is in its infancy. Such study depends on specimens, which are of the utmost importance to such work, yet the world's museums currently store relatively small and rather poorly representative holdings of most marine mammals, especially of wide-ranging species. Symptomatic of the problem of a dearth of study material is the strange fact that few marine mammals are presently considered polytypic (i.e. are subdivided into subspecies), and, to some extent, the incredible number of different genera that have been erected for a comparatively small number of species.

Especially over the last 25–30 years, 'traditional' biological classifications have been shaken by the arrival of cladistics (phylogenetic systematics) and molecular techniques, e.g. DNA-DNA hybridisation, among others. Such techniques are not without their critics but they have unquestionably led to an increasing abandonment, or at least upgrading or modernisation, of the so-called Biological Species Concept. Within the field of marine mammals the use of such techniques is producing surprising results.

The author and editor of this guide have spent a collective lifetime working with birds, where the discovery of new species continues at the rate of *c.*1–2 per annum. That such discoveries should occur in many comparatively remote and still-poorly collected regions of the world does not appear surprising to us, especially considering that many are relatively cryptic taxa which may even already be represented in museums but have lain unrecognised for a century or more. But, to consider that new species of great or baleen whales, 'giants' of the oceans, could have gone unnoticed is, on the face of it, remarkable. Nonetheless, new species of baleen whales (and, less surprisingly, beaked whales) are still being described through the use of both molecular analyses and, to a lesser extent, morphological work, and such techniques are also leading the way in defining our knowledge of the relationships between different 'stocks' of great whales and other cetaceans. Whilst some of the most recent work is open to different interpretation, we have attempted to 'point the way' for the benefit of our readers, and

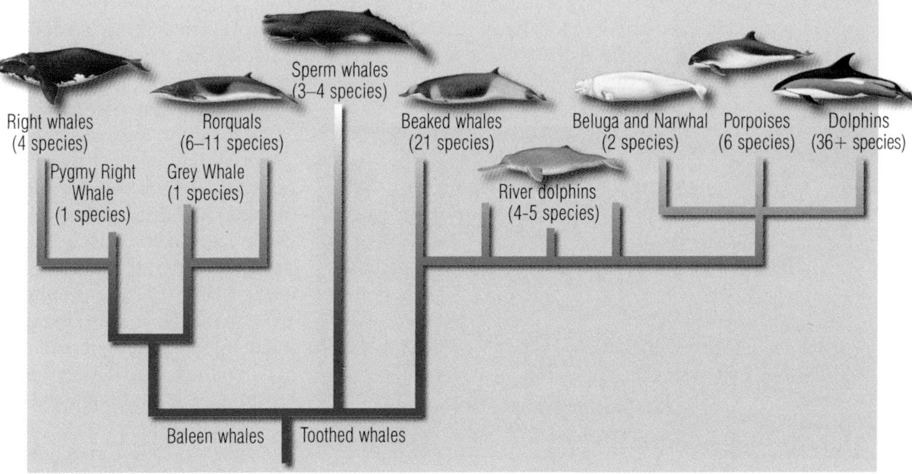

Fig. 2. Evolutionary relationships within the cetaceans.

thus have, for instance, treated Blue and Bryde's Whales as superspecies groups, whose taxonomy is very much in flux.

We rather suspect that a marine mammal guide 50 years hence might be rather different to the present book, as the array of taxonomic anomalies both thrown up by application of molecular techniques and awaiting such study is somewhat large, as a perusal of the **Taxonomy** subheadings within the different species accounts will demonstrate. It remains to be seen whether a broad range of new taxa, be they species or subspecies, are generally recognisable at sea as the result of such work, but in some cases morphological and ecological studies, such as those on Killer Whales, may provide the first or additional evidence of a lack of monophyly within taxa currently treated as basal. Whether amateur whale-watchers at the end of the present century will be able to identify all of the cetaceans and pinnipeds that might then be recognised is a particularly intriguing question. In addition to Rice, we also recommend to interested readers the checklists of marine mammals, and discussions of taxonomy, to be found in Berta & Sumich (1999) and Perrin *et al.* (2002), full details of which can be found in the bibliography.

Northern Minke Whale: until recently minke whales were treated as a single species, but appreciation of their molecular, ecological and morphological differences has led to the recognition of 2 (possibly 3) species and 2 distinctive populations of Northern Minke.

How to look for marine mammals

Even for the amateur there is now a plethora of opportunities to reach marine waters, where the chance of observing even rare species almost unknown to science until comparatively recently is quite real. However, not all of the marine mammals covered herein are strict inhabitants of the world's oceans. The river dolphins and some manatees are wholly or to a large extent riverine, and the majority of seals are most easily and best observed at their breeding sites on islands or (usually remote) continental beaches, with Caspian and Baikal Seals being confined to landlocked seas or lakes. Quite a number of remarkable marine mammals, including several species of dolphins and whales can be seen from land, some even at very close quarters.

Dolphin-watching in the Mekong River, Cambodia: 2 swimming Irrawaddy Dolphins in the foreground; boats are mostly paddled to avoid disturbance.

Nonetheless, to encounter real variety, pelagic trips, especially those that venture to

Dolphin- and whale-watch operators help to sustain the tourism industry worldwide. Here is a typical encounter of such an operation, providing an excellent opportunity to observe and learn about the animals, in this case a pod of Killer Whales off New Zealand.

deep continental shelf waters, provide the real 'icing on the cake'. Whilst not everyone can afford a several-week-long cruise to Antarctica or through the eastern tropical Pacific, there are many other opportunities to encounter marine mammals in their true environment, ranging from a few hours to a few days at sea. Some of the best 'areas' or 'sites' for marine mammal watching, principally for cetaceans, are described briefly after the species accounts, and we recommend readers search the Internet for additional details and updated information about such possibilities, either close to home or further afield.

Finding and observing marine mammals, especially at sea, can be a great challenge, and is strongly dependent on general weather and sea conditions. The best chances of finding cetaceans occur in calm seas, on wind-less and overcast days. Much is also dependent on the species involved (e.g. some spend most of their time underwater, others are endangered or threatened, and so on), season and even time of day, locality and the type of boat used (some species are very sensitive to large boats). However, a successful search is often also reliant on the skill of some of your group in spotting (often highly obscure) surfacing activities, which requires some practice, skill and motivation. Observers should therefore bear in mind that it is quite possible to see nothing, as when searching for marine mammals in the wild, success is far from guaranteed.

Excitement amongst passengers on a cruise vessel, observing inquisitive Humpback Whales.

It is important to be well prepared and equipped for a marine mammal watching trip, be it shore-based or at sea. It is worthwhile to emphasise a few key points. For pelagic trips, always assume that there is the possibility that you will be seasick and be prepared by carrying recommended medication with you. Also prepare for the worst weather by having plenty of layers of clothing available, a good waterproof and/or windproof jacket, and enough food and drinking water. A good-quality sun block is highly recommended. Good binoculars and, if conditions permit, a telescope are essential. Take careful notes; if in doubt record as much as you can see, rather than being data selective. In time and with experience, it will become apparent which are the most crucial features to record. The following section, which provides an overview of field identification, and the highlighted *italic* texts in the Identification boxes and the plates for each species are specifically designed to assist readers in rapidly keying into the general or specific characters crucial to, or strongly supportive, of species-level or group identifications. Lastly, there should never be a sense of defeat in letting an animal remain unidentified. Briefly or distantly seen fins or blows are likely to be unidentifiable, even by experts with years of experience.

Natural history of marine mammals

DISTRIBUTION AND MIGRATION

Marine mammals occur throughout the globe, from near the North Pole (one species of true seal and Polar Bear) to the summer limit of the Antarctic pack-ice. A small number can be considered cosmopolitan or virtually so, and many others are circumpolar in either the north or south, or are pantropical at low latitudes. Indeed, comparatively few species are highly restricted geographically: only a few Pacific eared seals which breed on a handful of islands, two true seals restricted to landlocked areas, the monk seals, the extinct Steller's Sea Cow, several of the riverine dolphins (which are some of the rarest cetaceans), Gulf of California Porpoise and the Franciscana, which inhabits inshore waters of SE South America.

Migrations are sometimes highly developed and remarkable, especially those of the baleen whales, which spend the summer feeding in cold seas, but fast (or feed very little) and breed in temperate or even warm-water ecosystems at much lower latitudes. Many toothed whales have reduced migratory tendencies, some even being more-or-less sedentary, but most make seasonal movements, usually inshore–offshore and vice versa, and several freshwater species exhibit quite well-defined movements in response to seasonal changes in water level. Many seals are very poorly known in the non-breeding period and their at-sea lives incredibly open to speculation. Some are known to wander widely, e.g. the South American Fur Seal, and others to make regular long-distance migrations, involving at least part of the population, e.g. Northern Fur Seal, whilst others appear relatively sedentary, e.g. the Galápagos endemics.

BEHAVIOUR

Many whales and dolphins have been comparatively well studied, especially using photo identification techniques which, particularly for large whales, permits individual recognition. Nonetheless, there are many gaps in our knowledge and for some groups of toothed whales, especially beaked whales, we still know very little, if anything, concerning their behaviour and ecology.

Many cetaceans, especially toothed whales and dolphins, travel in pods with incredibly strong social bonds, which appears to be the cause of mass-strandings. Nonetheless, the strongest bond is always between mother and calf. Pods may be fluid structures, stable but mixed groups of all ages and both sexes, or segregated by age and sex, and some animals, particularly male baleen whales, may spend comparatively long periods alone. Most social aggregations comprise a well-defined core group. In contrast, seals appear to be largely solitary or form only very small and loose aggregations at sea, and the function and form of any such associations can, for now, only be guessed at.

Hauled-out Northern Elephant Seals and Californian Sea Lions: both species are highly social at breeding and moulting sites, but much less so in the water; both also favour sandy beaches, which in this case has forced the smaller species to 'beach' themselves on the backs of the larger one for want of space.

Like pod structure, the surfacing and diving sequence of many cetaceans are quite well known, often specifically distinctive, and in many cases useful in species identification. Breaching and other surfacing displays or signalling, which are broadly shared by many cetaceans (although their biological significance is not always fully understood), often vary between species and can play an important role in identification (detailed in the identification boxes within the species accounts). Again, pinnipeds are especially poorly known, principally due to their rather undemonstrative behaviour at the surface and tendency to be more widely dispersed at sea. Even for better-known species, diving behaviour is not necessarily well known. Maximum and average dive timespans and depth are, for many species, based on rather few or small datasets. For some species, examination of the stomach contents of stranded animals provides the most detailed information concerning the usual depths at which they might forage, based on our knowledge of their prey species.

Spyhopping immature Sperm Whale. In many cetaceans, breaching and other surfacing displays are more frequent in young animals.

FEEDING

Very little is known of the pelagic behaviour of seals: here White-vented Storm-petrels Oceanites gracilis *are scavenging prey of a South American Sea Lion. Associations between seabirds and marine mammals are quite common at rich food sources.*

Virtually all marine mammals are carnivores, with the possible exception of the manatees. Cetaceans take tiny crustaceans to large fish and squid, and occasionally birds. Some even feed on other cetaceans, up to and including baleen whales! Many have quite broad, catholic diets, but others are relatively specialist. Sea otters may also be generalists but many of the seals are largely fish-eaters although some principally consume crustaceans and molluscs. In contrast, manatees are apparently mainly vegetarian, though they take some invertebrates and small fish, and Polar Bears take seals, occasionally toothed whales and seabirds, and also carrion. Prolonged seasonal fasts are a feature of several great whales, Polar Bear and Amazonian Manatee. One interesting facet of feeding in both cetaceans and pinnipeds is the extent to which some species associate with seabirds, particularly terns and tubenoses, especially in deep-sea and continental shelf-edge waters. Are such associations dictated by chance or do one or both groups search out the other at obvious rich feeding sources?

South African Fur Seal takes sardines in short, shallow dives.

REPRODUCTION

Unlike other facets of the lives of marine mammals, the breeding behaviour of seals is well known, largely because they come to land (or at least ice) to breed. This is in stark contrast to the majority of cetaceans which strictly breed in the water. Even so, most true seals exclusively mate in the water, only coming to land to give birth, using either sandy or rocky beaches, pack- or sea-ice or even caves. For most whales only general details of their reproductive cycles are known or, for the beaked whales and a number of other rare or only recently recognised species, wholly unknown. Whilst many great whales perform long-distance migrations, and some seals may also move far from their colonies during the non-breeding period, most toothed whales appear to be relatively opportunistic breeders, insomuch as they do possess well-established and particular mating and calving grounds, and many other seals are comparatively sedentary, breeding and feeding within rather well-defined ranges. Some species, especially seals and the Beluga may show highly developed faithfulness to breeding sites.

Mating Spinner Dolphins (♂ below): several ♂♂ may copulate with a single ♀ in a very short time (their mating system is probably promiscuous to polygynous, with degrees of polygyny).

Within the species accounts, the Ecology section describes the general reproductive system and cycle, to assist the understanding of an animals' range and appearance at a given time and place. It is also intriguing to consider the fascinating life histories of these animals whilst observing them. We strongly recommend observers with the desire to delve deeper into such subjects to consult the recent scientific publications by Berta & Sumich (1999) and Perrin *et al.* (2002), whilst, in particular, Reeves *et al.* (2002) also serves as a very accurate reference to these subjects.

STRANDINGS

Several species of cetacean are best known from beached animals, with our only significant knowledge of life history and biology coming from such unfortunates, whilst a handful of taxa are known solely from such events. Many thousands of animals are stranded, both alive or dead, on the world's beaches annually, and for many people this might be their first or only encounter with a cetacean. Although the phenomenon is well known, the mechanisms behind such events are not. Of course, some animals die at sea and are washed ashore, but live strandings are harder to explain. Several theories have been mooted: that changes in the Earth's magnetic field confuse the animals, that climatic events may cause them to panic (as may unusually loud noises), land noises and diseases may cause disorientation and that the animal's sonar system has failed. Indeed, there is a strong correlation between the number of cases on well-populated coasts where echolocation signals are may have been deflected. Increases in metal, chemical and, especially, acoustic pollution, even in deep waters, probably are also harmful. What is reasonably clear is that, once a single animal strands, its companion or companions often follow suit because of the strong social bonds operating in many species. Many of those that strand en masse are deep-ocean species, like pilot whales. However, many animals can be rescued and such operations exist in many countries, run by volunteers. We strongly encourage readers to join forces with such well-organised and professional cetacean rescue teams (contacts are easily found on the Internet).

Conservation

Within recent decades cetacean conservation has enjoyed some high-profile successes. Public attitudes towards whales and dolphins, in particular, have swung from moderate disinterest to popularity, in large part doubtless due to Hollywood films such as *Free Willy*, and their use, especially of dolphins, in 'live entertainment' in aquaria and zoos around the world, although these are still criticised by many conservationists. Nonetheless, within the course of a couple of generations, many societies have gone from being hunters to observers and conservationists, even forming huge and successful ecumenical industries for whale and dolphin watching.

Commercial whaling commenced *c.*1,000 years ago, but the heyday of sealing did not arrive until the late-18th century, especially in the ultra-rich Southern Ocean, and modern whaling was kick-started by the development of the first explosive harpoon in 1852 and then, in 1925, the invention of floating factory ships which obviated the need to process whales ashore and also subverted some of the mediocre regulations that existed -to limit hunting, e.g. on South Georgia.

Dugongs. Their numbers and range were both historically much larger, with hunting taking a particularly heavy toll in the 17th–19th centuries, although it persists to the present day in some areas. Incidental fishery bycatch and oil spills are also threats.

Hawaiian Monk Seal. This cow lost her pup due to the type of disturbance visible in the photo. Nets and plastic debris are hazards for young seals. Brought to the brink of extinction through indiscriminate hunting and commercial harvesting, military activities on certain islands during the last century also had negative impacts on this seal. The largest colony, at French Frigate Shoals, is currently declining.

Real efforts at protecting the large whales commenced in 1931, when Bowhead Whale was given a measure of legal protection. Further legislation followed, e.g. for Humpback and Blue Whales in 1966, but as late as 1984 for Sperm Whale. However, whaling still continued. Even the creation of the International Whaling Commission (IWC), in 1946, did little to alleviate the situation, as for the first 30 years of its existence it principally encouraged the industry, during which time an estimated two million plus whales were killed. A worldwide moratorium was agreed in 1982, although it only came into force four

Despite widespread legal protection, Irrawaddy Dolphin is killed for its oil whilst incidental bycatch in fishing nets is also significant, and explosives used for fishing may be particularly damaging. Habitat degradation and pollution are other concerns, and hydroelectric dams on the Mekong River threaten the freshwater Indochinese population. There seems little hope for the survival of this species.

years later, and in 1994 the IWC brokered a 50 million km^2 Southern Ocean Whale Sanctuary around Antarctica. Despite their slow reproductive rates, there is evidence that at least some baleen whales are responding favourably to protection and the relative cessation of whaling. Southern Right Whale populations have been increasing quite substantially for a number of years, but, in contrast, the North Atlantic and especially Pacific Right Whales, which were brought to the brink of extinction by commercial whaling, may never recover. And, despite the moratorium, commercial whaling continues, albeit on a small scale, with Japan and Iceland taking advantage of a loophole in the IWC agreement which permits limited numbers of whales to be taken for 'scientific research'; Norway refuses to accept the moratorium. Pressure against these three countries grew significantly in the 1990s but very recently Japan has taken control of the IWC, making a return to commercial whaling a very real and frightening possibility.

Subsistence whaling also continues, with communities in Russia, Iceland, Greenland, Alaska, Canada, Indonesia and other areas still permitted to take annual small quotas of large whales, and much larger numbers of Belugas, Narwhals and, especially, seals. Such activities have also drawn conservationist wrath, as not all indigenous hunts are necessary in terms of economics or nutrition, and, particularly in the case of seals, the 'inhumane' methods which have been utilised.

Belugas. Commercial whaling, principally in the 20th century, decimated stocks and hunting, which is still the most significant threat, continues to place small subpopulations at risk, e.g. in Greenland and perhaps Russia. Other threats include high contaminant levels, diseases and, locally, oil exploration, hydroelectric plants, vessel traffic and recreational sports.

Indeed, small-cetacean hunting is not confined to the high arctic but continues in many areas of the world, both commercially (to provide meat for human consumption and for crab fisheries) and by fishermen who blame cetaceans and seals for declining fish stocks.

Commercial hunts are most prevalent in Japan and Peru, although the latter banned dolphin hunting in 1990 and then stepped-up enforcement of existing legislation six years later.

However, currently the most invidious and startling worldwide threat to cetaceans and seals is the impact of fisheries, particularly drowning in nets, which may have accounted for millions of animals per annum. International regulations against drift-netting came into force in the early 1990s, although this had the knock-on effect of persuading many fishermen to switch to longlining with catastrophic results for seabirds, and international action, particularly the call for 'dolphin-friendly tuna', has also been successful in drastically reducing the numbers of cetaceans caught by tuna fisheries.

Other threats remain. Marine pollution is a source of general concern, although its effects on top predators are naturally greatest. Habitat change and loss is also significant, perhaps especially for riverine species. Dams and hydroelectric stations have a major detrimental effect on such environments and are amongst the principal threats facing river dolphins. Increasing human use of waterways and the high seas is also bringing many new threats. Oil and other chemical and heavy metal pollutants seriously affect marine mammals and their environments, but noise pollution may also wreak extensive damage on cetaceans, and may lead to increased numbers of strandings in some species. Physical collisions with boats are a significant source of mortality for many cetaceans, seals and manatees. Only recently has the magnitude of the numbers killed each year become apparent, which as always has the strongest impact on endangered species like the North Atlantic Right Whale.

Nonetheless, whilst threats to marine mammals remain great, the public desire to find solutions to such problems has never been greater. Whales and dolphins enjoy a higher public profile than ever before and more people are taking special pelagic trips in search of encounters with these mammals. As conservationists have been quick to note, such activities may pose threats as well, and it is important that whale-watchers take account of the guidelines for safe viewing (for both observers and the observed), in order to ensure that physical intrusion or even harassment do not occur. The closest permitted approach in a vessel varies between areas and species, but frequently is 100 m. This book aims to assist observers of marine mammals make accurate identifications of the animals they see, sometimes using features only visible given optimal views. But, respect for the guidelines and hence the animals welfare must come over and above securing a correct identification.

The conservation status of, and threats to, each of the world's marine mammals are summarised at the end of the book within the Conservation Checklist.

How to use this book

This guide seeks to create a user-friendly identification book to the marine mammals of the world for the layman and specialist alike, utilising many of the concepts that have gone into the development of the successful bird field guides of recent years. It is certainly true that many previous books, of undoubted quality, have sought to fill a similar niche. However, perhaps none has successfully brought those ideas to the page in the way that has made avian field guides so advanced, and we might add has made birds so popular.

Of course, this book goes beyond the conventional field guide in one respect, the liberal use of photographs in addition to illustrations. Other cetacean and pinniped guides have also relied heavily on such additional aids, but no previous guide has used comprehensive plates of age/sex and geographical variation, and carefully selected photographs with the sole and express purpose to assist readers in identifying animals at sea.

We have sought to produce a work that is above all accurate and easy to use. This has entailed jettisoning conventional taxonomic order for the species accounts. These form the bulk of the book, with cetaceans first, followed by sirenians (sea cows or manatees) and thereafter the seals and the few other, much smaller groups, namely the Polar Bear and sea otters. Each group of species is prefaced by a very short introduction to their systematics (which together with the checklist at the back provides readers with an overview of relationships) and identification. Of crucial importance is the *comparative plate*, whereby different species or taxa appear on the same page for the purpose of comparing their identification features, with short captions on each plate. For field users, we consider this to be very valuable.

There follows the individual species accounts. For field users, perhaps the most important part is the **Identification box** which, together with the relevant species plate, outlines the main features upon which observers must concentrate to achieve a correct identification. Use of *italics* is designed to assist readers key into the critical features. Italicised captions on the individual species plates highlight diagnostic or particularly useful features and/or those detectable on surfacing animals – thereby alerting observers to the key identification marks, and providing, at a glance, those features most important to record when faced by an unfamiliar animal. In many instances, the photographs and surfacing diagrams should assist observers to understand the appearance of key features at the surface. Other captions aim to explain variation which, together with the main text, affords a broader picture.

Thereafter, there is a **Similar species** section which, in some instances, is preceded by **Distinctive populations** wherein information concerning the identification of different species (in the case of two very closely related complexes), subspecies or 'stocks' is presented, especially in cases where these may be subject to taxonomic re-evaluation, or where species status for one or more subspecies or 'stocks' has been proposed. **Similar species** provides a further brief aid to the separation of similar forms, and frequently points out how age-/sex-related or racial variation may cloud identification. Thus, as will be emphasised many times, there is no 'shame' in leaving an animal unidentified to species.

Variation is subdivided into **Age/Sex**, wherein ageing, sexing and growth development are discussed and **Physical notes**, in which the range of full-grown adult lengths and weights (often given separately for ♂ and ♀) are presented, along with similar data for the newborn pup or calf. (Lengths presented in **Physical notes** and maximum figures specified in the comparison plates and opening sections are based on published material. However, the measurements on the species plates, usually close to the top end of the spectrum, relate to the *dimensions* of the painted animal relative to other animals on the same plate.) Further (optional) subheadings are **Other data**, where various information is presented to assist in ageing, sexing or identifying an animal to a specific taxon (but concentrating on characters that might be evaluated at sea), and **Taxonomy**, wherein ranges of any subspecies are presented, along with information concerning the results of any DNA work undertaken; alternative species (or even generic) classifications are also summarised. If a species is monotypic this section is usually omitted.

There follows **Distribution & population** in which the broad range is described (complementing the map), along with a summary of movements, regular migrations or vagrancy. The text rarely attempts to distinguish between at-sea sightings and strandings, except in extreme cases, and does not necessarily highlight relative abundance at the limits of a species' range, unless well-informed data are available. In many cases, data are still subject to refinement, making such statements liable to become quickly out of date. Each paragraph contains a subheading *Population*, wherein any significant recent estimates are presented. In most cases, conservation issues are relegated to the checklist at the end of the book.

Finally, the **Ecology** of each species, *where relevant to identification and distribution*, is subject to a brief résumé, usually opening with data on social structure, principally the number of animals and age/sex composition of pods (some of which may already have been detailed in the Identification box), and with subheadings describing: *Breaching* (for cetaceans only) and *Diving* (which for many species is still only partially known), as well as *Diet* (the main diet and sometimes feeding techniques), and closing with the basic facts concerning *Reproduction* and *Lifespan* (maximum longevity). Given the very tight restrictions on space, we generally do not provide information on numbers of calves (as in most species this is usually just one) or breeding success.

The rest of the guide comprises the introductory sections which include sections on watching and identifying marine mammals, their taxonomy and classification, their natural history and their conservation. The book concludes with a brief guide to some of the globe's best areas for watching marine mammals and a mini bibliography, featuring some of the best books available, principally, concerning cetaceans and pinnipeds. We have deliberately avoided listing papers published in the technical literature. References, as a whole, are very rarely mentioned in the species accounts or elsewhere, quite deliberately, as we have sought, throughout, to make this a book for field users.

Abbreviations used in this field guide:
ad(s) – adult(s)
subad(s) – subadult(s)
imm(s) – immature(s)
juv(s) – juvenile(s)
sp(p) - species
R - River
Is - Island(s)
♂ / ♂♂ – male/s
♀ / ♀♀ – female/s

The illustrations

One of the cornerstones of this work is an attempt to describe and illustrate forms that have rarely, if ever, been represented in previous works. Thus, the plates are the first-ever complete set of illustrations to show individual and geographical variation for all marine mammals, and the photographs have been chosen with similar thoughts in mind.

Marine mammals by their behaviour and habitat present a real challenge to piece together their unique anatomical forms, patterns and pigmentation. The plates are foremost intended to aid field identification and secondly to accurately depict anatomy. Attempting to illustrate all known races and ages proved difficult, as for some species few or no descriptions were available. As a rule each cetacean is represented by an adult female, but also a juvenile, immature or subadult and adult male in lateral and dorsal views. As a sense of form can be lost in lateral views, by including a dorsal view readers should gain a three-dimensional appreciation of each animal's overall structure. Field identification at a distance can prove very challenging, especially given light conditions and the angle of the animal to the observer. For instance, in sunny conditions bright sunspots can often give the impression of pale pigmentation whilst any obvious markings can appear amplified. It should be remembered that there is a wide array of subtle pattern and colour gradients in many species, related to age, sex and geographical variation. Italic captions on the plates illustrate diagnostic or particularly useful features and/or those detectable on surfacing.

Toothed whales, in particular older animals, often show conspicuous signs of interaction with their own species. Adding life-long scars from parasitic feeders such as cookie-cutter sharks, social interaction leaves frayed edges to fins and flukes, extensive tooth-rakes, and the cycle of shedding skin can often mask subtle markings and colour characteristics, making identification difficult. Generally, older males show far more wear and tear, and exaggerated physical features (e.g. more bulbous melon, thicker beak and tailstock and larger, more falcate dorsal fin). In most cases a relatively clean-skinned female and well-marked male are illustrated to indicate these differences.

Baleen whales, due to their massive size, can appear to have even less obvious markings. Above the waterline, observers may see subtle shading, blends and swirls of pigment that can help in identification and can even identify a particular stock or race. Those illustrated here are simply a sample of the variation that exists. Like toothed whales, they show considerable variation in dorsal fin size and shape. Overall length can be difficult to judge and observers should rely on a combination of above-water features and surfacing profile.

Seals, in particular fur seals, are notoriously difficult to identify on land or at sea. Given a combination of age, overall health and physical condition, fresh, bleached, moulting and wet coats, fur colour can change dramatically. Generally, a mature male and female, illustrating their respective sizes, with a dry coat are depicted. Identification of typical adult males and females in a single-species colony may appear straightforward but similar species can migrate huge distances and wander into these colonies.

The maps

A distribution map depicts the range of each living species. For most species, the quality and quantity of available distributional information is sketchy, and varies with location and season. Ranges in coastal and shelf waters are far better known than offshore waters, and, for example, the N Atlantic and eastern N Pacific are relatively well studied, whilst ranges in the S Atlantic and Indian Oceans are poorly understood. Similar contrasts exist away from the tropics due to seasonal fluctuations, with most data being from summer months when seas are calmer and days longer. These maps therefore serve only as a guide and marine mammals will continue to surprise us by appearing in unexpected locations. Given limitations in our current knowledge, the maps utilise the latest available information and, wherever possible, are based on sightings and illustrate the 'typical' range of a species. Extralimital or 'rare' sightings are therefore excluded. Sightings and stranding data were often used with known habitat preferences, using an overlay map of the mid slope of the continental shelf or high oceanic ridges at *c.*1,000 m depth. The latter is an important habitat boundary, generally marking a rapid decrease in water depth. In regions where sightings data are few, ranges are based solely or mostly on information from strandings. Thus, for example, some beaked whales known only from beached animals are assigned offshore distributions close to the stranding locations as dietary analysis suggests that they live solely in deep water.

The known or likely range is depicted in green, orange or blue, illustrating general occurrence/likely distribution, summer distribution, and winter distribution, respectively. Please note, the summer and winter ranges on the maps refer to the seasons appropriate to the hemispheres in which a particular species can be found. In addition, monthly occurrence is labelled regionally where such information is available. For example, '1–6' indicates that a species is present January–June. Known migration routes appear as arrows. Where possible, italicised scientific names show the distribution of a subspecies. To maximise the value of each map, red dots mark known hotspots for a given species. These are not exhaustive, but locate sites of established commercial whale-watch operators or land-based watching viewpoints. See map on inside back cover for the location and names of these hotspots.

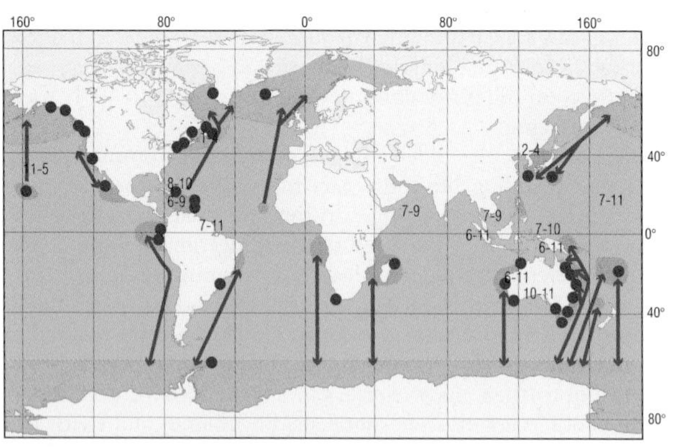

Humpback Whale, *Megaptera novaeangliae*

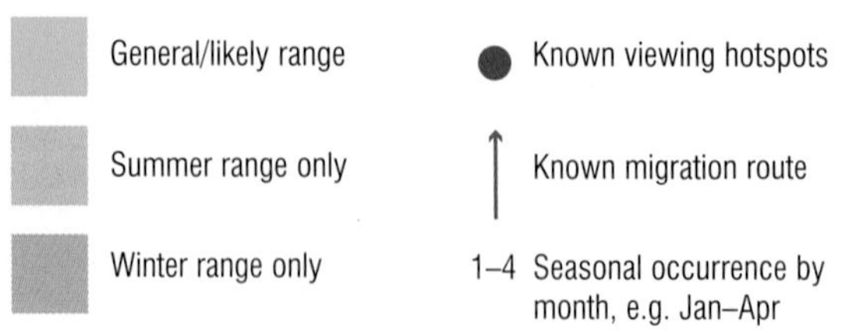

Sperm Whale

The toothed Sperm Whale is a truly unique cetacean, being placed in its own family, Physeteridae. Its bizarre shape attracts attention; the huge square head has a cavity large enough to hold a car. Sperm Whale is one of the most spectacular divers, reaching up to 3 km below the surface, hunting large squid using its spermaceti organ for echolocation in the darkness. Its highly complex social organisation is based on age and sex.

Sperm and Humpback Whales (see p. 25) are altogether different, the latter being a baleen whale. However, they are placed close together here, as they are among the most frequently encountered whales, and can appear superficially similar if seen briefly or at some distance, both being elongated and dark at the surface, when only small parts of the head and back may be visible.

Sperm Whale

Physeter macrocephalus

Cosmopolitan. Max 18.3 m.

Priority characters on surfacing

- Very long, log-like and usually finless body.
- Distinct *triangular or rounded hump ²/₃ of way along back*, followed by spinal ridge with 'knuckles'. Hump may appear fin-like in some.
- *Dark wrinkled skin* mainly dusky grey-brown (in some lights almost black or paler brown).
- *Broad, triangular-shaped and dark tail flukes*, often with ragged trailing edge and deeply notched (thrown vertical on commencing deep dive).
- Rarely visible: huge box-like head, with blunt snout and slight raised end; slit-like blowhole on left side at front of rostrum; off-white coloration around mouth and ventrally, especially in genital slit region; and disproportionately small, rounded flippers.

Typical behaviour at surface

- *Bushy blow always directed at low angle to left, as single nostril exhales forward and left (up to 5 m high but usually 1–2 m, for up to 5–8 min continuously every 10–30 sec)*. Against wind, blow can be directed upwards.
- Rather motionless or swims leisurely with very little of body visible (sometimes appears as if 2 animals present, as snout area and hump both protrude above back).
- On final blow, typically slightly raises snout and dorsal hump/fin, before briefly or partially submerging and accelerating in smooth, *well-exposed, steep arching roll, with tailstock and flukes raised vertically as it sinks*, leaving few ripples on surface.
- Usually visible at surface for *c.*10 min, typically diving from same location as it surfaced.
- Usually encountered singly in polar waters, in twos or in small, often well-dispersed groups of up to 20 in tropical waters.

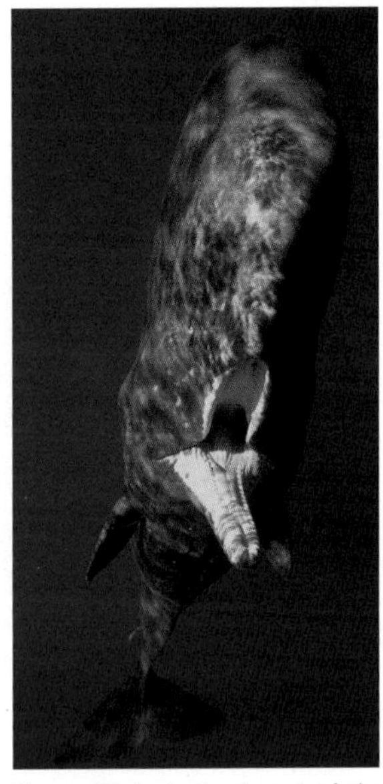

Sperm Whale is the largest of the toothed whales; its enormous box-like head has 20–26 thick, conical teeth on either side of its underslung lower jaw.

SIMILAR SPECIES

Virtually unmistakable. Both Sperm and ***Humpback*** similarly arch back on commencing dive, raising hump/fin (note latter's short stubby dorsal fin can appear hump-like), and both raise flukes. However, coloration and structure obviously dissimilar, and they have entirely different blow sequences. Unlike

Humpback, flukes clearly more triangular, deeper notched and uniformly dark below (Humpback can have all-dark underside to flukes). Beware also similar blows of some beaked whale spp.

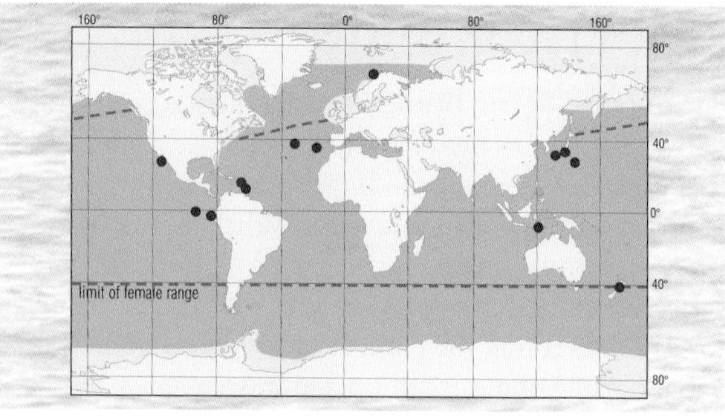

VARIATION

Age/sex Mature ♂ *c*.2× longer than ♀ and often has more narrow pale scars on head and back, relatively larger dorsal hump and head, and further-projecting snout. Tailstock and ventral keel behind anus also proportionately thicker. ♂ has more and larger teeth than ♀, but do not erupt until 12 yrs old. Calf averages paler/greyer. **Physical notes** ♂ 15–18.3 m and 43.5–55.8 tons; ♀ 8–17 m and 13.5–20 tons. Calf at birth 3.5–4.5 m and *c*.1 ton. **Other data** Fluke marks vary individually, according to age/sex and also geographically, and are caused by predators, whilst dorsal hump also varies: sometimes large, almost like a low fin, but occasionally absent. Individually identifiable by marks on trailing edges of tail flukes and shape of dorsal hump.

Sperm Whale has dark, wrinkled skin and a triangular or rounded hump (which appears fin-like in some).

DISTRIBUTION & POPULATION

Almost cosmopolitan, 60°N–70°S, with non-breeding ♂♂ periodically reaching polar regions, but avoids pack-ice. Cows and young generally move pole-wards in summer: in S Hemisphere, they

Logging Sperm Whales, note the very long, log-like bodies, and forward and leftward-directed blows.

Sperm Whale

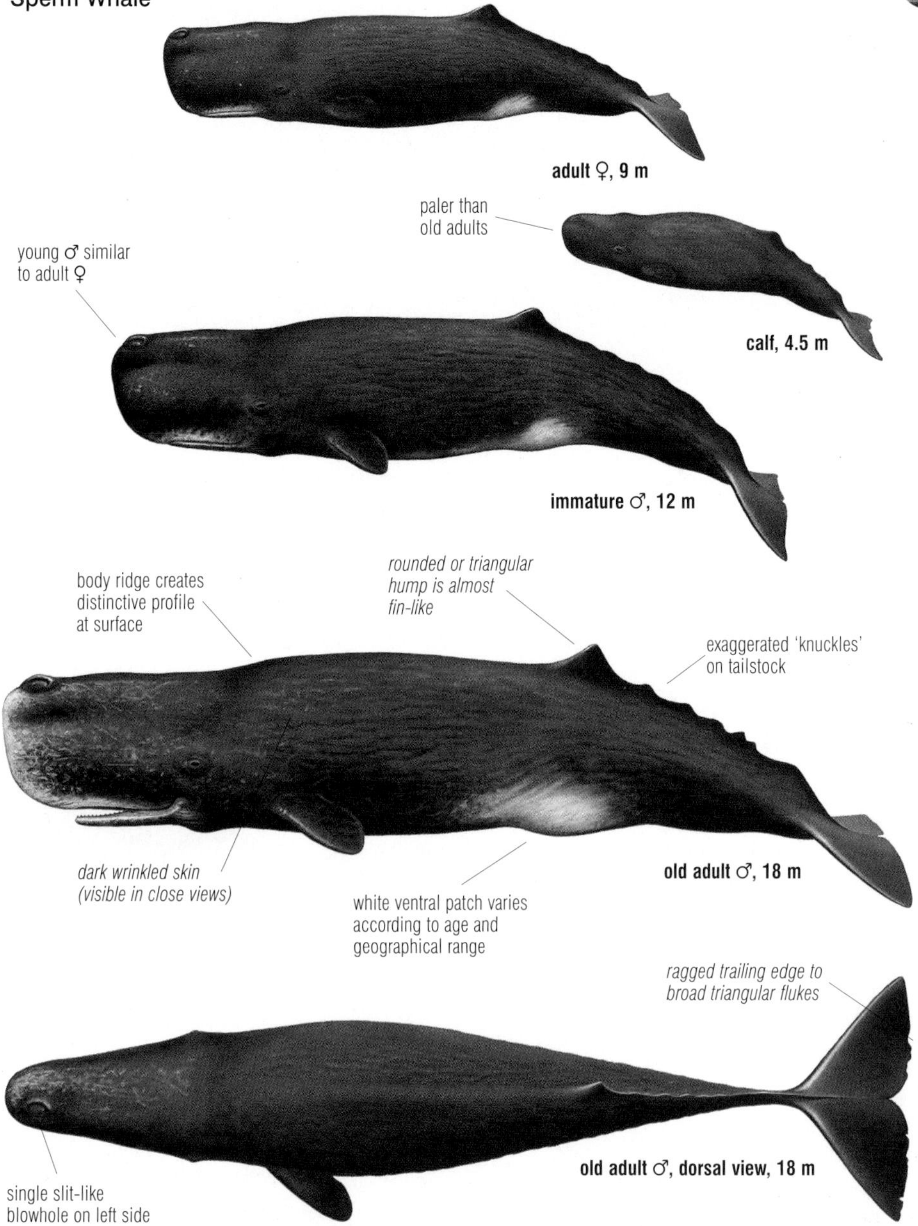

adult ♀, 9 m

paler than old adults

calf, 4.5 m

young ♂ similar to adult ♀

immature ♂, 12 m

body ridge creates distinctive profile at surface

rounded or triangular hump is almost fin-like

exaggerated 'knuckles' on tailstock

dark wrinkled skin (visible in close views)

white ventral patch varies according to age and geographical range

old adult ♂, 18 m

ragged trailing edge to broad triangular flukes

single slit-like blowhole on left side

old adult ♂, dorsal view, 18 m

Rather motionless when surfacing; bushy blow directed low, left and forwards; on final blow typically enters steep arching roll, with tailstock and flukes raised vertically on sinking into deep dive.

A Sperm Whale 'nursery' school comprising mothers and their offspring.

range south to Subtropical Convergence and in N Hemisphere north to the subarctic boundary and Subpolar Convergence. Often observed where continental shelf drops off dramatically and water depths reach 1,000–3,000 m. *Population* 1.9 million estimated in late 1970s, but more recently just 300,000.

ECOLOGY

'Nursery' schools of ♀♀ and their offspring form harems visited by single bull in mating season (older ♂♂ often solitary or in very small groups, and usually with others only in breeding season when bulls may move between groups of ♀♀). 'Bachelor' schools of younger ♂♂. Cows, calves and juvs in groups of 10–50 scattered over several km in non-breeding season. At surface indulges in much physical contact, rubbing and vocalising. Cows defend young against enemies, e.g. Killer Whales, by adopting marguerite formation, forming circle around young, with heads pointing inwards and tails towards danger. *Breaching* Full leap to more gradual and incomplete emergence; usually by juvs, and in poor weather, but sometimes by ♀ in presence of ♂. *Diving* Reaches up to 3 km below surface and can remain underwater for over 2 hrs. *Diet* Principally large squid in very deep water, in upwellings and at continental shelf. *Reproduction* ♂♂ not sexually active until at least 18 yrs old and 11–12 m long, and ♀♀ at 7–13 yrs (8.3–9.2 m). ♀♀ breed every 3–6 yrs, giving birth in tropical and temperate waters in summer and autumn, but ♂ calves on independence move to cooler waters where feeding better, whereas ♀ calves stay at lower latitudes. ♀♀ give birth to single calf, peak in May–Sep in N Hemisphere and Feb–Apr in S Hemisphere. Gestation 14–16 months and lactation 19–42 months; suckling (sometimes by ♀♀ other than mother) may continue 3.5 yrs, and some sporadically for as long as 13 yrs. *Lifespan* At least 60–70 yrs.

The tailstock and flukes are raised vertically on commencing deep dives.

Sperm Whale breaching.

Humpback Whale

The familiar Humpback is famous for its remarkable surface displays. One of the baleen whales, but unique amongst rorquals in being assigned its own genus, *Megaptera*. Characteristic are its long, almost wing-like flippers and numerous tubercles on the head and flippers. It performs some of the longest migrations of any mammal, feeding in polar waters and breeding in the tropics.

Though unmistakable, first-time observers should be aware of possible confusion with other large whales, e.g. Sperm Whale, which can appear superficially similar at the surface. On the other hand, researchers can recognise individuals using photo-identification techniques. It is important not to approach Humpbacks too closely, maintaining at least 100 m distance to the rear, as people have been killed when breaching whales have landed on their boats. In many countries, e.g. the USA, it is forbidden to follow these animals except on organised tours.

Head-on view of fluking Humpback Whale.

Humpback Whale flipper-slapping.

Humpback Whale

Megaptera novaeangliae

Cosmopolitan. Max 18 m.

Priority characters on surfacing

- *Large, uniquely shaped and mainly dark*, especially flattened, knobbly-marked rostrum and extremely long arm-like flippers, often visible underwater.
- *Dorsal fin varies in size and shape, from small triangular knob to larger 'sickle'*, and is situated nearly ⅔ of way along back on small raised platform.
- *Flukes (often lifted very high prior to diving) have characteristic serrated trailing edge and unique pattern, varying from entirely black to all white, on underside.*
- *Head rather slender and flat covered by rounded knobs* (and near tip of lower jaw); prominent double-blowholes and splashguard but inconspicuous single central rostrum ridge.
- Head and body black or grey, with variable amount of white on throat and belly, and sides.
- *White undersides to long flippers clearly visible in social activities.*
- Head, fore flippers and tail flukes often infested with barnacles.

Typical behaviour at surface

- *Blow bushy but highly visible* (2.5–3 m), relatively broad compared to overall height, and given 4–8× (3–6× on breeding grounds, but usually fewer between shallower dives or when travelling fast) at 15–90-sec intervals before diving; blow occasionally appears split and V-shaped with spray falling outwards.
- At surface: rostrum and prominent splashguard visible first, with blow, thereafter dorsal fin appears

SIMILAR SPECIES

Almost unmistakable given incredibly long flippers, knobbly head and uniquely serrated tail flukes. In commencing long dives, ***Sperm Whale*** typically also arches back and raises its flukes nearly vertically, whilst ***right whales*** often throw the flukes high, but all have very differently shaped and patterned flukes, being all dark with a straight trailing edge. Humpback blows occasionally appear V-shaped as in right whales.

VARIATION

Age/sex Perhaps estimable by overall size (♀ has grapefruit-like lobe behind genital slit). **Physical notes** 11–18 m and 24–40 tons, ♂ usually 1–1.5 m shorter than ♀. Calf at birth 4–4.6 m and *c.*1–2 tons (at 10–11 months is 7.5–10 m). **Other data** Pattern

The pattern on the underside of the flukes is highly variable and individually unique.

of white on underside of flukes individually unique. Underparts, including broad throat pleats, also vary individually: some all black but most have conspicuous white patch, often covering entire pleats, or only partial black in centre. Upper body usually black but a grey/ blue coloration sometimes apparent. Some, especially ♂♂, narrowly scarred whitish on upperparts and often have white marks behind eyes and on back and head. Distinctive tubercles very variable, on head, jaws, including chin and sometimes throat, and flippers often have large barnacles on their summits. **Taxonomy** Monotypic but Atlantic and Pacific Humpbacks have different flipper patterns. Former usually has largely white flippers with little black, whilst those in Pacific have black upperside and white underside; amount of white

along with part of body behind splashguard; after final blow, in preparing for deep dive, performs steeper arching roll of back, fin and tailstock, culminating in raised tailstock and flukes as submerges at variable angle, leaving quite obvious slick on surface. Flukes often not exposed in shallow dives.

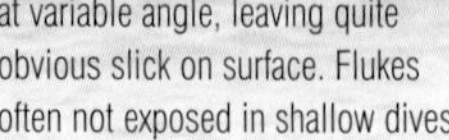

- Often very active at surface, breaching, spyhopping, lobtailing and tail- and flipper-slapping.

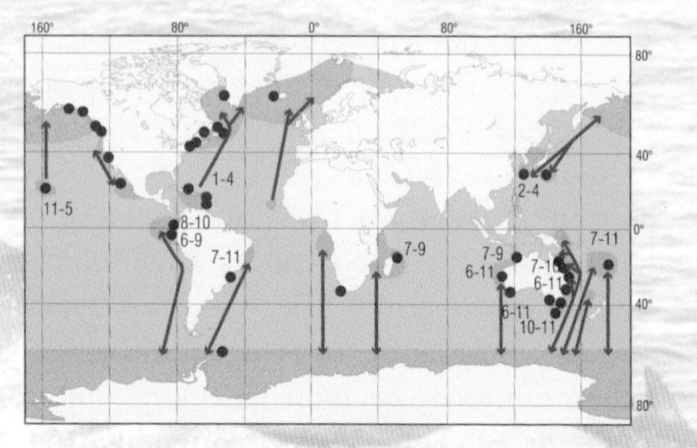

Surfacing Humpback Whales: note distinctive sloping back profile and stubby dorsal fin.

Tail-slapping Humpback Whale.

Humpback Whale

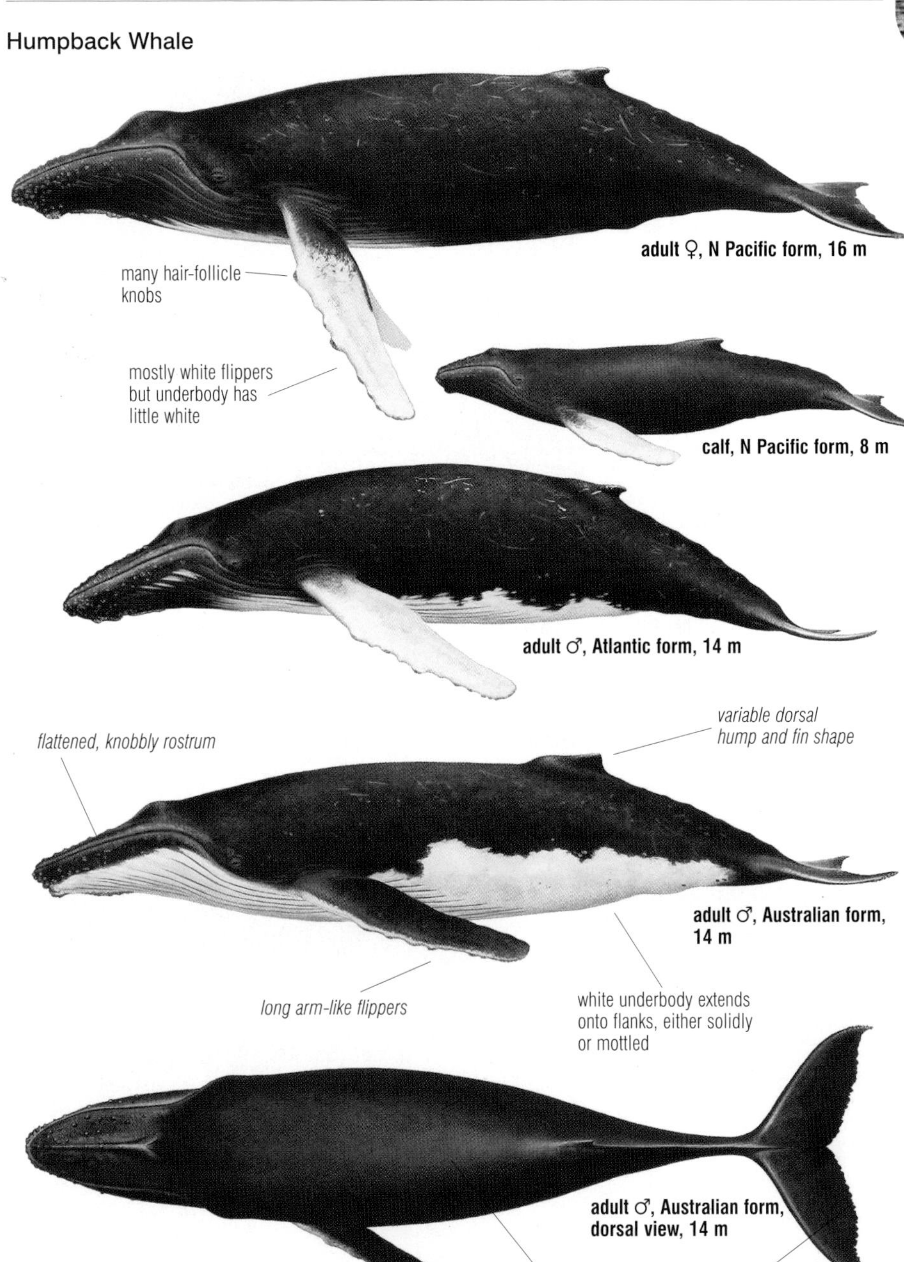

Rostrum and prominent splashguard visible first, with blow (bushy but highly visible), thereafter part of back and dorsal fin appear; in preparing for deep dive, performs steeper arching roll of back, fin and tailstock, culminating in raised tailstock and flukes.

on underbody corresponds to that on underflipper; S Hemisphere stocks generally intermediate or approach whiter N Atlantic animals. S Hemisphere populations named *M. n. lalandii*, with those in Australian and New Zealand waters accorded the name *M. n. novaezelandiae*, but neither proposal appears certainly warranted. Probably little gene-flow between N & S Hemisphere populations.

Spyhopping Humpback Whales.

DISTRIBUTION & POPULATION
Separate populations in N Pacific and N Atlantic and at least 9 subpopulations in Southern Hemisphere. Undertakes seasonal migrations of up to 16,000 km, from colder waters, where they feed in spring/summer, to tropical-water winter breeding grounds, where they mate, calve and usually do not feed, although some, e.g. in Arabian Sea, apparently resident. *Population* Recently estimated at 33,000–35,000 worldwide: 16,000–20,000 in N Hemisphere, chiefly western N Atlantic (Maine to Greenland) and eastern N Pacific (Bering Sea to Mexico), with at least 17,000 in S Hemisphere, of which 2,500 in Southern Ocean.

ECOLOGY
Groups of up to 12–15, sometimes larger in favoured feeding areas, but often just mother and calf. May group on breeding grounds, and ♂ accompanies cow/calf

Breaching Humpback Whale in full leap clear of water, the almost wing-like flippers outstretched.

Note characteristic surfacing profile and different stages of blow.

'pairs' and can be aggressive to other ♂♂ (probably promiscuous, competing for mature ♀♀). Breaching, lobtailing and flipper-slapping important in communication. Gives very long, complex, repetitive vocalizations in courtship. *Breaching* Full leap clear of water to leisurely surge in which less than ½ of body visible. Often lands on back but sometimes emerges dorsal side up and performs belly flop. *Diving* Lasts 3–15 min but sometimes up to 40 min, reaching *c.*150 m. *Diet* Feeds alone or cooperatively,

Humpback Whale preparing for deep dive, with steep arching roll of back and tailstock.

Humpback Whales lunge-feeding.

on small fish and krill, taken in shallow, spiral dives under shoal of food, containing it within a 'bubble net' (up to 45 m wide, engulfed by swimming through it at speed); frequently lunge-feeds in schools of small fish. *Reproduction* Sexually mature at 5–11 yrs (when 11.5–12 m, and reaches max size up to 10 yrs later). Winters in tropical oceans where cows bear single calf, every 2–3 yrs (occasionally successive yrs), in late autumn/early winter. Some ♀♀ may stay on summer feeding grounds. Gestation lasts 11–12 months, and calves associate with their mother for 1–2 yrs. Calving in N Hemisphere peaks Jan–Feb, but also Nov in Hawaii; in S Hemisphere peaks Jul–Aug. Calves weaned at 6–12 months and return to natal area, but may then wander between breeding areas. Mothers and calves remain longest on breeding grounds, with pregnant ♀♀ first to leave. *Lifespan* Up to 50 yrs.

Humpback Whales, mother and calf.

Underwater, a Humpback Whale with its flippers outspread almost appears to have wings.

Breaching Humpbacks often emerge sideways, with a half-turn, and land on their backs. Note individual variation in underbody coloration.

Grey Whale

One of the most familiar Pacific cetaceans, Grey Whale is placed in its own family, Eschrichtiidae, within the baleen whales (suborder Mysticeti). Given its distinctive morphological and ecological characteristics – unlike all other mysticetes it rears its young in warm shallow coastal areas, and is a bottom feeder in the arctic – such classification appears warranted. Although the N Atlantic population has been extinct for over 200 years, the protected eastern N Pacific population has recovered to pre-whaling levels. Grey Whale is especially known for its long seasonal migrations and is a key species of whale-watching trips from Baja California north to the Bering Sea.

Grey Whale

Eschrichtius robustus

N Pacific. Max 15 m.

Priority characters on surfacing

- Finless, medium-sized, mottled grey baleen whale (N Pacific only).
- *Lacks dorsal fin*, but has dorsal hump and series of 'knuckles' from hump to flukes (especially visible after final blow, when arching to dive).
- Robust body with relatively narrow, bowed head.
- *Grey body, marbled and blotched* (scarred) paler, with numerous pale barnacles and small parasitic crustaceans encrusted. Smaller calf more uniform and darker.
- *Triangular-shaped, blunt snout, long slightly arched mouthline*, whitish/yellowish baleen and indistinct longitudinal blowholes on top of head may be visible in very close views.
- Proportionately large tail flukes with convex, ragged trailing edge (notched in centre with pointed tips).
- Flippers small and paddle-shaped.

Typical behaviour at surface

- *Low heart- or V-shaped blow* (normally 3–4 m high, with spray falling inwards), 3–6× at 15–30-sec intervals. Only part of head and upper forebody visible when blowing.
- Usually makes short/shallow dives. *Large flukes thrown high into air on diving deeper*. Can be demonstrative, breaching and spyhopping.
- Occasionally inquisitive and 'friendly', and may approach boats.

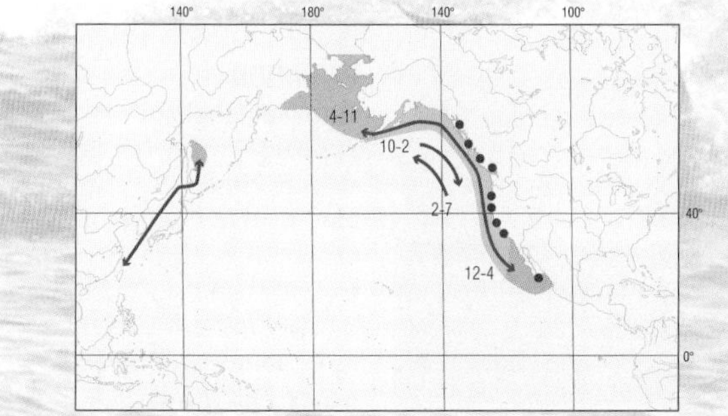

Grey Whale feeds mainly on the ocean floor, and may leave muddy trails.

SIMILAR SPECIES

Usually unmistakable. ***Humpback*** (which has similar blow) is blackish, not grey, and usually has obvious dorsal fin (although sometimes absent), different shape, with long flippers and tubercles on head, and different-coloured/shaped flukes. ***Sperm Whale*** which has superficially similar dorsal 'bump' is more uniform, lacking Grey's mottled appearance, and has different shape, blow and dive sequences. From ***North Pacific Right*** and ***Bowhead Whales*** by pale grey and mottled body coloration, and very different structure.

Grey Whale

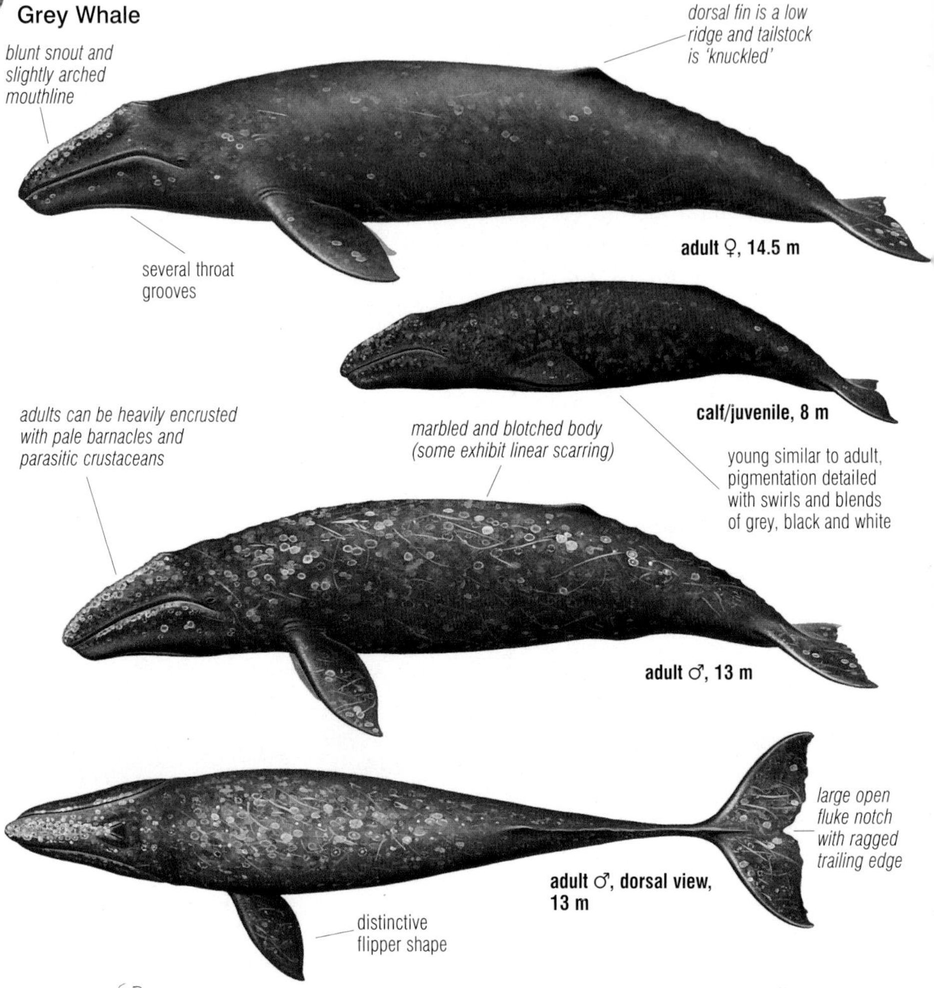

blunt snout and slightly arched mouthline

dorsal fin is a low ridge and tailstock is 'knuckled'

several throat grooves

adult ♀, 14.5 m

calf/juvenile, 8 m

young similar to adult, pigmentation detailed with swirls and blends of grey, black and white

adults can be heavily encrusted with pale barnacles and parasitic crustaceans

marbled and blotched body (some exhibit linear scarring)

adult ♂, 13 m

large open fluke notch with ragged trailing edge

adult ♂, dorsal view, 13 m

distinctive flipper shape

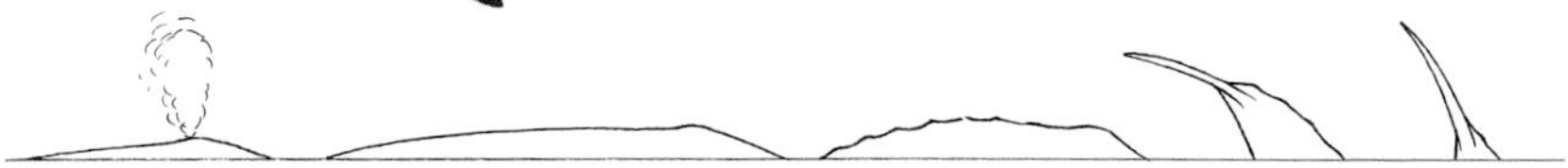

Only part of head and upper forebody visible when blowing; note sloping head; in preparing for deep dive, arches rear body and hump, and 'knuckles' emerge, before fluking.

In breaching, usually lands on back or side.

VARIATION

Age/sex Perhaps estimable by overall size (♀ slightly larger). Ad slate-blue marbled white or yellowish, with numerous barnacles and small parasitic crustaceans; calf darker and more uniform. **Physical notes** Full grown 12–15 m and 15–35 tons; newborn

4.6–5 m and *c.*½ ton. **Taxonomy** Monotypic, but E & W Pacific populations genetically distinct with virtually no gene-flow.

Grey Whales can be inquisitive; note pale baleen and skin mottled by barnacles and crustaceans.

DISTRIBUTION & POPULATION
Seasonal round-trip migrations of up to 20,000 km, feeding in Sea of Okhotsk, and off Alaska and in Bering and W Beaufort Seas, and giving birth in warmer waters. Generally Apr–Nov on feeding grounds, migrates south Oct–Feb, Dec–Apr on breeding grounds and Feb–Jul migrates north. ♀♀ (especially if pregnant) generally migrate earlier than ♂♂, and those with calves remain longer in breeding areas. *Population* Bulk in eastern N Pacific, estimated at *c.*21,000 (calving grounds chiefly off Baja California and Mexico). Remnant population in western N Pacific (calving grounds probably off S China) may number fewer than 100. N Atlantic population extinct by early-18th century.

Courting Grey Whales: note pale-mottled tail flukes with convex, ragged trailing edge.

ECOLOGY
Typical group 1–3, but larger in some feeding areas (up to 400) or on migration (16), and exceptionally 1,000 at a favoured breeding site. Highly active: spyhops, lobtails and breaches. Also quite frequently found in surf of very shallow water. *Breaching* Usually 2–3× in a row (but up to 40×); almost ¾ of body vertically erect and usually plunges sideways with enormous splash. *Diving* Reaches 170 m, but prefers 50–60 m-deep water; up to *c.*25 min, but mostly 3–10 min. *Diet* Principally benthic amphipods and similar organisms (by rolling on side, swimming slowly sucking up sediment, filtering it for food), but also midwater prey. *Reproduction* Sexually mature at 5–12 yrs when *c.*11–12 m, but continues to grow until *c.*40 yrs. Mates chiefly in warm waters, with groups consisting of a single ♀ attended by several ♂♂ observed in this period (late Nov–Dec). Both sexes may copulate with several partners. Cows give birth to a single calf every 2–3 yrs, in late Dec–early Mar (peaking Jan–Feb), following 11–13-month gestation, and calves are weaned at 7–8 months, remaining with mother for perhaps another 1–2 months. *Lifespan* 50+ yrs.

Only part of head and upper forebody are visible when blowing.

Right whales

In recent years, 2 species, Northern and Southern Right Whales, have been recognised, variably in the genera *Balaena* and *Eubalaena*, but, at least genetically, a third appears to be involved, as the N Pacific form (usually considered a subspecies of Northern Right Whale) is closer to Southern Right Whale than to the nominate form of Northern Right Whale, which in turn appears to be the most distinct of the 3 forms. Genetically they are distinctive and surely following separate evolutionary trajectories, but they seem to differ little morphologically. Also in this group is Bowhead Whale, which is placed in a separate genus, *Balaena*, and is essentially high arctic in distribution. All are baleen whales (suborder Mysticeti) of the family Balaenidae, characterised by their large, mostly dark rotund bodies, large heads with strongly arched mouthlines, in being finless with no central rostrum ridge, and broad spatulate flippers and broad flukes. N Hemisphere right whales are very close to extinction, despite decades of protection, but Southern Right Whale is steadily recovering from man's exploitation. Generally speaking, observers should find the group unmistakable, but depending on sea state and viewing conditions, closer views may be required to evaluate differences from other species, especially Humpback and Grey Whales. The 3 right whales are well separated geographically, whilst Bowhead Whale is wholly distinctive, generally larger, mostly uniformly darker and lacks right whales' pale callosities on head. All are usually readily separated from other large whales, principally by the lack of dorsal fin, V-shaped blow and overall shape and coloration.

A breaching Southern Right Whale crashes sideways to the surface; note extensive white below (highly variable).

Two fluking North Atlantic Right Whales; a third animal is surfacing between them, with its broad V-shaped blow visible.

Right Whales and Bowhead Whale

Generally identical to North Atlantic Right Whale but well separated geographically.

North Pacific Right Whale, p. 36, max 18.5 m

North Atlantic Right Whale, p. 36, max 18.3 m

Like other right whales has enormous rotund body, no dorsal fin or hump, is generally dark and large head has distinctive pale callosities, a strongly arched mouthline and narrow rostrum; notched and pointed flukes (with concave trailing edge) may be raised in diving, and has conspicuous surfacing behaviour.

Generally identical to the other right whales but averages smaller and is well separated geographically. (All forms of right whales show extensive individual variation in amount of white on undersides.)

Southern Right Whale, p. 36, max 17 m

Bowhead Whale, p. 40, max 19.8 m

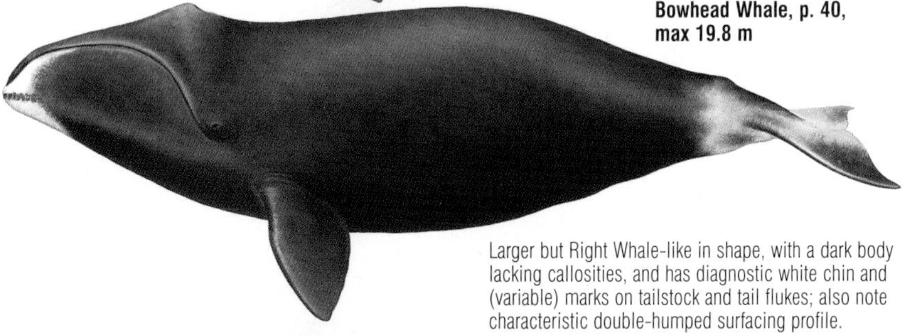

Larger but Right Whale-like in shape, with a dark body lacking callosities, and has diagnostic white chin and (variable) marks on tailstock and tail flukes; also note characteristic double-humped surfacing profile.

Surfacing North Atlantic Right Whale: head held high with sloping profile, and showing white callosities.

DISTINCTIVE POPULATIONS

Three geographically and genetically well-separated forms.

North Atlantic Right Whale *E. glacialis* N Atlantic (described in box).

North Pacific Right Whale *E. japonica* N Pacific: no external differences between this and previous form; probably averages a trifle larger than N Atlantic form.

North Atlantic Right Whale: huge, round head with narrow rostrum and strongly arched mouthline covered in callosities.

Southern Right Whale *E. australis* S Hemisphere: averages smaller than previous 2 forms and perhaps has slightly shorter baleen, as well as minor cranial differences and slightly different callosities (some have more on lower jaw and fewer on head).

SIMILAR SPECIES

All right whales are virtually unmistakable. Lack of dorsal fin should readily eliminate all other large whales except Bowhead. Limited risk of confusion, in poor views, with ***Humpback***, although latter has dorsal hump/fin, very long flippers, different body and head shape, different shape and pattern to tail flukes, and completely different surfacing/blowing technique. N Atlantic/Pacific Right Whales resemble only

North Atlantic Right Whale

Eubalaena glacialis

N Atlantic. Max 18.3 m.

North Pacific Right Whale

Eubalaena japonica

N Pacific. Max 18.5 m.

Southern Right Whale

Eubalaena australis

Southern Ocean. Max 17 m.

Priority characters on surfacing

- Large, *mostly dark, finless baleen whale* with enormous rotund body. Inquisitive and approachable behaviour eases identification.
- No central rostrum ridge, and splashguard and double-blowholes are relatively low.
- *Callosities form distinctive white patches on huge, round head.*
- *Flukes broad* with smooth, concave trailing edge, distinct central notch and pointed tips.
- *Distinctive head shape* with strongly arched mouthline, broad all-dark spatulate flippers and relatively short, narrow tailstock visible in close views.
- Black or dark brown, variably mottled grey, brown or blue, and some have irregular white blotches on belly.

Typical behaviour at surface

- *Rather obvious at surface*: broad back and, in particular, huge head quite exposed.
- *Emits broad V-shaped blows up to 5 m high* (jets often asymmetric in height), which sometimes appear as a single jet, especially if seen from side or in wind.
- Typically remains 1–3 min at surface, where blows 4–6× in preparing to dive; sinks head first, the body shortly afterwards and lastly the *tail flukes, which are often raised quite high and submerged at an angle*.
- Slow deliberate swimmer (often accelerating in short bursts); frequently inquisitive and approachable, and surprisingly demonstrative.

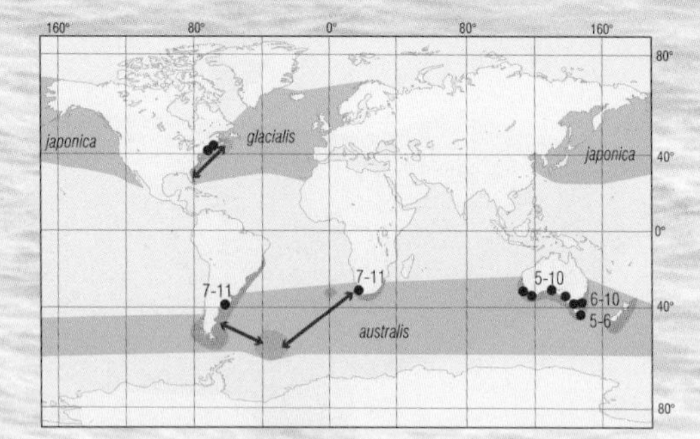

Southern Right Whale swimming in heavy seas; note well exposed forebody, sloping head covered in callosities and arched mouthline.

North Atlantic Right Whale, showing individually unique pattern of callosities.

Bowhead Whale, including similar V-shaped blow and well-exposed tail flukes on diving, but rarely overlap, and lack callosities on head, instead having extensive white on chin and often on tailstock and flukes, and blowholes situated on quite pronounced hump. Same true of ***Grey*** (in relation to N Pacific Right Whale), which is highly distinctive in structure, and has dorsal humps, very different coloration and surfacing/ blowing techniques.

VARIATION

Age/sex ♂ smaller (by *c.*1.5 m) and usually has more callosities. Calf, paler and greyer (some even born whitish), and lacks or has only indistinct callosities. Age development poorly known. **Physical notes** Max (*glacialis* and *japonica*) 15–17.1 m (♂) and 17.8–18.5 m (♀), or *australis* 11–17 m; 20–30 tons (all forms). Newborn (all forms) 4.5–6 m and *c.*1 ton. **Other data** Degree of mottling, scars, belly-patches and callosities on head of ads may individually identify an animal. Incidence of piebald individuals highest in S Atlantic (*australis*). **Taxonomy** Three genetically distinct and geographically allopatric species which are still often treated as 1 species. Genetic isolation of N and S Hemisphere populations may be also due to seasonal reproductive barrier (breeding cycle *c.*6 months out of phase), but gene-flow between subpopulations of *australis* also perhaps very low. DNA reveals that right whales in N & S Pacific are more closely related to each other than either is to N Atlantic species.

Southern Right Whale showing well-developed callosities.

DISTRIBUTION & POPULATION

North Atlantic Right Whale Principally from Nova Scotia (Canada) south to SE USA, where calves off Florida and Georgia in winter; apparently very few in NE Atlantic (mainly off Canaries and Iberia). Migratory or partially so, but still largely unknown where ♂♂ and non-calving ♀♀ concentrate in winter, whilst in summer/autumn both sexes congregate in Bay of Fundy; migrates in autumn and spring (during latter, aggregations occur mainly in Great South Channel, east of Cape Cod, and in Massachusetts Bay). *Population c.*300–400. **North Pacific Right Whale** N Pacific, from Sea of Okhotsk to Bering Sea and Gulf of Alaska (USA). May birth off Japan, but eastern population very poorly known. Occasionally recorded south to Baja California (Mexico). *Population c.*100, making it the most endangered great whale. **Southern Right Whale** Throughout Southern Ocean, chiefly at 20°S–60°S, mating and calving in winter in near-shore waters of Chile,

North Pacific Right Whale is on the verge of extinction: note head markings formed by numerous callosities.

Argentina, Brazil, S Africa, S Australia, W New Zealand and some S Hemisphere islands, migrating to Antarctic waters in summer, when generally south of 40°S and most in mid Southern Ocean, but some at edge of pack-ice, and various populations tend to cluster. Some exhibit greater degrees of residency at lower latitudes than formerly. *Population* *c.*7,000 in recent yrs and currently increasing.

ECOLOGY

Most data for Southern Right Whale. Groups of up to 12 (usually 2–3),

Southern Right Whale emits a broad V-shaped blow.

but loose associations of up to 100 at favoured feeding grounds. Inquisitive and often approachable, interacting peaceably with smaller cetaceans and pinnipeds. Group members often surface in turn rather than simultaneously. Significance of playful and even acrobatic actions, e.g. breaching, flipper-slapping, lobtailing and 'headstands',

Southern Right Whale, mother and calf.

not fully known but of high social significance. On breeding grounds bellows and moans. In courtship, surface activities involve several ♂♂ attempting to mate with 1 or more ♀♀ (may continue for 1 hr or more). *Breaching* Up to c.10× in series, rising almost vertically, then turning and descending backwards when *c.*⅔ of body out of water, and hits surface with strongly arched back. *Diving* Most dives last 10–20 min, but recorded underwater up to 50 min and to 184 m. *Diet* Mostly swims through or skims concentrated prey: chiefly plankton and some tiny crustaceans. *Reproduction* Sexually mature at 9–10 yrs old when *c.*15 m. Sperm competition important component of system (♀ can copulate with several ♂♂, even simultaneously). Bulls have largest recorded testes in animal kingdom, each pair weighing *c.*1 ton. ♀♀ calve every 2–4 yrs (3–5 yrs in northern forms), usually close inshore and in winter (May–Aug in southern form, Dec–Mar in northern forms). Weaned at 12 months (8–12 months in N Atlantic) and subsequently return to natal area. Gestation *c.*12–13 months in N Atlantic. On winter grounds, calves stay with ♀♀, isolated from ♂♂ in 'nursery', with well-developed ♀/calf bond. *Lifespan* May exceed 70 yrs.

Southern Right Whales fluking during social interaction. The flukes appear to differ due to the different angles and degree of submergence.

Forebody/head quite exposed at surface; sometimes, briefly more of rear back emerges at shallow angle; in smooth roll, sinks head first, the body shortly afterwards and, lastly, the tail flukes, which are raised at varying angles.

Right Whales

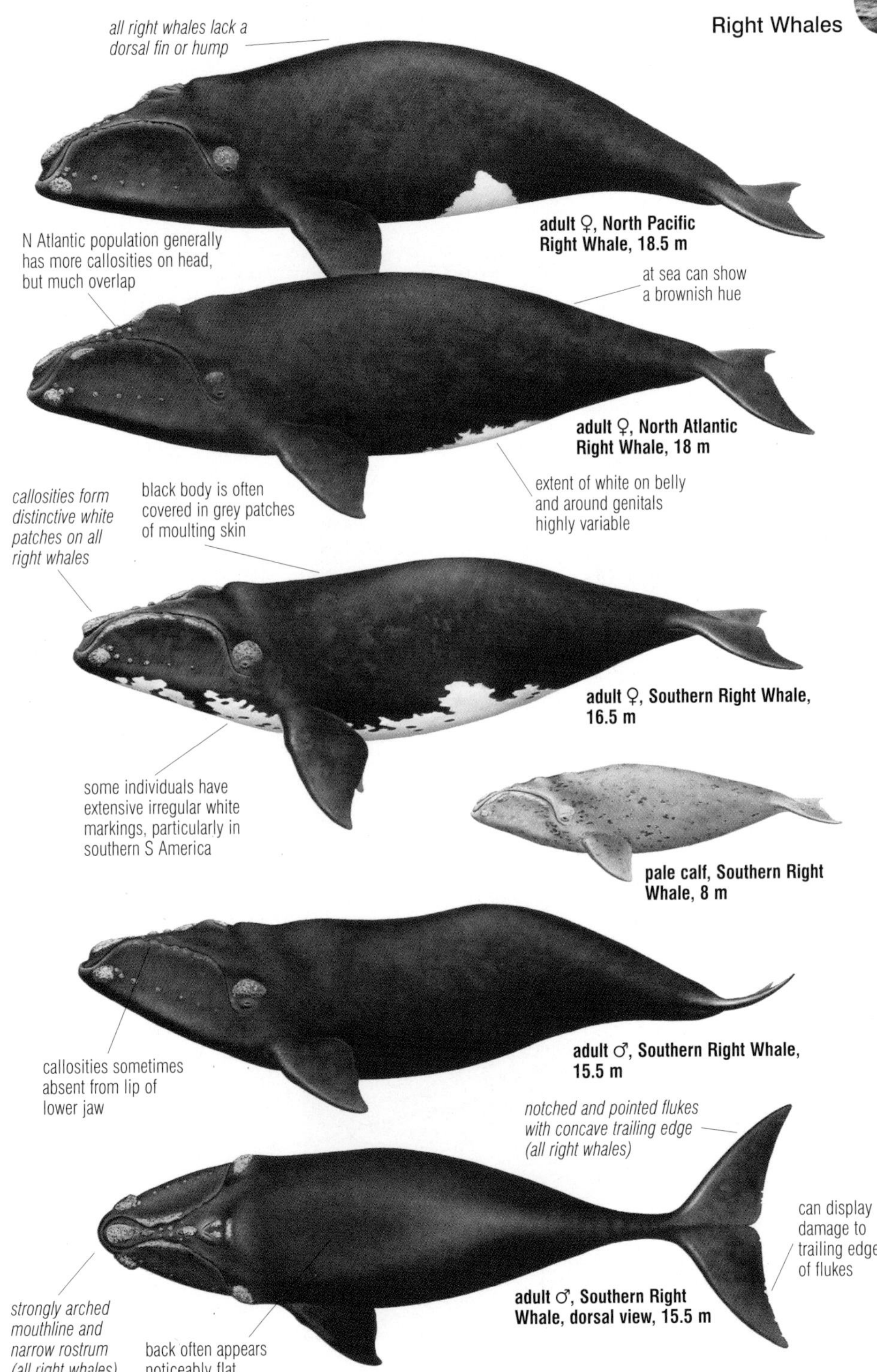

Bowhead Whale

Balaena mysticetus

High arctic. Max 19.8 m.

Priority characters on surfacing

- *Right whale-like*, with very large, dark body and diagnostic white markings, and characteristic surfacing profile.
- In comparison to northern right whales, less body visible above surface, but hump at front of head, rounded back and depression between them creates *double-humped* effect.
- *No dorsal fin* or hump, or central rostrum ridge, and also lacks pale callosities on head.
- *Diagnostic white chin and variable whitish/greyish area on tailstock and centre of tail flukes*. Former usually below surface but visible in close views and clear water, whilst pale tailstock/ flukes sometimes seen when lifted for dive.
- *Distinctive head size/shape* with strongly arched mouthline normally unseen below surface.

Typical behaviour at surface

- *Emits high, broad V-shaped blows of up to 7 m*, which may appear as a single jet, especially if seen from side or in wind (jets often asymmetric in height).
- Usually remains 1–3 min at surface, where blows 4–6× in preparing to dive, head first, with body still visible when starting smooth roll, and tail flukes last to disappear, usually raised vertically and submerging straight down, but often falling to right.
- Slow deliberate swimmer, but can be quite active at surface and often approachable. Often surfaces near same spot.

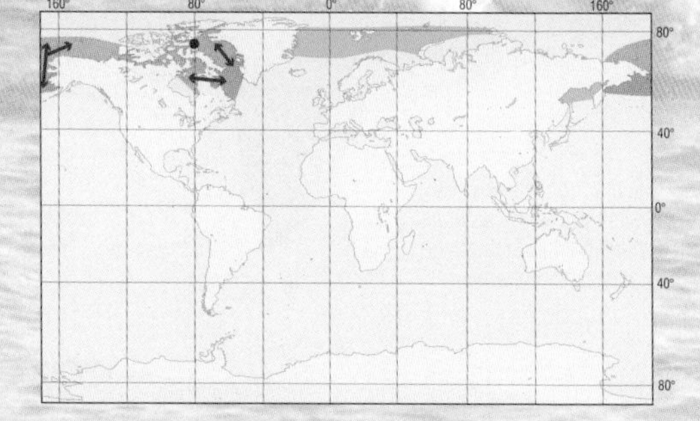

SIMILAR SPECIES

In range resembles only ***northern right whales***, but lacks callosities on head, and has distinctive white patch on chin and often on tailstock/ flukes, and different profile at surface. Their ranges barely overlap. Only in poor/brief views, might be confused with ***Humpback***, but latter has dorsal fin, different body and head shape, and different shape and, especially, pattern to tail flukes, as well as different surfacing/blowing technique. Lack of obvious dorsal fin, among many other characters, should readily eliminate all other large whales that may penetrate high-arctic latitudes.

Fluking Bowhead Whale showing variable whitish area on tailstock and centre of flukes.

On surfacing, note profile and characteristic elephant-like impression.

VARIATION

Age/sex ♀ averages larger than ♂ but not distinguishable at sea. Blowhole hump less developed in young, especially juvs, making double-humped surface shape less obvious or lacking altogether. Calf slimmer, paler and greyer, and lacks or has only indistinct whitish chin and often no white on tailstock/flukes. **Physical notes** 14–18 m (perhaps to 19.8 m) and 60–100 tons.

Bowhead Whale

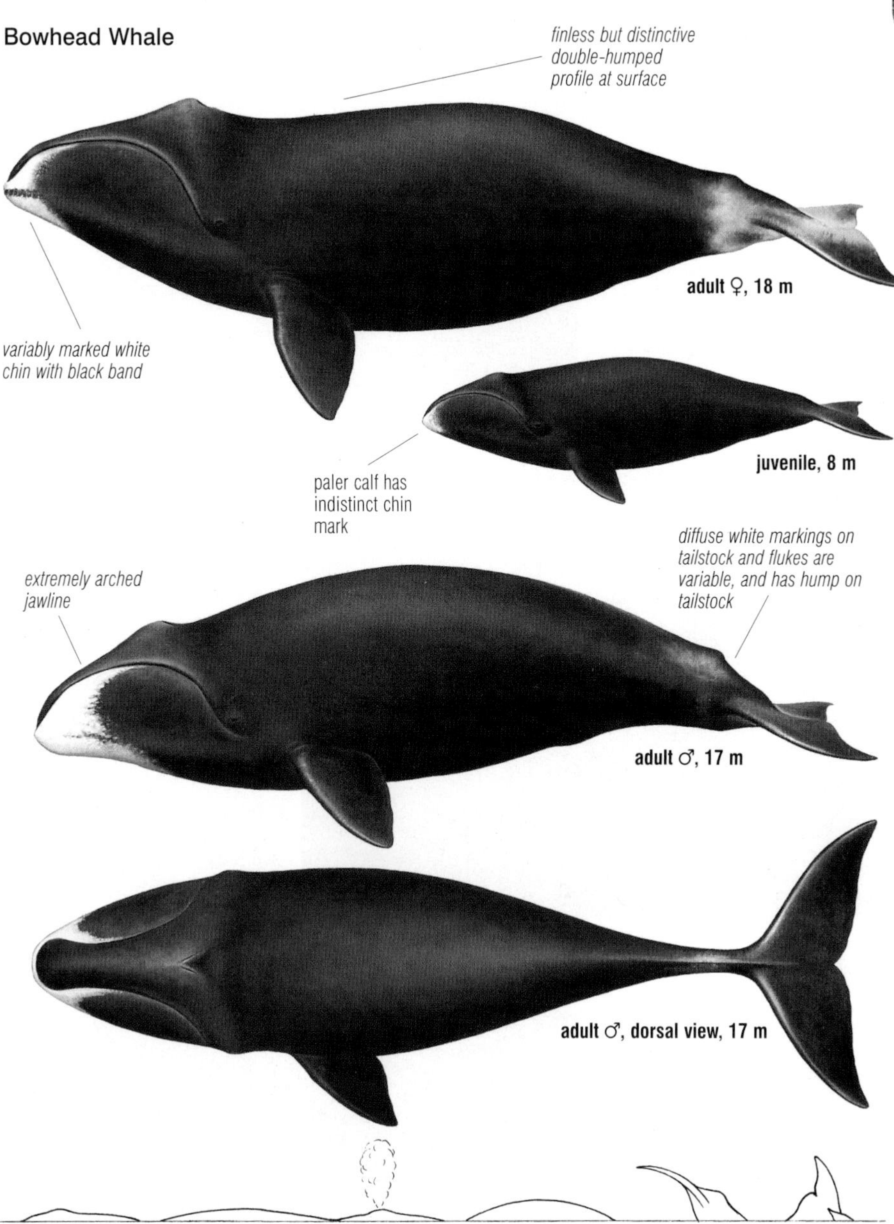

Double-humped appearance due to depression between head and back; in preparing to dive, sinks head first, with smooth roll, and tail flukes disappear last and are often raised at varying angles.

Newborn 4–5.2 m and *c.*1 ton.

DISTRIBUTION & POPULATION Circumpolar in arctic seas, closely associated with pack-ice and its seasonal movements. Range and general behaviour in winter very poorly known, but some populations perhaps resident. Recently, singles and small groups, probably from Davis Strait, seen off W Greenland. *Population* Overall *c.*10,000. Most (*c.*8,200) in Bering-Chukchi-Beaufort Seas, with other discrete populations, all numbering <350, in Sea of Okhotsk (Russia), Davis Strait/Baffin Bay, Hudson Bay (Canada) and Barents Sea.

Apparent social interaction. Note variably marked white chin with black band.

ECOLOGY

Groups of up to 14 (usually up to 6), but occasional loose associations of 60 at favoured feeding grounds. Mother/calf bond very strong. During summer feeding, segregates by age and sex, with mothers and calves migrating later in spring. Often associates with Belugas and Narwhals, and curious of objects in water. Breaching, flipper-slapping and lobtailing common, mostly in spring. *Breaching* In series, *c.*⅔ of body rises almost vertically from water, crashing on side. *Diving* Mostly less than 20 min, but can stay underwater up to 40 min and reach 200 m; can swim below ice and make breathing holes by breaking ice thicker than 1 m. *Diet* Catholic but prefers copepods, euphausiids and amphipods, taken by swimming or skimming through concentrated prey, from surface to seabed. *Reproduction* Sexually mature when 12–14 m long, at 12–15 yrs. Mating system little known, probably involving sperm competition (♀ can copulate with several ♂♂, which are highly vocal in this period), and presumably occurs in Jan–Feb. ♀♀ give birth to single calf every 3–4 yrs. Calves born during northern spring migration (Apr–Jun), after 12–14 months gestation and probably weaned at 9–12 months. *Lifespan* Perhaps exceeds 100 yrs.

Bowhead Whale: note double-humped appearance above the surface and, below it, the diagnostic white chin markings

Bowhead Whale surrounded by Belugas.

Pygmy Right Whale

The smallest baleen whale (suborder Mysticeti), it has a unique shape somewhat closer to rorquals and Grey Whale than to right whales, and is sufficiently genetically distinct to be placed in its own family, the Neobalaenidae. Apparently circumpolar in S Hemisphere, although seems scarce and to have a somewhat fragmented range, making it the least known of all the baleen whales and cetaceans in general. Very few people have seen this whale.

Pygmy Right Whale

Caperea marginata

S Hemisphere. Max 6.5 m.

Priority characters on surfacing

- Poorly known, the *smallest baleen whale*, with characteristic shape and surfacing behaviour.
- Proportionately rather large head and elongated rear body.
- *Sickle-shaped dorsal fin* proportionately low but pronounced.
- Dark grey or blue-grey dorsally and on sides; grey/white below.
- Variable pale chevrons behind head and small *narrow flippers (uniform above, lacking some Minkes' variable pale bands)*, but often difficult to observe.
- Tapered rostrum with small ridge, *arched mouthline and contrasting pale baleen plates* or other whiter elements also sometimes visible at very close range.

Typical behaviour at surface

- Blow fairly conspicuous, very small and oval in shape (similar to Antarctic Minke).
- Rarely more than a few sec at surface, and usually only snout breaks surface when swimming leisurely, at which times dorsal fin and back largely remain unseen (if latter exposed only very briefly and after blowhole disappears); flukes never raised clear of water.
- Slow swimmer, but sometimes more freely, in slow undulating movements, and capable of faster speeds when provoked.
- Rarely in large groups but sometimes associates with other cetaceans.

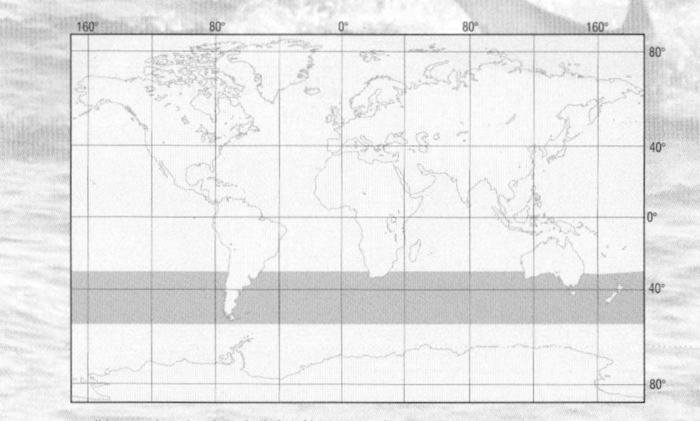

possible range based on latitude limits of known records

SIMILAR SPECIES

Considerably stockier than other, and the smallest of all, baleen whales. ***Antarctic*** and, mainly, ***Dwarf Minke Whales*** are main confusion risks, but Pygmy Right Whale has strongly arched jawline and lacks white in flippers (features which require confirmation for reliable separation). Distinctly smaller than ***Southern Right Whale*** and though shares arched mouthline, easily distinguished by more streamlined body, flatter rostrum with ridge, lack of callosities on head, paler and more blue-grey body, small sickle-shaped dorsal fin and smaller/narrower flippers.

VARIATION

Age/sex Perhaps estimable on size. Dorsal and sides become darker, usually with heavily pock-marked cookie-cutter shark bites on skin, and lower jaw appears more exaggerated with age. Calf proportionately slimmer with smaller head and is paler. **Physical notes** 5.5–6.5 m and 2.8–3.5 tons, and ♀ slightly larger than ♂. Newborn estimated at 1.6–2.2 m.

Pygmy Right Whale

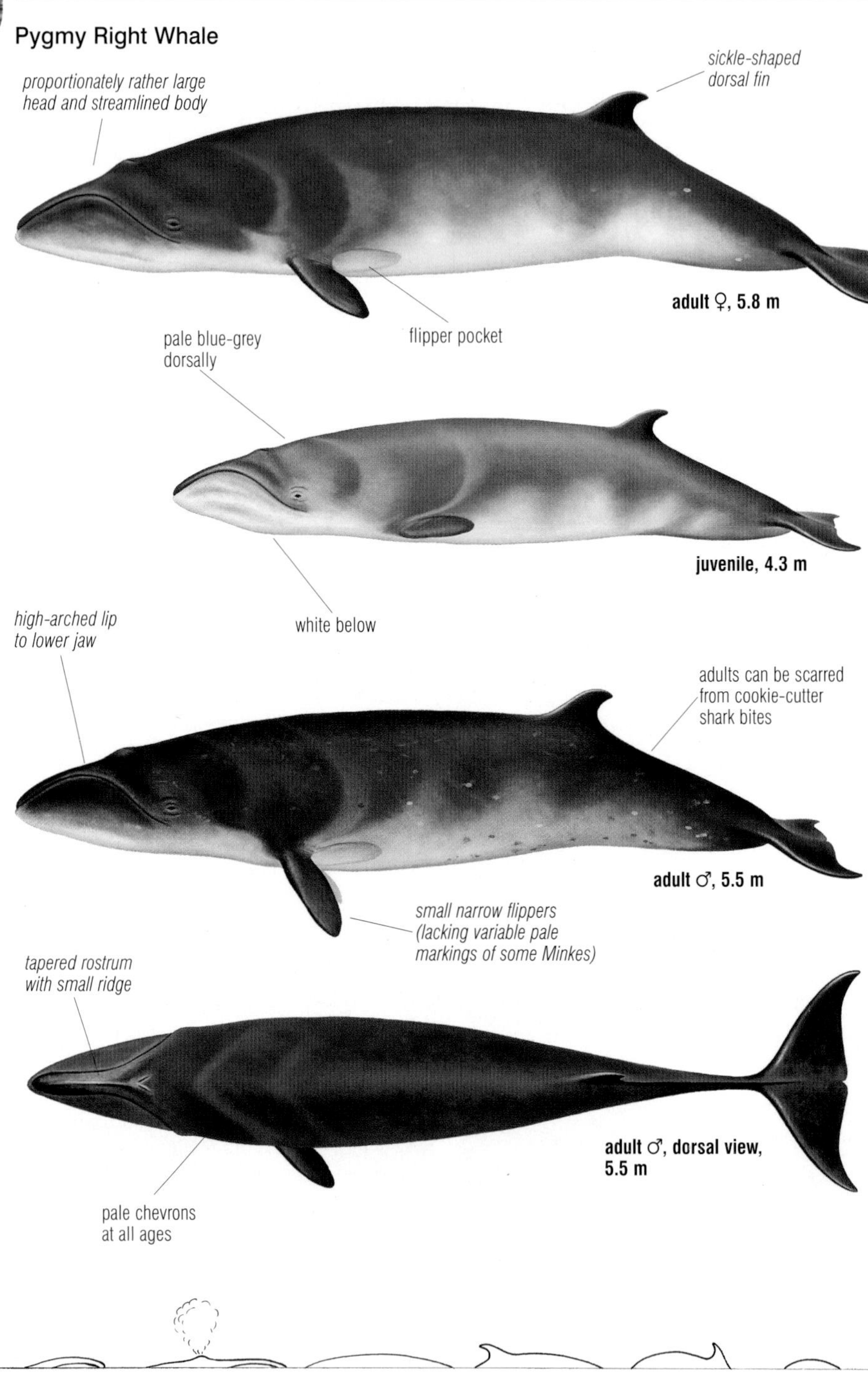

Only briefly surfaces, when usually only head appears; fairly conspicuous oval blow; when rolling to dive, dorsal fin may emerge very briefly, but flukes never raised clear.

DISTRIBUTION & POPULATION

The least-studied baleen whale in S Hemisphere with poorly known, perhaps rather fragmented, range; at least partially circumpolar. All records from 31°S to 55°S in waters of 5–20°C, with strandings in Tierra del Fuego, S Africa, S & W Australia and both main islands of New Zealand. At-sea records from Falklands, Crozet, S Atlantic and south of Australia. Perhaps never penetrates south of Antarctic Convergence. Some evidence that young visit inshore waters in spring/summer, but other populations perhaps resident (e.g. off Tasmania). *Population* Poorly known but probably not rare.

Pygmy Right Whale has a characteristic tapered rostrum with small ridge, and arched mouthline.

Back usually surfaces very briefly and after blow has disappeared; note tapered rostrum with small ridge and arched mouthline and pale chevrons behind head.

ECOLOGY

Groups of up to 10 but most sightings involve singles or pairs, though 30–80 reported. Observed with dolphins, Minke and pilot whales, and once a Sei Whale. *Breaching* Does not breach or lobtail, being rather undemonstrative. *Diving* Spends 40 sec to 4 min underwater, and usually surfaces only briefly. *Diet* Copepods, euphausiids and other tiny crustaceans. *Reproduction* Poorly known, with season possibly year-round. Gestation occupies *c.*12 months. *Lifespan* Unknown.

Pygmy Right Whale has a sickle-shaped dorsal fin which may show after blowhole disappears.

Blow fairly conspicuous, very small and oval; note arched mouthline.

Rorquals with streamlined bodies

These baleen whales are rorquals (Balaenopteridae) of, of which 6–8, possibly even 11 species, are recognised, depending on taxonomy. All except the Humpback are in the genus *Balaenoptera*. They exhibit enormous variation in size, from the smallest, minke whales, to the largest of all, the blue whales. A reasonably conservative systematic approach has been adopted, as clear-cut morphological or other differences, or evidence of reproductive isolation is often lacking in support of recent molecular findings. Most species are migratory or partially so, with some making very long migrations between warm-water breeding grounds and colder/polar waters where they feed voraciously, preparing for their lower-latitude fasts. Unfortunately, the larger species, especially blue whales, were seriously depleted by whaling; indeed some populations perhaps may never recover such was the scale of the slaughter.

External differences are undoubtedly more useful for species identification than dive sequences because the latter vary with circumstances. For instance, it is possible to reach a different impression or only see certain features, even of the same animal over a short period, and it also depends if an animal is travelling, floating or logging at the surface, or if it dives to feed after being near the surface for some time. Nevertheless, such features can provide valuable support, especially with experience. It is very important to know the distinctive and diagnostic features, and be able to assess them on the basis of only brief views of the dorsal fin and part of the back. As a rule, it is best to use a combination of characters rather than just one or two. Blue and Fin are huge or very large and long-bodied, Sei and Bryde's medium-sized (though still large), whilst minkes are noticeably smaller, although there is some overlap. A key field character is the dorsal fin, which in all species is about two-thirds of the way towards the tail (the shape varies individually, at least in some species), and its relative size tends to increase with diminishing overall length, whilst the larger the whale, the further it is positioned on the back. Thus, the fin emerges at a slightly different time after the rostrum

Breaching offshore Bryde's Whale (Brazil): the taxonomy of this complex is one of the most intriguing and complicated of all cetaceans. The photos below illustrate recent developments in our understanding of the variation shown by these taxa, but there is still much to be learned.

Bryde's Whale (off Bali, Indonesia) showing clear lateral rostrum ridges; this animal has a whitish right lower jaw (as in Fin Whale), hinting at the possibility of a regionally distinct form.

Pygmy Bryde's Whale (off Komodo, Indonesia): note white lower jaw, pale chevron on right side (as Fin Whale) and lack of lateral rostrum ridges; overall size was observed to be small (9–10 m) and identification was confirmed by genetics.

Rorquals with streamlined bodies

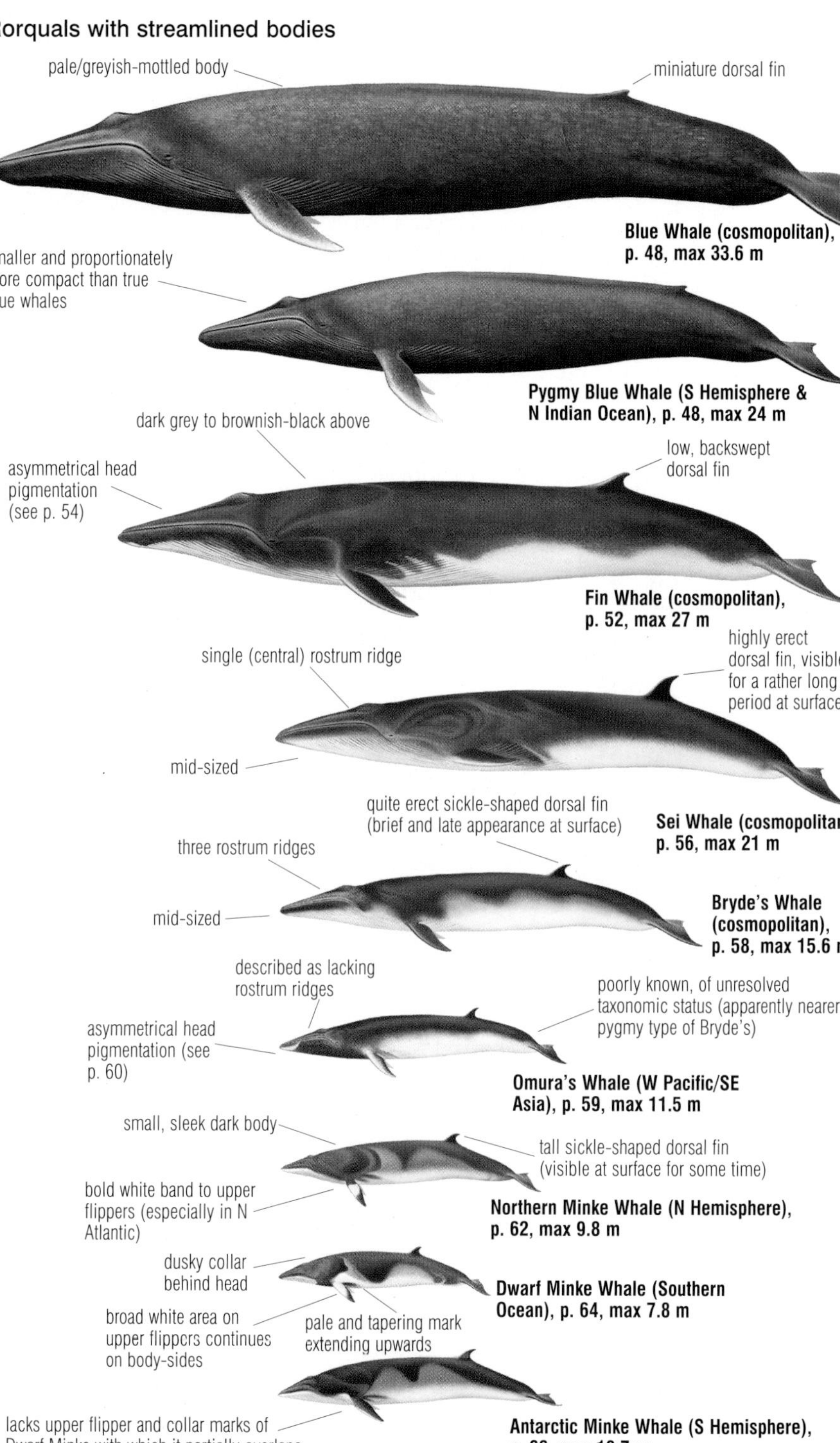

and blow between species. Fin height can sometimes be compared with the extent of exposed body above the surface. Blow height, shape and sequence (i.e. the number and intervals between blows) differ between species, but are variable, often difficult to evaluate and should not be regarded as primary identification features – height often decreases the longer a whale is at the surface, and may be affected by wind and waves. The combination of overall pattern (dive sequence) when a whale surfaces to breathe, and prepares to dive, when the body rolls, and fluking also differ. Other characters, e.g. head shape, rostrum ridges and splashguard/blowholes, as well as coloration or specific patterns, may also be visible and should take priority. Perceived colour often varies; pale grey animals can appear almost black in certain conditions.

Nominate Blue Whale feeding on krill; note the extended ventral pleats.

The tall columnar blow of a nominate Blue Whale.

Blue Whale

Balaenoptera musculus

Cosmopolitan. Max 24/33.6 m.

Priority characters on surfacing

- Gigantic but graceful, with huge head, heavy mid section and massive elongated rear body, though often very little visible above surface.
- *Diagnostic miniature dorsal fin* set well back on body, broad, very long tailstock and deeply keeled flukes, although all only briefly appear above surface, if at all.
- *Massive shoulder and splashguard* may appear prominent on surfacing, with splashguard almost as separate rounded hump in profile.
- *Pale/greyish-mottled coloration* (some bluer and darker).
- Head shape differs from other rorquals, being up to ¼ of total body length and very broad, with U-shaped rostrum from above.

Typical behaviour at surface

- *Blows tall and columnar* (dense and upright), reaching 9–12 m, every 10–20 sec, over 2–6 min before diving.
- Settles quietly into water without exposing rear body, tailstock or flukes. Typically, on sunny days body below surface appears as turquoise silhouette.
- Breaks surface with rostrum/ splashguard and shoulders, or with smooth mid-body

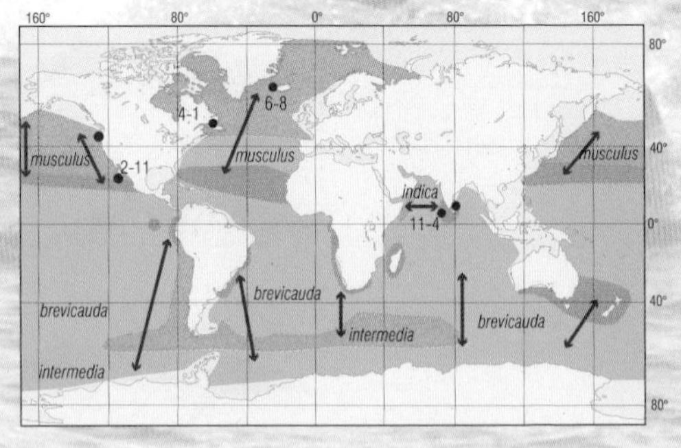

DISTINCTIVE POPULATIONS

Pygmy Blue Whale *B. m. indica/brevicauda* distinctly smaller, probably 15–20 m at maturity (some perhaps reach 24 m, but probably exceptional) and generally more compact, especially compared to true Blue

rolls. Splashguard/shoulders sometimes still visible when dorsal fin breaks surface, although latter more often seen after final blow and in preparation for deep dives.
- In deep dives, almost entire body sinks and dorsal fin briefly emerges, with strongly arched tailstock slightly above surface. Fluking usually low (frequent in some areas), fin occasionally seen.
- Characteristically, in evasive manoeuvre, accelerates with up to 50–60% of forebody visible, pushing a mass of water in front and to sides of head.

Mother and calf Blue Whale (nominate). Note huge head, mid section and elongated rear body.

Whale *B. m. musculus* of N Hemisphere, and *B. m. intermedia* of S Hemisphere. Apart from appearing 'blue' below surface, proportionately they seem quite rotund in middle ⅓ and even somewhat right whale-like. Pygmy Blue also typically has a proportionately shorter rostrum and very short and slender tailstock. Tip of rostrum also differs, being more rounded than true Blue Whales which have a longer, more curved rostrum with a more pointed tip. Small nub-like dorsal fin positioned on final ⅓ to ¼ of back, and *c.*3 m forward of flukes, highlighting how much shorter it is compared to true Blue Whales. Fluke width *c.*¼ of total body length and flippers proportionately long. Compared to true Blue Whales, in some areas less mottled and more uniform grey-blue. Pygmy Blue Whales are most frequently encountered in subantarctic waters of Indian and SW Pacific Oceans, and north in the Humboldt Current, but perhaps also to a limited degree in S Atlantic.

Blue Whale (nominate) flukes regularly in some areas, and usually rather low.

Nominate Blue Whale lunge-feeding; this species preys almost exclusively on krill.

SIMILAR SPECIES

Compare with ***Fin***, but Blue's blow usually denser and taller, and dorsal fin lower and less falcate (rarely visible). Arching on rolls less obvious and frequent than Fin and, unlike latter, sometimes slightly raises flukes prior to deep dives. More massive and can appear extremely broad and bulky compared to Fin; also paler and more mottled (blue to pale grey and mottled, rather than dark and sleek in Fin, with some overlap principally due to light conditions). In good views Fin's head is clearly narrower, and diagnostic white patch on right-hand side may be seen. Contrary to some literature, both may show an almost identical turquoise silhouette below surface. Much smaller ***Sei*** and ***Bryde's*** less heavily

Blue Whale

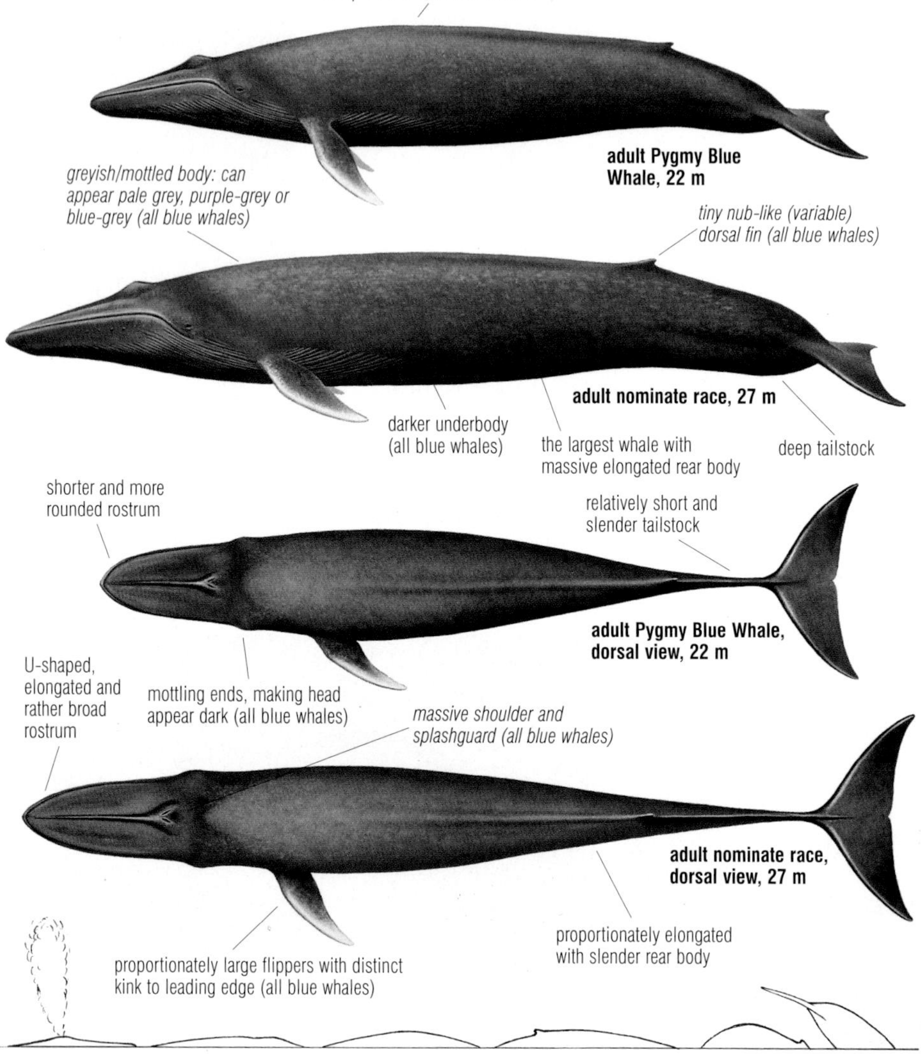

smaller and proportionately more compact than true blue whales

adult Pygmy Blue Whale, 22 m

greyish/mottled body: can appear pale grey, purple-grey or blue-grey (all blue whales)

tiny nub-like (variable) dorsal fin (all blue whales)

adult nominate race, 27 m

darker underbody (all blue whales)

the largest whale with massive elongated rear body

deep tailstock

shorter and more rounded rostrum

relatively short and slender tailstock

adult Pygmy Blue Whale, dorsal view, 22 m

U-shaped, elongated and rather broad rostrum

mottling ends, making head appear dark (all blue whales)

massive shoulder and splashguard (all blue whales)

adult nominate race, dorsal view, 27 m

proportionately large flippers with distinct kink to leading edge (all blue whales)

proportionately elongated with slender rear body

Tall, columnar blow; massive shoulder/splashguard emerge; in prepararing for deep dive, body rolls, tiny dorsal fin briefly emerges, and tailstock is strongly arached; flukes occasionally lifted.

built, with narrower heads and more prominent, less set-back dorsal fins, stronger dorsal/ventral contrast, and very different dive sequences/behaviour.

*Pygmy Blue Whale (*brevicauda*) breaks the surface with the rostrum/ splashguard and shoulders; blow dispersed by wind.*

Blue Whale (nominate) in smooth mid-body roll. Pale/greyish-mottled coloration and diagnostic miniature dorsal fin set well back.

Below: Fluking Blue Whale. Note underside pattern (cf. Fin Whale).

VARIATION

Age/sex Perhaps estimable by size. **Physical notes** 20–33.6 m and 80–150 (exceptionally 190) tons (the largest whale); ♀ slightly larger than ♂. Newborn 6–7 m and 2.5–4 tons. **Taxonomy** Varies in size and coloration, both individually and geographically. Status of the various forms highly controversial and information to permit at-sea identification lacking. However, at least Pygmy Blue Whale *B. m. brevicauda*, of S Hemisphere, may merit specific recognition. Other forms include *B. m. intermedia* (Southern Blue Whale) in S Hemisphere (north to 22°S off S America and 6°S off W Africa, though winter/breeding range almost unknown), *B. m. indica* (Indian Ocean Blue Whale) in N Indian Ocean, and nominate *B. m. musculus* (Northern Blue Whale) in N Hemisphere. *B. m. indica* seems morphologically and genetically close to, or even the same as, *brevicauda* (the name *indica* has priority). The N Indian Ocean whales, however, have a limited range and seem to undertake a rather unique migration. Hybrids: Blue × Fin recorded in N Atlantic (with fertile offspring), and possibly Blue × Humpback in S Pacific.

DISTRIBUTION & POPULATION

Separate populations in N Pacific, N Atlantic, Indian and Southern Oceans; mainly in cold waters (sometimes near polar ice) and open ocean, but also inshore, at edge of continental shelf, where feeds and possibly breeds. Migrates between summer feeding areas and warmer seas where winters and breeds. *Population* Perhaps fewer than 10,000, of which *c*.5,000 in S Indian Ocean and 710–1,255 in Antarctic waters, whilst in N Hemisphere largest numbers in NE Pacific, where *c*.3,000 (of which *c*.2,000 summer off California); *c*.400 in NE Atlantic, off Iceland and in adjacent waters, and 350+ in NW Atlantic.

ECOLOGY

Usually encountered alone or in twos. Migrates in groups of 2–3, rarely more; loose aggregations of up to 50 on feeding grounds,

*Pygmy Blue Whale (*brevicauda*) is relatively compact in structure and length.*

*Pygmy Blue Whale (*brevicauda*) has a pale-mottled body and tiny dorsal fin set well back.*

*Pygmy Blue Whale (*brevicauda*). On sunny days, a Blue Whale below the surface appears as a turquoise silhouette (Fin Whale can share this).*

Below: B. m. indica*, of the N Indian Ocean, seems identical to, and is apparently best regarded as, a Pygmy Blue Whale. During shallow rolls, the rostrum, splashguard and foreback are all visible.*

when recorded near Fin Whales. Aerial signals involve tail- and flipper-slapping. *Breaching* Very rare (usually at 45° angle, landing on belly/side), more frequent in young. *Diving* 5–20 min, reaching 150–200 m, but capable of deeper dives to 500 m (50 min); 10–20-min shallow dives at 12–20-sec intervals frequent. *Diet* Almost exclusively krill spp. at depths of less than 100 m, by gulp-feeding, consuming 3–8 tons daily. Most animals fast after leaving feeding grounds. *Reproduction* Sexually mature at 5–10 yrs old (reaches max size several yrs later, with some variation between populations). Breeds every 2–3 yrs. Mates from late autumn (peaking Jul in S Hemisphere, and continues until winter in N Hemisphere), and calves born in winter in warmer waters, following a 10–12-month gestation, and weaned at *c.*6–8 months. *Lifespan* Up to 90 yrs.

Fin Whale from the air. The blow is usually powerful and columnar, but can appear much more diffuse in certain conditions.

SIMILAR SPECIES

Main confusion risks ***Blue***, ***Sei*** and ***Bryde's Whales***. Evaluate sequential appearance of blow and dorsal

Fin Whale

Balaenoptera physalus

Cosmopolitan. Max 27 m.

Priority characters on surfacing

- Highly *elongated, streamlined rorqual* (the second largest after Blue Whale), essentially dark grey to brownish-black, but best separated by dorsal fin features, surfacing behaviour and asymmetrical head pigmentation.
- Comparatively *low, backswept dorsal fin* (tip pointed or rounded) on posterior ⅓ of back, appears above surface only after final blow (when blowholes/splashguard usually submerged).
- In relatively calm sea, look for *flattish V-shaped head* with narrow longitudinal rostrum-ridge and distinct blowhole splashguard.
- Diagnostic *creamy-white pigmentation on right side of lower jaw* (variably extending to upper jaw).
- Some may show darker line from flipper to eye and variable pale chevrons from flipper to shoulder, more prominent on right side of body. Flukes relatively small, triangular, notched and whitish below (but not usually visible at surface).

Typical behaviour at surface

- *Tall, usually narrow, upright blows* 4–8 m high (denser and taller than

all but Blue Whale), given 2–5× at intervals of 10–20 sec before diving.
- Blows occasionally appear vase-shaped, and sometimes given during slow surface travel.
- When surfacing, rises obliquely, head first and, following blows, vertically arches back in rolling to dive, exposing rear body and dorsal fin; flukes seldom visible.
- In steep dive, tailstock normally arched and disappears after the dorsal fin.
- Among the fastest-swimming great whales, but also travels leisurely just below or at surface, with back appearing quite flat.

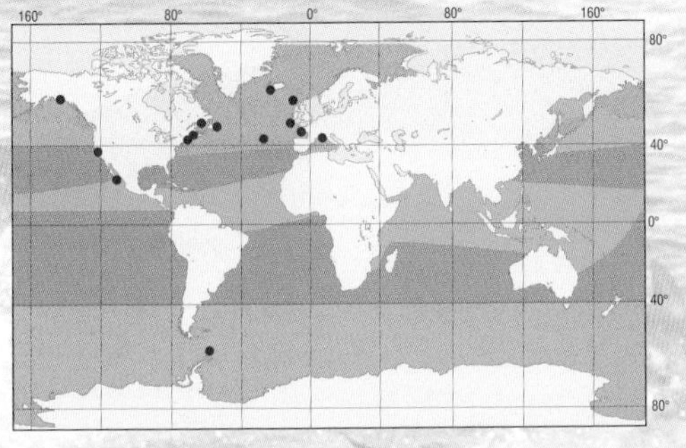

Fin Whale has a pointed, backswept dorsal fin, but shape is variable.

fin; also note steeply arched back/tailstock in deep dives (Sei, especially, does not, or only slightly, arches tailstock above the surface, unlike Fin). Fin Whale has a relatively small, backward-pointing dorsal fin (erect and very tall in Sei; highly variable but always has convex leading edge and intermediate in size in Bryde's; and Blue often has a nubbin). Check for asymmetrical head pigmentation and partially white baleen plates on right side (although usually visible only very briefly, if at all). Subsidiary features are: single longitudinal ridge on head and greyish-white chevron behind; blow characteristically vertical/narrow, taller and usually less bushy than Sei and Bryde's (which almost simultaneously or at briefer intervals, expose splashguard and dorsal fin on surfacing, whereas dorsal fin of Fin usually appears

The flukes are relatively small and whitish below (rarely visible as in photo).

well after head is submerged, although in smaller animals dorsal fin may appear soon after blow). In addition, Sei shows as much body as height of dorsal fin when preparing to dive, Fin twice as much (or more) body as height of dorsal fin.

Note the low, backswept dorsal fin, which usually appears after the head and blow have disappeared. The rear animal is about to deep dive, note the arched back and centrally placed dorsal fin.

Fin Whale

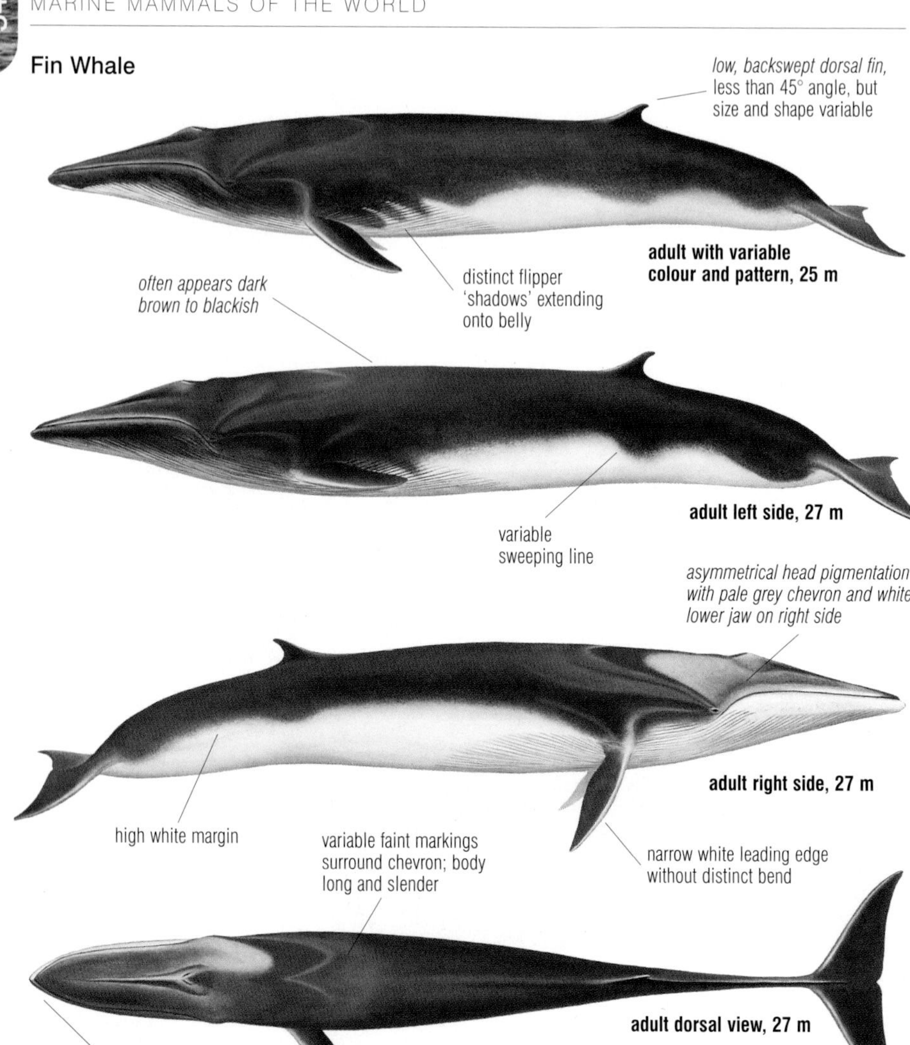

Head/forebody emerge first; blow columnar and usually well visible; back arched in rolling to dive, exposing long rear body and low dorsal fin; flukes seldom visible. In steep dive, tailstock normally arched and disappears after dorsal fin.

VARIATION

Age/sex Perhaps estimable by size; ads more frequently scarred on rear body. **Physical notes** 17–27 m and 30.4–81.2 tons, ♀ perhaps up to 5 m longer than ♂, and S Hemisphere animals typically larger. Newborn 6–7 m and 1–1.9 tons. **Taxonomy** Larger populations of S Hemisphere (also longer, narrower flippers) occasionally accorded the name *B. p. quoyi*, and apparently genetically isolated. Mediterranean population shows some degree of genetic isolation from those elsewhere in N Atlantic.

Fin Whale generally uses lunging and gulping methods to capture prey, and sometimes feeds at the surface, usually on its right side.

Hybridises with Blue Whale and hybrid ♀♀ fertile.

DISTRIBUTION & POPULATION
Chiefly deep offshore waters at temperate latitudes (fewer in tropics), with separate populations in N Atlantic, N Pacific and S Hemisphere. Migration routes poorly known, and different ages/sexes apparently move separately. *Population* Recently very roughly estimated at 119,000 (in S Hemisphere thought to have declined to 20% of original numbers, though now recovering slowly).

ECOLOGY
Usually 3–7, but up to 50–100 congregate at rich feeding grounds. Only strong social bond is between ♀ and calf. *Breaching* May leap (at varying angles, with large splash) but rarely given to spectacular behaviour. *Diving* Lasts 3–15 min (sometimes 30 min) and reaches 100–230 m (max 474 m). Series of 2–5 shallow, 10–20-sec dives may be followed by much longer period below surface. *Diet* Lunging and gulping, and sometimes at surface; often feeds on its right side, when left fluke may be visible above surface; often in association with dolphins and birds. Largely krill and other crustaceans, fish and squid, but varies seasonally and locally. *Reproduction* Sexually mature at 6–12 yrs old when 19–20 m. Breeds every 2–3 yrs. Largely mates in winter (Oct–Jan in N Hemisphere and mostly May–Aug in S Hemisphere), and gestation lasts 11–12 months. Gives birth in warmer waters and calves grow rapidly, being weaned at 6–7 months when ready to migrate to polar waters with ads. Records of ♀♀ with up to 6 foetuses, but unlikely that more than 1 would survive beyond birth and mother most probably cannot produce sufficient milk for more than this. *Lifespan* 85–90 yrs.

The head and forebody emerge first; look for the diagnostic whitish right side to the lower jaw, extending as a pale chevron on shoulder.

Long-bodied, the dorsal fin (foreground, with more rounded tip) usually emerges well after splashguard has sunk from view.

SIMILAR SPECIES

Look for tall, straight and erect dorsal fin (the peak often slightly bent back), uniformly dark head and relatively low blow with fin visible almost concurrently. Rarely arches tailstock clear above the surface and flukes only rarely visible. Chief confusion, especially at distance, is with ***Bryde's Whales***, which have sickle-shaped dorsal fin, whilst range may offer a clue, and differences in dive sequences and head ridges are useful (single longitudinal rostrum ridge separates Sei from Bryde's). ***Fin Whale*** usually has a taller, narrower blow, diagnostic white right lower jaw, more backward-set dorsal fin with front edge at angle of *c.*135° (not at a right-angle and falcate, as in Sei), and different dive sequence. Especially, unlike Fin (which typically strongly arches its back/tailstock in diving), Sei usually only slightly arches, and often appears to slip into a shallow dive, the dorsal fin submerging last. Viewed from above, head less pointed than in Fin but more so than in ***Blue***.

Sei Whale

Balaenoptera borealis

Cosmopolitan. Max 21 m.

Priority characters on surfacing

- Large slender rorqual with relatively tall dorsal fin.
- Compared to Fin and Bryde's, *dorsal fin taller, more erect and strongly sickle-shaped, often with tiny backward bend at apex*, and situated 2/3 of way along back.
- *V-shaped head with single central ridge*.
- Body slim and streamlined, but proportionately rather bulky.
- Head and body generally all dark bluish-grey to steely black.
- Very deep tailstock, small triangular-shaped flukes and short narrow flippers dark grey or bluish on both surfaces.
- Slight downward curve at snout tip, lower jaw variably darker, some have white streak behind eye but all these characters usually invisible.

Typical behaviour at surface

- Diffuse blow, up to 3 m high, given every 40–60 sec (or 20–30 sec) for 1–4 min before diving.
- *Dorsal fin visible for longer than other rorquals at surface; in shallow roll is visible almost simultaneously with blow* (only *c.*1 sec between their appearances).
- *Rolls low at surface* (and while diving, does not arch back/tailstock as much as Fin Whale), and dives usually shallow and short; may appear to sink below surface or slip into shallow dive, dorsal fin disappearing last, and never raises tail flukes.
- Often associated with large feeding frenzies of seabirds.

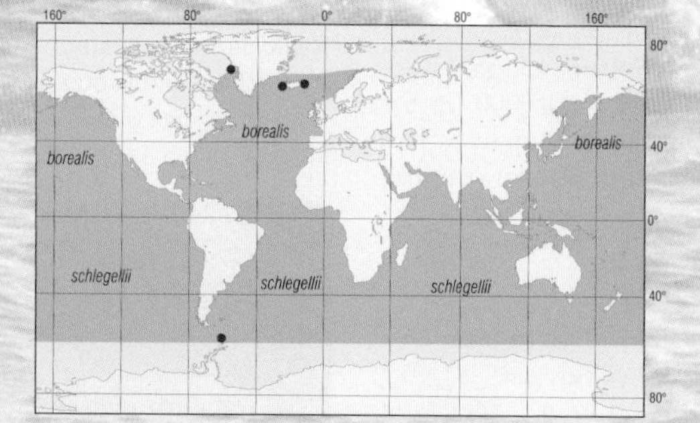

Sei Whale has a tall, erect and strongly sickle-shaped dorsal fin; note subtle but characteristic bend at apex of leading edge.

VARIATION

Age/sex Perhaps estimable by size (including of head); ads often typically mottled with numerous scars on body-sides (apparently mostly due to bites by cookie-cutter sharks and lampreys). **Physical notes** 12–21 m and 15.2–30.4 tons, ♀ usually larger; newborn 4.5–5 m and 0.65 tons. **Other data** *Throat grooves* Up to *c.*60 (fewer than Blue, Fin or Minke Whales), end just behind

The dorsal fin often emerges when splashguard/blow still visible (a characteristic shared mainly with minke whales), but surfacing technique varies with circumstances. Note tall dorsal fin and lack of lateral rostrum ridges of Bryde's Whale.

Sei Whale

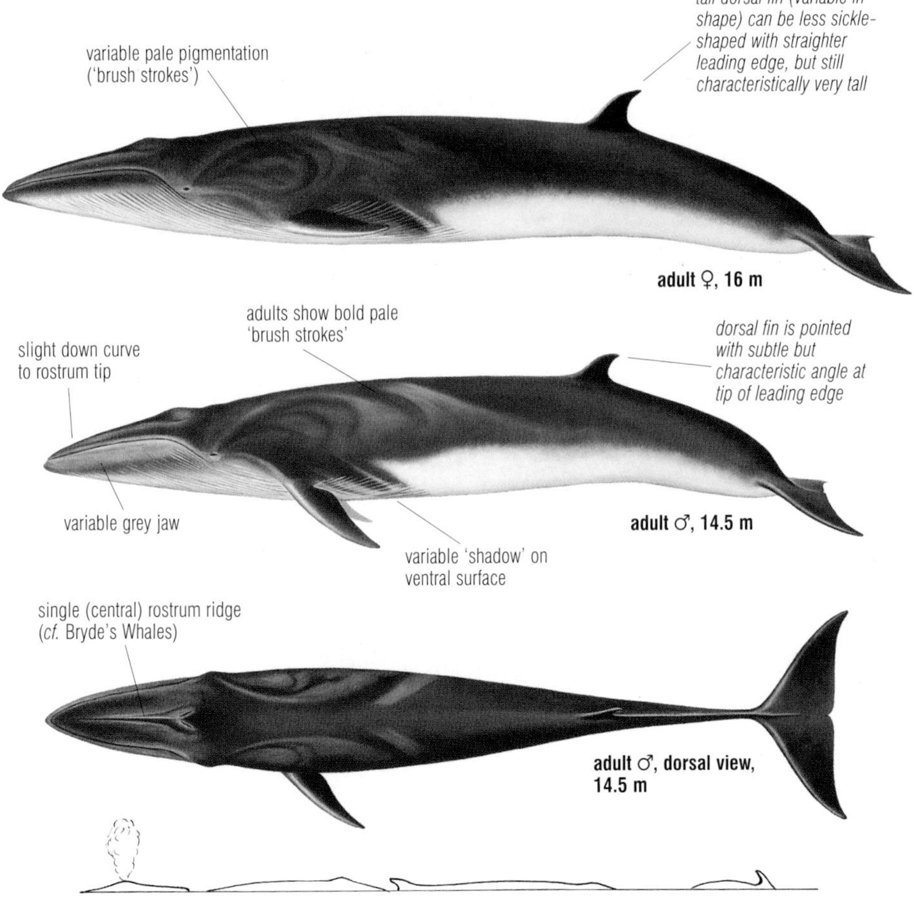

variable pale pigmentation ('brush strokes')

tall dorsal fin (variable in shape) can be less sickle-shaped with straighter leading edge, but still characteristically very tall

adult ♀, 16 m

slight down curve to rostrum tip

adults show bold pale 'brush strokes'

dorsal fin is pointed with subtle but characteristic angle at tip of leading edge

variable grey jaw

adult ♂, 14.5 m

variable 'shadow' on ventral surface

single (central) rostrum ridge (*cf.* Bryde's Whales)

adult ♂, dorsal view, 14.5 m

Head breaks surface often concurrently with part of back; blow columnar but low and diffuse; in shallow roll, erect dorsal fin well visible, often almost simultaneously with splashguard; fin disappears last, and never raises tail flukes.

flippers and usually form variable central white throat patch, becoming pale bluish-grey posteriorly. *Baleen plates* Mainly brownish-black, but some have a few paler plates at front of mouth, inviting confusion with Fin Whale. **Taxonomy** Polytypic: N (*B. b. borealis*) & S Hemisphere populations (*B. b. schlegellii*) genetically distinct and subtly differ in number of throat grooves and baleen plates, with *schlegellii* typically larger. Occasionally hybridises with Fin Whale.

DISTRIBUTION & POPULATION

Found in most waters, including subarctic and subantarctic in summer, with most migrating to warmer, lower latitudes (chiefly subtropical waters) to winter. In summer, does not reach as far north and south as other rorquals. *Population* Recently only *c.*23,000 in N Hemisphere (mostly N Pacific and C & NE Atlantic) and *c.*37,000 in S Hemisphere.

ECOLOGY

Usually alone or in pairs but also up to 5, rarely 30–50. 'Shy' of boats. *Breaching* At low angle, belly flopping into water. *Diving* Lasts 5–20 min but often comparatively close to surface. *Diet* Zooplankton, small schooling fish, squid. Usually feeds at dawn. One of the fastest-swimming great whales, and sometimes turns on side when feeding like Fin Whale. *Reproduction* Sexually mature 6–12 yrs old when 13–14 m (reaches max size several yrs later). ♀♀ give birth to single calf every 2–3 yrs with most calves born in winter (Jun in S Hemisphere). Gestation 11–13 months and weaned at 6–9 months, following arrival in cold-water feeding grounds (Nov–Dec in N Hemisphere). *Lifespan* Up to 70 yrs.

Sei with a more Bryde's Whale-like dorsal fin, but still characteristically tall/erect.

Typically appears to sink below surface or slips into shallow dive, the unmistakably erect dorsal fin disappearing last.

DISTINCTIVE POPULATIONS

Two, perhaps 3–4 distinctive forms apparently involved but field identification and relationships largely unresolved. **Offshore type/subspecies** (of 'ordinary form') Oceanic and at least partially migratory; external characteristics described in box. The name *brydei* (Bryde's Whale) may apply to this form, or *edeni*, depending on identity of the holotype specimen of *edeni*. **Inshore type/subspecies** (of 'ordinary form') Coastal, perhaps entirely resident, and externally very similar to preceding form, but averages

Bryde's Whale

Balaenoptera edeni

(Includes Omura's Whale *B. omurai*)

Cosmopolitan. Max 15.6 m.

Priority characters on surfacing

- Largish, streamlined rorqual, slightly smaller than Sei Whale.
- *Dorsal fin, on rear back, quite erect and strongly sickle-shaped* with deeply concave trailing edge.
- *Diagnostic 3 rostrum-ridges*, a broad central ridge and 2 narrower lines either side, visible only in close views.
- Dark smoky-grey dorsally (chocolate-brown or almost blackish in some lights) and slightly paler below, with some mottling or circular scars, especially on sides, and partially yellowish-white throat grooves.
- Relatively large flukes with slight concave trailing edge and usually whitish underside.

Typical behaviour at surface

- *Blow tall (3–4 m) and narrow*, reasonably conspicuous at distance; sequence irregular, typically 4–7 blows prior to dive.
- Typical surfacing technique is snout-first, with rostrum and even mouthline briefly visible; *fin visible well after blowhole has disappeared* from view, then a sharp body roll

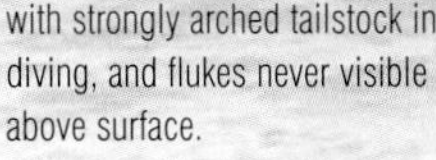

with strongly arched tailstock in diving, and flukes never visible above surface.

- When travelling, may blow once with head largely submerged, only slightly revealing back/fin before disappearing for a few min, surfacing again some 10s of metres ahead and performing same action (like minke whales).

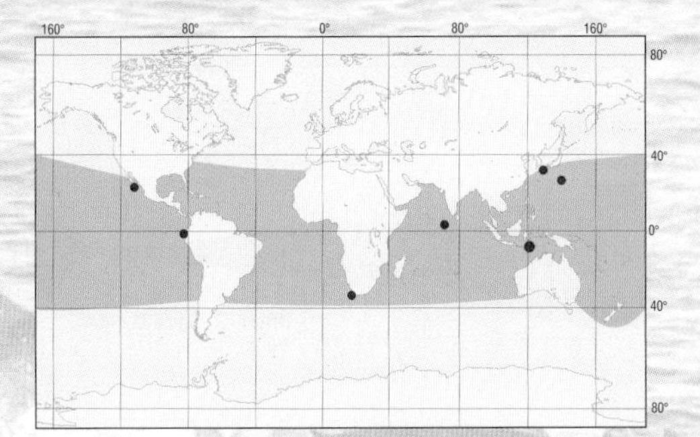

smaller and reportedly has less-extensive oval body scarring. Range poorly known (includes E Indian Ocean and SW Pacific). Again, either of the names *brydei* or *edeni* (Eden's Whale) may apply to this form, as a subspecies of the 'ordinary Bryde's Whale'. **Pygmy type** The recently described **Omura's Whale *B. omurai*** of W Pacific/ SE Asia (Sea of Japan, the Solomon Sea and E Indian Ocean, near Cocos Is) is putatively this type. Reportedly differs in anatomical and molecular criteria, and considerably smaller (9.6–11.5 m; ♀ at larger end of spectrum) than offshore type, but similar to small inshore type. Somewhat like much larger Fin Whale, with asymmetrical, bicoloured white throat grooves and baleen plates on right-hand side (left side greyer), and has larger number of grooves.

Bryde's Whales diagnostically have 3 rostrum ridges.

Lateral ridges on rostrum reportedly absent, but some animals may have them. Markedly small number of baleen plates which are short and broad with uncurled, stiff, greyish-white fringes. Genetic analyses did not include samples from the holotype of *B. edeni*, or small inshore form of 'ordinary' Bryde's Whales, and thus the species is of questionable status. The name *B. edeni* may apply to the specimens described as a new species, depending on the genetic identity of the holotype of that species. Alternatively, there may be two species of 'pygmy' Bryde's whales, i.e., 3 species overall, one with 2 distinctive subspecies.

Mother and calf: former turns on side to feed (behaviour shared with Fin and Sei Whales), exposing half of flukes (giving Killer Whale-like dorsal fin impression).

SIMILAR SPECIES

Bryde's have 3 parallel longitudinal ridges on head, unlike all other rorquals, which possess just 1; Omura's, however, appear to lack the 2 lateral ridges. Compared to similar ***Sei Whale*** dorsal fin more sickle-shaped and less erect, but also less backswept than distinctly larger ***Fin Whale***. Omura's distinctive also by combination of Fin Whale-like white right side to lower jaw and small size (but some Bryde's may also be asymmetrically ventrally, and may have obscure lateral rostrum ridges). Unlike Sei, has more conspicuous

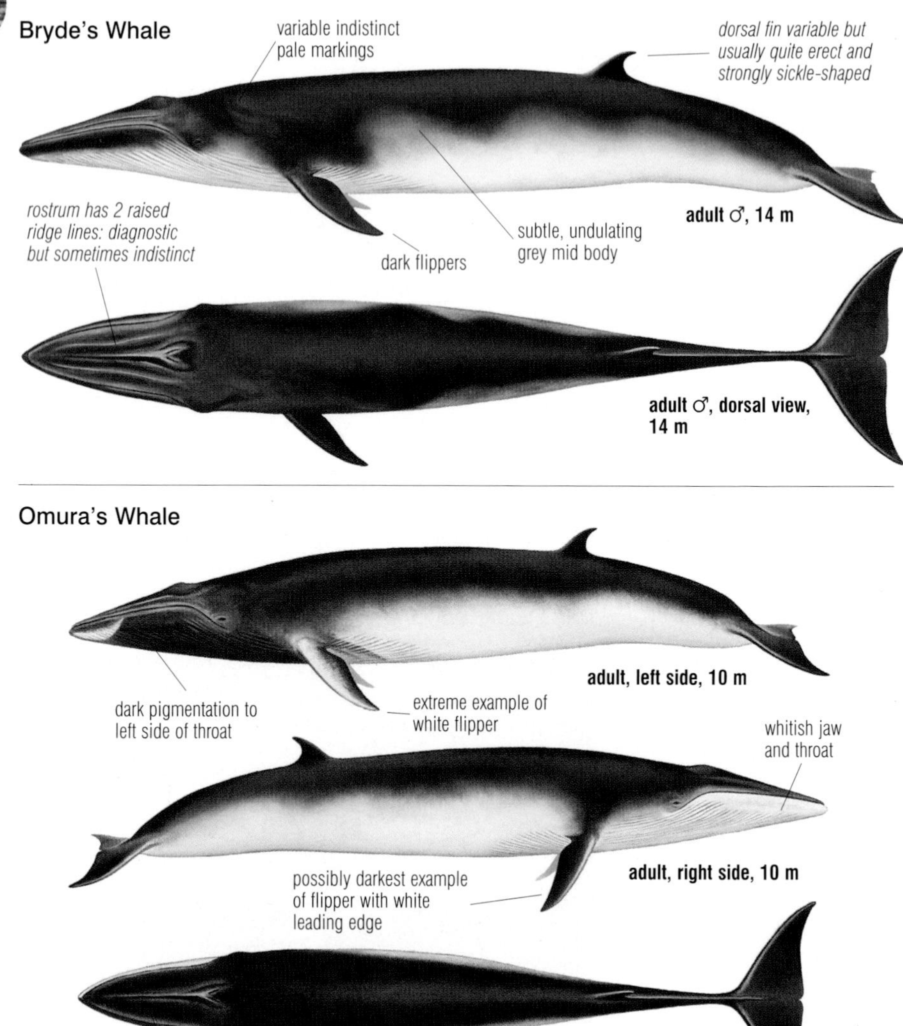

Bryde's/Omura's Whale: breaks surface with head at low angle; tall, narrow blow rather conspicuous; quite erect dorsal fin usually visible after splashguard is submerged; sharp roll in diving, with strongly arched tailstock; never flukes.

surfacing behaviour and blow, apparently due to its smaller size and being a deeper diver; in particular, has sharper descent, with strongly arched tailstock in preparing to dive. Surfaces less frequently than Sei and, in smooth body roll, blowhole tends to disappear before fin is visible. (No data concerning variation in surfacing behaviour amongst different forms of Bryde's and Omura's.) See ***minke whales***, which do not always appear clearly smaller, especially compared to smaller Bryde's and Omura's.

VARIATION

Age/sex No data on

Shape of dorsal fin varies individually with Bryde's, but is usually less erect than Sei and less backswept than Fin Whale, but some overlap with both (thus it is always best not to rely solely on fin shape and size).

separating different ages/sexes except by size. **Physical notes** 10–15.6 m and 12.1–20.3 tons; ♀ usually up to 1 m larger than ♂. Newborn 3.4–4 m and *c.*0.9 tons. **Taxonomy** Almost certainly involves at least 2–3 species which may overlap, are genetically distinct, and differ in cranial morphology, number and structure of baleen plates, and some ecological attributes. At-sea identification unknown and observers should take detailed notes/photographs of Bryde's Whales in near-shore tropical waters. For nomenclatural controversy surrounding *B. brydei* vs *B. edeni*, see Rice (1998), whilst these, and *B. omurai*, also discussed by Wada *et al.* (2003, *Nature* 426: 278–281), who claimed that the holotype of *B. edeni* is not of their new species. Note that in overall size and number of baleen *edeni* and *brydei* seem to be close to each other, but *omurai* reportedly has asymmetrical baleen like Fin Whale. Their relationship to Sei Whale also requires elucidation.

Sometimes, dorsal fin may emerge when splashguard still visible, like Sei (note also somewhat more Sei-like dorsal fin). This animal can be identified as an inshore Bryde's Whale by the lateral rostrum ridges and behaviour.

DISTRIBUTION & POPULATION

Tropical and warm-temperate waters, above 20°C, in Atlantic, Indian and W Pacific Oceans, and off New Zealand. Generally non- or partially migratory, rarely reaching subpolar and cold temperate seas (to 40°S and equivalent in N Hemisphere), but recently recorded off Denmark. Some tropical-water populations may be largely sedentary (e.g. off Japan and Mexico). *Population* (entire complex) Recently *c.*90,000, with 22,000 in NW Pacific, 8,000–9,000 in C Pacific and 13,000 in tropical E Pacific, but no truly comprehensive recent surveys. Pygmy-type perhaps very rare.

ECOLOGY

Details refer to all forms. Usually 1–7 but loose groups of 10–30 over several km in good fishing areas. Sometimes can be inquisitive of boats. *Breaching* In some areas (usually 2–3×), leaving water at steep (70–90°) angle, but infrequent in most of range. *Diving* Less than 2 min, but deeper dives up to 20 min recorded. *Diet* Feeds year-round. Gulp feeder that probably takes larger plankton and pelagic schooling fish; inshore form perhaps more dependent on schooling fish and offshore type on euphausiids. *Reproduction* Sexually mature at 8–13 yrs. Breeds every second year, in austral autumn off S Africa and late autumn/winter elsewhere in south, but perhaps year-round in some northerly and inshore populations. Gestation occupies *c.*11–12 months and calves are weaned at *c.*6 months. *Lifespan* Unknown.

Northern Minke Whale has a characteristic pale chevron with a well-defined dark leading edge.

Northern Minke Whale

Balaenoptera acutorostrata

N Hemisphere. Max 9.8 m.

Priority characters on surfacing

- *Small, streamlined rorqual* with slim, sleek dark body and fast, smooth surfacing movement.
- *Relatively tall sickle-shaped dorsal fin* situated nearly ²/₃ of way along back.
- *Triangular-shaped rostrum with highly pointed snout*; single sharp central rostrum ridge.
- Rather clear-cut straight borderline pigments to lower flanks and pale chevrons behind head.
- *Bold white band across centre of dark upper surface of flippers* (difficult to see).
- Upperside coloration varies, usually almost uniform dark grey-brown, often blackish, but true colour more greyish or brown.

Typical behaviour at surface

- *Blows rather weak*, very fine, disperse quickly and inconspicuous to invisible; vertical but rather bushy and mainly lower than 2 m (but up to 3 m); given 5–8× at intervals of less than 1 min.
- On surfacing, head usually appears at low angle, following blow and smooth body roll. *Fin may appear while splashguard is disappearing and while small blow is still settling.*
- Rolls quite high, humped and swift, and animal easily 'lost'; swimming speed varies but typically rather leisurely, just breaking surface once or twice to breathe.
- Arches almost vertically to deep dive, tailstock exposed rather high with dorsal fin still in view, but tail flukes usually below surface.
- May remain submerged for 15 min or more, but typically 6–12 min.
- Sometimes inquisitive around smaller boats but especially approachable when feeding.

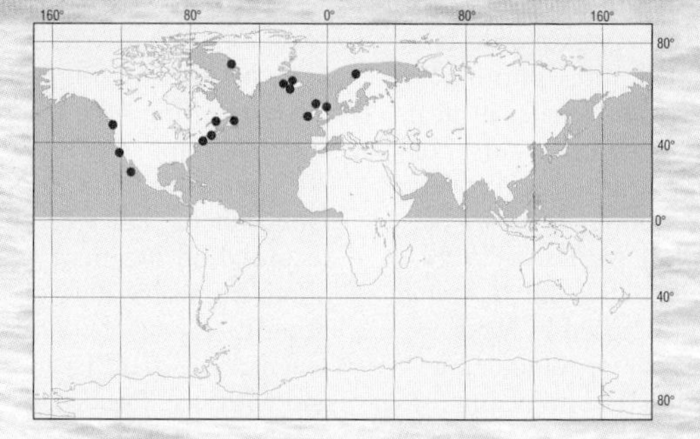

SIMILAR SPECIES

Well separated geographically from very similar ***Antarctic*** and ***Dwarf Minke Whales***, which differ in size, flipper and body-sides patterns, and baleen coloration/number, but pronounced individual variation. Compared to most other rorquals, especially ***Sei*** and ***Bryde's***, Minkes are usually appreciable smaller (not always easily judged), with slighter build and different surfacing behaviour (weak and less regular blow but, like Sei, dorsal fin appears simultaneously), single rostrum ridge (unlike Bryde's), and diagnostic but variable white band on upper flippers (in Pacific upper flippers can be grey), and some coloration differences on sides. Beware that pygmy-type Bryde's Whales are poorly known and could be confused in the Pacific. Unlikely to be confused with similar-sized ***beaked whales***, which often have somewhat similar dorsal fin, both in structure and location, including, e.g., ***Northern Bottlenose Whale***. However, unlike latter, has pointed flat head/rostrum, normally darker and almost unscarred body, straighter jawline, and other obvious differences in good views.

Northern Minke Whale: unless breaching, diagnostic bold white band across centre of flippers usually remains unseen below the surface.

Northern Minke Whale

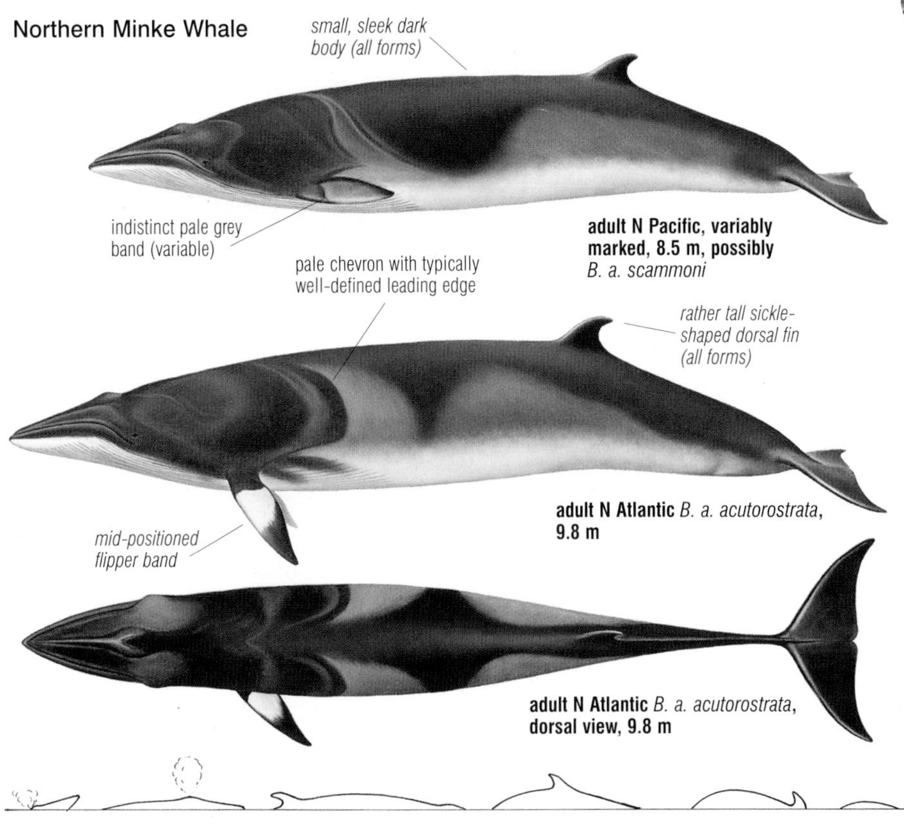

Snout emerges at low angle and blow is rather weak; fin may appear concurrently with splashguard and while small blow is still settling; often rolls quite high and arches almost vertically for deep dive, with exposed tailstock and dorsal fin still in view, but without fluking.

VARIATION

Age/sex Perhaps judged by overall size, although best done with experience and reference to other cetaceans. Calf darker with more rounded snout. **Physical notes** 7–9.8 m and 5–10 tons, ♀ *c.*0.5 m longer than ♂; newborn 2.4–3.5 m. **Taxonomy** The *B. acutorostrata* superspecies, which includes Antarctic Minke, forms a highly complex group of several forms, 3 of which are recognised here at species level. Northern Minke has 2 distinctive subspecies, nominate *acutorostrata* in the N Atlantic and (the apparently smaller/darker) *scammoni* in the N Pacific, and there is an additional, poorly known population, sometimes recognised as *thalmaha*, in Sri Lankan waters.

DISTRIBUTION & POPULATION

Widespread in N Hemisphere (mainly N Pacific and N Atlantic), both oceanic and coastal, from tropical, but mainly in temperate to polar, waters. Northern Minke frequents warmer waters in winter and moves north in summer, although in some areas it performs irregular seasonal movements. Often tends to segregate according to age/sex: in summer, ♂♂ migrate further north in open seas, ♀♀ remaining further south in coastal waters, and imms even further south. *Population* Presently *c.*185,000 in Atlantic with unknown numbers elsewhere.

ECOLOGY

Generally solitary or 2–3, less often small groups of 5–15, occasionally loose aggregations of up to 400 in productive feeding areas at high latitudes. Often spyhops around boats. *Breaching* Frequent, with almost clear leaps above surface. *Diving* Usually lasts 3–9 min but up to 20 min. *Diet* Gulp feeder (primarily krill, other crustaceans and small schooling fish), mainly near surface by lunging into school of prey, engulfing it while swimming; often turns on side when lunge-feeding.

During its high rolls the relatively tall sickle-shaped dorsal fin of Northern Minke Whale is apparent.

In Northern Minke Whale the dorsal fin may emerge while the splashguard is still visible.

Birds often gather in the area. Mostly feeds outside tropical and subtropical waters. *Reproduction* Sexually mature at 3–8 yrs old (when *c.*7 m) but reaches max size several yrs later. ♀♀ give birth to a single calf every 1–2 yrs, though reproductive interval probably *c.*14 months. Mating and calving seem to peak in Dec–Jun. Gestation lasts 10–11 months and lactation 4–6 months. *Lifespan* Up to *c.*50 yrs.

Breaching Dwarf Minke Whale. Note dusky half-collar (reaching throat) and mostly white upper flippers.

SIMILAR SPECIES

Especially similar to ***Northern Minke Whale*** but only overlaps with ***Antarctic Minke Whale***, which is larger and more poorly patterned above and on sides. Flipper pattern important: Dwarf Minke

Dwarf Minke Whale

Balaenoptera [*acutorostrata*] subspecies/allospecies

Southern Ocean. Max 7.8 m.

Priority characters on surfacing

- *Small, sleek rorqual* with surfacing behaviour similar to other Minkes.
- Elongated, with relatively *tall sickle-shaped dorsal fin* set *c.*²/₃ of way along back.
- Upperside uniform, dark grey-brown, often looking almost blackish, but really more greyish.
- Triangular rostrum with pointed snout and sharp central rostrum ridge, visible in close views from above.
- *Pale fore-flanks panel rather lower, but often extends upwards, tapering to a point on foreback*; rather clear-cut transition across lower flanks.
- Variable pale chevrons and dusky collar behind head, but mostly invisible below surface.
- *White area on upper flippers usually extensive and sharply demarcated, reaching to base of flipper, with only tip and trailing edge black, continuing as broad white shoulder patch behind flipper.*

Typical behaviour at surface

- *Blows rather vertical but diffuse and often hard to see*; normally less than 2 m high; given 5–8× at intervals of less than 1 min, but generally irregular.
- On surfacing, head usually appears at low angle, following blow and smooth body roll. *Fin may emerge while splashguard is disappearing and small blow is still settling.*
- Rolls quite high, humped and swift, and animal easily 'lost'; swimming speed varies but typically rather leisurely, just breaking surface once

or twice to breathe before diving.

- Arches almost vertically to deep dive, tailstock exposed rather high with dorsal fin still in view, but tail flukes usually below surface.
- May remain submerged for more than 15 min, and sometimes rather inquisitive towards smaller boats.

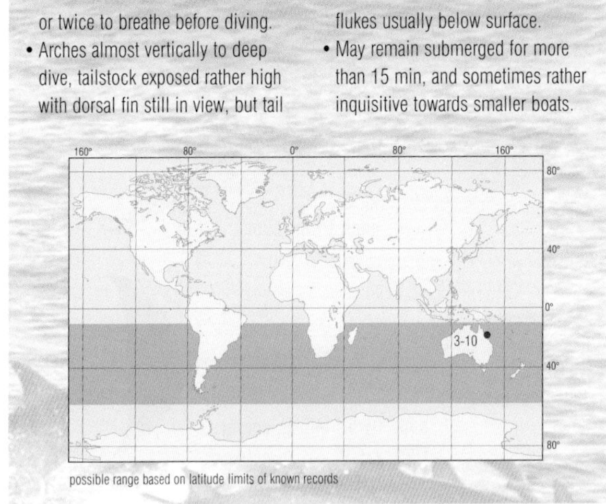

possible range based on latitude limits of known records

usually has an extensive solid white area across ⅔ of upper surface to base (leaving only sharply demarcated tip and trailing edge black), with a broad white shoulder patch behind flipper. In Antarctic Minke, flipper usually appears greyish above or has diffuse white central area which normally does not, or indistinctly, extends onto body. Compared to Antarctic Minke, pale flanks usually lower and more clear-cut, and white shoulder patch above flipper extends upwards as tapering greyish mark with forward-pointing ends. Also quite characteristic is that the top of rostrum/head and flanks are paler grey, bordered by a broad dusky collar from the eye and flipper across the neck (some may have an ill-defined, pale wavy pattern to the collar-sides, but others more uniform); in classic individuals the dusky half-collar is rather solid and broad and extends to the throat grooves. However, differences frequently clouded by individual variation and viewing conditions (characteristic white patches and flippers rarely visible above surface and then usually only partially or briefly). Belly often less pure white, affording greater contrast with white throat grooves (typically underside and flanks partially blotched or evenly coloured yellow, orange or even pink by diatoms and algae). Dwarf Minke distinguished from all other rorquals, including ***Sei/Bryde's***, by virtue of those characters listed under Northern Minke. Within range, beware confusion with similar-sized ***Pygmy Right Whale*** and perhaps some beaked whales, but in good views has straighter jawline, pointed and flat rostrum/head, almost unscarred body, and coloration differences.

VARIATION

Age/sex Probably mainly as Northern Minke. **Physical notes** Largest 7.8 m (♀) or 6.8 (♂), and newborn apparently up to 2.8 m. **Taxonomy** Dwarf Minke lacks a scientific name but in many respects (including genetically), it is apparently closer to Northern Minke of N Atlantic, but is restricted to Southern Ocean (where it overlaps to an unknown extent with Antarctic Minke).

DISTRIBUTION & POPULATION

Perhaps circumpolar in Southern Ocean (occasionally to 60°S)

Dwarf Minke Whale has characteristic pale chevrons behind head; note reflection of whitish flippers and shoulder, the latter extending upwards with forward-pointing ends.

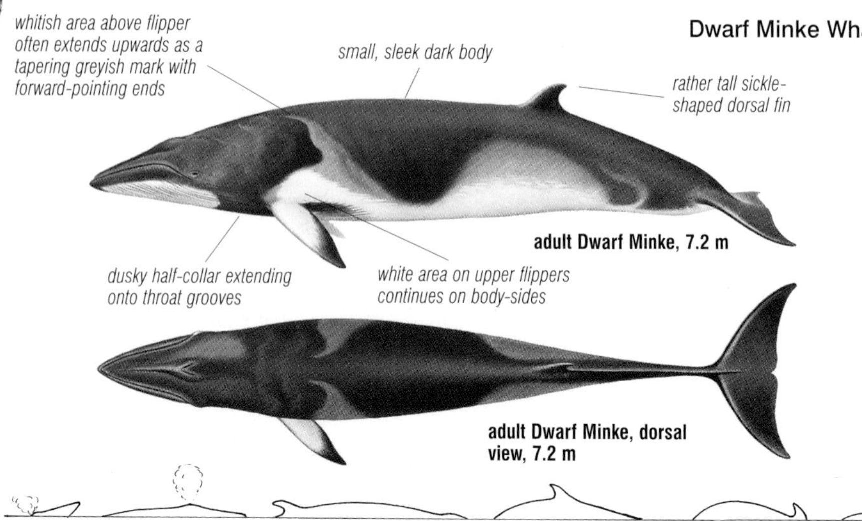

Snout emerges at low angle and blow is rather weak; fin may appear concurrently with splashguard and while small blow is still settling; often rolls quite high and arches almost vertically for deep dive, with exposed tailstock and dorsal fin still in view, but without fluking.

but most records off S Africa, Australia and the Indian Ocean, although occurs year-round to 7°S in Atlantic and to 11°S in Pacific. Sympatric with Antarctic Minke during austral summer and occurs off S Africa only in austral autumn/winter. *Population* No estimates, but considered relatively abundant by some sources.

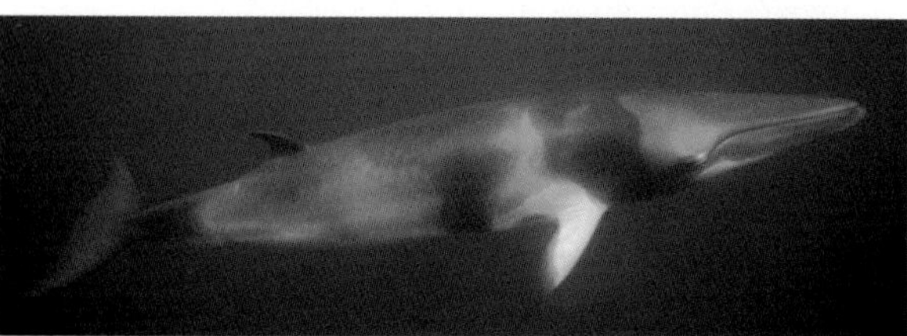
Dwarf Minke Whale has diagnostic whitish upper flippers (with black tip and trailing edge), continuing as a broad white band on body-sides.

ECOLOGY

Few or no specific data for this form, but most thought principally to be as Northern Minke. Observations suggest that it normally occurs solitarily or in pairs, occasionally up to 8.

SIMILAR SPECIES

Very similar to ***Northern*** and ***Dwarf Minke Whales***, but range overlaps only with latter. Flipper pattern varies individually but is an important feature and Dwarf Minke has white from belly reaching over insertion of flipper. Other differences, almost useless at sea, include larger/heavier build, head and back almost uniformly tinged paler/greyer (lighter

Antarctic Minke Whale

Balaenoptera bonaerensis

S Hemisphere. Max 10.7 m.

Priority characters on surfacing

- As other minkes, *small and streamlined*, with short surface periods and generally solitary, making them much less obvious than larger rorquals.
- Slim, sleek dark body, with *relatively tall sickle-shaped dorsal fin* (positioned nearly 2/3 of way along back) visible during brief surfacing and rolling.
- Upper surface almost uniform dark grey-brown, often blackish, but actually more greyish.
- Triangular rostrum, pointed snout and sharp central rostrum ridge perhaps visible if close.
- *Border between dark dorsal and*

paler thoracic flank area rather high and forms rather ill-defined, undulating transition; also variable pale chevrons behind head in good views.

- *If visible, upper surface of flipper appears mostly greyish* (may show variable whitish central area but diffuse or indistinct; white leading edge in some).

Typical behaviour at surface

- *Blow medium height, columnar and thin, but usually visible*; vertical but rather bushy, and normally 2–3 m; given 5–8× at intervals of less than 1 min.
- On surfacing, head usually appears at low angle, following blow and smooth body roll. *Fin may emerge while splashguard is disappearing and small blow is still settling.*
- Rolls quite high, humped and swift, and animal easily 'lost'; swimming speed varies but typically rather leisurely, just breaking surface once or twice to breathe before diving.
- Arches almost vertically to deep dive, tailstock exposed rather high with dorsal fin still in view, but tail flukes usually below surface.
- May remain submerged for 15 min or more.
- Sometimes rather inquisitive around smaller boats but especially approachable when feeding.
- Often travels in packs, sometimes in 100s in rich feeding areas; throws up rooster-tails when travelling fast.

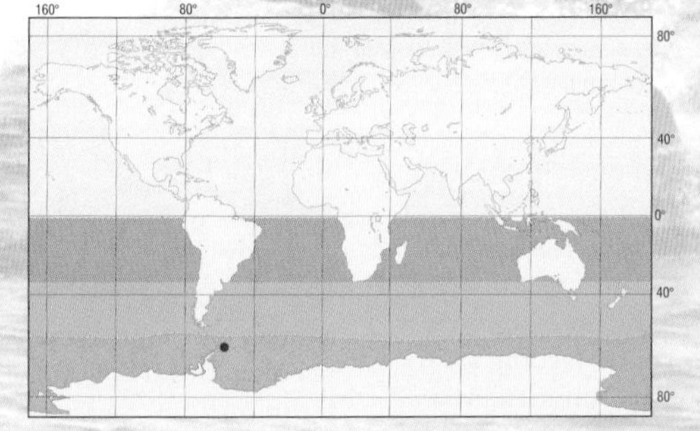

bluish-grey), but much individual variation, and in most conditions dorsal areas appear equally dark or black. Also tends to have more ill-defined and undulating transition between dark dorsum and pale/whitish flanks and belly, with border between them higher on flanks (but individual variation may render this of little use). Above-mentioned differences refer only to typical individuals. Antarctic Minke distinguishable from all other rorquals, and from some similar-sized beaked whales, using characters discussed under Northern Minke.

Antarctic Minke Whale in smooth, long body roll, revealing sickle-shaped dorsal fin while small blow still settling.

Spyhopping Antarctic Minke Whale. Note undeveloped dusky half-collar (not reaching throat or below flipper level).

VARIATION

Age/sex Probably mainly as Northern Minke. **Physical notes** Poorly studied: 7.2–10.7 m and 5.8–9.1 tons; ♀ up to 1 m longer than ♂. Newborn 2.4–2.8 m. **Other data** *Baleen plates* Unlike other Minkes, asymmetrical with more anterior white plates on right jaw and remaining baleen duskier. In Antarctica often has a yellowish diatom wash. **Taxonomy** Antarctic Minke is the main S Hemisphere, and largest, form within the Minke Whale complex which also comprises Northern Minke (N Hemisphere, the second-largest form) and Dwarf Minke (the smallest form, which has traditionally been considered a 'dwarf'

Antarctic Minke Whale

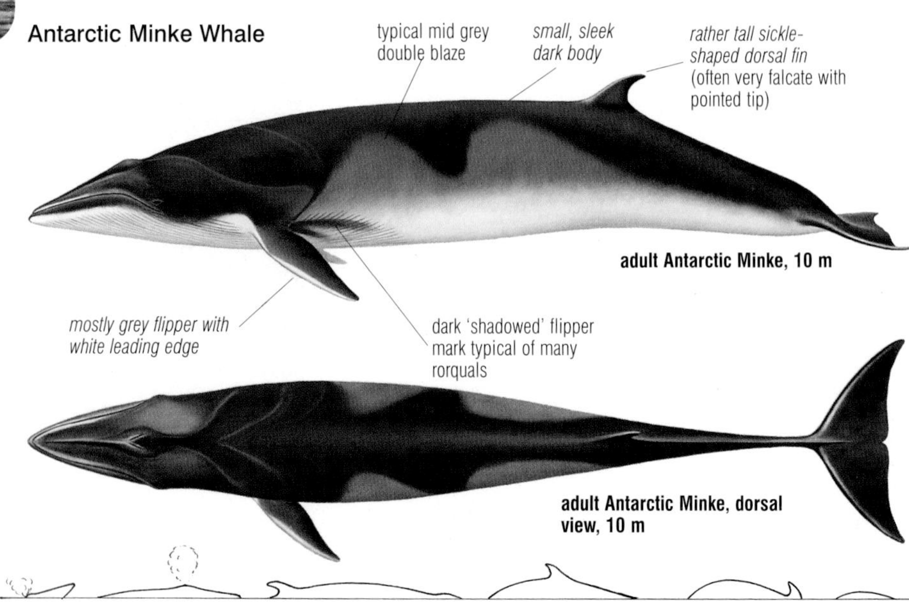

Snout emerges at low angle and blow is rather weak; fin may appear concurrently with splashguard and while small blow is still settling; often rolls quite high and arches almost vertically for deep dive, with exposed tailstock and dorsal fin still in view, but without fluking.

form of Northern Minke and overlaps widely with Antarctic Minke at lower latitudes in the Southern Ocean).

DISTRIBUTION & POPULATION Circumpolar and pelagic in S Hemisphere (65–20°S in Atlantic), from pack-ice to tropical S Atlantic, Indian and less so into S Pacific Oceans (e.g. fairly scarce in New Zealand and Tasmanian waters). Often in shallow temperate coastal seas. Breeds in austral winter, principally at 10–30°S, but recorded once to Suriname in N Hemisphere, and occasionally in Antarctica, at this season. Mature ♂♂ and pregnant ♀♀ migrate to Antarctic feeding areas for austral summer, even reaching 78°S in Ross Sea, but others rarely penetrate below 42°S at this season. Sexual segregation reported, at least temporally. Some migrate between waters near equator and coastal Antarctica. *Population* Recently estimated at 510,000–1.4 million, although perhaps as few as 380,000.

ECOLOGY Principally as Northern Minke. *Diet* Chiefly krill in Antarctica. *Reproduction* Gives birth every 1–2 yrs, though actual reproductive interval is probably as Northern Minke, *c.*14 months. Long mating season, from late austral winter to early summer (Jun–Dec, peaking Aug–Sep); calves born in warmer waters, mostly in late May–Aug.

Spyhopping Antarctic Minke Whales in the partially frozen sea of Eastern Antarctica

Killer Whale

One of the most familiar and distinctive of all cetaceans is a true oceanic dolphin, despite its vernacular name, and therefore a member of the Delphinidae. Together with several other dark-bodied and beakless but smaller species, some collectively referred to as 'blackfish', it forms a rather distinctive subgroup within the subfamily Orcininae or Globicephalinae. Ongoing research may soon prove the existence of more than one species of killer whale, but for now all forms and populations are considered a single, rather variable species.

Calf and ♀ Antarctic Killer Whale, Type C of E Antarctic: note narrow, forward-slanting eye-patch.

Killer Whale

Orcinus orca

Cosmopolitan. Max 9.8 m.

Priority characters on surfacing

- Rather large, round-bodied, mostly dark cetacean.
- *Tall dorsal fin* is centrally positioned (up to 1.8 m and forms sharp triangle in ad ♂, up to 0.9 m and slightly curved in ♀/young)—pods usually contain at least 1 ♂.
- *Mainly black with contrasting white throat to abdomen and rear flanks.*
- Grey-white patch ('saddle') behind dorsal fin, and black upperbody contrasts sharply with white underparts including chin and eye-patch.
- *Huge conical head* with poorly defined, blunt beak.
- Flippers are large rounded paddles (obvious when breaching or spyhopping).

Typical behaviour at surface

- Blow tall but bushy, often quite conspicuous in windless conditions. Breathes every 10–35 sec during series of a dozen short dives, followed by a longer/deeper dive.
- Fast swimmer with unpredictable movements and behaviour; sometimes inquisitive and approachable.
- Sociable, pods (2–50 individuals) often travel in tight unison, particularly in coastal areas.
- Sometimes associates with other cetaceans.

DISTINCTIVE POPULATIONS

Off western N America (Washington state to Alaska) and around Antarctica, 3 forms recognised, differing in dorsal fin shape, pigmentation, dialect (which maintains pod discreteness between sympatric groups), DNA, physiology and behaviour. Similar ecotype variation may occur elsewhere.

NE Pacific forms Three largely sympatric ecotypes: 1) coastal fish-eaters ('residents'), medium-sized groups often with dark pigments in saddle ('open saddle'); 2) mammal-eaters ('transients'), small groups, no 'open saddle'; 3) 'offshore', large school size type, smaller body size,

Adult ♂ Antarctic Killer Whale, Type A, is circumpolar in offshore, ice-free waters: note medium-sized, horizontal white eye-patch, and no 'cape'.

Killer Whale – Antarctic forms

Killer Whale – NE Pacific forms

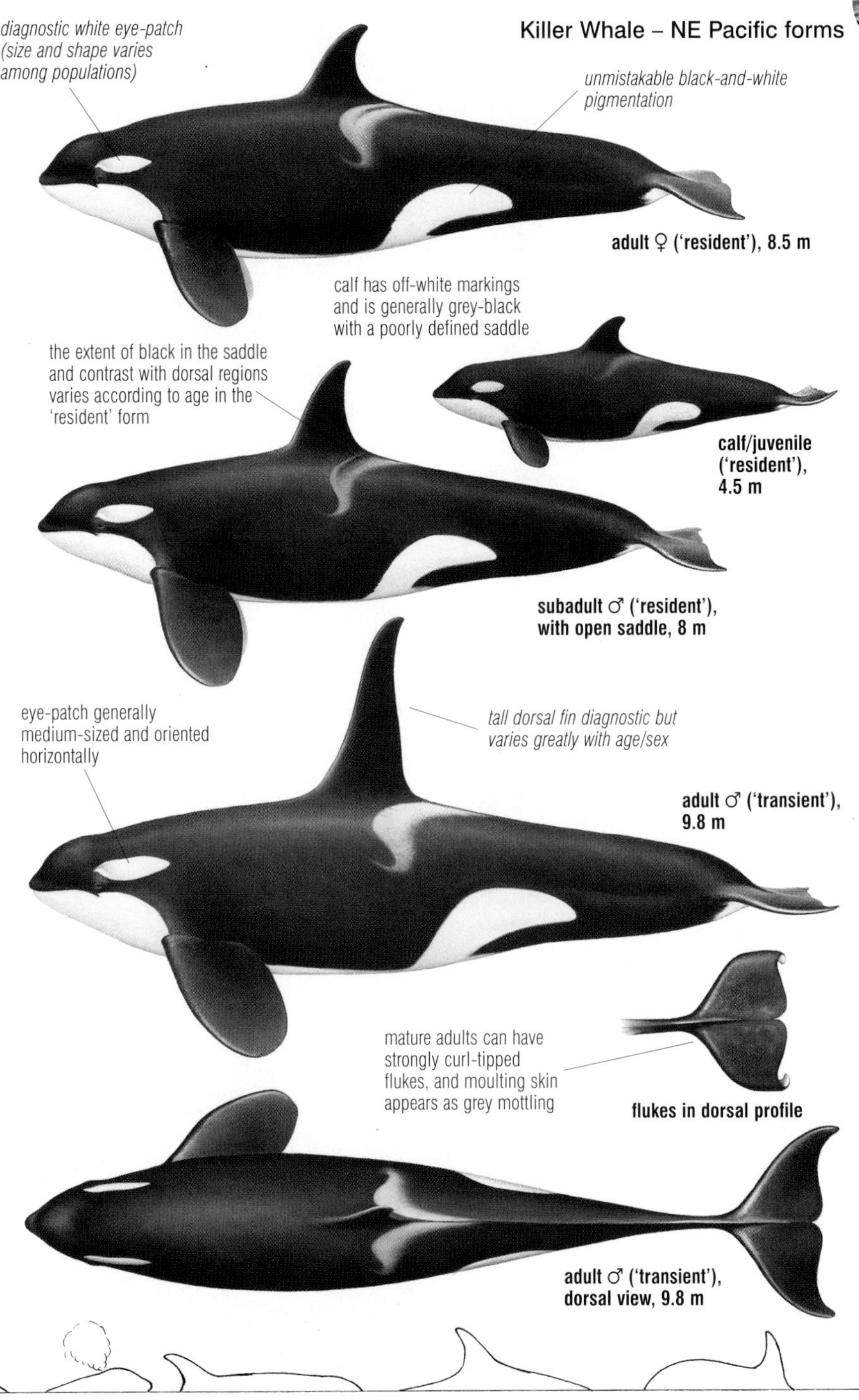

Blow bushy but quite tall; often makes series of short dives, surfaces and rolls rather high, followed by longer/deeper dive; fast and often erratic; huge variation in overall and dorsal fin sizes.

some with 'open saddle', dietary habits unknown. **Antarctic forms** The 3 Antarctic ecotypes appear to possess much more pronounced morphological and biological differences, and may be biological species. 'Type A' has medium-sized, horizontal white eye-patch roughly parallel to body axis; lacks a dorsal cape; inhabits offshore, ice-free waters; is circumpolar in distribution and preys predominantly on Antarctic Minke Whales. 'Type B' similar, but oval eye-patch at least twice as large; clear-cut dorsal cape; inhabits inshore waters, closely associated with continental pack-ice (frequent around Peninsula); seals predominate in diet but also takes Antarctic Minkes and Humpbacks. 'Type C' most distinctive, having narrow, sloping diagonal white eye-patch that slopes downward at front; distinct dorsal cape; inhabits inshore pack in E Antarctica, where feeds on Antarctic toothfish. In Antarctica, presumably only types B and C possess white patches stained yellow-orange by diatoms, and chocolate-brown appearance to dark areas of body. Forms with cape have distinctive 2-toned look when seen in good light, with eye-patch positioned in paler grey area. No reliable data on size, but types B and C may be 'dwarf' forms.

Antarctic Killer Whale (probably adult ♀), Type B of inshore continental pack-ice: note huge oval eye-patch (at least twice as large as Type A); distinct border between black forecape and grey sides; white areas stained yellow-orange by diatoms, dark areas yellowish/brown.

'Resident' Killer Whale (probably adult ♀) of coastal NE Pacific: segregated genetically and by behaviour, and variable 'open saddle' (though lacking here).

Below: 'transient' Killer Whale (mature ♂) of coastal NE Pacific: mammal-eaters that travel in small schools and lack an 'open saddle'.

'Offshore' Killer Whale, probably subadult ♂♂, NE Pacific: relatively small animals.

Killer Whale (probably immature ♂), Pacific, in the tropics.

VARIATION

Age/sex Overall size and shape and height of dorsal fin useful in ageing/sexing. Head more smoothly rounded in ad (subtly more conical in young). Calf as ad but saddle reduced and dorsal fin even lower and more falcate than imm/♀, and white areas often tan to orange-yellow.

SIMILAR SPECIES

Distinctive shape, black-and-white coloration, tall, sword-shaped and strikingly visible dorsal fin, and spectacular behaviour almost unmistakable. At distance (especially in groups with no ad ♂), ♀♀/young could be mistaken for similar-sized whales, due to their less distinctive dorsal fin, but head shape and coloration are unique, and dorsal fin still distinctly taller than all similar-sized cetaceans. Compare also ***False Killer Whale***, ***pilot whales*** and ***Risso's Dolphin*** for possible confusion with young animals.

Breaching Killer Whale (mature ♂) of the inshore NE Pacific ecotype, probably a 'resident'.

Killer Whale killing Northern Elephant Seal pup (off California, probably the 'transient' ecotype).

Physical notes ♂ 7–9.8 m and 3.8–5.5 tons, ♀ smaller in overall size (4.5–8.5 m), flipper length and dorsal fin height; newborn 2.1–2.6 m and *c.*160–200 kg.
Taxonomy Traditionally considered monotypic, but distinctive morphological, behavioural and genetic differences described among sympatric populations and more than 1 species may be involved, at least in the eastern N Pacific and Antarctica. Around Antarctica 2 names proposed: '*O. (o.) glacialis*' (probably referable to Type C) and '*O. (o.) nanus*' (possibly Type B); Type A is probably the (nominate) worldwide form.

DISTRIBUTION & POPULATION
The most widespread cetacean, but commonest in cold-temperate coastal areas. Cosmopolitan, reaching to edge of pack-ice at both poles, usually within 800 km of land. Migrations, principally in response to changes in favoured prey abundance, occasionally long, e.g. between Alaska and California, USA.

Killer Whales (probably adult females), similar to Antarctic Type A, patrolling Crozet Island Beach, S Indian Ocean.

Antarctic Killer Whales, Type A (Patagonia), challenging bull Southern Elephant Seal.

'Resident' Killer Whales, coastal NE Pacific (British Columbia) usually occur in medium-sized pods; from left to right mature ♀ or ubadult ♂ and 2 full-grown adult ♂♂; a calf c.*1yr old on the far right.*

Population No global estimate. Most subpopulations thought to number in the 100s or low 1,000s, but in Antarctica (perhaps optimistically) estimated at 70,000, and *c.*8,500 thought to occur in tropical E Pacific, *c.*2,000 off Japan and 2,850 off Alaska. In Europe, most frequent off Iceland, Norway and the Faeroes.

Killer Whale (California, probably 'transient' ecotype) killing Pacific White-sided Dolphin.

Killer Whale (mature ♂), similar to Antarctic Type A, taking South American Sea Lion pup in Argentina.

ECOLOGY

Mammal-eating forms in smaller groups (e.g. 5–10) than fish-eaters (e.g. 20–200+); herds of 10s recorded, albeit scattered over several km. Groups usually mixed sex, with calves and juvs, and oldest ♀ often dominant. Pods usually contain at least 1 mature ♂, but some ♂♂ solitary. Frequently spyhops, tailslaps and flipper-slaps. Can be highly vocal, with some strong dialectical differences known. *Breaching* Graceful leap, crashing into water on back, stomach or side, and juvs perform more

Female Killer Whale with her stillborn calf, Norway.

adventurous manoeuvres. *Diving* Breathes every 10–35 sec during series of *c.*12 short dives, followed by dive lasting up to *c.*17 min; max depth 260 m. *Diet* Overall catholic, but usually specialises regionally, and populations in same region may be segregated by diet. *Reproduction* Sexually mature at *c.*15 yrs (♂) or *c.*9 yrs (♀); breeds every 3–8 yrs. Gestation 15–18 months. ♀♀ give birth to single calf, largely in autumn to spring (varies regionally), but in some areas may occur year-round; calves nursed for at least 1 yr, some not being weaned until 2 yrs old. *Lifespan* Up to 90 yrs.

Killer Whale: an infrequent view of the underside of the flukes.

Three spyhopping Antarctic Killer Whales, Type C (inshore pack-ice of E Antarctic): note narrow, slanting white eye-patch.

Pilot whales – the large 'blackfish'

Relatively large and oceanic members of the Delphinidae of the subfamily Globicephalinae, pilot whales are often referred to as 'blackfish'. The subfamily also includes Pygmy Killer, Melon-headed and False Killer Whales, Risso's Dolphin, and perhaps Killer Whale. Pilot whales are very similar, generally beakless with a rounded bulbous melon-like forehead, but most characteristic is their distinct broad-based, backswept dorsal fin and very long pectoral flippers, both set well forward. Their blackish bodies are only inconspicuously marked, with a diagonal stripe that slopes downward at the front, a pale 'saddle' just behind the dorsal fin and an 'anchor-shaped' ventral patch. Among the most familiar whales, they form large pods which periodically strand en masse and frequently associate with other species. Large drives are organised in some areas (e.g. the Faeroes) to 'push' the whales shorewards in order to hunt them.

A young pilot whale with its relatively indistinct dorsal fin (being more pointed) could be confused with False Killer Whale, but adults are unmistakable. Bottlenose dolphins often associate with pilot whales, but the main identification issue is the separation of the two pilot whales from each other, and this can prove impossible in areas where they overlap in distribution.

Calf and ♀ Short-finned Pilot Whale: typically both pilot whales have a falcate, backswept dorsal fin (set forward with very long base), thick tailstock, bulbous melon, quite long, sickle-shaped flippers with sharply-pointed tips; also note paler grey diagonal eyestripe.

Pilot Whales

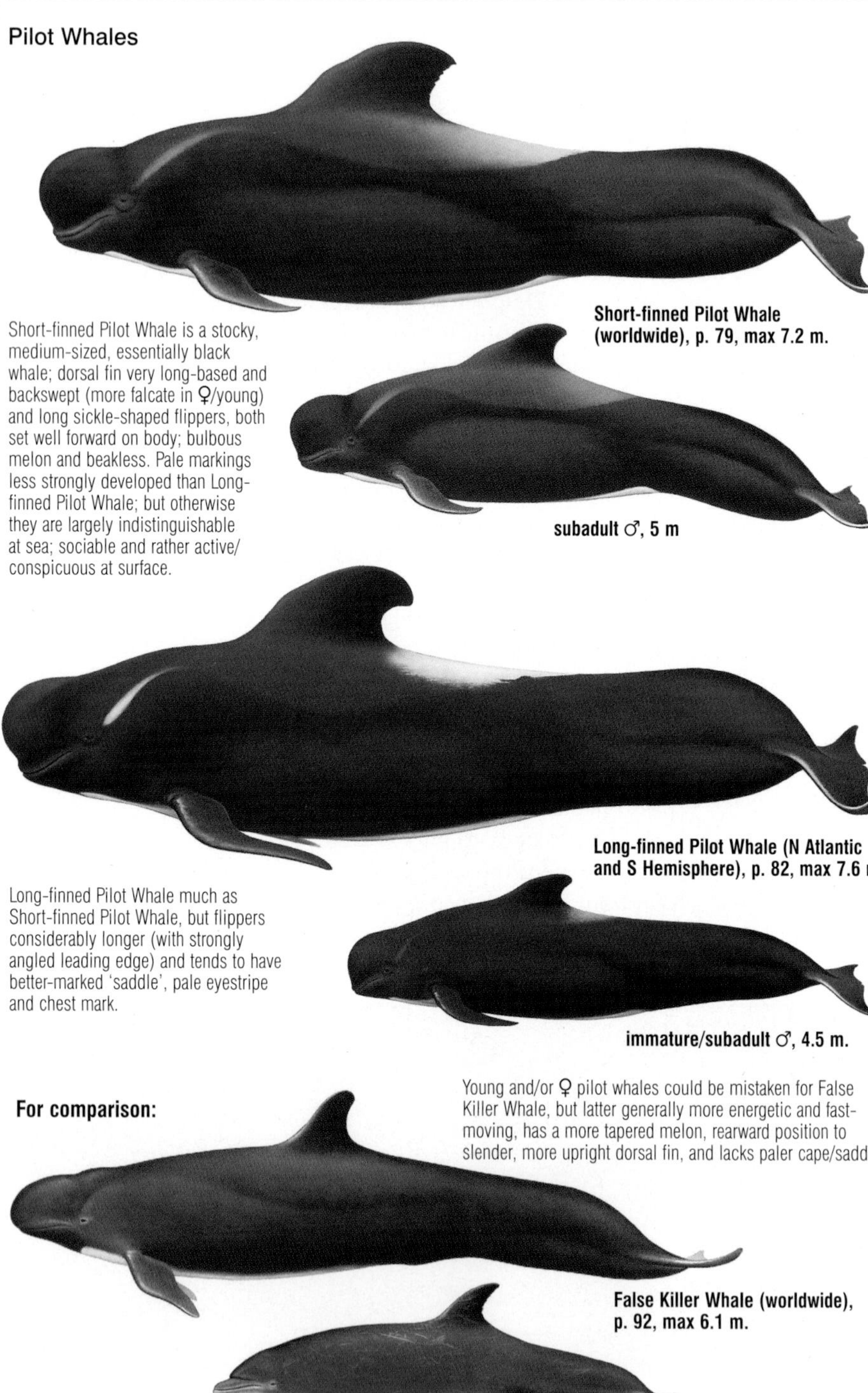

Short-finned Pilot Whale (worldwide), p. 79, max 7.2 m.

Short-finned Pilot Whale is a stocky, medium-sized, essentially black whale; dorsal fin very long-based and backswept (more falcate in ♀/young) and long sickle-shaped flippers, both set well forward on body; bulbous melon and beakless. Pale markings less strongly developed than Long-finned Pilot Whale; but otherwise they are largely indistinguishable at sea; sociable and rather active/conspicuous at surface.

subadult ♂, 5 m

Long-finned Pilot Whale (N Atlantic and S Hemisphere), p. 82, max 7.6 m.

Long-finned Pilot Whale much as Short-finned Pilot Whale, but flippers considerably longer (with strongly angled leading edge) and tends to have better-marked 'saddle', pale eyestripe and chest mark.

immature/subadult ♂, 4.5 m.

For comparison:

Young and/or ♀ pilot whales could be mistaken for False Killer Whale, but latter generally more energetic and fast-moving, has a more tapered melon, rearward position to slender, more upright dorsal fin, and lacks paler cape/saddle.

False Killer Whale (worldwide), p. 92, max 6.1 m.

Pods of pilot whales often associate with Bottlenose Dolphins.

Bottlenose Dolphin, large offshore form (worldwide), p. 155, max 4.1 m.

Short-finned Pilot Whale

Globicephala macrorhynchus

Temperate to tropical waters. Max 7.2 m.

Priority characters on surfacing

- *Stocky, medium-sized*; much as Long-finned Pilot Whale, sharing characteristic fin shape.
- *Dorsal fin set forward*, c.1/3 *of way back from head, low and falcate, appears backswept*, with very long base relative to height, although shape and size vary strongly with age/sex.
- *Bulbous melon* (varies with age/sex) and no or tiny beak.
- Body *essentially black* but may appear browner/greyer when close.
- Several paler grey marks: diagonal stripe behind eye, a diffuse 'saddle' just behind dorsal fin (may be lacking or difficult to see) and anchor-shaped patch on chest.
- Tail flukes may be raised prior to deep dive (concave trailing edges, midpoint notch and sharply pointed tips); *flippers quite long and sickle-shaped* with sharply pointed tips.

Typical behaviour at surface

- Very *sociable and frequently associates with other species* (mostly smaller dolphins).
- Surfaces to breathe leisurely, with slow swimming and rolls, sometimes logging or floating motionless; blows low and bushy but quite distinct in calm weather.
- Often permits close approach, though ads often shyer than calves.
- Sometimes slaps flukes on surface (lobtailing) and spyhops.
- Travels in lines in scattered subgroups and individuals; when not travelling, rafts in tight groups.

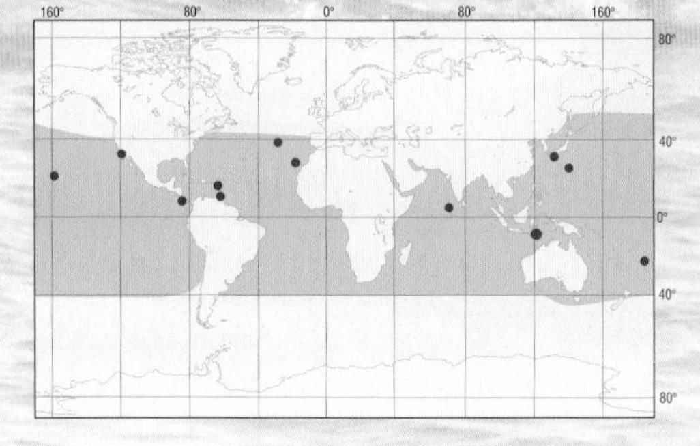

SIMILAR SPECIES

At sea usually indistinguishable from ***Long-finned Pilot Whale***, although range very helpful for separating them. Northern limit of Short-finned and southern of Long-finned potentially overlap, but latter usually in colder temperate waters of N Atlantic and S Hemisphere, whilst in N Pacific only Short-finned now present. Long-finned tends to have more conspicuous 'saddle', and pale eyestripe and chest mark reduced, but these features vary individually and difficult to appreciate, whilst bulbous melon larger in older ♂. Flippers average shorter, less than *c.*15% of overall length (*c.*25% in Long-finned), with gentle-curved edges, but again, difficult to determine at sea. Dead animals may be identified by number of teeth and flipper length, but some overlap between them. Much experience and prolonged views needed to separate them in overlap zone. Could also be confused with other, smaller blackfish, namely ***False Killer Whale***, but less likely with ***Pygmy Killer*** and ***Melon-headed Whales***. However, dorsal fin shape and position, and overall larger size with stronger globular-shaped head, as well as different behaviours, identify pilot whales from all these.

Short-finned Pilot Whales: adult ♂ at rear; foreground possible ♀ and calf. Adult ♂♂ have much larger, more lobe-shaped dorsal fin than ♀ or juveniles.

VARIATION

Age/sex Ad ♂ larger, and develops larger and more swollen head with better-defined melon, which becomes more globular in older ♂, and may overhang snout; dorsal fin also highly characteristic, being strongly hooked with thicker leading edge; deepened tailstock with post-anal keel. Body may be scarred. Young quite slender and dorsal fin smaller/narrower and

Short-finned Pilot Whale

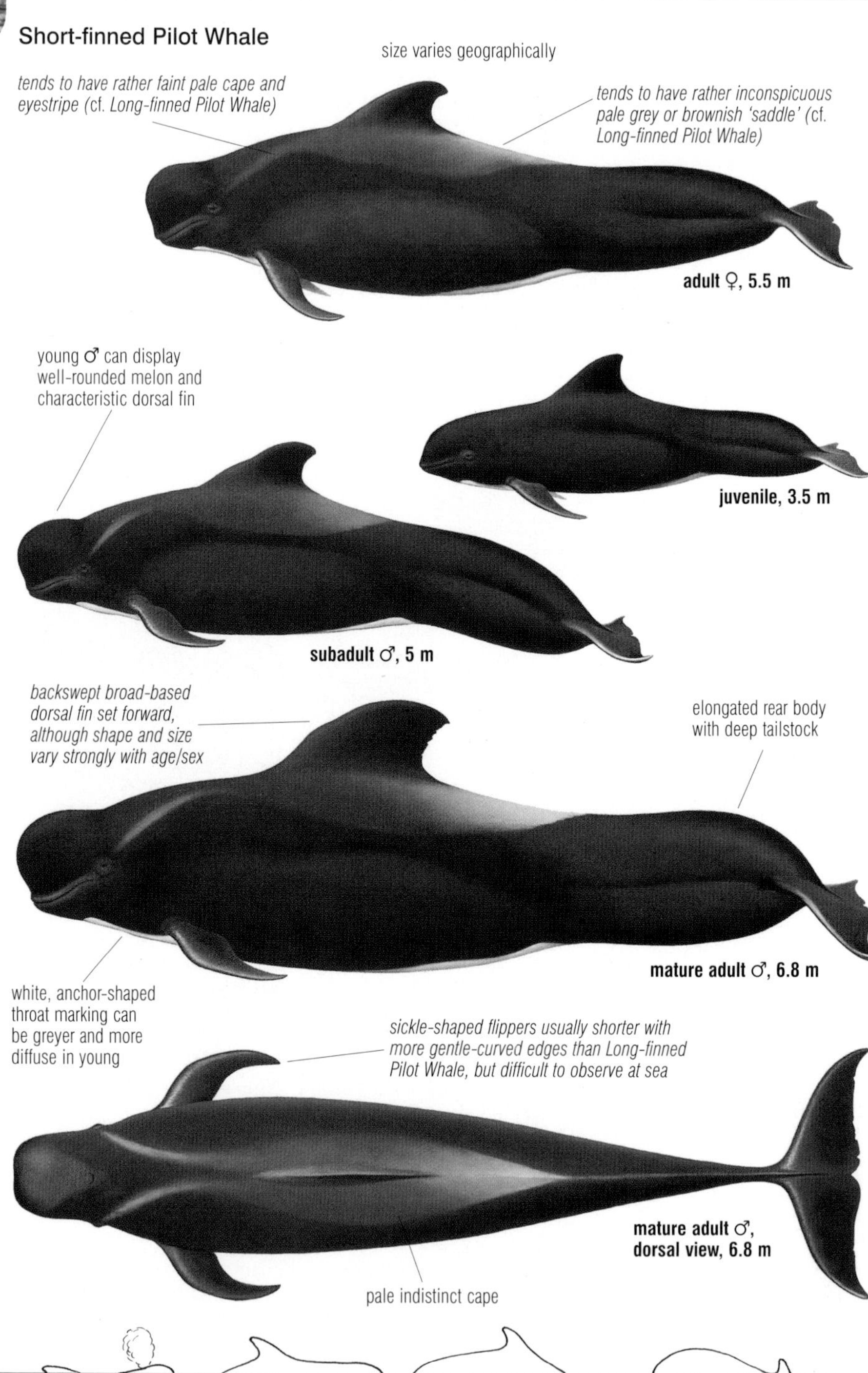

Surfaces well above surface, often effortlessly; blows low and bushy (obvious in calm weather); often in tight pods; note variable dorsal fin; makes steeper arching rolls to deep dive (with sharp bend of thick tailstock), sometimes raising flukes in finale.

Mixed age/sex pod of Short-finned Pilot Whales. Typically logs in calm seas; note 2 bulls (1 in foreground) with characteristic broad-based dorsal fin.

more central on back. Calf averages slimmer and more uniform brown. **Physical notes** Full-grown ad 3.6–7.2 m (most < ♂ 6.8 m and ♀ 5.5 m) and 1–4 tons. Newborn 1.4–1.9 m and *c.*60 kg. **Taxonomy** Two distinct geographic forms off Japan differ in size, morphology and DNA, and breeding cycle, but not yet recognised taxonomically.

DISTRIBUTION & POPULATION

Generally abundant in tropical and warm-temperate seas of all major mid-latitude oceans, reaching 25°S off both coasts of S America, to S Africa, W & S Australia and New Zealand, and north to New Jersey (USA), Madeira and Canaries (more exceptionally Bay of Biscay), Japan and Vancouver (Canada). Absent from Mediterranean, but common in Caribbean. Sea-current changes which affect prey availability may cause local N–S movements, but some populations strictly resident. *Population* No overall estimate, but probably at least 150,000 in tropical E Pacific and 18,000–19,000 off Japan.

ECOLOGY

Groups typically 15–50, sometimes several 100s, of mixed age/sex, with usually 1 ad ♂ to every 8 ad ♀♀, which usually remain within natal school for life, but ♂♂ move between family groups to mate. Schools in active travel form long lines up to 0.6 km long. *Breaching* More frequent than Long-finned Pilot Whale. *Diving* May remain underwater for up to 27 min, reaching 800–900 m. *Diet* Squid predominant, but octopus and fish also taken; mostly feeds at night. *Reproduction* Sexually mature at *c.*9 (♀) and 13–16 (♂) yrs old. Cows give birth to single calf every 6–9 yrs. Gestation *c.*15–16 months and calves weaned at 24–42 months. Older ♀♀ give birth less often, but may breed until over 40 yrs old, caring for their final calf for as long as 15 yrs. Season varies regionally. *Lifespan* Up to 63 yrs.

Spyhopping Short-finned Pilot Whale.

Surfacing ♀ and calf: colour ranges from black, in poor light, to brownish, in direct sun; in good light, eyestripe (calf) and pale saddle behind dorsal fin (cow) can be visible.

DISTINCTIVE POPULATIONS

Two geographically and genetically well-separated forms.

Nominate *G. m. melas* N Atlantic: described in box.

Race ***G. m. edwardii*** S Hemisphere: differs chiefly in having more distinctive 'saddle' and eye blaze.

SIMILAR SPECIES

Could be confused with almost identical and partially overlapping ***Short-finned Pilot Whale*** of warmer waters, but see latter. Other similar species are ***Killer*** and ***False Killer Whales***. Former, given reasonable views, readily identified by white markings and very different fin shape of at least some pod members. Long-finned Pilot Whale, particularly young and/or ♀♀, could be mistaken for False Killer Whale which is generally more active, energetic and fast-moving, has a more tapered melon, rearward position to slender, more upright dorsal fin and lacks paler saddle.

VARIATION

Age/sex ♂ averages up to *c.*1 m longer than ♀. Dorsal fin in ad ♂ almost flag-like with deeply concave trailing edge, thick rounded tip and forms less upright triangle than ad ♀; sickle-shaped in young. Melon often better developed in ♂, especially older animals, when may overhang upper jaw. Most ads have some scarring. Calf as ad but uniformly paler. Young also paler (often slightly spotted) and have pointed, more dolphin-like, dorsal fin positioned further forward. **Physical notes** ♂ 4–7.6 m and up to 3 tons, ♀ 3.8–5.7 m and 2–2.5 tons.

Long-finned Pilot Whale

Globicephala melas

Temperate to subpolar waters. Max 7.6 m.

Priority characters on surfacing

- *Stocky, medium-sized* with characteristic lobed dorsal fin.
- *Dorsal fin set forward, c.1/3 of way back from head, low, falcate and backswept*, with very long base relative to height.
- *Bulbous melon* (varies with age/sex); imperceptible beak.
- *Body essentially blackish* but may show browner/greyer tones at close range.
- Several pale marks, often with whiter and *better-marked diagonal eyestripe, 'saddle' behind dorsal fin* and anchor-shaped ventral patch (all difficult to observe and vary individually).
- Tail flukes may be raised prior to deep dive (concave edge, pointed tips and median notch); *flippers longer than previous species* with strongly angled leading edge forming sickle-shaped 'elbow'.

Typical behaviour at surface

- Very *sociable and commonly associates with smaller cetaceans.*
- Quite visible on surface (blow low, up to 1 m, but can be quite distinct in calm weather).
- Swims leisurely and rolls slowly, often fairly inactive at surface, logging or floating motionless, mostly dorsal fin and blowhole exposed; sometimes lobtailing or spyhopping.
- Surfacing groups often approach slow-moving vessels, though ads tend to be shyer than calves and young generally more active.

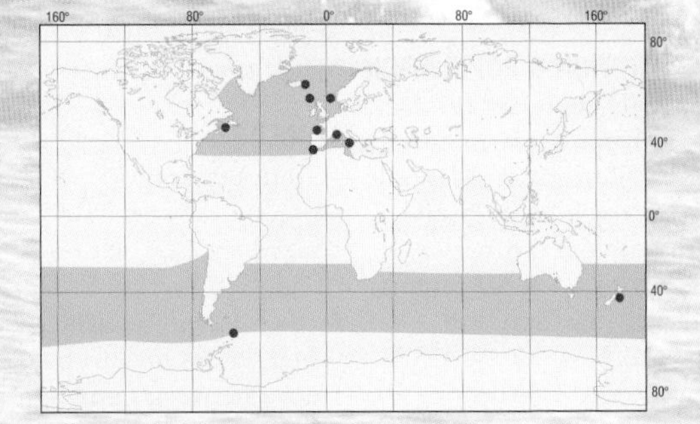

Long-finned Pilot Whale: stocky, essentially blackish, with bulbous melon and forward-set, backswept dorsal fin characteristic of pilot whales, but separation from Short-finned generally impossible at sea.

Long-finned Pilot Whale

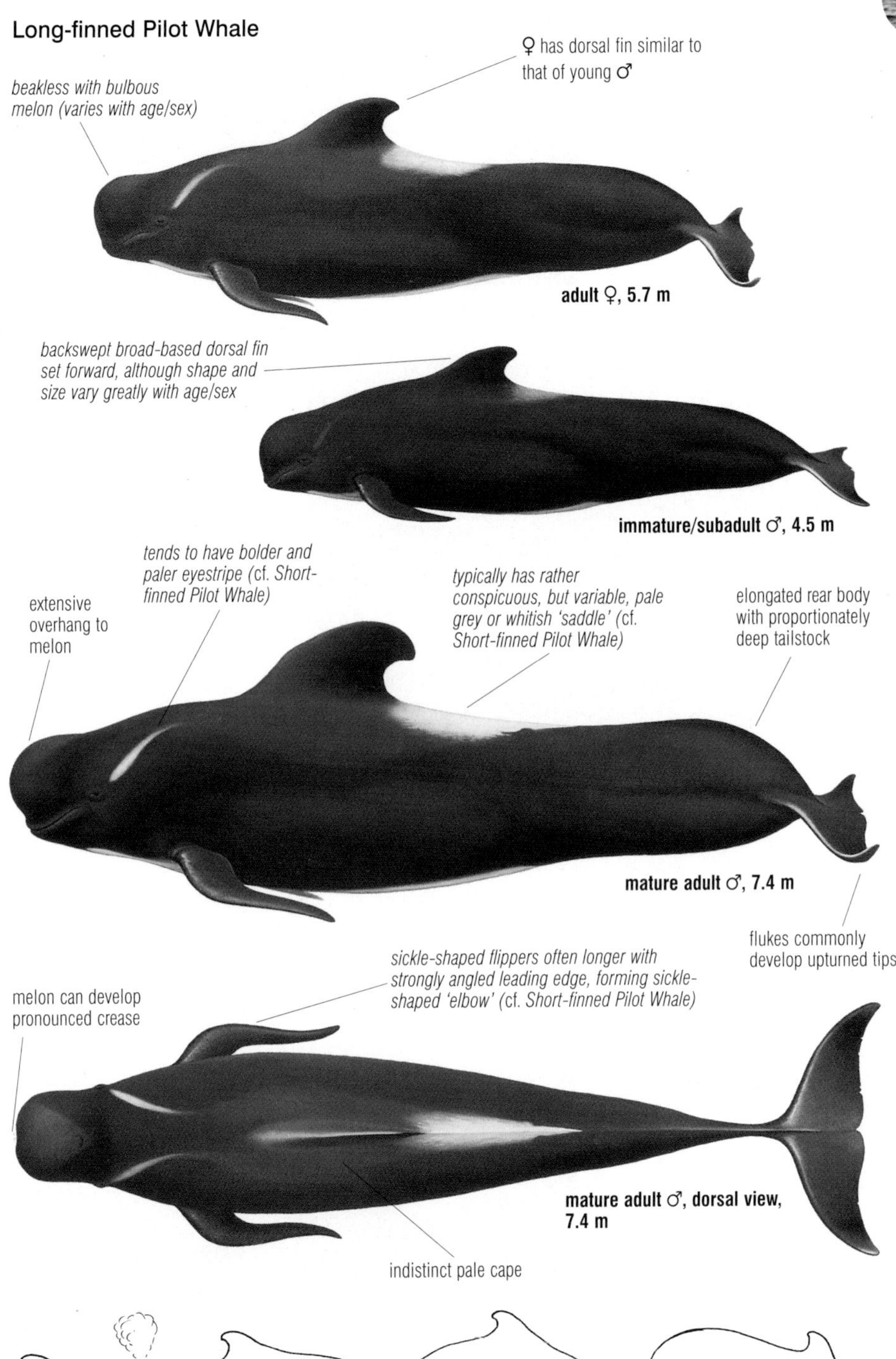

Often surfaces well clear of surface; blows low and bushy (obvious in calm weather); often in tight pods; note characteristic but variable dorsal fin; prior to deep dives, steep arching rolls of back and tailstock, and sometimes raises flukes in finale.

Newborn 1.75–2 m and *c.*75–80 kg. **Taxonomy** Two races occasionally treated as species, with an unnamed form in western N Pacific known from subfossil record.

Calf (foreground) and ♀ Long-finned Pilot Whale.

DISTRIBUTION & POPULATION
S Hemisphere (*G. m. edwardii*), where particularly associated with Humboldt and Benguela Currents, and the Falklands, but circumpolar. Reaches 14°S but generally replaced by previous species in tropical and subtropical seas. Disjunct population in N Atlantic, from N Carolina (USA) and Azores north to Greenland and Barents Sea (nominate). Prefers deep waters. Largely nomadic and penetrates almost to sea-ice (has reached 68°S in C Pacific, though generally not below 60°S). Largest aggregations in winter and spring in continental shelf waters, closer inshore in summer/autumn. *Population G. m. edwardii* perhaps 200,000 in Antarctic waters, 10,000–20,000 of nominate form in western N Atlantic and possibly as many as 775,000 elsewhere in north.

Long-finned Pilot Whale, showing 'anchor-shaped' ventral patch and long flipper with strongly angled leading edge.

ECOLOGY
Often in loose aggregations of several 100s or even 1,000, but usually fewer than 50. Social pattern little known but pods often contain more ♀♀; structure usually stable. Groups tighter on move, or being chased, than if feeding. *Breaching* Almost fully vertical, usually falling back on fore-sides; more frequent in young. *Diving* Usually *c.*10 min (max *c.*16 min) and can reach at least 600 m, but more commonly 30–60 m. *Diet* Fish and squid; frequently taken in deep water, mostly at night, but also inshore. *Reproduction* Sexually mature at *c.*8 (♀) to *c.*13 yrs (♂).Cows give birth to a single calf every 3–6 yrs, mostly Apr–Sep in N Atlantic, Oct–Apr in S Hemisphere. Gestation 12–16 months and calves weaned at 18–44 months (may overlap with next pregnancy). Older ♀♀ help care for calves of other ♀♀, once they become infertile (at 40–55 yrs old). *Lifespan* Up to 60+ yrs.

Long-finned Pilot Whales: typical tight logging pod with bull (second animal): the farthest animal has the relatively obvious whitish saddle.

Small 'blackfish' whales and Risso's Dolphin

Pygmy Killer Whale: separation from Melon-headed Whale difficult, but note paler/greyer body, narrower cape with more extensive dark area on rounder head.

Pygmy Killer, Melon-headed and False Killer Whales and Risso's Dolphin, together with the pilot whales and perhaps Killer Whale, form a rather distinctive group traditionally classified as the Globicephalinae, although a recent molecular study suggests that Killer Whale might be better placed with Irrawaddy Dolphin in the subfamily Orcininae. Despite their vernacular names, they are all oceanic dolphins and all are small to almost mid-sized, with the largest, False Killer Whale, rather similar in size to pilot whales. They are largely pantropical and overlap broadly in range (especially in the Pacific), with Risso's Dolphin also further north and south in temperate waters, and all are generally rather sociable. Until very recently all, except Risso's Dolphin, were best known from strandings, but in recent years observers have started to become better acquainted with these animals at sea.

Melon-headed Whales: similar to overlapping Pygmy Killer Whale but usually far more gregarious, and best identified by its all-black coloration, thin white lips, dark cape that dips low below dorsal fin, and black 'bandit' mask.

Risso's Dolphin is included here because it is not always distinctly pale and scarred; some appear darker with a smaller fin and less square-shaped head. Pygmy Killer, Melon-headed and False Killer Whales are darker grey or more blackish, but latter is distinctly larger, thus Pygmy Killer and Melon-headed are most similar in size and appearance. The comparison plate also includes Bottlenose and Rough-toothed Dolphins as they often have a tall dorsal fin and dark coloration. Note that young pilot whales can look confusingly smaller, slighter and have a more falcate dorsal fin, and thus superficially resemble False Killer Whale; also, the tall fin of Risso's Dolphin can recall that of young Killer Whales.

The vernacular names of Pygmy Killer Whale and Melon-headed Whale are rather confusing as the former has the more rounded, melon-like head, whilst the latter has a more pointed/conical or triangular head shape, and above all, is not a whale but a dolphin. A better name for the species might be Electra Dolphin which derives from its scientific name and reflects its energetic and erratic behaviour.

Unlike the similar Pygmy Killer Whale, the Melon-headed Whale has more pointed beak (especially in young) and lacks a white chin; in good light, dark cape that dips low below dorsal fin is diagnostic. Often travels in large herds, throwing up lots of whitewater.

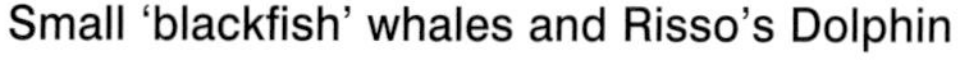

Small 'blackfish' whales and Risso's Dolphin

Pygmy Killer Whale (worldwide), p. 87, max 2.6 m

Small, beakless dolphin with narrow black cape, white lips and chin, rounded and shorter head, relatively tall (variable) falcate or more pointed dorsal fin, and short/round flippers; elusive and occurs in small pods, and only occasionally bow-rides.

Melon-headed Whale (worldwide), p. 89, max 2.8 m

Small/slim, beakless dolphin, with even darker dorsal and facial areas, cape dips below dorsal fin, but has only narrow white lips (difficult to see); blunt-tipped head may appear more triangular in dorsal view, and has tall falcate dorsal fin, in some with rounded apex (but much overlap with Pygmy Killer Whale), whilst flippers sharper pointed; highly gregarious and sometimes bow-rides.

False Killer Whale (worldwide), p. 92, max 6.1 m

Large, beakless dolphin, distinctly larger and more elongated than above two species; relatively tall curved dorsal fin (on mid-back), blunt conical head, no visible cape, and long elbow-shaped forward-set flippers; sociable, frequently acrobatic and sometimes bow-rides.

Risso's Dolphin (worldwide), p. 94, max 4 m

Robust dolphin, with tall falcate dorsal fin, bulbous head and bulging face; pale grey, adults often heavily scarred, with almost whitish body; in small pods and active at surface, especially (darker) young.

For comparison:

Pods of some of the above species sometimes associate with other dolphins, and broadly overlap in range with oceanic Bottlenose Dolphins and, at a glance, may appear confusingly darker with a similar dorsal fin.

Bottlenose Dolphin, large offshore form (worldwide), p. 155, max 4.1 m

Also has a relatively tall dorsal fin and is largely dark, but is unmistakable in close views.

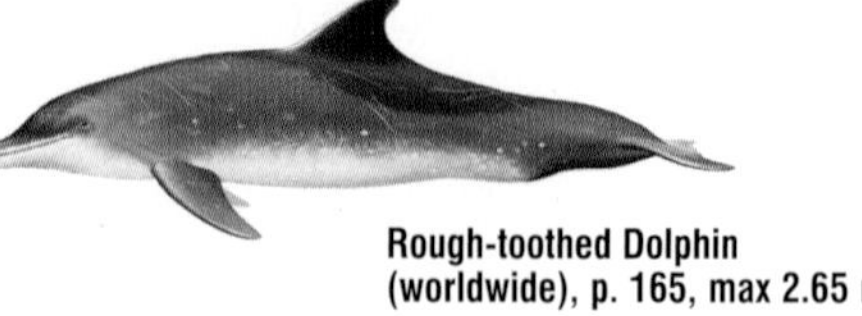

Rough-toothed Dolphin (worldwide), p. 165, max 2.65 m

Pygmy Killer Whale

Feresa attenuata

Tropical and subtropical waters. Max 2.6 m.

Priority characters on surfacing

- Overall, a *darkish small dolphin* with noticeably robust body, *rounded head and no beak*.
- Proportionately tall, slightly pointed and *falcate dorsal fin*.
- *Narrow blackish cape with only shallow sweep near dorsal fin.*
- Except in good light, often appears confusingly uniform grey/ blackish.
- Variable white scratches and scars on body.
- White chin to 'lips' (variable) and white belly patch normally difficult to see or invisible.
- *Flippers moderately long with rounded tips*; noticeably slimmer rear body.

Typical behaviour at surface

- Normally *in small groups* which roll synchronously, shoulder-to-shoulder.
- Evasive, tends to avoid boats (only occasionally bow-rides) and mainly found in deep water.
- In calm seas may raft at surface showing just part of dorsal areas, especially melon to fin.
- Usually a slow, sluggish swimmer but, occasionally, rather fast, porpoising clear of water, especially when feeding.
- Rarely acrobatic but occasionally leaps clear of water during signalling and social behaviours.

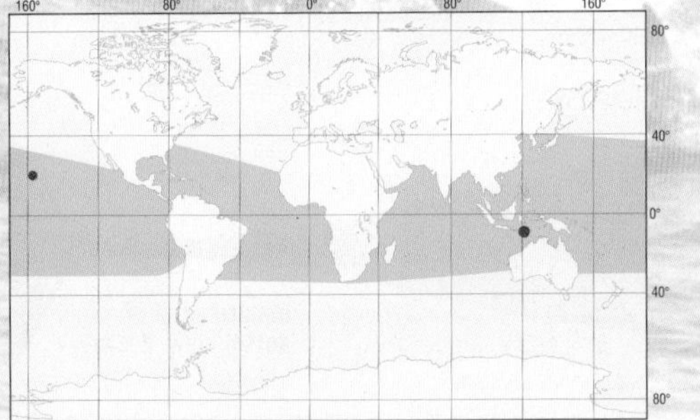

SIMILAR SPECIES

Most likely confusion is with ***Melon-headed Whale*** and separation difficult unless following observed: extent of blackish cape and paler/greyer rest of body; more rounded head with melon-like forehead (rather than narrower head with sloping forehead) and less-pointed flippers that are perhaps proportionately shorter; also most have some pale scars and white on chin (lacking in Melon-headed). Much less gregarious than Melon-headed and school size may prove useful in identification. Unlike superficially similar ***False Killer Whale***, Pygmy Killer is smaller with compact body, more rounded head, relatively larger dorsal fin and different flipper shape, whilst white on 'lips' and, sometimes, chin diagnostic. Distinctive white belly patch difficult to see (usually smaller and greyer on Melon-headed and lacking or virtually so in False Killer). Unlikely to be confused with pale/scarred ad ***Risso's Dolphin*** which

Pygmy Killer Whale: note rounded head with broad white lips (and sometimes chin), irregular white ventral patch and round-tipped flippers.

Pygmy Killer Whale

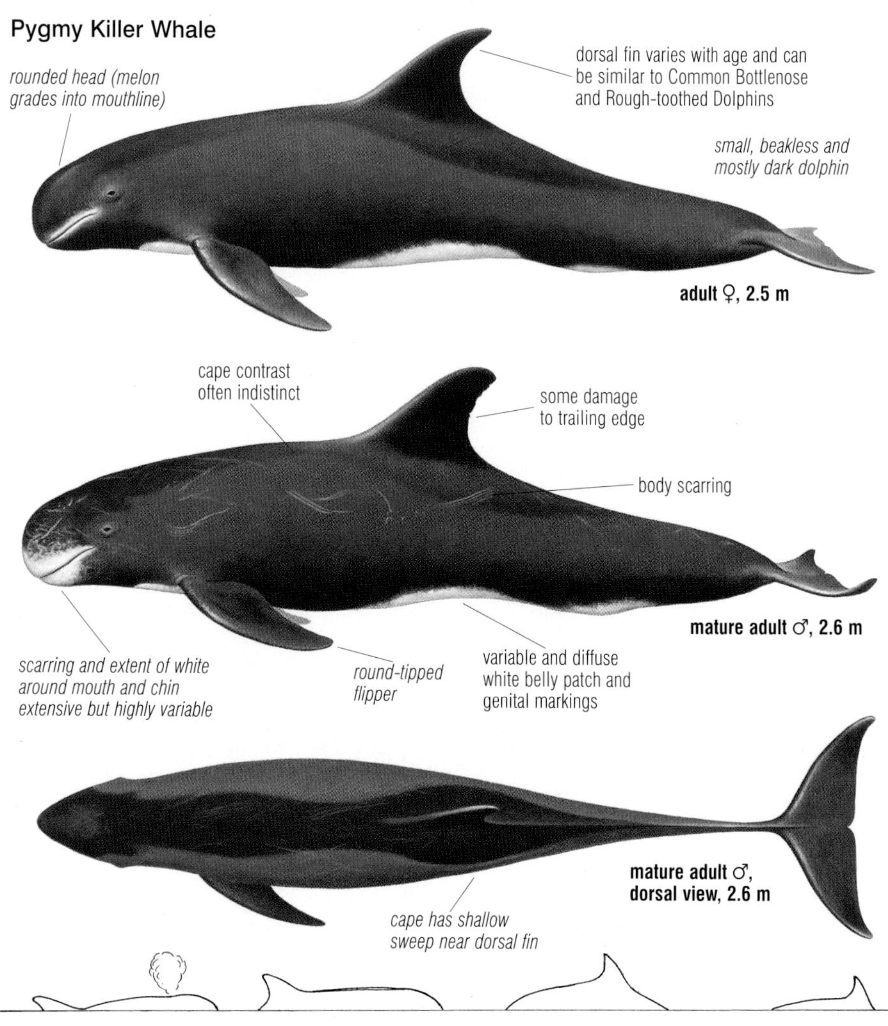

Surfaces rather low, usually in small groups which roll synchronously, but occasionally a more lively swimmer, especially when feeding; note more rounded head profile.

also differs structurally, but young Risso's darker and less distinctive. Mainly when distant and due to small size, Pygmy Killer could be overlooked among dolphins, but is beakless and colour, structure and behaviour should readily confirm identity.

VARIATION

Age/sex Sexes apparently overlap in size, but forehead lump less developed in young; in some ads can develop as more extensive melon, even appearing somewhat forward-leaning in profile. Body of ads, especially mature ♂, scarred. Calf perhaps slimmer and more uniform. **Physical notes** 2.1–2.6 m and 110–170 kg. Newborn *c.*80 cm.

DISTRIBUTION & POPULATION

Tropical and subtropical seas of all major oceans, usually in deep, warm waters, and rarely near land, except around oceanic islands, reaching north to Florida (USA), Senegal (W Africa), Arabia and Japan, and south to N Argentina, S Africa, N Australia and Peru. Perhaps most frequent and common in tropical E Pacific, off Hawaii, and Japan. No seasonal migrations reported. *Population* No

Pygmy Killer Whales with Humpback Whale; note rounded head shape, robust body and white lips (often difficult to observe).

lobtail. Sometimes utters growling sounds at surface. *Breaching* Occasional, high above surface. *Diving* No data. *Diet* Apparently mostly cephalopods and small fish, but perhaps occasionally also *Stenella* dolphins and Short-beaked Common Dolphin. *Reproduction* Age of sexual maturity estimated when reaches *c.*2 m. Breeding data extremely few. Calves presumably born in summer. *Lifespan* Unknown.

overall estimate, but 40,000 considered present in E tropical Pacific.

ECOLOGY

Usually in groups of <50 (typically 15–25), but sometimes 100, which swim in coordinated lines but bunch in alarm. Only occasionally bow-rides, sometimes beside Rough-toothed Dolphins in Hawaii, but usually does not associate with other cetaceans. May spyhop and

Pygmy Killer Whale: note rounded melon-shaped head, white lips and robust forebody with round-tipped flippers.

Melon-headed Whale

(Electra Dolphin)

Peponocephala electra

Tropical waters. Max 2.8 m.

Priority characters on surfacing

- Rather small/slim, *beakless dark dolphin* with torpedo-shaped body.
- Conical, *blunt-tipped head* shape (in profile appears narrow, tapered or slopes to point).
- *Tall, falcate dorsal fin* may recall Common Bottlenose Dolphin.
- Medium to dark overall; *darker/blacker cape dips low below dorsal fin*, but other features inconspicuous or rarely visible at sea (*cf.* Pygmy Killer Whale).
- Look for *narrow white 'lips', darker facial area* and *sharply pointed flippers*. Indistinct greyish-white belly patch rarely visible.

Typical behaviour at surface

- *Highly gregarious* (*cf.* Pygmy Killer Whale).
- In some regions, normally avoids boats and chiefly far from land. In others, e.g. Maldives, Seychelles, Hawaii and Philippines, where occurs close to shore, readily bow-rides.
- If undisturbed can be quite demonstrative on surface.
- Fast swimmers, porpoising regularly in low leaps with much spray, making most features

SIMILAR SPECIES

Main confusion is with ***Pygmy Killer Whale***. Also quite similar to ***False Killer Whale*** but latter distinctly larger with different shape, bent flippers, proportionately smaller dorsal fin and more rounded head, and lacks white on lips or white belly patch, and has different behaviour. See ***Risso's Dolphin*** which normally has much taller dorsal fin and ads are heavily scarred, but young less distinctive. Could be confused with dark dolphins but is beakless. Possible confusion with ***Burmeister's Porpoise*** which is similarly dark and performs jerky, splashing leaps, but is distinctly smaller, more compact and coastal, and less tropical, forms smaller schools and has very different dorsal fin.

VARIATION

Age/sex ♂ develops comparatively longer flippers, taller dorsal fin and broader tail flukes, and some show pronounced ventral keel rear of the anus. Some ads develop quite substantial

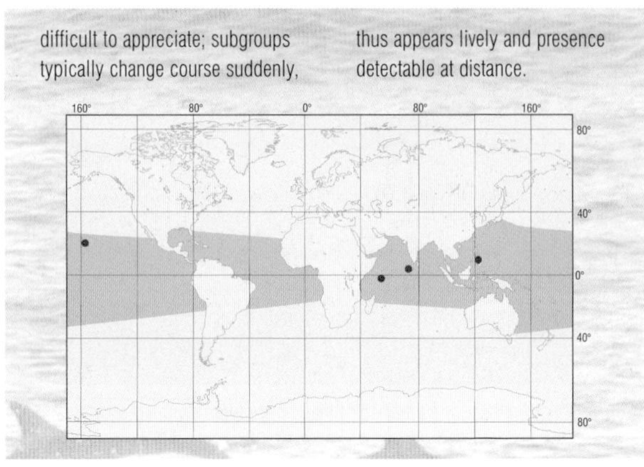
difficult to appreciate; subgroups typically change course suddenly, thus appears lively and presence detectable at distance.

Melon-headed Whale

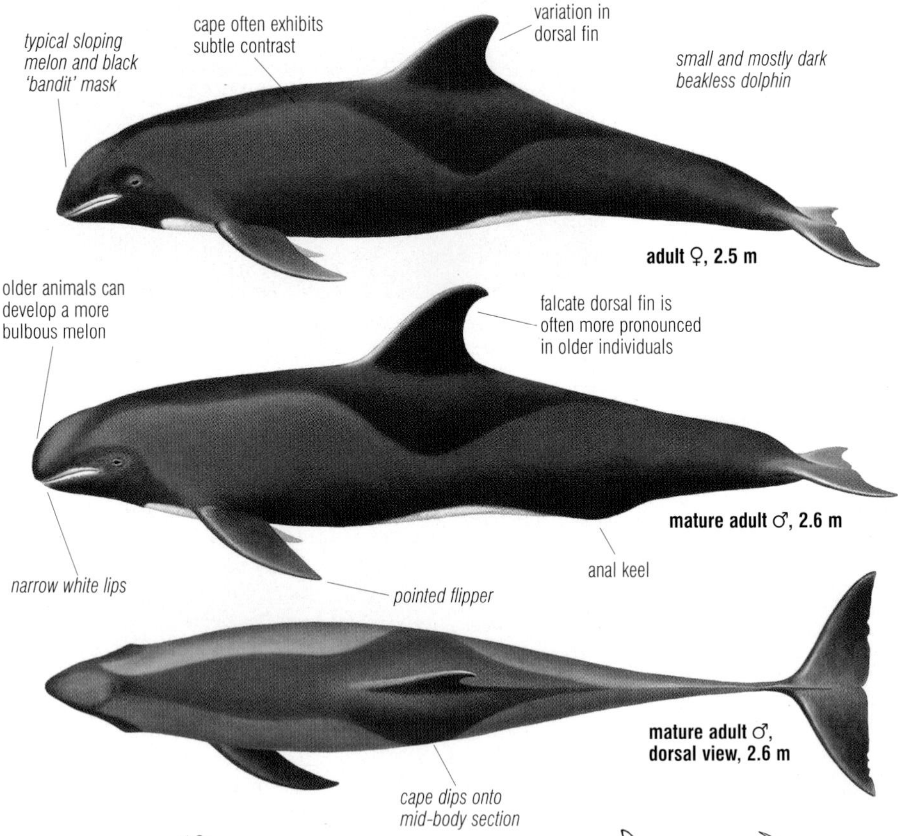

typical sloping melon and black 'bandit' mask

cape often exhibits subtle contrast

variation in dorsal fin

small and mostly dark beakless dolphin

adult ♀, 2.5 m

older animals can develop a more bulbous melon

falcate dorsal fin is often more pronounced in older individuals

mature adult ♂, 2.6 m

narrow white lips

pointed flipper

anal keel

mature adult ♂, dorsal view, 2.6 m

cape dips onto mid-body section

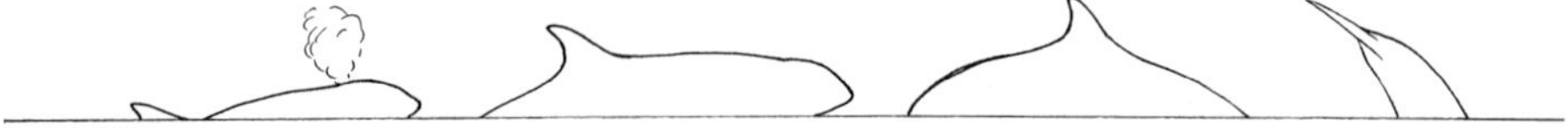

Typically energetic, porpoising low (often appears to skim surface with two-thirds of body); frequently in huge pods that suddenly change course; note more triangular head profile.

Melon-headed Whale: note somewhat pointed head, narrow whitish lips, and (often hard to see) black 'bandit' mask.

bulbous forehead. **Physical notes** 2.1–2.8 m and up to 210 kg. Newborn *c.*1 m and *c.*15 kg.

DISTRIBUTION & POPULATION

Cosmopolitan in pantropical oceans, with most records between 20°N and 20°S. Occasionally in more temperate regions, with extralimitals recorded in S Africa and NW Europe (during warm-water incursions), but regularly occurs north only to the USA, W Africa, Arabia (rare) and S China Sea. Most frequent in the Maldives, Philippines (especially off Cebu), Hawaii, various islands in S Pacific, off E Australia and throughout transequatorial Pacific. *Population* Estimated at 45,000 in tropical E Pacific, with *c.*4,000 in N Gulf of Mexico, but almost no other data.

ECOLOGY

Typically in tight-knit schools of 100–500, exceptionally 1,000–2,000, albeit comprising much smaller subgroups. Mass-strandings indicate pronounced social cohesion even in larger schools. Strong association with Fraser's Dolphin, and occasionally accompanies Rough-toothed, Spinner or Bottlenose Dolphins. *Diving* No data. *Diet* Primarily pelagic fish, squid and, occasionally, crustaceans. *Reproduction* Sexual maturity 3–7 (♂) or 4–12 (♀) yrs. Gestation *c.*1 yr and calving Aug–Dec, Apr and Jun in S Hemisphere, at least Jul–Oct in N Hemisphere. *Lifespan* Up to 47 yrs.

Although Melon-headed Whales usually 'charge' through the water in dense herds, they sometimes raft at the surface; note blackish colour, relatively large dorsal fin and sloping forehead.

Melon-headed Whales: the dark cape dips low below the dorsal fin and is important for separating this species from Pygmy Killer Whale, which has an almost straight cape; note very narrow pale lips and relatively large dorsal fin.

SIMILAR SPECIES

Combination of long/slender body, conical head, shape of dorsal fin (although quite variable) and flippers, and behaviour, are important. At least twice as long as ***Pygmy Killer*** and ***Melon-headed Whales***, and lacks whitish lips, with different shape (especially head and flippers), overall darker and more uniform body, and small puffy blows. Usually clearly darker (lacking white patches on flanks) than same-sized ♀/young ***Killer Whale*** which may otherwise appear similar at distance. Distinguishable from distant pilot whales by slender head and body, sickle-shaped dolphin-like dorsal fin on mid-back (rather than more forward and rounded), and more acrobatic/demonstrative behaviour. Separation from ***Risso's Dolphin*** (noticeably taller dorsal fin, squarer head and ads heavily scarred) and ***pilot whales*** (backswept, broader-based fin set forward on back and more bulbous head) usually easy, especially if typical behaviour observed. In close views, several other characters listed under these confusion species may also prove useful.

False Killer Whale

Pseudorca crassidens

Tropical waters. Max 6.1 m.

Priority characters on surfacing

- *Long-bodied, dark and beakless*; distinctly larger than previous 2 species with characteristic longer elbow-shaped flippers.
- *Almost entirely blackish/slate grey* (*no visible cape*) with unscarred body, but some have slightly paler/greyer head and sides (pale W on chest usually invisible).
- Rather erect, *falcate dorsal fin* that is shaped like a parallelogram with a flat top, set on mid-back (*cf.* pilot whales).
- Blunt, conical head has low but quite pronounced melon-like forehead; tip of upper jaw slightly overhangs lower jaw, giving slightly round-beaked impression.
- *Flippers rather long, strongly bent* and pointed, and set forward on body.

Typical behaviour at surface

- The only blackfish that *frequently bow-rides* (usually in coastal waters, but note *Pygmy Killer* and *Melon-headed Whales* also do so in some regions). Blow fairly conspicuous and bushy.
- School size varies from fewer than 10 to 100s, typically scattered over several km.
- Typically *fast-moving and energetic*; often travels fast and low showing little more than a splash and a dorsal fin, but at time leaps gracefully clear of water (in low, flat arcs, rising at varying angles).
- Often associates with other cetaceans, especially Bottlenose Dolphin.
- Often very acrobatic and may raise head and much of body above surface.

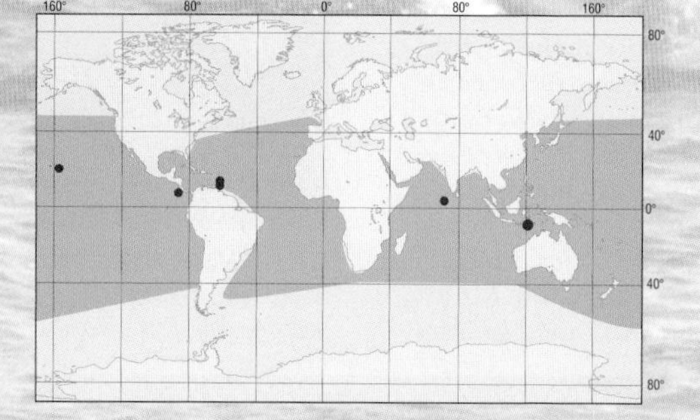

False Killer Whale is an all black, elongated, beakless dolphin; note no evident cape, the pronounced melon and falcate dorsal fin on the mid-back.

False Killer Whale

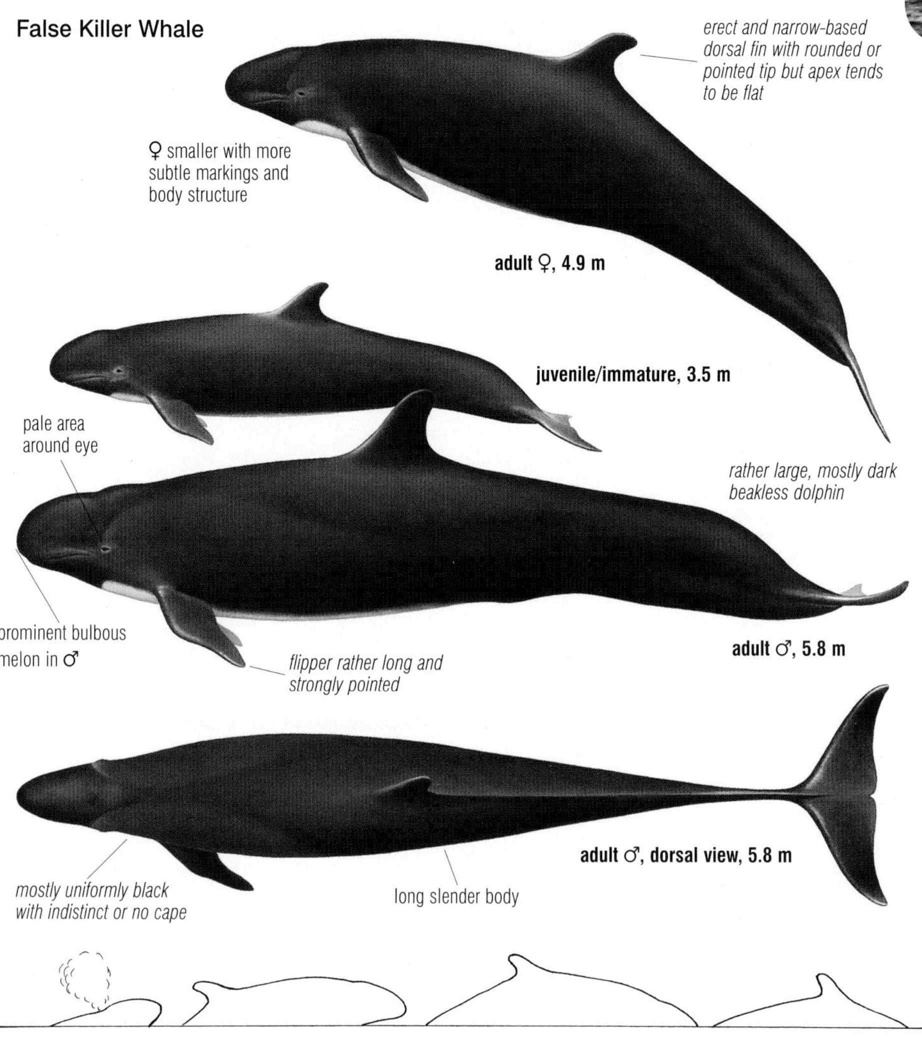

Powerful and graceful above surface; sometimes porpoises fast with sudden turns; erect dorsal fin on mid-back and conical head profile visible, sometimes also the characteristic flippers.

VARIATION

Age/sex Perhaps estimable by overall size, although difficult to appreciate at sea, and older ♂ has more forward-projecting forehead melon, whilst young tend to be uniformly paler. **Physical notes** ♂ 3.7–6.1 m; ♀ 3.5–5 m, and 1.01–2.03 tons. Newborn 1.5–1.9 m and *c.*80 kg. **Taxonomy** Monotypic genus, although some evidence for geographic differences in skull morphology. Genetic data suggest strong regional population structure in C Pacific.

DISTRIBUTION & POPULATION

Widespread between 50°N and 52°S, reaching south to New Zealand, Peru, C Argentina, S Africa and much of N Indian Ocean, and north to Sea of Japan, British Columbia (Canada), Maryland (USA) and Bay of Biscay (exceptionally Scotland and Norway), and penetrates both Red and Mediterranean Seas. Deep water (200 m to at least 2,000 m), except where range approaches land. Seasonal migrations suspected in western N Pacific and winter strandings suggest some movements.

Population Most estimates from Pacific, where 16,500 north of 25°N, 40,000 in tropical east and 500+ off Hawaii, with several 100s in Gulf of Mexico.

False Killer Whales resting at the surface: note the small but visible blow, long black body, and falcate dorsal fin with a flat top, often distinctively parallelogram-like.

Bow-riding False Killer Whales: powerful, fast porpoising in flat arcs clear of water; note overall, head, dorsal fin and flipper structures.

ECOLOGY

Small groups of 10–50 and, sometimes, larger herds of 300 (mass-stranding of 800) usually contain both sexes and all ages; strongly bonded and may associate with other cetaceans. Usually forms smaller and well-scattered groups when travelling, and perhaps when hunting. *Breaching* Frequent, twisting in mid-air to land on its side. *Diving* Estimated to reach 500 m. *Diet* Principally fish and cephalopods, also smaller dolphins; may attack larger whales. *Reproduction* Sexually mature 8–14 yrs. Breeds year-round, though may peak in late winter (Jan–Mar) and calves nursed 18–24 months, with intervals of up to 7 yrs between births. Single calf. Gestation *c.*11–16 months. *Lifespan* Up to 63 yrs.

Easily identified by the blunt head, pale body and large dorsal fin, old Risso's Dolphins become heavily scarred and even almost pure white.

SIMILAR SPECIES

At first glance, might be confused with ***bottlenose dolphins*** and ***pilot whales***, with which it can coexist, but former has beak, and latter is larger with different dorsal fin structure, amongst other obvious differences. Esp. young, confusingly

Risso's Dolphin

Grampus griseus

Tropical/temperate waters. Max 4 m.

Priority characters on surfacing

- Heavily scarred, very broad, pale body with bulbous head (beakless) and conspicuously erect fin. Very young juvs 2-tone grey with conspicuous cape.
- Numerous *pale scratches and scars* on mature animals, with head and back often whiter, albeit with much variation (generally paler with age, but young still uniformly coloured).
- *Very tall falcate dorsal fin* on mid-back.
- Overall somewhat compact but very robust body.
- *Bulbous head and bulging face*, but melon square in profile with abrupt forehead.
- Long, pointed flippers may be visible.
- Darker sides, dorsal fin, flippers and flukes.
- Peculiar, deep V-shaped crease from blowhole to tip of rostrum, but difficult to see or only visible in head-on view at close range.

Typical behaviour at surface

- Blow very indistinct between typically short dives and surfaces at 45° angle; flukes often visible when diving.
- Normally in *groups of 5–50+*. May form lines when hunting. Sometimes associates with other species, principally Bottlenose Dolphin.
- Often active at surface: rarely porpoises like other dolphins, and may bow-ride or swim alongside vessel (but more usually ignores boats and travels rather slowly).
- *Young (darker) animals more demonstrative*, and more frequently spyhop (revealing entire head and body down to flippers), lobtail, flipper-slap and breach.

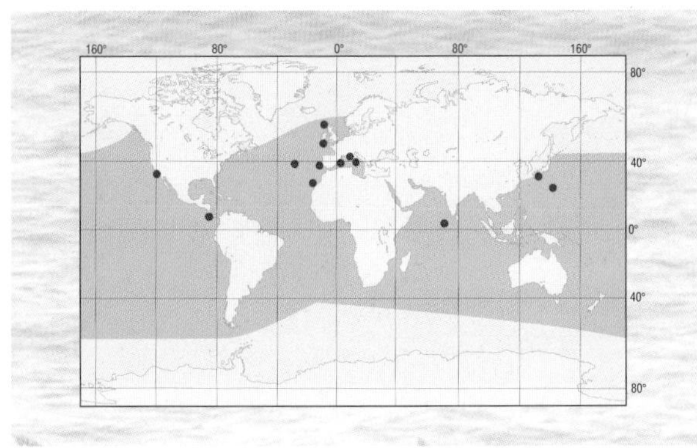

darker, almost unscarred and frequently misidentified by inexperienced observers as either ***Pygmy Killer***, ***Melon-headed*** and ***False Killer Whales***, particularly in suboptimal viewing conditions, although young Risso's rarely seen alone (thus note presence of typical scarred ads in pod). The other three species are usually appreciably darker and differ in structure and surfacing

Risso's Dolphin

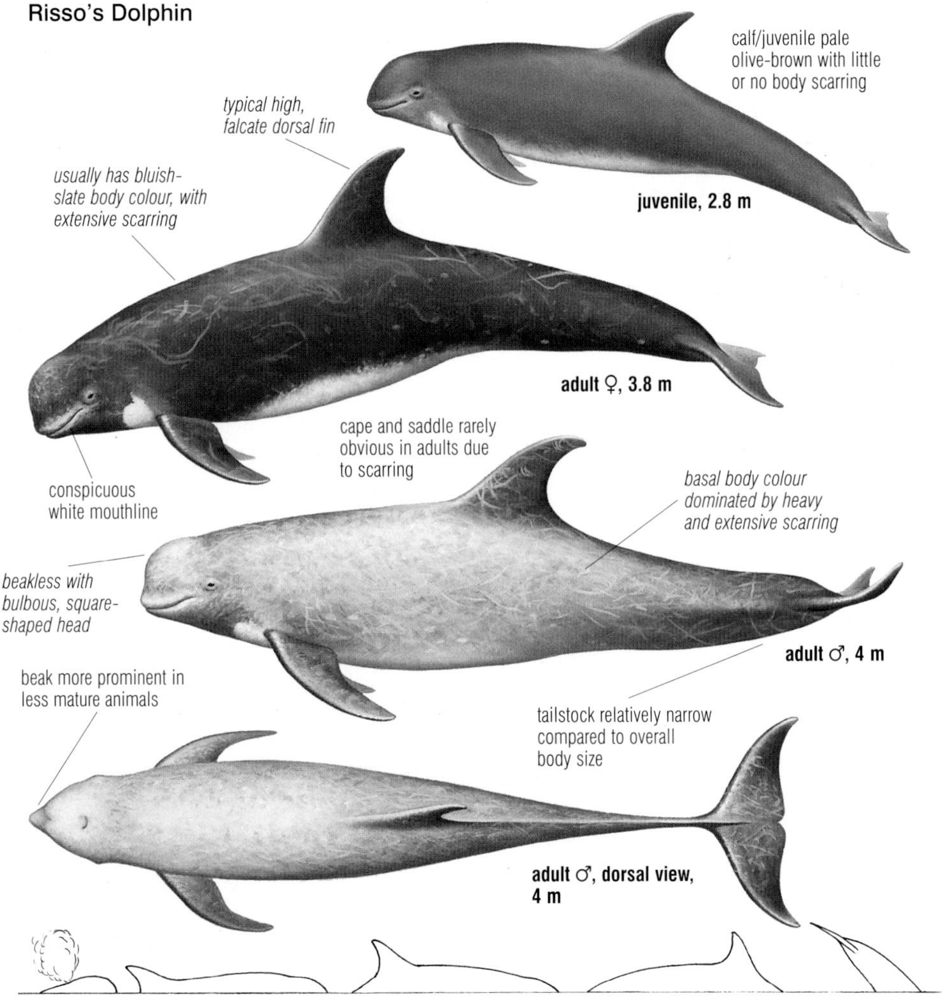

calf/juvenile pale olive-brown with little or no body scarring

typical high, falcate dorsal fin

juvenile, 2.8 m

usually has bluish-slate body colour, with extensive scarring

adult ♀, 3.8 m

cape and saddle rarely obvious in adults due to scarring

conspicuous white mouthline

basal body colour dominated by heavy and extensive scarring

beakless with bulbous, square-shaped head

adult ♂, 4 m

beak more prominent in less mature animals

tailstock relatively narrow compared to overall body size

adult ♂, dorsal view, 4 m

Usually surfaces rather low, when robust body and bulbous head may partially emerge, but very tall falcate dorsal fin always conspicuous; flukes may appear in high/fast porpoising or in diving or other social circumstances.

behaviour. Tall dorsal fin may recall ♀/young ***Killer Whale*** or ***White-beaked Dolphin***, and extensive scarring and whitish skin shared by some ***beaked whales***, but several characters, especially beak shape, should eliminate confusion. Extreme older individuals may appear almost all white and could momentarily be misidentified as ***Irrawaddy and Australian Snubfin Dolphins*** (much-reduced dorsal fin and other features).

Risso's Dolphin, showing variation in scarring and whitening of body: combination of highly erect falcate dorsal fin, grey-and-white scarred body and bulbous (beakless) head make the species unmistakable.

Surfacing ♀ and calf Risso's Dolphin: note 2-tone grey body and conspicuous cape of the calf.

VARIATION

Age/sex Young generally darker with no scarring, being initially olive-buff dorsally and creamy-white ventrally. With age (especially oldest) become much paler, with whiter head (only tip of beak and area around eye dark, and often have extensive scarring). **Physical notes** 2.6–4 m and 300–500 kg, ♀ may be slightly smaller and body size may vary regionally. Newborn 1.1–1.7 m and *c.*20 kg.

DISTRIBUTION & POPULATION

Probably abundant and occurs worldwide, south to Argentina, Chile, S Africa, Australia and New Zealand, and even penetrates Mediterranean and Black Seas. Records from *c.*60°N to 60°S, usually seaward of continental shelf and oceanic island slopes. Some undertake seasonal movements, moving to cooler waters in summer. Prefers deep and continental shelf waters (0–1,000 m) of 15–30°C. *Population* No overall estimates, but probably *c.*175,000 in tropical E Pacific, 85,000 in western N Pacific and E China Sea, and *c.*30,000 each off E & W coasts of USA.

ECOLOGY

Mean group size 10–30 (varies regionally) but solitary individuals or pairs also occur; 100s may gather in an area. Composition fluid though subgroups may exhibit higher degree of fidelity. *Breaching* See box. *Diving* Usually 1–2 min, then up to 12 exhalations at 15–20-sec intervals, but may dive for 30 min and reach at least 300 m. *Diet* Chiefly octopus, cuttlefish, squid and krill, taken in continental shelf areas and mostly at night. *Reproduction* Poorly known: may calve year-round (though Dec–Jun peak in N Atlantic/Mediterranean) with gestation 13–14 months. *Lifespan* At least 30 yrs.

Risso's Dolphins are usually only seen porpoising when being chased by a predator (e.g. Killer Whale); the white scars, blunt head, mottled coloration and very tall dorsal fin are conclusive.

Beluga and Narwhal

Highly distinctive toothed whales (Odontoceti) which constitute a separate family, Monodontidae, and keen observers in search of Narwhal will need to make a high-arctic cruise. They are like large dolphins in size, but each has several striking features, especially the white coloration of Beluga, its highly flexible neck, head and 'lips', and musical vocalisations, whilst the spotted Narwhal has an extraordinary twisted tusk in males, used in contests between rivals, the tusks making a 'clacking' sound; they are perhaps the source of the unicorn legend.

Beluga

Delphinapterus leucas

Arctic and subarctic waters. Max 5.5 m.

Priority characters on surfacing

- Medium-sized, rather elongated but stocky and generally unmistakable in range.
- *Overall pigmentation white to whitish-grey.*
- No dorsal fin, but low serrated darkish ridge/hump on rear back.
- Small/narrow head with quite pronounced bulbous melon and very short beak.
- 'Blubbery' or lumpy sides due to supple, often wrinkled fat-folded skin.
- Variable yellowish tone often apparent, especially on larger animals (local/seasonal).
- Calves dark grey to brownish-grey; imm progressively whiter/spotted with age.
- Flukes have strong convex trailing edge.
- Small, rounded flippers are mobile; head and neck also have considerable flexibility, enabling animals to turn/nod their head quite sharply.

Typical behaviour at surface

- Habitually spends some time at surface. Usually performs 5–6 shallow dives in 1 min, with *c.*3 sec per breath (blow rather inconspicuous), followed by deeper, longer dive. Spyhopping and tail-slapping common.
- Slow swimmer, but highly manoeuvrable and agile, with gently undulating motion in raising head above surface, affording somewhat 'seal-like' impression (rarely leap).
- Sociable, usually in parties of 5–10, but gatherings of several 1,000s known; attracted to river mouths and adapted to shallow, complex coastlines, where capable of manoeuvring through partially ice-covered water.

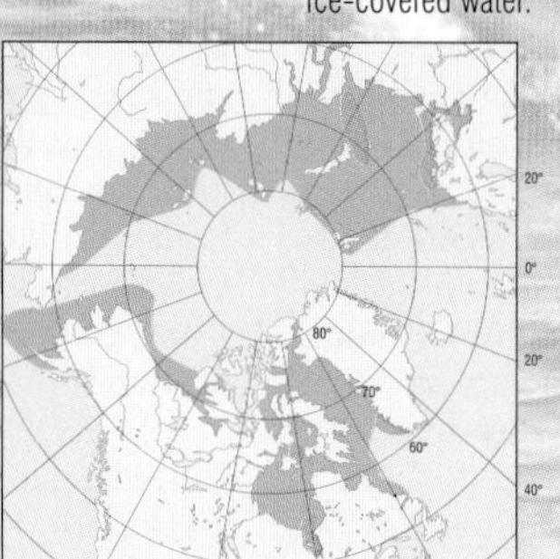

Spyhopping Beluga, the head and neck are very flexibile, enabling animals to turn/nod the head quite sharply.

SIMILAR SPECIES

Within range, unlikely to be confused but note that ***Narwhal*** which overlaps in much of range has quite similar shape and size. Especially young and ♀ Narwhals could be mistaken for young Belugas, but usually accompanied by ads. Narwhal's blotchy/speckled grey/brown pattern, and tusks in ♂♂ usually permit straightforward separation. Older ad ***Risso's Dolphin*** can be sufficiently scarred to appear almost all white and could be mistaken for Beluga, but has much more southerly range and a high dorsal fin.

Beluga

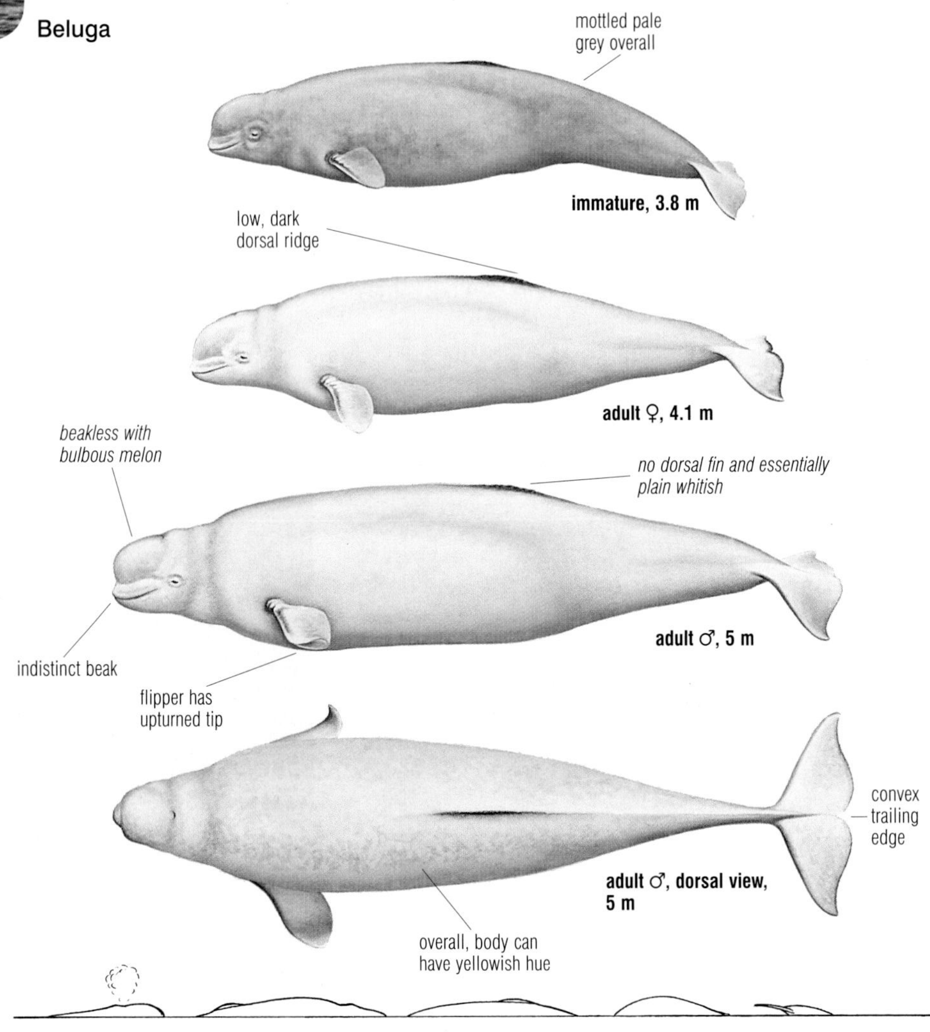

Sluggish but manoeuvrable swimmer, with low gentle surfacing (head sometimes slightly raised above surface); blow rather low and inconspicuous; flukes sometimes lifted at low angle.

VARIATION

Age/sex Full-grown ♂ up to 25% larger/heavier, with larger head and upcurled flippers at tip/rear margin (♀'s flippers flat or only slightly convex). Convex rear margin to flukes more pronounced with age and may have dark trailing edge. Calf dark ash-grey to bluish, sometimes with brownish-red tone. Becomes progressively whiter, gradually and patchily altering to brilliant white when *c.*7–9 yrs old, although dorsal ridge, edges of flippers and flukes may retain dark pigment throughout life. Prior to late-summer moult, ads can acquire a yellowish cast to body. **Physical notes** Largest ad ♂ 5.5 m and ♀ 4.1 m, and weigh 400–1,500 kg, but 2 tons apparently exceptional. Calves average *c.*1.5–1.6 m and *c.*80 kg at birth. **Other data** Considerable neck flexibility and rather mobile head with bulbous melon capable of radical changes in shape, and has rich repertoire of sounds (hence the name 'sea canary'). **Taxonomy** Considerable geographic variation in body size with smallest physically mature

Belugas are highly playful, here one animal dives and another surfaces.

♂ *c.*3.5 m and ♀ 3.2 m in Hudson Bay and N Quebec, intermediate-sized animals in Cumberland Sound, Alaska, the St Lawrence estuary, White and Kara Seas, and the largest, in W Greenland and Sea of Okhotsk, averaging 4.8 m and 3.9 m, respectively.

DISTRIBUTION & POPULATION
Virtually circumpolar in high arctic, mainly at 50–80°N. Summers in bays and estuaries (and may penetrate up to 1,000 km up wide rivers), but as these freeze in autumn they move to edge of pack-ice or into areas of shifting ice up to 1,100 km from land. Most movements rather short and some populations, e.g. in St Lawrence R, Canada, resident. ♀♀, particularly, extremely faithful to natal area. *Population* Currently 110,000+, of which 40,000 in Beaufort Sea, 28,000 in NE Canada, 25,000 in Hudson Bay and 18,000 in Bering Sea.

ECOLOGY
Tight groups, frequently of same sex/age (♀♀ and calves in smaller pods than ♂♂), and aggregations in some favoured feeding areas can number 1,000s. ♂♂ may migrate ahead of ♀♀ and young, but groups often fluid. Inquisitive and surface-signalling frequent. Highly diverse vocal repertoire, which may possess human-like quality. *Breaching* Very rare. *Diving* Capable of reaching 800–1,000 m and remaining below surface for 25 min. *Diet* Principally a bottom-feeder and often hunts cooperatively; fish, cephalopods, crustaceans and large zooplankton all commonly taken. *Reproduction* Sexually mature at 4–7 (♂) to 6–9 (♀) yrs old. Gives birth every 3 yrs. Mating principally late Feb–May; gestation 12–14.5 months. Young born close to arrival in warmer, coastal waters. Calves dependent for at least *c.*2 yrs. *Lifespan* Up to 50+ yrs.

Adult Belugas and their offspring (calves are smaller and grey).

Surfacing Belugas: habitually social and spend much time at surface, often off shallow coasts and river mouths, and may form large seasonal gatherings.

SIMILAR SPECIES

Might be confused with overlapping ***Beluga*** which is rather similar in size and shape; both lack dorsal fins and have rounded heads. Mainly greyish, young Narwhals can resemble imm Belugas, and very old ♂ Narwhal extensively white over entire body. However, Narwhal's mottled coloration and ♂'s long tusk usually render it unmistakable, although old ♀♀ can be almost white and lack a tusk. They occur in same areas and sometimes in partially mixed groups, but usually there are at least some characteristic ads or ♂♂ to enable swift identification.

VARIATION

Age/sex ♂ longer and heavier than ♀ with long left-hand tusk and more extensively white with age, whilst short flippers and flukes upturned at tips/margins. Calf/juv uniform grey to brownish-grey, becoming blackish grey-brown and subsequently developing whitish spots on lower flanks, belly and rear, but transitional pattern varies individually and with age/sex. **Physical notes** Largest ad ♂ 4.7 m (excluding tusk) and ♀ 4.2 m, and 0.8–1.6 tons. Newborn 1.6 m, weighing *c.*80 kg. **Other data** *Teeth* 2, both in upper jaw: in ♀ almost always embedded in upper jaw bone, but in ♂ left tooth normally grows as anticlockwise-twisted tusk,

Narwhal

Monodon monoceros

High Arctic. Max 4.7 m.

Priority characters on surfacing

- Medium-sized, highly distinctive whale of high-arctic waters.
- Stocky-bodied but has relatively small, bulbous head and slight or no beak.
- No dorsal fin (but slight dorsal ridge present).
- *Mature ♂ develops 3 m-long twisted tusk* on front of head that spirals to shiny white point.
- *Darker-capped appearance*; in close views, *variable black and greyish mottling* on paler, cream/whitish ground colour distinctive; lower flanks and belly purer white.
- Older animals whiten considerably, but some black marks still present above and on sides.
- Odd-shaped flukes with strongly convex trailing edge, deeply notched and tips may curl upwards, whilst leading edge usually also slightly concave.
- Comparatively short blunt flippers located close to head.
- Young more uniform grey to brownish-grey, more or less mottled.

Typical behaviour at surface

- Shy and wary of boats.
- May float motionless at surface with part of back, tusk or flipper visible; occasionally, entire groups leap and dive in unison. When feeding or in rough seas, submerges for long periods and spends little time at surface.
- Rather fast, erratic swimmer. Fairly acrobatic and demonstrative, but seldom leaps clear of water.
- Gregarious, in parties of 2–10, frequently in very large groups of 100s (occasionally 1,000s).

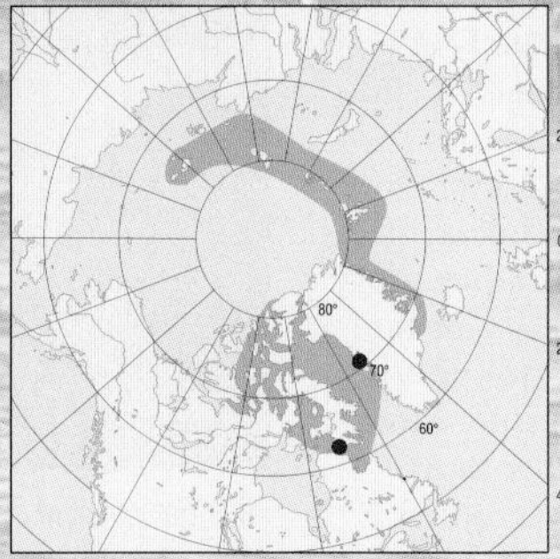

Two mature ♂ Narwhals, sparring with tusks crossed like swords, when a 'clacking' sound may be audible.

The left tooth of a mature ♂ Narwhal usually grows 2–3 m long; body whitens with age but diagnostic dark blotches and patches are still present dorsally, affording a dark-capped appearance.

2–3 m long; occasionally ♀♀ with a tusk (up to 1.2 m) or ♂♂ with right-hand side tusk or even 2 tusks are observed (right one slightly smaller). Tusk first erupts at 2–3 yrs old, and is used in display between ♂♂, which become scarred around head. Tusks of jousting ♂♂ crossed like swords, and a 'clacking' sound is audible during such sparring matches when tusks may splinter.

DISTRIBUTION & POPULATION
Discontinuous but widespread in high arctic, with most in extreme NE Canada, Greenland and Barents Sea, at 65–85°N. Migrates according to ice formation and melt, penetrating receding pack-ice in spring and moving to deep-water offshore wintering areas from early autumn, but these migrations only recently revealed by satellite tracking.

Narwhal's strongly convex flukes are distinctly blotched (cf. flukes of Beluga).

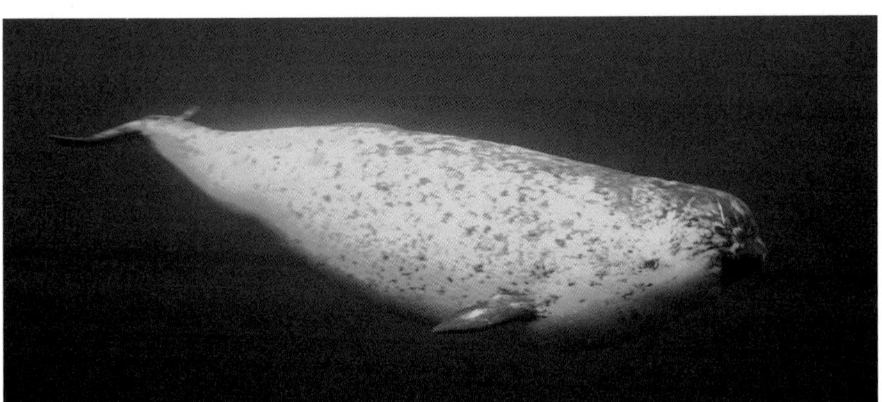

Narwhal: the combination of relatively white body and lack of tusk suggests an adult ♀.

Narwhal

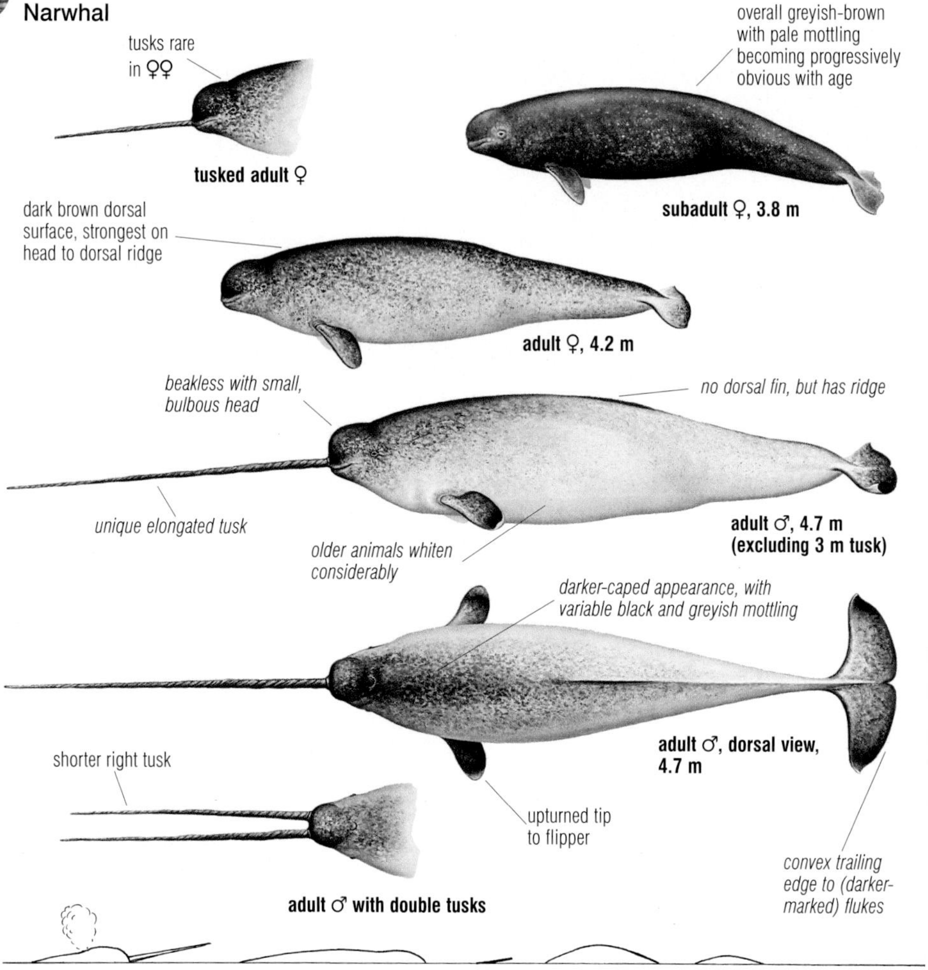

tusks rare in ♀♀

tusked adult ♀

overall greyish-brown with pale mottling becoming progressively obvious with age

subadult ♀, 3.8 m

dark brown dorsal surface, strongest on head to dorsal ridge

adult ♀, 4.2 m

beakless with small, bulbous head

no dorsal fin, but has ridge

unique elongated tusk

older animals whiten considerably

adult ♂, 4.7 m (excluding 3 m tusk)

darker-caped appearance, with variable black and greyish mottling

adult ♂, dorsal view, 4.7 m

shorter right tusk

upturned tip to flipper

convex trailing edge to (darker-marked) flukes

adult ♂ with double tusks

Shallow, smooth surfacing, with head (including tusk in adult ♂) and part of back breaking surface; smooth rolls in diving; seldom leaps clear of water.

Extralimitals recorded NW Europe, Russia and Alaska. *Population* Probably 50,000+, of which 35,000 are in Baffin Bay, Canada. A declining population, *c.*1,400, in Hudson Strait is the most accessible to whale-watching boats, with 300 in E Greenland.

ECOLOGY

Hundreds may congregate in rich feeding areas and migrate en masse. Some groups mixed, especially on migration, but usually segregated by age and sex, with ♀♀ and calves, and juvs and ad ♂♂ keeping separate. Ads show strong inter-annual site fidelity to summering and wintering areas. Above-surface signalling and underwater 'clicking' sounds frequent. *Breaching* Very rare, but occasionally lunges above surface when swimming. *Diving* Mostly 7–20 min and can reach 1,160 m. *Diet* Takes pelagic fish, squid and shrimp, and various bottom-dwellers. *Reproduction* Sexually mature at 5–8 (♂) or 11–13 yrs (♀).Cows give birth to single calf every 2–3 yrs. Mating late winter (Mar–May) and peaks Apr. Gestation 14–15 months. Calvings mostly Jul–Aug. Weaned at *c.*1 yr, but dependent for another 8–12 months. *Lifespan* 25–50 yrs.

Beaked whales

The second-largest cetacean family (Ziphiidae) with 21 species, but the least familiar, being strictly oceanic, deep-diving whales with inconspicuous surfacing behaviour. Most sightings are very brief and a matter of luck. Some species have never been identified at sea and most are best known from strandings. Generally, they have a well-defined beak, small triangular dorsal fin set well back, and small flippers, a single pair of throat grooves which converge anteriorly, and the flukes generally lack a central notch. Generally only in adult males do the teeth erupt from the gums (often colonised by soft barnacles); females and juvs are effectively toothless. Size, shape and position of the teeth is the primary difference between many beaked whales. males use tusk-like teeth as weapons in intra-specific combat, and inflict linear scars. Recent years have seen increased interest in the group, leading to improved knowledge of the identification and taxonomy of several species, and recognition of new species.

The 6 genera include the mesoplodont beaked whales (genus *Mesoplodon*), with most species – 14, all small to medium-sized; and the bottlenose and similar whales of the genera *Hyperoodon* and *Indopacetus* – all large, rotund animals with a distinctive, rounded melon. *Berardius* comprises 2 large species unique in having 2 visible pairs of teeth in both sexes, and a rounded melon and very long beak. *Tasmacetus* consists of a single, rather large species, the only beaked whale with a complete set of functional teeth in both sexes. *Ziphius* also consists of a single species with the most extensive geographic range of all ziphiids. It typically lacks a distinct beak and adult males have a single pair of teeth at the tip of the lower jaw.

Familiarise yourself with those species that might be expected within a given region and the features useful for identification, although many species' ranges are known rather imperfectly and vagrants can appear almost anywhere. Most species are very difficult to observe, let alone identify at sea. In some cases you are likely to be able only to place an animal in 1 of the 5 main groups highlighted above. However, under optimal conditions, Cuvier's Beaked Whale (*Ziphius*) and the bottlenose (*Hyperoodon*) and *Berardius* beaked whales are sufficiently distinctive to be identified. (Continued on p. 107.)

Breaching Cuvier's Beaked Whale: identified by robust body, pale head and stubby beak; orange patches are probably the result of diatoms (often much more extensive than shown here). Breaching is considered to be rare in this species.

Gray's Beaked Whales in typical breathing roll of most Mesoplodonts, with beak often emerging first at steep angle.

Blainville's Beaked Whales descending to deep waters (dives can last 20–45 min and regularly reach c.1,000 m deep).

Northern latitude beaked whales (mature ♂♂)

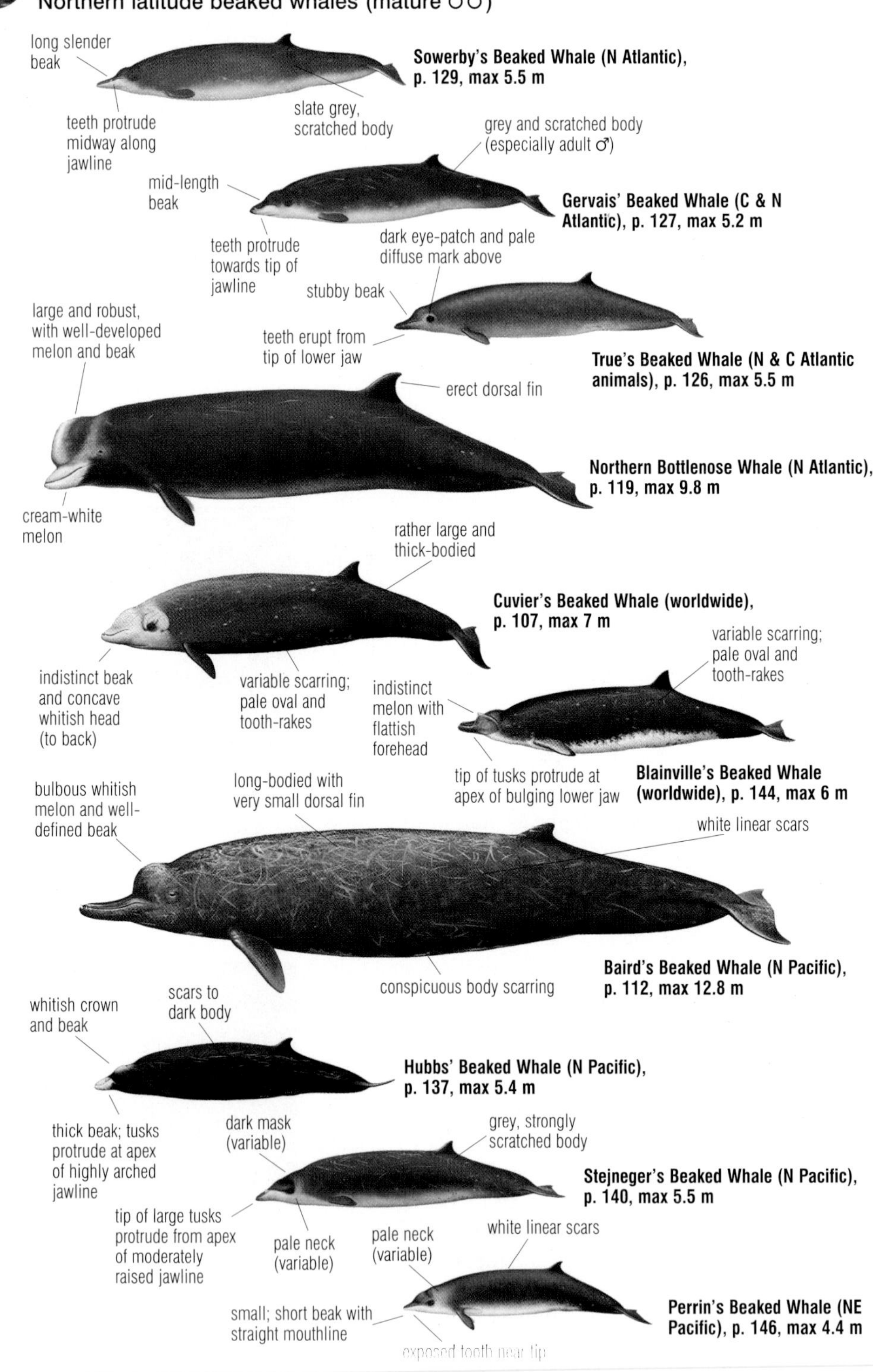

Middle latitude beaked whales (mature ♂♂)

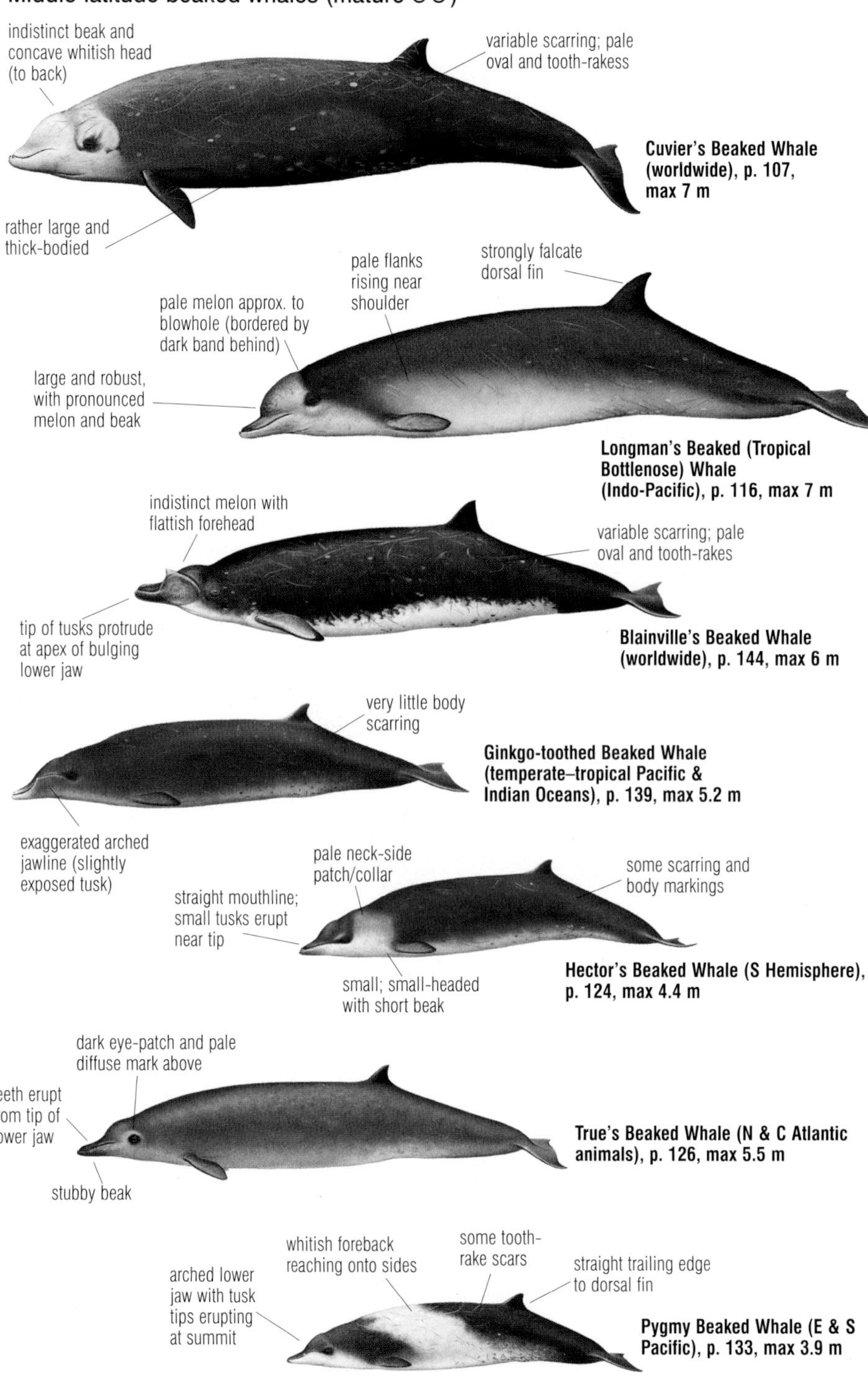

Cuvier's Beaked Whale (worldwide), p. 107, max 7 m

Longman's Beaked (Tropical Bottlenose) Whale (Indo-Pacific), p. 116, max 7 m

Blainville's Beaked Whale (worldwide), p. 144, max 6 m

Ginkgo-toothed Beaked Whale (temperate–tropical Pacific & Indian Oceans), p. 139, max 5.2 m

Hector's Beaked Whale (S Hemisphere), p. 124, max 4.4 m

True's Beaked Whale (N & C Atlantic animals), p. 126, max 5.5 m

Pygmy Beaked Whale (E & S Pacific), p. 133, max 3.9 m

Southern latitude beaked whales (mature ♂♂)

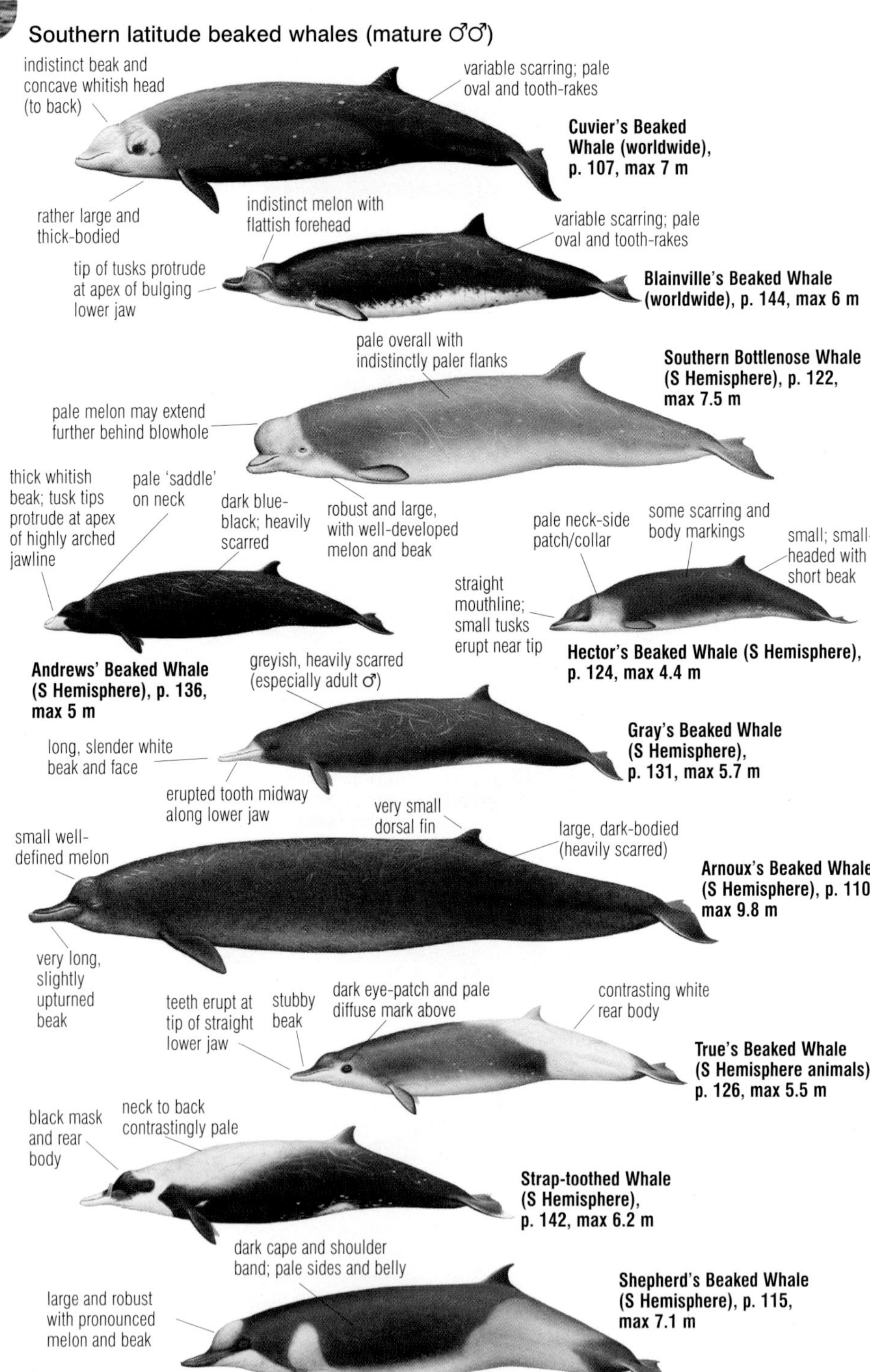

Longman's Beaked Whale (*Indopacetus*) may also be identifiable, but there may be some overlap in range between Southern Bottlenose and Longman's Beaked Whales. Gray's Beaked Whale (*Mesoplodon*) is another relatively distinctive species. Mesoplodonts frequently can be identified to species only by the teeth of mature males. Most species avoid boats or surface only very briefly, but in very calm seas may log at the surface, permitting the head shape, beak length, mouthline and erupted teeth of adult males to be observed. Some species also differ in coloration and fin shape, but for many there is insufficient evidence to be confident such features are truly diagnostic. Modern digital photography and video make it possible to document animals at long ranges or during fast travel, and subsequently confirm the features on-screen.

Cuvier's Beaked Whale

Ziphius cavirostris

Worldwide. Max 7 m.

Priority characters on surfacing

- The most frequently seen beaked whale, with distinctive coloration (dark grey to reddish-brown, with some countershading) and head shape.
- *Medium-sized or largish* with robust, rotund and mostly brownish body.
- *Back typically has large pale area* (less pronounced in ♀♀) *with many pale scars* (linear or oval in ♂♂, none or oval in ♀♀), and falcate/ triangular dorsal fin.
- When swimming fast, head partially clear of water, has *concave whitish face*, almost *beakless look* (with characteristic 'smile') and large slit-like blowhole at very close range.
- Body colour may appear more reddish-brown in bright sunlight, due to diatom infestation.
- Mature ♂ has 2 small teeth erupted at tip of lower jaw (may be visible in close views).

Typical behaviour at surface

- Blow often inconspicuous or invisible (2–3× at 20–30-sec intervals), bushy, usually less than 1 m high and projects slightly forward and left.
- Arches back in vertical descent to deep dive. Rarely breaches.
- Considered not particularly approachable, but often seen close to boats.
- *Normally in small groups (1–3) or alone*.

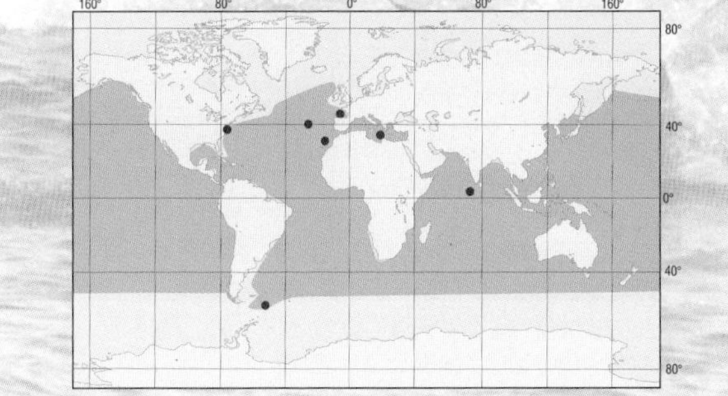

Cuvier's Beaked Whale: the apparently limited scarring and dusky top of head and sides suggest a younger animal.

SIMILAR SPECIES

Could be confused with any beaked whale with overlapping distribution, although Cuvier's has unique head shape of smooth-sloping forehead, indistinct beak and no obvious melon. The white dorsal region in mature ♂♂, and to a lesser extent in ad ♀♀, usually extends from the face to back, and old ♂♂ can appear almost all white. Cuvier's also larger than most *Mesoplodon* spp, but smaller than bottlenose whales. Young more easily confused with other ziphiids, as they lack whitish head, although head shape and lack of an obvious beak are still distinctive. Sometimes even ads can be difficult to identify at sea. In poor visibility, could be confused with ***Risso's Dolphin*** (although latter has large dorsal fin), and extremely pale/white older animals with ***Belugas***, but there is relatively little overlap in range and the latter lacks a dorsal fin.

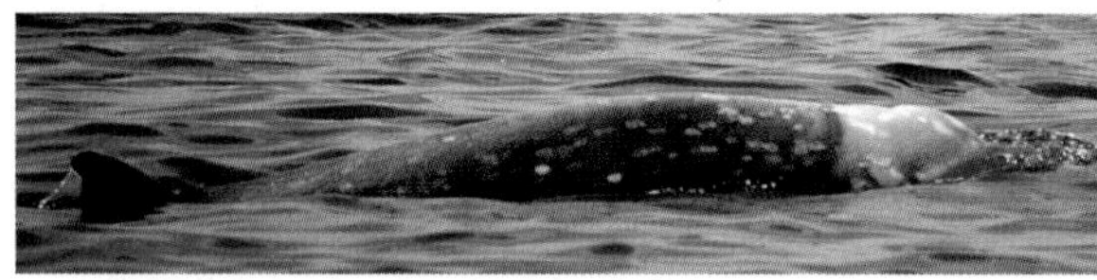

Pale oval scars frequent most animals at lower/warmer latitudes (also seasonally in other regions); lack of pale area on back and tooth-rake scars suggest a mature ♀; this animal was also seen to lack protruding teeth.

Cuvier's Beaked Whale: an adult ♂ identified by the long linear scars over much of the body.

heads. **Physical notes** 4.7–7 m and 2.03–3.4 tons (no significant sexual dimorphism). Newborn 2–2.7 m and *c.*250–300 kg. **Other data** *Teeth* Ad ♂ has 2 cone-like teeth at tip of lower jaw. Teeth visible when mouth closed and may become worn down in older animals. In ♀♀/young, teeth concealed by gums. Some have supernumerary teeth (i.e. 2 pairs versus normal single pair).

DISTRIBUTION & POPULATION

Tropical, subtropical and temperate waters, prefers continental slope and deep oceanic waters. Occurs north to the Aleutians and Massachusetts (USA), the Shetlands (UK), and south to Tierra del Fuego, S Africa, New Zealand and, occasionally, Antarctic waters, penetrating Gulf of Mexico, Caribbean and Mediterranean Seas. Resident populations may occur in parts of N Hemisphere, perhaps including Bay of Biscay. *Population* No estimates.

Cuvier's Beaked Whale: the limited scarring, both linear and oval, indicates a subadult (but note, in some areas all individuals lack cookie-cutter scars).

ECOLOGY

Often alone or in groups of 3–12, (up to *c.*25). Lone animals perhaps older males. Pods of 5–10 darker animals often also contain 1 old ♂, which may move between groups. Generally avoids boats, but can be inquisitive, logging or moving slowly near vessels. *Breaching* Rare. *Diving* Usually

VARIATION

Age/sex Ad ♂ has long linear and white oval scars; ad ♀ and juvs only latter. Both sexes paler with age, especially ad ♂ (in which white pigmentation extends further posteriorly). Younger animals usually darker and greyer. Calves also darker (including beak), distinctly paler below, and have rounded, more dolphin-like

Cuvier's Beaked Whale: the lack of scarring indicates a subadult; note well-defined pale head and almost beakless appearance (with characteristic 'smile' and goose-beak profile).

Cuvier's Beaked Whale

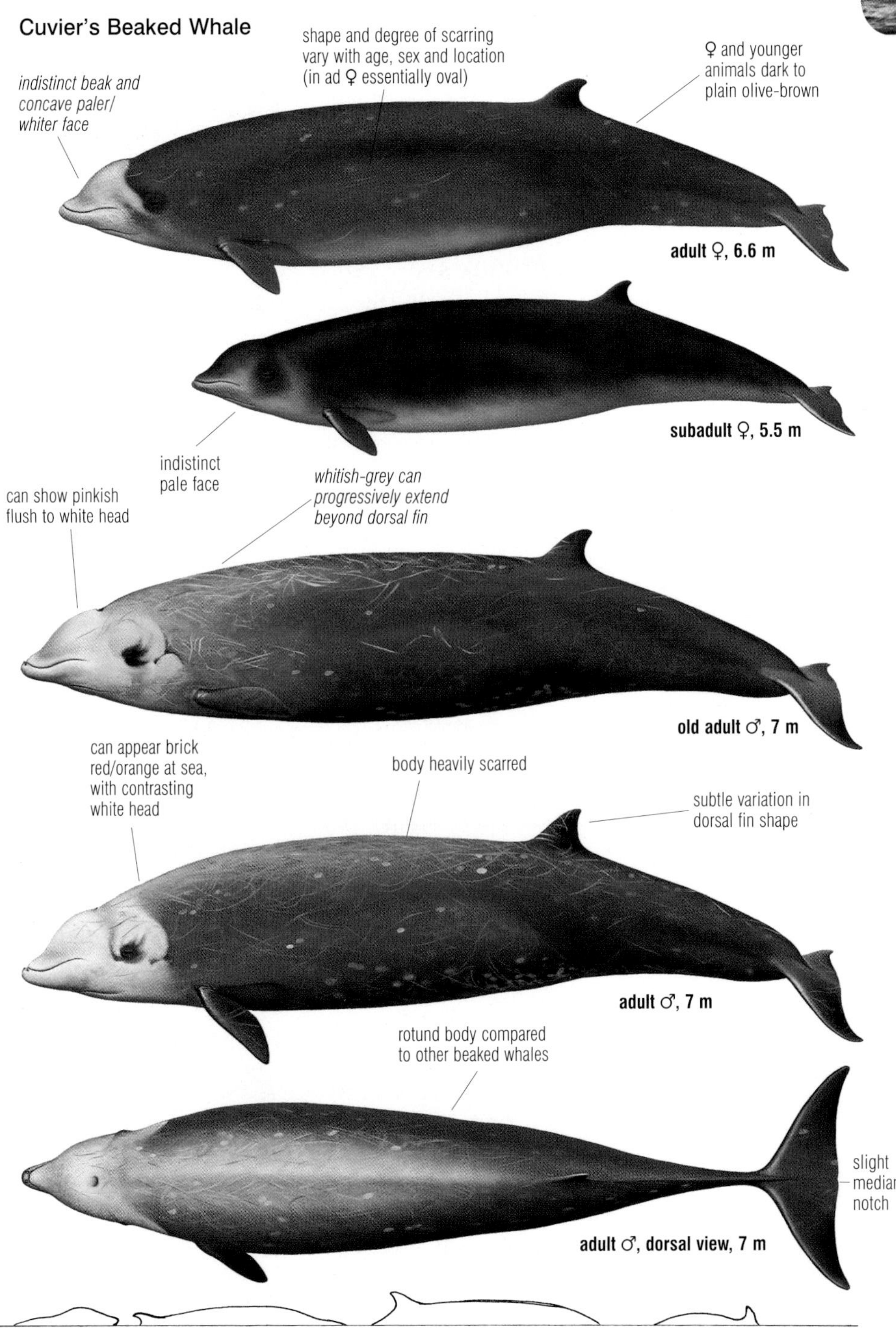

On surfacing, head partially visible (note unique concave almost beakless look), and body may emerge quite high; dorsal fin usually emerges as head disappears; arches back in vertical descent in deep diving; blow usually inconspicuous.

20–40 min. *Diet* Squid and, less frequently, fish in deep waters; perhaps some crustaceans. *Reproduction* Appears to calve all year. *Lifespan* Up to *c.*60 yrs.

Cuvier's Beaked Whale: extremely pale head and dorsal areas, extensive linear scarring, and 2 cone-like teeth readily distinguish this as a mature ♂; note goose-like head profile.

SIMILAR SPECIES

Main confusion risk is with ***Southern Bottlenose Whale*** which overlaps in range and is far commoner, and has a massive melon, short stubby beak, prominent dorsal fin and is usually brownish. In contrast, Arnoux's Beaked Whale has a low melon, long beak and small dorsal fin. Both sexes of Arnoux's have visible teeth and become heavily scarred. In *Hyperoodon,* only ad ♀♀ have emergent teeth and little or no scarring. ***Baird's Beaked Whale*** is externally similar but occurs only in N Pacific. Possible confusion with *Mesoplodon* spp (which usually are smaller with slimmer heads and lack a visible blow), especially compared to younger and paler Arnoux's. See also ***Cuvier's Beaked Whale***.

VARIATION

Age/sex Ads generally paler and more heavily scarred with age. Young apparently more uniform and less heavily scarred. **Physical notes** 7.8–9.8 m and 7.1–10.1 tons. Newborn *c.*4–4.5 m. **Other data** *Teeth* Both sexes have 2 pairs of triangular teeth in lower jaw. Pair nearest tip of jaw larger, whilst smaller pair usually concealed in gum until later life. In older animals, teeth may be so worn down as to be invisible. **Taxonomy** Unclear whether Arnoux's and Baird's Beaked Whales are separate species or mere geographic variants, although available genetic evidence suggests that they separated several MYA. There may also be slight differences in cranial osteology. Mature *B. arnuxii* perhaps somewhat smaller than *B. bairdii*.

Arnoux's Beaked Whale

Berardius arnuxii

S Hemisphere. Max 9.8 m.

Priority characters on surfacing

- *Large*, proportionately elongated beaked whale.
- *Dark slate grey* or blue-black to pale brown; *melon and, sometimes, dorsal paler*.
- Contrasting heavy *white scars on dorsal surface and upper flanks* (especially older ads).
- Relatively small head with *prominent long beak and moderately steep melon; lower jaw protrudes beyond upper*.
- *Noticeably small fin* (triangular or slightly rounded and falcate) set well back on body.
- Ventral surface paler and slightly mottled.
- Tail flukes (may be slightly raised on diving) triangular, almost straight-edged and unnotched.
- Both sexes have *2 pairs of teeth at tip of lower jaw* (only larger apical pair nearest tip erupt), but very difficult to detect at sea.

Typical behaviour at surface

- Rather slow swimmer with very little of body exposed above surface. Generally shy of boats.
- *Blow low (to 2 m), bushy*, angled forward (perhaps slightly left) and diffuse, but can be quite distinct, even at distance, similar to bottlenose whales; blows *c.*15× prior to dive.
- Beak sometimes appears first on surfacing, when small dorsal fin may also be visible, but melon not always obvious.
- *Cruises at surface in very tight groups*, which may surface and breathe in unison.

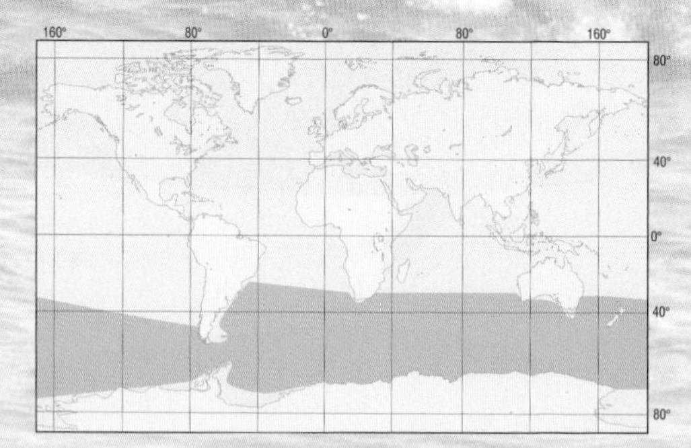

Arnoux's Beaked Whale

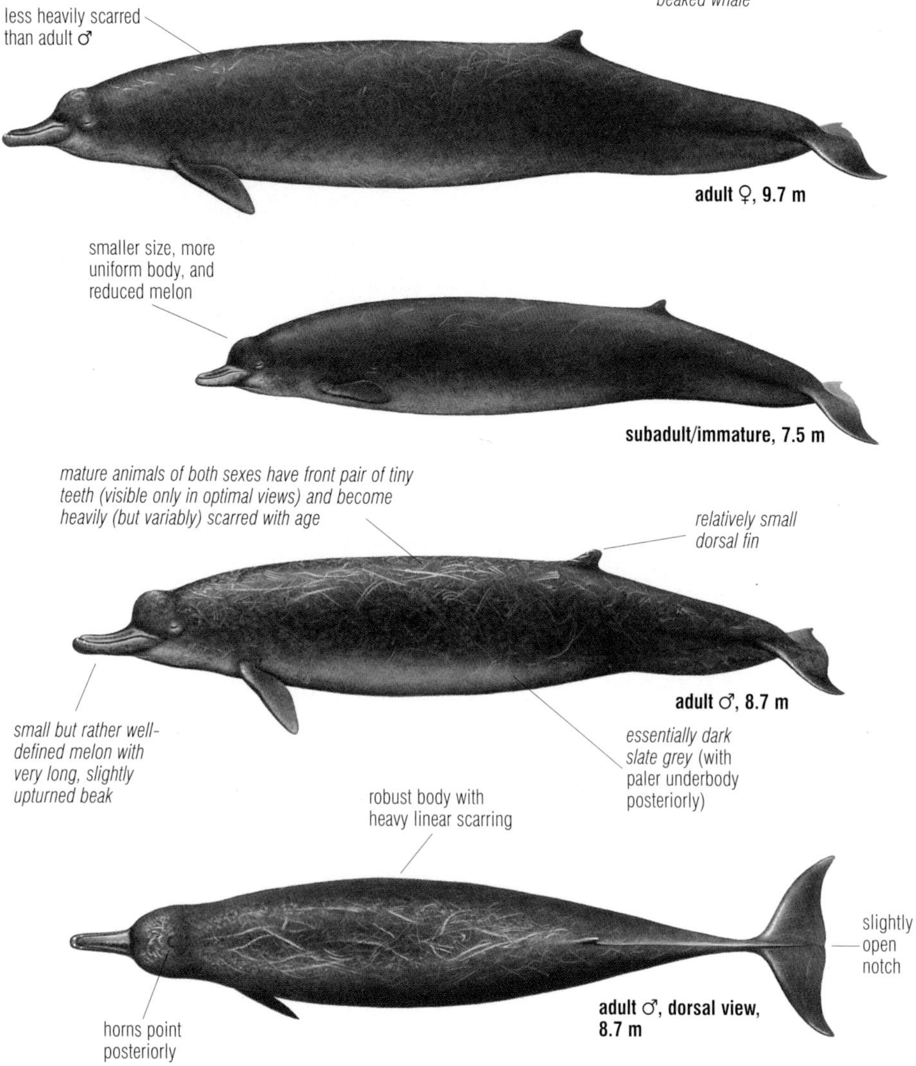

large, dark-bodied beaked whale

less heavily scarred than adult ♂

adult ♀, 9.7 m

smaller size, more uniform body, and reduced melon

subadult/immature, 7.5 m

mature animals of both sexes have front pair of tiny teeth (visible only in optimal views) and become heavily (but variably) scarred with age

relatively small dorsal fin

small but rather well-defined melon with very long, slightly upturned beak

adult ♂, 8.7 m

essentially dark slate grey (with paler underbody posteriorly)

robust body with heavy linear scarring

slightly open notch

horns point posteriorly

adult ♂, dorsal view, 8.7 m

Surfaces beak first (usually appears much longer than here) in shallow but steep roll, long back and dorsal fin emerge after melon has disappeared (latter rarely detected); blow low and diffuse, mostly angled forward, but can be quite obvious.

Note very long, blue–black body; tiny fin set well back.

DISTRIBUTION & POPULATION Rare in Southern Ocean, between 24°S (mainly 34°S) and 78°S, reaching pack-ice, exceptionally north to SE Brazil, and seems commonest in Cook Strait and perhaps Ross Sea. Most strandings in New Zealand and the Chathams (Dec–Mar), but also in Australia, S Africa, southern S America, the

Falklands, S Georgia and Antarctic Peninsula. Probably also occurs in S Indian Ocean. Movements, if any, unknown. *Population* No estimates.

ECOLOGY

Occurs singly or in tight groups of 6–10, but up to 80 observed (in subgroups of 8–15). *Breaching* May leap almost clear of water. *Diving* Usually 12–25 min but sometimes over 1 hr. *Diet* Squid, octopus and fish in deep waters. *Reproduction* No data, though a ♀ stranded in Dec was pregnant. Probably similar to Baird's Beaked Whale. *Lifespan* Unknown.

Mature Arnoux's Beaked Whale breaking the icy surface with beak, revealing its diagnostic blackish slate grey body, prominent beak and moderately steep melon.

Breaching is common behaviour for Baird's Beaked Whale.

SIMILAR SPECIES

Could be confused with ***Hubbs'*** and ***Stejneger's Beaked Whales*** which overlap in range, but Baird's is more widespread, distinctly larger/more robust and has

Baird's Beaked Whale: small, almost triangular dorsal fin with rounded tip.

Baird's Beaked Whale

Berardius bairdii

N Pacific. Max 12.8 m.

Priority characters on surfacing

- *Large, longish robust body.* The largest beaked whale, restricted to deep offshore waters of northern N Pacific. May be relatively approachable in regions where not hunted.
- Rounded head with distinct *bulging forehead* (melon higher and whiter with age).
- *Small, almost triangular dorsal fin* with rounded tip set far back.
- May appear brownish or warm brown at sea (true coloration more greyish), but heavily scarred animals look overall paler.
- Grey/white spots and blotches below; *variable pale linear scars/scratches chiefly on older animals*.
- *Long beak* with lower jaw projecting beyond upper.
- *Front teeth protrude in ads of both sexes* (visible in optimal conditions).
- Short/round flippers and dark flukes (with slight central notch and somewhat concave trailing edge), but usually barely visible, even when very close.

Typical behaviour at surface

- Surface periods short, at most 5 min; *low circular 'puffy' blow often visible at long distance*; forehead and, often, beak appear first, and

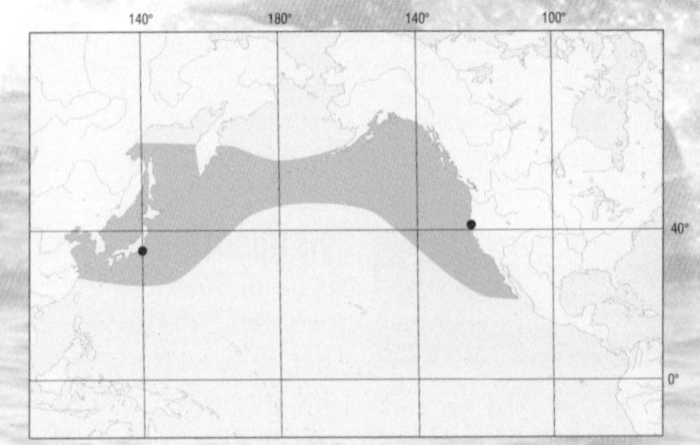

blowhole normally disappears before dorsal fin emerges.
- Rather social, *often in tight groups* that typically surface/log and blow in unison; groups at surace often swim sideways exposing half of flukes.
- Spyhopping and lobtailing apparently frequent, and perhaps habitual.

a large, distinct melon, long beak, with different tooth position and form, and a visible blow. All 3 differ in head coloration, but at-sea identification of lone young problematic. Confusion also possible with ***Cuvier's Beaked Whale*** which broadly overlaps Baird's in range, but differs in head/beak shape and colour, and ***Longman's Beaked Whale*** which may overlap at lower latitudes.

VARIATION

Age/sex Pale coloration varies with age and sex. Calves slimmer and more uniformly dark above with whiter underparts and a shorter beak. **Physical notes** Largest ads 10–12.8 m, and

Baird's Beaked Whale

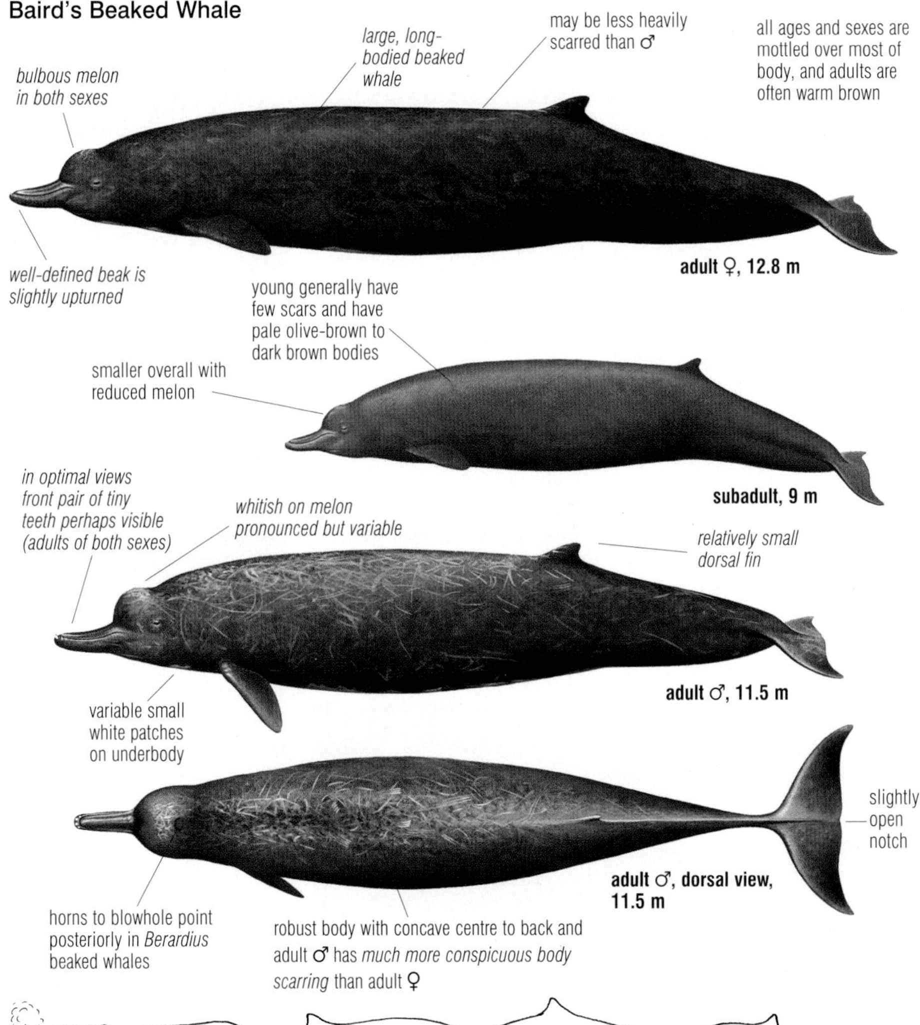

Low 'puffy' blow (mostly angled forwards and left) often visible; surfaces beak first or only melon is visible, and in shallow roll, long back and small dorsal fin emerge after melon has disappeared; may arch for deep dive.

Typical tight group of Baird's Beaked Whales (often surface and blow in unison): note whiter melon and grey-brown, heavily scarred body.

10–15 tons. Newborn is *c.*4.5 m. **Other data** *Teeth* Ads have 2 pairs of teeth in lower jaw; apical pair larger, second pair may not erupt. In old age teeth can wear down to gum level.

DISTRIBUTION & POPULATION

N Pacific, principally in deep water and only near shore where continental shelf is narrow, from Sea of Japan and Baja California (*c.*30°N) north to Sea of Okhotsk and S Bering Sea (62°N), where may enter drift-ice. Appears to perform local movements in response to food availability (e.g. along Pacific coast of Japan). *Population* Few data. Perhaps more than 10,000, of which possibly 6,800 off Japan, where hunted, and 400 of W USA (excluding Alaska).

ECOLOGY

Tight groups of 2–9, occasionally up to 30; usually more mature ♂♂ in groups than ♀♀. Mass-strandings noted. *Breaching* Common, a low/medium graceful arc, landing on side (often repeatedly, several animals simultaneously). May swim sideways exposing half of the flukes. *Diving* Usually 11–30 min, sometimes over 1 hr, regularly reaches 1,000 m, perhaps even 3,000 m. *Diet* Cephalopods, deep-sea and pelagic fish. *Reproduction* Sexually mature at 6–11 (♂) or 10–15 yrs (♀). Calving mainly Mar–Apr. Cows give birth to a single calf every 3+ yrs. ♂♂ may help care for weaned calves. *Lifespan* Up to 84 yrs.

Baird's Beaked Whale: low 'puffy' blow angled forwards and left often reveals presence, even at long range.

Small, almost triangular dorsal fin (set well back) usually emerges after forebody has disappeared.

SIMILAR SPECIES
Could be confused with any overlapping, similar-sized beaked whale, although coloration of Shepherd's possibly distinctive. Any at-sea record requires photographic documentation for verification. Larger than most *Mesoplodon* spp with a steeper melon and distinctive flank pattern. *Cf.* ***Southern and Longman's Beaked Whales***, ***Arnoux's*** and ***Cuvier's Beaked Whales***.

Shepherd's Beaked Whale

(Tasman's Beaked Whale)

Tasmacetus shepherdi

S Hemisphere. Max 7.1 m.

Priority characters on surfacing

- *Large, robust beaked whale*, which is elusive and rare.
- *Diagnostic colour pattern includes diagonal dark shoulder band and cape, contrasting with pale sides and belly.*
- Dark brownish-black above and creamy-white below.
- Pale head patch (variable).
- Small, falcate dorsal fin (with *narrow pointed tip* in at least some), set far back.
- *Steep, rounded melon and prominent dolphin-like beak* (slender with straight mouthline).
- Full dentition in upper and lower jaws (both sexes); *in ad ♂ pair of larger apical teeth protrude from gum of lower jaw.*

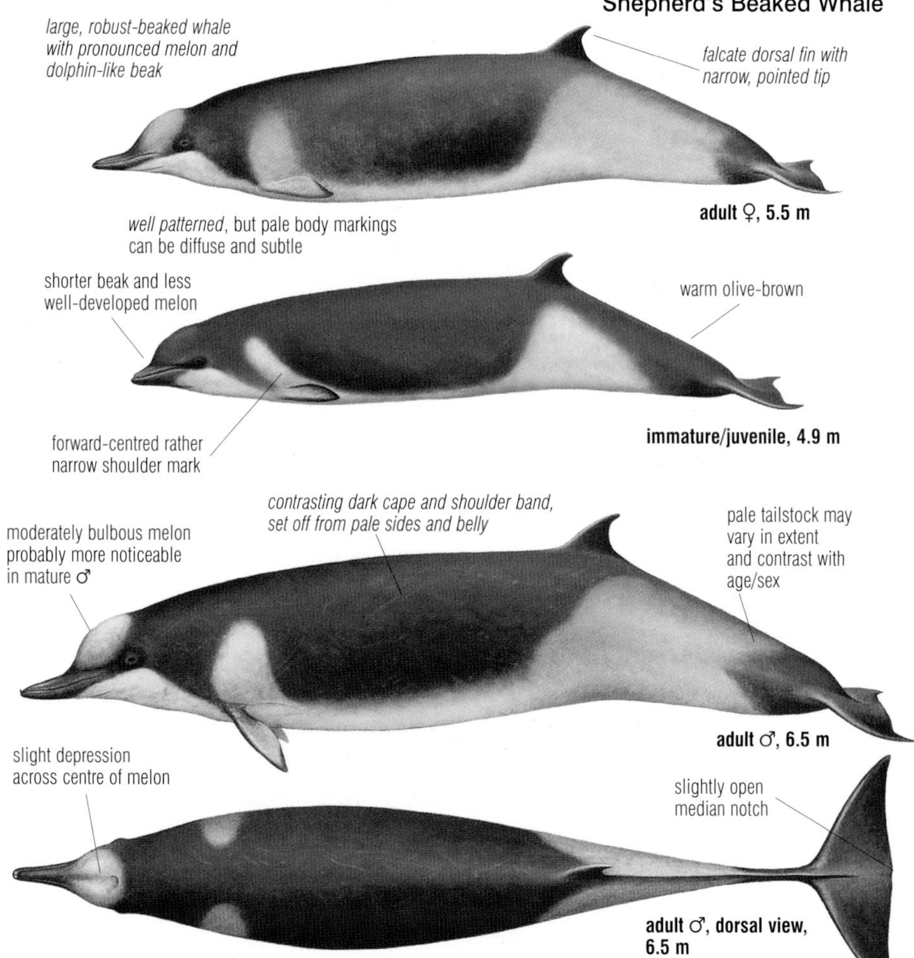

VARIATION

Age/sex Ad ♂ probably more heavily scarred with age. Melon better developed and offset more sharply from beak in older animals, which may also have paler forehead and crown. Juv similar colour to ad, but less or no scarring. **Physical notes** 6–7.1 m and *c.*2.32–3.48 tons. Newborn *c.*3m. **Other data** *Teeth* Only beaked whale with complete set of functional teeth in both jaws. Only ad ♂ has larger pair of tusks at tip of lower jaw.

Typical behaviour at surface
- Among the least-known cetaceans, most information being from strandings. Very few sightings at sea.
- Surfacing behaviour perhaps similar to some *Mesoplodon*, possibly never gregarious.

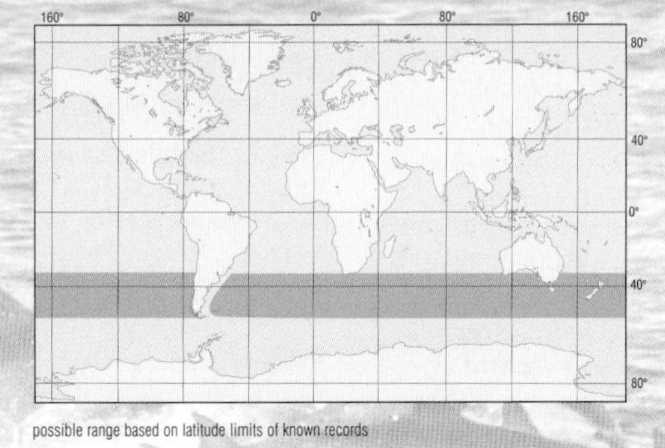

possible range based on latitude limits of known records

DISTRIBUTION & POPULATION

Probably circumpolar in cold-temperate waters of S Hemisphere, south of 30°N. Most records from New Zealand, but also Juan Fernández Is, Chile, Tierra del Fuego, Argentina, Tristan da Cunha, S Africa, S Australia and the Chathams. Putative sightings from western S Atlantic, New Zealand and Antarctic waters. *Population* No estimates.

ECOLOGY

May be solitary or occur in small groups. *Breaching* No information. *Diving* No data. *Diet* Perhaps eats more fish than other mesoplodonts.

SIMILAR SPECIES

Cf. ***Cuvier's Beaked Whale***. May overlap with ***Southern Bottlenose Whale*** in south of range and they may be extremely difficult to differentiate at sea, but note larger group size of present species. Melon meets rostrum at *c.*90° in *Southern Bottlenose Whale* and at *c.*75° in *Longman's Beaked Whale*, and also note extent of pale coloration (and darker borders) around melon region and flanks. Confusion also possible with rare ***Shepherd's Beaked Whale*** in southern waters, which is similar size, with similar pale melon and dusky 'shoulder'. Confusion with ***Mesoplodon*** spp possible but most are smaller, lack a bulbous melon and have less robust bodies. Optimal

Longman's Beaked Whale

(Tropical Bottlenose Whale)

Indopacetus pacificus

Indian Ocean and tropical Pacific. Max 6–7 m.

Priority characters on surfacing
- Generally, the *only bottlenose-like whale in tropical/subtropical waters of Indian and Pacific Oceans.*
- *Large, robust animal.*
- *Dorsal fin relatively large, erect, strongly falcate and set well back.*
- *Moderate to well-developed bulbous melon with long robust beak.*
- *Paler melon coloration extends to about blowhole.* Whitish patch behind eye may also be visible. Dark back coloration extends laterally as *broad dusky band* towards flipper.
- *Dull buff-brown, tan or greyish-brown*, darker dorsally and paler ventrally, but becoming paler, even whitish, with age.
- *High whitish thoracic panel* bordered in front by slightly darker transverse band.
- White or yellowish spots, or oval scars, mainly on sides and belly. Ad ♂ may have extensive pale linear scars.
- *Robust, dolphin-like beak* and projecting white or pink lower jaw; dark upper jaw.
- Two small, roughly conical teeth at tip of lower jaw.

Typical behaviour at surface
- Can be *gregarious*, sometimes associating with other species, e.g. pilot whales, in tight-knit groups. Can be elusive, fast-swimming, but sometimes shows interest in boats.
- Surfacing behaviour similar to *Hyperoodon* spp. Blow bushy,

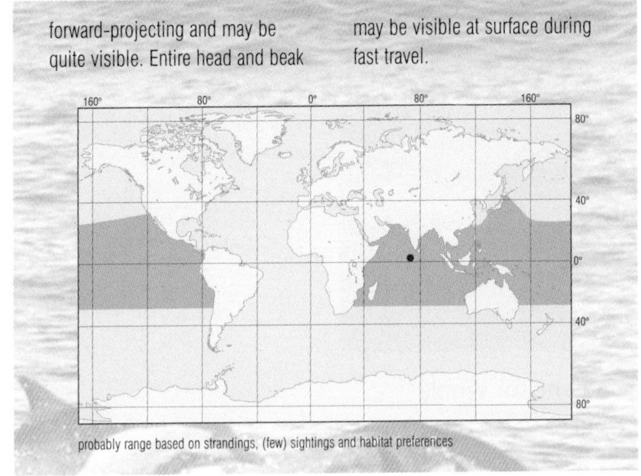

views essential for reliable identification, especially with young, and caution is always recommended.

VARIATION

Age/sex When older melon better developed and more perpendicular to beak. Juv has less-developed melon, darker upperparts, contrasting whitish lower flanks and belly, and pale melon. **Physical notes** Known from only *c.*6 strandings (juvs and ad ♀♀), and sightings at sea. Max size of ad ♂ *c.*6 m. Ad ♀ may be slightly larger. A neonate calf was 2.9 m and 228 kg. **Other data** *Teeth* 2, small, conical teeth at apex of lower jaw, probably erupt from gum only in ad ♂. **Taxonomy** Described originally as a *Mesoplodon* but removed to its own genus, *Indopacetus*, based on osteological features. Long known from only 2 beach-cast skulls, the recent discovery of 4 new specimens allowed links to be made to previously unidentified animals observed at sea and a more thorough knowledge of the species' characteristics.

DISTRIBUTION & POPULATION

Poorly known and probably rare overall, although not uncommon around Maldives. Perhaps found in deep-water regions throughout tropical Pacific and Indian Oceans, to S Africa and the Arabian Sea, with strandings in Somalia and N Australia, the Maldives, Kenya, S Africa and S Japan. *Population* No estimates.

ECOLOGY

Usually in pods of 15–20, occasionally up to 100; composition unknown, but appear close-knit. Also observed near Bottlenose and Spinner Dolphins. *Breaching* Occasional. *Diving* Lasts 14–33 min. *Diet* Unknown. *Reproduction* Calving may occur Sep–Dec in S Africa. *Lifespan* Unknown.

The rather gregarious Longman's Beaked Whale here surfacing in tight formation. Distant animals can be difficult to separate from overlapping Cuvier's Beaked Whale (check of head and beak shape often essential).

Longman's Beaked Whales: note shallow 'puffy' melon (pale extends to about blowhole and is bordered behind by slightly darker band), and higher and better-defined pale thoracic panel.

Longman's Beaked (Tropical Bottlenose) Whale

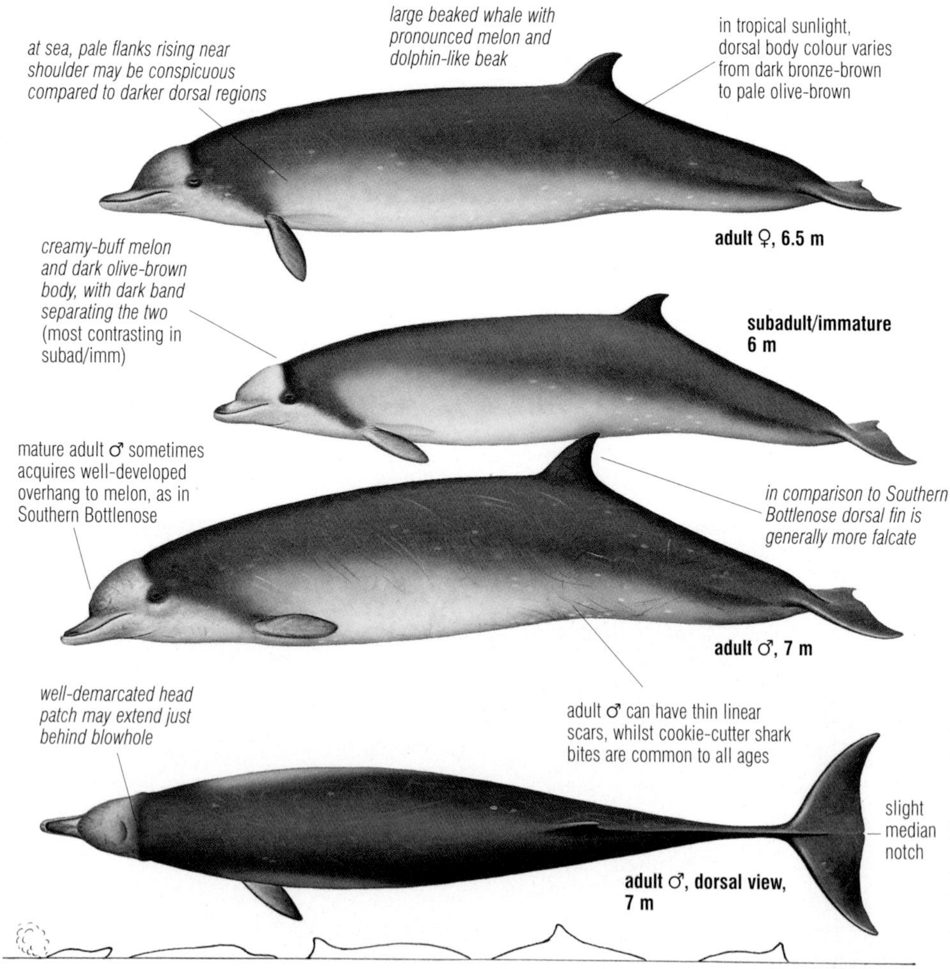

at sea, pale flanks rising near shoulder may be conspicuous compared to darker dorsal regions

large beaked whale with pronounced melon and dolphin-like beak

in tropical sunlight, dorsal body colour varies from dark bronze-brown to pale olive-brown

adult ♀, 6.5 m

creamy-buff melon and dark olive-brown body, with dark band separating the two (most contrasting in subad/imm)

subadult/immature 6 m

mature adult ♂ sometimes acquires well-developed overhang to melon, as in Southern Bottlenose

in comparison to Southern Bottlenose dorsal fin is generally more falcate

adult ♂, 7 m

well-demarcated head patch may extend just behind blowhole

adult ♂ can have thin linear scars, whilst cookie-cutter shark bites are common to all ages

slight median notch

adult ♂, dorsal view, 7 m

Surfacing roll often quite high, bushy low blow (slightly angled forward) perhaps visible; dorsal fin may emerge when melon just disappearing but usually well before; in fast travel forebody, including entire head and beak, break surface; does not arch as steeply as Cuvier's in preparing to deep dive.

Northern Bottlenose Whale

Hyperoodon ampullatus

N Atlantic. Max 9.8 m.

Priority characters on surfacing

- *Robust, large* beaked whale, with well-developed melon and distinct appearance at surface.
- Highly *bulbous melon* (flatter in older ♂), and short, *stubby beak*, melon typically visible on surfacing; small teeth at tip of lower jaw in ad ♂ usually not visible.
- *Dorsal fin erect* and often pointed, triangular to slightly falcate and set well back.
- Chocolate-brown to olive-brown above, paler flanks, ♂ *buff or cream-white on head* with age.

Typical behaviour at surface

- Surfaces for up to 10 min, frequently logs and swims quite fast, *rolls quite high*, with head sometimes very briefly visible. Dives usually long (up to 2 hrs).
- *Bushy blow* to *c.*1 m high (every 30–40 sec), angled slightly forward and normally quite visible.
- Rarely lifts flukes before diving.
- May (rarely) appear to lift flukes prior to deep dive, but lobtailing sometimes frequent.
- Occurs singly or in groups.

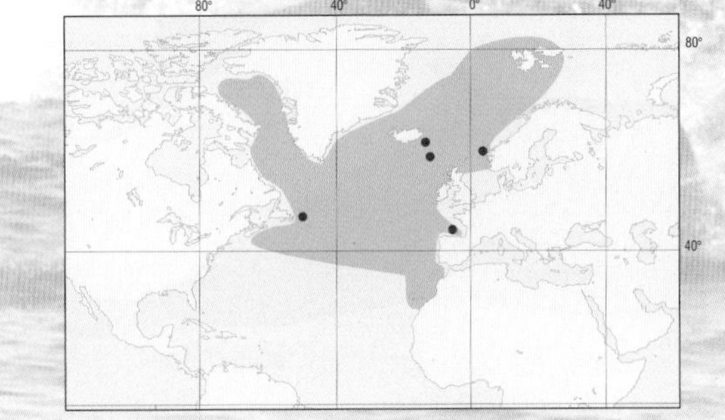

SIMILAR SPECIES

Distinctive melon profile and beak size, and body coloration, all often visible above surface. May be confused with ***Northern Minke Whale*** at distance, as shape and position of dorsal fin quite similar. May also superficially resemble pilot whale, although good views of coloration and distinct beak, bulbous melon and dorsal fin render it unmistakable. Other beaked whales in range (e.g. ***Cuvier's*** and ***Sowerby's***) usually smaller with less bulbous melons and/or different beak shape, though both Cuvier's and Northern Bottlenose can appear pale-headed. Young Northern Bottlenose, Southern Bottlenose, Longman's and Shepherd's Beaked Whales similar, but well separated geographically.

Northern Bottlenose Whale ♀ and calf: bulbous melon and robust body evident; note also stubby beak of calf and longer beak of adult ♀.

Northern Bottlenose Whale, probable female and calf: note the calf's stubbier beak and paler head, surrounded by a dark facial band.

VARIATION

Age/sex In ♂ melon becomes more developed with age; forehead very steep and flat. Extensive white forehead (may extend as irregular patch back to eyes) usually attributed to older ♂♂. Young ♂♂ intermediate between sexes in head features. Calf and juv darker, black to brown dorsally and greyish-white ventrally, with shorter beak and less-developed melon. Distinctive notches and marks on dorsal fin acquired with age, which with melon shape and 'saddle' may assist individual identification. **Physical notes** Ad ♂ 7.5–9.8 m, ♀ 5.8–8.7m; 5.8–7.5 tons. Newborn *c.*3–3.5 m and *c.*300 kg. **Other**

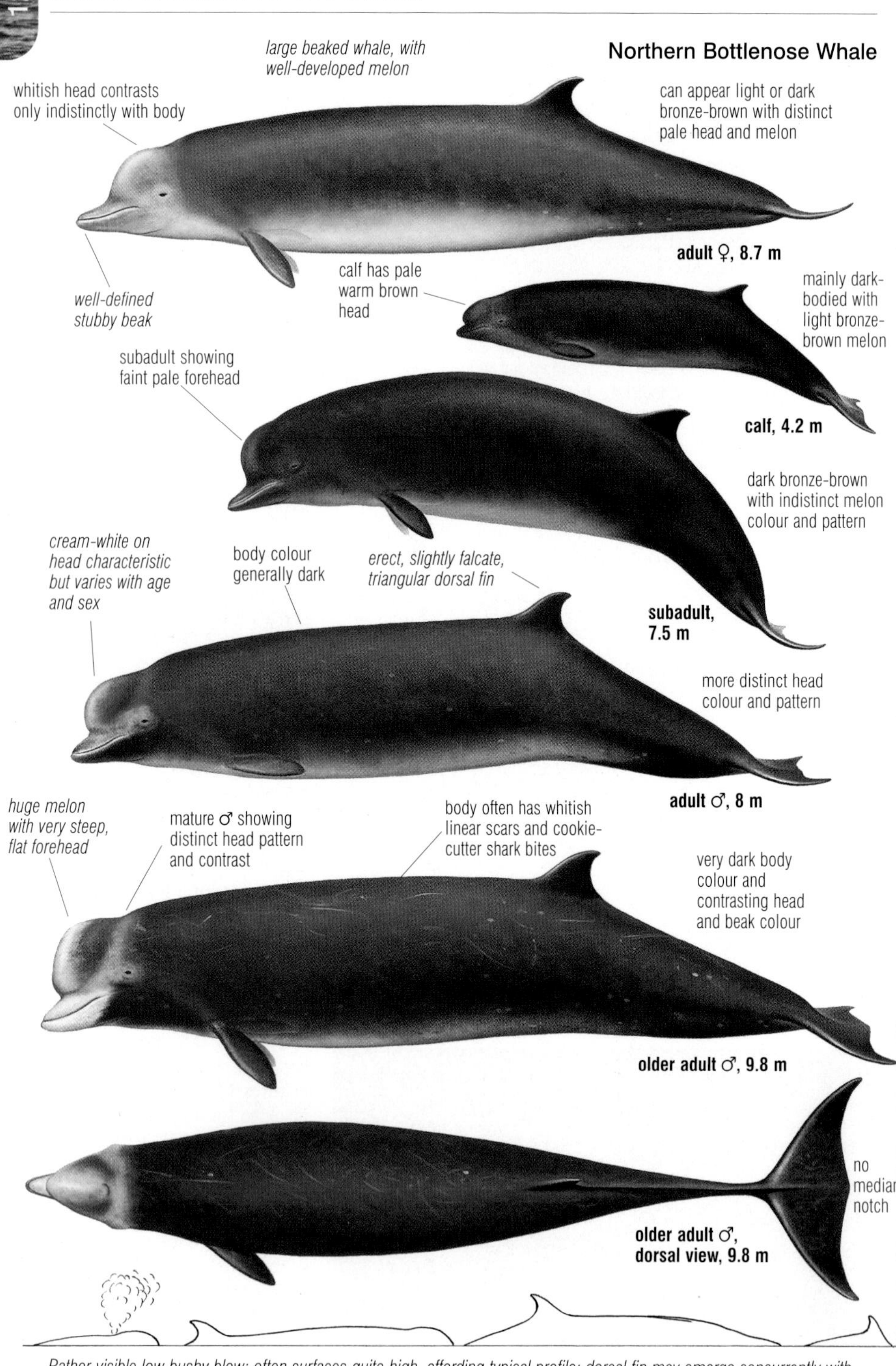

Rather visible low bushy blow; often surfaces quite high, affording typical profile; dorsal fin may emerge concurrently with melon but usually disappears well before; large melon and sometimes beak briefly visible; arches steeper for deep dive.

Juvenile Northern Bottlenose Whale: note prominent melon and stubby beak.

belly-first like rorquals. *Diving* <10 min, but also regularly in excess of 1 hr, reaching at least 1,500 m. *Diet* Mostly squid in very deep waters, but juvs may feed closer to surface. *Reproduction* Sexually mature at 7–11 yrs. Gives birth once every 2+ yrs. Most calves born Apr–Jun (–Aug), following gestation of at least 1 yr, and young weaned after another 12+ months. *Lifespan* At least 37 yrs.

data *Teeth* Ad ♂ has single pair of small, conical teeth at tip of lower jaw; in ♀/juv hidden in gums. **Taxonomy** Monotypic, but overall length and distribution of mtDNA haplotypes differ between some populations, suggesting some measure of geographic isolation.

Northern Bottlenose Whales: may closely approach boats; adult ♂ (foreground) has huge melon with very steep flat forehead like the end of a barrel; the animal behind has prominent dorsal fin, pointed and falcate.

DISTRIBUTION & POPULATION

Cold-temperate waters of N Atlantic, from Davis Strait and Labrador Sea east to Barents Sea, and south to Gulf of St Lawrence and New England (USA), the North and Baltic Seas, and rarely the Azores and Canaries. Recorded year-round off Nova Scotia, Canada, yet appears to be seasonal in Faeroes and Bay of Biscay, where numbers peak late summer. *Population* Those in eastern and central N Atlantic placed at 40,000 recently. 'The Gully' population, off Nova Scotia, numbers *c.*130.

Lobtailing Northern Bottlenose Whale: flukes lack a median notch.

ECOLOGY

Most groups 4–10, but up to 20; pods may loosely aggregate. Most groupings rather ephemeral and comprise exclusively mature ♂♂, ♀♀, and young, or a mix of ages/sexes. Ad ♂♂ may form long-term bonds. *Breaching* Not uncommon, usually forward, sometimes dolphin-like but can land

Breaching Northern Bottlenose Whale: note robust body.

SIMILAR SPECIES

No overlap with similar Northern Bottlenose Whale. May overlap with ***Longman's Beaked Whale*** in warmer waters and might be confused with ***Arnoux's Beaked Whale*** in Antarctic waters, as well as with ***Cuvier's Beaked Whale*** or even ***Dwarf and Antarctic Minke*** and ***Long-finned Pilot Whales***, but note tan coloration. A good view of the head, with its distinct melon and beak, however, renders the species unmistakable. ***Mesoplodon*** spp in range usually smaller with less bulbous melons and longer beaks, but beware of possible confusion with young animals.

VARIATION

Age/sex Typically ad ♂ paler, greyish/brown with prominent whitish bulbous melon, beak and lower foreface to belly. Ad ♀♀ may be darker with less bulbous melon. White on head of both sexes increases with age. Scarring on ad ♂♂ also increases with age. Calf/juv dark grey-brown with more dolphin-like head and inconspicuous melon. **Physical notes** 6–7.5 m (but probably not max size) and 6.9–8.1 tons; ♂ probably larger than ♀. Newborn 2.7–3.6 m. **Other data** *Teeth* Ad ♂ has single pair of conical teeth at tip of lower jaw that may become worn down with age, in ♀/juv hidden in gums. Some individuals have supernumerary teeth (i.e. 2 pairs vs normal single pair).

Southern Bottlenose Whale

Hyperoodon planifrons

S Hemisphere. Max 7.5 m.

Priority characters on surfacing

- *Large, robust beaked whale*, with distinct bulbous melon.
- *Pale tan coloration* and *tall, sickle-shaped dorsal fin* set far back.
- *Bulbous forehead* (most obvious in old ♂), and stubby dolphin-like beak, but latter usually unseen.
- *Extensive pale scars* above and on sides (especially old ♂) and often has whitish spots on abdomen and sides.
- *Head, beak and (ill-defined) underbody all usually paler; pale melon border may extend further behind blowhole* (cf. Longman's Beaked Whale).
- Pair of small teeth at tip of lower jaw may be visible in ad ♂.
- Tail flukes usually unnotched and deeply concave.

Typical behaviour at surface:

- Following deep dive may surface for 10 min.
- *Bushy blow (c.1 m) projects slightly forward* and may be visible in favourable conditions.
- When swimming fast head projects well above surface and may fully breach on surfacing.
- Tail flukes may be raised in social and signalling behaviours or (rarely seen) prior to deep dive.
- Normally in small groups and rarely seen near boats.

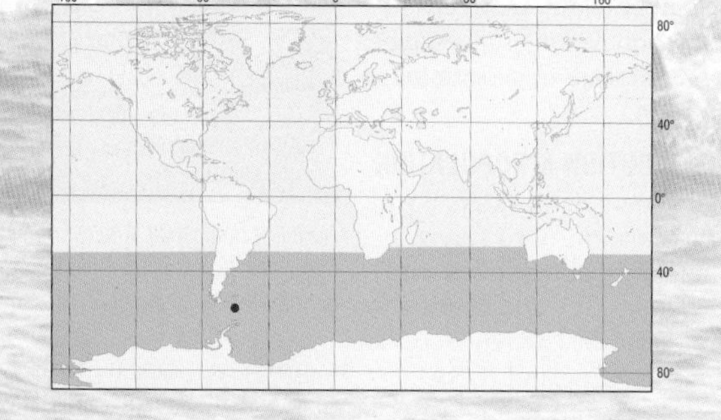

Breaching Southern Bottlenose Whale: note large body, bulbous melon, stubby beak, overall uniformly pale coloration with even paler head, and tall, sickle-shaped dorsal fin set well back. Lack of scarring indicates a young animal.

DISTRIBUTION & POPULATION

Circumpolar in deep waters of Southern Ocean, rarely

Southern Bottlenose Whale

pale flanks far less contrasting than in Longman's Beaked Whale

moderately tall, erect dorsal fin

body coloration often appears pale olive-brown or golden in sunlight

adult ♀, 7.4 m

slightly darker dorsally

much like Northern Bottlenose, ♀ can exhibit narrower beak and less bulbous melon

immature, 6 m

large beaked whale, with well-developed melon and pronounced beak (size and shape varies with age and sex)

adult ♂ can have whiter head

commonly has many linear scratches and cookie-cutter shark bites

adult ♂, 7 m

in comparison to Longman's Beaked Whale, pale melon border may extend further behind blowhole

slight median notch

adult ♂, dorsal view, 7 m

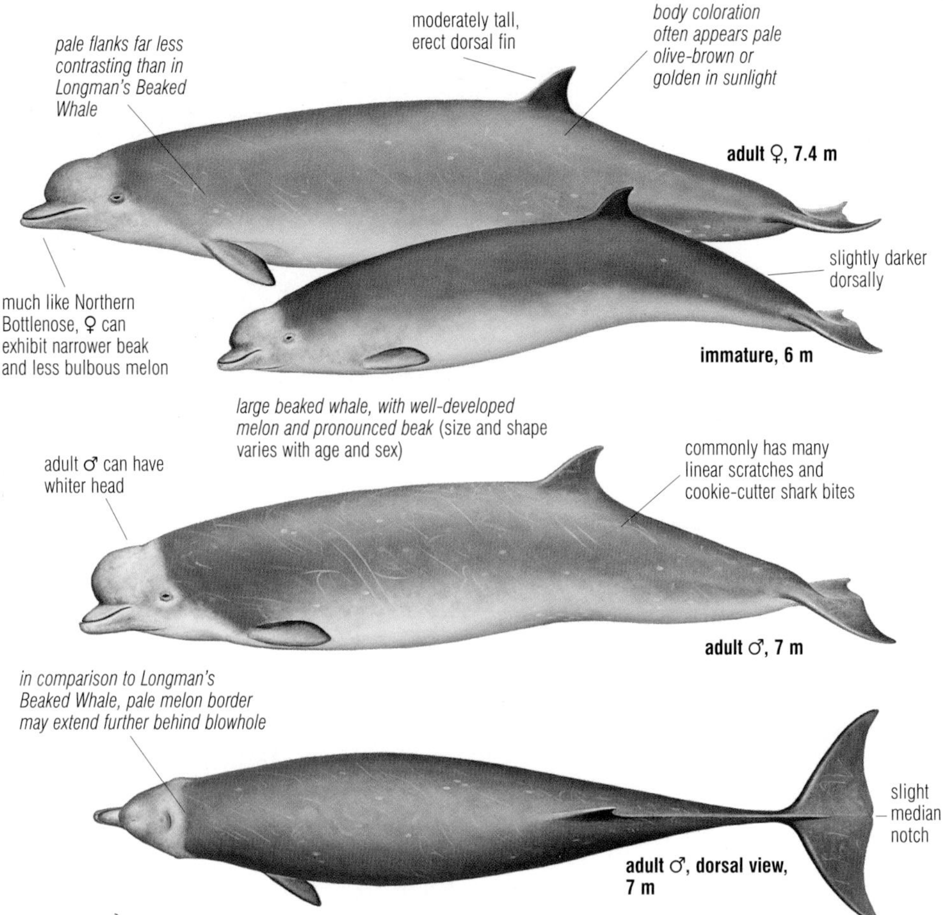

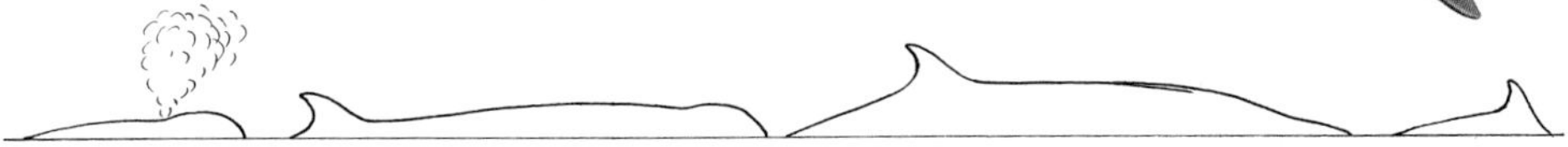

Often surfaces quite high (low bushy blow visible); dorsal fin may emerge concurrently with melon but usually disappears well before; large melon and sometimes beak briefly visible; arches steeper for deep dive.

north to *c.*30°S and usually some south of 58°S, with sightings off New Zealand, S Australia, S Africa and S America (Brazil to Chile), subantarctic islands off S America and Antarctic continent (73°S) in summer. More northerly records probably strays or misidentified Longman's Beaked Whales. May move

Southern Bottlenose Whales: the slightly small dorsal fin and unscarred body suggest immatures or ♀♀.

to warmer waters in winter. *Population* No robust abundance estimates, but sighted frequently in some Antarctic regions.

ECOLOGY

Usually in groups of 1–3 (rarely more than 10 in Antarctic waters); few records of up to 25. *Breaching* Occasional, mostly by younger animals. *Diving* Probably as Northern Bottlenose. *Diet* Squid, with fewer fish and other invertebrates. *Reproduction* Calving apparently in spring or early summer. *Lifespan* Unknown.

Southern Bottlenose Whale is large, robust; the pale greyish basal colour with numerous scars suggest subadult or mature ♂, and the bulbous melon appears prominent.

Hector's Beaked Whale

Mesoplodon hectori

S Hemisphere. Max 4.4 m.

Priority characters on surfacing

- *Small beaked whale*, with typical mesoplodont body form. Very rarely seen.
- *Short, dolphin-like beak, may be pale grey or white* (straight mouthline and lower jaw pale).
- *Small head with slight melon development*.
- May have variable *dusky mask and eye-patch*, and *pale grey or whitish neck-sides and collar (or half-collar)* appear constant species-specific characters.
- Dorsal surface dark grey or brownish-grey, paler ventrally.
- *Variable pale body scars on ad ♂.*
- Small triangular, round-tipped dorsal fin.
- *Ad ♂ has 2 small, triangular teeth near tip of lower jaw.*

Typical behaviour at surface

- Found mainly in offshore waters, generally shy of vessels.

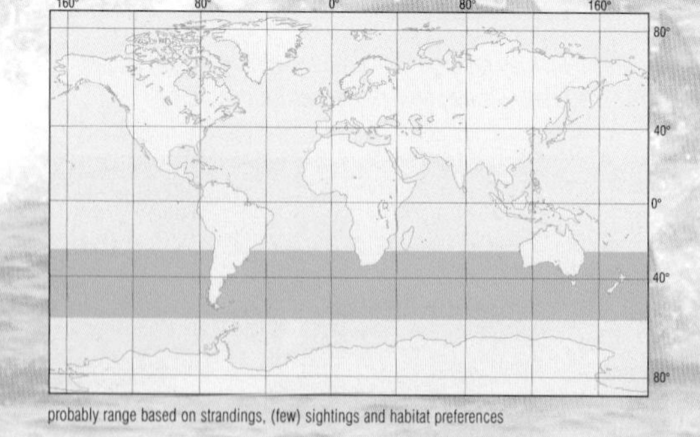

probably range based on strandings, (few) sightings and habitat preferences

SIMILAR SPECIES

Probably difficult to distinguish from other small S Hemisphere mesoplodonts, e.g. ***True's*** (also has apical teeth). *Cf.* ***Blainville's***, ***Gray's***, ***Andrews'*** and ***Ginkgo-toothed Beaked Whales***. If visible, ad ♂'s combination of small head, stubby pale beak and diagnostic placement of flattened teeth at tip of lower jaw are useful field marks.

VARIATION

Age/sex Aside from dentition, ♀/juv may be more uniform with fewer or no scars. Calf presumably much as ♀ but perhaps paler. **Physical notes** 3.9–4.4 m and *c.*1.01–2.03 tons. Newborn 1.9 m. **Other data** *Teeth* Ad ♂ has single pair of triangular teeth set at tip of lower jaw, in ♀/juv hidden by gum.

DISTRIBUTION & POPULATION

Cool–temperate S Hemisphere waters, apparently circumpolar. Most records from New Zealand but also Tasmania, W Australia, S Africa southern S America (north to Brazil) and the Falklands. *Population* No estimates.

ECOLOGY

Largely unknown. *Diet* Chiefly squid in deep waters.

Hector's Beaked Whale

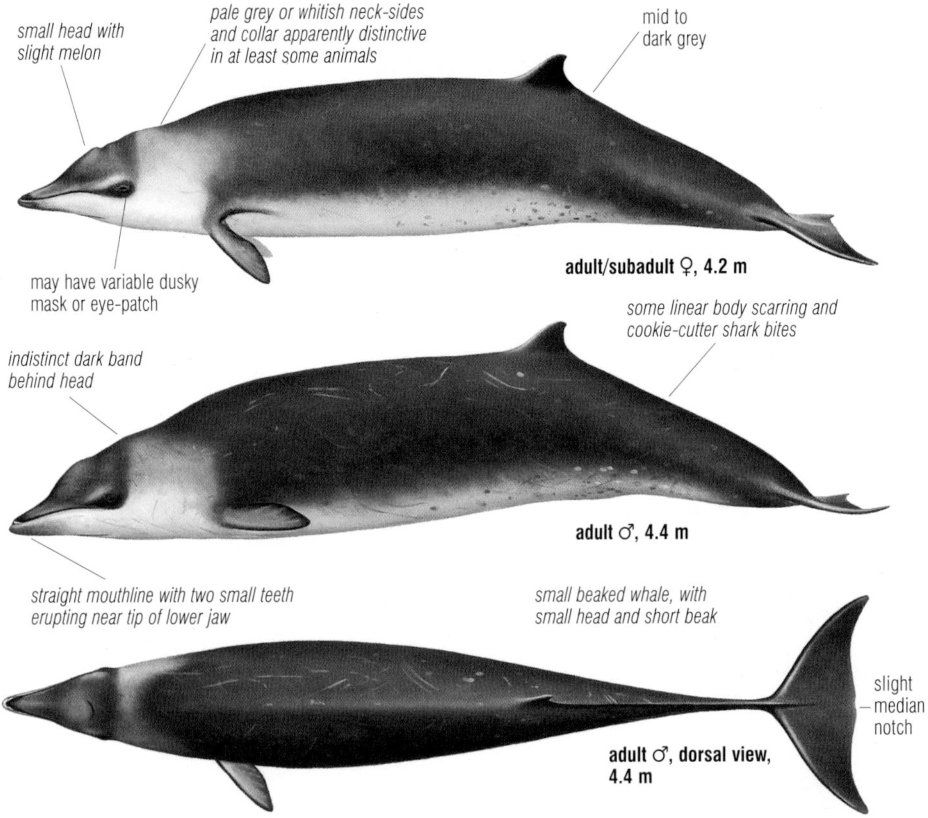

small head with slight melon

pale grey or whitish neck-sides and collar apparently distinctive in at least some animals

mid to dark grey

may have variable dusky mask or eye-patch

adult/subadult ♀, 4.2 m

some linear body scarring and cookie-cutter shark bites

indistinct dark band behind head

adult ♂, 4.4 m

straight mouthline with two small teeth erupting near tip of lower jaw

small beaked whale, with small head and short beak

slight median notch

adult ♂, dorsal view, 4.4 m

Beak often emerges first at steep angle (blow normally invisible); in usual slow surfacing roll, dorsal fin may emerge as head begins sinking; arches steeper for deep dive.

A very rare photograph of a breaching Hector's Beaked Whale; it is not known if the dark eye-patch and large white patch on the neck-sides shown here are useful for identifying this species in the wild.

SIMILAR SPECIES

Little known and only very rarely positively identified at sea, although S Hemisphere form should be easier to identify due to its contrasting white tailstock, flukes and dorsal fin, being quite distinct from N Atlantic form. Nonetheless, except in optimal or comparative views, may not be reliably separable from several congeners (in north ***Sowerby's*** and ***Gervais' Beaked Whales***, in south several species), especially young animals. Confusion risks chiefly other *Mesoplodon* but *cf.* ***Cuvier's***.

True's Beaked Whale

Mesoplodon mirus

C & N Atlantic, S Africa and Australia. Max 5.5 m.

Priority characters on surfacing

- *Small, elongated beaked whale.* Rare.
- *Gently sloping forehead* and mid-sized, *stubby, dolphin-like beak* with straight mouthline.
- May have *dark area around eye, contrasting with paler cheeks* and lower jaw.
- C Atlantic and southern animals differ. Former medium-grey dorsally and pale grey ventrally. Latter dark grey/bluish grey-black to almost blackish on upperside.
- *Mature ♂ may have white linear scars on back and sides.*
- Small, falcate or triangular dorsal fin with concave trailing edge (set well back).
- *Mature ♂ has 2 small triangular teeth, set at extreme tip of lower jaw.*

Typical behaviour at surface

- Little known. As other *Mesoplodon*, may come to surface in slow breathing roll, and porpoise with shallow leaps in fast travel.
- Generally unobtrusive at surface. Small groups and pairs.

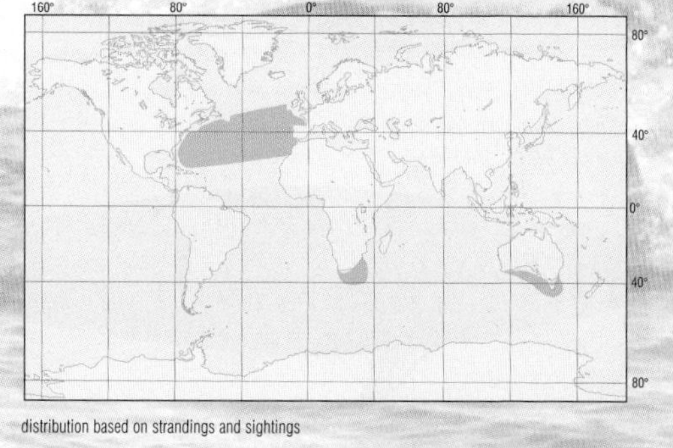

distribution based on strandings and sightings

Probable True's Beaked Whale (N Atlantic): note relatively small size, uniform pale grey pigmentation, stubby, dolphin-like beak and gently sloping forehead.

VARIATION

Age/sex Little known. May be limited apart from differences in tooth development. ♀/young possibly paler and less patterned on head, and lack scars. **Physical notes** 4.8–5.5 m and *c.*0.89–1.5 tons. Newborn *c.*2.2 m and *c.*136 kg. **Other data** *Teeth* 2 small triangular teeth, protruding from tip of lower jaw in ad ♂, but concealed in ♀/young.

DISTRIBUTION & POPULATION

Principally warm-temperate waters of N Atlantic, from Nova Scotia, Canada and Ireland south to Florida, the Bahamas and Canaries, with sightings in Bay of Biscay. Also recorded in warm-temperate waters of S Hemisphere, off S Africa and southern Australia. Movements, if any, unknown. *Population* Perhaps naturally rare like many other *Mesoplodon* spp.

ECOLOGY

Largely unknown but group size perhaps 1–6. *Breaching* Series of complete breaches recorded, landing on side (see photo). *Diet* Presumably mostly squid in deep waters.

Probable True's Beaked Whale (N Atlantic): note small dark eye-patch. The white tip on the beak appears to be a tooth, but True's lacks large teeth. The short beak eliminates Sowerby's.

True's Beaked Whale

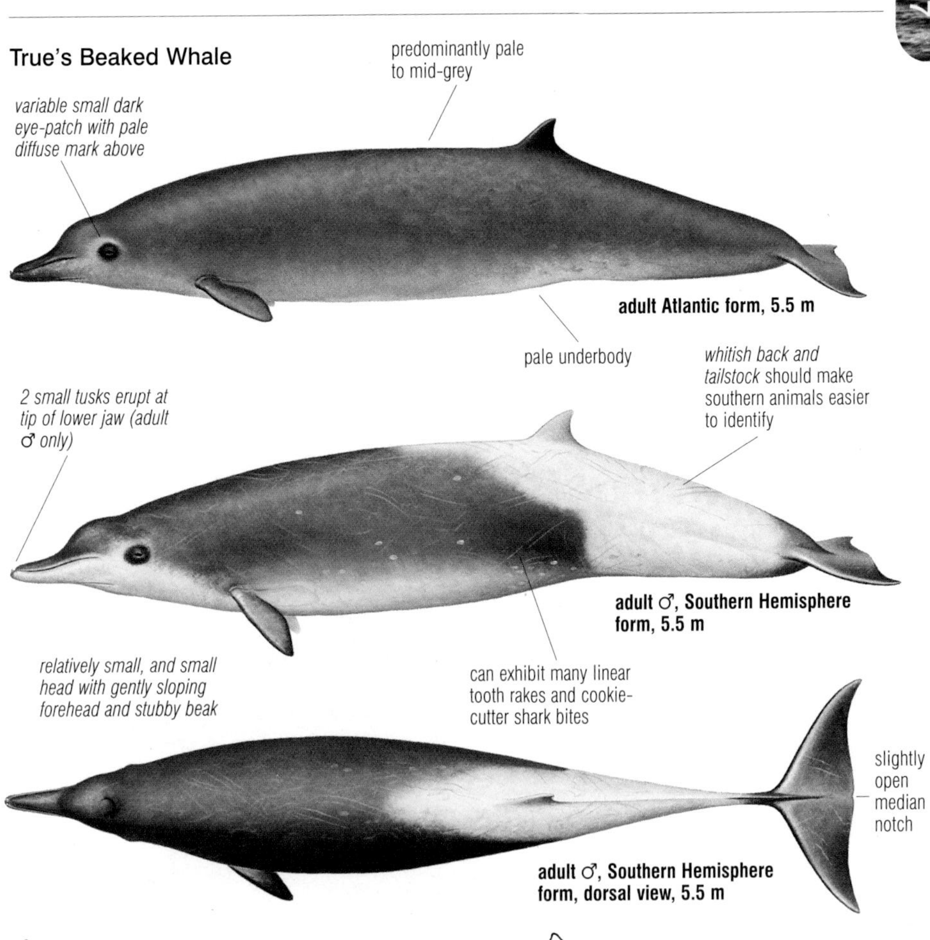

Beak and melon break surface (blow usually extremely weak); in usual slow surfacing, dorsal fin may emerge as head begins sinking; arches steeper for deep dive.

Gervais' Beaked Whale

Mesoplodon europaeus

C & N Atlantic. Max 5.2 m.

Priority characters on surfacing

- *Medium-sized* beaked whale of C and N Atlantic. Rarely seen at sea and may avoid vessels.
- Rather robust, with *small/narrow head, mid-length beak* and indistinct melon.
- *Dorsal fin very small and variable, shark-like or more curved with a rounded tip.*
- Chiefly bluish-grey to grey dorsally, contrastingly paler below. Some grey/white spots below, and *variable pale linear scars*, especially on ad ♂.
- *Teeth of ad ♂ small and triangular, and set slightly back from tip of lower jaw. Tooth position and size important for identification*, but difficult to see.

SIMILAR SPECIES

Reliable identification at sea extremely difficult, especially for ♀♀/young. Most similar is ***Sowerby's Beaked Whale*** but *cf.* ***Blainville's*** and ***True's Beaked Whales***, all of which can sometimes be separated by combination of dental features (ad ♂♂ only), curve of mouthline (again, mostly adult ♂♂), minor differences in coloration and, to some extent, by range. Range also overlaps with larger, more robust and distinctive ***Cuvier's Beaked Whale*** and ***Northern Bottlenose Whale***.

VARIATION

Age/sex Perhaps by overall size (ad ♀ possibly larger on average) and dentition. Pale markings vary with age and sex (see Sowerby's). Some ad ♀♀ have white ano-genital patch and more pale areas on head. Calf slimmer and more uniformly dark above, with whiter underparts that darken with age, and shorter beak. **Physical notes** Ad 4–5.2 m and 1–2.6 tons.

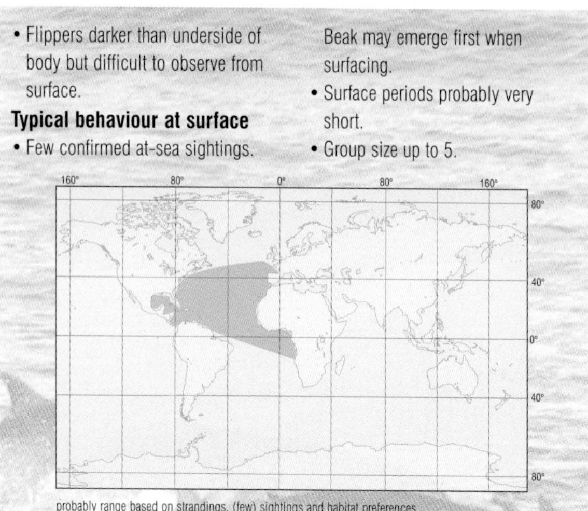

- Flippers darker than underside of body but difficult to observe from surface.

Typical behaviour at surface

- Few confirmed at-sea sightings. Beak may emerge first when surfacing.
- Surface periods probably very short.
- Group size up to 5.

probably range based on strandings, (few) sightings and habitat preferences

Gervais' Beaked Whale

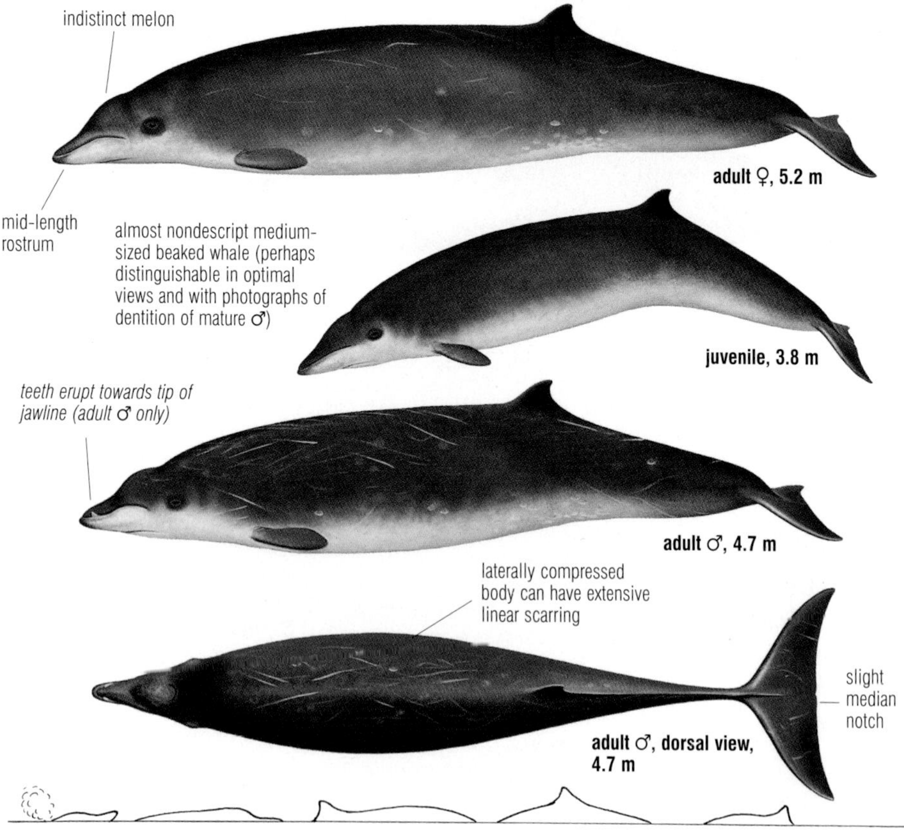

indistinct melon

mid-length rostrum

adult ♀, 5.2 m

almost nondescript medium-sized beaked whale (perhaps distinguishable in optimal views and with photographs of dentition of mature ♂)

juvenile, 3.8 m

teeth erupt towards tip of jawline (adult ♂ only)

adult ♂, 4.7 m

laterally compressed body can have extensive linear scarring

slight median notch

adult ♂, dorsal view, 4.7 m

Beak and melon emerge, blow perhaps normally invisible; in shallow roll, dorsal fin may emerge as head is sinking; arches more steeply for deeper dive.

Newborn 1.6–2.2 m and *c.*80 kg. **Other data** *Teeth* Single pair of medium-sized triangular teeth in lower jaw, set 7–10 cm back from tip. Teeth may curve outward, but comparatively small size makes at-sea viewing difficult. In ♀/juv teeth hidden by gums.

DISTRIBUTION & POPULATION
Tropical and warmer temperate waters of Atlantic, principally north of the equator and extending occasionally to cold-temperate seas. Most southerly records from Ascension Is. Most records from western N Atlantic, in the Caribbean, Gulf of Mexico and north almost to Canada and Iceland (rare). Fewer records from eastern N Atlantic, off W Africa, the Canaries and NW Europe. Movements, if any, unknown. *Population* No estimates.

ECOLOGY
Almost unknown.

Sowerby's Beaked Whale

Mesoplodon bidens

N Atlantic. Max 5.5 m.

Priority characters on surfacing

- *Small to medium-sized, narrow-bodied* beaked whale of N Atlantic.
- *Small head, long slender beak and low, convex forehead bulge.*
- May have some pale grey-brown coloration on head/beak, *otherwise chiefly slate grey* and paler below, and perhaps darker in young.
- *Small curved dorsal fin* with rounded tip (set well back).
- *Pale oval spots on ads, and ♂ especially also has pale linear scars* and scratches (less conspicuous than in congeners).
- *Single pair of triangular teeth, erupt midway along beak (adult ♂ only).*

Typical behaviour at surface

- *Periods at surface may be short* (*c.*1 min or a few mins), with *c.*5 rapid breaths, blow normally invisible or extremely weak.
- May surface with beak emerging first from water at steep angle.
- Both flippers and flukes largely invisible on surfacing, though tail-slapping recorded.
- Group size up to 10 animals.

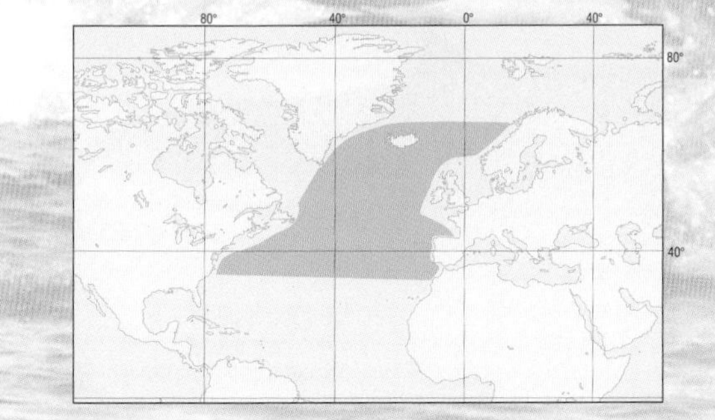

SIMILAR SPECIES
May be confused with any other ***Mesoplodon*** in range, but note extremely long beak and flat head, and position of teeth in Sowerby's. ***Gervais' Beaked Whale*** similar but generally more southerly. ***Blainville's Beaked Whale*** (somewhat wider overlap in range, but usually more heavily scarred) and ***True's Beaked Whale*** (apparently rare in Sowerby's range) also similar, being separated mainly by shape of mouthline (curved in latter) and by teeth of ad ♂♂ (in True's at tip of lower jaw, in Blainville's middle of lower jaw and mostly covered by bone and gum tissue). Tooth characteristics should be used only in optimal views and with caution. Probably most young and ♀♀ indistinguishable at sea. ***Cuvier's Beaked Whale*** also overlaps in range, but is larger, more robust with a considerably shorter beak and whiter head. ***Northern Bottlenose Whale*** in N Atlantic generally markedly larger and robust, and has bulbous, well-defined melon, among other characters.

Mature ♀ Sowerby's Beaked Whale: note low, convex forehead bulge, long slender beak and unscarred body (an attendant calf was present).

VARIATION

Age/sex Perhaps by size (♂ presumably larger on average than ♀) and dentition. Pale linear scars and other markings increase with age, mainly in ad ♂♂. Calf slimmer and more uniformly dark, with shorter beak and poorly developed melon. **Physical notes** Ad 4.4–5.5 m and 1–1.3 tons. Newborn 2.4–2.7 m and *c.*170 kg. **Other data** *Teeth* Single

The beak often emerges first at a steep angle; note small head, long slender beak and low, convex forehead bulge.

Sowerby's Beaked Whale

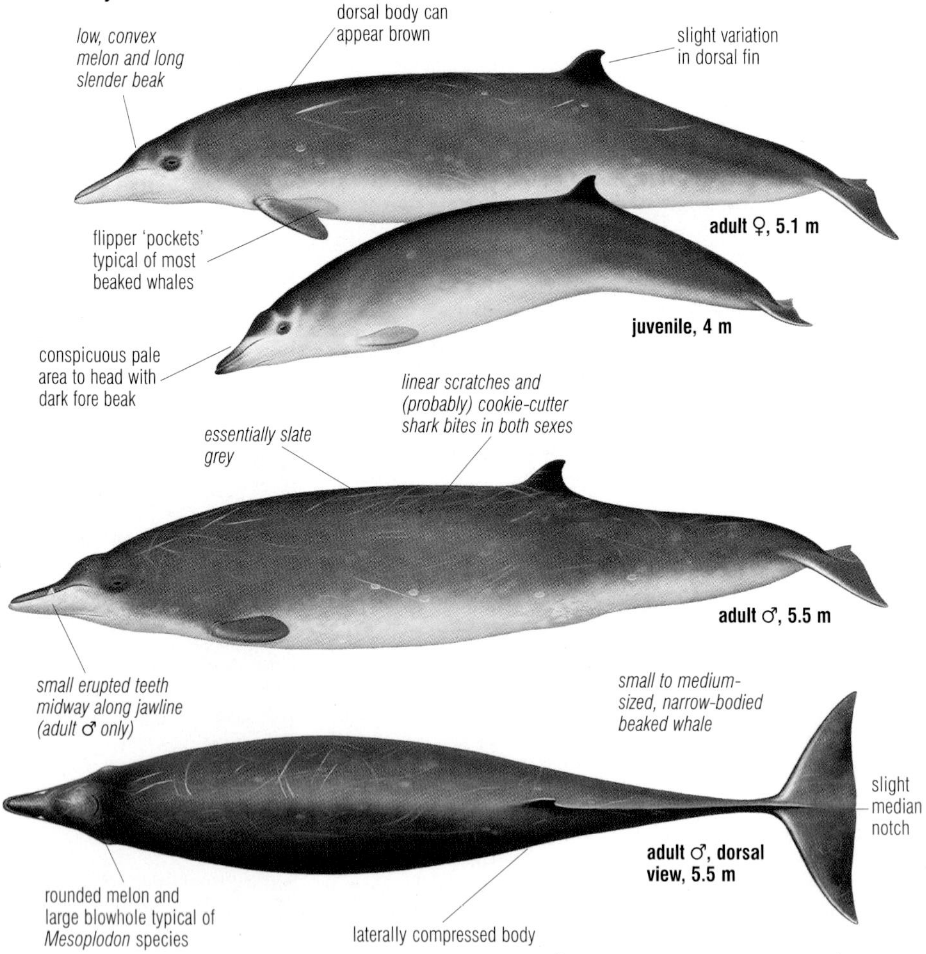

low, convex melon and long slender beak

dorsal body can appear brown

slight variation in dorsal fin

flipper 'pockets' typical of most beaked whales

adult ♀, 5.1 m

juvenile, 4 m

conspicuous pale area to head with dark fore beak

linear scratches and (probably) cookie-cutter shark bites in both sexes

essentially slate grey

adult ♂, 5.5 m

small erupted teeth midway along jawline (adult ♂ only)

small to medium-sized, narrow-bodied beaked whale

slight median notch

adult ♂, dorsal view, 5.5 m

rounded melon and large blowhole typical of *Mesoplodon* species

laterally compressed body

In slow breathing roll beak (usually much longer than diagram) often emerges first at steep angle (blow normally invisible or weak); dorsal fin may emerge about same time as head begins to sink; arches steeper for deep dive.

pair midway between tip of beak and corner of mouth that erupt only in ♂.

DISTRIBUTION & POPULATION
Cool and warm-temperate continental shelf and deep offshore waters of N Atlantic, north to Labrador and Norwegian Sea, reaching south to Massachusetts (USA) and Canaries. More records from E Atlantic than W. Single stranding in Gulf of Mexico assumed extralimital. Movements, if any, unknown. *Population* No estimates.

ECOLOGY
Typically in groups of 8–10, of mixed age/sex. *Breaching* Apparently rare. *Diving* Up to 28 min (usually 10–15 min) and to 1,500 m. *Diet* Squid presumed to be most important constituent, but takes some fish. *Reproduction* Probably sexually mature after 7 yrs old. *Lifespan* Unknown.

Sowerby's Beaked Whale preparing for a deep dive: abundant scarring indicates an adult, and the long, linear scars are suggestive of an adult ♂.

Gray's Beaked Whale

Mesoplodon grayi

S Hemisphere. Max 5.7 m.

Priority characters on surfacing

- *Medium-sized* beaked whale with elongated body and contrasting white face.
- Dark bluish-grey, brownish-grey or black dorsally, paler to whitish ventrally.
- *Conspicuous long slender white beak diagnostic* (most pronounced in ads), and face may also be white.
- Characteristic *small narrow head*, with indistinct melon.
- Pointed dorsal fin with concave trailing edge.
- *Variable pale linear scarring on body (especially ad ♂)*, also white round–oval scars and whitish-yellow blotches ventrally.
- Straight mouthline.
- Ad ♂ has *single pair of triangular teeth* in lower jaw, *c.½ way from tip*. Tooth size and degree of curvature from beak varies.

Typical behaviour at surface

- Beak often emerges first when surfacing, at *c.*50° angle; usually swims slowly and rolls smoothly, but may leap low or appear to accelerate with low short pushes during fast travel.
- Breaches at shallow angle (occasionally lifting body as far as flukes, even becoming entirely airborne several times in succession).
- Sometimes in small groups which may breach simultaneously.

SIMILAR SPECIES
Other mesoplodonts with overlapping ranges. Given good views, the long, snow-white beak is distinctive (ads). Identification of juvs more difficult and could be confused with juv ***Strap-toothed Whale***. Ad ♂ of both species, however, wholly distinctive. Also ***Blainville's***, ***Andrews'***, ***True's***, ***Hector's*** and ***Ginkgo-toothed Beaked Whales*** which in some circumstances can be eliminated by combination of length and shape of beak, dentition and overall coloration.

VARIATION
Age/sex Aside of dental differences, sexes apparently mostly alike. However, there is evidence that some ad ♀♀ are more like young (see artworks). In general, subad/imm paler and less greyish, and more uniform on sides and below (with fewer yellowish spots around navel), often with some dark areas on head, and has less obvious pale beak. Ad ♀/juv have fewer or no linear scars. Calf even paler/more uniform than subad/imm with clearer dark eye-patch and forehead, whilst beak is indistinctly paler. Variation requires further study. **Physical notes** 4.5–5.7 m and *c.*1.01–1.5 tons. Newborn 2–2.4 m.

Other data *Teeth* Ad ♂ has single pair of triangular teeth of variable width in mid lower jaw, in ♀/juv hidden by gum. Both sexes often have tiny vestigial teeth towards back of upper jaw, not present in other mesoplodonts. **Taxonomy** Proposed monotypic genus, *Oulodon*, for this species rarely supported. Those observed in E tropical Pacific have white lower and dark upper jaws.

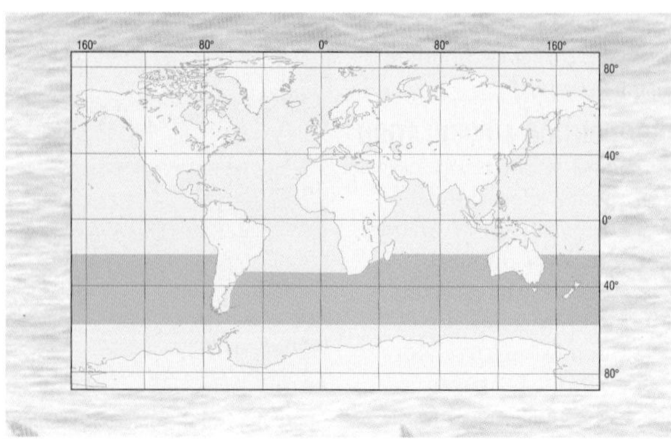

Gray's Beaked Whale

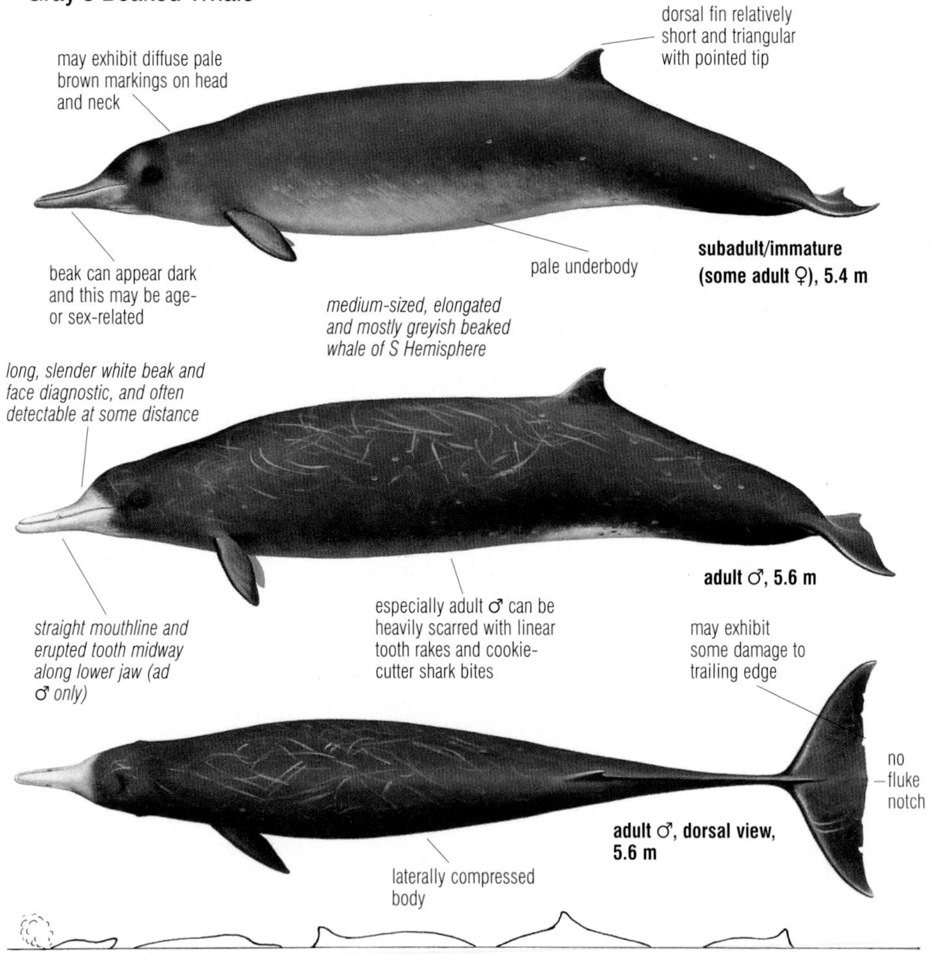

may exhibit diffuse pale brown markings on head and neck

dorsal fin relatively short and triangular with pointed tip

beak can appear dark and this may be age- or sex-related

pale underbody

subadult/immature (some adult ♀), 5.4 m

medium-sized, elongated and mostly greyish beaked whale of S Hemisphere

long, slender white beak and face diagnostic, and often detectable at some distance

adult ♂, 5.6 m

straight mouthline and erupted tooth midway along lower jaw (ad ♂ only)

especially adult ♂ can be heavily scarred with linear tooth rakes and cookie-cutter shark bites

may exhibit some damage to trailing edge

no fluke notch

adult ♂, dorsal view, 5.6 m

laterally compressed body

Beak (usually appears much longer than here) often emerges first at steep angle (blow normally invisible); in usual slow surfacing roll, dorsal fin may emerge as head begins sinking; arches more steeply for deeper dive.

DISTRIBUTION & POPULATION
Circumpolar south of 30°S, known primarily from strandings in New Zealand, as well as southern Australia, S Africa, the Falklands and Tierra del Fuego. Single stranding record from N Atlantic (Netherlands) considered stray. *Population* No estimates. Appears widespread and reasonably common in Southern Ocean.

Gray's Beaked Whale: lack of whitish beak/face and dark eye-patch suggest a young animal.

Gray's Beaked Whales, mother and calf: the latter still has a stubby beak and stronger head pattern.

ECOLOGY
Singly or in small groups of 2–6. Only ziphiid for which regular mass-strandings noted. *Breaching* See box. *Diving* Deep diver given food preferences. *Diet* Squid and fish. *Reproduction* Calving off New Zealand appears to occur late spring–summer. *Lifespan* unknown.

Gray's Beaked Whales often break the surface at a steep angle; the background animal is exposing the extremely long, all-white beak (diagnostic in adults).

Pygmy Beaked Whale

Mesoplodon peruvianus

E tropical and S Pacific, and off California. Max 3.9 m.

Priority characters on surfacing

- *The smallest beaked whale.* Small number of specimens from Pacific, range unclear.
- Small *dorsal fin is triangular.*
- At least some ad *♂♂ distinctive, with whitish swath on foreback onto sides*, bordered by broad (but ill-defined) dark shoulder patch, cape and rear body; some have *heavy linear tooth-rake*

SIMILAR SPECIES
Recent photographs suggest not all ad ♂♂ are distinctively patterned, in some the pale areas are light greyish brown, but it is unknown if such variation relates to age. Both the text and artworks are based on very little material, and further work is required.

Confusion risks with ♀♀/young chiefly involve other *Mesoplodon* that overlap in range (e.g. Perrin's in E North Pacific), but combination of small size, more triangular (less curved) dorsal fin, short beak with curved mouthline and head shape and overall coloration offer clues. Without optimal viewing conditions, comparative views and photographic documentation, identification of ♀♀/young, of such rare species at sea is unreliable.

VARIATION

Age/sex Little known (see Priority characters on surfacing and Similar species). **Physical notes** 3.4–3.9 m. Newborn *c.*1.5 m. **Other data** *Teeth* 2 small conical teeth at apex of arch of lower jaw, difficult to observe at sea. **Taxonomy** Strong evidence that *Mesoplodon* sp 'A', an unidentified ziphiid known only from sightings in the E tropical Pacific represents *M. peruvianus.*

scars, exaggerating pattern.

- Narrow, smoothly sloping forehead (perhaps with slight melon) *tapering to stubby beak.*
- ♀♀ / young seem far more nondescript, mostly dark to pale grey-brown (some perhaps have paler cape) and unscarred; head variably has pale sides and darker forehead, sometimes blackish-brown, affording mask-like appearance, especially around eyes; lower flanks and underparts paler grey to whitish.
- *Curved mouthline with small teeth set in mid jaw, but at most only slightly visible in ad ♂*; latter also appear to have more pronounced small melon.
- Melon and mouthline seem much reduced in ♀♀/ young

Typical behaviour at surface

- In shallow breathing rolls first hauls head and part of forebody slightly out of water, whilst triangular dorsal fin emerges last, and may also porpoise in low arc-shaped leaps.
- Chiefly offshore and *found in pairs*; sometimes approachable.

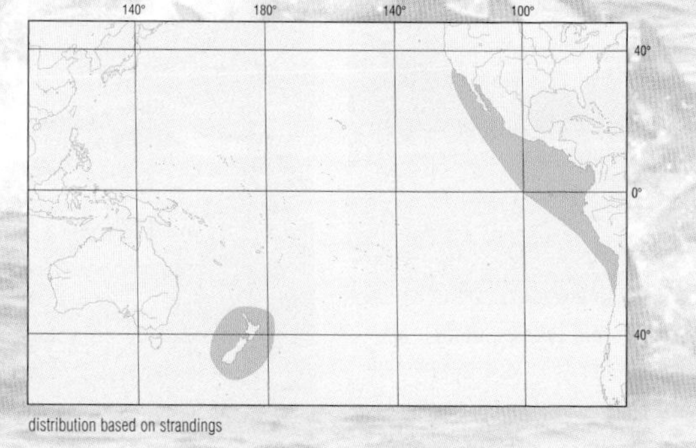

distribution based on strandings

DISTRIBUTION & POPULATION

Known primarily from SE Pacific waters off Peru, south to Chile (11–29°S), and records also from Mexico, C California and New Zealand suggesting a wider range. Sightings presumably of this species available for most waters between Peru and Mexico. Movements, if any, unknown. *Population* No estimates.

ECOLOGY

Largely unknown but usually in small, tight groups of up to 8. Lobtailing, spyhopping and other surface activities uncommon. *Breaching* Once observed to breach 3× in succession. *Diet* Squid and fish in deep waters.

Probable Pygmy Beaked Whale, eastern tropical Pacific, based on combination of small size and small, triangular dorsal fin (usually with a straight trailing edge); overall pigmentation (no scars or patterning) suggests ♀♀ and/or young; orange tinge to head is probably due to diatoms.

Pygmy Beaked Whale

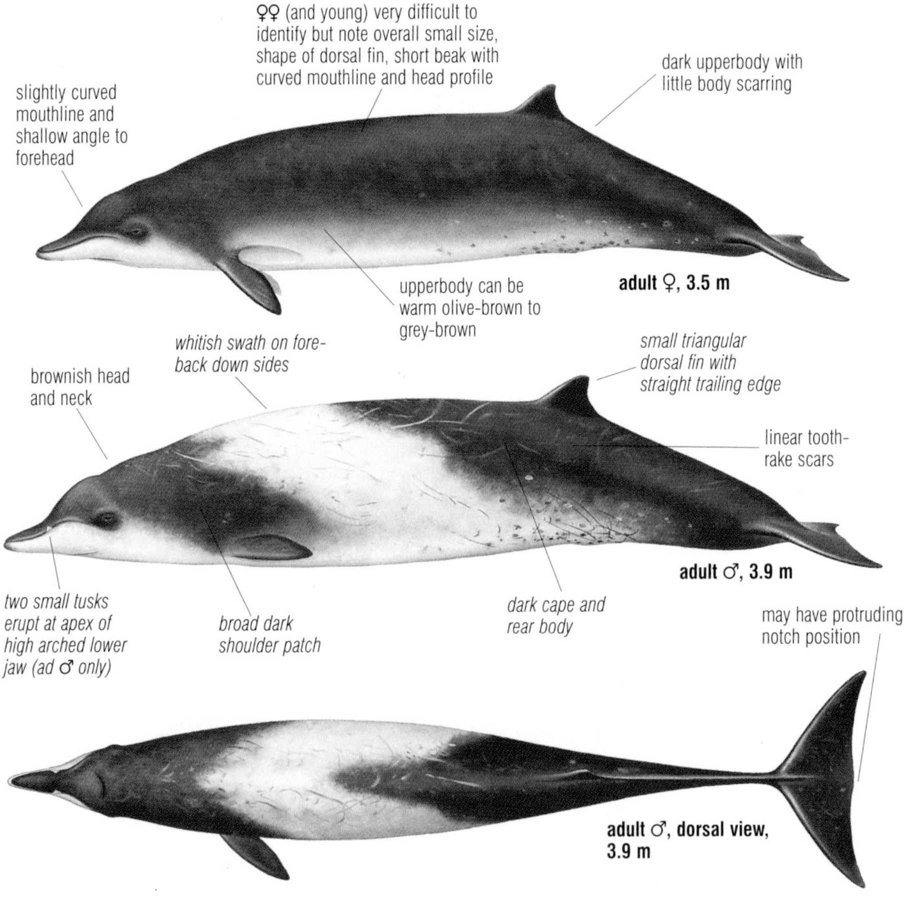

♀♀ (and young) very difficult to identify but note overall small size, shape of dorsal fin, short beak with curved mouthline and head profile

slightly curved mouthline and shallow angle to forehead

dark upperbody with little body scarring

upperbody can be warm olive-brown to grey-brown

adult ♀, 3.5 m

whitish swath on fore-back down sides

brownish head and neck

small triangular dorsal fin with straight trailing edge

linear tooth-rake scars

adult ♂, 3.9 m

two small tusks erupt at apex of high arched lower jaw (ad ♂ only)

broad dark shoulder patch

dark cape and rear body

may have protruding notch position

adult ♂, dorsal view, 3.9 m

Beak and forebody often emerge first (blow usually invisible); in usual slow surfacing roll, dorsal fin may emerge just after head begins sinking; arches slightly more steeply for deep dive.

Pygmy Beaked Whale, probably adult ♀: note characteristic triangular dorsal fin.

Adult ♂ Pygmy Beaked Whale, showing the distinctive whitish swath and scars on foreback and to lower sides.

Andrews' Beaked Whale

Mesoplodon bowdoini

S Hemisphere. Max 5 m.

Priority characters on surfacing

- *Smaller beaked whale* with rather robust body. Following is based on stranded individuals.
- *Dark blue-black*, some have brownish tone and greyer 'saddle'.
- Variable *white scratches (especially in ad ♂), scars and oval patches*; may show pale patch in front of eyes.
- *Short thick beak is predominantly white*.
- Insignificant forehead melon, but *strongly arched mouthline* (with elevated 'lower cheeks' that may even extend slightly above the rostrum level).
- Two broad *teeth protrude from central mouthline in ad ♂*.
- *Small, triangular and pointed or blunt-tipped dorsal fin* set ⅔ of way along back.

Typical behaviour at surface

- Unknown.

SIMILAR SPECIES

Unknown at sea. Even in close views perhaps difficult or impossible to identify from overlapping and mainly dark, similar-sized congeners, e.g. ***Blainville's Beaked Whale***. However, ad ♂ has conspicuous white-tipped beak, strongly arched lower jaw and heavy scarring; ♀ and young probably indistinguishable from other *Mesoplodon* of this age/sex class. Presumed range may help distinguish it from some similar species. *Cf.* ***Strap-toothed***, ***Gray's***, ***Hector's*** and ***Ginkgo-toothed Beaked Whales***.

VARIATION

Age/sex Old ad ♂♂ generally heavily scarred and white on beak (and often on base/top of melon, and/or just in front of eye) more pronounced and extensive; ♀♀/young apparently more uniformly slate grey to greyish-brown, respectively, with paler flanks and belly (flippers darker than surroundings) and usually only lower jaw prominently whitish with ill-defined

Andrews' Beaked Whale

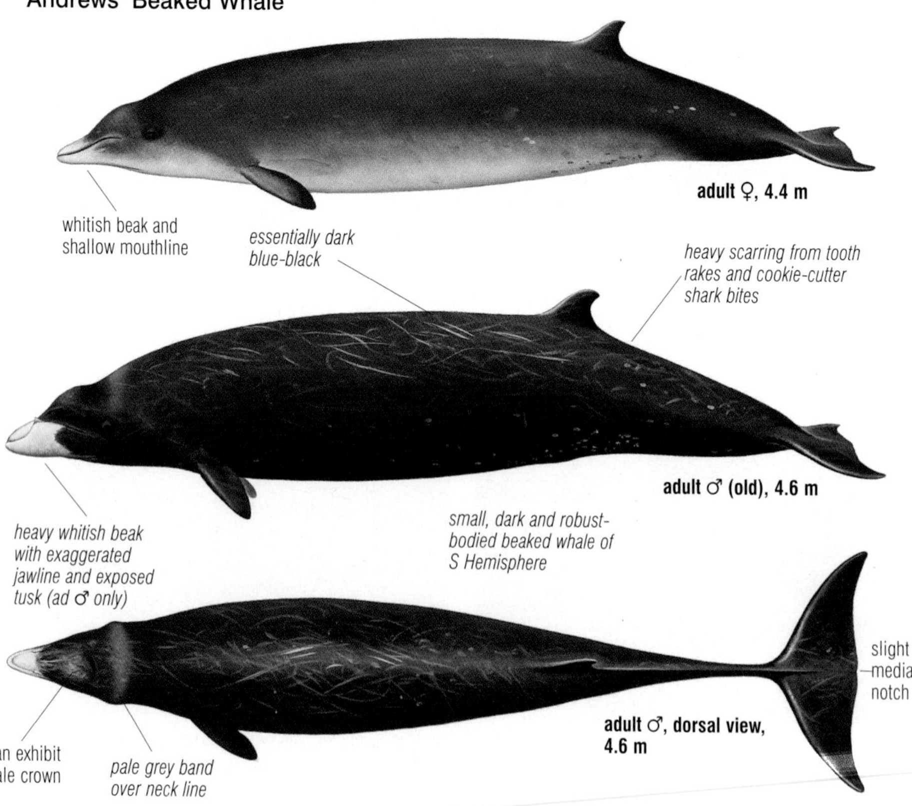

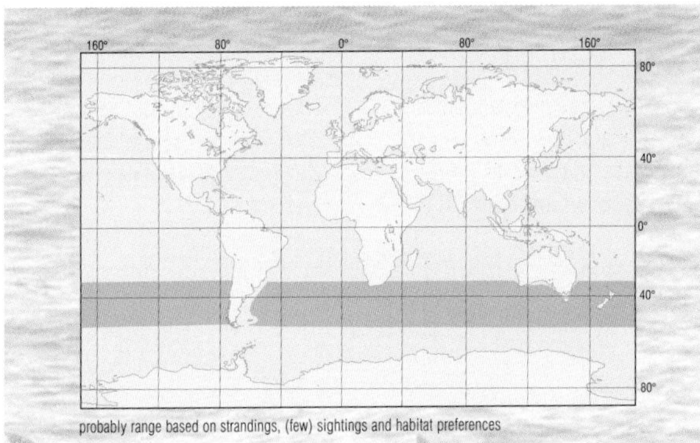

probably range based on strandings, (few) sightings and habitat preferences

patches above eyes. **Physical notes** Ad ♂ *c.*3.4–4.4(-5?) and ad ♀ *c.*3.6–4.9 m, and 1.1–1.5 tons (both sexes). Newborn *c.*2.2 m. **Other data** *Teeth* Ad ♂ has single pair of large, flattened tusk-like teeth at apex of lower jaw arch, curving slightly outwards above upper jaw. In ♀/juv hidden in gums. **Taxonomy** Sometimes considered sister-species of Hubbs' Beaked Whale.

DISTRIBUTION & POPULATION

Probably circumpolar north of Antarctic Convergence, between 32°S and 54°S. Considered rare in cool-temperate waters around New Zealand, and off southern and W Australia. *Population* No estimates.

ECOLOGY

Largely unknown. *Diet* Presumably chiefly mesopelagic squid in deep waters. *Reproduction* Only breeding data from New Zealand, where calving seems to occur in summer/autumn.

Spade-toothed Beaked Whale

Mesoplodon traversii

S Hemisphere. Max 5.5 m?

Priority characters on surfacing

- Recently redescribed beaked whale known from 2 skulls and 1 jawbone from both sides of S Pacific, yet to be seen alive.
- Possibly a medium-sized beaked whale, but no information on coloration.
- Skull morphology similar to Andrews' and Ginkgo-toothed Beaked Whales.

Typical surfacing behaviour

- Unknown.

SIMILAR SPECIES

Most likely to be mistaken with the several overlapping *Mesoplodon* spp in S Pacific, perhaps especially Strap-toothed Beaked Whale. External appearance unknown, making comparison impossible.

VARIATION

Age/sex Unknown. **Physical notes** May reach 5–5.5 m. **Other data** *Teeth* 2 large spade-shaped teeth, similar to Strap-toothed Whale but apparently shorter and more robust. Teeth erupt only in ad ♂. **Taxonomy** Bahamonde's Beaked Whale *M. bahamondi* now recognised as synonymous with *M. traversii.*

DISTRIBUTION & POPULATION

Known only from a lower jaw and teeth from Chatham Is, New Zealand, a partial skull from Juan Fernández Is, off Chile, and a second partial skull from White Is, New Zealand.

ECOLOGY

Unknown.

Hubbs' Beaked Whale

Mesoplodon carlhubbsi

N Pacific. Max 5.4 m.

Priority characters on surfacing

- One of the *most localised beaked whales*; rare; at least ad ♂ distinctive.
- *Medium-sized beaked whale*, with proportionately elongated body.
- *Ad ♂ has white 'cap' on melon around blowhole.*
- *Stocky white beak* (less obvious in ♀).
- *Deeply curved mouthline.*
- *Large pale teeth exposed about midway along lower jaw.*
- *Ad ♂ dark grey to black with*

SIMILAR SPECIES

Might be confused with other beaked whales in range, *cf.* ***Ginkgo-toothed***, ***Stejneger's***, ***Blainville's*** and even ***Baird's*** and ***Cuvier's***. Note relative beak length, tooth position and gape shape, and coloration of any heavily scarred animals. Although ad ♂ Hubbs'

Beaked Whales generally distinctive, beak/dental features and distinctive white cap of ad should be confirmed, preferably photographically, for this rare species. Identification at sea of ♀/young perhaps impossible.

VARIATION

Age/sex Ad ♂ dark grey to black, with extensive white linear scars and variable white 'cap' around blowhole. Entire lower beak or at least front of upper jaw also white. Forehead hump reduced or often lacking in ♀/young, which are reportedly paler grey and less marked (fewer

extensive white linear scarring.

- ♀/young medium grey and less marked (fewer/no scars and lack white cap); paler below.
- *Medium-sized, falcate, pointed dorsal fin* set well back.

Typical behaviour at surface

- Like most ziphiids, prefers deeper offshore waters, surface periods short, does not approach boats. May haul head out of water slightly on surfacing.

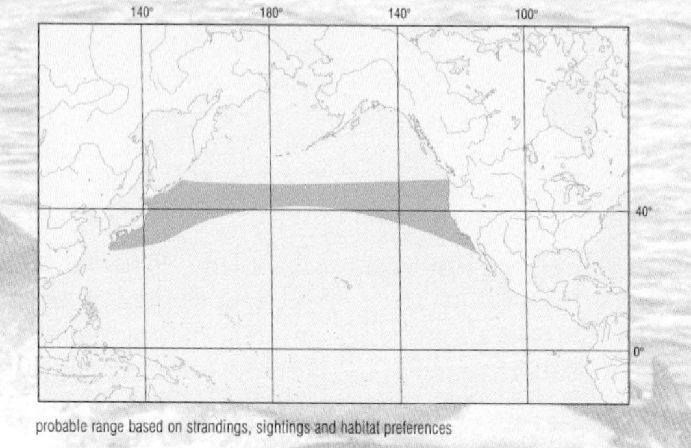

probable range based on strandings, sightings and habitat preferences

Hubbs' Beaked Whale

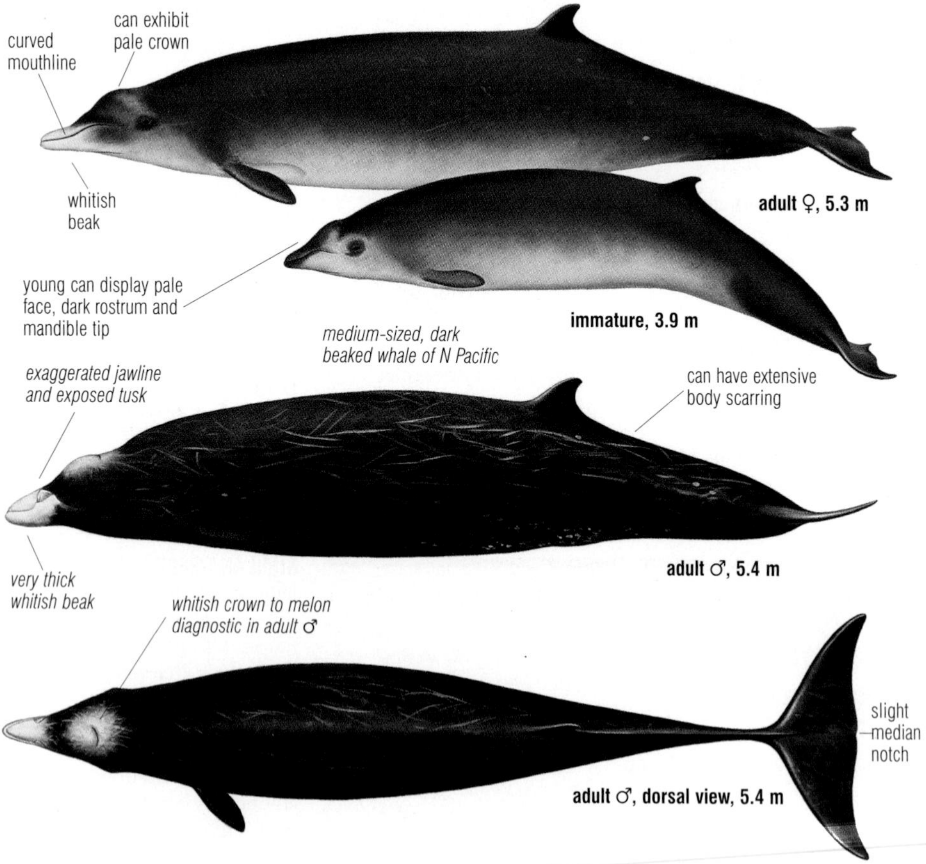

curved mouthline

can exhibit pale crown

whitish beak

adult ♀, 5.3 m

young can display pale face, dark rostrum and mandible tip

immature, 3.9 m

medium-sized, dark beaked whale of N Pacific

exaggerated jawline and exposed tusk

can have extensive body scarring

very thick whitish beak

adult ♂, 5.4 m

whitish crown to melon diagnostic in adult ♂

slight median notch

adult ♂, dorsal view, 5.4 m

scars, white of beak limited and less contrasting, white on melon perhaps absent), with quite pronounced paler undersides. Calf probably uniformly darker. **Physical notes** Ad 5–5.4 m and 1–1.5 tons. Newborn 2.5 m or less. **Other data** *Teeth* Single pair of large, white triangular teeth project from apex of lower jaw arch in ad ♂. In ♀/juv hidden by gums.

DISTRIBUTION & POPULATION

Temperate waters of N Pacific, off NE Honshu (Japan) and from British Columbia (Canada) south to S California (USA). Movements, if any, unknown. *Population* No estimates.

ECOLOGY

Almost unknown. Usually recorded in groups of 1–3. *Diet* Principally mesopelagic squid and fish. *Reproduction* Calving perhaps mainly in summer.

Ginkgo-toothed Beaked Whale

Mesoplodon ginkgodens

Temperate/tropical Pacific and Indian Ocean. Max 5.3 m.

Priority characters on surfacing

- *Very rare medium-sized beaked whale* with robust, compact body.
- *♂ may be very dark*, perhaps marine-blue, with white blotching mainly around navel; ♀ less dark and has even paler belly.
- *Uniquely among mesoplodonts, body usually unscarred.*
- *Small, rounded melon* with long forehead and *mid-length beak perhaps paler distally.*
- *Mouthline strongly arched.*
- Ad ♂ has *single pair of wide, triangular teeth at midpoint of lower jaw. Teeth largely hidden and only tips visible*, and do not project above top of upper jaw.
- *Pointed dorsal fin, which may have falcate trailing edge,* is set *c.*2/3 of way back.

Typical behaviour at surface

- Mainly in deep, offshore waters, and generally shy of vessels.
- Surfacing periods probably brief, making identification even more difficult.
- Probably occurs in small groups.

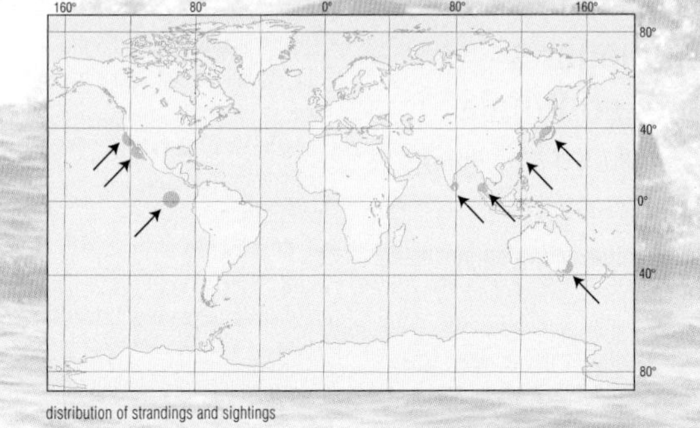

distribution of strandings and sightings

SIMILAR SPECIES

At-sea sightings extremely rare. Even at close quarters, difficult to separate from other dark-coloured beaked whales, although if heavily scarred animal seen this probably rules out Ginkgo-toothed Beaked Whale. Most confusion likely with ***Blainville's***, which has similar arched mouthline, but is paler grey-brown dorsally and whiter ventrally, with a flatter head. ***Hubbs'*** also has arched mouthline but has diagnostic white cap and beak. Also ***Stejneger's*** and ***Andrews' Beaked Whales***. Identification of ♀/young very difficult, even of dead animals.

VARIATION

Age/sex Difficult, aside from dental differences (teeth perhaps only visible in full-grown ♂); ♀/young may be paler. Calf presumably much as ♀ in coloration. **Physical notes** 4.5–5.3 m and *c.*1.5–2.03 tons. Newborn *c.*2.1–2.4 m. **Other data** *Teeth* Ad ♂ has single pair of large, broad, roughly triangular (tusk-like) teeth at apex of lower jaw arch; only tips emerge and do not project above top of upper jaw. Generally wider than other mesoplodonts, although some Gray's Beaked Whales may be similar. In ♀/juv teeth hidden in gum tissue. Arch of jaw more subtle.

DISTRIBUTION & POPULATION

Principally temperate–tropical N Pacific (especially Japan) and Indian Oceans. Records few but widespread, including Guam, Australia, New Zealand, Sri Lanka, the Maldives and Strait of Malacca. In E Pacific, California and the Galápagos. *Population* No estimates, probably uncommon.

ECOLOGY

Almost unknown. *Diet* Mesopelagic squid and possibly fish in deep waters.

Ginkgo-toothed Beaked Whale

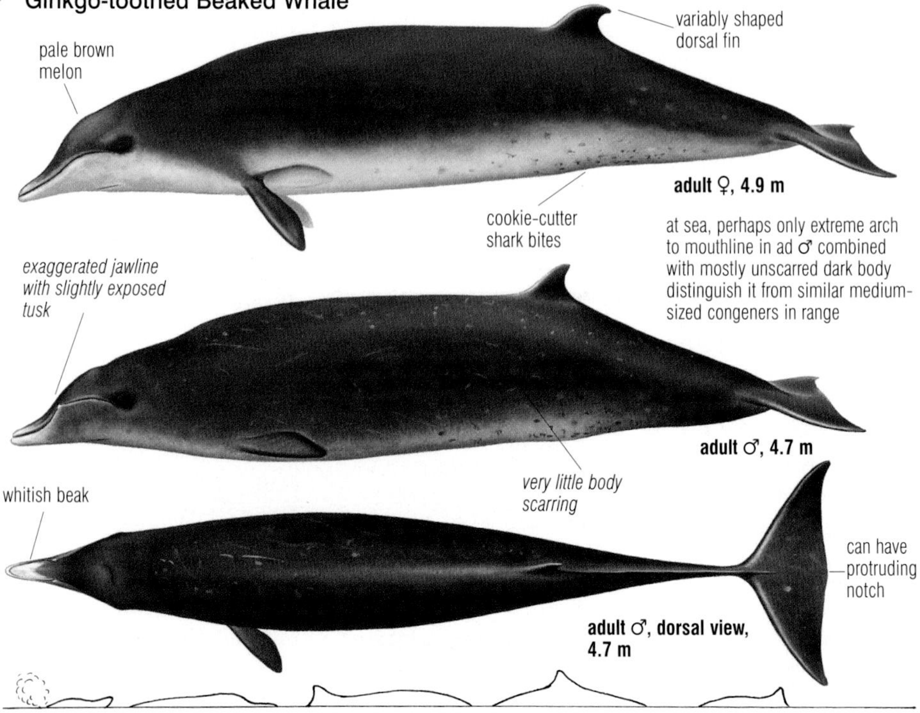

pale brown melon

variably shaped dorsal fin

adult ♀, 4.9 m

cookie-cutter shark bites

at sea, perhaps only extreme arch to mouthline in ad ♂ combined with mostly unscarred dark body distinguish it from similar medium-sized congeners in range

exaggerated jawline with slightly exposed tusk

adult ♂, 4.7 m

very little body scarring

whitish beak

can have protruding notch

adult ♂, dorsal view, 4.7 m

Beak and melon emerge, blow normally invisible; in shallow roll, dorsal fin may emerge as head is sinking; arches more steeply for deeper dive.

SIMILAR SPECIES

Partial overlap with ***Blainville's***, ***Ginkgo-toothed*** and ***Hubbs' Beaked Whales*** in range, but mature ♂♂ of all separable in close views. Stejneger's is a cold-water species of higher latitudes. As such, at least in Alaskan waters, Blainville's can be eliminated by range. *Cf.* ***Perrin's Beaked Whale*** which may overlap at lower latitudes and shares characteristic pale neck-sides, but ad ♂ differs in head pattern and note structure of jawline and teeth. ***Cuvier's*** and ***Baird's*** (distinctly larger) are most frequent other ziphiids in range of Stejneger's. Separated from Baird's by much smaller size, lack of melon, arched

Stejneger's Beaked Whale

Mesoplodon stejnegeri

N Pacific. Max 5.5 m.

Priority characters on surfacing

- *Small beaked whale of northern N Pacific.*
- Rather long, spindle-shaped appearance; *small head with smooth-sloping forehead*, tapering to mid-length beak (no obvious melon).
- Some animals appear to be more strongly patterned,with *variable ill-defined pale collar to neck* and darker elements to face (apparently pronounced in ad ♂).
- *Arched mouthline; ad ♂ has 2 enormous tusk-like teeth erupting midway along beak.*
- Small triangular-shaped dorsal fin, slightly falcate and set far back on body.
- *Largely black, dark grey or brown* upperbody, gradually becoming paler below.
- *Ad ♂ has white linear scars/ scratches*, mainly above; variable pale spots/blotches below and on sides.
- Whitish starburst-like pattern on underside of flukes, at least in some animals.

Typical surfacing behaviour

- Normally in small tight groups of 5–15 swimming in unison (mixed ages/sexes). Surfacing periods usually short when indistinct blow may be visible.
- Shy and difficult to approach (rarely seen at sea).

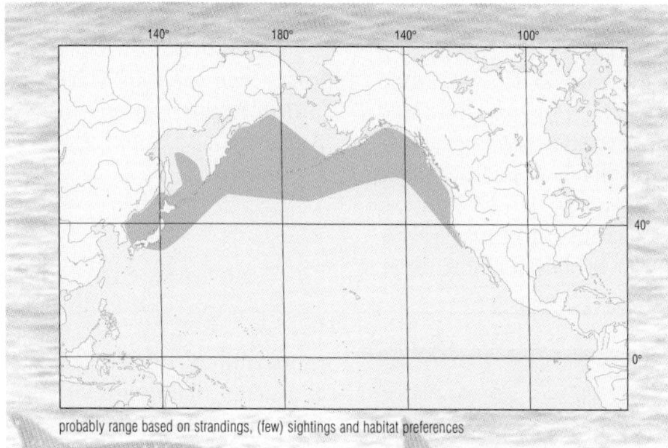

probably range based on strandings, (few) sightings and habitat preferences

mouthline and large tusk-like teeth erupting from mid jaw. However, at-sea identification of beaked whales often difficult and, as always, ♀/young less well marked and more problematic.

VARIATION

Age/sex Ad ♀ probably larger on average with straighter mouthline. Ad ♂ has large triangular teeth. Pale scars vary with age and sex, but most numerous on old ♂. Few linear scars on ♀. Calf has shorter beak and, reportedly, pale streaks on neck. **Physical notes** Largest ad ♂ 5.25 m and ♀ 5.5 m, and 1–1.5 tons. Newborn 2.1–2.3 m. **Other data** *Teeth* Pair of huge white teeth erupt from middle of lower jaw in ad ♂, but not in ♀/young.

Stejneger's Beaked Whale

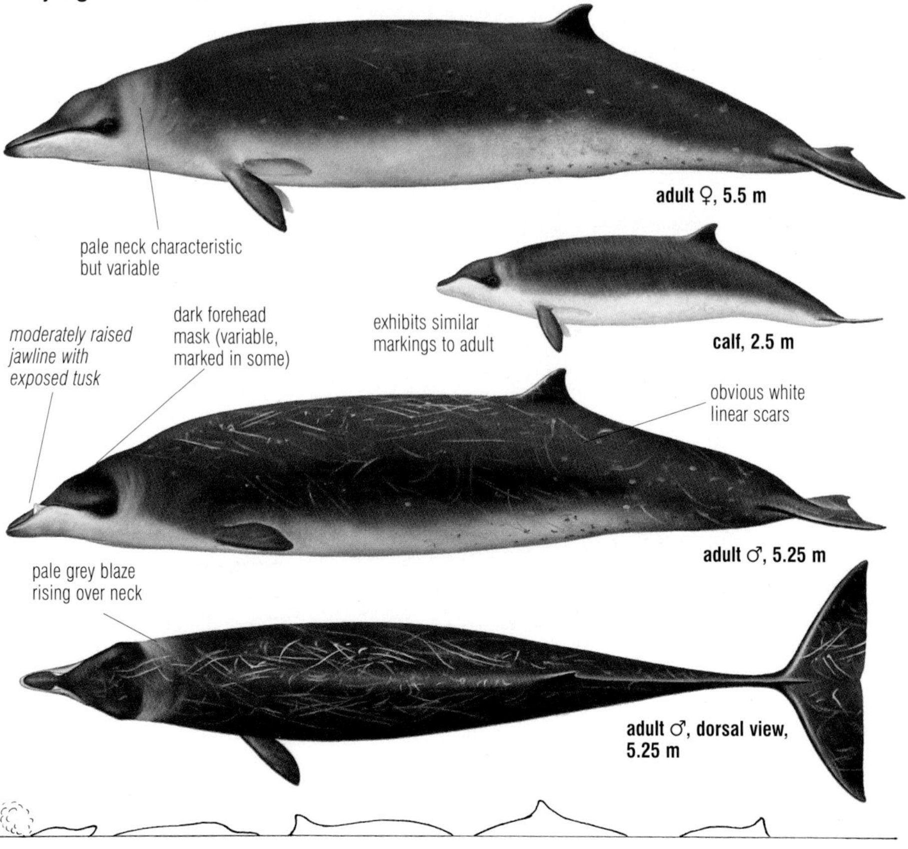

adult ♀, 5.5 m

pale neck characteristic but variable

exhibits similar markings to adult

calf, 2.5 m

moderately raised jawline with exposed tusk

dark forehead mask (variable, marked in some)

obvious white linear scars

adult ♂, 5.25 m

pale grey blaze rising over neck

adult ♂, dorsal view, 5.25 m

In slow breathing rolls, beak and head break surface (blow usually unseen); dorsal fin may emerge as head begins sinking; arches more steeply for deep dive.

DISTRIBUTION & POPULATION

Cool-temperate and subarctic waters of N Pacific and SW Bering Sea, principally in deep-slope waters, but recorded south to Japan (especially Sea of Japan) and C California. *Population* No estimates.

ECOLOGY

Tight, cohesive groups of 3–4, even up to 15, with mix of age/sex classes. *Breaching* Undescribed. *Diving* Typically 5–6 shallow dives, followed by 10–15 min underwater, and may reach 1,500 m. *Diet* Principally deep-sea squid. *Reproduction* Data scarce, but off Japan at least some calve in Mar–May, and in Alaskan waters in Apr–May and Sep. *Lifespan* Unknown.

Strap-toothed Whale

Mesoplodon layardii

S Hemisphere. Max 6.2 m.

Priority characters on surfacing

- *Medium-sized beaked whale, the largest Mesoplodon*, with distinct black-and-white pattern (both sexes). Distinctive but difficult to approach.
- *Black mask and shoulder patch* (from flipper) contrast with *white back/shawl and neck.*
- Predominantly dark brown or bluish-black below, and on rear and sides; ad ♂ has numerous white linear scars.
- *Beak is long and mostly pale.* Modest forehead and melon.
- *Ad ♂ has 2 strap-like tusks that project above upper jaw* and may curve around upper jaw in older ♂.
- Low, falcate dorsal fin set far back on body.
- Grey or white patches around genital slit.

Typical behaviour at surface

- Beak breaks surface first (at 45° angle), then part of head briefly revealed to exhale (blow inconspicuous); little of back and low dorsal fin usually visible.
- May log at surface and habitually swims slowly; rarely shows flukes above water before diving; may dive by rolling over sideways.
- Recorded in groups of up to 5.

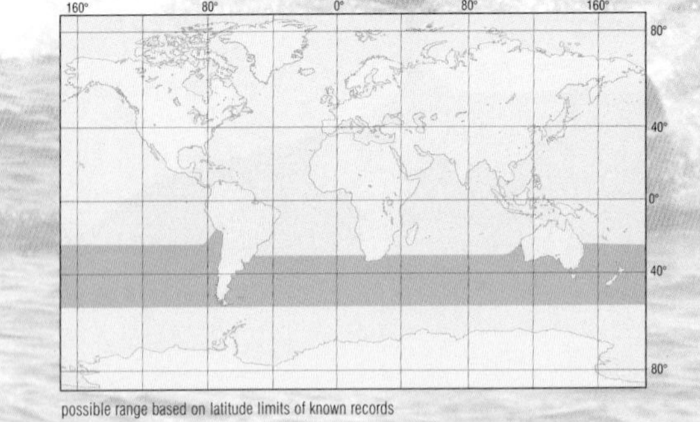

possible range based on latitude limits of known records

SIMILAR SPECIES

Given distinct coloration (ads of both sexes) and bizarre tusks of ad ♂, among the easiest beaked whales to identify. Inconspicuous surfacing behaviour may reduce usefulness of these features. Pale head and anterior part of back not always obvious. Teeth, although large, may be difficult to observe, as positioned at border between black and white areas of beak. Imms more difficult to identify, appearing mainly greyish and superficially similar to ***Gray's Beaked Whale*** (overlapping range).

VARIATION

Age/sex Full-grown ad ♂ has at least partially exposed whitish teeth in mid lower jaw; longer and more curved with age. Calves generally paler and similarly patterned to ads, but pigmentation reversed, having pale facial mask, flippers, sides and rear body, with dark foreback, collar, abdominal patch and beak. Calf and ♀ have fewer or no scars. **Physical notes** 5–6.2 m and *c.*1.1–3.4 tons (largest *Mesoplodon*). Newborn 2.2–2.5 m. **Other data** *Teeth* ♂ has 2 very long tusks (up to 30 cm) that curl backward and inward, and sometimes overlap on rostrum. Juv/♀ lacks erupted teeth though young ♂ may have smaller, exposed triangular-shaped teeth.

DISTRIBUTION & POPULATION

Southern Ocean, south of 30°S and north of Antarctic Convergence. Most records from New Zealand and southern Australia; also southern S America (north to Uruguay), S Africa, Indian Ocean (Kerguelen) and the Falklands. May occur south of 38°S year-round, whilst occurrences north of 38°S are seasonal. *Population* No estimates.

Strap-toothed Whale

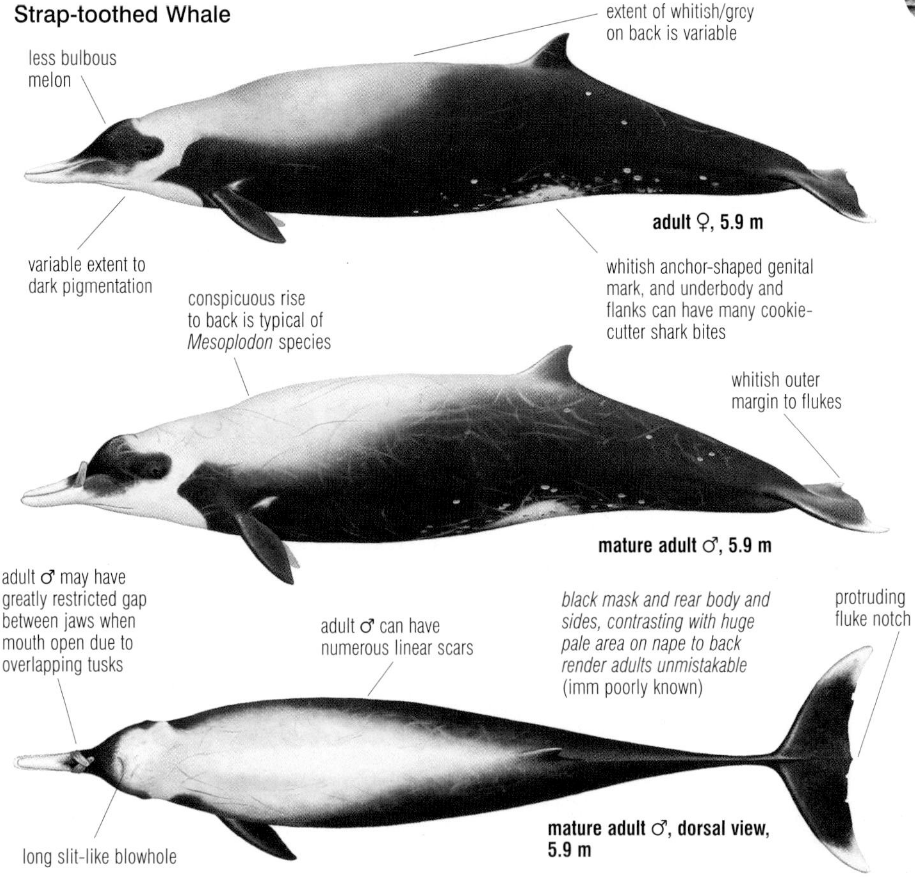

extent of whitish/grey on back is variable

less bulbous melon

adult ♀, 5.9 m

variable extent to dark pigmentation

whitish anchor-shaped genital mark, and underbody and flanks can have many cookie-cutter shark bites

conspicuous rise to back is typical of *Mesoplodon* species

whitish outer margin to flukes

mature adult ♂, 5.9 m

adult ♂ may have greatly restricted gap between jaws when mouth open due to overlapping tusks

adult ♂ can have numerous linear scars

black mask and rear body and sides, contrasting with huge pale area on nape to back render adults unmistakable (imm poorly known)

protruding fluke notch

mature adult ♂, dorsal view, 5.9 m

long slit-like blowhole

In slow breathing roll, beak and melon visible (blow normally too weak to be seen); dorsal fin may emerge as head begins sinking; arches more steeply for deep dive.

Breaching Strap-toothed Whale: note long white beak (dark at the base) and dark melon contrasting with the pale back. The bull's strap-shaped teeth can be difficult to see because they project where the black meets the white on the beak.

ECOLOGY

Almost unknown. *Breaching* Series of complete breaches recorded; may fall back into water on side (see photo). *Diving* Deep diver given food preferences. *Diet* Small, deep-water squid, probably captured by intense suction.

Blainville's Beaked Whale

Mesoplodon densirostris

Worldwide. Max 6 m.

Priority characters on surfacing

- *Medium-sized* beaked whale with large dolphin-like body.
- *Flattish forehead* and indistinct melon, *falcate dorsal fin* set *c.*$^2/_3$ back may be prominent.
- *Strongly arched lower jaw, forms bulges around beak base,* which in profile appears proportionately long and thick.
- Ad ♂ has *pair of large teeth at apex of arch of lower jaw*, angled forward and raised above level of top of upper jaw, but *only tips emerge* (may be encrusted with soft barnacles).
- Generally brownish to dark bluish slate grey, paler greyish below and on face-sides.
- *Ad ♂ extensively scarred—head and anterior dorsal area may appear 'wrinkled'.*

Typical behaviour at surface

- Can emerge beak first on surfacing, head may be partially exposed on breathing; inconspicuous blow projected low and forward.
- Sometimes performs shallow dives at 15–20-sec intervals, may slap beak on surface.
- Usually encountered in small groups.

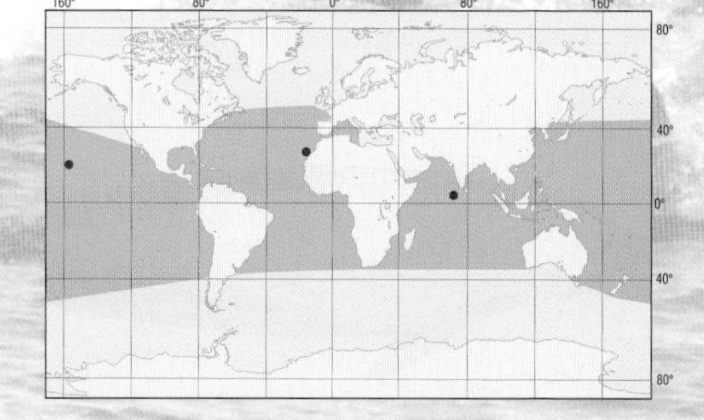

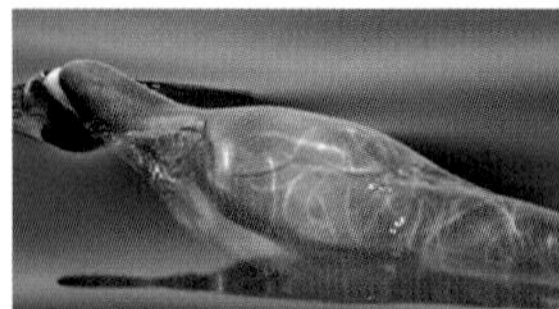

Blainville's Beaked Whale: the shallow arch of the jawline and linear scratches suggest that it is an immature ♂.

SIMILAR SPECIES

Unless viewing conditions very good, confusable with several overlapping congeners. ♀/juv very difficult to identify if not accompanied by ad ♂. Many features described or illustrated often difficult to observe at sea. Combination of medium size, high-arched mouthline (even just visible in ♀) and raised, forward-pointing tusk-like teeth of ad ♂, together with colour and scarring patterns, may enable identification.

Calf and ♀ Blainville's Beaked Whale.

VARIATION

Age/sex Massive tusk-like teeth, angled forwards, and strongly arched bulging lower jaw of ad ♂ distinctive. Only tips of teeth emerge from jaw/gum tissue. Arch of mouth in ♀/young less extreme, often have paler flanks merging with whitish underparts, less flattened head, and are more uniform above with less mottling and fewer scars. **Physical notes** 4.5–6 m and 0.7–1.03 tons. Newborn 1.9–2.6 m and *c.*60 kg. **Other data** *Teeth* Ad ♂ has single pair of massive teeth at apex of strongly arched lower jaw, but only tips emerge. In ♀/juv teeth hidden in gums.

Bull and adult ♀: former extensively lined with linear scratches (and has the eartufts-like appearance due to barnacle infestation on erupted tusks) and the latter marked with pale round cookie-cutter shark bites.

DISTRIBUTION & POPULATION

Widespread in warm-temperate and tropical seas, north to Nova Scotia (Canada), Iceland, UK (extralimital), Japan and C

Blainville's Beaked Whale

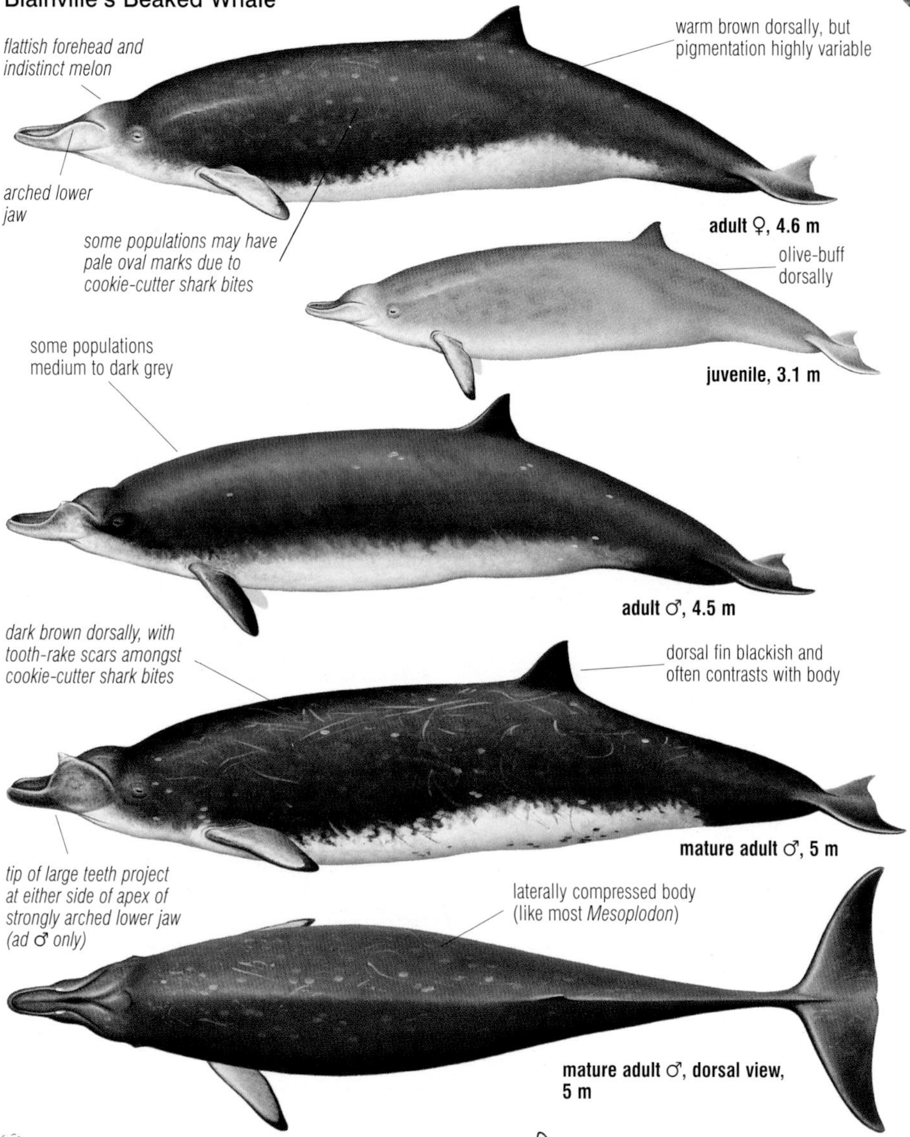

flattish forehead and indistinct melon

warm brown dorsally, but pigmentation highly variable

arched lower jaw

some populations may have pale oval marks due to cookie-cutter shark bites

adult ♀, 4.6 m

olive-buff dorsally

juvenile, 3.1 m

some populations medium to dark grey

adult ♂, 4.5 m

dark brown dorsally, with tooth-rake scars amongst cookie-cutter shark bites

dorsal fin blackish and often contrasts with body

mature adult ♂, 5 m

tip of large teeth project at either side of apex of strongly arched lower jaw (ad ♂ only)

laterally compressed body (like most *Mesoplodon*)

mature adult ♂, dorsal view, 5 m

Breaks surface at shallow angle (blow usually hardly invisible); dorsal fin may emerge as head begins to sink or has already disappeared (however, may also appear to accelerate with 'half-porpoise' in shallow leap); arches more steeply for deeper dive.

Mature ♂: dorsal fin low, triangular and wide-based, only slightly falcate; pale lines above are tooth-rake scars from agonistic behaviours with other ♂♂.

Mature ♂ Blainville's Beaked Whale seen head-on: the tusk projects from the right-hand side at the apex of the strongly arched lower jaw; the left side is encrusted with barnacles.

California, and south to extreme S Brazil, C Chile, S Africa, southern Australia and New Zealand. Furthest range extents of associated with warm-water currents. No evidence for seasonal movements. *Population* No estimates; probably not rare.

ECOLOGY

Occurs singly or as groups of 3–7, but up to 12 reported. Groups may include a single ad ♂ or consist only of ♀♀ and juvs. *Breaching* Occasional. *Diving* Usually 20–45 min, and regularly reaches 1,000 m. *Diet* Squid and small fish in deep waters. *Reproduction* Unknown. *Lifespan* Unknown.

Presence of cookie-cutter shark bites but lack of linear scratches and shallow arch of jawline suggest that it is an adult ♀; orange coloration on beak and head is probably due to diatoms.

The rather uniform body (few scratches) suggests a young animal.

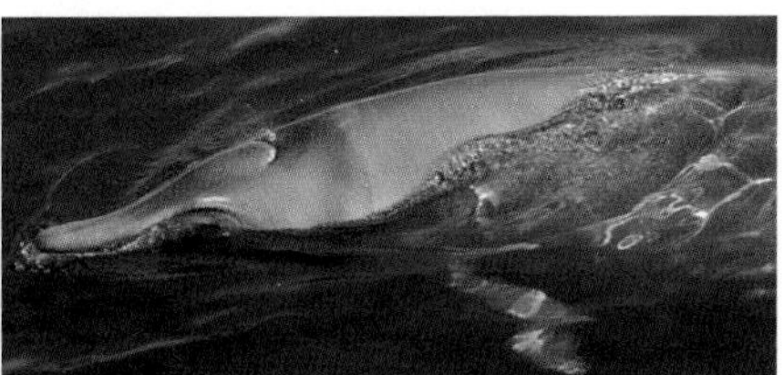

Often predominantly greyish; the virtually unscarred body and shallow-arched jawline suggests a young animal, and rusty-brown tinge is apparently due to diatoms.

SIMILAR SPECIES

Confusion most likely with several overlapping *Mesoplodon* spp in E & C Pacific (***Hubbs', Ginkgo-toothed***, ***Stejneger's***, ***Blainville's*** and ***Pygmy Beaked Whales***). At sea, still barely known, making even vague comparisons impossible. If seen in Californian waters or a mature ♂ with fully erupted teeth is observed, reliable separation may be possible. Unlike all above-mentioned species, teeth at tip of lower jaw (rather than midway/rear) and mouthline straighter. Only **Hector's Beaked Whale** (which it was overlooked as in past) has similar teeth, but is well

Perrin's Beaked Whale

Mesoplodon perrini

California/NE Pacific.
Max 4.4 m.

Priority characters on surfacing

- *Small, typical-shaped mesoplodont* with generally nondescript coloration.
- *Relatively small head, melon forms small bulge*; long, thick body with deep tailstock.
- *Rostrum short* (like Hector's and Pygmy Beaked Whales), with rather *straight mouthline*.
- Generally dark grey dorsally grading to white ventrally, including lower jaw and throat regions, and a white patch around umbilicus.
- *Slightly darker face* (from corner of mouth, encompassing eye and rostrum, forming extended but ill-defined mask) may be a feature of the species.
- *Small, triangular and slightly curved dorsal fin* set ⅔ of way along back.
- *Teeth of ad ♂ large and triangular, at tip of lower jaw*; probably distinctive in close view.
- No clear notch in dark grey flukes (pale grey ventrally with diffuse darker edges); small flippers, medium to dark grey dorsally and white ventrally.
- Ad ♂ may have white linear scars on back and flanks.

Typical behaviour at surface

- Still largely unknown at sea (presumably not dissimilar from congeners).

distribution based on strandings

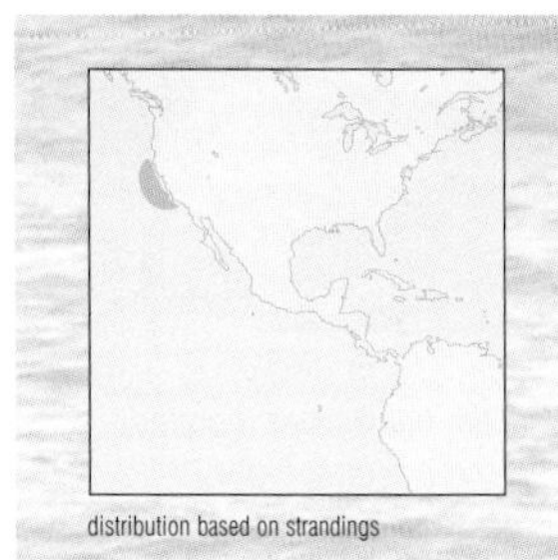

separated geographically, Hector's being confined to S Hemisphere.

VARIATION

Age/sex Perhaps by size and dentition; pale scars on back and flanks and other markings documented on 1 ad ♂. Calf slimmer and rostrum appears shorter and stubbier than in ads. Calves also more uniformly pale to dark grey dorsally and white ventrally. **Physical notes** Ad ♂ 3.9 m and ad ♀ 4.43 m. Calf 2.1 m. **Other data** *Teeth* Single pair of large triangular teeth at apex of lower jaw, erupt from gum only in ad ♂, slightly above top of upper jaw.

DISTRIBUTION & POPULATION

Known only from 5 strandings and 1 possible sighting in California. Might be expected in much of eastern N Pacific, in waters of 1,000 m+ depth, but extent of distribution unknown. *Population* Unknown.

ECOLOGY

Largely unknown. *Diet* Presumably chiefly mesopelagic squid in deep waters, like other *Mesoplodon*.

Perrin's Beaked Whale

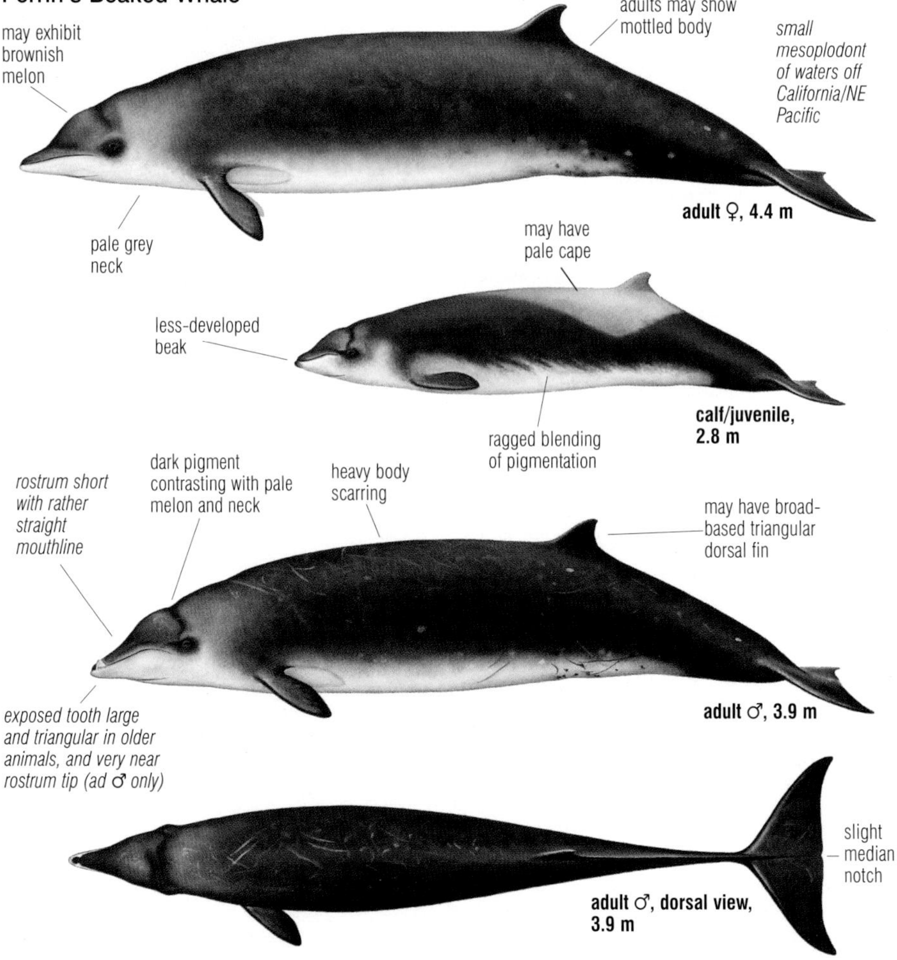

may exhibit brownish melon
adults may show mottled body
small mesoplodont of waters off California/NE Pacific
pale grey neck
adult ♀, 4.4 m
may have pale cape
less-developed beak
ragged blending of pigmentation
calf/juvenile, 2.8 m
rostrum short with rather straight mouthline
dark pigment contrasting with pale melon and neck
heavy body scarring
may have broad-based triangular dorsal fin
exposed tooth large and triangular in older animals, and very near rostrum tip (ad ♂ only)
adult ♂, 3.9 m
slight median notch
adult ♂, dorsal view, 3.9 m

Pygmy and Dwarf Sperm Whales

These toothed whales, perhaps closely related to Sperm Whale, are placed in their own family, Kogiidae. Very small, which combined with their asocial behaviour, unobtrusive surfacing techniques and preference for deep water, makes them among the least observed of all cetaceans. They are rather shark-like with a pointed rostrum, a small underslung jaw and a pigmented line behind the eyes that appears like a gill slit. Frequent strandings in some areas implies that they are commoner than presently known, being scarcely seen at sea, where their separation is often very difficult. Like Sperm Whale they have a single blowhole, positioned slightly to the left, as well as a spermaceti organ. Unlike Sperm Whale, they employ a 'squid tactic' by expelling dark reddish-brown liquid from a sac in the lower intestine which clouds the water and conceals their escape. They also sink below the surface very slowly.

Pygmy Sperm Whale has a smaller, backswept (hooked) and more rounded dorsal fin, set further back.

Pygmy Sperm Whale, tends to float higher on surface than Dwarf and here showing the distinct hump on back; note fin shape variation.

SIMILAR SPECIES

Could be confused with overlapping in range and very similar ***Dwarf Sperm Whale***, and identification requires much caution. Pygmy has a smaller, more rounded (less erect and pointed) dorsal fin (less than 5% of total length), set much further back, and swims higher in water than Dwarf. Thus, a useful proportional discrimination is form, with a relatively smaller/lower dorsal fin in relation to the more extensive exposed length of back (the opposite in Dwarf). However, shape, height and position of dorsal fin all vary, and to some degree overlap with Dwarf, making these not wholly reliable characters. Furthermore, usually has a distinct hump on rear back

Pygmy Sperm Whale

Kogia breviceps

Temperate to tropical waters.
Max 3.5 m.

Priority characters on surfacing

- Very *small compact*, rather robust, shark-like toothed whale; very like Dwarf Sperm Whale.
- Head usually unseen, but typically shows *distinct hump at rear of back*.
- *Tiny, hooked but essentially rather rounded dorsal fin, set well behind mid-back.*
- Dark blue-grey or olive-brown wrinkled skin (wrinkles hard to see), with paler, sometimes pinkish-tinged undersides.
- Squarish, short head with snout overlapping tiny underslung lower jaw.
- False gill forms bracket-shaped mark at rear of head, just behind eyes.
- Tiny pale circular mark above/around eye.
- Broad, short flippers set high and far forward, near head; flukes broad and slightly notched.

Typical behaviour at surface

- Typically rises to surface slowly and *floats motionless* with blowhole to foreback above water; *sinks below surface* like a stone, but occasionally rolls in diving.
- Very difficult to detect, except in extremely calm seas. Undemonstrative, but may permit close approach by boats.
- Slow deliberate swimmer, with sluggish appearance and blow invisible (or almost so).
- Uses same 'squid tactic' as Dwarf Sperm Whale.

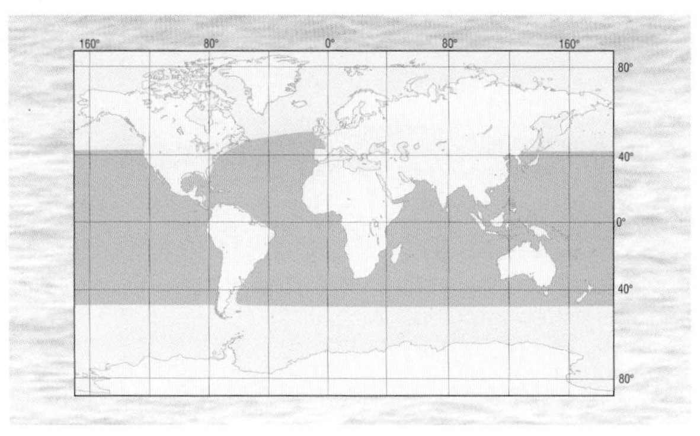

(much flatter profile in Dwarf). Pygmy also reaches slightly greater overall lengths, but impossible to evaluate at sea. Only rarely observed alive at sea, but among the most frequently stranded small whales in some areas. Like Dwarf Sperm Whale, when stranded it appears slightly shark-like owing to shape of tiny jaw and false gills behind eyes.

Pygmy Sperm Whale

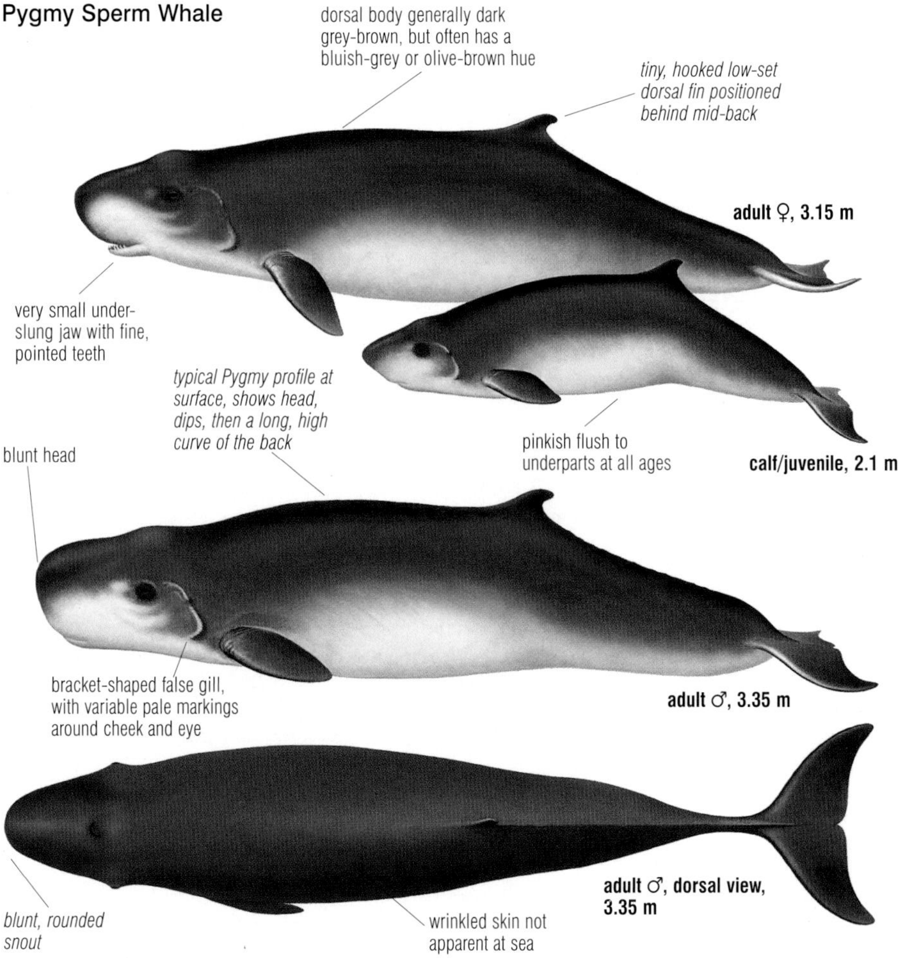

dorsal body generally dark grey-brown, but often has a bluish-grey or olive-brown hue

tiny, hooked low-set dorsal fin positioned behind mid-back

adult ♀, 3.15 m

very small under-slung jaw with fine, pointed teeth

typical Pygmy profile at surface, shows head, dips, then a long, high curve of the back

pinkish flush to underparts at all ages

calf/juvenile, 2.1 m

blunt head

bracket-shaped false gill, with variable pale markings around cheek and eye

adult ♂, 3.35 m

adult ♂, dorsal view, 3.35 m

blunt, rounded snout

wrinkled skin not apparent at sea

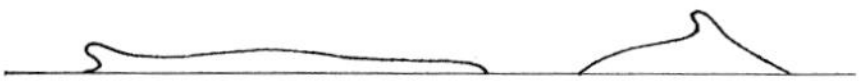

Surfaces slowly and logs motionless; sinks, but occasionally rolls to dive; note humped profile to back, and lower, backswept, rounded dorsal fin.

VARIATION

Age/sex Probably only minimal size difference between sexes; juvs have slightly more pointed head, becoming squarish and blunter with age. **Physical notes** Ads reach 3.5 m and 315–450 kg; newborn *c.*1.2 m and 50 kg. Very similar to Dwarf Sperm Whale; they were not recognised as different until 1966. No geographical variation described.

DISTRIBUTION & POPULATION

Widespread in tropical and temperate seas, principally beyond continental shelf. Records from Nova Scotia (Canada), NW Europe, the Azores to Uruguay and S Africa (in Atlantic), and from Japan and Hawaii to the Tasman Sea and Chile (in Pacific), as well as the Indian Ocean. Migrations, if any, unknown. *Population* Largely unknown, but 3,000+ off California.

Cow and calf Pygmy Sperm Whale showing distinct profile with hump on back; note low backswept dorsal fin.

ECOLOGY

Usually alone or in groups of up to 6–7, of mixed age/sex. *Breaching* Occasional, leaps vertically and falls tail first or on belly. *Diving* No data. *Diet* Mid- and deep-water cephalopods, fish, and occasionally crustaceans. *Reproduction* Both sexes sexually mature at 4–5 yrs. Gestation 9–11 months, and mating and calving season *c.*7 months (probably peaking Mar–Aug). Weaned at *c.*1 yr, by which time ♀♀ may be pregnant again. *Lifespan* Up to 22 yrs.

DISTINCTIVE POPULATIONS

At least genetically, 2 distinctive ocean-based populations, in Atlantic and Indo-Pacific. Unknown, however, if their external characteristics differ and whether at-sea identification is possible in potential overlap areas, or how they differ from Pygmy Sperm Whale. Studies are needed.

SIMILAR SPECIES

Easily confused with ***Pygmy Sperm Whale***. Very similar, but relative size and shape of dorsal fin (taller and more pointed in Dwarf; smaller, more lobed in Pygmy) very useful with experience. In optimal views, taller, more dolphin-like dorsal fin set closer to mid-back (slightly variable), flatter back profile, more pointed head and less body exposed at surface can, in combination, identify typical individuals. Beware that quite erect

Dwarf Sperm Whale

Kogia sima

Temperate to tropical waters. Max 2.7 m.

Priority characters on surfacing

- Very *small, compact*, toothed whale very similar to Pygmy Sperm Whale.
- *Prominent, falcate, pointed dorsal fin*, slightly closer to mid-back than in Pygmy Sperm.
- Back flatter in profile.
- Dark blue-grey to olive-brown wrinkled skin (wrinkles very difficult to see), and paler, sometimes pinkish-tinged, below.
- Shark-like head, as Pygmy Sperm, but has more pointed snout, giving slightly conical (rather than squarish) head profile. Snout extends beyond tiny underslung lower jaw.
- False gill just behind eye and pale circular mark above eye (as Pygmy Sperm).

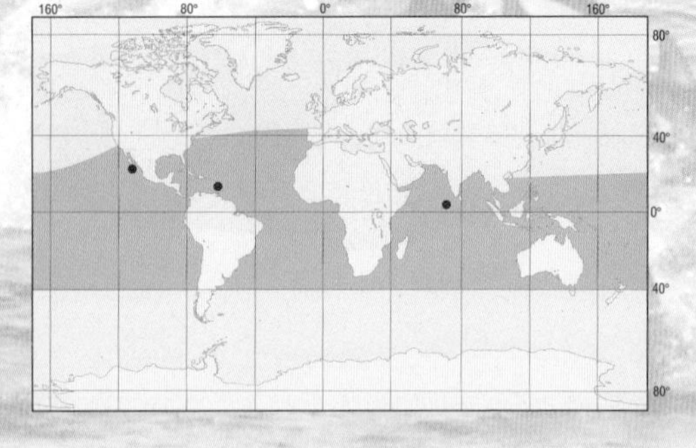

- Broad, short flippers set high and far forward, and flukes broad and slightly notched (as Pygmy Sperm). Many field marks may be impossible to assess at sea.

Typical behaviour at surface

- Very difficult to detect, except in extremely calm seas; may permit approach by boats.
- *Slow swimmer, usually floating motionless at surface*, like Pygmy Sperm, but body perhaps even less exposed. Blow invisible.
- Typically *rises to surface slowly and sinks from view* (as Pygmy Sperm).
- Uses same 'squid tactic' as Pygmy Sperm Whale.

dorsal fin is not unlike that of ***Bottlenose Dolphin***, but diving and swimming behaviours wholly different. Like ***Pygmy Sperm Whale***, rarely positively identified at sea, being best known from strandings, when it is often mistaken for a shark due to distinct upper jaw, 'bulging' eyes, and 'pseudo-gills' on rear head.

VARIATION

Age/sex Probably only minimal difference in size between sexes. **Physical notes** Ads reach 2.7 m and 135–272 kg; newborn *c.*1 m and 40–50 kg. **Taxonomy** No geographical differences described but height and position of dorsal fin vary, and in extreme cases overlap with Pygmy Sperm Whale. Recent genetic results suggest isolation between Atlantic and Indian/Pacific Ocean populations; this may lead to future recognition of 2 species.

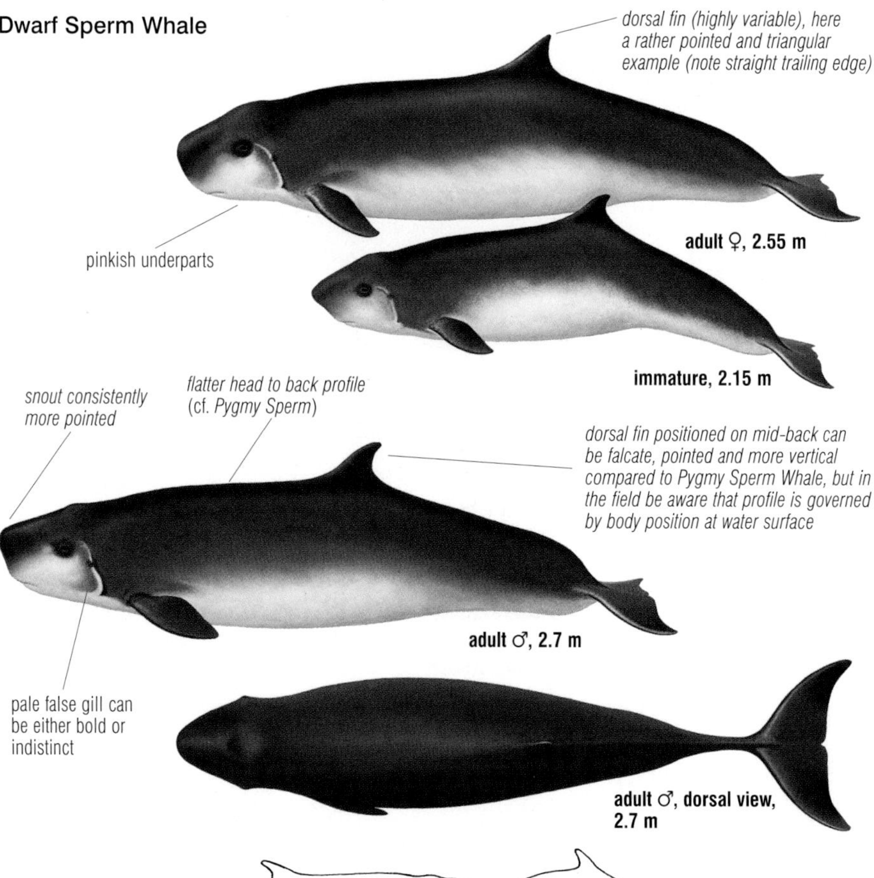

Surfaces slowly and logs motionless; sinks to submerge, but occasionally rolls to dive; note flatter back, with rather forward-set, higher and pointed dorsal fin.

DISTRIBUTION & POPULATION
Cosmopolitan in tropical and temperate seas, but apparently more coastal than previous species, being principally observed in warmer shelf-edge and continental slope waters. Probably locally fairly common (e.g. in Maldives). Records from Virginia (USA), the Mediterranean and NW Europe to S Brazil and S Africa (in Atlantic), and from Japan and British Columbia (Canada) to New Zealand and Chile (in Pacific). Also Indian Ocean, from S Africa to Oman, Indonesia and Australia. Migrations, if any, unknown. *Population* No overall estimate, but perhaps 11,000 in tropical E Pacific and a few 100s in Gulf of Mexico.

Dwarf Sperm Whale (Indian Ocean), floating motionless at surface: note erect dorsal fin on mid-back (also less hooked or backswept) with straighter trailing edge; also flatter back and more pointed snout.

Logging Dwarf Sperm Whale (Pacific): an extreme example of an animal with highly erect and rather falcate dorsal fin.

ECOLOGY
Usually alone or in groups of up to 10 of mixed age/sex. Above-surface activity scarce. Rarely approaches boats. *Breaching* As Pygmy Sperm. *Diving* Probably to at least 300 m. *Diet* As Pygmy Sperm, but feeds in shallower waters. *Reproduction* The few breeding data are very similar to those for the previous species, but off S Africa, most births are in summer (Dec–Mar). *Lifespan* Unknown.

Breaching Dwarf Sperm Whale (Atlantic): note characteristic head and shape of dorsal fin.

Logging Dwarf Sperm Whales (Pacific): dorsal fin shape varies extremely (in foreground note characteristic erect, pointed fin set rather forward); note also low appearance at surface and flatter back.

Cow and calf Dwarf Sperm Whales (Pacific): the former has a pointed, triangular dorsal fin; note wrinkled skin.

Bottlenose and similar plain dolphins

Bottlenose and humpback dolphins belong to a variable group of oceanic dolphins (subfamily Delphininae) that also includes *Stenella*, *Delphinus* and *Lagenodelphis*. Included here, Rough-toothed Dolphin (subfamily Stenoninae) is often seen with bottlenose dolphins and they share some characters. *Tursiops* is a rather widespread genus, but *Sousa* is restricted to tropical and warm-temperate latitudes, and inshore waters. Like several dolphins, Common Bottlenose has both coastal and offshore populations which usually differ morphologically. These ecologically separate populations may represent the first stage in the process of speciation.

Indo-Pacific Bottlenose Dolphins at the surf line during the annual sardine run, off S Africa; note enormous dorsal fins.

Common Bottlenose Dolphin, especially, appears to 'befriend' man in many regions and frequently seems to perform aerial behaviours for the benefit of observers. (You should not swim with wild dolphins except in certain well-regulated circumstances, and do not touch animals as this could cause stress or even an aggressive response.) Indeed, Common Bottlenose Dolphin was well known to both the ancient Greeks and Romans. The genus name *Tursiops* means 'dolphin-like' and suggests that bottlenose dolphins were amongst the 'original' or prototype dolphins.

All species are rather distinctive but can be confusing, especially in poor conditions or if seen very briefly (though they all frequently bow- or wake-ride, except *Sousa*). Overall impression, especially size, coloration and degree of cape contrast and spotting, is often strongly dependent on population, age and sex. Identification should be based on a combination of features.

Breaching Indo-Pacific Humpback Dolphin (Hong Kong): note absence of hump but large, triangular dorsal fin (with straight trailing edge); finer spotting and pinker body suggest a mature animal.

Some potential identification pitfalls should be mentioned. Remember, not all *Tursiops* are approachable, especially in oceanic waters, and they can be one of the more difficult species for inexperienced observers to identify – look for the shoulder blaze in the cape of *Tursiops*. Not all Common Bottlenose are obviously larger and chunkier (Indo-Pacific Bottlenose, Humpback and Rough-toothed Dolphins are broadly similar to subtropical/tropical and/or

Pale dolphins

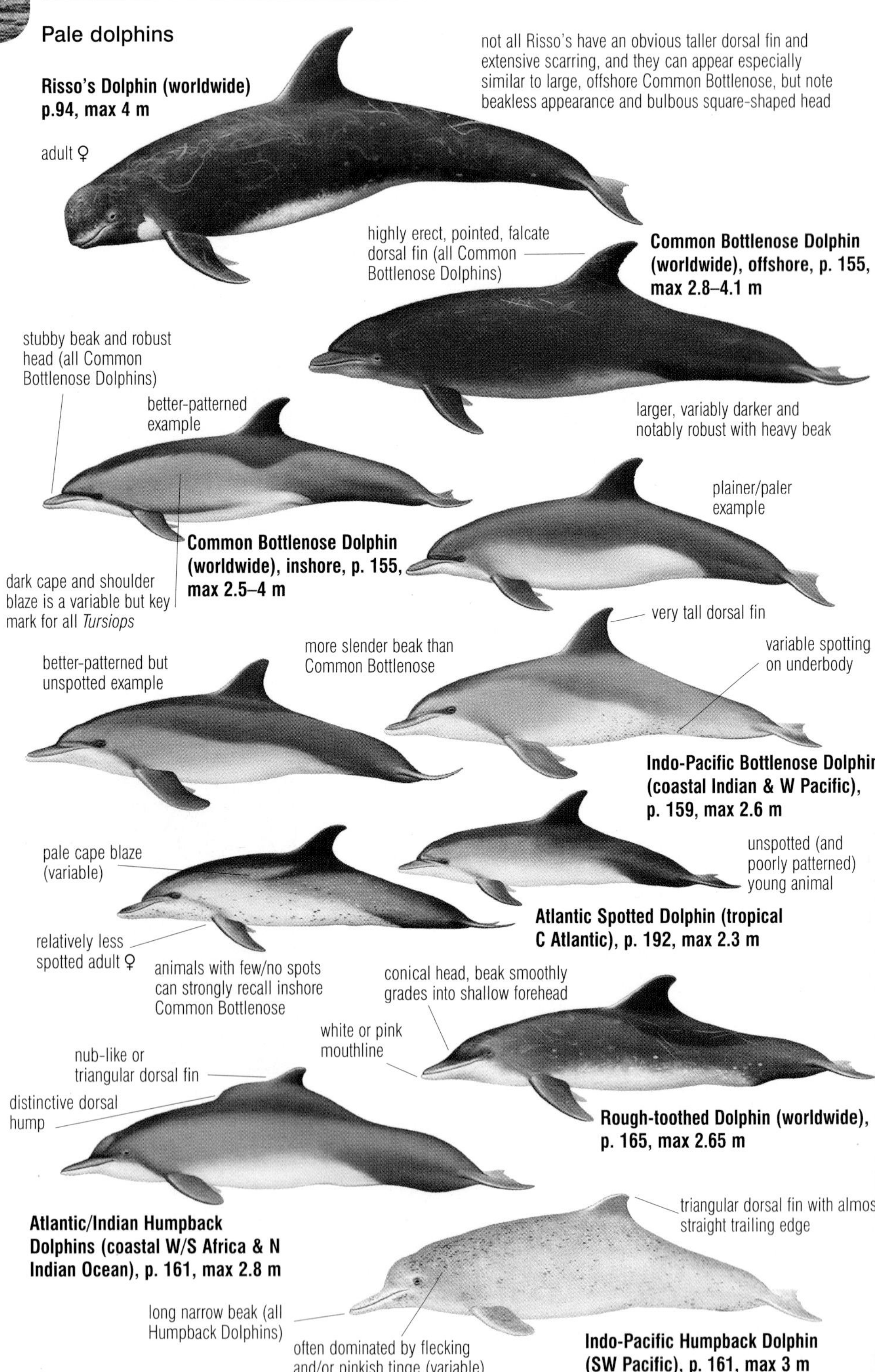

inshore populations of Common Bottlenose). It is also not always easy to detect Common Bottlenose's stubby beak, distinctly separated from the large melon by a crease. Indo-Pacific Bottlenose's smaller melon, longer and more delicate beak, and generally paler coloration (with a better-defined cape and whiter, and in some extensively spotted, underbody) are not always detectable, making confusion with Common Bottlenose highly likely. The low sloping forehead and pale lips of Rough-toothed Dolphin are not always immediately apparent when bow-riding, and not all are distinctly darker and slimmer than bottlenose dolphins. Both spotted dolphins can be rather spotless, especially the chunkier Atlantic Spotted, whose dark dorsal cape with distinct pale blaze can be subdued or absent, and thus bear a close resemblance to the smaller/tropical Common Bottlenose. Also, not all humpback dolphins are distinctively coloured or possess a clear triangular fin with a basal hump.

Lastly, adult Risso's Dolphin is not always obviously paler and scarred, and its characteristically beakless, square-headed appearance is not always apparent, whilst it shares with the bottlenose dolphins the tall fin; indeed, they are sometimes seen together.

Common Bottlenose Dolphins: some populations show a distinct 3-part colour pattern; note darker cape contrasting with paler grey flanks and whiter abdomen.

Common Bottlenose Dolphin

Tursiops truncatus

Worldwide tropical to temperate waters. Max 4.1 m.

Priority characters on surfacing

- Among the largest dolphins, *notably robust and chunky*, but typically rather featureless.
- *Dorsal fin high, central, broad-based and falcate* with pointed tip (shape very variable).
- Size varies, with some populations larger/chunkier than others.
- *Moderate-length, stubby beak (distinctly set off from robust head by a crease)*; often has white-tipped lower (and sometimes upper) jaw.
- *Rather uniform*, being mostly dark (some even blackish) or pale bluish- or brownish-grey; *often with darker dorsal cape*, from apex of melon to behind fin (mainly visible on bow-riders).
- Paler lower sides, whiter belly (especially younger animals), may exhibit *cape/shoulder blaze* (variable, mainly seen on bow-riders).
- Subtle facial and throat markings, and eye–flipper stripe hardly visible on most animals.
- Flippers longish and pointed, and tail flukes pointed.

Typical behaviour at surface

- Strong swimmer and spends much time at surface.
- *Typically in small groups and often associates with other cetaceans.*
- *Playful, frequently bow- or wake-rides* large whales or boats.
- Tail-slaps, head-slaps, nose-outs, aerobatics and throwing kelp into air frequent.

Common Bottlenose Dolphin is a robust, largely grey dolphin; note the stubby beak separated by a crease from the large round head.

DISTINCTIVE POPULATIONS

Many populations segregate into smaller inshore and larger offshore animals, but intermediate or converse examples occur. The following phenotypes occur in the Atlantic, but these are reversed in the E tropical Pacific.

Inshore Smaller with proportionately larger flippers and longer/slender beak, and generally paler with darker cape and/or better-marked pale cape/ shoulder blaze (features that also characterise some warm-water stocks). **Offshore** Larger, stockier and more uniformly dark, with proportionately smaller flippers and stubbier beak (features that also characterise cold-water populations).

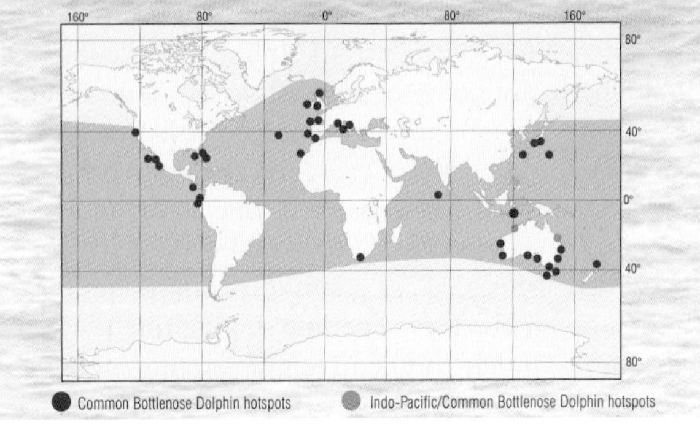

Playful Common Bottlenose Dolphins, here in impressive and 'synchronised' aerobatics. White belly is common in some populations, but not others.

SIMILAR SPECIES

Some are relatively less robust with slimmer body and beak, especially in tropical waters, and have similar size and shape to ***Striped Dolphin***. Overlaps with many other greyish dolphins and easily mistaken for ***Indo-Pacific Bottlenose Dolphin***, either ***spotted dolphin*** (which can be confusingly unspotted, especially Atlantic Spotted) or ***Rough-toothed Dolphin*** (which can have similar fin), and separation from the ***humpback dolphins*** or dolphins of the genus *Sotalia* is not always straightforward. With good views, however, Common Bottlenose Dolphin is distinctive with a very different dorsal fin shape compared to *Sousa* spp. Absence of obvious markings, the high dorsal fin, well-pronounced mid-length beak and thick head (separated by a crease), larger size, shoulder blaze in dark cape, and highly inquisitive, active behaviour, are conclusive. Could also be confused with ***Risso's***

Leaping ♀ and calf Common Bottlenose Dolphin: note stocky belly, stubby beak, and rather dark body with ill-defined dark cape and pale shoulder blaze; dorsal fin erect, central and falcate; note grey belly.

Common Bottlenose Dolphin

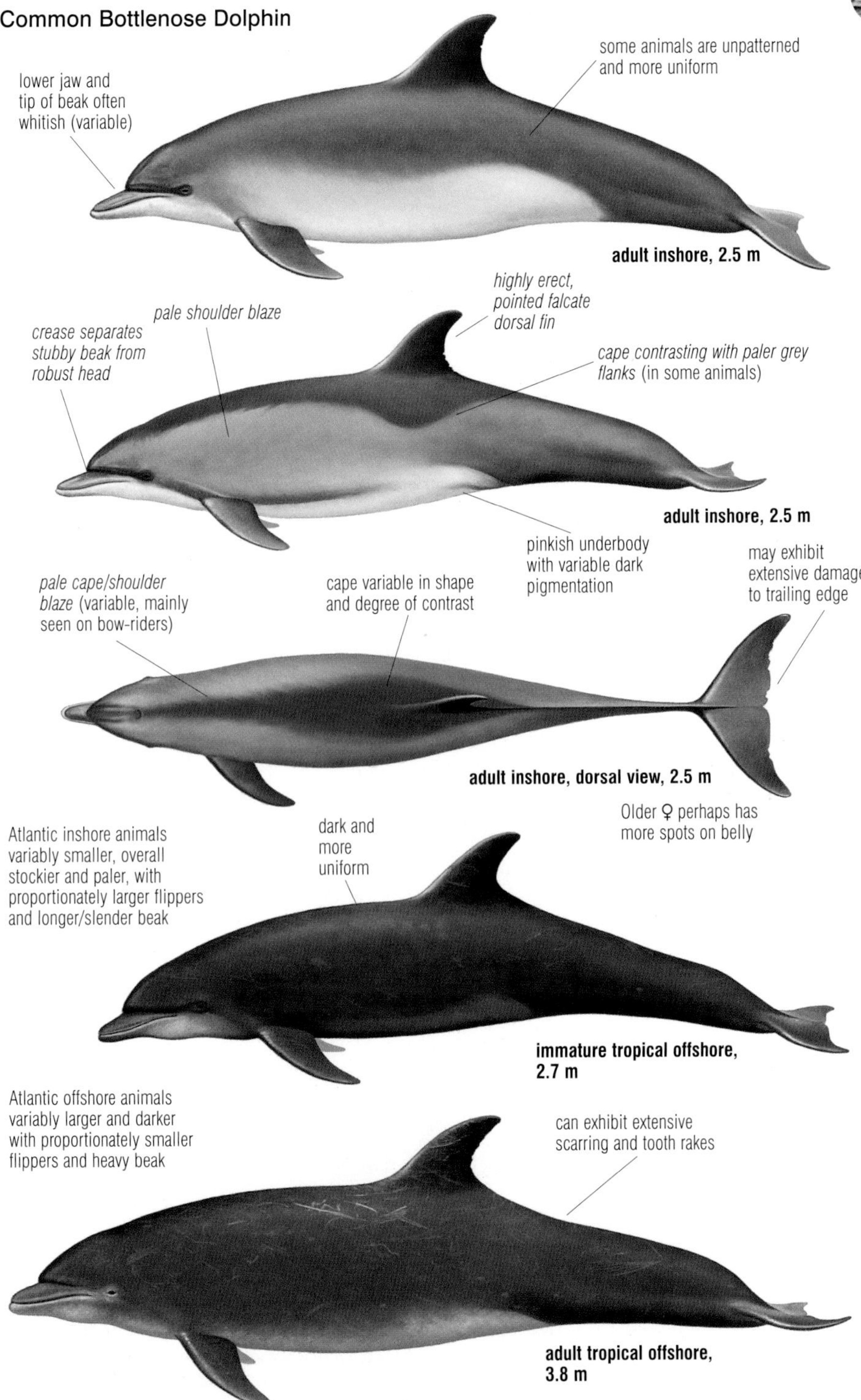

Common Bottlenose Dolphin (Caribbean): overall smaller, slimmer and paler body, slightly darker cape, with proportionately larger flippers and longer/slender beak, are characteristics of these animals.

Dolphin*, *White-sided Dolphin or even young ***pilot whales***, but such confusion generally only occurs given poor views.

VARIATION

Age/sex Size/shape varies greatly between and within regions. Coloration varies too, mainly individually but also geographically, with some all grey and others having conspicuous white belly and/or darker cape. ♀ often with calf; may show mammary slits. Ad ♂ may have more extensive body and fin scarring. Young darker. **Physical notes** Full-grown ads 1.9–4.1 m and 150–650 kg (smallest populations up to 2.5 m and 250 kg), ♂ typically slightly larger. Newborn 0.84–1.4 m and 15–30 kg. Considerable variation in beak length/width. **Taxonomy** Inshore and offshore forms in many areas, but variation between inter-ocean populations even completely reversed. Significant genetic differentiation noted, even between neighbouring populations, and several species possibly involved. Up to 20 forms described, but geographical variation so poorly understood that present subspecific limits appear of very limited value.

DISTRIBUTION & POPULATION

Cosmopolitan outside polar regions, north to Iceland, south to Patagonia and New Zealand. Offshore populations undertake seasonal movements of up to 4,200 km but inshore groups largely resident, although some move in response to El Niño Southern Oscillation events. *Population* No overall estimates.

ECOLOGY

Typical group size up to 15 but as many as 1,000 may occur and lone individuals frequent. Basic social units include nursery groups and mixed-sex juvs. *Breaching* Frequent, up to several metres above surface. *Diving* Usually 3–4 min, but up to 12 min (reaching 535 m) in offshore populations. *Diet* Fish, krill and other crustaceans; some (offshore) take squid. Cooperatively herd fish, disorienting them by leaping and pushing them shorewards. May take advantage of small-scale human fisheries. *Reproduction* Sexually mature at 5–13 (♀) and 8–15 yrs old (♂). Calves every 2–6 yrs and births often peak in warmer months. Gestation *c.*12 months and calves dependent for at least 6–12 months (lactation may last 3–7 yrs), and sometimes cared for by other ♀♀. Strong ♀ to calf bond persists until next birth. *Lifespan* Up to 52 yrs.

Typical high, graceful and effortless leaps of Common Bottlenose Dolphins; they are almost always happy to accompany a passing vessel.

Indo-Pacific Bottlenose Dolphin

Tursiops aduncus

Coastal Indian, SW and NW Pacific Oceans. Max 2.6 m.

Priority characters on surfacing

- *Very similar to Common Bottlenose Dolphin*, especially smaller animals, but perhaps slightly smaller and slimmer.
- *Head somewhat smaller* with less robust/convex melon and perhaps *longer, thinner beak*.
- *Dorsal fin proportionately taller*, but also centrally placed, very broad-based and falcate.
- *Generally greyish to milky brown, with rather variable but in some rather contrasting darker cape* (shoulder blaze usually ill-defined and indistinct).
- *Whiter and variably spotted below* (spots vary mainly with age, and ad can be extensively spotted, unlike Common Bottlenose; however, many/most individuals in a pod are unspotted or only very indistinctly so).
- Facial marks and eye–flipper stripe even less distinct than in Common Bottlenose.
- Flippers perhaps proportionately larger than in Common Bottlenose.

Typical behaviour at surface

- Sociable and shares many behavioural characteristics with Common Bottlenose; they often associate, and with other dolphins. In many areas, however, less playful, frequently shy of boats and only in few places (or only for short periods) approachable, inquisitive and bow-rides; less frequently leaps high above water or breaches.

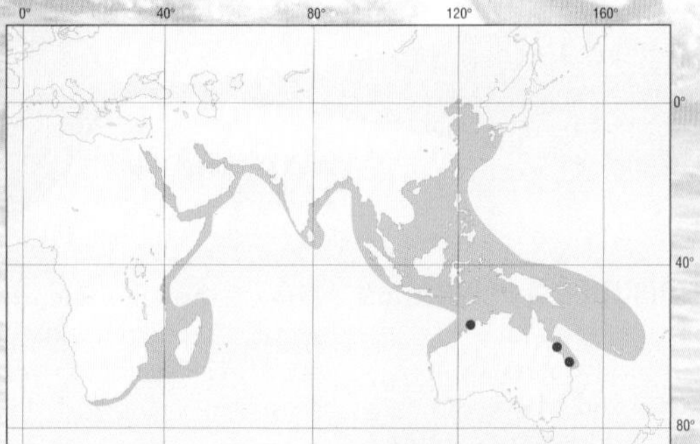

SIMILAR SPECIES

Overlaps in range with several other greyish dolphins, but most likely to be confused with ***Common Bottlenose Dolphin*** as they form mixed pods in some areas. However, Indo-Pacific is generally more elusive and less playful, with more sluggish and less obvious surfacing behaviour than Common Bottlenose. With experience, Indo-Pacific is usually appreciably slimmer with a smaller melon and narrower, better-defined beak (with more parallel edges and delicate mouthline), and dorsal fin is proportionately taller and broader based. Also usually (though much overlap) paler and some have a better-marked cape and whiter underparts, which in ads can be extensively spotted – typically only a few animals within a pod are heavily spotted. ***Pantropical Spotted Dolphin*** is similarly spotted (or unspotted) and has dark cape, but its body and beak are even more slender and elongated, with a shorter dorsal fin, and dark cape more contrasting and spotted in ads. Pantropical Spotted also occurs further offshore and is more acrobatic. Similar-sized ***humpback dolphins*** also overlap in range, but have a dorsal hump (except in SE Asia/ Australia) and shorter dorsal fin, longer/slender beak, and are more greyish-pink, sometimes all pink and/or more extensively spotted.

VARIATION

Age/sex Young darker and more uniform. Greater

Indo-Pacific Bottlenose: the presence of at least 1–2 mature animals in a pod with extensive spotted underparts offers a more reliable distinction.

Indo-Pacific Bottlenose Dolphin

dorsal fin tall and broad-based

long slender beak

cape can be indistinct

adult ♀, 2.5 m

variable spotting on underbody

some have better-defined dark cape (but much individual variation and overlap with Common Bottlenose)

body typically pale grey, but can be very similar to Common Bottlenose

adult ♂, 2.6 m

proportionately large flipper

pink flush to underbody, some populations being slightly spotted

adult ♂, dorsal view, 2.6 m

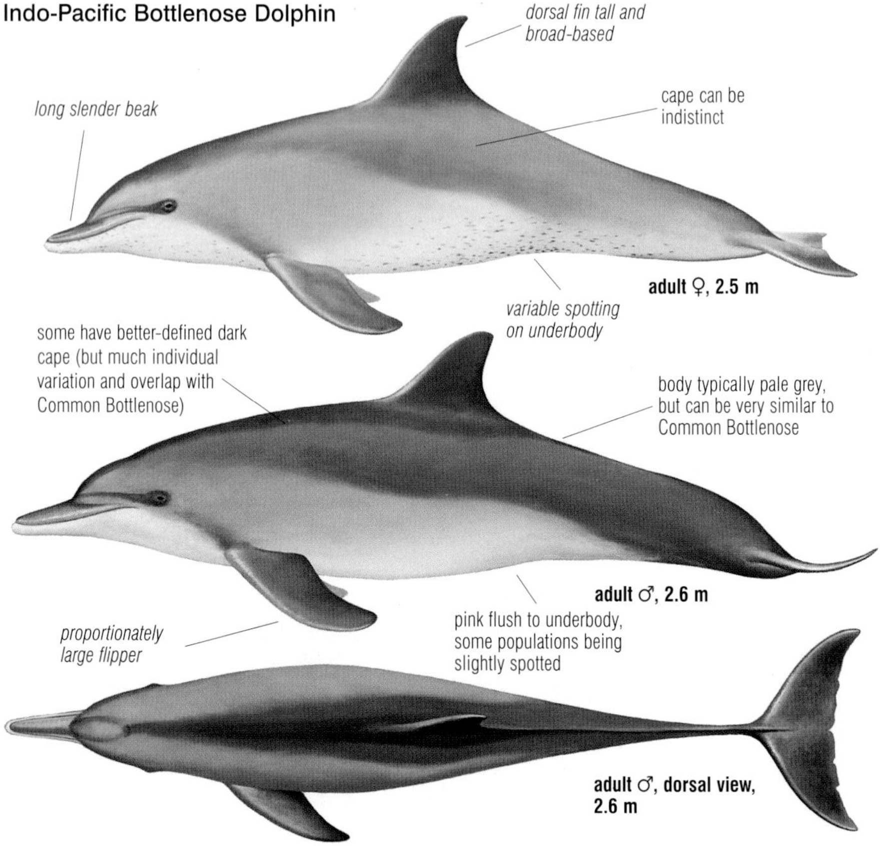

contrast between dorsal and ventral parts, and spotting on latter age-dependent, generally increasing with age but much variation. **Physical notes** Full-grown ads reach 2.6 m and 230 kg, with ♂ perhaps averaging slightly larger. Newborn 0.84–1.1 m and 9–21 kg. **Taxonomy** Significant genetic differentiation and larger number of teeth, as well morphological differences described above, have led to separation from Common Bottlenose; genetically, Indo-Pacific Bottlenose appears closer to some *Stenella*.

DISTRIBUTION & POPULATION

Coastal, tropical and subtropical waters, from S Africa and Madagascar north and east along entire rim of Indian Ocean, including Indonesia, much of N Australasia south to New South Wales, and north to S Japan. Occurs in Red Sea and Persian Gulf. Movements, if any, poorly known, though some groups regularly return to same areas. *Population* No overall estimate.

ECOLOGY

Concentrations may occasionally number 1,000, but typical pod size 5–15. In some areas, regularly in mixed schools with Common Bottlenose and

Indo-Pacific Bottlenose Dolphins (New Caledonia) showing dark cape (with rather distinct pale shoulder blaze) and dorsal fin variation.

Indo-Pacific Bottlenose Dolphin (New Caledonia) surfacing in calm sea: beak hardly breaks surface but still appears narrower and longer than in Common Bottlenose.

Humpback Dolphins. *Breaching* Less frequent and repetitive than Common Bottlenose. *Diving* Much as Common Bottlenose. *Diet* Cephalopods and fish, principally taken around reefs and the seabed. *Reproduction* Mating and calving peak in late spring/summer (year-round in some areas). Gestation *c.*12 months and calves weaned at 1.5–2 yrs, but may remain with cow another 1–3 yrs. ♀♀ usually breed every 4–6 yrs. *Lifespan* 40+ yrs.

Indo-Pacific Humpback Dolphin

Sousa chinensis

Pacific Humpback Dolphin
S. c. chinensis
SW Pacific, China to Australia

Indian Humpback Dolphin
S. c. plumbea
S Africa to Sri Lanka

Atlantic Humpback Dolphin

Sousa teuszii

Coastal W Africa

Max 3 m.

Priority characters on surfacing

- Relatively large robust dolphin, with *strong geographical and individual variation*.
- *Distinctive dorsal fin and basal hump* important characters, but E populations lack hump.
- *Rather long beak* clearly separated from round, high forehead melon.
- *Variable (tiny to very large) ridges on midline of back to tailstock* (at least on many ads) afford rather ragged appearance (at close range).
- Body *grey to nearly white or pinkish-white, occasionally even uniform pink*.
- Young mostly medium/pale grey with pinkish-white underparts, but variable.
- Variable fine dark spots and flecks over much of body, except dorsal fin and abdomen, but many older animals almost uniform.
- Blotchy dark eye-patch (mainly in Asia).

Typical behaviour at surface

- *Small pods; slow swimmer*, but often difficult to approach and *does not usually bow-ride*.
- Tends to surface with characteristic pause at top of roll.
- Surfaces every 40–60 sec but can be submerged for several min. Breaches, lobtails and spyhops, and may swim on its side waving its flippers.
- Inhabits tropical to warm-temperate coastal waters, often entering rivers and mangroves. Sometimes occurs with bottlenose dolphins.

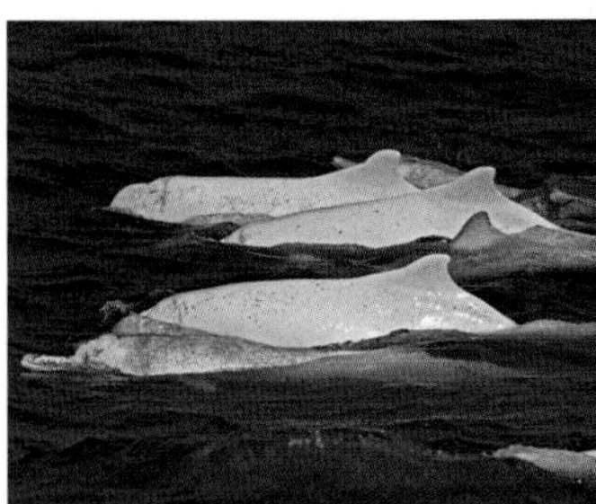

Indo-Pacific Humpback Dolphin (Hong Kong): note lack of hump; larger, triangular dorsal fin with almost straight trailing edge; greyish-white and pinkish colour, with older animals less and more finely spotted (but much individual variation).

DISTINCTIVE POPULATIONS

Two species, one with 2 subspecies and further variations between local populations, as well as by age and, sometimes, sex.
Pacific Humpback Dolphin *S. c. chinensis* (SW Pacific, from China to Australia) Dorsal fin relatively large and triangular with straight or slightly angled trailing edge, without basal hump, but fin often has long base sloping forward and back. Heavily spotted

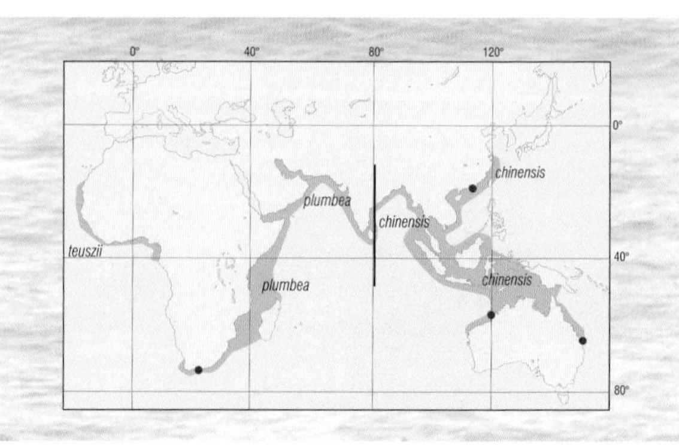

or flecked on greyish-white background, sometimes with pinkish hue, and older animals generally have less and finer spotting, but in SE Asia young very dark grey (even black), becoming paler with age. ♂ retains more spots than ♀, which is frequently more uniform and pinker. However, those in Australia usually greyer, becoming slightly whiter much later in life, often less pinkish and with fewer spots in all stages. Develops quite distinct, blotchy dark eye-patch, mainly in Asian animals.

Indian Humpback Dolphin *S. c. plumbea* (S Africa to N Indian Ocean east to Sri Lanka) Dorsal

Pacific Humpback Dolphin (South China Sea)

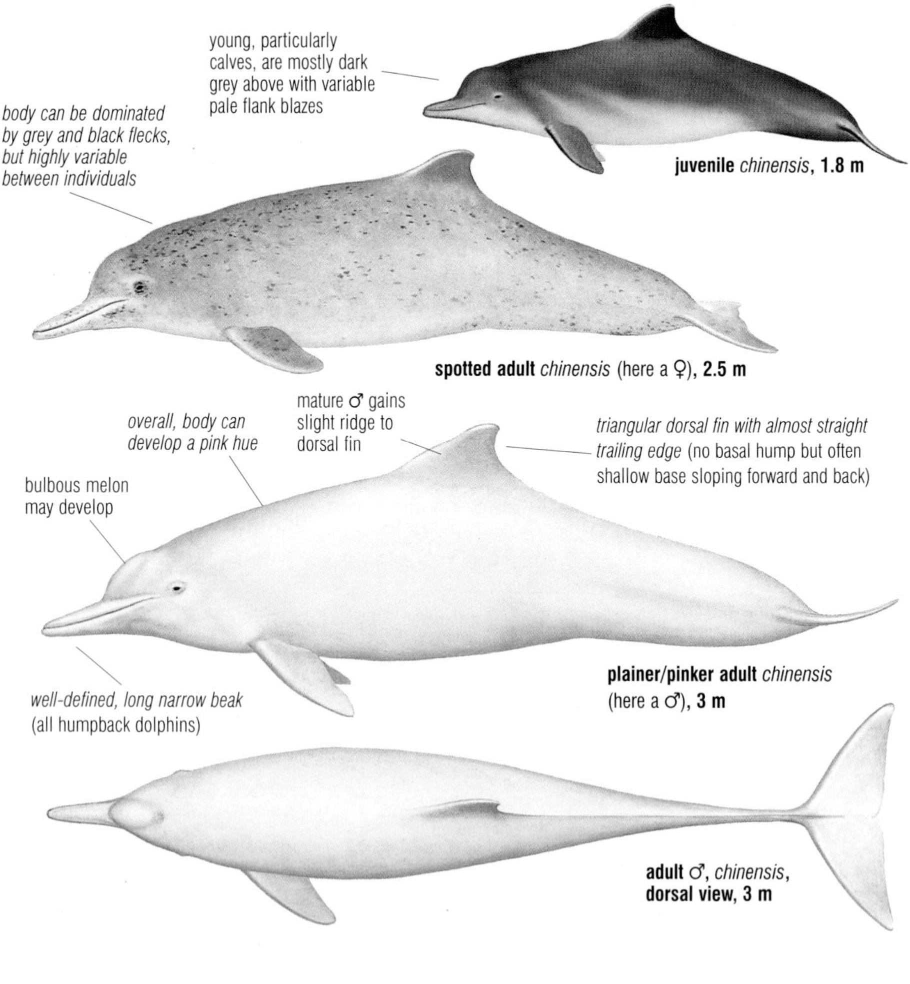

young, particularly calves, are mostly dark grey above with variable pale flank blazes

juvenile *chinensis*, **1.8 m**

body can be dominated by grey and black flecks, but highly variable between individuals

spotted adult *chinensis* (here a ♀), **2.5 m**

overall, body can develop a pink hue

mature ♂ gains slight ridge to dorsal fin

triangular dorsal fin with almost straight trailing edge (no basal hump but often shallow base sloping forward and back)

bulbous melon may develop

well-defined, long narrow beak (all humpback dolphins)

plainer/pinker adult *chinensis* (here a ♂), **3 m**

adult ♂, *chinensis*, **dorsal view, 3 m**

Indo-Pacific Humpback Dolphin (Hong Kong): note steel-grey colour of calf compared to pink coloration of ♀.

(except in most Asian waters), range of pale ash-grey or grey-brown, often whitish and/or pinkish, colorations, and variable spotting. Strong variation in body pigmentation; some, generally young, animals much greyer and uniform, and might be confused with ***bottlenose dolphins***, especially in poor conditions, but dorsal fin and behaviour quite different. No overlap with similar river dolphins.

fin smaller, less triangular and more nub-like; slightly falcate, appearing backswept on tall basal hump, which can be nearly absent in young, but develops with age. Uniformly pale plumbeous or brownish-grey and possess no or an indistinct pinkish tint and, at most, only faint flecks on sides and dorsal areas. Those off E/S Africa greyer and even less spotted.

Indian Humpback Dolphin (S Africa): probably mature ♀ and calf, with small slightly falcate dorsal fin on tall basal hump (but less developed compared to mature ♂).

Atlantic Humpback Dolphin *S. teuszii* (W Africa) Dorsal fin and basal hump very similar to Indian Humpback or hump even more pronounced. Coloration much as latter but perhaps darker, greyer and usually has very few spots. Variable: both very dark and very pale individuals. Generally darker with age; the dorsal fin, however, becomes paler.

SIMILAR SPECIES

Unlikely to be confused given combination of robust body, rounded melon, slender beak, unique dorsal fin/hump

Indian Humpback Dolphin (S Africa): probably mature ♂, with small backswept dorsal fin on tall basal hump, and generally pale grey body.

VARIATION

Age/sex Strong age-related variation in body pigmentation, which varies with population. Most distinct are Chinese animals which change from uniformly dark/medium grey in calf, to whitish-grey, heavily spotted in imm (with some pinkish hue) and finally whiter and pinker and less/finer spotted in ad. In this population, ♂ tends to retain more spots than ♀. Elsewhere calf also dark grey, becoming mainly dull greyish, less white, with almost no pink tinge and spots may not develop at all. Beak and fin of most

Indian and Atlantic Humpback Dolphins

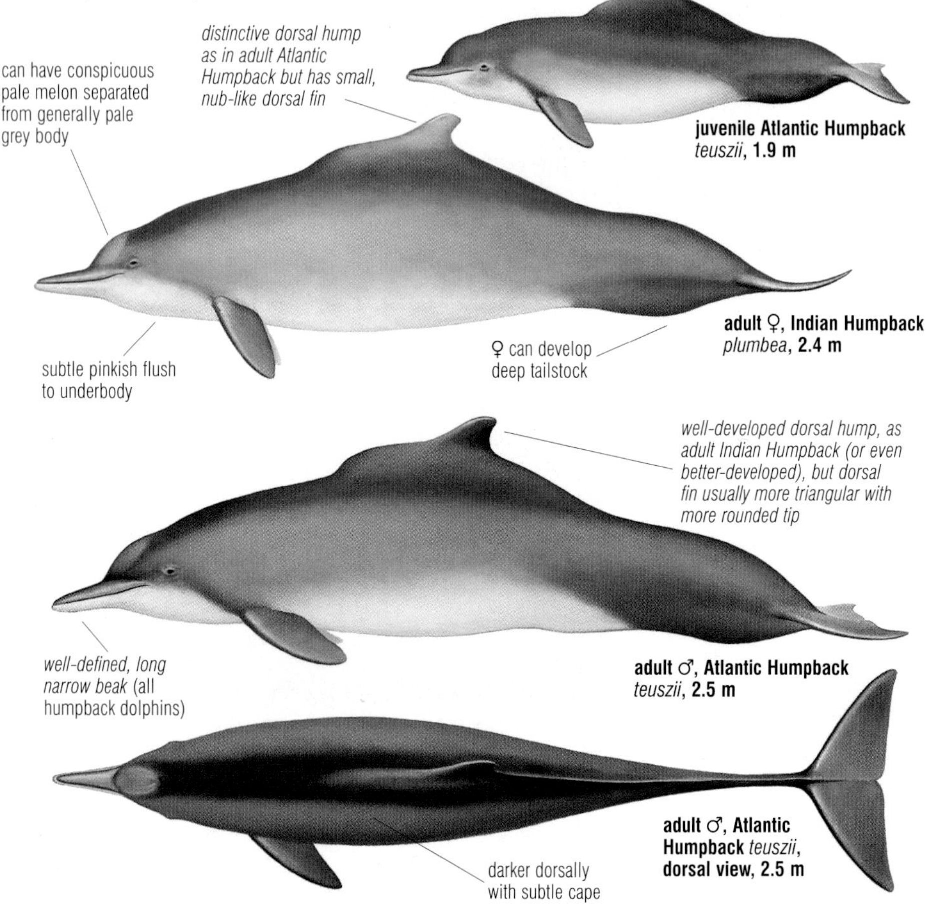

hump also very prominent in young

juvenile Atlantic Humpback *teuszii*, **1.9 m**

can have conspicuous pale melon separated from generally pale grey body

distinctive dorsal hump as in adult Atlantic Humpback but has small, nub-like dorsal fin

subtle pinkish flush to underbody

♀ can develop deep tailstock

adult ♀, Indian Humpback *plumbea*, **2.4 m**

well-developed dorsal hump, as adult Indian Humpback (or even better-developed), but dorsal fin usually more triangular with more rounded tip

well-defined, long narrow beak (all humpback dolphins)

adult ♂, Atlantic Humpback *teuszii*, **2.5 m**

darker dorsally with subtle cape

adult ♂, Atlantic Humpback *teuszii*, **dorsal view, 2.5 m**

become paler with age. Size apparently useful for ageing/sexing in some areas. **Physical notes** Full-grown ad 1.8–3 m and 250–285 kg. Newborn *c.*1 m and 14+ kg. **Taxonomy** Two species, one of them polytypic. External differences predominantly clinal, with spotting and white/pink skin decreasing east–west, and those west of Persian Gulf greyer and plainer, whilst dorsal fin characters change abruptly in E India (and hump disappears east of Sumatra). Those in SE Asia intermediate between *S. c. chinensis* and *S. c. plumbea* in other characters. Note: most Indian Ocean and coastal African animals very similar in colour and dorsal fin (but differ in skull morphology and genetically), and thus differ from SW Pacific populations.

Atlantic Humpback Dolphin (W Africa), probably immature: note obvious hump; dorsal fin appears triangular with rounded tip

Atlantic Humpback Dolphin (W Africa), mature, probably ♂: very similar to Indian Humpback but hump even more pronounced and is darker grey.

DISTRIBUTION & POPULATION
Atlantic Humpback is local and fragmented in coastal W Africa, from S Morocco to Gabon/Angola, whilst Indo-Pacific Humpback ranges from S Africa and Madagascar north and east to India, N & E Australia and the E China Sea. Bays, estuaries, mangroves and sandbanks, usually in waters shallower than 25 m. Has wandered to the Mediterranean (via the Suez Canal) and up the Ganges R, but mostly resident. *Population* Few estimates, although 1,000 in Pearl R estuary (near Hong Kong) and 450+ in Alagoa Bay (S Africa).

ECOLOGY
Typically in groups of 3–7, occasionally up to 44; composition fluid. Imms usually form groups with at least 1 ad. Sometimes follows trawlers or tides. *Breaching* Occasional. *Diving* Usually less than 1 min, but up to 5 min recorded. *Diet* Small fishes, squid and octopus, often on seabed or around reefs. *Reproduction* Sexually mature at *c.*10 yrs old. Cows give birth to a single calf, year-round but mainly spring/summer (Mar–Aug in Hong Kong), with gestation 10–12 months. Calves usually weaned at 2 yrs old, but take solids from 6 months. Inter-calving interval probably 3 yrs. *Lifespan* 40+ yrs.

Rough-toothed Dolphin

Steno bredanensis

Worldwide tropical to sub-tropical waters. Max 2.65 m.

Priority characters on surfacing

- *Relatively large*, powerful, long reptilean body with tapering head.
- *Diagnostic whitish-pink tip to beak and, often, lips* (usually extends onto lower jaw).
- *Long beak poorly defined*, but characteristically smoothly tapers from blowhole with no demarcation, or crease, between melon/snout.
- *Conical head shape*, from flippers to tip of rostrum, and relatively large eyes, afford slight reptilian appearance.
- *Dorsal fin prominent, falcate to triangular*, centrally positioned and often has white scars.
- Narrow, pale border sets dark cape off from lateral field. Cape seen best on bow-riding individuals; often has large, irregular, white (or pink) genital patches.
- White scratches and spots may cover much of body.
- Flippers proportionately very large and set rather far back.

Typical behaviour at surface

- Often associates with, e.g., bottlenose, spotted and spinner dolphins, and pilot whales.
- Usually sluggish and does not porpoise even in fast travel; often swims in a phalanx (several shoulder-to-shoulder), also regularly swims with tip of beak and chin out of the water.
- Normally in small groups (5–10) and often associated with flotsam in water.
- Makes usually shallow leaps; *sometimes bow- or wake-rides*, but less commonly than other dolphins. Usually unobtrusive at surface.

Younger Rough-toothed Dolphins have a greyish lower jaw, whilst adults have a white lower jaw and white lips.

SIMILAR SPECIES
Characteristic cone-shaped head and beak, diagnostic whitish-pink beak tip and lips, prominent falcate dorsal fin on long, dark reptilean body with narrow cape and, often, distinct white scars make Rough-toothed

difficult to confuse with other dolphins, but most likely to be mistaken for ***bottlenose dolphins***, with which it sometimes occurs, but distinctive sloping forehead and white lower jaw usually permit easy separation. Some Common Bottlenose possess superficially pale elements on beak (and conversely a few Rough-toothed may

160°
80°
0°
80°
160°
80°
40°
0°
40°
80°

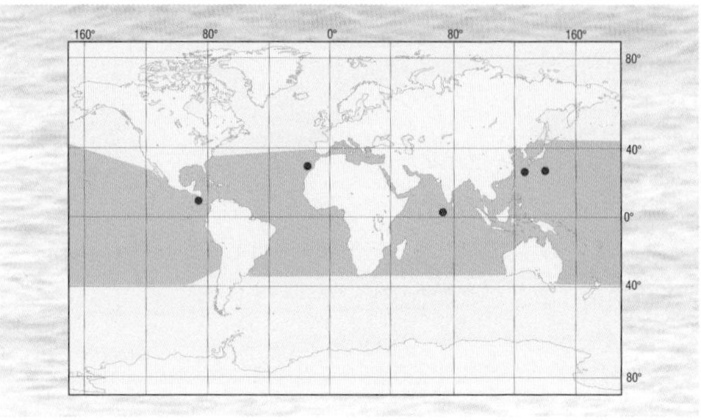

Rough-toothed Dolphin

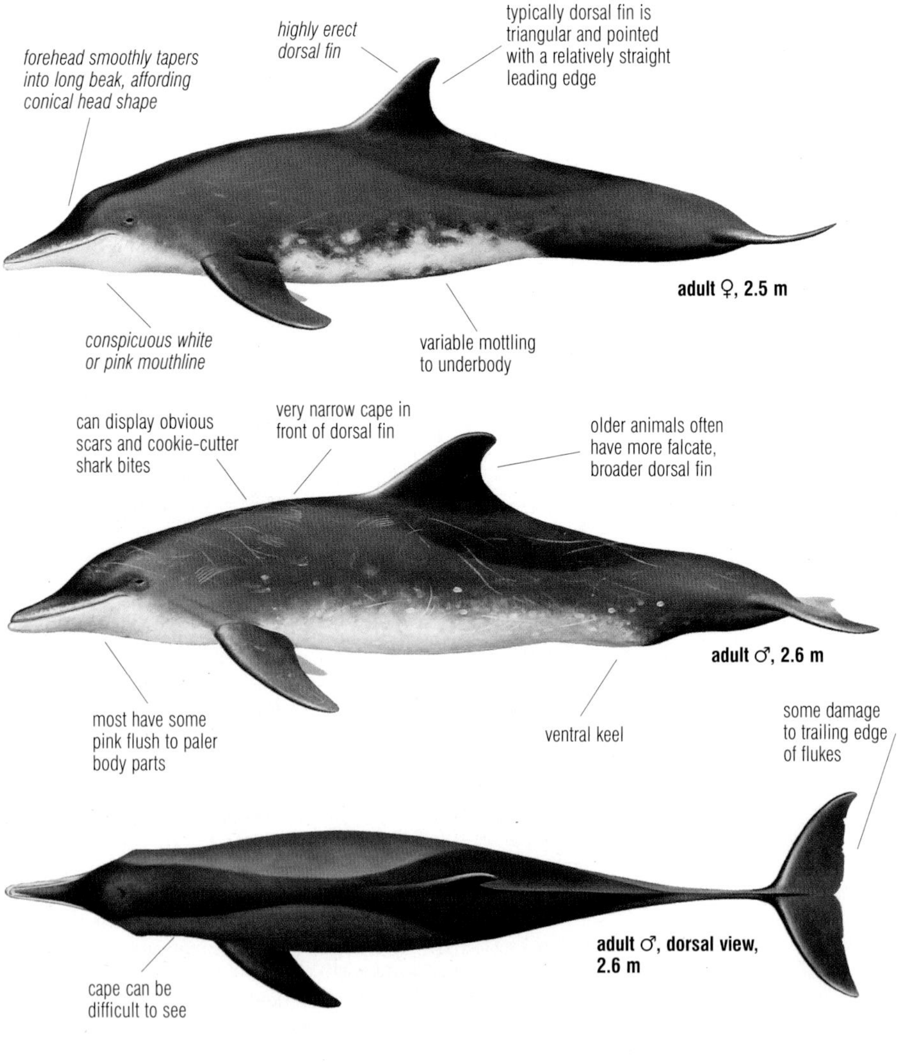

highly erect dorsal fin
typically dorsal fin is triangular and pointed with a relatively straight leading edge
forehead smoothly tapers into long beak, affording conical head shape
adult ♀, 2.5 m
conspicuous white or pink mouthline
variable mottling to underbody
can display obvious scars and cookie-cutter shark bites
very narrow cape in front of dorsal fin
older animals often have more falcate, broader dorsal fin
adult ♂, 2.6 m
most have some pink flush to paler body parts
ventral keel
some damage to trailing edge of flukes
adult ♂, dorsal view, 2.6 m
cape can be difficult to see

Slow, shoulder-to-shoulder surfacing is very common amongst Rough-toothed Dolphins, a species which could be said to have invented synchronised swimming; note large dorsal fin and smooth-sloping forehead.

lack them), and therefore shape of head/beak takes priority. Only at long distances could it be overlooked as, or resemble, ***spinner*** or ***spotted dolphins***.

VARIATION

Age/sex Sexes largely alike but ♂ slightly larger with pronounced keel or post-anal hump. Individual variation in strength of dark cape, whilst ads, presumably mostly mature ♂♂, most likely to possess more scratches/spots (mainly caused by cookie-cutter sharks, but probably also intraspecific interactions). Extent of white on underparts partly geographically dependent, and older individuals have more extensive whitish-pink lips that more often extend onto jaws. Ads more mottled, whereas young, especially calf, darker and more uniform. Other facial marks sometimes apparent, e.g. darker eye-stripe/patch. **Physical notes** Full-grown ad 2.1–2.65 m and 90–160 kg. Newborn probably *c.*1 m.

DISTRIBUTION & POPULATION

Deep tropical and warm temperate waters worldwide, reaching north to SW (exceptionally NW) Europe, Virginia (USA) and C Honshu (Japan), and south to Rio Grande do Sul (Brazil), N New Zealand and N Chile. Few records from Indian Ocean, except from the Maldives. Penetrates the Mediterranean, and apparently resident in many areas. *Population* Only estimate comes from E tropical Pacific, where perhaps 150,000, with 850 in N Gulf of Mexico.

ECOLOGY

Close-knit groups of 10–20, rarely 50–300. Regularly consorts with other species. *Breaching* Occasional, in a low, rather flat manoeuvre, but more rarely high. *Diving* Up to 15 min and to at least 70 m. *Diet* Mainly fish and cephalopods, sometimes taken cooperatively; may regularly take very large dolphinfish that associate with flotsam. *Reproduction* Almost unknown. Age of sexual maturity 10–14 yrs. *Lifespan* Up to 36 yrs.

Rough-toothed Dolphin has a large dorsal fin, tapering, reptilian head with whitish-pink lips, and proportionately very large flippers.

Narrow-beaked oceanic dolphins

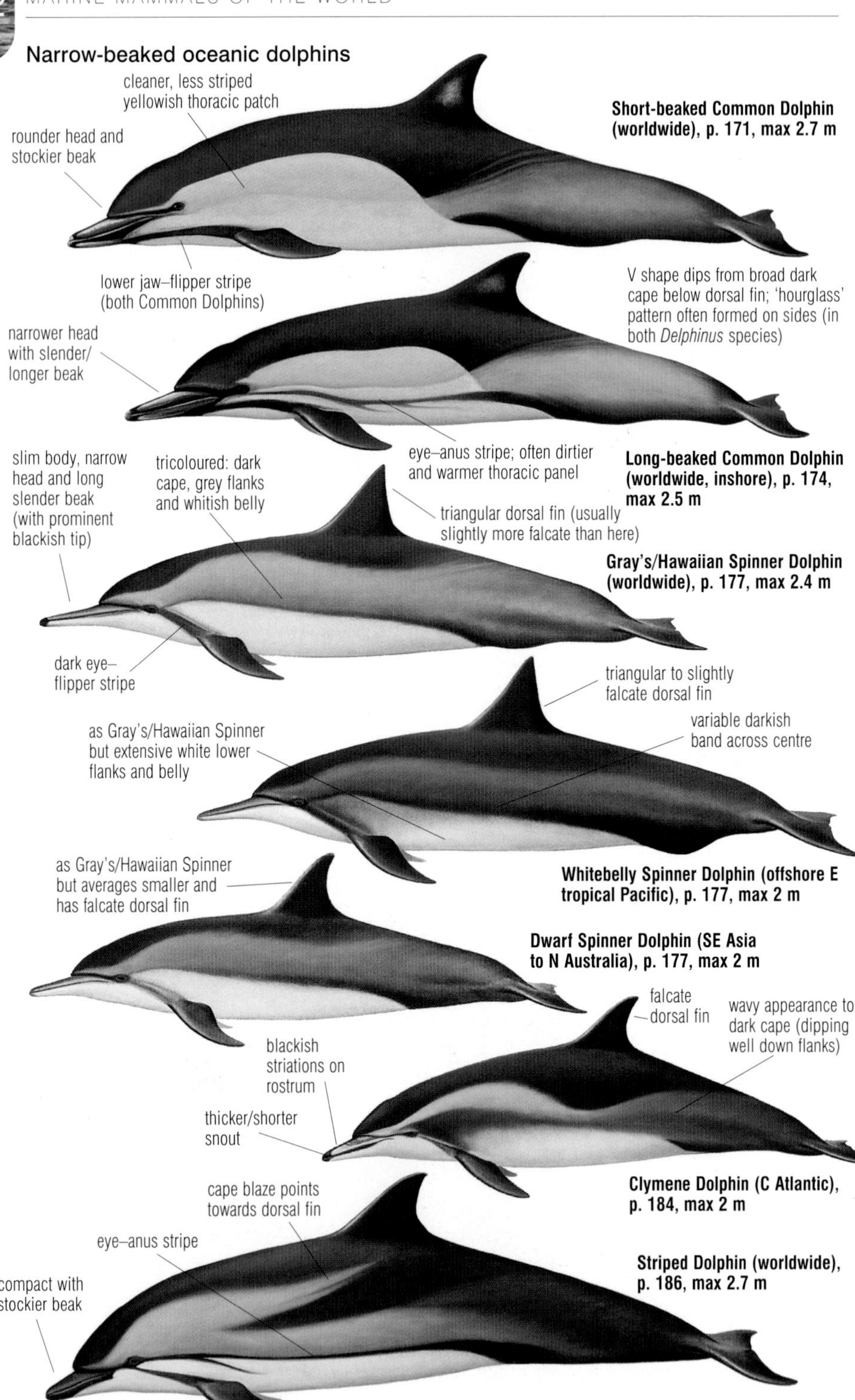

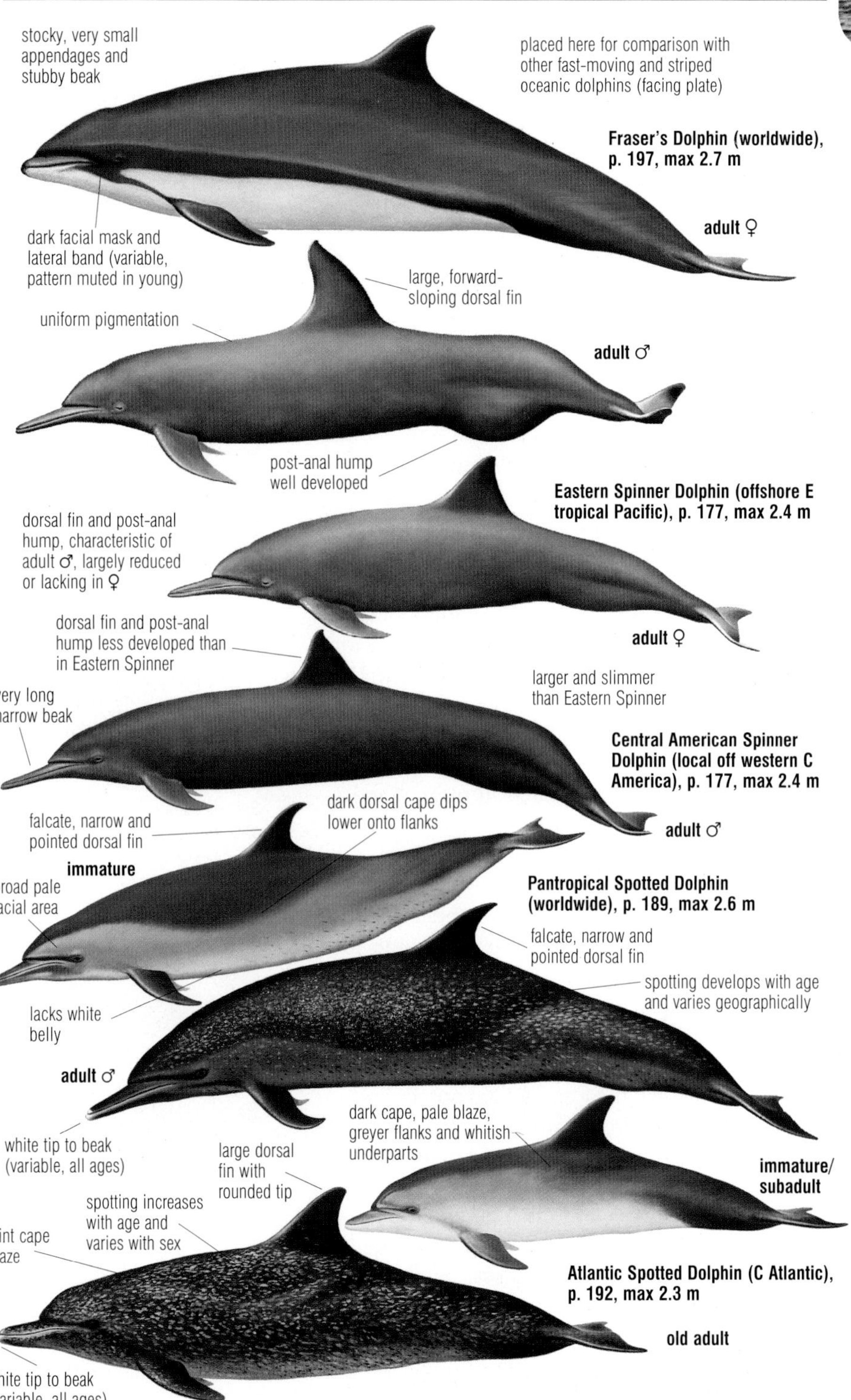
stocky, very small appendages and stubby beak
placed here for comparison with other fast-moving and striped oceanic dolphins (facing plate)
Fraser's Dolphin (worldwide), p. 197, max 2.7 m
adult ♀
dark facial mask and lateral band (variable, pattern muted in young)
large, forward-sloping dorsal fin
uniform pigmentation
adult ♂
post-anal hump well developed
Eastern Spinner Dolphin (offshore E tropical Pacific), p. 177, max 2.4 m
dorsal fin and post-anal hump, characteristic of adult ♂, largely reduced or lacking in ♀
adult ♀
dorsal fin and post-anal hump less developed than in Eastern Spinner
larger and slimmer than Eastern Spinner
very long narrow beak
Central American Spinner Dolphin (local off western C America), p. 177, max 2.4 m
adult ♂
dark dorsal cape dips lower onto flanks
falcate, narrow and pointed dorsal fin
immature
broad pale facial area
Pantropical Spotted Dolphin (worldwide), p. 189, max 2.6 m
falcate, narrow and pointed dorsal fin
spotting develops with age and varies geographically
lacks white belly
adult ♂
white tip to beak (variable, all ages)
dark cape, pale blaze, greyer flanks and whitish underparts
large dorsal fin with rounded tip
immature/ subadult
spotting increases with age and varies with sex
faint cape blaze
Atlantic Spotted Dolphin (C Atlantic), p. 192, max 2.3 m
old adult
white tip to beak (variable, all ages)

Narrow-beaked oceanic dolphins

This very distinctive group of dolphins of the genera *Delphinus* and *Stenella* (subfamily Delphininae) is characterised by its habit of leaping, and some are among the most beautifully and strikingly patterned of all dolphins. Geographical variation is often marked, with several distinct or variable populations, and some species have coastal and open-ocean populations. 'Common Dolphin' was previously considered a single, highly variable species, but recent research has led to Short-beaked Common Dolphin *D. delphis* and Long-beaked Common Dolphin *D. capensis* being treated as separate species. Their ranges partly overlap, but Short-beaked is principally oceanic, whereas Long-beaked is more tropical and prefers continental shelf and coastal waters. The other complex also essentially comprises cosmopolitan tropical and subtropical species, namely the various spinner dolphins, the closely related Clymene Dolphin (of the Atlantic), the spotted dolphins – Pantropical Spotted Dolphin (worldwide) and Atlantic Spotted Dolphin (also confined to the Atlantic) – whilst Striped Dolphin is cosmopolitan at tropical and temperate latitudes.

You should not expect to identify to species level every single dolphin or pod, and observers should strictly stick to diagnostic characters (preferably in combination), even if this means leaving some animals undetermined, especially in areas where several species can occur. Familiarity and experience will naturally lead, in time, to easier and more accurate identifications, which often initially rest on dorsal fin shape. However, these species are not always demonstrative, and do not always bow- or wake-ride. It is important to practice accurately evaluating the key features on these fast-leaping dolphins. Note: features seen below the surface can often be misleading.

Some of these (different species in different areas) share or 'switch' characteristics, whilst the overall impression of a species, especially its size and coloration, including the stripes, thoracic panel, cape, tailstock and any spotting, is often strongly dependent

Spinner Dolphins, S. l. longirostris, *(Hawaii), in typical tight-knit surfacing group.*

Above and below: Dwarf Spinner Dolphins S. l. roseiventris *(off Bali, Indonesia) are distinctive by their smaller size and, especially, the more strongly falcate dorsal fin than the nominate; tricoloured pattern usually well pronounced.*

on population, age and sex. Three species 'pairs' demand most caution in their identification: the two common dolphins, the spinners/Clymene Dolphin, and the two spotted dolphins. Spinner and Pantropical Spotted Dolphins often mix and, especially, poorly marked individuals or in less-favourable conditions can be readily confused. The two spotted dolphins are highly variable, being often confusingly unspotted. Atlantic Spotted more recalls Common Bottlenose Dolphin. Separation of the common dolphins from the rest should prove straightforward, but in certain lights the foresides of other species can confusingly appear to have almost as large a thoracic panel as on common dolphins. Only Spinners/Clymene spin.

Porpoising Short-beaked Common Dolphins; the species often occurs in large, boisterous schools.

Short-beaked Common Dolphin

Delphinus delphis

Tropical to temperate Atlantic/Pacific. Max 2.7 m.

Priority characters on surfacing

- Medium-sized, rather chunky dolphin with huge foreside thoracic panel.
- Dorsal fin tall, triangular, falcate and pointed; can be all dark or have paler or white centre.
- Broad dark cape extends to rear sides; *V-shape dips from side of cape below dorsal fin and 'hourglass' pattern often forms* on animals with grey wash to tailstock.
- Highly demarcated *yellowish-buff or pale golden thoracic panel, bordered below by whiter flanks*.
- *Shorter (but still moderately long) beak and more rounded melon than Long-beaked.*
- Black eye spot/stripe stands out vividly; *narrow, often well-defined dark beak–flipper stripe;* stripe forward of the vent muted or lacking (often well developed in Long-beaked).
- Pale beak base and generally more *open facial appearance, with pale line above and sometimes in front of eye an important feature*.

Typical behaviour at surface

- Fast swimmer, usually in large, boisterous schools that whip the surface as they porpoise.
- Often associates with other marine mammals and feeding frenzies of birds.
- Aerially acrobatic, with flipper-slapping, lobtailing, bow-riding, breaching and sometimes somersaulting.

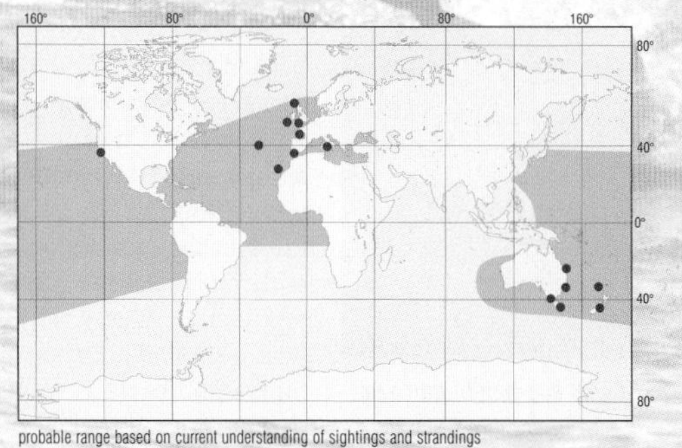

probable range based on current understanding of sightings and strandings

Short-beaked Common Dolphin (N Atlantic): note black eye-patch clearly separated from beak–flipper stripe; in Long-beaked, the eye-patch is usually embedded in the lateral or flipper stripes.

DISTINCTIVE POPULATIONS

Several populations in the E Pacific, including northern, central tropical and southern populations. As more data accumulate, more morphologically distinguishable populations will undoubtedly be identified there and in other regions.

SIMILAR SPECIES

Both common dolphins share beak–flipper (rather than eye–flipper) stripe, dark V-shaped 'saddle' (dipping from side of cape below dorsal fin), well-defined yellowish thoracic panel on foresides, and 'hourglass' or 'crisscross' flank pattern (often absent if tailstock lacks grey and difficult to appreciate at sea), which are among the best features for excluding other oceanic and similar-sized *Stenella* dolphins, *cf.* Striped, Spinner and Clymene Dolphins, and Pantropical and Atlantic Spotted Dolphins.

Short-beaked Common Dolphin is overall less slender with a more rounded head, shorter and stockier beak than Long-beaked; unique criss-cross coloration forms hourglass pattern; white in dorsal fin is variable but usually absent in warmer water populations.

Shorter and stockier beak is principal difference from ***Long-beaked Common Dolphin***, but often difficult to appreciate and beware individual/geographical variation and that juv Long-beaked has shorter beak. Bicoloured thoracic panel of Short-beaked usually has broader yellowish upper layer and whitish belt on lower flanks that extends above dark beak–flipper stripe (but monotone thoracic panel frequent). Most Short-beaked tend to have narrower dark lower jaw–flipper stripe which does not continue beyond flipper or very faintly so (broader beak–flipper and, although variable, eye–genital stripe in Long-beaked). Short-beaked always has very clean thoracic patch with obvious black eye-patch; in every school of Long-beaked many have a bold black ventral stripe that intrudes lower half of thoracic patch. In addition, ventral stripe usually sufficiently broad that eye-patch appears embedded within it, affording face a consequently dirtier appearance. Generally, Short-beaked has a more open facial expression (perhaps with more conspicuous black spectacles and paler beak), cleaner, less striped sides, and is overall less slender with a more rounded head.

Short-beaked Common Dolphin: note obvious black eye-patch; narrower dark lower jaw–flipper stripe and lack of lateral stripes behind flipper point, with cleaner and broader yellowish thoracic panel.

VARIATION

Age/sex To some extent, ♂ has slightly broader black blaze just above genital region (narrower/paler in ♀), and young smaller and often paler. Calf even less contrastingly patterned. **Physical notes** Those off California 1.7–2 m (♂), 1.6–1.9 m (♀), and 70–110 kg (but up to 235 kg reported); much higher figures probably refer to *D. capensis*, but E tropical Pacific and eastern N Atlantic populations large; ♂ averages slightly larger and heavier. Newborn probably *c.*0.7–1 m and *c.*10 kg. **Taxonomy** Previously considered conspecific with Long-beaked Common Dolphin. Black Sea population named *D. d. ponticus.* At least 3 geographically separate populations in NE Pacific identifiable by body length and cranial features. Overall pigmentation, especially on face, beak and area between flipper and beak, as well as darkness of tailstock and dorsal fin vary individually

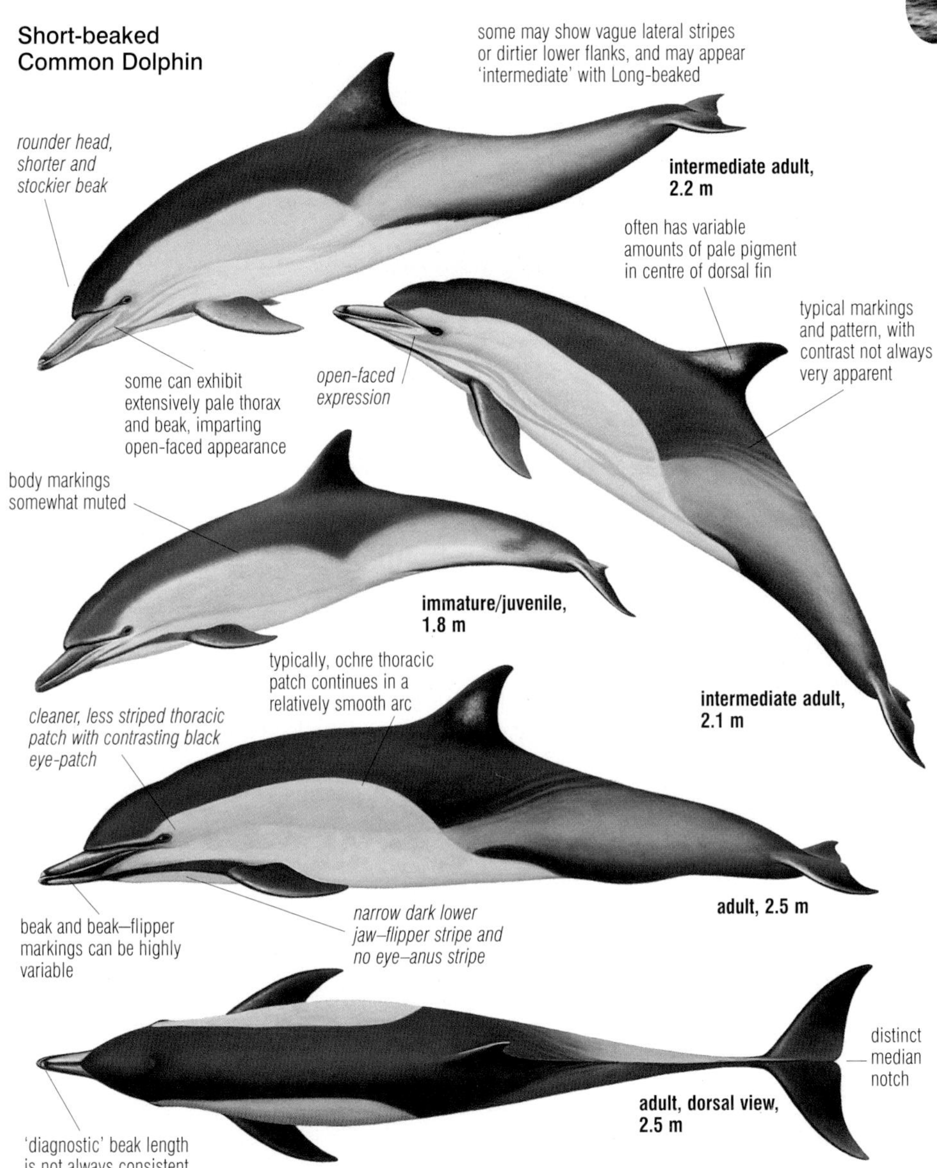

and, to some extent, between different populations. Flippers and flukes dark grey or black, but in eastern N Atlantic, flippers often paler, frequently with white patches.

DISTRIBUTION & POPULATION

Widespread mainly in warm-temperate or subtropical waters, and perhaps absent from Indian Ocean. Many populations undertake seasonal movements and may follow warm-water currents. Principally offshore. *Population* No overall estimates, but plausibly 100,000 off NW Europe, 100,000s off western N America and 3 million in E Pacific.

ECOLOGY

Much as Long-beaked, but can aggregate in 1,000s. *Breaching* Frequent, sometimes somersaults. *Diving* Most dives reach *c.*90 m and last *c.*3 min but to

260 m and 8 min. *Diet* As Long-beaked; principally feeds nocturnally in some areas. *Reproduction* Sexually mature by (2) 6–7 (♀) or 5–7 (12) yrs old (♂). Breeds mainly Jun–Sep, gestation lasts 10–11 months, lactation *c.*19 months and inter-calving interval is 2–3 yrs; ♀♀ with calves often remain longer at lower latitudes, and breeding less seasonal in tropical waters. *Lifespan* Up to 35 yrs.

Young Short-beaked Common Dolphin: juveniles of Long-beaked and Short-beaked have muted coloration and shorter beaks than adults, making them difficult to distinguish; however, schools rarely, if ever, mix.

Long-beaked Common Dolphin calf and ♀: variable vent stripe (subdued in this ♀) meets flipper–gape stripe and eye-patch, giving face a darker or dirtier appearance; note calf's muted pattern.

DISTINCTIVE POPULATIONS

Indo-Pacific Common Dolphin *D. c. tropicalis* (Indian Ocean to SE Asia) Extremely long, narrow beak, and more teeth, and clean thoracic patch like Short-beaked Common Dolphin.

SIMILAR SPECIES

Especially in close views and favourable sea conditions, easily distinguished from *Stenella* spp by broad flipper stripe, vent stripe reaching to anus, dark V-shaped pattern below dorsal fin, well-defined ochre thoracic panel and so-called 'hourglass' pattern. May be confused with Clymene Dolphin in Atlantic, as cape

Long-beaked Common Dolphin

Delphinus capensis

Warm/tropical near-shore waters. Max 2.5 m.

Priority characters on surfacing

- Slender with longer beak than otherwise near-identical Short-beaked Common Dolphin.
- *Long beak and slender head*, with flatter melon, afford Spinner Dolphin-like appearance.
- Dorsal fin tall, triangular, falcate and pointed (all dark, occasionally with some pale areas).
- Broad *dark cape dips at sides in V-shape* below dorsal fin.
- *Thoracic panel on foresides duller, more evenly ochre (rather than yellowish, often with whitish lower area) than Short-beaked.*
- *Dark beak–vent stripe (unlike Short-beaked)* and often reaches gape, merging with black eye-patch, giving face much darker appearance (dirtier in some with greyer vent stripe).
- *'Hourglass' pattern often seen* on animals with a faint grey wash to tailstock.
- *Face duskier; thoracic panel does not continue above eye and pale line in front of eye indistinct or lacking* (*cf.* Short-beaked).

Typical behaviour at surface

- Usually in large, boisterous pods which surface like Short-beaked and perform similar acrobatics.
- Inhabits more inshore waters than Short-beaked, but forms similar associations.

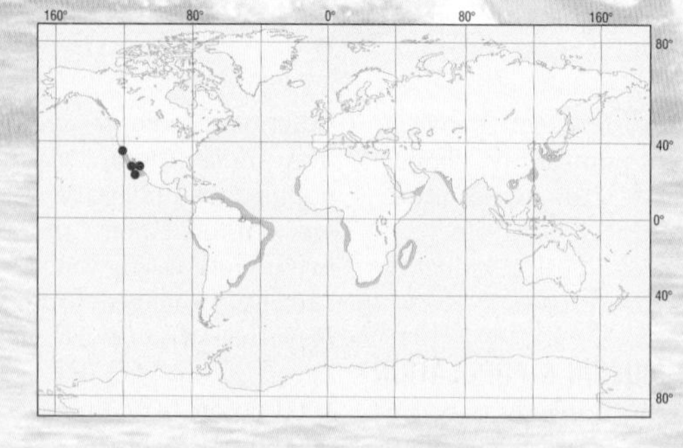

Long-beaked Common Dolphin

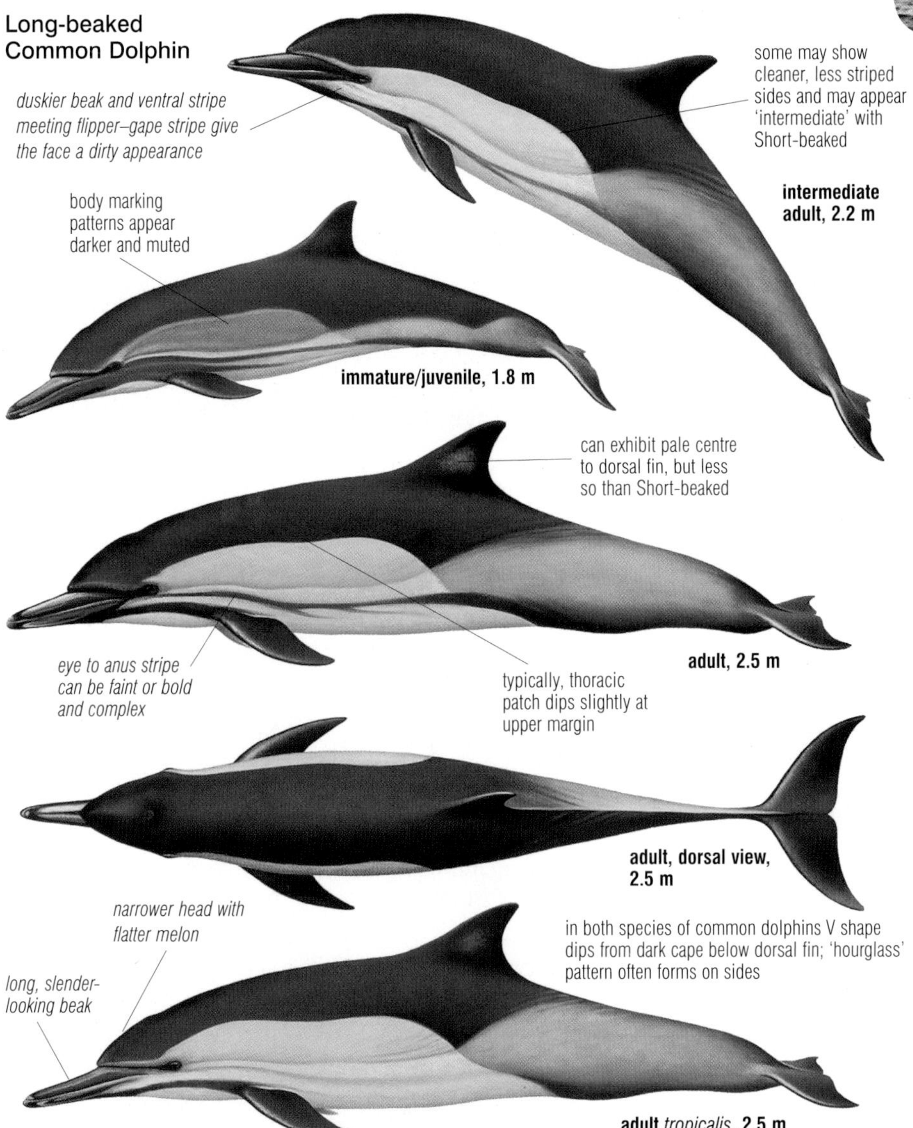

in that dolphin extends low on the side to yield almost an hourglass-like appearance, but in close views Clymene can be seen to have 'moustache' on beak and small separation between cape and ventral field. Separation from ***Short-beaked Common Dolphin*** more difficult. Longer, more slender beak and flatter melon are best distinguishing marks, but also slimmer bodied. Other marks apply to most, but not all, Long-beaked. Usually has broader streak between lower jaw–flipper that, with dark band from eye to vent, forms diagnostic broad dark belt bordering pale thoracic area, which is more restricted and duller ochre. Normally has broader black patch on lower jaw, pale thoracic panel does not extend above eye and pale line in front of eye indistinct or lacking (together with darker beak, forms less open, duskier face). Furthermore,

Long-beaked Common Dolphins often form very large schools. The vent–gape stripe is highly variable: often indistinct and greyish in juveniles and some adults, at least some show a heavy black band on the sides.

coloration overall somewhat muted, and pale area on dorsal fin only occasionally present, or faint and more restricted. Long-beaked usually nearer shore than Short-beaked. Much individual and geographical variation in pigmentation, especially on face and sides.

VARIATION

Age/sex Much as Short-beaked Common Dolphin. **Physical notes** Full-grown ads 2–2.5 m (♂), 1.9–2.2 m (♀) and 80–150 kg (up to 235 kg reported), with ♂ slightly heavier. Newborn *c.*0.8–1 m and probably *c.*10 kg. **Taxonomy** Polytypic. Until recently regarded as conspecific with Short-beaked Common Dolphin. *D. c. tropicalis* (Indo-Pacific Common Dolphin) sometimes treated specifically, but recent study places it firmly in *D. capensis*. All other described forms probably represent only local variation.

DISTRIBUTION & POPULATION

Warm-temperate and tropical oceans, north to S Japan and C California and south to S Africa and N Argentina. *Population* No overall estimates but most of the 15,000–20,000 *Delphinus* off eastern S Africa are this form.

ECOLOGY

Concentrations of 100–500 usually due to many smaller pods (typically of 10–30) coalescing. Some segregation by age/sex. May overlap with Short-beaked, but mixed schools unconfirmed. *Breaching* As Short-beaked. *Diving* Up to 8 min, usually 10 sec–2 min and can reach 280 m. *Diet* Chiefly small schooling fish, squid and krill. *Reproduction* Calving mainly spring/autumn; gestation 10–11 months with 1–3 yrs between births. Near-term pregnant and lactating ♀ may be separated from rest of population.

Long-beaked Common Dolphin: note long, narrow beak giving head a tapered look; intersection of thoracic patch and dorsal cape forms distinctive V below dorsal fin in both species of common dolphins.

Spinner dolphins

One of the most taxonomically complex groups which, especially in the E tropical Pacific, varies considerably, whilst in the Atlantic they are sympatric with their very close relative, Clymene Dolphin. They present a considerable identification challenge to identify and to study. The main plate (pp. 168–169) depicts all the principal variants but each distinct population is illustrated separately, with the full range of variation, on the following plates. All are extremely acrobatic spinning in mid-air by twisting their bodies on a longitudinal axis, landing with a large splash. They also breach more normally and perform somersaults like their close relatives. Highly social, they often coexist with Pantropical Spotted Dolphins at feeding frenzies of yellowfin tuna and seabirds.

Typical tight underwater formation of Spinner Dolphins, S. l. longirostris, *Hawaii.*

Spinner Dolphin

Stenella longirostris

Worldwide warm waters.
Max 2.4 m.

Priority characters on surfacing

- Strong geographical variation in body size, shape and colour, but all share the following.
- Medium to small, *highly streamlined slim body*.
- *Head elongated*; forehead sloping into *extremely long, slender beak* set off by a crease.
- *Tall, upright dorsal fin on mid-back usually more or less triangular or slightly falcate*, in some slightly forward.
- Tricoloured, with dark cape, pale grey sides and whitish belly, but Eastern and Central American Spinners basically monotone, and Whitebelly has a bipartite pattern.
- *Dark eye–flipper stripe and dark upper jaw, lips and tip of beak.*
- Tailstock of ad ♂ may be much deeper, with enlarged post-anal keel.
- Medium-length flippers have sharply pointed tips.
- Small, medium grey flukes.

Typical behaviour at surface

- Often in large groups, sometimes with Pantropical Spotted, yellowfin tuna and seabirds.
- *Fast, highly acrobatic dolphin, leaping up to 3 m, and may spin in mid-air* (body twisted longitudinally up to 7× in single leap) and up 14× in series.
- Near-shore populations often inquisitive around boats and will more often bow-ride.

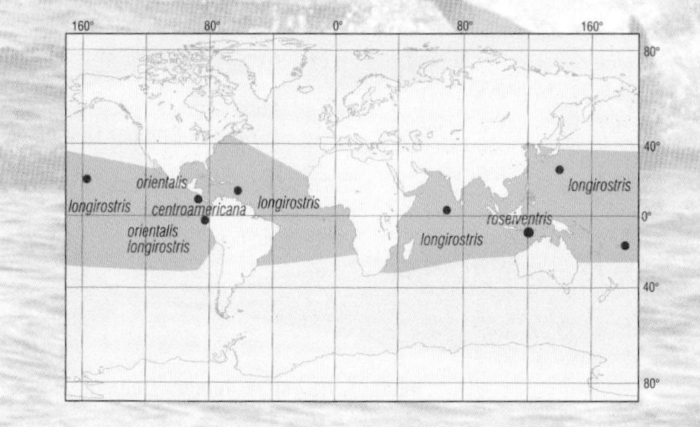

DISTINCTIVE POPULATIONS

Four subspecies described which may vary further between populations, as well as by age and minor sexual differences.

Gray's (Hawaiian) Spinner Dolphin *S. l. longirostris* (Worldwide, except E tropical Pacific) Dark grey cape, pale grey sides and white belly; dark flippers and facial markings often obvious; dorsal fin slightly/moderately falcate; more robust than other forms; post-anal hump of ad ♂ poorly defined.

*Spinner Dolphin (*S. l. longirostris, *Hawaii): note tricoloured pattern, with dark cape, pale grey sides and whitish belly; also dark eye–flipper stripe and very long beak; spinning behaviour, shown here, is diagnostic.*

Gray's (Hawaiian) Spinner Dolphin including Whitebelly Spinner Dolphin

Central American and Dwarf Spinner Dolphins

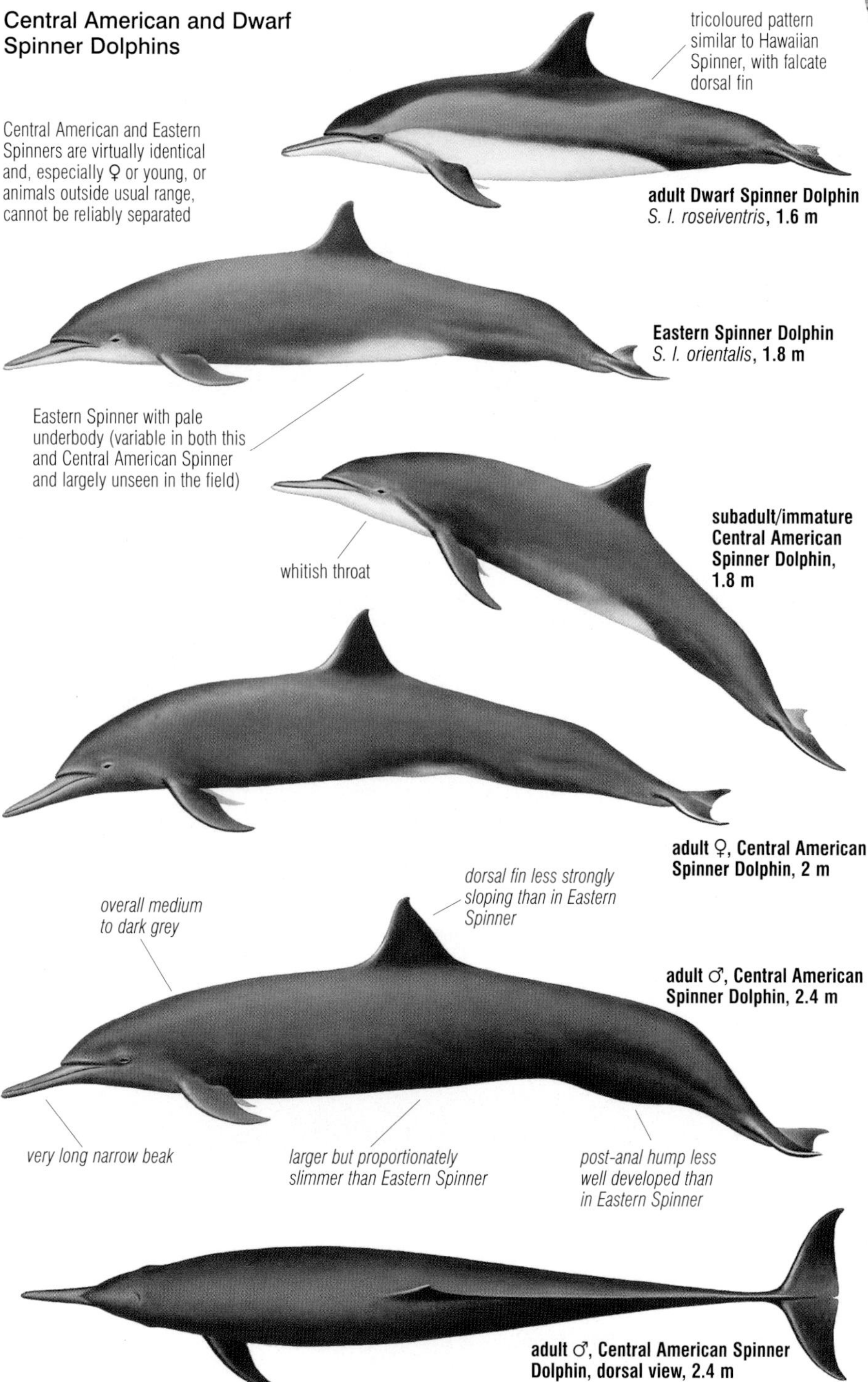

adult Dwarf Spinner Dolphin *S. l. roseiventris*, **1.6 m**

Eastern Spinner Dolphin *S. l. orientalis*, **1.8 m**

subadult/immature Central American Spinner Dolphin, 1.8 m

adult ♀, Central American Spinner Dolphin, 2 m

adult ♂, Central American Spinner Dolphin, 2.4 m

adult ♂, Central American Spinner Dolphin, dorsal view, 2.4 m

Eastern Spinner Dolphins

Spinner Dolphins, S. l. longirostris, *♀ and calf (Hawaii): dark upper jaw and blackish beak tip are often noticeable when bow-riding* (cf. *Pantropical Spotted Dolphin*).

Spinner Dolphin S. l. longirostris (*Maldives, Indian Ocean*) *shows considerable colour pattern variation; this one for example, has relatively subdued patterns.*

Eastern Spinner Dolphin *S. l. orientalis* (E tropical Pacific east of 145°W and from Baja California, Mexico, south to equator) Almost uniform darkish to medium grey (paler/whiter area around genitals and axilla variable); dorsal fin triangular or sloped forward, especially in older ad ♂, which has deep tailstock and large post-anal hump; overall less robust.
Central American Spinner Dolphin *S. l. centroamericana* (Local in 150 km zone off western C America) Nearer *S. l. orientalis* being almost uniform grey; also similar in dorsal fin and post-anal hump, but former less strongly sloping in older ad ♂ and latter less well developed. Larger and proportionately slimmer (with perhaps slightly longer/narrower beak) than Eastern.
Dwarf Spinner Dolphin *S. l. roseiventris* (Gulf of Thailand, Malaysia to N Australia) Closer to *S. l. longirostris* but averages smaller.
Whitebelly Spinner Dolphin Hybrid *longirostris* × *orientalis* (Offshore E tropical Pacific) Many intermediate phenotypes but typically robust, with clear or moderate darkish cape and white lower flanks and abdomen; often a narrow darkish divide between these areas (the predominant morphotype in some areas). Dorsal fin variable, slightly falcate to slightly sloping; post-anal hump of ad ♂ small to moderate. Facial and flippers markings obscured.

Adult ♀ or immature ♂ (limited post-anal hump) Eastern Spinner Dolphin (S. l. orientalis, *E tropical Pacific) is all grey, sometimes with a white ventral patch, and an erect, triangular dorsal fin.*

Adult ♂ Eastern Spinner Dolphin (S. l. orientalis, *E tropical Pacific) has a distinctively forward-sloping dorsal fin and well-developed post-anal keel.*

SIMILAR SPECIES

Range closely overlaps ***Pantropical Spotted Dolphin*** and they often mix, e.g. in E tropical Pacific latter often found in pods of Eastern and Whitebelly dolphins. Especially latter could be confused, owing to more falcate dorsal fin and superficially similar 2-toned appearance, with dark dorsal cape and paler lower flanks and abdomen (like

*Group of Eastern Spinner Dolphins (*S. l. orientalis*, E tropical Pacific) moving at high speed from a research vessel; this subspecies often associates with Pantropical Spotted Dolphins, yellowfin tuna and seabirds.*

young Pantropical Spotted). However, in close views, Pantropical Spotted has dark cape extending even lower, pale greyish sides, more backswept dorsal fin, stubbier beak with whitish tip, and gape–flipper stripe. Both are aerial and highly acrobatic. In Atlantic, spinners most likely to be confused with ***Clymene Dolphin*** and both ***spotted dolphins***, which share geographical range, behaviour and appearance, but pattern of head and body (including Clymene's dark cape reaching lower flanks on mid body, and above eye, affording a wavy appearance, and 'moustache' on basal rostrum), and general shape (shorter snout and more falcate dorsal) distinguish them. In distant views, Spinners might also be confused with other dolphins, especially the ***common dolphins*** and ***Striped Dolphin***, but coloration and behaviour quickly eliminate them.

Eastern Spinner Dolphins S. l. orientalis *(E tropical Pacific): the almost uniform middle animal also lacks a forward-sloping dorsal fin suggesting an adult ♀; the furthest animal seems to be a juvenile given the shorter beak and whitish throat.*

Eastern Spinner Dolphins S. l. orientalis *(E tropical Pacific): the furthest animal is an adult ♂ with a strongly forward-sloping dorsal fin.*

VARIATION

Age/sex Perhaps by overall size, with ♂ slightly larger. Calf slimmer and more uniform. **Physical notes**

Central American Spinner Dolphin, S. l. centroamericana, *is a longer, lankier version of the Eastern Spinner which inhabits the continental shelf-break off W Central America. It only rarely performs such acrobatics, especially in daylight.*

Full-grown ad 1.75–2.4 m and 75 kg (those in C Pacific and Atlantic usually largest, with Eastern Spinner smaller than Central American Spinner; dwarf form smallest). Newborn 70–85 cm and probably *c.*10 kg. **Taxonomy** Polytypic, with at least 4 races.

DISTRIBUTION & POPULATION

Cosmopolitan in tropical and subtropical seas, generally between 30°N and 30°S. Ranges north to New Jersey (USA), Senegal, S Honshu (Japan) and Hawaii, and regularly south to Paraná (Brazil), (perhaps) St Helena, S Africa and Queensland (Australia). Vagrant to New Zealand. Some populations largely resident. *Population* No overall estimate, but at least 1.5 million in E Pacific.

ECOLOGY

Gregarious, sometimes in 1,000s in ocean, but usually just 100s or even 10s in near-shore waters. Inshore schools increase in size in late afternoon in preparation for nocturnal feeding, breaking into smaller units in day. *Breaching* See box. *Diving* Recorded to 600 m. *Diet* Chiefly small mesopelagic fish; dwarf population principally takes bottom- and coral-dwelling fishes and invertebrates.

Central American Spinner Dolphins S. l. centroamericana *(off western C America): note forward-sloping dorsal fins which give the mistaken impression they are swimming from left to right.*

Whitebelly Spinner Dolphins (E tropical Pacific): hybrid form occuring where longirostris *meets* orientalis *which shows many intermediate phenotypes.*

Reproduction Sexually mature at 4–7 (♀) to 7–10 yrs (♂). Breeds year-round with different populations exhibiting seasonal peaks. Probably promiscuous to polygynous, with degrees of polygyny and sexual dimorphism regionally correlated. Gestation *c.*10–11 months and calves weaned at 1–2 yrs. Inter-calving interval *c.*3 yrs. *Lifespan* Up to 23 yrs.

Some populations of Spinner Dolphins, S. l. longirostris *(E tropical Pacific), have a contrasting, tripartite colour pattern with a distinct black stripe between the white (sometimes pink) belly and the grey sides, hence they may appear superficially like Whitebelly Spinner Dolphin.*

*Clymene Dolphin has a tripartite pattern like Spinner (*S. l. longirostris*) but a shorter beak and stockier appearance; the dark cape dips well below dorsal fin; ill-defined duskier band on sides is characteristic.*

SIMILAR SPECIES

Most likely to be confused with ***Short-beaked Common Dolphin*** or several *Stenella* spp, especially ***Spinner Dolphin*** which has similar behaviour (including spinning leaps) and general appearance. ***Clymene*** usually has decidedly stockier snout (with perhaps more contrasting black tip and upper ridge), slightly more rounded forehead, rather more falcate dorsal fin (more triangular in spinners, but much variation and overlap), and is overall smaller and more robust. The dark cape dips usually well below fin and again slightly above eye affording the cape a wavy appearance compared to Spinner Dolphin; diagnostic blackish striations on rostrum, forming so-called 'moustache', variable and generally visible only on bow-riders. Although spins longitudinally, less acrobatic and frequent than Spinners.

Clymene Dolphin

Stenella clymene

Tropical and subtropical Atlantic. Max 2 m.

Priority characters on surfacing

- *Less elongated with shorter beak and slightly rounder forehead than similar Spinner Dolphin.*
- *Dark cape dips below dorsal fin, almost reaching white underside; also usually dips slightly above eye affording more S-shape to cape.*
- Below dark grey cape, paler grey flanks, white chin and (often pinkish-tinged) belly.
- *Dorsal fin small, slightly falcate and centrally positioned.*
- *Mid-length beak with distinctive black tip* that continues narrowly to base.
- Dark, ill-defined band sometimes develops on mid body (can be quite confusingly marked).
- Dark grey eye–flipper stripe, which broadens downwards.
- Dark and pale eyestripes and dark nasal marking forms 'moustache' on beak (visible on bow-riders).
- Dark, slender, sharply pointed flippers; slightly enlarged post-anal keel below tailstock.

Typical behaviour at surface

- Frequently in pods of fewer than 50, often with similar-sized dolphins.
- Approaches boats, capable bow-riders, but rather shy in some areas.
- Fast swimmer and often spins awkwardly, with usually only 1 rotation (*cf.* 5+ in Spinners).

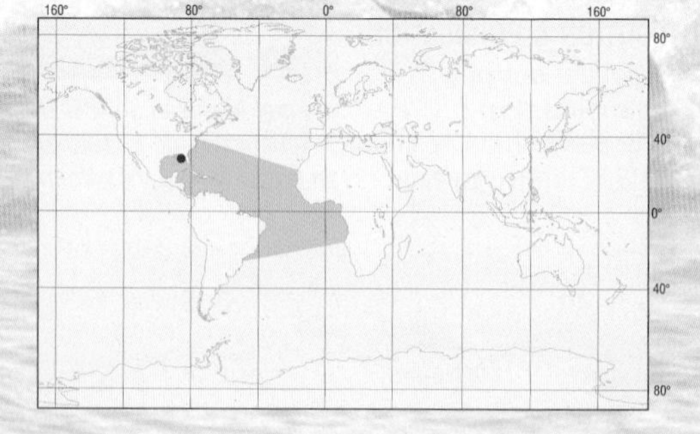

Clymene Dolphin

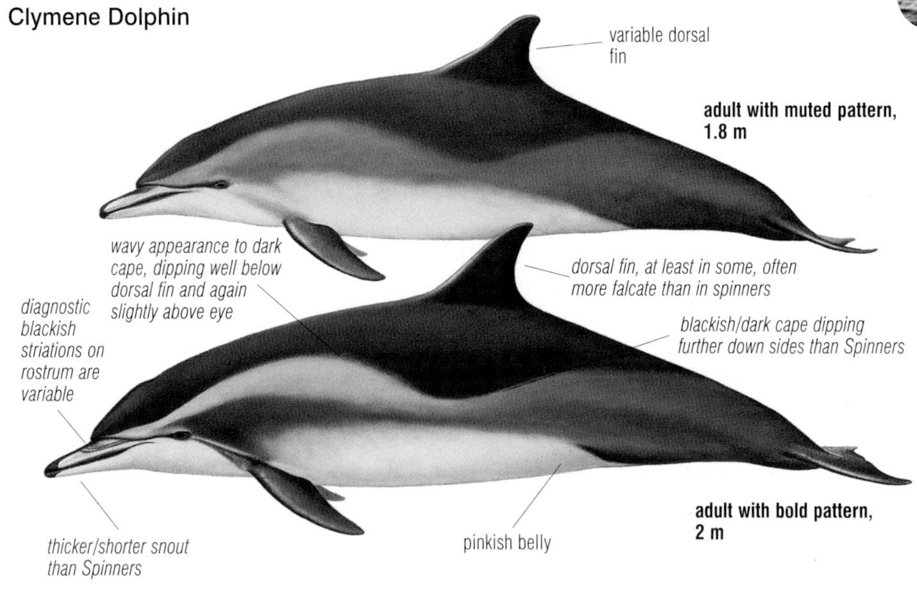

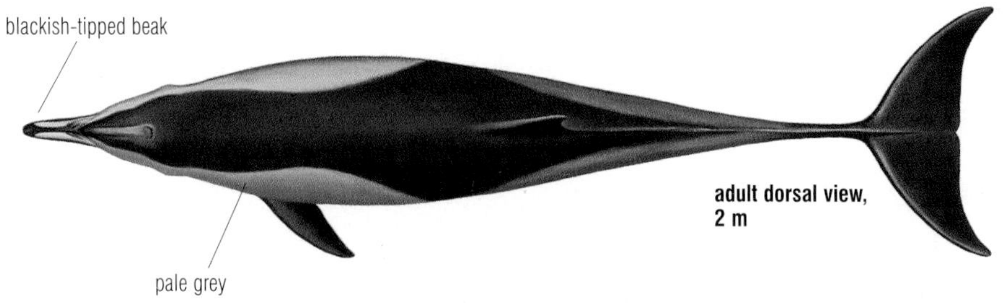

For separation from ***Striped Dolphin*** see that species. ***Common dolphins*** best distinguished by distinct yellowish-buff thoracic panel, dark cape that forms a V below fin and chin–flipper stripe. ***Pantropical*** and ***Atlantic Spotted Dolphin***s, especially unspotted animals could be confused, but both more robust, with at least some of pod spotted (although beware mixed pods with present species), and have small whitish tip to beak without black tip; both are acrobatic, but only perform somersaults, not longitudinal spins of Clymene and Spinner Dolphins.

Clymene Dolphin: this duskier variant would, if seen alone, prove difficult to identify. Note the black-tipped beak, like Spinner Dolphin, but shorter and stouter.

VARIATION

Age/sex ♂ averages larger. Calf slimmer and more uniform. **Physical notes** Full-grown ad 1.75–2 m and 50–90 kg. Newborn probably *c.*80 cm and *c.*10 kg. **Taxonomy** Until 1981 considered conspecific with Spinner Dolphin, but skull morphology and mtDNA suggest that Clymene Dolphin is more closely related to Striped Dolphin.

DISTRIBUTION & POPULATION

Perhaps widespread in the tropical Atlantic, from New Jersey (USA) and Senegal south to Santa Catarina (Brazil) and Gulf of Guinea. Movements, if any, unknown. *Population* Unknown but seems naturally uncommon, and only a single area of abundance yet identified, the N Gulf of Mexico, where *c.*5,500.

ECOLOGY

Occasional recorded in 100s. To some extent, pods appear sexually segregated. *Breaching* Frequent, reaching as high as Spinner Dolphins and capable of rotating on their own long axis, landing on their sides or backs, though does so less frequently; many fewer rotations than Spinners. Unique roto-tailing behaviour, leaping clear of water and making circular tail motions. *Diet* Mesopelagic fish and squid, apparently mostly taken at night. No other data on life history and ecology.

Leaping ♀ and calf Striped Dolphin, showing distinctive narrow cape blaze in front of dorsal fin.

SIMILAR SPECIES

Lateral stripe and cape blaze particularly useful in separation from other white-bellied oceanic dolphins (*Stenella* and *Delphinus*). Beware that markings vary to some extent geographically, can be very weak or lacking. Check as many pod members as possible. Striped Dolphin rarely mingles with other dolphins (occasionally with common dolphins) and less frequently shares feeding frenzies with seabirds (than Pantropical Spotted and Spinner Dolphins). ***Pantropical Spotted***

Striped Dolphin

Stenella coeruleoalba

Worldwide tropical and temperate waters. Max 2.7 m.

Priority characters on surfacing

- *Mid-sized, fast-moving dolphin*; robust body, medium beak and rounded melon.
- Dorsal fin (subtriangular to falcate) is central and tall.
- *Dark grey cape and prominent black eye–anus stripe* (at least on strongly marked animals).
- Pale V-shaped stripes behind and above eye, with *cape blaze pointing towards dorsal fin* (variable and not always easy to see).
- *Bluish-grey blaze on upper flanks to below dorsal fin, and white to pinkish underparts.*
- Black central stripe encircles eye and broadens on sides to anus.
- Black eye–flipper stripe; another, narrower and shorter line behind eye (variable).

Typical behaviour at surface

- Highly gregarious (less so in Atlantic); fast, energetic swimmer.
- Bow-rides only in some areas; may approach boats if with Short-beaked Common Dolphin but in general *infrequently associates with other dolphins or seabirds*.
- Agile and capable of amazing acrobatics: somersaults, tail-spins and back somersaults.

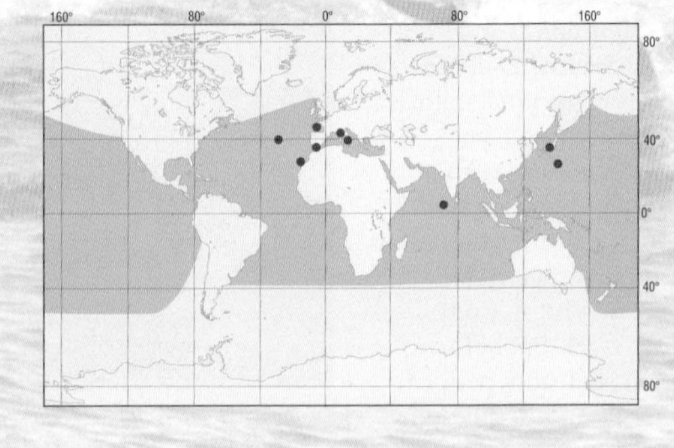

eliminated by lack of white belly and all-dark appearance at distance; ***Spinner*** has more triangular fin, usually lacks eye–anus stripe, spinning behaviour; much longer beak and long, thin body, affording it a long lean look vs stouter body and shorter beak of Striped. ***Short-beaked and Long-beaked Common Dolphins*** lack central body stripe (in most populations) and cape blaze, instead having criss-cross side pattern. ***Clymene Dolphin*** which overlaps in range,

Striped Dolphin: note distinctive but highly variable cape blaze, which can be very thin, indeed almost invisible, or form a broad, conspicuous band.

Striped Dolphin

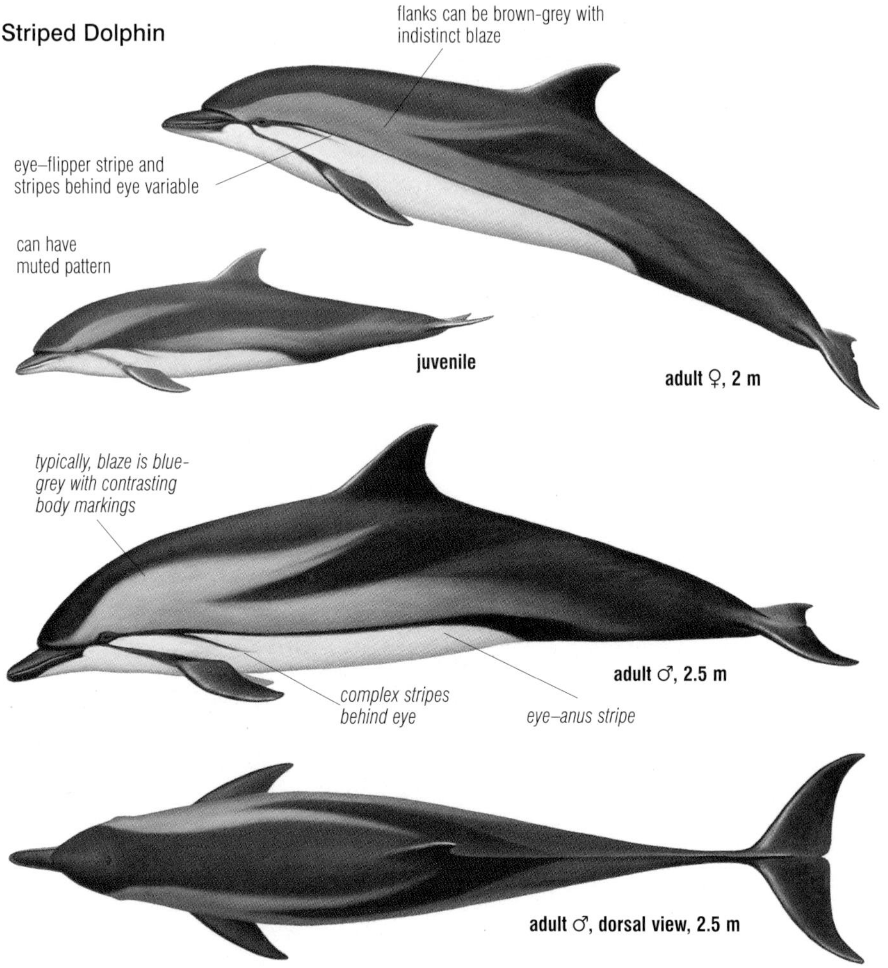

flanks can be brown-grey with indistinct blaze

eye–flipper stripe and stripes behind eye variable

can have muted pattern

juvenile

adult ♀, 2 m

typically, blaze is blue-grey with contrasting body markings

adult ♂, 2.5 m

complex stripes behind eye

eye–anus stripe

adult ♂, dorsal view, 2.5 m

Striped Dolphins: note chunky body, stubby beak and distinctive eye-to-anus stripe; some animals (as on the right) have a more muted pattern.

behaviour and appearance readily eliminated as lacks clear-cut dark central body and pale cape blaze, and has characteristic dark cape dipping just below fin. ***Fraser's Dolphin*** has superficially similar eye–anus stripe, but separated by smaller equilateral dorsal fin and flippers, lack of shoulder blaze, shorter/thicker snout and schooling characteristics.

VARIATION

Age/sex Perhaps by overall size, with ♂ larger. Age development poorly known. Calf averages slimmer and more uniform. **Physical notes** Full-grown ♂ 1.8–2.7 m, ♀ 1.9–2.4 m, and weight 90–156 kg. Newborn 0.9–1.0 m and 20 kg.

DISTRIBUTION & POPULATION

Cosmopolitan in tropical and temperate waters, generally beyond continental shelf, exceptionally ranging north to Greenland, more usually the UK, Denmark, the Sea of Japan and Washington state (USA), and south to Argentina, S Africa, W Australia and New Zealand. Indian Ocean range poorly known, but relatively common in the Maldives. Widespread and the commonest small cetacean in the Mediterranean. Movements generally follow warm currents. *Population* No overall estimate but perhaps 2 million in E tropical Pacific, 570,000+ off Japan, 62,000 in western N Atlantic and 100,000+ in Mediterranean.

ECOLOGY

Forms dense groups of 20–50, occasionally 100s. Composition varies from just ads, only juvs or mix of ages. May further subdivide into breeding and non-breeding groups. *Breaching* Frequent and very high, sometimes rapidly rotating tail. *Diving* Recorded to 700 m. *Diet* Small schooling fish and cephalopods throughout water column. *Reproduction* Sexually mature at 7–15 yrs. Mating system unknown. ♀♀ give birth to a single calf chiefly in summer/autumn. Gestation lasts 1 yr, lactation 12–18 months, and intervals between calvings 3–4 yrs. *Lifespan* Up to 58 yrs.

Porpoising Striped Dolphins: note compact build, distinctive cape blaze and eye–anus stripe; belly is bright white or sometimes quite pinkish.

Pantropical Spotted Dolphin

Stenella attenuata

Worldwide tropical or warm waters. Max 2.6 m.

Priority characters on surfacing

- *Medium-sized dolphin with slender, streamlined body, and medium–long narrow beak.* Generally a *dark dolphin with a darker cape*, but often appears all dark at distance. Only very young have pale bellies.
- *Dark dorsal cape reaches lower on flanks* in front of dorsal fin and tapers on head. No cape blaze.
- *Dorsal fin narrowest of any dolphin, also falcate and normally pointed.*
- Ad spotted/mottled to varying degree, but this only visible in close views.
- *Many animals unspotted*, particularly young, but distinct geographical variation in spotting, which also increases with age.
- *Lips and beak tip usually brilliant white.*
- Dark gape–flipper and eyestripes.

Typical behaviour at surface

- Abundant, highly gregarious, fast and acrobatic, frequently bow-rides.
- Two main forms: *coastal* form in groups less than 100, but *offshore* herds reach 1,000s.
- *Often associates with spinner dolphins, yellowfin tuna and seabirds.*

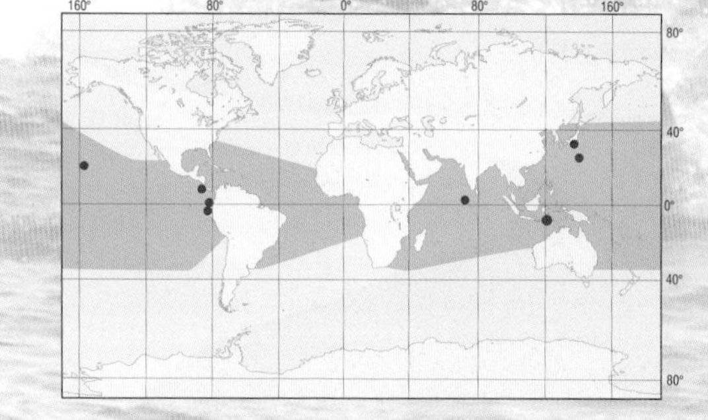

Adult ♂ Pantropical Spotted Dolphin (coastal, E tropical Pacific): coastal form larger and stockier, with much more extensive spotting that nearly obscures cape.

VARIATION

Age/sex Ad ♂ has conspicuous bulge behind anus. Generally, spots larger and more numerous with age and, in oldest animals, tend to merge, appearing more uniform grey, almost obliterating cape. Calf more uniform, whilst juv/imm spotted below, thereafter extending above. **Physical notes** Full-grown ♂ 1.6–2.6 m, ♀ 1.6–2.4 m, and weigh 90–119 kg. Newborn 80–85 cm but weight unknown. **Taxonomy** Polytypic,

SIMILAR SPECIES

Separated from most other similar-sized, long-beaked oceanic dolphins by lack of white belly and presence of dark cape; white tip to beak (variable), also sometimes useful. Especially take care in E tropical Pacific where this species occurs with confusingly darker and more uniform forms of ***spinners***, which have different dorsal fin shape, facial/beak and lateral markings, which features should be used in combination. Separation from ***Atlantic Spotted Dolphin*** (in the Atlantic) is discussed under the latter; also consider (distant) ***common dolphins*** (qv).

Beware that both ***bottlenose dolphins*** have superficially similar white tips to their beaks (and Indo-Pacific Bottlenose can be mottled on the belly), but distinguished by heavier body and size, with much stouter beak, larger head, and much broader and taller dorsal fin; they also usually lack a contrasting dorsal cape, but often have variable cape blaze that Pantropical Spotted lacks.

Adult Pantropical Spotted Dolphin (offshore, E tropical Pacific), possibly ♂: slimmer build and finer spotting on cape and flanks characterise offshore animals; dorsal fin distinctive, being very narrow, pointed and falcate.

Pantropical Spotted Dolphin

Pantropical Spotted Dolphins (offshore, E tropical Pacific): immature (foreground) with typical dark, contrasting cape extending low on flanks; in adult (possibly ♀) note extensive spotting on dark cape, reducing contrast. Both show characteristic broad pale grey face and narrow beak with whitish tip.

with 2–4 races probably diagnosable but not all described. *S. a. attenuata* worldwide in tropical and warm waters, except E tropical Pacific; S. *a. graffmani* ('Eastern Pacific Coastal Spotted Dolphin') limited to within 185 km of coast in E tropical Pacific; *S. a.* subsp. ('Hawaiian Spotted Dolphin') inshore waters of Hawaii; *S. a.* subsp. ('Eastern Pacific Offshore Spotted Dolphin') intermediate offshore waters, over 30 km out, of E tropical Pacific. Spotting varies geographically and between inshore/offshore populations. In E tropical Pacific *coastal form* larger and stockier, with thicker beak and more extensive spotting than *offshore form* (e.g. most ads appear unspotted at a distance in Hawaii and Gulf of Mexico).

DISTRIBUTION & POPULATION

Cosmopolitan in tropical and warm-temperate seas, reaching north to Massachusetts (USA), Cape Verdes, N Indian Ocean, N Honshu (Japan) and Hawaii, and south to Uruguay, St Helena, S Africa, New Zealand and C Chile. Appears to move inshore in autumn/winter and offshore in spring. *Population* Probably in excess of 3 million worldwide, with ⅔ of these in E tropical Pacific and 400,000 off Japan.

ECOLOGY

Highly social, occurring in 1,000s, though mostly in groups of *c.*10–20, with different pods often in close contact. Each school may comprise cows with young, juvs or ad ♂♂, and composition appears fluid, except in case of all-♂ groups. *Breaching* Frequent, high arching leaps, especially by juvs. *Diving* Up to 3.4 min recorded, but probably capable of much more sustained dives. *Diet* Small pelagic fish, cephalopods and crustaceans, mostly near surface or in mid waters. *Reproduction* Sexually mature at mean 9 (♀) or 12 yrs (♂). Breeds year-round, with several seasonal peaks. Gestation lasts 11–12 months, with calves weaned at 1–2 yrs (though take solids at 3–6 months). Cows give birth to a single calf every 2.5–4 yrs. *Lifespan* Up to 46 yrs.

Pantropical Spotted Dolphin (coastal, E tropical Pacific): young have a paler belly and little or no white spotting on cape/sides, making dorsal cape more obvious. Note lack of cape blaze.

Adult/subadult Pantropical Spotted Dolphins (E tropical Pacific, apparently offshore) showing individual variation in cape contrast and amount of spotting. At distance they appear all dark with very narrow dorsal fins.

SIMILAR SPECIES

Unspotted individuals may be confused, especially with smaller/coastal ***Common Bottlenose Dolphins*** (due to present species' relatively stronger snout, pronounced melon and crease between them, and overall chunky appearance). Differences in size and shape offer good clues, but experience required to discern these. Heavy spotting also characteristic of well-marked Atlantic Spotted, but check if any bottlenose present, or whether just juvs or weakly-spotted Atlantic Spotted in pod. Also, usually has clearer cape than bottlenose, becoming greyer laterally and whiter below.

Very like ***Pantropical Spotted Dolphin***, but Atlantic Spotted has taller, more erect dorsal fin (tip often more rounded) and much heavier spotting in areas where both occur, and cape blaze quite evident on bow-riders; unlike Pantropical, pigmentation tripartite (not bipartite): dark cape, greyer laterally and whiter ventrally. Atlantic

Atlantic Spotted Dolphin

Stenella frontalis

Warm, tropical waters of Atlantic. Max 2.3 m.

Priority characters on surfacing

- *Robust*, relatively compact and often distinctly spotted; superficially resembles bottlenose dolphins in shape or somewhat intermediate between latter and Pantropical Spotted.
- *Tall falcate dorsal fin*.
- *Beak moderately long, but rather chunky*; pale beak tip and lips.
- *Melon rather pronounced*; distinct crease between latter and beak.
- Much age-related *variation in spotting*, but always tends to have dark cape, greyer lateral and whiter ventral areas, and usually several well-spotted animals in a school.
- *Pale cape blaze meets dark cape just below and in front of fin* (variable), reminiscent of Striped Dolphin.
- With age, dark spots form on paler lower body and whitish spots increase dorsally.
- Grey eye–flipper stripe (variably gape–flipper).
- Broad-based flippers, curved with pointed tips.

Typical behaviour at surface

- Fast swimmer; often attracted to fast-moving boats and rides bow waves.
- Highly acrobatic; typically leaping out of water and falling back with large splash.

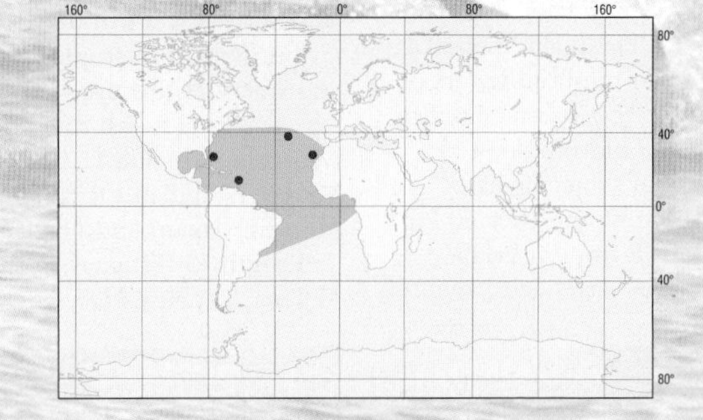

Adult ♀♀ and calves of Atlantic Spotted Dolphins: in older animals the cape is usually obscured by heavy spotting, which usually emphasises the blaze (e.g. animal on far right); calves are more uniform greyish with unspotted, whitish underparts.

Atlantic Spotted Dolphin

large dorsal fin is variable, but has rounded tip

modest dark and pale spotting increases with age

dark cape with pale blaze (below and in front of dorsal fin), greyer flanks and whitish underparts are important in identification of lightly spotted and unspotted animals

adult ♀, 2 m

unspotted muted pattern

immature/subadult, 1.6 m

dark cape obscured by spotting and faint blaze reaching onto cape

white tip to beak (variable)

pale belly

old adult ♂, 2.3 m

adult ♂, dorsal view, 2.3 m

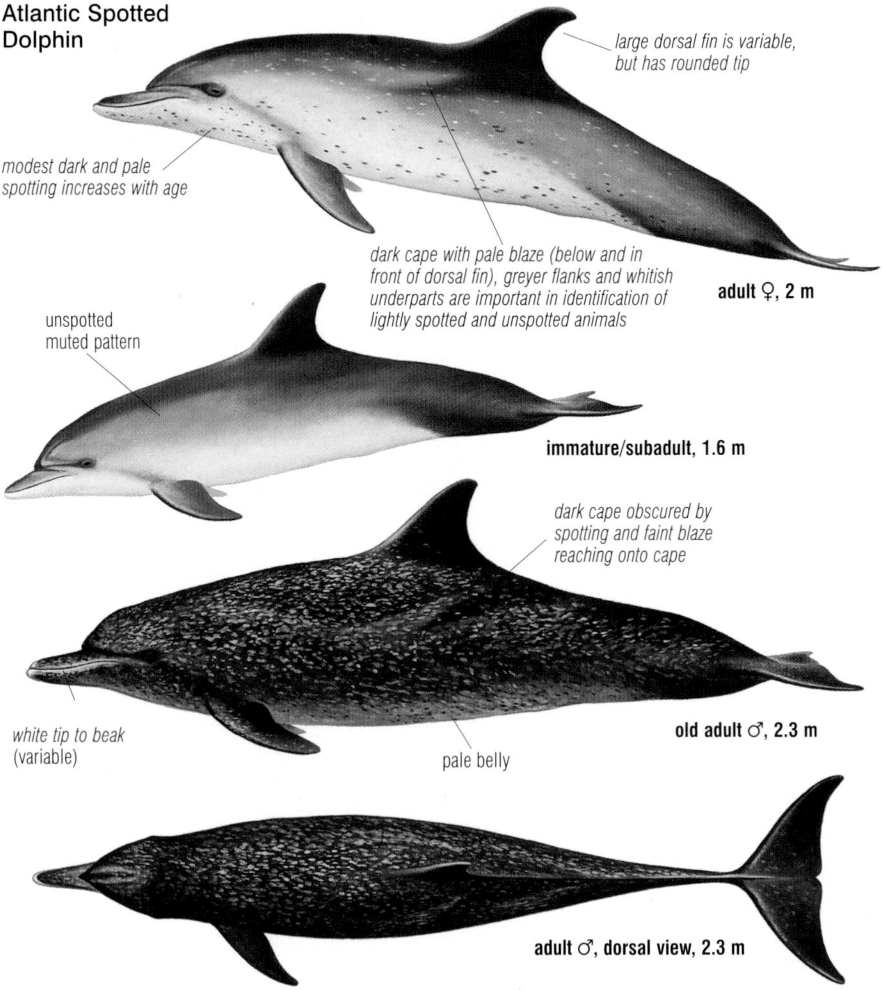

Spotted also averages larger and chunkier with less extensive cape.

Spinner and ***Clymene Dolphins*** (and ***Striped*** and ***common dolphins***) all overlap to some extent with Atlantic Spotted, and if seen poorly could be confused, but differences in overall shape, beak length and coloration usually identify them.

Atlantic Spotted Dolphins: mating has social as well as reproductive value among rampantly promiscuous dolphins; note age-related variation in the amount of spotting.

VARIATION

Age/sex ♂ averages larger. Calf slimmer and

more uniform, without spots. Much variation in pattern and spotting, which progressively increases with age; imm in transition rather slender and partially spotted, but has clearly dark cape, pale grey sides, variable blaze below fin and whiter belly; in some advanced heavily spotted, ads cape margin and spinal blaze obscured. Populations of almost unspotted animals exist, complicating issue. **Physical notes** Full-grown ad 1.6–2.3 m and 100–143 kg. Newborn 0.9–1.1 m. **Taxonomy** Monotypic, but oceanic and coastal populations; former often smaller and has fewer spots, and generally less spotted in E Atlantic.

Atlantic Spotted Dolphins showing age-related variation in amount of spotting; with maturity the cape is largely obliterated but, as in the lower animal, the spotting tends to emphasise the blaze. Spotting is more heavily developed in older ♂♂, which are also darker. Oceanic populations are much less heavily spotted and can look very similar to bottlenose dolphins.

DISTRIBUTION & POPULATION

Widespread in warm-temperate and tropical waters of Atlantic, from Cape Cod (USA) and the Azores south to Rio Grande do Sul (Brazil), Gabon and St Helena. Often in waters 20–250 m deep, but regionally much deeper. At least in Bahamas, strongly resident. Rarely seen mid ocean and only very infrequently, if ever, penetrates Mediterranean. *Population* No overall estimate, although 50,000+ off E USA and a few 1,000s in N Gulf of Mexico.

ECOLOGY

Normally <50 in a group (inshore pods chiefly 5–15), but up to over 200; may segregate by age/sex. Occasionally in mixed schools with Common Bottlenose Dolphins. *Breaching* Frequent, high above surface and seeming to 'hang' in mid-air before crashing down. *Diving* Usually less than 2 min and to 10 m, but up to 6 min and 40–60 m recorded. *Diet* Small fish, cephalopods and deep-water invertebrates, sometimes taken cooperatively. *Reproduction* Sexually mature at 8–15 yrs in ♀♀. Breeding poorly known, but ♀♀ nurse young for 3+ yrs (occasionally 5), and mean inter-calving interval is 3–4 yrs. *Lifespan* Unknown.

Young Atlantic Spotted Dolphin: combination of dark cape with pale spinal blaze, grey flanks and whitish underparts closely recalls Tursiops *species, but note the longer beak.*

Short-beaked oceanic dolphins

Very distinctive oceanic dolphins of the family Delphinidae, some have been classified in the subfamily Delphininae, others in the subfamily Lissodelphinidae, and others are *incertae sedis* within the Delphinidae. All are short-beaked and strongly patterned dolphins, but for the sake of identification they can be grouped by similarity and geographical region. Some species are rather familiar to man, particularly White-beaked Dolphin in the North Sea, Pacific White-sided Dolphin (e.g. off California), Peale's Dolphin (Argentina) and Dusky Dolphin (New Zealand), but Hourglass and Fraser's Dolphins are found in more remote areas, and the latter was only described as recently as 1956. The better-known species are typically acrobatic and strongly social, and are frequently inquisitive and perform demonstrative behaviours around boats. Observers should prepare by familiarising themselves with those species most likely to be seen in a given area, and which are the principal confusion species, e.g. in several parts of the Southern Ocean, Peale's, Hourglass and Dusky Dolphins may occur together. All are very fast-swimming dolphins which often leap clear of the water. It is recommended to focus on the diagnostic marks and not always the overall pattern or impression. In tropical waters, only Fraser's is to be expected. All are rather similar in size and shape, with a short beak and most have a well-developed dorsal fin, making it important to home in on the specific pattern of the body-sides, specifically how the patches, stripes or blazes are connected or disconnected, fin coloration, and possible behavioural differences.

Breaching White-beaked Dolphin (N Atlantic): in its range virtually unmistakable, with massive dorsal fin and distinctively marked sides.

Short-beaked oceanic dolphins

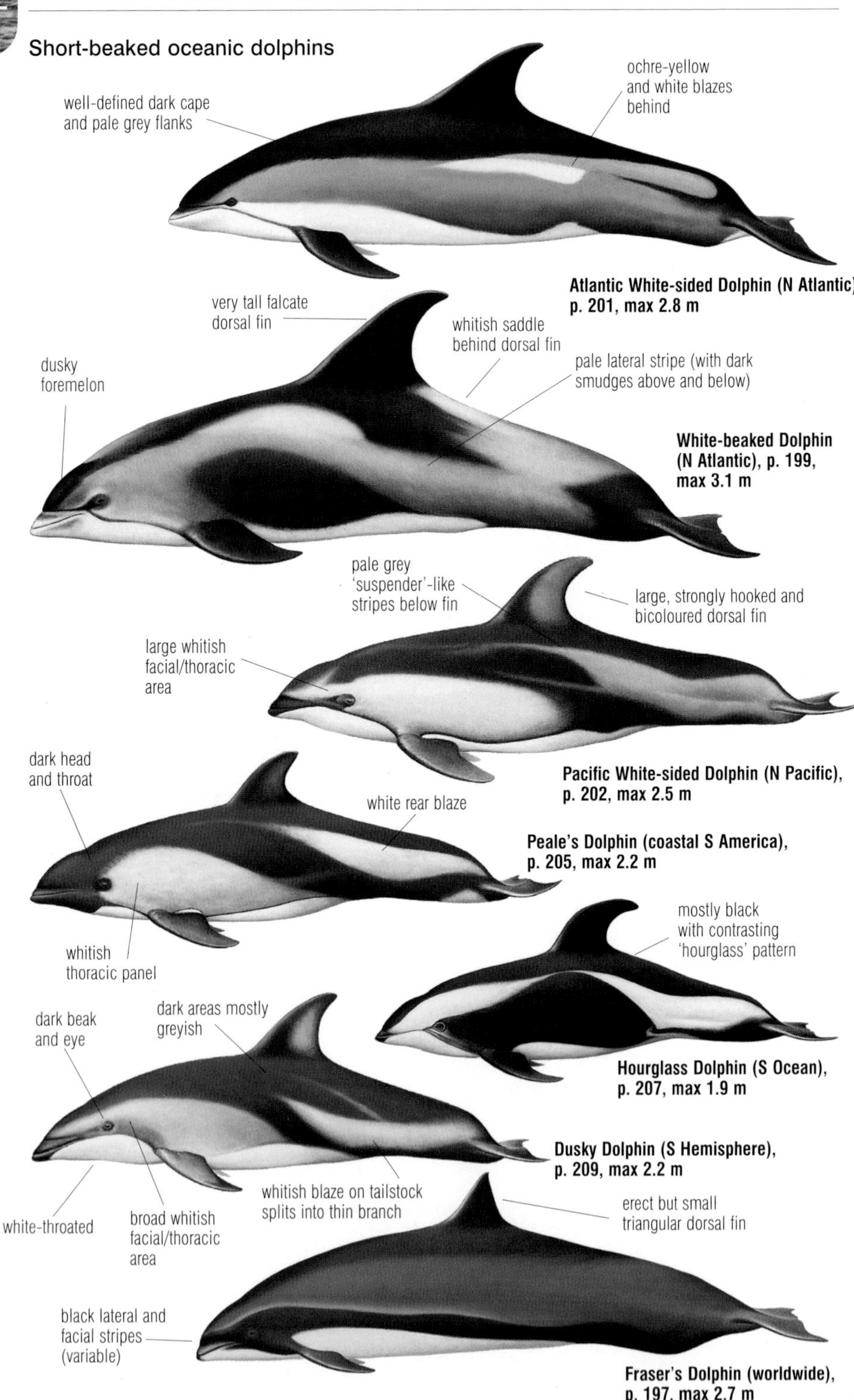

Fraser's Dolphin

Lagenodelphis hosei

Worldwide, warm and tropical waters. Max 2.7 m.

Priority characters on surfacing

- Distinctive, with a stocky body and extremely small appendages. Colour pattern variable, sometimes striking.
- *Dorsal fin proportionately short and triangular* or slightly falcate.
- *Beak short and stubby but well defined.*
- *Dark lateral stripe* from face to anus can be vivid black in some older ads, but is pale grey in young, and is absent in some populations.
- *Facial mask* merges with dark beak–flipper stripe, highly distinctive in ad ♂.
- Dark lateral stripe and *facial markings weaker in ♀ and rarely apparent in young.*
- Blue-grey to dark brownish-grey upperparts (cape indistinct), and paler lower sides and belly. Young duller and, in particular, often have pinkish-tinged bellies.

Typical behaviour at surface

- *Aggressive swimmer, with pods creating much splashing*, and tends to be in large groups of high tens, 100s or even 1,000s.
- Often mixes with other species, e.g. Melon-headed Whales and Short-finned Pilot Whales.
- In some areas shy and difficult to approach and rarely playful, but usually more approachable and even bow-rides.

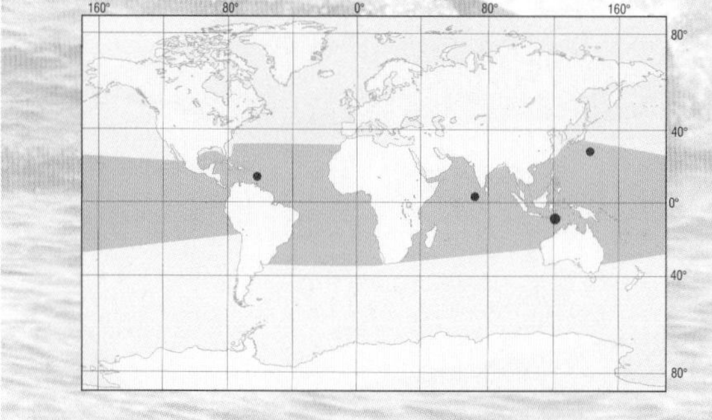

SIMILAR SPECIES

Given good views, Fraser's unique body shape with very short beak and distinctive coloration (at least of some animals in a pod), as well as behaviour, should usually eliminate any confusion. However, ***Common***, ***Bottlenose***, ***Striped*** and ***Whitebelly Spinner Dolphins*** may have a superficially similar body-side stripe, but that in Fraser's is much broader than in any of these species.

VARIATION

Age/sex ♂ generally larger with slightly less falcate fin and better developed post-anal hump. Much individual variation within pods, both age and sex-related, in lateral and beak–flipper stripes and facial markings. Width and intensity of markings generally increase with age. Duller calves have these subdued or almost lacking, the body being pale pinkish-brown and pinkish-white (obscure, ill-defined dusky marks on foreparts), before maturing into ♀-like stage, when develop more striking appearance, but ♀♀ and similar young ♂♂ never attain broad or well-defined dark black markings, nor bluish-grey tinge to skin, as ad ♂♂. **Physical notes** Full-grown ads reach 2.1–2.7 m and 160–210 kg. Newborn *c.*1 m and probably *c.*20 kg. **Taxonomy** Recently described (1956), but not seen alive by Western scientists until the early 1970s. Population in Philippines is genetically distinct from that exploited in Japan.

DISTRIBUTION & POPULATION

Cosmopolitan, principally in deep tropical waters, from 30°N to 30°S, but may occur close to shore where continental shelf particularly narrow, e.g. in

Fraser's Dolphins are often seen in tightknit herds that leave distinct wake. Chunky dolphins with very stubby beak and small dorsal fin and flippers. Front animals adults, probably ♀♀ (well-defined but narrow lateral and beak–flipper stripes, and facial markings); further 3 smaller youngsters (muted markings).

Fraser's Dolphin

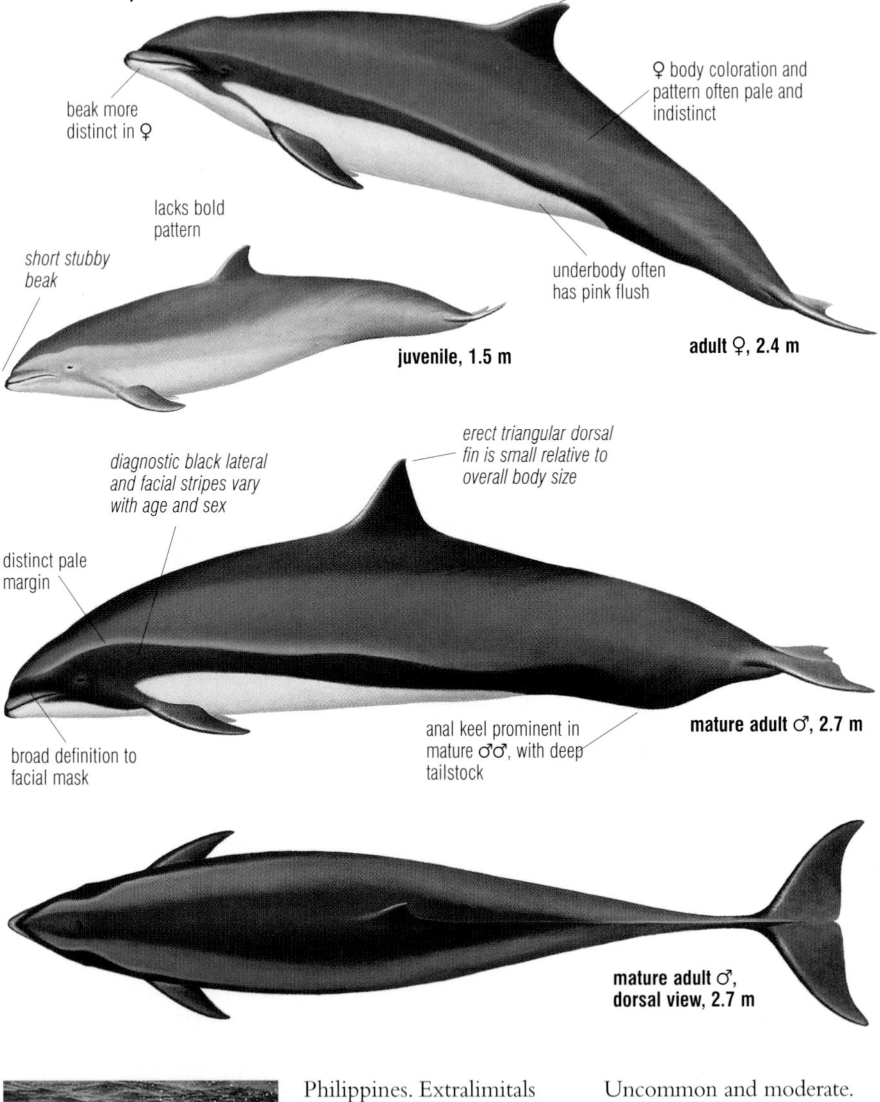

dorsal fin often falcate

♀ body coloration and pattern often pale and indistinct

beak more distinct in ♀

lacks bold pattern

short stubby beak

underbody often has pink flush

juvenile, 1.5 m

adult ♀, 2.4 m

erect triangular dorsal fin is small relative to overall body size

diagnostic black lateral and facial stripes vary with age and sex

distinct pale margin

broad definition to facial mask

anal keel prominent in mature ♂♂, with deep tailstock

mature adult ♂, 2.7 m

mature adult ♂, dorsal view, 2.7 m

Adult ♂ Fraser's Dolphin: broad black lateral and beak–flipper stripes and facial markings; note almost non-existent beak.

Philippines. Extralimitals stranded in S Australia, France, W Scotland and Uruguay. Movements, if any, unknown. *Population* More than 100,000 estimated in E Pacific, but overall numbers unknown.

ECOLOGY

Social organization largely unknown but pods contain mixed ages/sexes. *Breaching* Uncommon and moderate. *Diving* Few data. *Diet* Feeds to 600 m on mesopelagic fish, crustaceans and cephalopods; also feeds at surface with terns. *Reproduction* Sexually mature at 5–10 yrs. Gestation 10–12.5 months, with calving in Japan peaking spring and autumn (summer in S Africa). ♀♀ breed every 2 yrs. *Lifespan* Unknown.

White-beaked Dolphin

Lagenorhynchus albirostris

N Atlantic, temperate to subpolar waters. Max 3.1 m.

Priority characters on surfacing

- *Highly robust*, short-beaked dolphin, with strikingly marked sides and prominent fin.
- *Dorsal fin tall and falcate (especially in ad distinctively hooked), with pointed tip and positioned centrally.*
- Black to dark grey cape sweeps around base of fin, and *pale grey or white area of variable extent on upper flanks in front of fin, and behind fin over back and tailstock.*
- *Diagnostic pale grey-and-white saddle, just behind fin*, broadening at rear around deep tailstock.
- Characteristic stubby, *mostly white beak* (variable), set-off from sloping melon.
- Belly and cheeks white; may show dark beak–flipper stripe.
- *Dark melon enhanced by pale grey and flecked collar* (variable); black flipper.

Typical behaviour at surface

- *Less demonstrative than many small oceanic dolphins* but often fast and powerful, and leaping and breaching frequently recorded.
- Pods of up to 30 not uncommon, sometimes much larger herds. Commonly bow-rides.
- Sometimes associates with rorquals and *forms mixed schools with Atlantic White-sided Dolphins when feeding.*

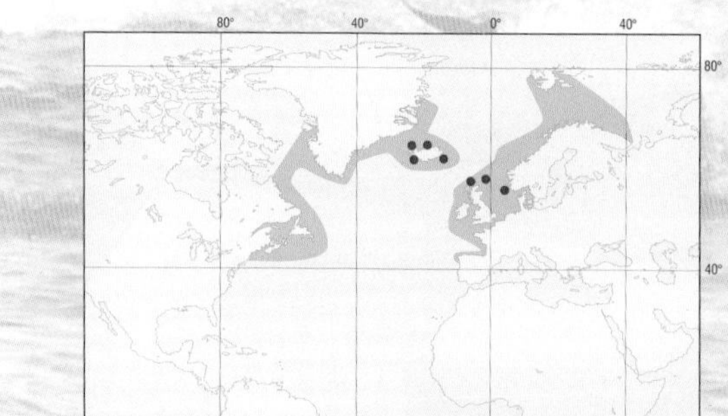

Due to contrasting black-and-white markings and relatively tall dorsal fin, a distant White-beaked Dolphin can resemble a short-finned ***Killer Whale***. Latter much larger, with much taller fin and very different markings and behaviour.

VARIATION

Age/sex ♂ averages larger and has taller fin and thicker tailstock. Calf slimmer and more uniform pale grey above, has narrower, ill-defined whitish-grey upper-flank blaze and saddle, much narrower greyish lateral stripe, and more extensive whitish belly and lower flanks. **Physical notes** Full-grown ad 2.3–3.1 m and 180–354 kg (♀ apparently to max 306 kg). Newborn 1.1–1.2 m and probably *c.*40 kg. **Taxonomy** Lip and beak generally white, particularly in E Atlantic, but may be dark in W Atlantic. A recent molecular phylogeny of the Delphinidae listed the species as *incertae sedis*, hinting that more remains to be understood concerning its relationships, although the analysis was based on a single gene.

SIMILAR SPECIES

Most likely to be confused with ***Atlantic White-sided Dolphin*** (as roughly same size with similarly small beak), but latter lacks white saddle behind dorsal fin and white beak, and flank patterns very different in ads. Observers should bear in mind that some have the white beak partially tinged dirty grey (and Bottlenose can have a white tip to the beak), occasionally extensively darker, and blazes on sides and saddle often vary in width and extent. Calves and young even more similar.

White-beaked Dolphin: short beak (here mostly dark with white tip), dark face, pale lateral stripe (with dark smudges above and below), and whitish saddle behind huge dorsal fin are useful identification features.

White-beaked Dolphin

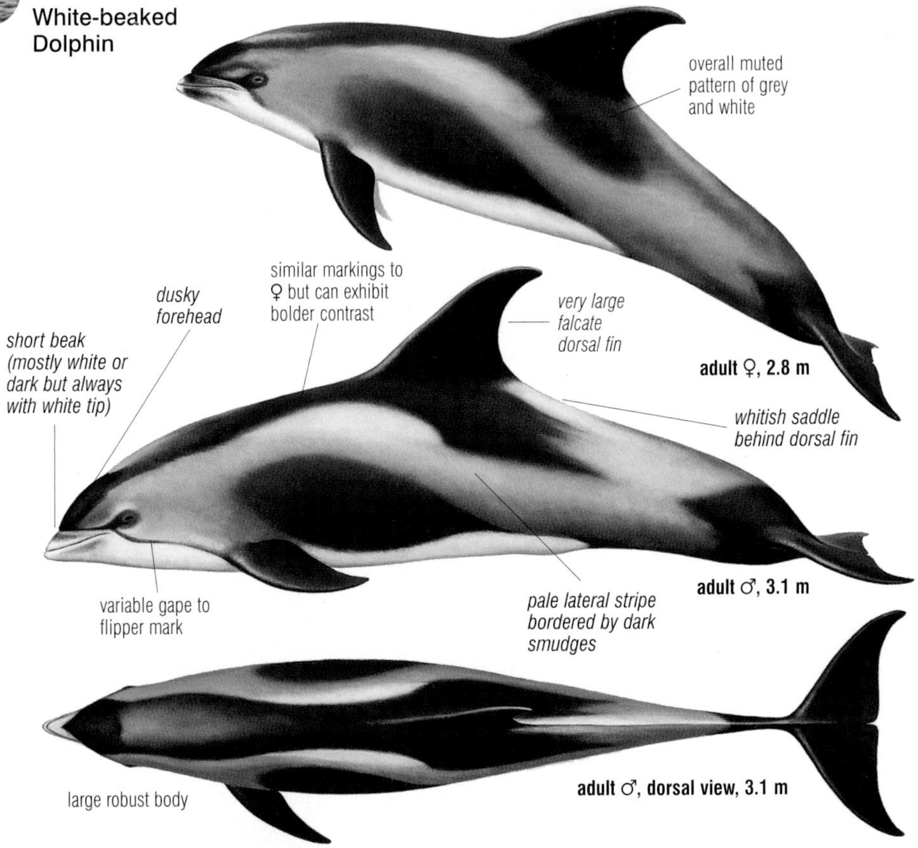

overall muted pattern of grey and white

adult ♀, 2.8 m

short beak (mostly white or dark but always with white tip)

dusky forehead

similar markings to ♀ but can exhibit bolder contrast

very large falcate dorsal fin

whitish saddle behind dorsal fin

variable gape to flipper mark

pale lateral stripe bordered by dark smudges

adult ♂, 3.1 m

large robust body

adult ♂, dorsal view, 3.1 m

White-beaked Dolphin: huge dorsal fin with diagnostic whitish saddle behind.

DISTRIBUTION & POPULATION

Temperate and cold shelf waters of N Atlantic where broadly overlaps Atlantic White-sided Dolphin, though latter mainly occurs in deeper waters. From Cape Cod (USA), Iberia and even the Baltic (irregular and rare) north to Greenland, Svalbard and extreme W Barents Sea. Moves south and offshore in winter with increasing extent of ice, but resident in some seas, e.g. off Britain. *Population* No estimate but overall numbers possibly in the low 100,000s, with most in NE Atlantic.

ECOLOGY

Groups 5–50 but pods of several 100s recorded, exceptionally 1,500. Ads with calves and juvs form separate pods. *Breaching* Quite common: may involve forward or side leaps, occasionally falling backwards. *Diving* Few data. *Diet* Fish, crustaceans and octopus, often taken cooperatively and near seabed. *Reproduction* Sexually mature at 7–12 yrs. Data limited to calving period (mainly May–Aug), and gestation is *c.*11 months. *Lifespan* Unknown.

Atlantic White-sided Dolphin

Lagenorhynchus acutus

N Atlantic temperate/subpolar waters. Max 2.8 m.

Priority characters on surfacing

- Short-beaked dolphin with stocky appearance, prominent dorsal fin and well-marked sides.
- Dorsal fin black, rather tall and strongly sickle-shaped (placed centrally).
- *Very short stubby beak with black upper jaw.*
- Black to dark grey cape reaches upper sides, contrasting with *broad grey lateral flank stripe.*
- *Diagnostic, long white, then ochre, blaze, almost to tailstock,* usually visible if porpoising or bow-riding.
- Contrasting whitish lower jaw, throat and belly to genital region.
- Dark eye-patch, beak–eye and face–flipper stripes (hard to see on fast-moving or distant dolphins).

Typical behaviour at surface

- *Less demonstrative than many oceanic dolphins; rather shy and only infrequently bow-rides.*
- Fast swimmer and may breach and lobtail.
- Pods normally large, involving tens or low hundreds of animals.
- *Sometimes associates with White-beaked Dolphins,* and occasionally with rorquals.

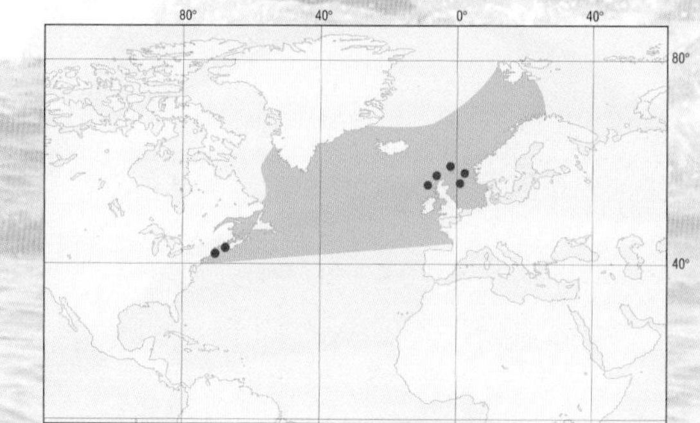

VARIATION

Age/sex ♂ averages larger and has deeper tailstock. Calf slimmer and more uniform. **Physical notes** Full-grown ad 1.9–2.8 m (max for ♂ 2.8 m and ♀ 2.5 m) and 165–230 kg. Newborn 1.1–1.2 m and probably weighs 20–35 kg. **Taxonomy** A recent molecular phylogeny of the Delphinidae listed the species as *incertae sedis*, hinting that more remains to be understood concerning its relationships, although the analysis was based on a single gene.

DISTRIBUTION & POPULATION

Temperate and cold waters of N Atlantic from N Carolina to W Greenland, and Bay of Biscay to Svalbard. Occasional further south, even to the Azores, and almost reaches Baltic. Prefers deep-slope continental shelf and canyon waters. Some move to higher latitudes in summer, and also moves inshore at this season. Off N America, numbers in south of range notably increase in winter/spring. *Population* No

SIMILAR SPECIES

Most likely to be confused with heavier ***White-beaked Dolphin***, but they are readily distinguished by coloration differences, especially latter's huge flank patches, white saddle behind fin and, usually, mostly white beak. Range to lesser extent overlaps with other species in N Atlantic, including ***Short-beaked Common Dolphin***, but given good views easily separated by size, shape, beak length and coloration.

Atlantic White-sided Dolphins: note diagnostic white and ochre blazes on sides; black back behind dorsal fin permits separation from White-beaked when low in water.

overall estimate, but at least 42,000 off N America.

ECOLOGY

Groups typically 30–150 with larger aggregations of up to 500 not uncommon, particularly at favoured food sources or on migration. Social structure largely unknown but some segregation by age/sex noted. Often associates with Fin and Humpback Whales in Gulf of Maine, and forms mixed schools with White-beaked Dolphin off W Europe. *Breaching* Frequent, leaping well clear of surface. *Diving* Surfaces to breathe every 10–15 sec, with max dive 4 min. *Diet* Wide variety of fish, also squid; feeds cooperatively on fish near surface. *Reproduction* Sexually mature at 6–12 yrs. Peak calving May–Aug in NE Atlantic but perhaps more prolonged in west. Gestation *c.*11 months. Calves weaned at 18 months. Probably breeds every 2 yrs, although ♀♀ that were both lactating and pregnant have been noted. *Lifespan* Up to 27 yrs.

Atlantic White-sided Dolphin

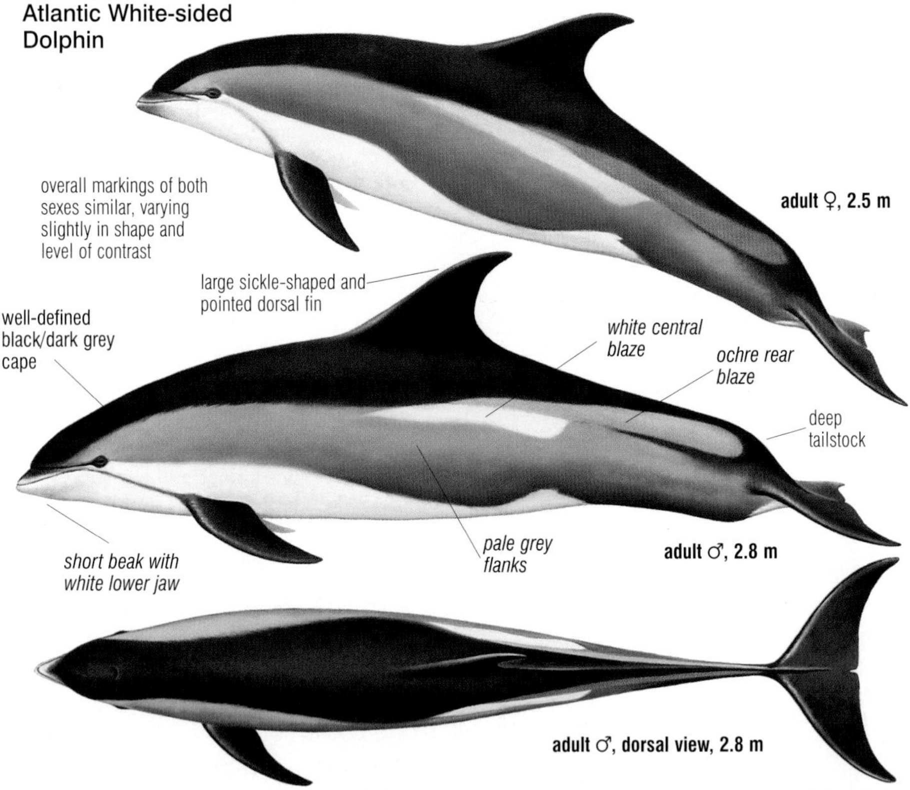

overall markings of both sexes similar, varying slightly in shape and level of contrast

adult ♀, 2.5 m

large sickle-shaped and pointed dorsal fin

well-defined black/dark grey cape

white central blaze

ochre rear blaze

deep tailstock

short beak with white lower jaw

pale grey flanks

adult ♂, 2.8 m

adult ♂, dorsal view, 2.8 m

SIMILAR SPECIES

Most likely to be confused with the ***common dolphins*** as all have a thoracic patch and habitually occur in large schools, but only at long range as they are readily differentiated by coloration, shape and size of beak and shape of dorsal fin (e.g. common dolphins have

Pacific White-sided Dolphin

Lagenorhynchus obliquidens

Temperate/subpolar waters of N Pacific. Max 2.5 m.

Priority characters on surfacing

- Beakless, robust appearance, with prominent dorsal fin and well-marked sides, unique within N Pacific range.
- *Dorsal fin diagnostically tall, recurved and strikingly bicoloured* with at least rear ½ pale (placed centrally), and older ads may have the fin distinctively lobed (appears hooked).

- Very short stubby beak with blackish lips.
- *Black to dark grey, and (usually even blacker) broad lateral fields* bordered below by *conspicuous whitish-grey thoracic patch*.
- *Narrow pale grey 'suspender'-like stripes* separate dark of cape/lateral fields, and sweep down from head and broaden into *pale tailstock panel*.
- Top of snout/narrow forehead pale (distinctive head-on) and merge with thoracic patch; contrasting whitish lower jaw, throat and belly to genital region.
- Large flippers with slightly rounded tips and, like dorsal fin, dark at front edge.
- Narrow dark eye-patch and face–flipper–anus stripes (hard to see on a fast-moving or distant dolphin).

Typical behaviour at surface

- Frequently in groups of tens (very large herds of 100s or even 1,000s not uncommon).
- Fast active swimmer, often acrobatic and playful, leaping, flipping or somersaulting, landing on belly or sides with large splash and also backward-leaning.
- Tends to approach boats, commonly bow-riding.
- Sometimes associates with other cetaceans, e.g. Northern Right Whale and Risso's Dolphins and large rorquals.

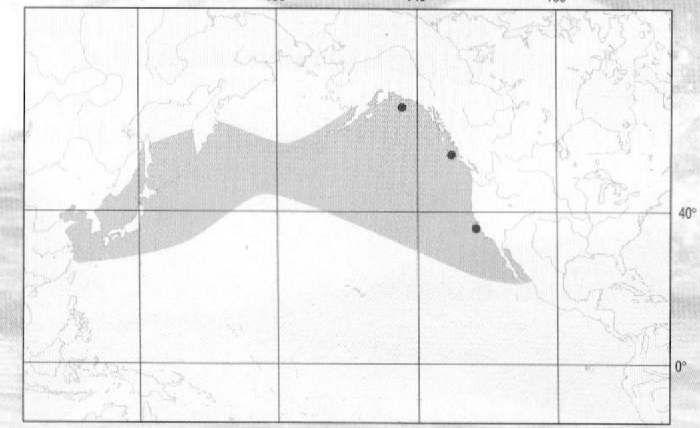

pronounced beak and V-shaped saddle below fin). Also overlaps with ***Dall's Porpoise***, but latter has different fin shape (smaller and triangular), and different overall structure and pattern on body-sides, as well as behaviour.

VARIATION

Age/sex ♂ averages larger and has deeper tailstock. Calf slimmer and less contrastingly patterned, fin slightly more triangular and tailstock indistinctly keeled. **Physical notes** Full-grown ad 1.7–2.5 m and 85–181 kg. Newborn 0.8–1.2 m and probably weighs *c.*15 kg. **Other data** Fin shape varies considerably in height and degree of curvature, and is often more rounded than pointed; pigmentation also varies, especially pattern on body-sides. **Taxonomy** Monotypic though 2–3 populations distinguished in NE Pacific. Recent mtDNA studies indicate species is better placed in *Sagmatias*.

Highly sociable and acrobatic Pacific White-sided Dolphins: note very stubby beak, obvious whitish-grey thoracic patch and narrow whitish forehead (distinctive head-on).

Pacific White-sided Dolphin

slight variation in dorsal fin

both sexes can exhibit muted pattern

very short beak

adult ♀, 2.2 m

typically has large pale grey thoracic patch reaching over eyes

very large, strongly hooked and bicolored dorsal fin

medium grey tailstock

adult ♂, 2.5 m

prominent white throat

pale grey 'suspender'-like stripes

adult ♂, dorsal view, 2.5 m

stocky and robust body

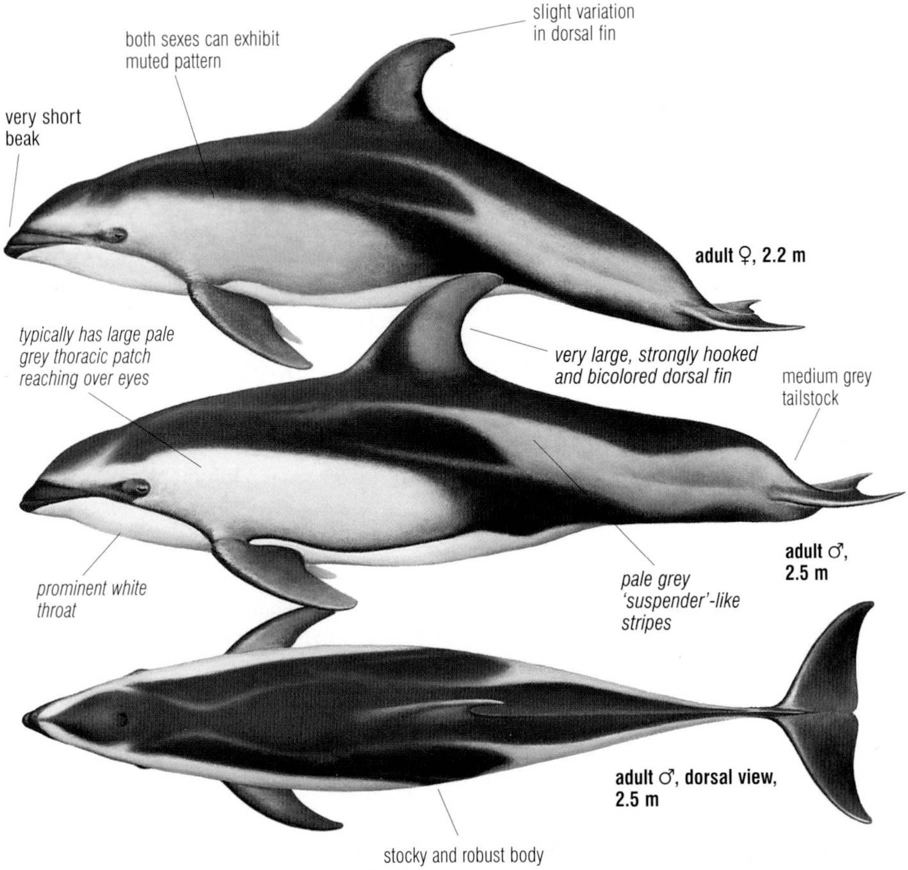

DISTRIBUTION & POPULATION

Temperate and cold waters of N Pacific, from S Bering Sea and S Sea of Okhotsk south to the Gulf of California (Mexico) and Taiwan. Prefers continental shelf waters at least seasonally. Some move to lower latitudes in winter (Nov–Apr) and, in British Columbia (Canada), at least, to inshore waters at same season. *Population* No overall estimate. Perhaps 26,000 off California, Oregon and Washington in 1990s.

ECOLOGY

Highly gregarious with social structure poorly known.

Pacific White-sided Dolphin, showing hooked and strikingly bicoloured dorsal fin; narrow pale grey 'suspender'-like stripes and contrasting thoracic patch; an avid bow-rider.

Small groups of ♂♂ form long-lasting associations. Wide variety of aerial behaviours. Feeds cooperatively on fish near surface, such frenzies often attracting seabirds. *Breaching* Frequent, leaping well clear of surface (see box). *Diving* No data. *Diet* Small schooling fish inshore, and cephalopods (mainly squid) and mesopelagic fish in deep water. *Reproduction* Sexually mature at 7–10 yrs. Peak calving Apr–Aug. Gestation 10–12 months. Calves weaned at 6 months. Probably breeds every 2–3 yrs. *Lifespan* 46+ yrs.

Pacific White-sided Dolphins: note stubby beak typical of the genus, large hooked dorsal fin and complex patterns on side (diagnostic).

Peale's Dolphin

Lagenorhynchus australis

Coastal S America. Max 2.2 m.

Priority characters on surfacing

- Medium-sized, *beakless coastal dolphin with robust body.*
- Tall facate dorsal fin (indistinctly 2-toned with paler greyish trailing edge).
- Very short, somewhat pointed beak grades into gently sloping forehead.
- Dark grey or black face and back contrast with *conspicuous whitish-grey thoracic patch* from eye to mid body, and *rear blaze reaching to tailstock.*
- *Dark on face usually ends abruptly at chin*, and varies on beak; paler or darker eye-patch may be apparent in close views.
- Whiter chest/abdomen (perhaps bordered above by variable dark lower-flank stripe).
- On some a narrow longitudinal streak reaches back from above eyes.
- Shiny white patch at upper base of flippers (difficult to see).

Typical behaviour at surface

- *Usually in small groups.*
- Often swims slowly, with usually only blowhole and small part of back exposed, but also capable of long, low leaps, interspersed with acrobatic higher jumps.
- Bow-rides; infrequently spyhops and breaches.
- Not always easy to appreciate distinctive pattern on side.

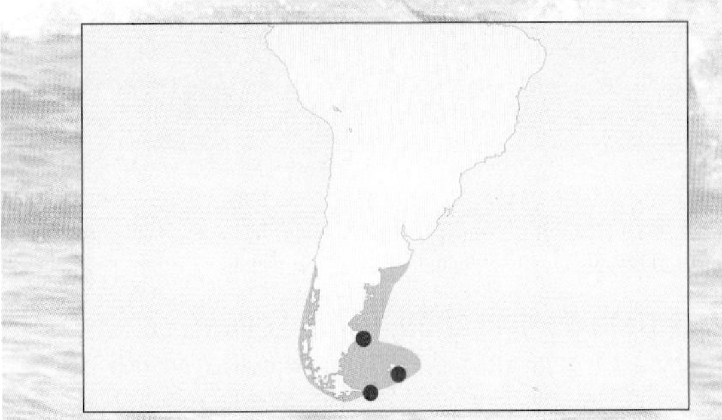

Breaching Peale's Dolphin: tall, falcate dorsal fin, and blackish face, throat and back contrast with white thoracic patch and rear blaze on tailstock.

SIMILAR SPECIES

Peale's shares range and, to some degree, shape, behaviour and coloration with ***Hourglass Dolphin*** (but latter more offshore, and distinguished by 2 conspicuous white patches on flanks) and, especially, ***Dusky Dolphin***. From latter, close views sometimes required to observe all-dark foreface (paler/open face with dark beak–eyestripe of Dusky) and overall blacker/darker appearance of Peale's. Additionally, variable, black stripe/border below thoracic patch and small, shiny white, oval-shaped patch at base of

Peale's Dolphin

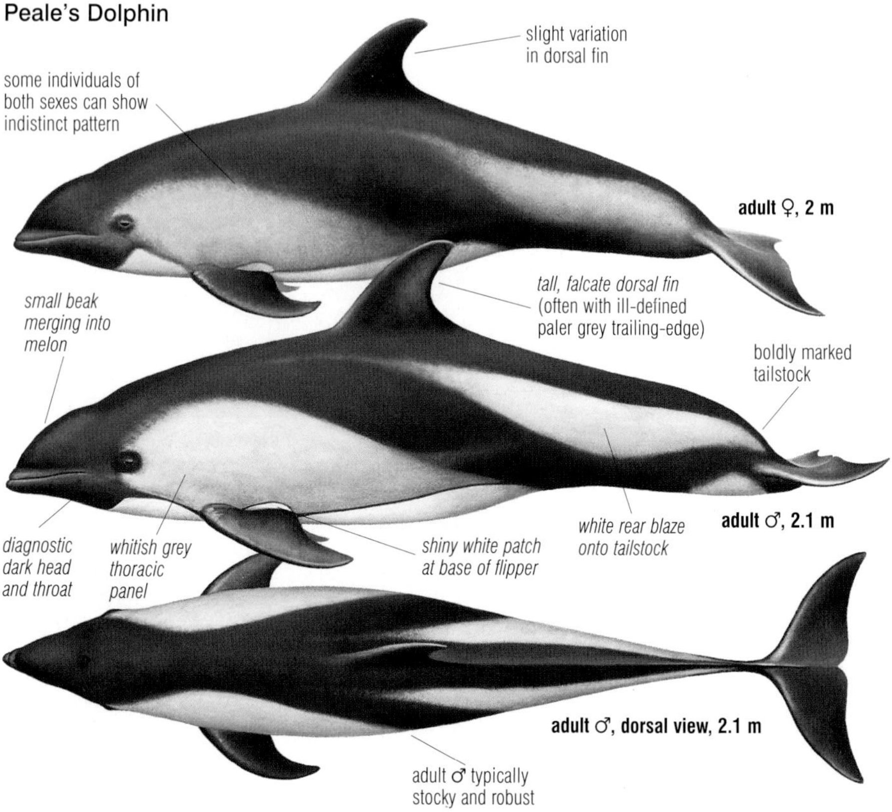

slight variation in dorsal fin

some individuals of both sexes can show indistinct pattern

adult ♀, 2 m

small beak merging into melon

tall, falcate dorsal fin (often with ill-defined paler grey trailing-edge)

boldly marked tailstock

diagnostic dark head and throat

whitish grey thoracic panel

shiny white patch at base of flipper

white rear blaze onto tailstock

adult ♂, 2.1 m

adult ♂, dorsal view, 2.1 m

adult ♂ typically stocky and robust

darker flippers are features of Peale's, but difficult to see. They also slightly differ in shape (e.g. thicker head and overall heavier appearance in Peale's) and behaviour (smaller, less-agile pods usually a feature of Peale's).

Peale's Dolphins are usually more coastal than their congeners: note blackish head (ending abruptly on chin), white thoracic panel and rear blaze on tailstock.

VARIATION

Age/sex ♂ averages larger. Young separable by size and are overall paler grey with less-distinct boundary between thoracic and flank patches. Flippers of older animals may have knobs on leading edge. **Physical notes** 1.3–2.2 m and 100–115 kg. Newborn *c.*1 m. **Taxonomy** Recent mtDNA studies indicate that it should be placed in the genus *Sagmatias*.

DISTRIBUTION & POPULATION

Restricted to near-shore, usually shallow, waters of southern S America, often at entrance to fjords, mainly south of 40°S and regular off the Falklands, reaching at least

59°S in Drake Passage. Exceptionally, north to 33°S in Pacific and 38°S in Atlantic. Probably largely resident though some may move inshore in austral summer, and sightings of animals similar to (or this) species recently made off Cook Is in Pacific. *Population* No estimates.

ECOLOGY

Typical group size 2–20 but may form temporary schools of 30–100 in summer/autumn. Often associates with Commerson's Dolphin and, less regularly, other dolphins. Head-slapping observed. *Breaching* Partial single spins. *Diving* Up to 2.5 min (typically less than 30 sec) with 3 short dives usually followed by longer period underwater. *Diet* Small cephalopods, crustaceans and bottom-dwelling fish. Regularly feeds in kelp zone and may cooperatively herd small fish. *Reproduction* Calving may last Oct–Apr. *Lifespan* Unknown.

Hourglass Dolphin

Lagenorhynchus cruciger

Southern Ocean. Max 1.9 m.

Priority characters on surfacing

- Small oceanic dolphin, strikingly patterned black and white.
- *Tall, markedly hooked dorsal fin* (positioned centrally).
- Beak extremely short and stubby, and mostly black.
- *White 'hourglass'* divides blackish upperbody from long flank stripe to eye.
- White fore blaze broadest above flippers, passing above eye to cover head-sides (merging with white of throat/chest between eye and beak).
- Posterior white blaze covers tail-stock, tapering towards dorsal fin.

Typical behaviour at surface

- Normally in small groups, larger herds infrequent.
- Typically fast swimmer with long low leaps. *Often travels very close to surface with only dorsal breaking surface, raising a splash in front.*
- Enthusiastic bow-riders, often leaping as they race towards the bow or stern.
- Sometimes associates with other cetaceans, especially Long-finned Pilot Whale.

SIMILAR SPECIES

Body pattern and surfacing behaviour make it usually unmistakable, and within range superficially only resembles ***Dusky*** or ***Peale's Dolphins***, but, as name suggests, body pattern differs strikingly. Hourglass has a tall, sometimes strongly hooked, all-dark dorsal fin and is the only small oceanic dolphin with such a fin in southern polar waters.

VARIATION

Age/sex Perhaps partially differ by coloration and overall size, but difficult to appreciate at sea. Ad ♂ has much larger, more lobed dorsal fin than ♀ which has a smaller, more pointed fin. Fins seen on some individuals probably develop at onset of physical maturity. **Physical notes** 1.42–1.87 m and 73.5–120 kg. Newborn <1.1 m. **Taxonomy** Recent mtDNA studies indicate that it should perhaps be placed in genus *Sagmatias*, although more data are required.

DISTRIBUTION & POPULATION

Cold-water, circumpolar oceanic species, most frequent in subantarctic and Antarctic seas at 45°S–68°S, though recorded north to 33°S off Chile. Sightings least frequent in S Atlantic, at 0–40°W, and S Pacific, at 80–150°W. Probably makes seasonal movements, north in winter and south in summer. *Population* A total of 144,300 south of Antarctic Convergence in summer in early 1990s.

Hourglass Dolphins: note striking pattern formed by fore and rear white blazes; ♂♂ (left animals) have larger, more hooked dorsal fin compared to ♀ (at right).

ECOLOGY

Groups usually 4–8 but occasionally 60–100. May accompany larger cetaceans including baleen whales, e.g. Fin Whales. *Breaching* Often high above surface. *Diving* No data. *Diet* Small fish, small squid and crustaceans. Often feeds amongst large flocks of seabirds and in plankton slicks. *Reproduction* Unknown but calves seen Jan–Feb. *Lifespan* Unknown.

Hourglass Dolphin

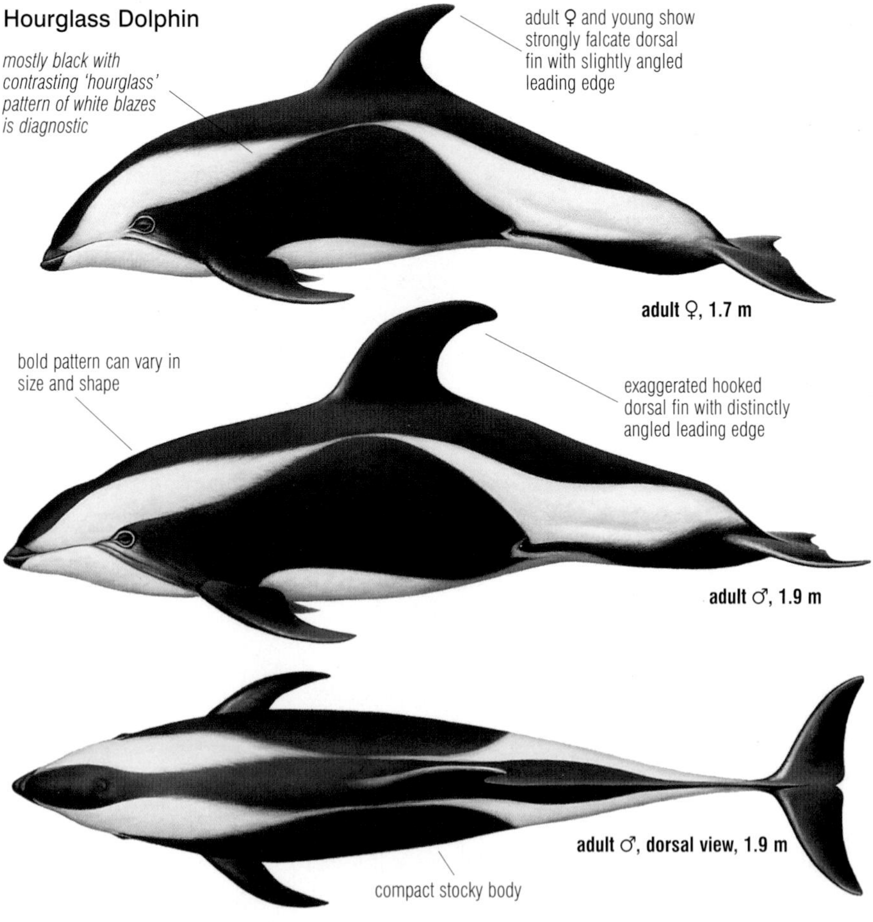

mostly black with contrasting 'hourglass' pattern of white blazes is diagnostic

adult ♀ and young show strongly falcate dorsal fin with slightly angled leading edge

adult ♀, 1.7 m

bold pattern can vary in size and shape

exaggerated hooked dorsal fin with distinctly angled leading edge

adult ♂, 1.9 m

adult ♂, dorsal view, 1.9 m

compact stocky body

Dusky Dolphin

Lagenorhynchus obscurus

S Hemisphere. Max 2.2 m.

Priority characters on surfacing

- Medium-sized, compact dolphin, virtually beakless with distinctive coloration and fin.
- *Tall, moderately falcate and pointed dorsal fin, characteristically 2-toned* (with variable paler trailing edge).
- *Pale-faced appearance* with forehead gently sloping into short, blunt, dark-tipped beak.
- Bluish-black to dark grey dorsally, with *dark band across rear flanks from below dorsal fin to tailstock*.
- Prominent *whitish blaze on sides of tailstock*, which visibly branches into *pale greyish stripes near base of dorsal fin*.
- White below and *whitish-grey thoracic patch on lower foresides*, encompassing face and head-sides, and tapering towards belly.
- Dark eye-patch and eye–flipper stripe often apparent.

Typical behaviour at surface

- *Highly gregarious, usually in groups of 15–500*, but sometimes even larger herds.
- Fast active swimmer; *highly acrobatic with high jumps and twists*, and may leap several dozen times, with entire group following first to breach.
- Inquisitive around boats and frequently bow-rides.
- May associate with other cetaceans as well as seabirds.

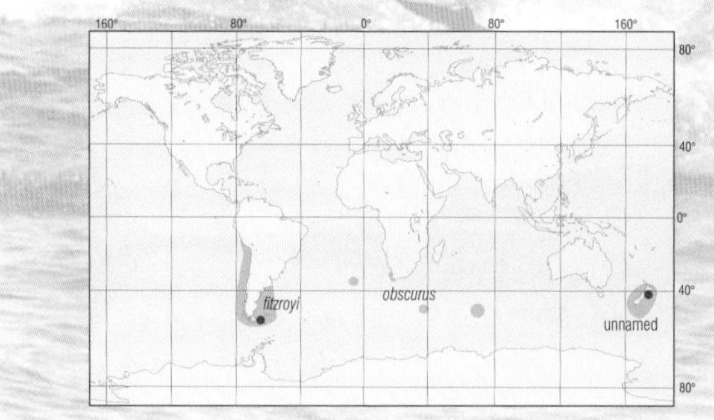

Taxonomy Polytypic: *L. o. fitzroyi* in S American waters and *L. o. obscurus* off S Africa, with an unnamed form in New Zealand, vary in size and weight; those off S America apparently largest. Sometimes considered conspecific with Pacific White-sided Dolphin, but ecological and biological parameters, and mtDNA studies, indicate species status is warranted, and molecular evidence suggests that the species should be placed in genus *Sagmatias*.

DISTRIBUTION & POPULATION

Three disjunct populations: off New Zealand, Chatham, Auckland and Campbell; SW Africa, the Prince Edwards and Amsterdam (doubtfully Kerguelen and Crozet); and S America north to Peru and N Argentina, including the Falklands. Records from Gough (S Atlantic) not identified to subspecies, and sporadic reports from S Australia and Tasmania recently verified. Some populations appear to undertake seasonal

SIMILAR SPECIES

Within range only resembles larger and more robust Peale's Dolphin, but latter has dark face and throat, and only a single whitish flank stripe, and is less demonstrative and gregarious. Less likely to be confused with Hourglass Dolphin.

VARIATION

Age/sex ♂ averages larger. Calf slimmer and paler. **Physical notes** 1.5–2.2 m and 69–90 kg. Newborn 0.55–0.91 m and 3–10 kg.

Dusky Dolphins (off Kaikoura, New Zealand): pale-faced appearance with broad thoracic area, dark eye and beak tip; whitish blaze on tailstock, with thinner divide near dorsal fin.

Dusky Dolphin

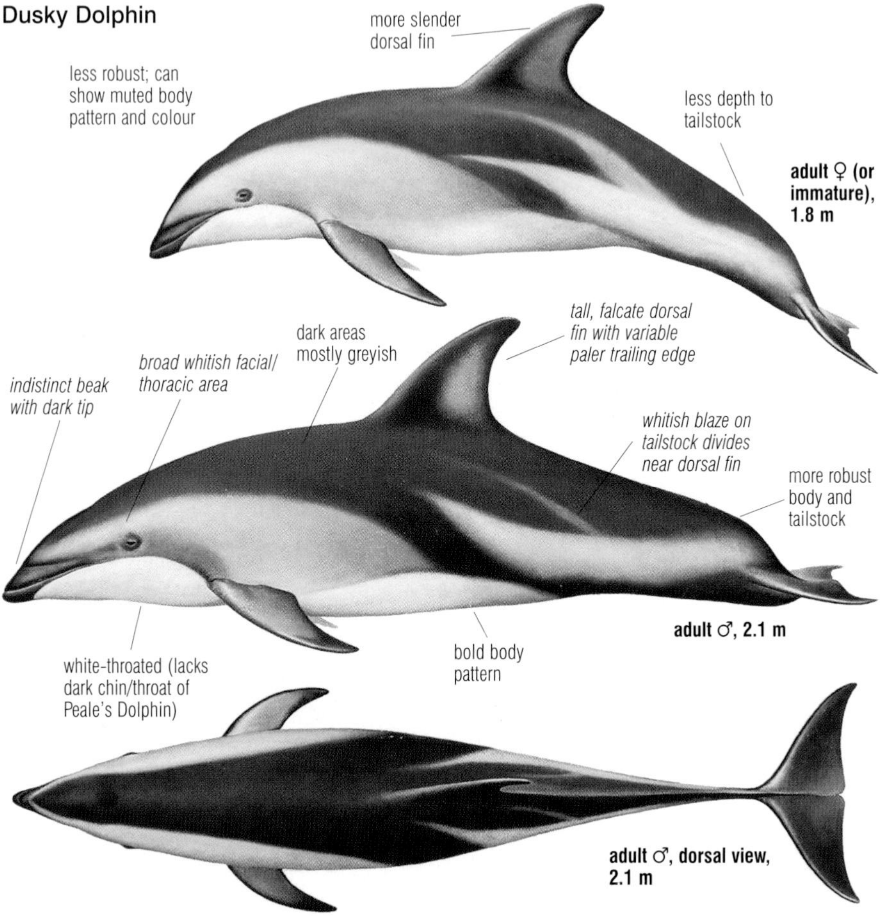

more slender dorsal fin

less robust; can show muted body pattern and colour

less depth to tailstock

adult ♀ (or immature), 1.8 m

tall, falcate dorsal fin with variable paler trailing edge

dark areas mostly greyish

broad whitish facial/ thoracic area

indistinct beak with dark tip

whitish blaze on tailstock divides near dorsal fin

more robust body and tailstock

adult ♂, 2.1 m

white-throated (lacks dark chin/throat of Peale's Dolphin)

bold body pattern

adult ♂, dorsal view, 2.1 m

Dusky Dolphins: note virtually beakless appearance, large dorsal fin with paler trailing edge and pattern on sides.

Dusky Dolphins often form large tightknit herds, here in impressive formation off Kaikoura (New Zealand).

movements of up to 780 km, generally south in summer and north in winter, but others chiefly resident (e.g. off Argentina). *Population* No overall estimates but at least 7,000 off C Patagonia alone in mid 1990s.

ECOLOGY

Typical group 6–20 in winter, but in rich coastal waters 100s or even 1,000s may aggregate in summer, or winter off New Zealand. May consort with other dolphins, e.g. Southern Right Whale Dolphin, and pilot whales. *Breaching* In arc-shaped leaps returning head-first, slamming body against surface; or by high somersaults (tumbling in air). Other surface-signals frequent. *Diving* Frequently to at least 150 m. *Diet* Small fish, squid, krill and other crustaceans, often taken cooperatively. *Reproduction* Sexual maturity apparently varies regionally, from 4–6 to 7–10 yrs. Calves born midwinter (mainly Aug–Oct off Peru and Nov–Feb off New Zealand); in Argentina summer is prime birth season. Gestation 11–13 months and young may be nursed 12–18 months. Inter-calving interval 2–3 yrs. *Lifespan* Up to 36 yrs.

Bow-riding Dusky Dolphins can be highly acrobatic: race fitzroyi, *off Peru.*

Cephalorhynchus dolphins

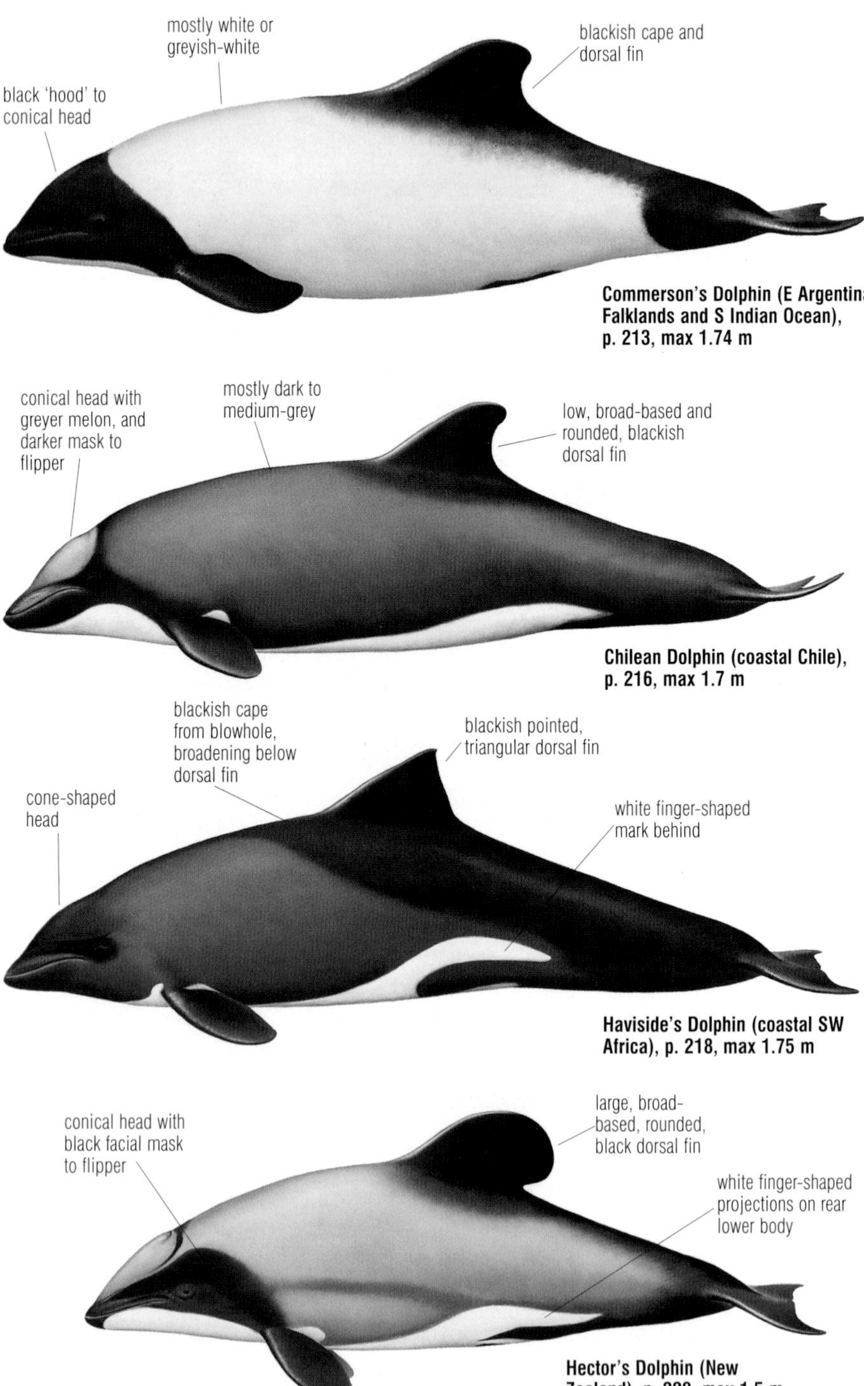

Commerson's Dolphin (E Argentina, Falklands and S Indian Ocean), p. 213, max 1.74 m

Chilean Dolphin (coastal Chile), p. 216, max 1.7 m

Haviside's Dolphin (coastal SW Africa), p. 218, max 1.75 m

Hector's Dolphin (New Zealand), p. 220, max 1.5 m

Cephalorhynchus dolphins

This group of dolphins is essentially restricted to coastal waters of the S Hemisphere (at temperate latitudes), and forms a subfamily, Cephalorhynchinae (although one molecular phylogeny places them in the subfamily Lissodelphininae). All are very small, dumpy and short-beaked, and most have a rounded dorsal fin with a long base and are rather strongly patterned. They are also mostly isolated geographically from each other, and thus unlikely to be confused. The genus *Cephalorhynchus* is a rather poorly known group; only the New Zealand species has been subject to particularly intensive study, largely due to its unfavourable conservation status and the greater number of cetacean specialists working in the country. Whilst Hector's Dolphin is probably the most threatened of the species, all have been hunted for both food and bait. Although poorly known, all are inquisitive and attracted to boats, except Chilean Dolphin.

Commerson's Dolphin

Cephalorhynchus commersonii

Local off E Argentina, Falklands and in S Indian Ocean.
Max 1.74 m.

Priority characters on surfacing

- Unmistakable, stocky and strikingly black-and-white delphinid. Chiefly coastal waters.
- *Largely white, except mainly black face and narrow cape*, which extends on rear 1/3 of body from dorsal fin to flukes.
- *Dorsal fin large, though rather low and rises at shallow angle, usually rounded.*
- *Conical blunt head* with gently sloping forehead and little or no beak.
- Black face connected to flippers by broad black band, which reaches onto chest.
- Isolated white throat and black patch on white belly (latter varies with age/sex).
- Tail flukes slightly notched and round-tipped, and flippers small and rounded.
- Distinct age-/sex-related and geographical variation in purity of white and black pattern.

Typical behaviour at surface

- Resembles a porpoise but is a *true dolphin in action and behaviour*, making coloration far more striking. Fast active swimmer, frequently bow-rides, swimming upside-down or spinning underwater, and breaches or leaps, even surfing on inshore waves.
- Small groups are the norm.

Commerson's Dolphins (Falklands), adult in foreground and (greyer) young behind.

DISTINCTIVE POPULATIONS

Two disjunct populations, off South America and the Falklands, and around Kerguelen archipelago, S. Indian Ocean.

SW Atlantic Described in box.

Kerguelen Markedly larger

and white areas variably tinged greyer (and some ads resemble young of Atlantic population), except central belly, which is purer white. Black of face and dorsal area usually more extensive and somewhat less clearly demarcated, whilst white throat more asymmetric and restricted. The black, so-called 'widow's peak', behind the blowhole is more poorly

Adult Commerson's Dolphin (Kerguelen, S Indian Ocean): larger than S American animals with greyer tinge to body (but much variation) and black areas usually more extensive and/or less clearly demarcated.

defined or lacking. Beak better defined and flippers more tapered.

SIMILAR SPECIES

Coloration wholly distinctive given a reasonable view but in poor light could be confused with ***Spectacled Porpoise***, although dorsal fin shape and coloration differences should be readily apparent. Could also be confused with ***Chilean Dolphin***, but latter mostly dark grey.

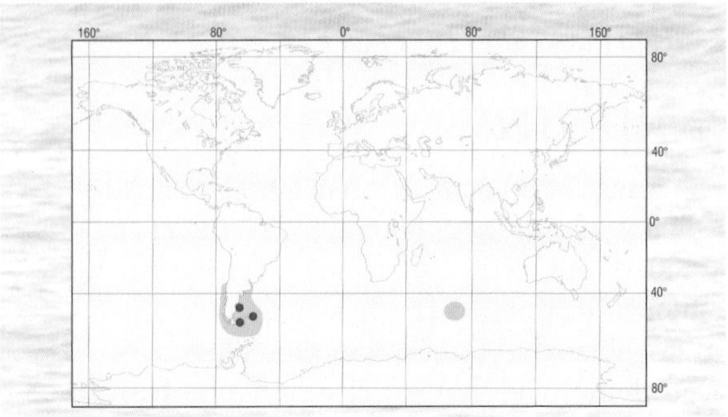

VARIATION

Age/sex ♂ smaller by 5–10%. Shape of ragged, black central belly patch varies, being more oval in ♂ and U-shaped in ♀. Imm smaller and intermediate between ad and calf, chiefly whitish-grey, black and brown. Calf distinctive, being initially all brown with muted pattern. With age, black areas as ad but less sharply defined, with brownish-grey and black marks merging into largely whitish-grey body. **Physical notes** Full-grown ad 1.2–1.74 m and 35–86 kg (off South America to 1.5 m and 66 kg; off Kerguelen 1.74 m and 86 kg). Newborn 0.55–0.75 m and 4.5–7 kg. **Other data** Black 'widow's peak' smudge behind blowhole and pigmentation on tailstock individually unique (SW Atlantic population). **Taxonomy** Monotypic, but 2 disjunct populations: that around Kerguelens geographically isolated with skeletal and genetic differences, and may deserve separate taxonomic status. No data concerning the recently discovered population around Heard.

DISTRIBUTION & POPULATION

Cold, shallow temperate waters of extreme southern S America (north to 34°S in Argentina and 50°S

Commerson's Dolphins (Argentina): usually in small groups and approachable in coastal waters.

Commerson's Dolphin

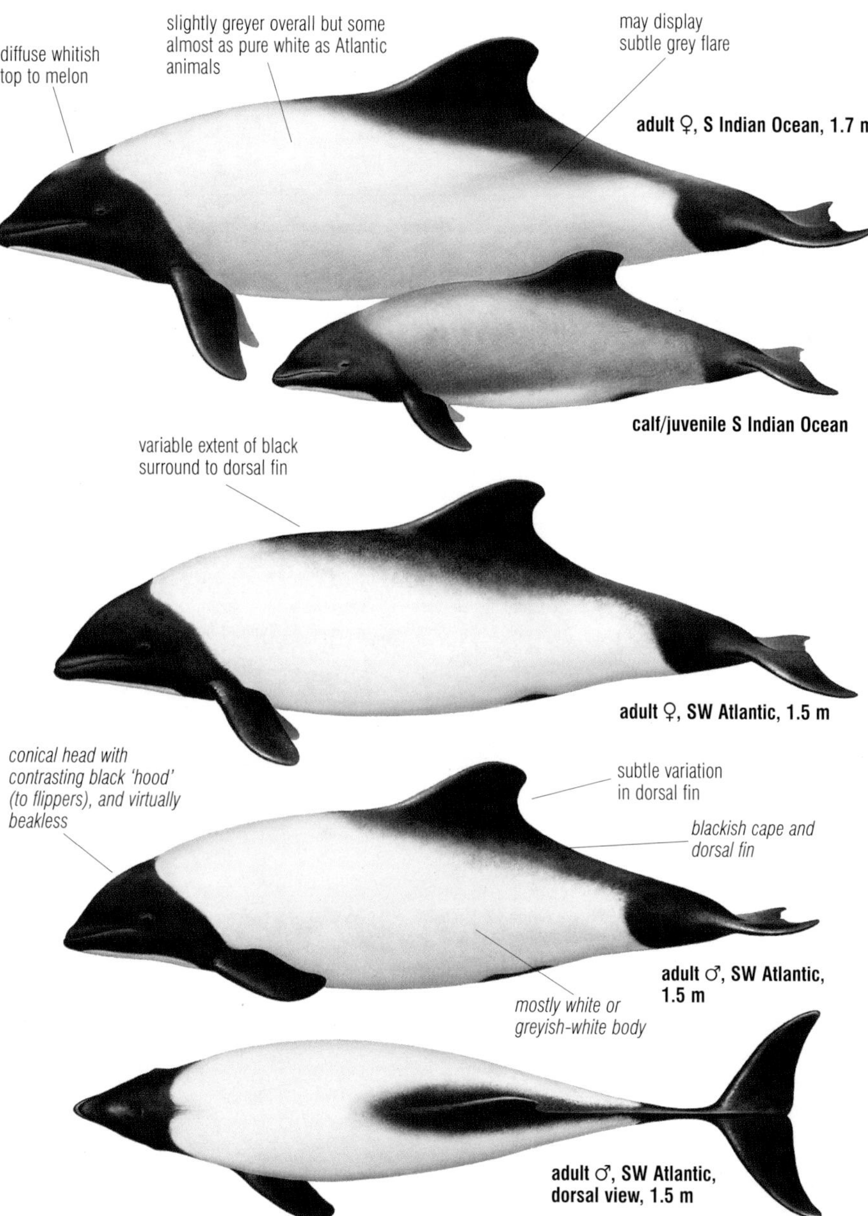

in Chile), south to 61°S in Drake Passage, the Falklands, Kerguelen (where most frequent in Golfe du Morbihan) and Heard Is. Largely sedentary but appears less common inshore in austral winter and spring (Jun–Dec in Kerguelen). *Population* No overall estimate but seems common off Patagonia, Tierra del Fuego (where *c.*3,200 in 1984) and the Falklands.

ECOLOGY

Typical group size up to 15 (mostly 2–12) but groups of

100+ form seasonal, feeding or breeding aggregations. Some large groups contain up to 30% calves. Associates with Burmeister's Porpoise, Peale's and Chilean Dolphins. *Breaching* Very frequent: in 1 study, 6 individuals did so on 65–70 occasions in 17 min. *Diving* 15–20 sec, breathing 2–3× between dives. Longer/ deeper dives known but no data. *Diet* Small fish, crab, octopus, krill and other crustaceans, possibly largely taken inshore, in kelp beds, and near seabed. Sometimes herds fish close inshore. *Reproduction* Sexually mature at 5–8 yrs. Peak calving early in austral summer (Oct–Mar), with gestation 10–12 months. *Lifespan* 18+ yrs.

Chilean Dolphin

Cephalorhynchus eutropia

Chilean coastal waters. Max 1.7 m.

Priority characters on surfacing

- *Small, stocky, beakless* and largely dark coastal dolphin. Restricted to Chile.
- Large but rather low, *rounded dorsal fin* and *conical head* with sloping forehead and very short, poorly-defined beak.
- *Generally grey body* (may seem brown or black at distance).
- Greyer fore face, enhances *broad black mask, and dark lower jaw continues as black band to flippers*, with distinctive white throat and narrow whitish mouthline.
- Blackish, ill-defined lateral band at border of slate-black sides, heightening contrast with white below. There is often a bold white axilla mark at the base of the flipper.
- Large white patch on belly, from behind flippers to genital area, and narrow grey patches around genital area, which vary sexually and individually.
- Tail flukes notched with pointed tips, and flippers small and rounded.

Typical behaviour at surface

- *Undulating swimming motion*, somewhat sea lion-like.
- Usually unobtrusive but occasionally investigates boats, bow- or waist-riding.
- Pods usually small.

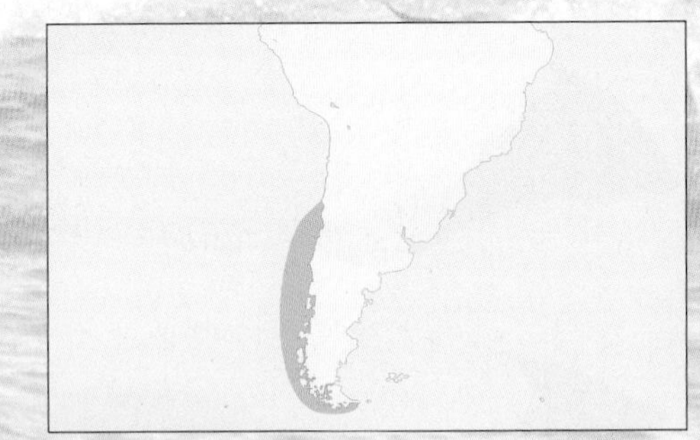

Chilean Dolphin: small and greyish with conical head and poorly-defined beak; also large rounded dorsal fin, greyer melon, darker mask and band to flippers.

SIMILAR SPECIES

Dorsal fin shape distinguishes it from overlapping and superficially similar ***Burmeister's*** and ***Spectacled Porpoises***, and distant ***Commerson's Dolphins***, especially brownish young, can appear confusingly darker.

VARIATION

Age/sex Sexes differ in their genital patches, whilst calf slimmer and more uniform. **Physical notes** Full-grown ad 1.2–1.7 m and 30–63 kg. No data on calf.

DISTRIBUTION & POPULATION

Coastal Chile north to Valparaíso and south to Tierra del Fuego and Cape Horn, and occasionally adjacent Argentine waters. Mainly sedentary but less common inshore in austral winter. Prefers areas of rapid tidal flow and shallow waters at entrance to fjords. *Population* No estimates but probably in low 1,000s.

Chilean Dolphins: note large blackish dorsal fin contrasting with grey body, which can identify the species even at some distance.

ECOLOGY
Typical group size 2–15 but 20–50, especially in north, and concentration of possibly 4,000 reported in past. May associate with Peale's Dolphin. Herds fish using circular or zigzag movements. Often associates with feeding seabirds. *Breaching* Uncommon, with moderate-height full leaps observed but no other details. *Diving* No data. *Diet* Small schooling fish, squid, krill and other crustaceans. *Reproduction* Calves observed Oct–Apr. *Lifespan* Unknown.

Chilean Dolphin

Haviside's Dolphin: note narrow blackish cape broadening below dorsal fin.

SIMILAR SPECIES

Unmistakable in range: the only other small cetaceans present are noticeably larger dolphins, with falcate dorsal fins, prominent beaks and different colorations, which should be readily apparent.

VARIATION

Age/sex Slight differences in shape of white belly patch between sexes, especially where it meets anus. Calf generally as ad but slimmer and more uniform. **Physical notes** Full-grown ad 1.2–1.75 m and 40–75 kg. Newborn 0.8–0.85 m and 9–10 kg. **Other data** Several predominantly white individuals recorded.

Haviside's Dolphin

Cephalorhynchus heavisidii

Coastal SW Africa. Max 1.75 m.

Note: Named after Captain Haviside, the species name has been frequently been mispelled as Heaviside's Dolphin. Under the rules of nomenclature the spelling of the scientific name cannot be changed.

Priority characters on surfacing

- Compact, stocky and beakless coastal dolphin; restricted to SW Africa.
- *Cone-shaped head with indistinct beak*, but *dorsal fin triangular and pointed*.
- *Largely grey, with blackish-blue cape* from blowhole, only broadening below dorsal fin.
- *Dark oval area around eye or over much of face*, grading into uniformly paler rest of fore parts.
- Dark rear sides and tailstock, with variable paler horizontal streak.
- Brilliant white trident-shaped ventral patch, with extended 'arms' that project as a *finger-shaped mark on both sides of lower rear body*.
- Small bold white axilla either side of the flipper base, the dorsal patch forming an extension to the whitish chest patch.
- Tail flukes distinctly notched with pointed tips, and small flippers tapered but have blunt tips.

Typical behaviour at surface

- *Rather shy and rarely active* or boisterous, though sometimes porpoises at high speed and occasionally bow- and wake-rides, when may follow small vessels for long periods.
- Normally in small pods.

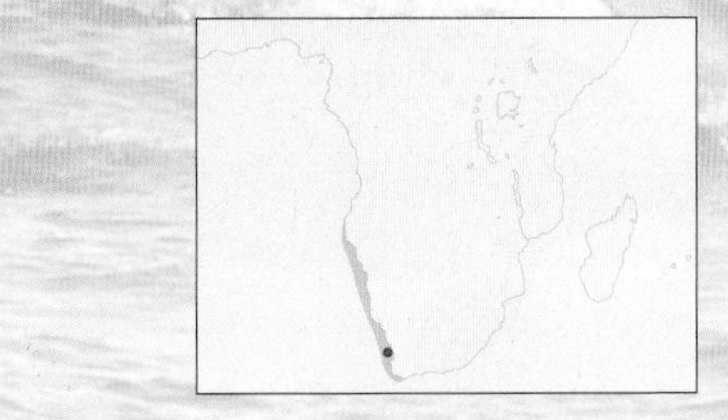

Haviside's Dolphin: conical head, blackish cape and triangular dorsal fin, and white finger-shaped mark on lower rear body render it unmistakable.

Haviside's Dolphin

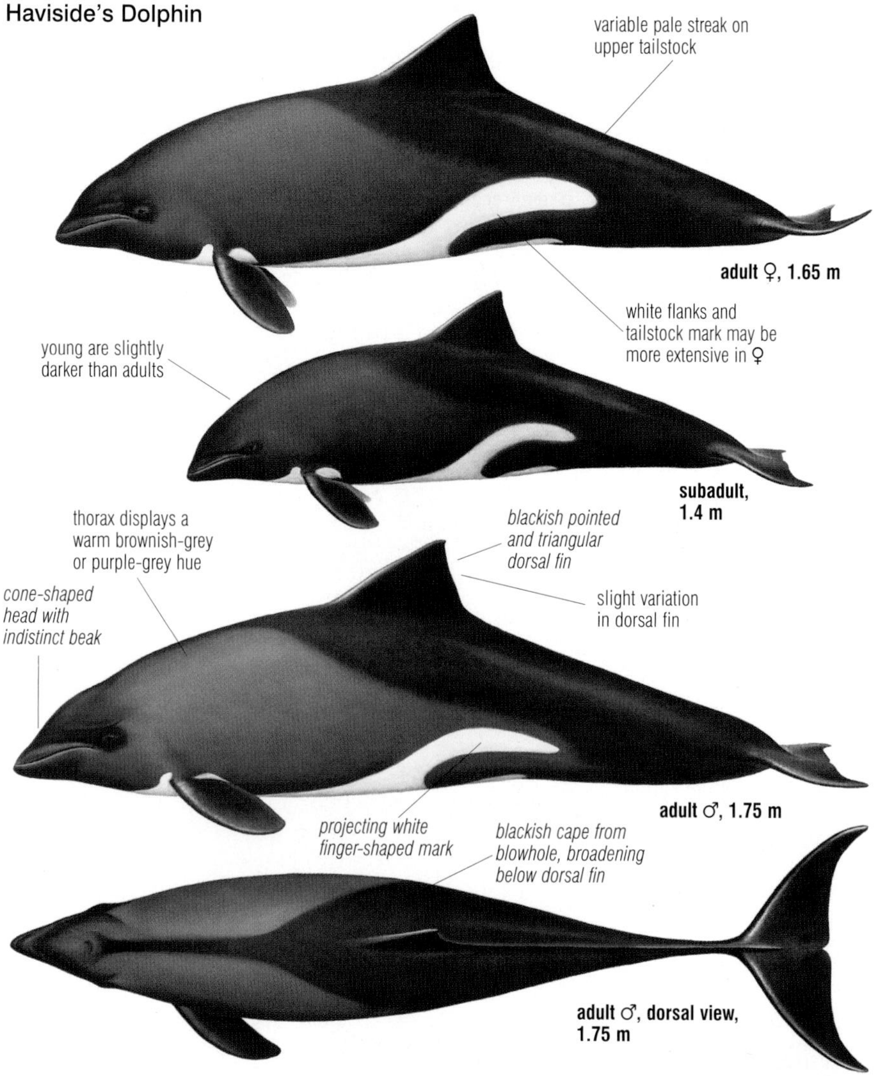

variable pale streak on upper tailstock

adult ♀, 1.65 m

white flanks and tailstock mark may be more extensive in ♀

young are slightly darker than adults

subadult, 1.4 m

thorax displays a warm brownish-grey or purple-grey hue

blackish pointed and triangular dorsal fin

cone-shaped head with indistinct beak

slight variation in dorsal fin

adult ♂, 1.75 m

projecting white finger-shaped mark

blackish cape from blowhole, broadening below dorsal fin

adult ♂, dorsal view, 1.75 m

DISTRIBUTION & POPULATION

SW Africa, from Cape of Good Hope north to Cape Cross, NC Namibia. Largely resident in near-shore areas, usually in waters shallower than 100 m, although recorded up to 45 nautical miles from shore. *Population* No estimates.

ECOLOGY

Typical group size up to 10, but aggregation of 20–30 noted. Sex and age composition unknown but speculated to be fluid. *Breaching* Frequent: sometimes performs rapid, forward somersaults up to 2 m high, which end with dolphin slapping surface with its tail. *Diving* No data. *Diet* Bottom-dwelling fish, squid, octopus, cephalopods and crustaceans. *Reproduction* Calves seen Oct–Jan. *Lifespan* Unknown.

Haviside's Dolphin can occasionally be more active and acrobatic; note the brilliant white trident-shaped ventral patch.

SIMILAR SPECIES

Unmistakable given limited range and striking combination of characters. Small size, contrastingly large, black, rounded dorsal fin, flippers and broad facial mask eliminate any possible confusion (no similar species in range), and has very different behaviour from other dolphins off New Zealand, including being strongly coastal.

VARIATION

Age/sex ♂ 5–10% smaller, although difficult to evaluate at sea, and has larger dark grey oval-shaped patch around genital slit (reduced in ♀) placed further forward; calf or younger imm clearly smaller and has less-developed convex dorsal fin, colour/pattern overall darker and subdued and 4–6 pale bands on each side of body between flipper and tailstock (which disappear at *c*.6 months). Young become progressively paler. **Physical notes** Full-grown ad 1.2–1.53 m and 35–65 kg. Newborn estimated at 0.6–0.75 m and *c*.9 kg.

Hector's Dolphin

Cephalorhynchus hectori

Coastal waters of New Zealand. Max 1.5 m.

Priority characters on surfacing

- *New Zealand endemic*; the smallest dolphin.
- *Medium grey with contrasting black rounded dorsal fin* (broad base with convex tip and trailing edge, appears to lean backwards).
- *Compact body* tapers into *cone-shaped head and blunt snout* affording beakless appearance.
- Striking body pattern: *black snout and broad triangular mask* narrows above dark flipper and sometimes continues as ill-defined stripe between dark blue-grey sides and white underparts. Forehead and back greyish.
- White trident-shaped ventral patch with *finger-shaped projections on rear lower body*, and small bold white axilla behind flipper (difficult to see).
- White ventral area separated from clear white throat by variable black area between flippers; also a small dark grey genital patch (smaller or less apparent in some ♀♀).
- Black, round-tipped, large flippers, and slightly notched, point-tipped tail flukes.

Typical behaviour at surface

- Typically has leisurely, *low surfing motion*, barely disturbing surface.
- Rarely bow-rides but often investigates slow-moving or stationary boats.
- Not very sociable, normally in pods of 2–8.

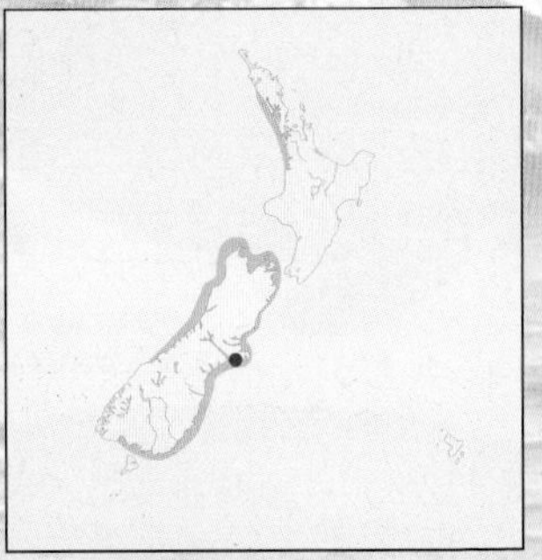

Breaching Hector's Dolphin: the smallest dolphin, showing its complex underbody pattern.

Taxonomy Polytypic, with recent recognition of N Island stock as *C. h. maui*, and those of S Island as nominate, differing in structure, skeletal features and mtDNA. Furthermore, east- and west-coast S Island populations appear genetically distinct, and there is an apparently isolated population in Te Wae Wae Bay, on S Island.

DISTRIBUTION & POPULATION

Coastal waters (less than 75 m deep) of New Zealand,

Hector's Dolphin

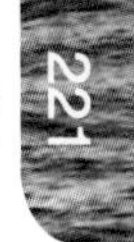

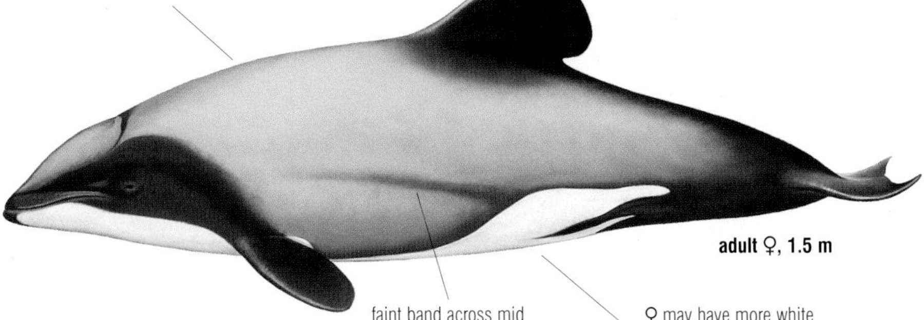

adult ♀, 1.5 m

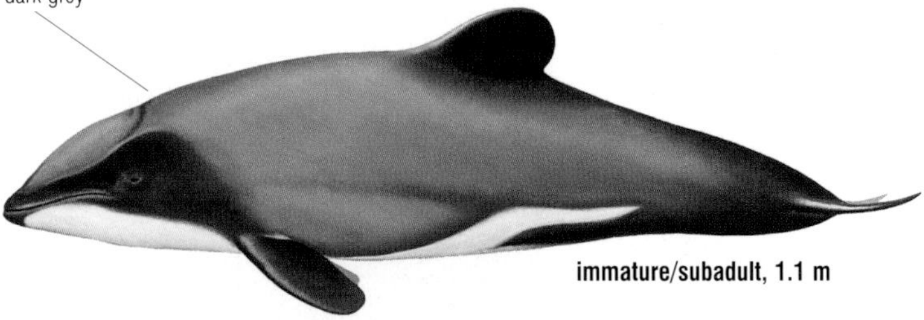

immature/subadult, 1.1 m

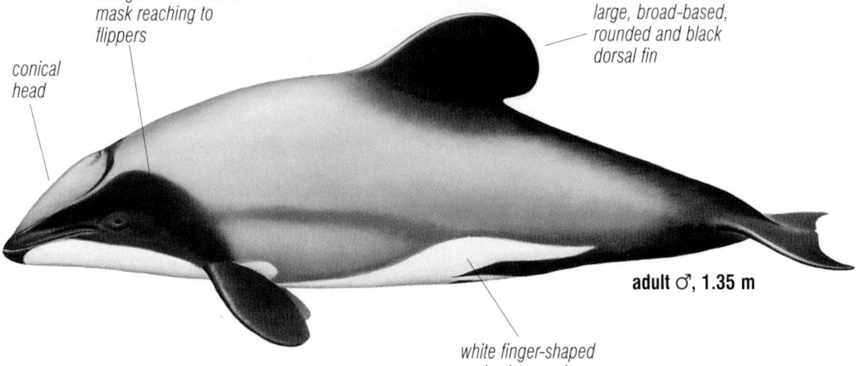

adult ♂, 1.35 m

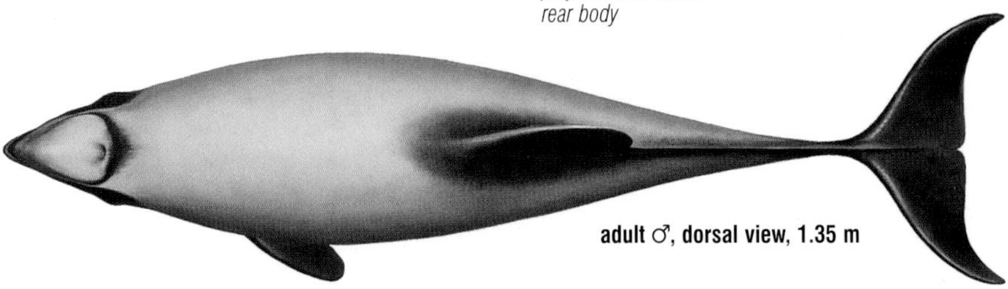

adult ♂, dorsal view, 1.35 m

Hector's Dolphins are restricted to very shallow coastal bays in New Zealand.

where most common on east and west coasts of S Island and only a very small population (perhaps <100) on west coast of N Island. Movements of up to 30 km reported: favours areas further offshore in winter, although always prefers river mouths. *Population* S Island *c.*7,300 in recent years, of which *c.*5,400 on west coast.

Mother and calf Hector's Dolphins: above the surface the pale body and contrasting large, rounded black dorsal fin are conclusive.

ECOLOGY

Typical group size up to 30 but 100 reported. Associations in different subpopulations relatively fluid. Spyhops and lobtails.

Hector's Dolphin is unmistakable given the large, rounded black dorsal fin, conical head, black mask reaching to the flipper, and white finger-shaped marks on the lower rear body.

Breaching Regular, with 3 types: horizontal, vertical and 'noisy'. *Diving* Surfaces frequently, usually at intervals of less than 30 sec, with *c.*6 short dives followed by 1 of *c.*90 sec. *Diet* Small, surface and mid-water schooling fish, squid, krill and other crustaceans. *Reproduction* Sexually mature at 6–9 yrs. Mating and calving early Nov–mid Feb and gestation lasts 10–11 months. Lactation lasts at least 6 months. Mature ♀♀ calve every 2–4 yrs and young remain with ♀ for 1–2 yrs. *Lifespan c.*20 yrs..

Right Whale dolphins

Northern and Southern Right Whale Dolphins are among the most distinctive oceanic dolphins, in shape and coloration resembling no other cetaceans. The former is restricted to the N Pacific, and the latter circumpolar in the Southern Ocean. The genus *Lissodelphis*, of which they are the sole members, is often thought to represent a subfamily, Lissodelphinae (of the family Delphinidae), although one molecular revision of the dolphins classified the genus within the Lissodelphinae, together with the genera *Cephalorhynchus* and some *Lagenorhynchus*. They have highly streamlined bodies with no dorsal fin or break between short beak and head, and are largely shiny black or contrastingly black with a white underside. Given their spindle-like shape, coloration and behaviour, they are unlikely to be confused with any other dolphins, and both (despite some colour variation) differ strikingly in coloration, and are well separated geographically. Strongly gregarious, right whale dolphins are capable of very high-speed travel, porpoising rapidly, and frequently associate with other cetaceans.

Northern Right Whale Dolphins in extremely fast travel: the slender body, lack of a dorsal fin and mostly black coloration make this species unmistakable.

Northern Right Whale Dolphin

Lissodelphis borealis

N Pacific. Max 3.1 m.

Priority characters on surfacing

- Unmistakable, *largely shiny black dolphin with extremely slender body and no dorsal fin*; N Pacific only.
- *Short, smoothly curved narrow beak and low, gently sloping forehead.*
- Principally black; irregular white band from throat to fluke notch widens on chest.
- White spot just behind tip of lower jaw.
- *Tailstock very narrow* with small, point-tipped flukes (white ventrally and dark dorsally with pale grey trailing edge) and narrow, pointed flippers (partially or all black).
- Young have muted coloration of dark grey and pale brownish-grey.

Typical behaviour at surface

- Fast, graceful swimmers, *usually in large pods* and frequently mixed with Pacific White-sided Dolphins.
- When travelling fast, *groups create much surface disturbance with their low-angle leaps* and belly flops. Very long bounces recorded, as far as 7 m in one leap!
- Usually appears smaller than real size. *Most likely to be seen porpoising in calm seas.* When moving slowly at surface, only exposes small part of top of head and back.

Northern Right Whale Dolphin often shows considerable colour variation; this individual has more extensive white on underbody than most.

SIMILAR SPECIES

Readily distinguished by slender, finless body, unlike all other N Pacific small cetaceans, but, surprisingly, a distant porpoising sea lion could present a brief confusion risk.

VARIATION

Age/sex ♀ smaller and ventral white band broadens slightly around genitals. Calf slimmer and overall greyish-brown or, sometimes, cream and remains so for 1 yr, before becoming black with a clear white ventral area and white tip to lower jaw. **Physical notes** Full-grown ad 2–3.1 m, up to 2.3 m (♀) and 3.1 m (♂), and weighs 60–113 kg. Newborn 80–103 cm. **Other data** A so-called 'swirled' variant with more extensive white ventral areas has been recorded in several areas.

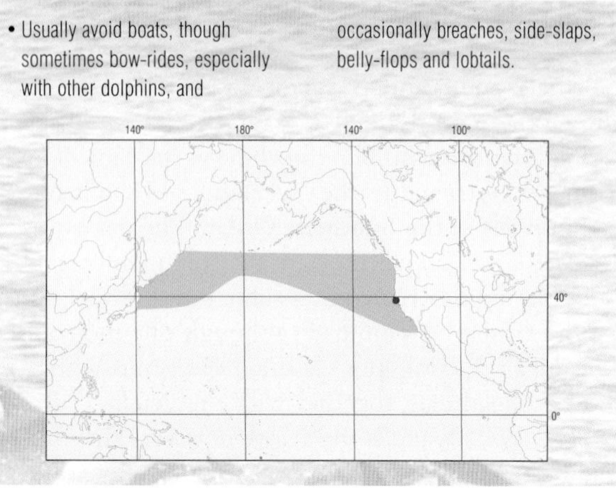

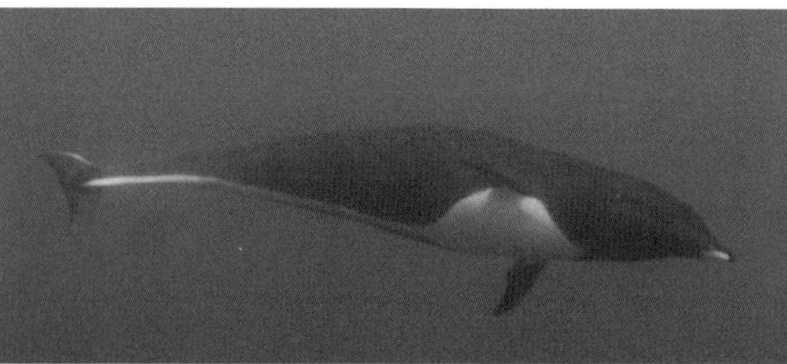

Northern Right Whale Dolphin: note white pattern on underbody.

DISTRIBUTION & POPULATION

Widespread in N Pacific, from Japan and Kamchatka and Gulf of Alaska south to N Baja California (Mexico), usually in deep continental shelf waters and occasionally reaching further south with incursions of cold water. In mid Pacific mainly between 34°N and 47°N. In the east, some seasonal movements have been noted, north and offshore in summer. *Population* Poorly known, although 14,000 estimated off western N America.

ECOLOGY

Very large pods of up to 2,000–3,000 comparatively frequent. Associates with at least 14 species, including Pacific White-sided and Risso's Dolphins, and Short-finned Pilot Whales. *Breaching* Fairly common. *Diving* Up to 6.5 min. *Diet* Principally small fish (especially lanternfish) and squid. *Reproduction* Sexually mature late in 9th yr. Most calve in Jul–Aug in N Pacific, with gestation lasting 1 yr, and most ♀♀ breeding every 2+ yrs. *Lifespan* Up to 42 yrs.

Northern Right Whale Dolphins have an obvious arrow-like profile and perform long, low-angle leaps.

Northern Right Whale Dolphin

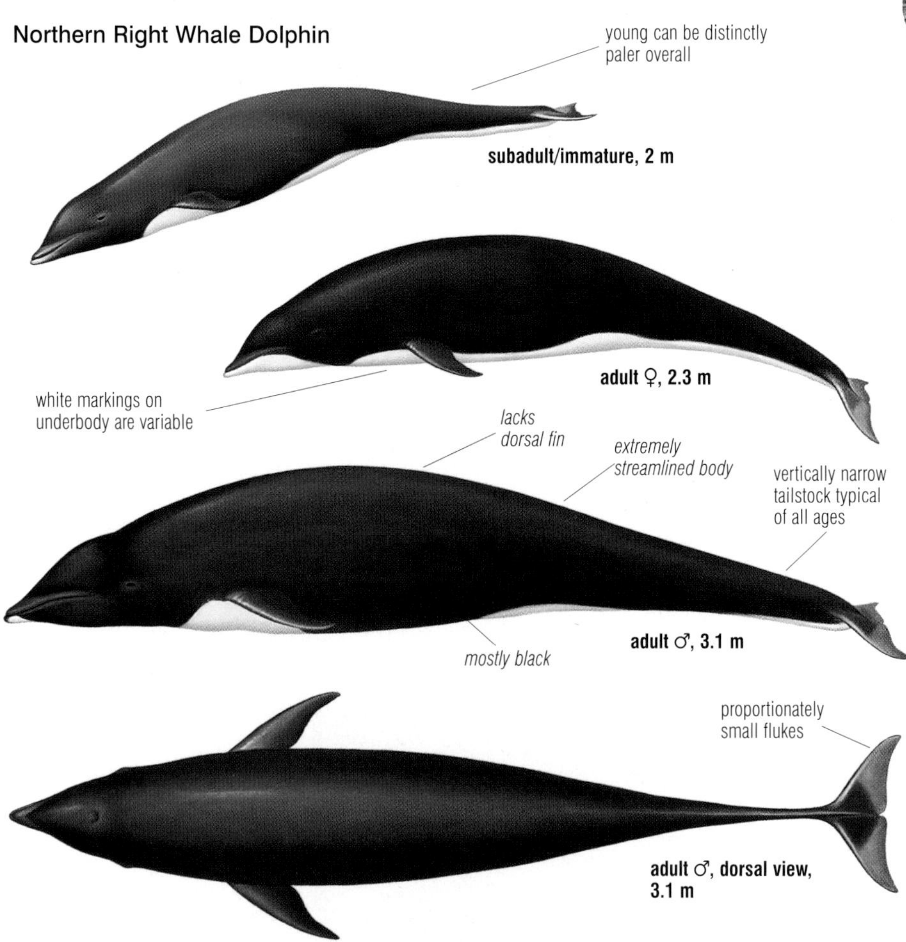

Southern Right Whale Dolphin

Lissodelphis peronii

Southern Ocean. Max 3 m.

Priority characters on surfacing

- Unmistakable, with *contrasting black upperside and white below*, and noticeably streamlined body and *lack of dorsal fin* eliminates all other dolphins in Southern Ocean.
- *Short, well-defined and smooth-curved beak*, and low, gently sloping forehead.
- Dorsal coloration jet black, from forehead, passing between eyes and mouth corners, and sweeps up past flipper to back, before levelling-off at tail.
- Snout and lower forehead whitish (to just below blowhole level); rest of lower body white, except rear edge of flippers, which is black.
- Flippers small, falcate and pointed; some all white, others have a narrow dark leading edge and some a broader dark leading edge.
- *Tailstock extremely narrow*; small flukes have curved trailing edge, pointed tips and distinct notch; white ventrally, and dark grey,

SIMILAR SPECIES

Unique body shape and pigmentation unmistakable within range, although ***Spectacled Porpoise*** may prove a confusion risk for the inexperienced observer. Smaller than Northern Right Whale Dolphin and has more white on head and sides.

VARIATION

Age/sex ♂ averages larger and smaller/slimmer young separable by size, whilst newborn calves are dark grey/brown and only attain ad coloration at 1 yr. **Physical notes** Full-grown ad 1.8–3 m and 60–116 kg. Newborn probably 0.8–1.0 m. **Other data** Some individual variation reported within pods, as some animals pigmented with more white or black, often producing irregular patterns, and others abnormal altogether.

DISTRIBUTION & POPULATION

Circumpolar and generally common in subantarctic to temperate waters north of Antarctic Convergence, at 25–65°S, reaching 12°30'S off western S America and 23°S off Namibia. Northward movements in winter and spring off Chile, otherwise largely sedentary. Prefers deep water and is common off New Zealand, SW Africa, in the Falkland Current and off Chile. *Population* No estimates.

ECOLOGY

Often travels in large herds of up to 1,000+ though 100–200 more typical; social composition unknown. Most frequently associates with Long-finned Pilot Whale and *Lagenorhynchus* dolphins. *Breaching* Uncommon. Diet Small fish, krill and squid. No other data.

fading to white on leading edge.

Typical behaviour at surface

- Typically in pods of <100, often with Dusky or Hourglass Dolphins or pilot whales.
- Fast, energetic swimmer, typically *porpoises like penguins*, with bouncing motion of *low-angle leaps* clear of water at great speed.
- When swimming slowly, only exposes a small part of top of head and back when surfacing to breathe; thus, if not porpoising, hard to see.
- May bow-ride, but sometimes avoids vessels. Breaching, belly flopping, side-slapping and lobtailing or fluke-slapping all recorded.

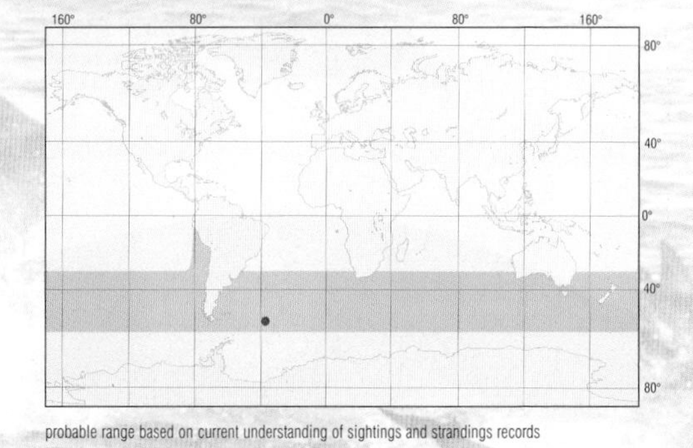

probable range based on current understanding of sightings and strandings records

Left: Southern Right Whale Dolphin is one of the most attractive of all cetaceans: shape and coloration make it unmistakable.

Below: Southern Right Whale Dolphins often occur in large spread-out herds whose porpoising, at distance, may appear penguin-like.

Southern Right Whale Dolphin

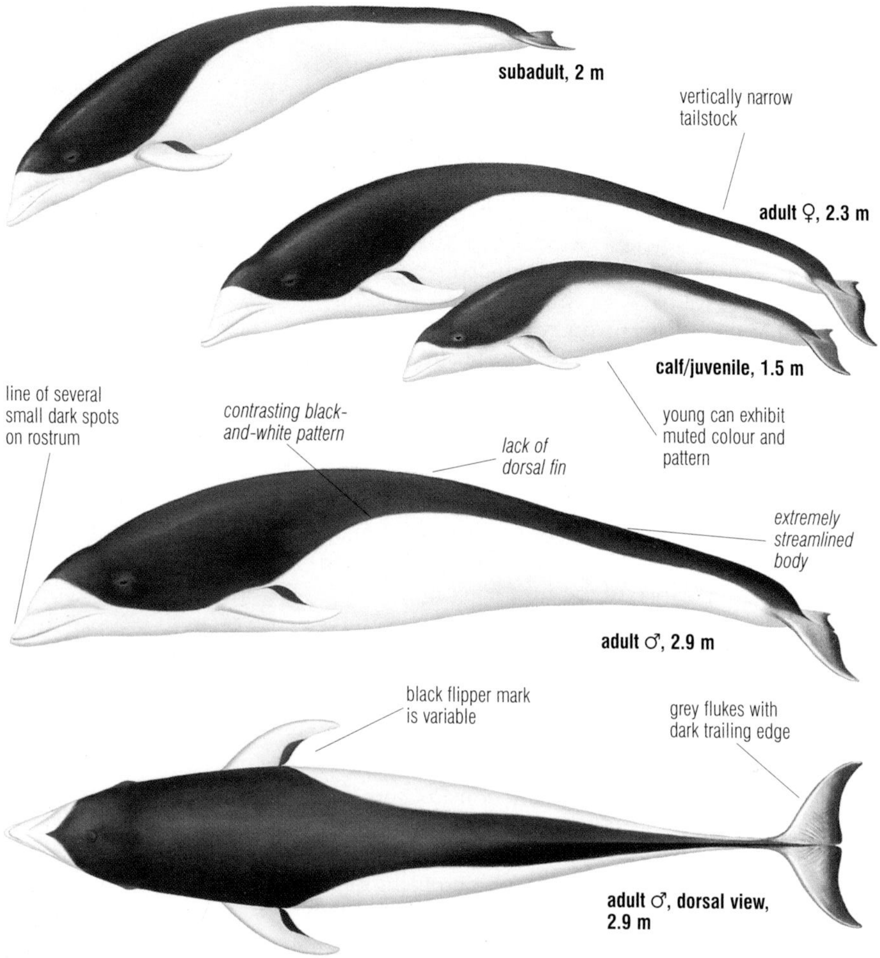

subadult, 2 m

vertically narrow tailstock

adult ♀, 2.3 m

calf/juvenile, 1.5 m

young can exhibit muted colour and pattern

line of several small dark spots on rostrum

contrasting black-and-white pattern

lack of dorsal fin

extremely streamlined body

adult ♂, 2.9 m

black flipper mark is variable

grey flukes with dark trailing edge

adult ♂, dorsal view, 2.9 m

Southern Right Whale Dolphins (in typical long, low leaping behaviour): black-and-white coloration and lack of dorsal fin make identification straightforward.

River dolphins and Tucuxi

Primarily riverine-adapted cetaceans with very long beaks, well-developed teeth and strong sense of echolocation (some species are virtually blind). Most are very pale-coloured, with small or indistinct dorsal fins, which may appear as just a hump on the back. Exceptional is the Franciscana which is marine and has a better-developed fin. Also included here is the Tucuxi due to overlap with Amazon River Dolphin (in rivers) and Franciscana (in coastal waters). Apart from these, the river dolphins are essentially well separated geographically. In South-East Asia, Chinese River Dolphin is restricted to the Yangtse River (and is the sole member of the family Lipotidae), whilst Ganges and Indus River Dolphins are, as their names suggest, almost entirely restricted to single river systems within the Indian subcontinent (and form a separate family, Platanistidae). Amazon River Dolphin (the only representative of the Iniidae) is almost restricted to Amazonia, where it is sympatric with the Freshwater Tucuxi, which superspecies also occurs on the Atlantic coast of Central and Southern America (and is a member of the Delphinidae, being placed in the subfamily Steninae or, based on DNA analysis, in the tiny subfamily Stenoninae with the Rough-toothed Dolphin). Finally, the Franciscana occurs along southern Atlantic coasts of South America (and is also placed in its own family, the Pontoporiidae). River dolphins offer an extremely interesting problem for evolutionary historians. The different species apparently adapted to freshwater environments at different times and as a result of convergent evolution, with similar adaptations occurring independently in the Tucuxis and Irrawaddy Dolphin. However, river dolphin is an ambiguous term which some scientists feel should be abandoned as the grouping is not monophyletic and all of the closely related extinct species were in fact marine. The modern-day species are also at considerable risk, the Indian subcontinent taxa due to hunting and habitat degradation, and Chinese River Dolphin is now the rarest cetacean on Earth, apparently heading inexorably towards extinction, whilst Franciscana has also declined. Only Amazon River Dolphin (and the Tucuxi) are still reasonably common, but even they have been subject to greater hunting pressure and habitat change in recent years.

Freshwater Tucuxi (Amazon River, Colombia) is noticeably smaller than Marine Tucuxi. The pale blaze across the mid-flanks is highly variable but usually does not continue onto the tailstock, unlike the latter. Here, both the mid-flank blaze and thoracic band are pronounced.

Marine Tucuxi (coastal S Brazil): these compact dolphins can be sometimes highly acrobatic and demonstrative. Note extensive pale thoracic band across the flanks (right animals).

Franciscana: note very long pointed beak and low, broad-based dorsal fin; some animals are rather grey looking (cf. image on p. 232). Highly threatened coastal species (mainly incidental bycatch in gillnets and industrial fishing and also habitat degradation.

River dolphins and Tucuxi

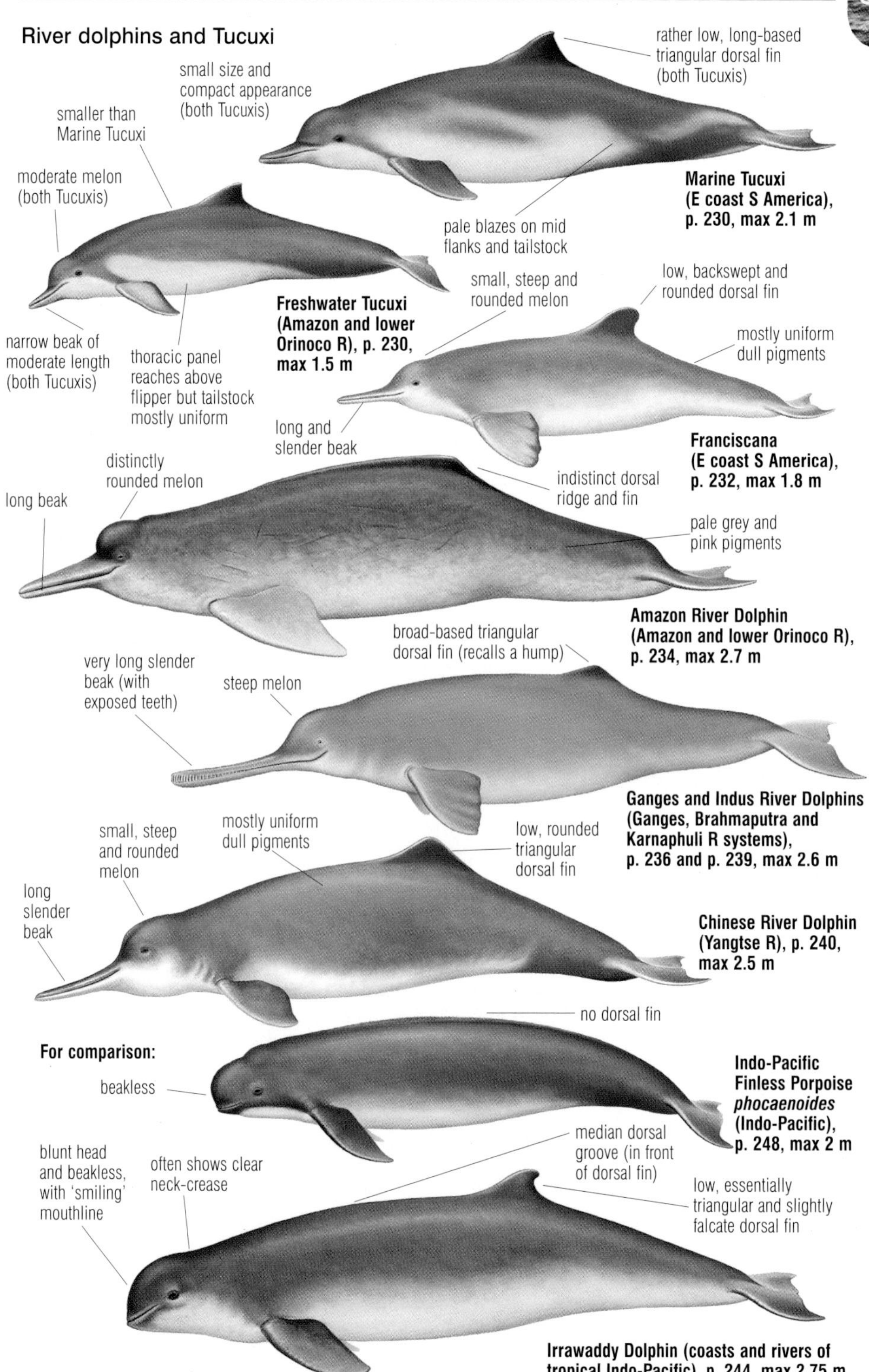

Freshwater Tucuxi (Amazon R, Colombian border): small dumpy appearance, almost uniform flanks and tailstock; pinkish underbody extends to slightly above flippers.

Tucuxi

Sotalia fluviatilis

Coastal waters and estuaries of E South America. Max 2.1 m.

Priority characters on surfacing

- *Small, compact dolphin*, rather chunky and in shape *superficially resembles much larger bottlenose dolphins*. Two forms: a true riverine and a marine animal (latter *c*.30% larger).
- *Dorsal fin rather low and triangular* with a long base and often slightly hooked.
- *Snout of moderate length and rather narrow*.
- *Distinct melon* and gently sloping forehead. Dark eye accentuated by black lids.
- Uniform pale to medium grey, bluish-grey or brownish-grey, becoming pale grey or white on lower flanks and belly, and much of *ventral area tinged pinkish*.
- Broad flippers concolorous with upperbody.
- Broad, somewhat vague stripe from eye to flipper and other *ill-defined dusky smudges and pale flashes behind flippers*.

Typical behaviour at surface

- Mostly in very small pods, but schools of up to 20 (in fresh water) or 50 (in marine waters).
- *Fast active swimmer and can be very acrobatic* (spyhops, lobtails, flipper-slaps, vertical and horizontal leaps, and breaching all frequent).
- Short dives. Generally quite timid and shy, keeps away from boats.
- Marine form occasionally schools with bottlenose dolphins.

DISTINCTIVE POPULATIONS

Marine and freshwater populations differ mainly in size, ecology, behaviour and DNA. Some dental differences and body-sides patterns have been noted, but their consistency and the extent of individual variation are not fully understood. Evidence that the 2 forms overlap needs verification.

Freshwater Tucuxi (Amazon R, Colombian border): based on its uniform pigments this appears to be a young animal.

Freshwater Tucuxi *S.* (*f.*) *fluviatilis* Riverine form (main rivers of Amazon basin). Principal differences from *guianensis* are smaller size, somewhat darker cape and plainer grey flanks (above the whitish thoracic panel-like area from belly to above flipper) and tailstock. **Marine Tucuxi** *S.* (*f.*) *guianensis* Inshore marine form is larger, has more teeth in upper jaw and some have muted pale blazes on sides, across upper flanks and on tailstock.

SIMILAR SPECIES

Could be confused with greyish, especially young ***Amazon River Dolphins***, but differences in dorsal fin and head shapes, and behaviour readily distinguish them. Coastal animals hard to separate from similar-sized ***Franciscana*** or much larger ***Common Bottlenose Dolphin***. Franciscana has much longer beak, squarish (rather than pointed) flippers

Marine Tucuxi (coastal S Brazil): note clear whitish thoracic band extending above flipper, pale grey sides and faint darker cape.

Tucuxi

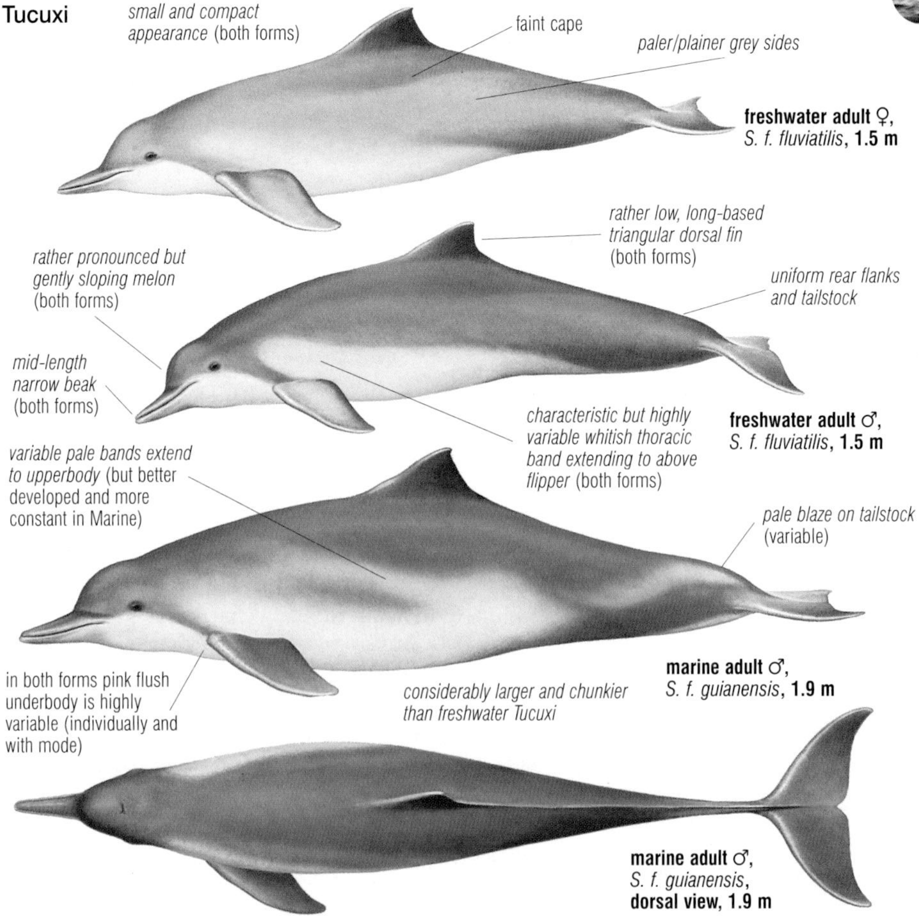

small and compact appearance (both forms)

faint cape

paler/plainer grey sides

freshwater adult ♀,
S. f. fluviatilis, **1.5 m**

rather low, long-based triangular dorsal fin (both forms)

rather pronounced but gently sloping melon (both forms)

uniform rear flanks and tailstock

mid-length narrow beak (both forms)

characteristic but highly variable whitish thoracic band extending to above flipper (both forms)

freshwater adult ♂,
S. f. fluviatilis, **1.5 m**

variable pale bands extend to upperbody (but better developed and more constant in Marine)

pale blaze on tailstock (variable)

in both forms pink flush underbody is highly variable (individually and with mode)

considerably larger and chunkier than freshwater Tucuxi

marine adult ♂,
S. f. guianensis, **1.9 m**

marine adult ♂,
S. f. guianensis,
dorsal view, 1.9 m

Marine Tucuxi (coastal S Brazil) is noticeably larger than Freshwater Tucuxi, usually with clear pale blazes on mid-flanks and tailstock.

and generally more uniform body-sides, whilst larger/heavier Common Bottlenose Dolphin has taller, more falcate dorsal fin.

VARIATION

Age/sex ♂ perhaps averages smaller. Calf slimmer and more uniformly grey. Pinkish ventral coloration may be partially seasonal. **Physical notes** Max length of full-grown ads 2.1 m (♀) and 1.9 m (♂) in marine form (1.5 m both sexes of riverine form), and weigh at least 45 kg. Newborn 0.7–0.8 m (marine 0.8–1.0

m). **Taxonomy** Polytypic, with 2 races (see above). Further study may reveal that they are separate species, as already suggested by first genetic results.

Marine Tucuxi (Baía Norte, Santa Catarina, S Brazil): both forms of Tucuxi are small compact animals, with a rather low, triangular and often slightly hooked dorsal fin, rather pronounced melon and narrow mid-length beak.

DISTRIBUTION & POPULATION
Widespread and rather common in eastern C & S America. *S. (f.) guianensis* from Nicaragua (perhaps Honduras) along northern and eastern seaboard of S America south to Santa Catarina (Brazil), often congregating in shallow estuaries and bays. Usually resident. *S. (f.) fluviatilis* inhabits lakes, streams and large rivers throughout virtually the entire Amazon and lower Orinoco R basins, from Brazil to SE Colombia, E Ecuador and NE Peru, with short-distance movements due to changing water levels. *Population* Few estimates.

ECOLOGY
Interactions noted with Bottlenose and Amazon River Dolphins, sometimes feeds near latter. *Breaching* Frequent, in low arc, occasionally a somersault. *Diving* Shallow dives lasting 11 sec–3 min. *Diet* Amazonian form mostly takes fish, whilst coastal animals take schooling and bottom-dwelling fish, some cephalopods, shrimps and flounders. Mostly feeds in pairs or cooperative subgroups, especially the marine form. *Reproduction* Freshwater animals have gestation of *c.*10 months, with most Brazilian populations mating Jan–Feb and calving Oct–Nov. Coastal populations calve year-round, with gestation period of 11–12 months and 22–23 months between births. *Lifespan* Up to 35 yrs.

Franciscanas: note extremely long slender beak (breaking surface at low angle) and dull grey-brown pigmentation; usually a sluggish deliberate swimmer that shows little of itself at surface.

SIMILAR SPECIES
Young Franciscana can only be confused with ***Tucuxi***, but is identified by the very long beak and more rounded dorsal fin.

Franciscana

Pontoporia blainvillei

E coast of S America.
Max 1.8 m.

Priority characters on surfacing

- *Small, very pale dolphin*; primarily marine.
- *Beak extremely long and slender and forehead steep and rounded.*
- *Dorsal fin low and rounded*, with broad base, convex tip and trailing edge, appears backswept. Dorsal ridge continues to tailstock.
- Slightly contrasting darker cape, otherwise dull pale brownish to grey above, and paler or somewhat yellowish-grey below and on lower flanks.
- Skin may lighten in winter and with age; some older animals predominantly white.

- Flippers proportionately large, broad and spatulate, with undulating trailing edge.
- Eyes small but very well developed.

Typical behaviour at surface

- *Smooth movements*, shows little of itself at surface, although long beak may break surface at 45°, and rarely leaps or splashes.
- Social and foraging behaviour observable in very shallow coastal waters; fond of rippled sand, even lying in shallows on hot, sunny days.
- Solitary but often found in groups of up to 15. In general, appears to avoid boats.

VARIATION

Age/sex ♂ averages smaller. Calf has considerably shorter beak and is slimmer and even more uniform in coloration. **Physical notes** Full-grown ♂ up to 1.63 m and ♀ 1.77 m (minimum possibly 1.2 m) and 29–53 kg. Newborn 59–75 cm and 7.3–8.5 kg. **Taxonomy** Monotypic, although 2 forms which differ in their mtDNA and skull morphology exist, a smaller northern (Rio de Janeiro to Santa Catarina) and larger southern one (Rio Grande do Sul to Argentina).

DISTRIBUTION & POPULATION

Coastal waters from SE

Franciscana

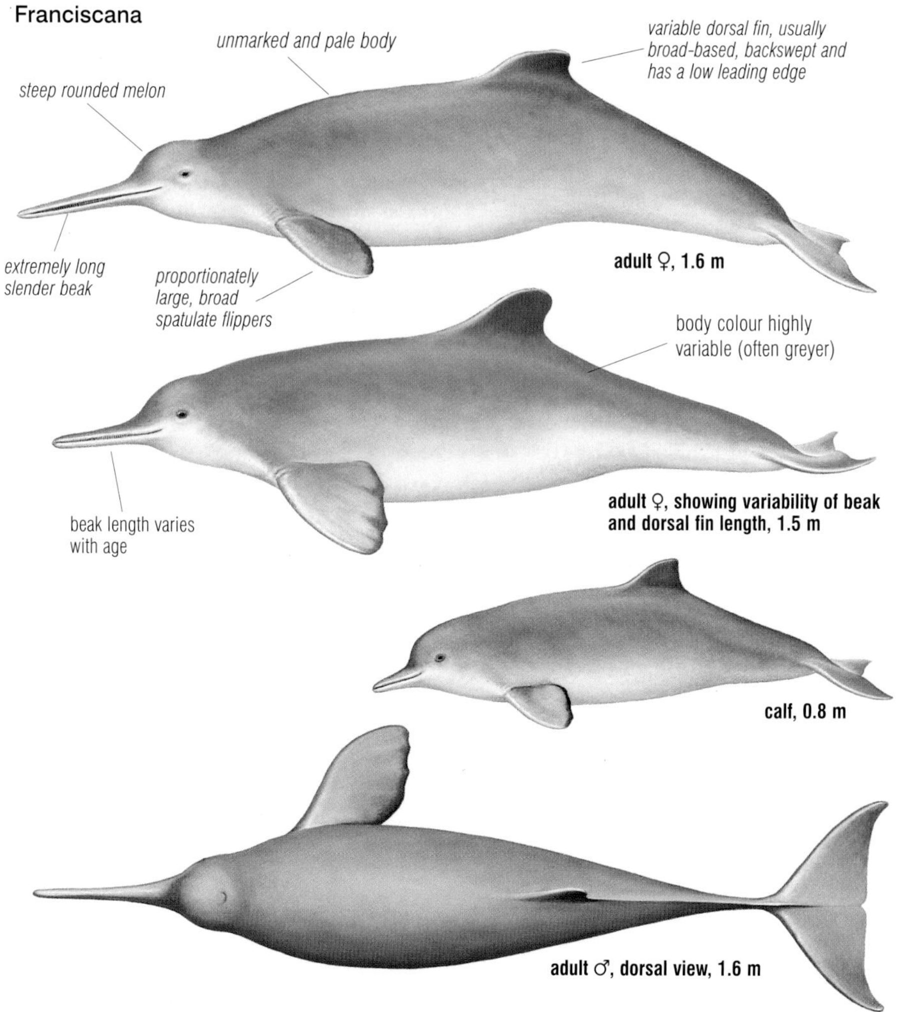

adult ♀, 1.6 m

adult ♀, showing variability of beak and dorsal fin length, 1.5 m

calf, 0.8 m

adult ♂, dorsal view, 1.6 m

Brazil (north to Espírito Santo) to NC Argentina (reaching Golfo San Matías and, formerly, Peninsula Valdés). Movements unknown. *Population* Unknown but a rather imprecise estimate of 42,000 off Rio Grande do Sul (Brazil) and common in La Plata estuary (Uruguay/ Argentina).

ECOLOGY

Social structure poorly known (see box). *Breaching* No data. *Diving* Almost entirely restricted to shallow water less than 30 m deep. Intervals between dives usually less than 30 sec, rarely over 1 min. *Diet* Mostly takes bottom-feeding fishes, as well as squid, octopus and shrimps.

Reproduction Reaches sexual maturity at 2–4 yrs. Mating occurs Jan–Feb and gestation occupies 10–11 months, calving mainly Nov–Dec, with young weaned at 8–9 months (but take solids from 3 months). Gives birth every 2 yrs. *Lifespan* Usually up to 15–20 yrs.

Amazon River Dolphin showing characteristic long beak, distinct rounded melon, broad-based dorsal ridge, and grey and pink coloration.

Amazon River Dolphin (Boto)

Inia geoffrensis

Amazon and Orinoco R basins of S America. Max 2.7 m.

Priority characters on surfacing

- *True river dolphin, large-bodied, rather robust*, with long beak and steep bulbous forehead.
- *Obscure dorsal fin, but quite noticeable broad-based dorsal ridge*.
- *Very long beak* with short bristles on upper and lower jaws, and *bulging melon* with variable chubby-cheeked appearance.
- Generally *off-white to blue-grey or vivid pink* above and paler below; some entirely pink.
- Young mostly uniform dark grey.
- Large, paddle-like flippers with blunt tips, flukes have a concave, often ragged, trailing edge, and eyes relatively small, though all these characters are rarely seen.
- Can turn head at rather sharp angle, and also appears capable of changing colour, becoming pinker when active and grey when relaxed.

Typical behaviour at surface

- *Slow swimmer*, surfaces at a shallow angle, *showing top of head and dorsal ridge fin.* Blow may reach 2 m and often heard before animal is seen (recalls a human sighing).
- Mostly singly or in pairs. Often occurs near Tucuxis, but do not associate. May approach boats but normally avoids them.
- Ads rarely jump clear of water but race across surface; young sometimes leap up to 1 m and often 'play', rolling over to reveal their pink bellies and flippers. Commonly slaps tail flukes on surface.

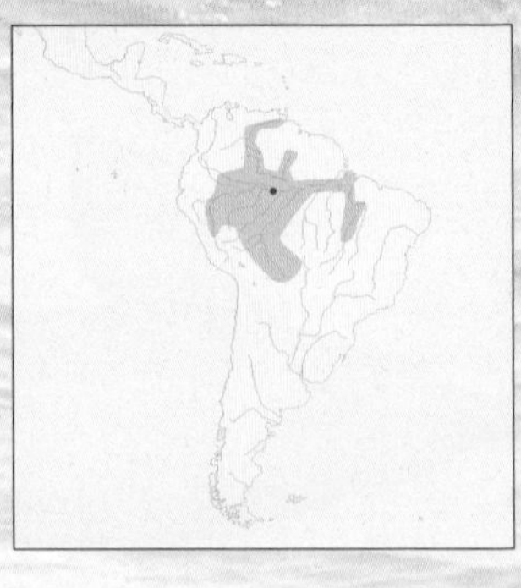

SIMILAR SPECIES

The only dolphin that overlaps in range is ***Tucuxi***, which is much smaller, has a taller dorsal fin and noticeably sprightly behaviour. Amazon River Dolphin tends to be found closer to shore than Tucuxi, which prefers deeper water in centre of rivers.

VARIATION

Age/sex ♂ larger with considerably more bulbous melon. Calf slimmer, more uniform and greyer, and older animals develop pink blotches on upperbody, with exception of blowhole region and mid-back, and some are virtually white in adulthood. **Physical notes** Full-grown ♂ reaches 2.7 m, ad ♀ 2.3 m, and both sexes weigh 85–185 kg. Newborn 76–82 cm and probably *c.*7

Amazon River Dolphin (Boto)

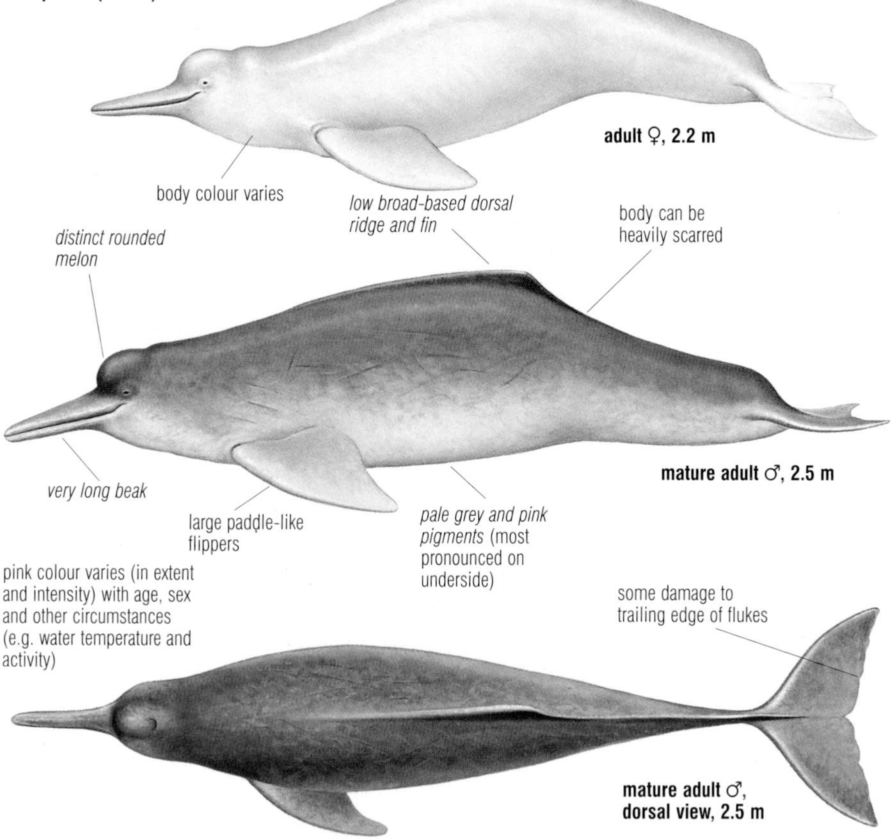

adult ♀, 2.2 m

body colour varies

low broad-based dorsal ridge and fin

body can be heavily scarred

distinct rounded melon

very long beak

large paddle-like flippers

pale grey and pink pigments (most pronounced on underside)

mature adult ♂, 2.5 m

pink colour varies (in extent and intensity) with age, sex and other circumstances (e.g. water temperature and activity)

some damage to trailing edge of flukes

mature adult ♂, dorsal view, 2.5 m

kg. **Taxonomy** Polytypic: *I. g. geoffrensis* (throughout most of Amazon R basin), *I. g. humboldtiana* (in Orinoco R basin), and *I. g. boliviensis* (on upper Madeira R, Brazil/Bolivia, from Porto Velho to Guajará-Mirim) which is sometimes accorded species status. No known external differences between them.

Amazon River Dolphins are usually slow, but capable of bursts of speed; note the broad-based dorsal ridge and very small and low dorsal fin.

DISTRIBUTION & POPULATION Widespread from S Venezuela and Guyana to E Colombia, E Ecuador, NE Peru, N Bolivia and much of Amazonian Brazil, including most major rivers and seasonally (Dec–Jun) even enters flooded forest. In dry season (Jul onwards) concentrates in main river channels. *Population* No complete estimates but appears not uncommon in many areas.

ECOLOGY

Occasional gatherings of up to 15 in dry season. *Breaching* Rare, may reach up to 1 m. *Diving* Most dives last 30–40 sec (up to 1.5 min). *Diet* Varies according to water levels. Up to 43 fish spp recorded, also crustaceans, molluscs and small turtles. May feed cooperatively and larger fish are torn to pieces rather than swallowed whole. Mostly feeds early morning and late afternoon, and flocks of terns may accompany them. Sometimes feeds near Tucuxi or Giant Otter *Pteronura brasiliensis*, and even man. *Reproduction* Sexually mature at *c.*5 yrs or when 2 m (♂) and 1.6 m (♀). In Brazil gestation lasts 10–11 months, with most calving in May–Jul at peak of high water (but in Venezuela most calve at end of low-water period). Calves weaned at 1 yr and ♀♀ give birth every 2–3 yrs. *Lifespan* Up to 36 yrs.

Amazon River Dolphin is capable of moving effortlessly through shallow water using its long flexible neck, very long beak and large paddle-like flippers; the animals are virtually blind with well-developed echolocation.

Amazon River Dolphin (in evasive acceleration): in close views the rib-like, highly flexible skin may be obvious.

SIMILAR SPECIES

Largely unmistakable, but might be confused with several other small cetaceans that occasionally reach river mouths, including ***Finless Porpoise*** (which lacks dorsal fin and long beak), ***Irrawaddy Dolphin*** (lacks long beak) and much larger ***Bottlenose*** and ***Indo-Pacific Humpback Dolphins*** (which have taller dorsal fins).

VARIATION

Age/sex ♀ larger with proportionately longer beak which may curve upwards and sideways. Calf slimmer and more uniform grey, subsequently developing paler

Ganges River Dolphin

Platanista [gangetica] gangetica

Ganges, Brahmaputra and Karnaphuli River systems. Max 2.6 m.

Priority characters on surfacing

- *True river dolphin*, with robust appearance and unique shape to very long beak.
- *Dorsal fin a very low, broad-based, triangle, more of a hump than fin*, set ⅔ back on body.
- *Largely grey*, greyish-blue to blue or even chocolate-brown, and often has slightly darker dorsal surface and pinkish tone to belly.
- *Very long slender beak, with elongated sharp front teeth exposed even in closed mouth*, laterally compressed and broader at tip.
- Steep melon but head relatively small; characteristic slit-like blowhole in shallow longitudinal ridge on melon; flexible neck.
- Eyes extremely small, positioned just above corners of mouth, which in profile curves up at top of jaw, giving smiling appearance. Almost blind.
- Flippers broad and paddle-like, usually with flat trailing edge but sometimes scalloped like fingers, whilst flukes distinctly concave on rear edge.

Typical behaviour at surface

- Small groups but often solitary or in pairs. Usually slow but capable of bursts of speed.
- Rarely leaps, but can be rather active and demonstrative. *Beak often lifts clear of surface and may swim on its side*. When startled may breach, re-entering water head first, followed by a lobtail movement and distinct splash.
- Vocalises constantly (echolocation clicks); breathing sounds like a sneeze.

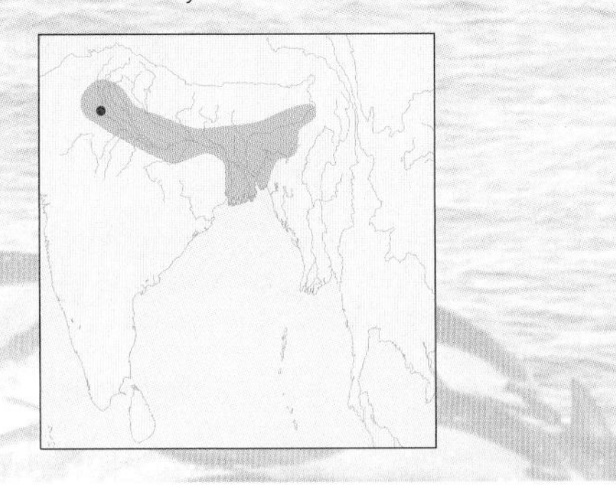

throughout Ganges, Brahmaputra, Megna, Sangu and Karnaphuli R basins, from India into Nepal and Bangladesh. Usually downstream of channel convergences, around meanders and islands. *Population* At least a few 100s and probably several 1,000s. Range has contracted considerably since 19th century, it being nearly extinct in Nepal, considerably reduced in India, with several subpopulations extirpated or nearly so, and only significant populations on the lower Sangu R, in Bangladesh, and the Ganges/Brahmaputra delta.

belly with slight pinkish hue. **Physical notes** Full-grown ♂ reaches 2.2 m, ad ♀ 2.6 m and both sexes 70–90 kg (probably up to 108 kg or even more). Newborn 65–90 cm and probably *c.*7.5 kg. **Taxonomy** Often regarded as conspecific with near-identical Indus River Dolphin, but separated geographically and by some internal differences.

DISTRIBUTION & POPULATION

Formerly occurred

Ganges River Dolphin may breach, re-entering head first, followed by a lobtail movement and distinct splash; note very low, broad-based triangular dorsal fin, greyish-blue pigments, and broad paddle-like flippers.

Ganges River Dolphin usually surfaces slowly but is capable of bursts of speed; note the steep melon and unique, crocodile-like, very long slender beak.

ECOLOGY

Breaching Occasional; re-enters water head first. *Diving* Mean dive time 30–90 sec but can last several min. *Diet* Principally shrimps and fish, from riverbeds. Pairs may forage cooperatively. *Reproduction* ♂ reaches sexual maturity when 1.7 m and ♀ when 2 m. Gestation *c.*1 yr, with extended calving, mainly early winter and early summer. Young weaned at less than 1 yr, and take solids after 1–2 months. *Lifespan* To at least 28 yrs.

Ganges and Indus River Dolphins

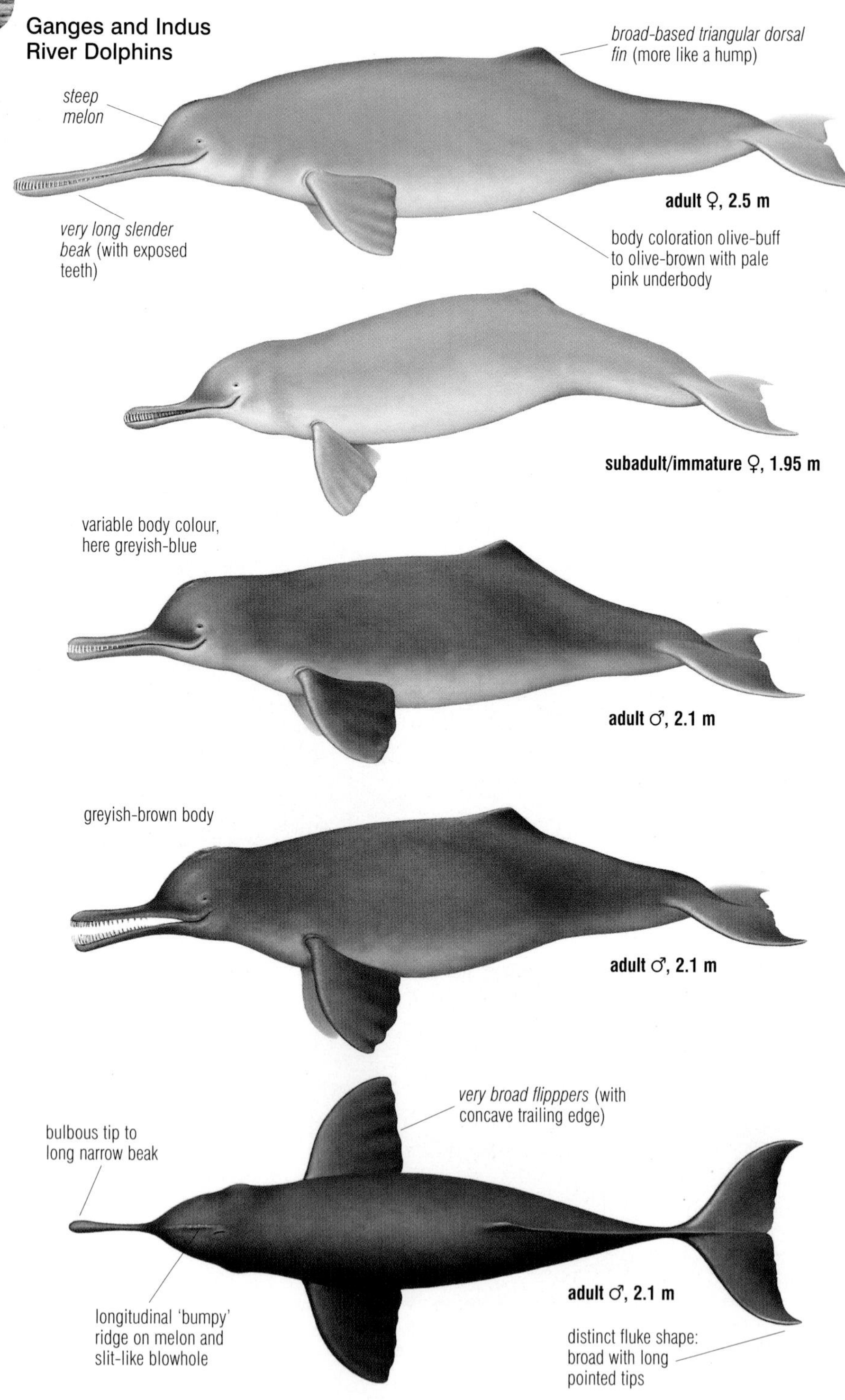

Indus River Dolphin

Platanista [gangetica] minor

Indus River. Max 2.5 m.

Priority characters on surfacing

- *True river dolphin*, identical to Ganges River Dolphin. Extremely rare.
- *Very long slender beak with many elongated sharp front teeth visible.*
- Small head; *obvious forehead melon* and shallow, longitudinal blowhole; flexible neck.
- *Very low, broad-based, triangular dorsal hump*, set 2/3 back on body.
- *Mostly grey*, grey-brown or dull brown, often slightly darker dorsally and pinker below.
- As Ganges River Dolphin, eyes poorly developed and just above corners of mouth.
- Flippers broad and paddle-like (usually with flat trailing edge, but sometimes has finger-like undulations), whilst flukes distinctly concave at rear edge.

Typical behaviour at surface

- Shy and retiring. Often solitary or in pairs. Usually slow but capable of bursts of speed. Usual time between surfacing 30–90 sec, but can be several minutes.
- Rarely leaps, but sometimes more demonstrative and *often swims on side. Beak (and sometimes almost entire head) often lifted above surface* and may breach with large splash in distress or because of danger, but flukes otherwise rarely visible.
- Vocalises constantly (echolocation clicks); breathing sounds like a sneeze.

VARIATION

Age/sex ♀ larger with proportionately longer beak. Calf slimmer and more uniform grey. **Physical notes** Full-grown ads 1.5–2.5 m and 70–90 kg; no data on newborn. **Taxonomy** Increasingly treated as conspecific with near-identical Ganges River Dolphin under name of South Asian River Dolphin. Separated geographically, and by relative prominence of nasal and maxillary crests, and blood protein composition, but these are generally considered insignificant to warrant species-level recognition.

DISTRIBUTION & POPULATION

Confined to Indus R and its tributaries where 3 meta-populations (the largest between the Guddu and Sukkur barrages, in SC Pakistan, which was declared a reserve in the 1970s), and range now just 700 km (20% of its historic extent). *Population* Estimated at 1,000+ in 2001.

ECOLOGY

No known differences from Ganges River Dolphin.

SIMILAR SPECIES

No overlap with ***Bottlenose*** and ***Indo-Pacific Humpback Dolphins***, ***Irrawaddy Dolphin*** and ***Finless Porpoise***. However, these are all easily differentiated given reasonable views: by the presence of a more obvious dorsal fin in much larger bottlenose and humpback dolphins; complete lack of a beak in Irrawaddy Dolphin; and absence of a dorsal fin in Finless Porpoise.

This Indus River Dolphin was rescued by local people. Although we have generally avoided using such photos in this guide, we have included this example to heighten public awareness of this very rare species.

SIMILAR SPECIES

Finless Porpoise is the only other small cetacean in the Yangtse R, China, but is readily distinguished as it lacks a dorsal fin and is generally darker.

VARIATION

Age/sex ♀ larger with proportionately longer beak and larger skull. Beak lengthens with age. Calf slimmer and more uniform grey. Facial pattern individually variable. **Physical notes** Full-grown ♂ reaches 2.3 m and 135 kg, and ♀ 2.5 m and over 240 kg (overall range 1.8–2.6 m and 100–240 kg). Newborn 80–91 cm and 2.5–4.8 kg.

DISTRIBUTION & POPULATION

Restricted to 1,700 km of middle and lower Yangtse R, and formerly its tributary lakes during flood periods. Range has contracted noticeably since 1940s, disappearing from Funchun R in late 1950s, and known from only 5 areas in 1990s,

Chinese River Dolphin (Baiji)

Lipotes vexillifer

Yangtse R, China. Max 2.5 m.

Priority characters on surfacing

- *Rather stocky river dolphin* with long slender beak. Critically Endangered.
- *Long, narrow, slightly upturned beak and rounded melon with steep forehead.*
- *Low, triangular stubby dorsal fin* (set c.$^{2}/_{3}$ back on body).
- Chiefly pale *bluish-grey to brownish-grey upperbody and pale grey to white underbody.*
- Pale patches on sides of face and rear body.
- Tiny eyes but not as small as those of *Platanista*.
- Large, rounded paddle-like flippers, and flukes distinctly notched, greyish above and almost white below.

Typical behaviour at surface

- Pods of 2–5 historically, with aggregations of up to *c.*15 recorded.
- *Elusive and easily disturbed.*
- At surface, *often only top of head, dorsal fin, and small part of back are exposed.*

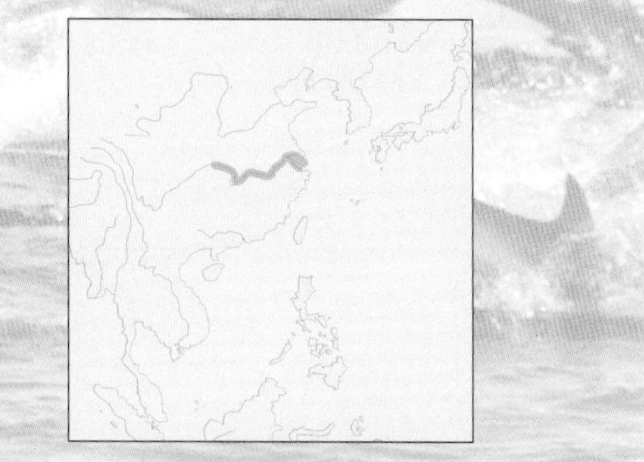

The Critically Endangered Chinese River Dolphin has a long slender beak, small rounded melon, and low triangular dorsal fin set well back, and large, rounded, paddle-like flippers.

Chinese River Dolphin (Baiji)

subadult, 1.9 m

small triangular dorsal fin set well back

shallow rounded melon

pale bluish-grey to brownish-grey

adult ♂, 2.3 m

long slender beak

rounded, paddle-like flippers

subtle flaring to pale underbody

melon can show pronounced ridge

adult ♂, dorsal view, 2.3 m

all downstream of Dongting Lake. Typically found at channel convergences, around sandbanks and below meanders. Makes both local and longer-range movements of up to 200 km. *Population* Estimates largely guesswork. Just 13 in 1997 (400 in 1979–80 and 300 in 1989) and continually declining.

ECOLOGY

Most common group size was 2–5 (with occasional amalgamations of subgroups reported), but no aggregations larger than 10 reported since 1980s. Sometimes rests in deepwater currents for 5–6 hrs. *Breaching* No data. *Diving* Intervals between dives generally 30–40 sec, followed by longer period of 200 sec. *Diet* Freshwater fish up to 9 cm long. *Reproduction* Age of sexual maturity 4–6 yrs. Most calving Feb–Apr and gestation 10–11 months. *Lifespan* At least 24 yrs.

Australian Snubfin and Irrawaddy Dolphins

As recently as 2005 the Australian Snubfin Dolphin, which was initially considered a population of the monotypic Irrawaddy Dolphin, was described to science. Thus, the Irrawaddy superspecies now comprises: Irrawaddy Dolphin of freshwater and marine habitats from the Bay of Bengal through South-East Asia, South Indonesia and the Philippines, whilst Australian Snubfin Dolphin is apparently an exclusively marine (largely coastal) form that occurs mainly off Northern Australia and to some extent in Papua New Guinea.

Both species lack a beak and are rather uniform, and thus superficially recall the partially sympatric but smaller Finless Porpoise, which lacks a dorsal fin. They are members of the Delphinidae and closely related to several 'blackfish', but placed in their own subfamily or in the same subfamily as Killer Whale. Here, however, for the sake of convenience for field users, the Australian Snubfin and Irrawaddy Dolphins are placed after the river dolphins and before the porpoises.

Irrawaddy Dolphin (Mekong River, Cambodia) in low, horizontal and very splashy leap.

Australian Snubfin Dolphin

Orcaella heinsohni

N Australia to Papua New Guinea. Max 2.7 m.

Priority characters on surfacing

- Robust, low fin, rounded melon, virtually beakless and long flexible neck.
- *Small, triangular, slightly falcate dorsal fin, with rather pointed tip, set on mid-back.*
- *Smooth back* (lacks or has only very indistinct median dorsal groove of Irrawaddy Dolphin and Finless Porpoise).
- *Generally slate to pale blue-grey* (or almost whitish-grey): may appear subtly 3-toned, with *slightly darker cape*, white abdominal field and intermediate pale grey to brownish-grey area on sides.
- *Blunt head with round forehead*; straight mouthline angled upwards, affording 'smiling' appearance, and often shows *clear necks crease*.
- Large spatulate flippers with curved leading edge and rounded tip; small, notched flukes have shallow concave trailing edge and pointed tips.

Typical behaviour at surface

- Normally in small groups.
- Shy and retiring, does not bow-ride; when alarmed may dive for prolonged periods.
- *Chiefly coastal and shallow waters*, including lagoons and river mouths.
- *Slow, not particularly active, keeps low at surface and often not easy to detect.*
- Occasional low leaps, or spyhops, lobtails and rolls sideways waving flipper; groups may suddenly perform playful jumps and sideways leaps with much splashing.

SIMILAR SPECIES

Fortunately, most probably no overlap or contact with very similar ***Irrawaddy Dolphin***, although in close views they can be separated by the latter's diagnostic (but variable) median dorsal groove and tendency to have a lower, more rounded dorsal fin, as well as 2-toned coloration (tripartite with darker cape in Australian Snubfin).

If seen poorly could be confused with ***Dugong*** or much smaller ***Finless Porpoise***, but neither has dorsal fin. Overlaps with ***bottlenose*** and ***Indo-Pacific Humpback Dolphins*** but lacks prominent beak and has different dorsal fin structure and altogether different behaviour.

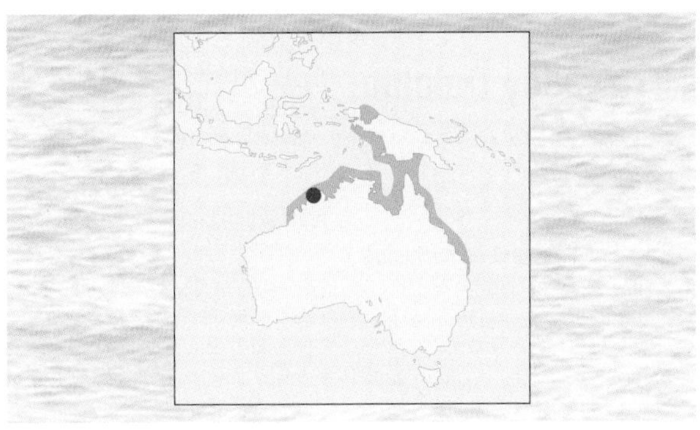

requires confirmation, particularly within the Indonesian archipelago.

DISTRIBUTION & POPULATION

Confirmed records from Broome, W Australia, Northern Territory, and the Queensland coast south

Australian Snubfin Dolphin, showing rounded melon and smooth back (only subtle median dorsal groove).

to the Brisbane R, with 1 record from Daru, Papua New Guinea. Inhabits mainly protected, shallow, coastal waters, especially adjacent to rivers and creeks. *Population* No overall estimate, but a group of 200 is thought to live off Townsville, NE Australia.

ECOLOGY

Apparently mostly as Irrawaddy Dolphin (see p. 244), but unknown if spits water from mouth like freshwater population of Irrawaddy Dolphin.

VARIATION

Age/sex ♂♂ apparently grow larger than ♀♀, but age development unknown. Smaller calf generally greyer. **Physical notes** Full-grown ad 1.86–2.7 m (♀♀ to 2.3 m), and 114–133 kg. Length and mass of newborn as Irrawaddy Dolphin. **Taxonomy** Monotypic and until very recently regarded as unnamed population of Irrawaddy Dolphin, but Australian and Asian animals differ in height and shape of the dorsal fin, lack of a median dorsal groove but presence of a dorsal cape in present species; their DNA and several osteological and dental features also differ. Nevertheless, further study of behavior, general biology, ecology and vocalizations is recommended, and animals from some regions, e.g. Papua New Guinea, are poorly known. The apparent gap in distributions (separated by deep oceanic waters) of the 2 species

Australian Snubfin Dolphins: note darker cape and sharper triangular dorsal fin.

Australian Snubfin Dolphin

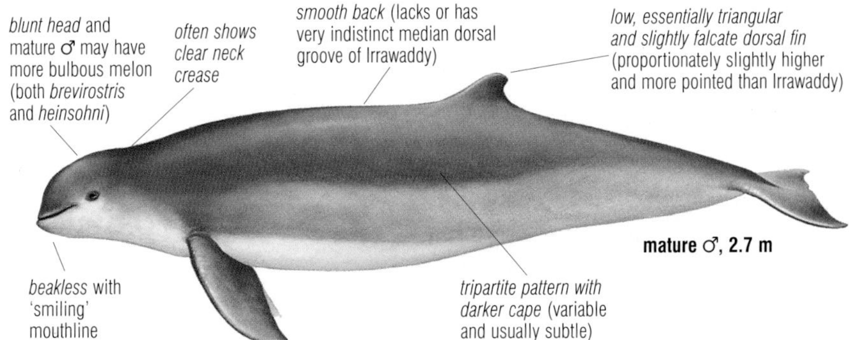

SIMILAR SPECIES

As Australian Snubfin Dolphin.

VARIATION

Age/sex ♂ apparently averages larger, but age development unknown. Smaller calf generally greyer. **Physical notes** Full-grown ad 1.73–2.75 m and 90–130+ kg. Newborn 0.9–1 m and 10–12 kg. **Taxonomy** Monotypic but variable (see Australian Snubfin Dolphin). Genetic data indicate presence of 2 well-defined subpopulations in Asia: in the Mekong R, Cambodia and S Laos, and elsewhere (from marine and freshwater sites in Thailand, Indonesia and Philippines), but apparently no clear separation between freshwater and marine populations. The Mahakam R (E Kalimantan) population has not been named, but possesses several variant and potentially taxonomically informative characters. The name '*fluminalis*' has been applied to *Orcaella* dolphins from the Ayeyarwady R, but there seem to be few data to support this for now.

Irrawaddy Dolphin

Orcaella brevirostris

Coasts and rivers of tropical Indo-Pacific. Max 2.75 m.

Priority characters on surfacing

- Robust, low fin, rounded melon, virtually beakless and long flexible neck.
- *Small, triangular and slightly falcate dorsal fin, with blunt rounded tip, set on mid-back.*
- *Mostly uniform slate to pale blue-grey*, with paler ventral field extending to underside of flippers (some can appear overall whitish above); lacks dorsal cape of Australian Snubfin Dolphin.
- *Blunt head with round forehead*; straight mouthline angled upward, affording 'smiling' appearance, and often has *clear neck crease*.
- *Median dorsal groove in front of dorsal fin* diagnostic (but variable).
- Large spatulate flippers with curved leading edge and rounded tip; small, notched flukes have shallow concave trailing edge and pointed tips.

Typical behaviour at surface

- Normally in small groups.
- Shy and retiring, does not bow-ride; when alarmed may dive for prolonged periods.
- Chiefly coastal and shallow waters, including lagoons, river mouths (estuarine and brackish waters), and freshwater rivers.
- *Slow, not particularly active, keep lows at surface and often not easy to detect.*
- Frequently (but solely or mainly in freshwater populations) *spits water from mouth*, which can be detected from some distance.
- Occasional low leaps, or spyhops, lobtails and sideways rolls waving flipper; groups may perform more playful jumps with much splashing.

DISTRIBUTION & POPULATION

Coastal waters and rivers (fragmented and small populations) from Bay of Bengal, W India, through Indochina, Malaysia, Indonesia and the Philippines (Malampaya Sound, Palawan). Landlocked populations reach at least 1,500 km inland on the Irrawaddy River, Myanmar; on Mekong River – up to 690 km upstream in Vietnam, Cambodia, S Laos, and on Mahakam River –Semayang Lake system – up to 560 km upstream in E Kalimantan, Indonesia. *Population* No overall estimate, but generally threatened, declining and

Irrawaddy Dolphin (Mekong River, Cambodia) spitting water, which it apparently uses as a method to disorientate fish.

Irrawaddy Dolphin

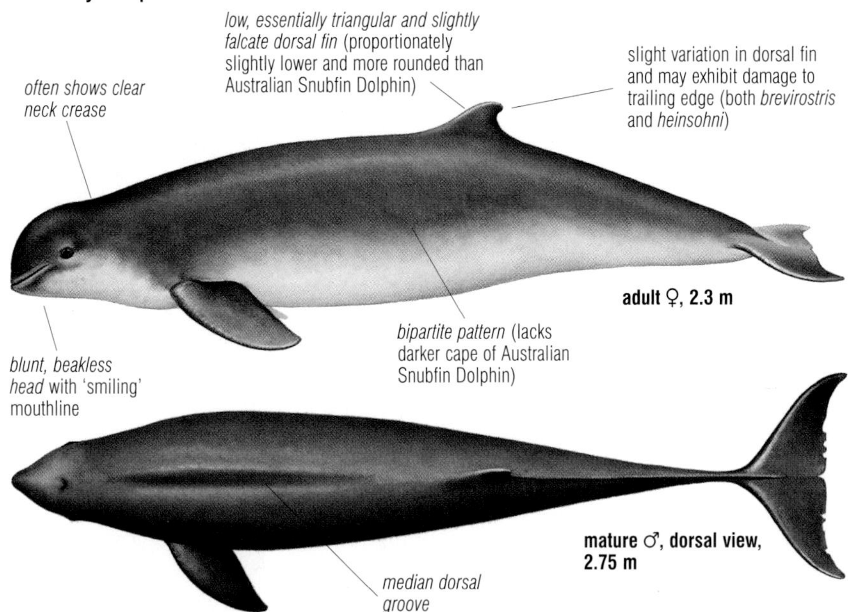

some subpopulations likely to become extinct in near future.

ECOLOGY

Group size usually just 2–3, but occasionally 10–15. *Breaching* Low, horizontal leaps or vertical jumps, just clearing surface, falling back sideways or backwards. *Diving* 0.5–12 min, usually 30 sec–3 min. *Diet* Fish, shrimps and cephalopods, usually taken near seabed or in open water, and sometimes cooperatively; spits water from mouth, apparently to confuse schools of fish. *Reproduction* Age of sexual maturity unknown, but ad size achieved at 4–6 yrs. Most births Dec–Jul, with gestation lasting *c.*14 months. Fully weaned at 2 yrs, but takes solids from 6 months. *Lifespan c.*30 yrs.

Irrawaddy Dolphin (Mekong River, Cambodia) sometimes makes more demonstrative, higher leaps; note blunt (beakless) head with 'smiling' mouthline.

Irrawaddy Dolphin (Mekong River, Cambodia) showing variation in body colour; note also triangular dorsal fin and median dorsal groove in front of it.

Porpoises

Porpoises are a very distinctive group of cetaceans, somewhat dolphin-like, small and beakless, with 6 species belonging to 3 genera – *Neophocaena*, *Phocoena*, *Phocoenoides* – collectively the family Phocoenidae. They are closely related to dolphins and were formerly considered a subfamily of the Delphinidae, but have spatulate or peg-like (not conical) teeth and several different anatomical and structural characteristics. Porpoises are largely continental shelf animals and favour temperate seas in both hemispheres.

Finding and identifying porpoises often requires skill, patience and some luck. They are generally inconspicuous at the surface and rarely perform acrobatics like dolphins. With the exception of Dall's, which is the fastest swimmer and regularly bow-rides, they tend to avoid boats and humans in general. The plate depicts each of the porpoises, but due to the generally very limited degree of overlap between them (only Dall's and Harbour Porpoises in North Pacific), confusion is much more likely with several dolphins. An example of such a pitfall, Irrawaddy Dolphin vs Finless Porpoise, appears on the comparison plate opposite. As always, it is best to concentrate on the diagnostic characters (preferably in combination), and with familiarity and experience these animals usually become easier to recognise. Some forms vary both individually and geographically, and also take account of sea and weather conditions which can affect overall appearance. The following characters are useful: overall size and shape, size of fin, and general shape of head/snout, but most important is the pattern around the head/face, across the body-sides and flippers, and the presence and nature of the demarcation between dorsal and lateral/ventral pigmentations. Note also possible behavioural differences, as well as range.

Breaching Burmeister's Porpoise showing typical blunt, beakless head and large, blunt-tipped flippers. Porpoises are generally elusive and undemonstrative, hence this behaviour is very rarely documented in photos.

Adult ♀ Spectacled Porpoise; typically fast and powerful, skimming surface with extensive splashing; note diagnostic long-based triangular fin and characteristic pale, diffuse 'saddle' below fin.

Yangtse Finless Porpoise (Yangtse River, China) can porpoise fast and low across the surface. It typically appears very dark; note the comparatively well-defined narrow dorsal ridge.

Porpoises

compact build with triangular dorsal fin
small, stocky with very tall triangular and falcate dorsal fin
very rare, usually difficult to detect
extensive pale foresides and flanks (often with mottled border)
Harbour Porpoise (N Atlantic and N Pacific), p. 252, max 1.9 m
traingular, strongly backswept dorsal fin (set at rear back)
Gulf of California Porpoise (Vaquita) (Gulf of California), p. 254, max 1.5 m
pale face with dark lips and eye
all dark, appearing black or dark grey
Burmeister's Porpoise (Coastal waters of S America), p. 255, max 2 m
robust body
distinctive white patterns
huge, round dorsal fin in adult ♂
Dall's Porpoise (N Pacific), p. 257, max 2.4 m
black-and-white pattern
all species are beakless with blunt face; surfacing behaviours are usually inconspicuous
Spectacled Porpoise (Southern Ocean), p. 250, max c.2.3 m
dorsal ridge narrow and prominent in Yangtse but broad and flat in Indo-Pacific
no dorsal fin
Chinese Finless Porpoise (W Pacific), p. 248, max 2 m
extreme white animal (in some populations off Japan to China Sea)
overall appearance and sometimes surfacing behaviours can appear superficially like Finless Porpoise but has dorsal fin and is usually clearly larger
usually medium-to dark grey
Indo-Pacific and Yangtse Finless Porpoises (N Indian and SW Pacific Ocean), p. 248, max 2 m
For comparison:
Irrawaddy Dolphin (Indo-Pacific), p. 244, max 2.75 m

DISTINCTIVE POPULATIONS

Three subspecies differ in dorsal denticulations, osteology and external proportions. Skull morphology varies intra-subspecifically. Morphological differences clouded by local variation and apparent clinal variation, as well as much individual, age and (minor) sexual variation.

Indo-Pacific Finless Porpoise *N. p. phocaenoides* (coastal and riverine waters of S China Sea and Indian Ocean) See box. Dorsal ridge comparatively broad and flat.

Yangtse Finless Porpoise *N. p. asiaorientalis* (Yangtse R and southern E China Sea where overlaps with next) Ads darker grey, sometimes nearly black, like young of other taxa. Dorsal ridge narrow and very prominent.

Chinese Finless Porpoise *N. p. sunameri* (Japan, Korea, Yellow Sea and southern E China Sea) Probably nearer *asiaorientalis* but dorsal ridge often even narrower. Ad is pale grey in coloration.

Finless Porpoise

Neophocaena phocaenoides

Warm, coastal Indo-Pacific waters. Max 2 m.

Priority characters on surfacing

- Streamlined porpoise, distinctive in being *finless and beakless*. Coastal and riverine.
- *Predominately grey*, with paler throat area and around genitals.
- Flat dorsal area with ridge of wart-like tubercles from mid-back to tailstock.
- *Rounded forehead* rises steeply from snout, slight bulbous melon often overhangs upper lip, and short mouthline curves slightly upwards.
- Rather flexible body, especially neck. Flukes rather broad with concave trailing edge; flippers large and rounded. Tiny dark eyes obvious on pale animals.
- Morphology varies regionally, especially animals in Japan to S China Sea.

Typical behaviour at surface

- Usually in singles, twos, or small groups.
- *Usually swims just below surface*, making sudden, darting movements, causing some disturbance when rising, and tends to roll onto side.
- Sometimes leaps from water, shows tail or spyhops, but only occasionally breaches.
- Does not bow-ride and shy of boats in most areas, except those in Yangtse R.

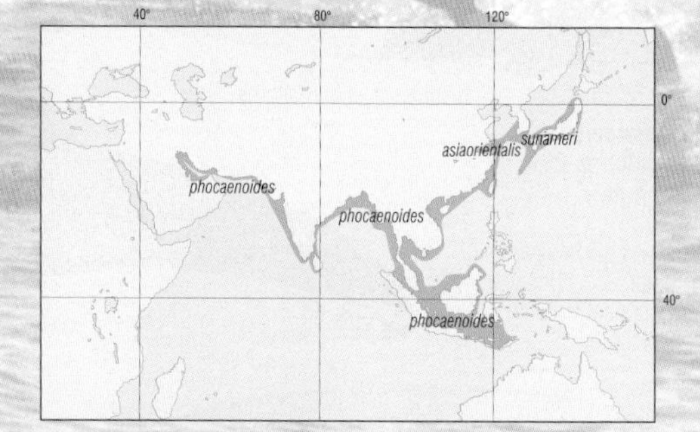

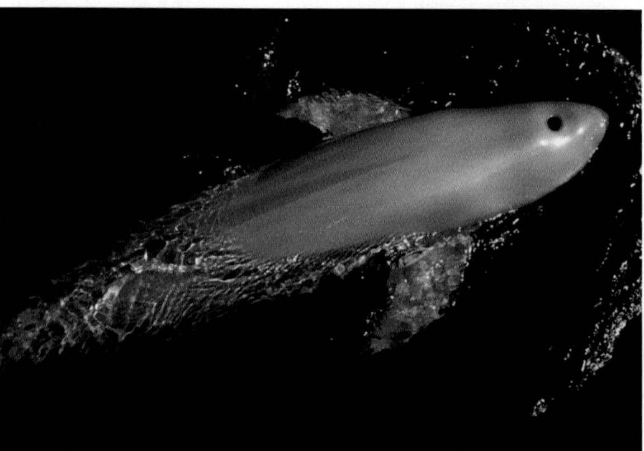

Chinese Finless Porpoise (Japan): pale grey in colour; dorsal ridge is narrow and very prominent.

SIMILAR SPECIES

In most of range, the smooth, finless back and beakless head make this small cetacean easily distinguished from similar-sized species, namely ***Irrawaddy*** and the ***river dolphins*** (qv). Unlikely to be confused with any other porpoises.

VARIATION

Age/sex ♂ slightly larger and proportionately heavier, including melon. Older animals paler grey than imms and considerably so than juvs. Those in Japan become

Finless Porpoise

almost white as ads, whilst in S China Sea and elsewhere they are charcoal grey. Calf slimmer, darker and often almost blackish, except paler dorsal areas (but in S China Sea pale grey to cream at birth). **Physical notes** Full-grown ad 1.2–2 m and 70–100 kg. Newborn 68–80 cm and *c.*7 kg. **Taxonomy** Polytypic with 3 races; regional differences in body size and morphology, and Yangtse R animals apparently a separate population. Two species, in tropical and the other in temperate waters, perhaps involved, both with geographical variants (e.g. in Japan up to 5 local populations identified on the basis of skull morphology and mtDNA).

DISTRIBUTION & POPULATION

Widespread in coastal waters from upper Persian Gulf east through Indo-Malaya, the Greater Sundas, Sulawesi, and north to Korea and Japan (reaching 38°N). Regularly enters estuaries and tidal, mangrove creeks, and even resident in middle Yangtse R and associated freshwater lakes, e.g. Poyang and Dongting, 1,600 km inland. Also penetrates Indus and Brahmaputra R. Some northerly populations make short-range migrations in winter, but resident in most areas. *Population* No overall estimate, but at least 2,000 in 2 areas of Japan in recent yrs.

ECOLOGY

Aggregations of up to *c.*50 recorded. *Breaching* Rare, vertically, falling sideways. *Diving* Typically breathes 3–4× between dives of up to 3 min (usually 20 sec). *Diet* Varied, opportunistically taking bottom and surface-dwelling fish, shrimp, squid, cuttlefish and octopus. *Reproduction* Those in coastal Japan and Inland Sea give birth in May–Jun, and Apr–May on Yangtse R; earlier in some tropical-water populations, mostly Nov–Dec. Gestation *c.*11 months and calves weaned at 6–7 months. Cows probably mainly breed every 2 yrs. *Lifespan* Up to 33+ yrs.

Indo-Pacific Finless Porpoises (Hong Kong): medium to dark grey, no dorsal fin, and has comparatively broad and flat dorsal ridge.

Adult ♂ Spectacled Porpoise, showing diagnostic black-and-white pattern and huge rounded dorsal fin.

SIMILAR SPECIES

Unmistakable: no other similar-sized cetacean has such sharply demarcated black-and-white pattern

Spectacled Porpoise

Phocoena dioptrica

S Hemisphere, offshore islands. Max 2.3 m.

Priority characters on surfacing

- Unmistakable 2-toned, stocky porpoise with highly distinctive (but variable) dorsal fin.
- Typical porpoise shape, being *small-headed and virtually beakless.*
- *Huge, broad-based and rounded dorsal fin* (particularly ad ♂).
- Glossy *blue-black upperside sharply demarcated from white underside.*
- Mouthline short and straight with black lips, white spectacles and ill-defined dark gape–flipper stripes, but all hardly visible at sea.
- Narrow but clear white band on top of tailstock; distinctly notched, point-tipped flukes with white/pale grey undersides.
- Flippers small with rounded tips and either all dark or greyish-white with grey edges.

Typical behaviour at surface

- *Very inconspicuous on surfacing,* but often fast in water, when white underside frequently visible, and *arches back strongly on diving, when dorsal fin prominent.*

- Typical porpoise: slow roll at surface, then swims rapidly just below surface.
- Normally avoids boats; group size small, apparently mostly singles and pairs.

160°
80°
0°
80°
160°
80°
40°
0°
40°
80°

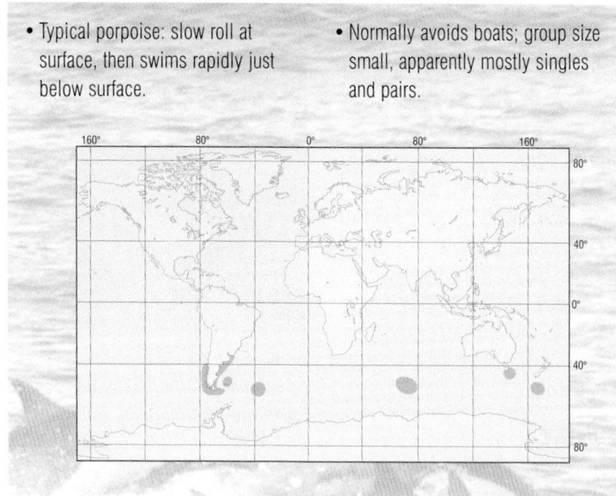

midway across flanks, but beware confusion with distant ***Commerson's*** and ***Black Dolphins*** and ***Burmeister's Porpoise***, though all are strikingly different in dorsal fin shape and other colour features, whilst superficially similar ***Southern Right Whale Dolphin*** lacks dorsal fin.

VARIATION

Age/sex ♂ averages larger and has noticeably larger, rounded dorsal fin; shorter and a shallow triangle in ♀,

Spectacled Porpoise

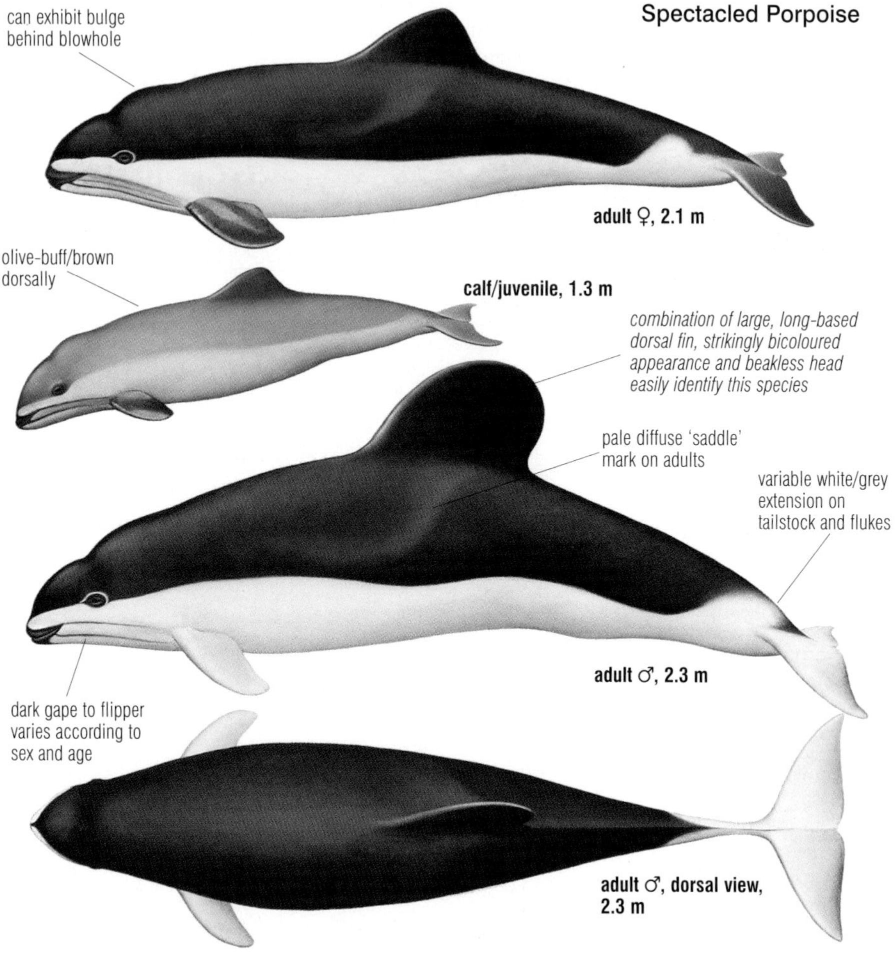

can exhibit bulge behind blowhole
adult ♀, 2.1 m
olive-buff/brown dorsally
calf/juvenile, 1.3 m
combination of large, long-based dorsal fin, strikingly bicoloured appearance and beakless head easily identify this species
pale diffuse 'saddle' mark on adults
variable white/grey extension on tailstock and flukes
adult ♂, 2.3 m
dark gape to flipper varies according to sex and age
adult ♂, dorsal view, 2.3 m

and same shape but smaller in respective young, which are less pure white below, whilst dark stripe from lips to flippers often fades with age. Calf dark grey dorsally and pale grey ventrally, with darker streaks including well-defined mouth–flipper stripe. **Physical notes** Full-grown ad 1.24–2.3 m (max ♀ 2.1 m) and 90–115 kg. Newborn 50–100 cm. **Taxonomy** Formerly classified as *Australaphocaena dioptrica*.

DISTRIBUTION & POPULATION

Probably circumpolar in cold temperate waters of 5–10°C, but known mainly from Atlantic coast of S America, exceptionally north to 32°S in Brazil, and regular in the Falklands, S Georgia (and south in Drake Passage to at least 59°S) and S Indian Ocean islands of Kerguelen and Heard, as well as in Australian and New Zealand subantarctic regions (once in Tasmania). Principally oceanic. *Population* No estimates but apparently uncommon away from Patagonia.

ECOLOGY

Typical group size 1–3, occasionally up to 10. *Breaching* No data. *Diving* Insufficient data. *Diet* Fish, krill and small squid (but dataset tiny). *Reproduction* Age of sexual maturity *c.*2 yrs in ♀ and 4 yrs in ♂. Calves mostly born Nov–Feb, gestation 11 months and lactation 6–15 months. *Lifespan* Unknown.

Adult ♂ (rear), and ♀ and calf Spectacled Porpoises; young/♀ have a more triangular, but still diagnostically large, long-based and rounded dorsal fin.

Harbour Porpoise (N Atlantic): note small blunt head, and well-demarcated cape and tailstock.

SIMILAR SPECIES

Behaviour usually inconspicuous, but characteristic roll and, if seen well, small size and small triangular dorsal fin, make it relatively easily distinguished from various overlapping dolphins. ***Dall's Porpoise*** overlaps in N Pacific, but its black-and-white coloration and different dorsal fin shape should identify it (beware, hybrid Dall's × Harbour Porpoise, although many are rather distinctive). When no obvious clue as to size, dorsal fin of ***Minke Whale*** can appear confusingly similar.

Harbour Porpoise

Phocoena phocoena

N Atlantic and N Pacific.
Max 1.9 m.

Priority characters on surfacing

- Chunky, compact, but *rather small porpoise*, with rotund body and *blunt head*.
- Short broad-based, *triangular dorsal fin set just beyond midpoint of back* (long sloping leading edge and blunt tip).
- Generally *dark grey dorsally with paler foresides*, white throat and ventral surface; variable grey blotches across foresides to flanks.
- Thin (and difficult-to-see) dark grey gape–flipper stripe.
- Small rounded head slopes to mouth (short beak); straight mouthline slants upwards.
- Flippers small and fairly rounded; slight dorsal ridge extends from dorsal fin to tailstock; flukes all dark with concave trailing edge, median notch and blunt tips.

Typical surfacing behaviour

- Retiring and rarely bow-rides, but sometimes attracted to slow-moving boats.

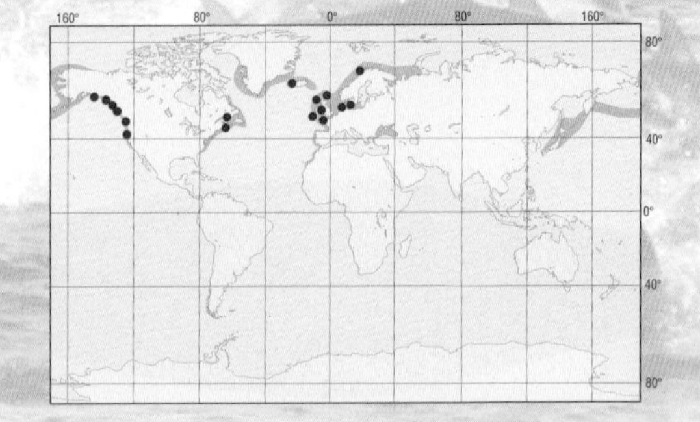

- Normally in small loose groups, mother–calf 'pair' or alone.
- Slow swimmer, usually inconspicuous, *surfacing in rolling motion, occasionally with vigorous vertical leap out of water*.
- Unobtrusive breathing sequence makes species difficult to observe in all but calmest seas.
- Often rests or basks on surface, particularly in calm weather.
- Breaches and other leaps, and tail-slaps (most often given when socialising) are rare.

VARIATION

Age/sex ♀ slightly larger (*c*.10–15 cm longer); young tend to be darker. Calf slimmer and more uniform. **Physical notes** Full-grown ads 1.3–1.9 m and 50–70 kg (animals of over 2 m recorded). Newborn 67–90 cm and *c*.5 kg. **Taxonomy** Polytypic with 3–4 races: *P. p. phocoena* (N Atlantic, W Africa), *P. p. relicta* (Black Sea, Sea of Azov), *P. p.* subsp (NW Pacific) and *P. p. vomerina* (NE Pacific) differ mainly in skull and jaw morphology, and mtDNA. Geographic differences in frequency of tubercles, e.g. Black Sea population has fewer than Atlantic population.

DISTRIBUTION & POPULATION

Inhabits shelf areas (rarely in seas deeper than 200 m), including estuaries, wide rivers and harbours, of N Atlantic, from the USA and W Africa to W Greenland and Barents Sea, and penetrating the North, Baltic and Black Seas, and N Pacific, from N California and C Japan north to the Chukchi Sea. Range generally discontinuous. Some populations, especially in largely land-locked seas, apparently strictly resident. *Population* No overall estimate, but *c*.340,000 in NW European waters in 1994.

Harbour Porpoise

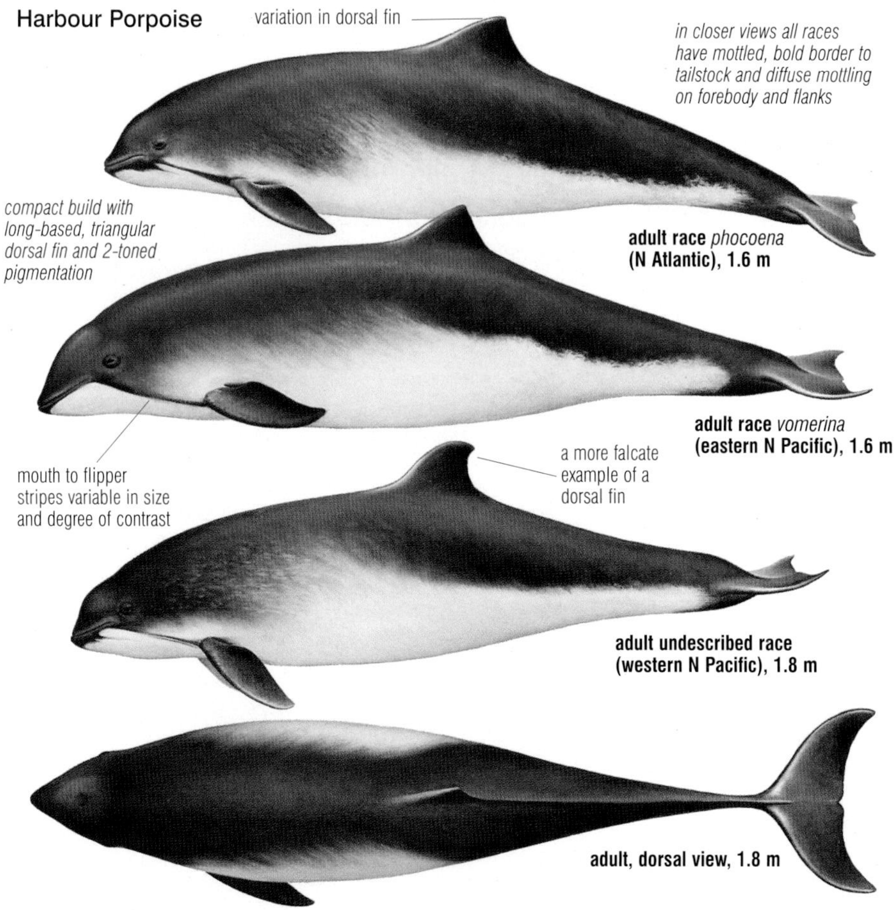

ECOLOGY
Most frequently in groups of 2–8, with concentrations, mostly post-breeding, of 10s (possibly >100) infrequent. *Breaching* Rare, vertically, falling sideways. *Diving* Normally *c.*3 min (6–12 min recorded) and up to 90 sec at surface; max depth 220 m. *Diet* Forages near seabed, taking schooling fish, cephalopods and small crustaceans. *Reproduction* Sexually mature at 3–5 yrs. Most calves born May–Aug. Gestation lasts 10–11 months and calves weaned at 4–8 months. Lactation and pregnancy frequently overlap, with many cows enduring pregnancies several yrs in succession and mating commencing 1.5 months after calving. *Lifespan* Up to 24 yrs.

Harbour Porpoises (nominate phocoena, *Atlantic) are compact with a short, long-based triangular dorsal fin and paler foresides merging into whiter ventral areas.*

SIMILAR SPECIES
Might only be confused at distance, due to its tall dorsal fin, with ***Bottlenose*** and ***Long-beaked Common Dolphins*** (both overlap). Differences in body coloration and shape, and lack of beak, as well as in behaviour, distinguish present species.

VARIATION
Age/sex ♀ averages slightly larger. Calf generally slimmer and more uniformly dark. **Physical notes** Full-grown ♂ to 1.45 m and ♀ 1.5 m and weigh 30–55 kg. Newborn 70–78 cm and 7.5 kg.

DISTRIBUTION & POPULATION
Restricted to upper Gulf of California (Sea of Cortez), Mexico, within 25 km of shore and in waters less than 50 m deep, being most frequent in Colorado R delta. Formerly extended further south along Mexican mainland. *Population*

Gulf of California Porpoise (Vaquita)

Phocoena sinus

Gulf of California. Max 1.5 m.

Priority characters on surfacing
- *Among the smallest cetaceans.*
- Like all porpoises, *stocky and compact, with a blunt, near-beakless head.*
- *Dorsal fin tall, triangular and clearly falcate* (whitish spots on leading edge become small bumps in full-grown ad).
- *Medium to dark grey, becoming paler on lower sides* and whiter still ventrally; in certain lights can appear tawny or brownish.
- *Pale face contrasting with blackish-grey lips and eye*; dark grey gape–flipper stripe broader distally (variable), but all are difficult to see.
- Large, broad-based flippers, curved and have pointed tips; flukes notched and pointed.

Typical behaviour at surface
- Smooth movements, relatively inconspicuous, slow surfacing. *Shows little of itself at surface and often stays underwater for rather long periods.*
- Shy and retiring, and avoids boats.
- Normally in small pods of up to 7.
- *Very rare and local.*

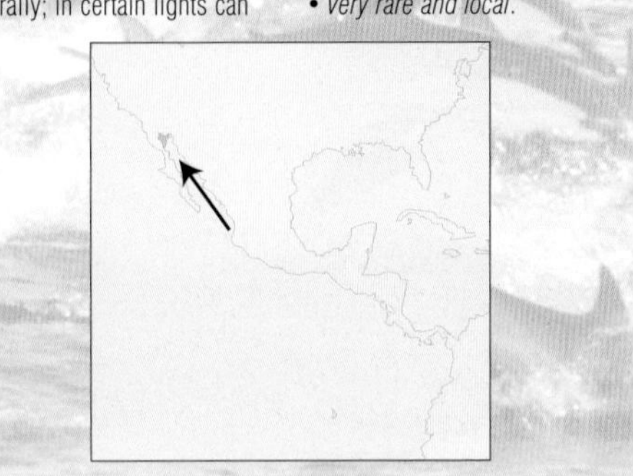

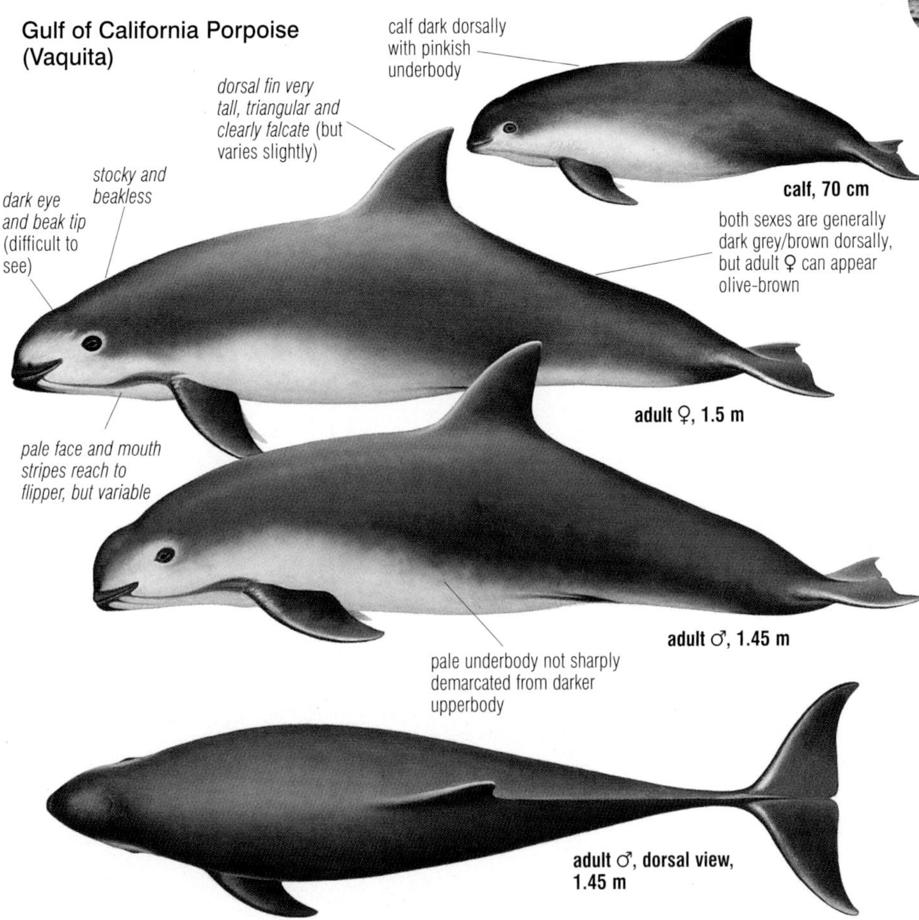

Currently estimated at just 500–600, and much reduced due to habitat alteration and commercial fishing.

ECOLOGY

Most frequently occurs singly or in pairs, occasionally groups up to 10, but aggregations appear very short-lived. *Breaching* Unknown. *Diving* Poorly described. *Diet* Small bottom-feeding fish and squid. *Reproduction* Sexually mature at 3–6 yrs. Gestation *c.*11 months, with most calving in Feb–Apr (peak late Mar/early Apr). Cows probably do not breed annually. *Lifespan* 21+ yrs.

Burmeister's Porpoise

Phocoena spinipinnis

Coastal waters of S America. Max 2 m.

Priority characters on surfacing

- All dark with shallow backswept dorsal fin and low-profile swimming behaviour.
- *Stocky compact body, blunt beakless head* (flat forehead) and upturned mouthline.
- *Triangular and strongly backswept dorsal fin* (angled low with long, leading edge and short convex trailing edge) *set well beyond*

SIMILAR SPECIES

Separated from superficially similar ***Chilean Dolphin*** by shallower, backswept and rearward dorsal fin (in latter is round, set high on mid-back), and by different surfacing behaviour. Chilean Dolphin also has grey forehead and pure white throat and belly. Distinctive differences in dorsal fin shape, coloration and surfacing behaviour readily separate it from overlapping ***Spectacled Porpoise*, *Commerson's Dolphin*** and ***Franciscana***. However, if seen badly, could be confused with fur seals and sea lions, which often raise their flippers (and can appear like dorsal fin of Burmeister's Porpoise).

midpoint of back.

- *Body black or deep grey*; ventrally paler grey with 2 abdominal stripes.
- Dark lips, eye-patch and dark grey chin–flipper stripe (wider on left side of body).
- Broad-based and blunt-tipped large flippers, distinctly notched, point-tipped tail flukes (variably paler on underside).

Typical behaviour at surface

- Inconspicuous on surface, but at times moves jerkily.
- *Shy, easy to overlook and groups tends to scatter when approached.*
- Uninterested in vessels and does not porpoise or bow-ride when approached.
- Usually in small groups.

VARIATION

Age/sex ♀ averages 5 cm larger, and pattern of abdominal stripes varies sexually; tubercles on leading edge of dorsal fin become sharper with age. Slimmer calf much like ad in coloration. **Physical notes** Full-grown ads reach 2 m and 105 kg; Atlantic animals perhaps slightly larger than those in Pacific, where some indications that it forms a separate population. Newborn 86 cm (mean).

Burmeister's Porpoise, showing all dark body with triangular and strongly backswept dorsal fin (with low angled and long leading edge) set far at the back.

DISTRIBUTION & POPULATION

To 50 km off South America, discontinuously from Tierra del Fuego to N Peru (at 5°S) and S Brazil. Commonest inshore, occasionally frequenting estuaries and the kelp-line. Probably more common on Pacific coast where seems numerous. May move north–south or inshore–offshore seasonally, at least in some areas (in others, e.g. Beagle Channel, appears resident). *Population* No estimates or information concerning threats or trends.

Burmeister's Porpoise surfaces low and rolls leisurely, showing typical shape and angle of dorsal fin.

ECOLOGY

Typical group size <8 but up to 70 may occur together. *Breaching* Rare, vertically, falling sideways. *Diving* Unrecorded in waters deeper than 60 m; dives of 1–3 min common. *Diet* Fish, krill and other crustaceans. *Reproduction* Calving perhaps early autumn, and ♀♀ may give birth annually. Gestation estimated 11–12 months and conception and parturition may peak Feb–Mar. *Lifespan* At least 12+ yrs.

Burmeister's Porpoise

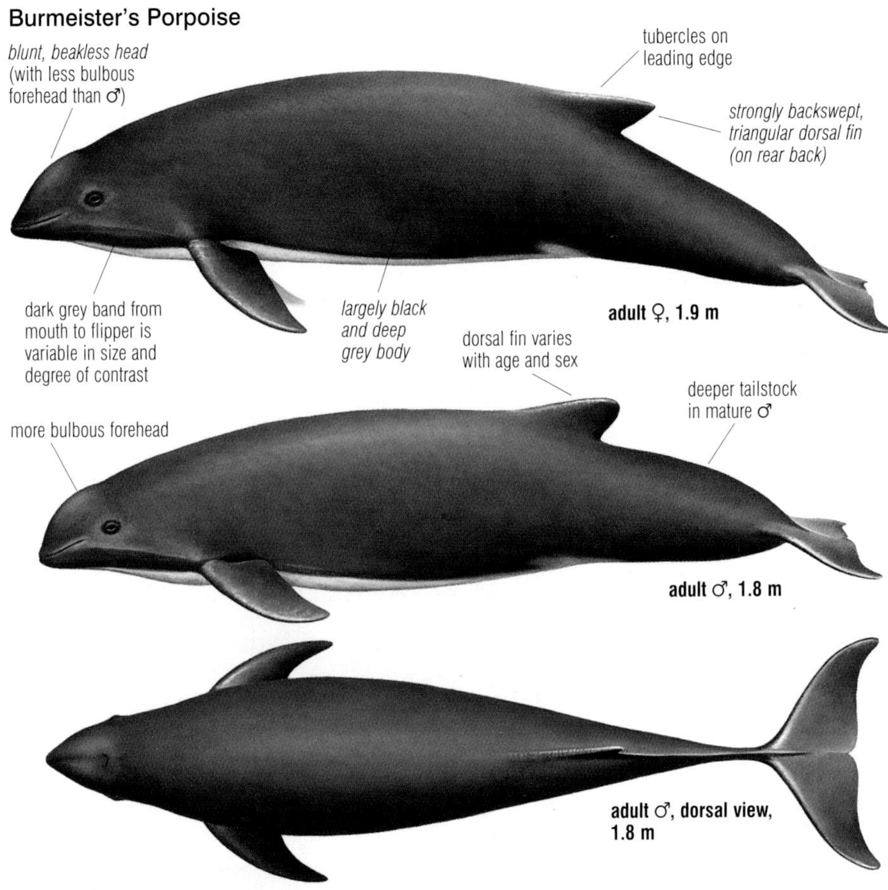

Dall's Porpoise

Phocoenoides dalli

N Pacific. Max 2.4 m.

Priority characters on surfacing

- *Robust though compact, and hyperactive in nature*, being energetically dolphin-like on surface. Regular in deep offshore waters.
- *Relatively small, short-beaked head* (rather flat forehead or slight melon; from above, appears triangular), with upturned mouthline.
- Broad-based *triangular dorsal fin with white to pale grey 'frosting'* on upper part.
- *Chiefly black with bright white flank–ventral patch* (extending to mid belly and midway along sides).
- Small/round flippers near head; notched flukes with variable white trailing edge.
- Two colour types: *dalli*-type (described above) and *truei*-type

SIMILAR SPECIES

In range might only be confused with ***Harbour Porpoise***, especially if seen poorly or when slow rolling at surface, but well differentiated in dorsal fin shape and coloration, as well as by their completely different surfacing behaviours (at high speeds only Dall's throws up 'rooster tail').

VARIATION

Age/sex ♂ averages larger,

has wider distance between anal and genital openings, and deeper post-anal hump. Slimmer calf has similar, but muted, coloration, with dark and pale grey, instead of black and white, and lacks pale areas on fin and flukes. **Physical notes** Full-grown ♂ reaches 2.4 m and ♀ 2.1 m (minima for both sexes 1.7 m), and 170–220 kg. Newborn *c*.1 m and 11 kg. **Other data** Beside 2 classic morphs, *dalli*-type and *truei*-type, intermediates and mostly greyish or even all-black and other variants known. **Taxonomy.** Two major colour types: *dalli*-type frequent in N Pacific, whilst *truei*-type is only in W Pacific. Both forms controversial and previously often thought to represent races or even species, but some recent studies consider them mere colour morphs which vary in frequency between populations. Hybrids: Dall's × Harbour rather frequent (see latter).

(larger flank patch extends to level of flipper).

Typical behaviour at surface

- Apparently the fastest-swimming small cetacean, reaching 55 km/h in short bursts.
- *On rapidly surfacing often slices surface, producing characteristic trail of spray off tail, with none of the body visible.*
- Sometimes moves slowly and rolls at surface, creating little or no disturbance.
- Mostly in small fluid groups.
- *Regularly bow-rides in jerky zigzags* before suddenly disappearing; often appears beside fast-moving vessel (but loses interest if speed is less than 20 km/h).
- Breaching, porpoising, and other aerial behaviours rare.

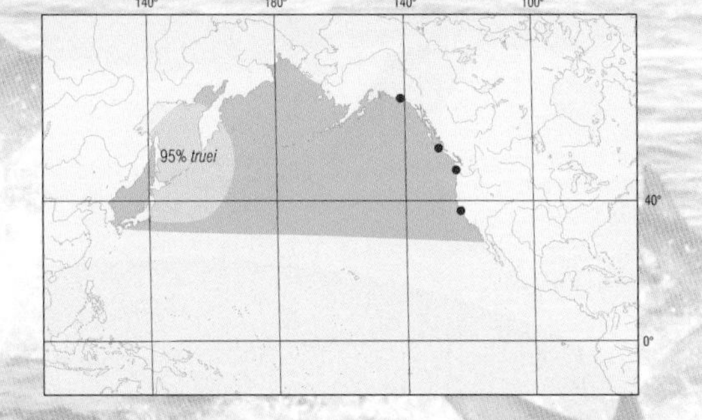

DISTRIBUTION & POPULATION

Cool-temperate waters of N Pacific, from US/Mexico border and C Japan north to Bering and Okhotsk Seas. Of the 2 morphs, *dalli*-type occurs throughout, but *truei*-type restricted to W Pacific between 35°N and 54°N. In W Pacific appears to migrate north in summer and south in winter, but performs inshore–offshore movements in parts of E Pacific. *Population* Reasonably abundant, with 50,000 off W USA, 80,000 in Alaskan waters, more than 100,000 off Japan and several 100,000s in Sea of Okhotsk.

ECOLOGY

Usually in groups of <20, but exceptional aggregations

Dall's Porpoise often swims just below surface; note robust body, short-beaked head and distinctive pattern.

of several 100s or even 1,000. Frequently associates with Pacific White-sided Dolphin. *Breaching* Rare, vertically, falling sideways. *Diving* May reach 500 m. *Diet* Takes fish and cephalopods, mainly at night. *Reproduction* Sexually mature from 3.5 yrs. Gestation lasts 10–12 months and calves probably weaned <4 months. Most births apparently in summer, mainly Jun–Sep. *Lifespan* Up to 22 yrs.

Dall's Porpoises rolling in calm sea, showing forward-projecting dorsal fin ('frosted' whitish-grey), white thoracic panel (left animal) and exaggerated, deep tailstock (right animal).

Dall's Porpoise

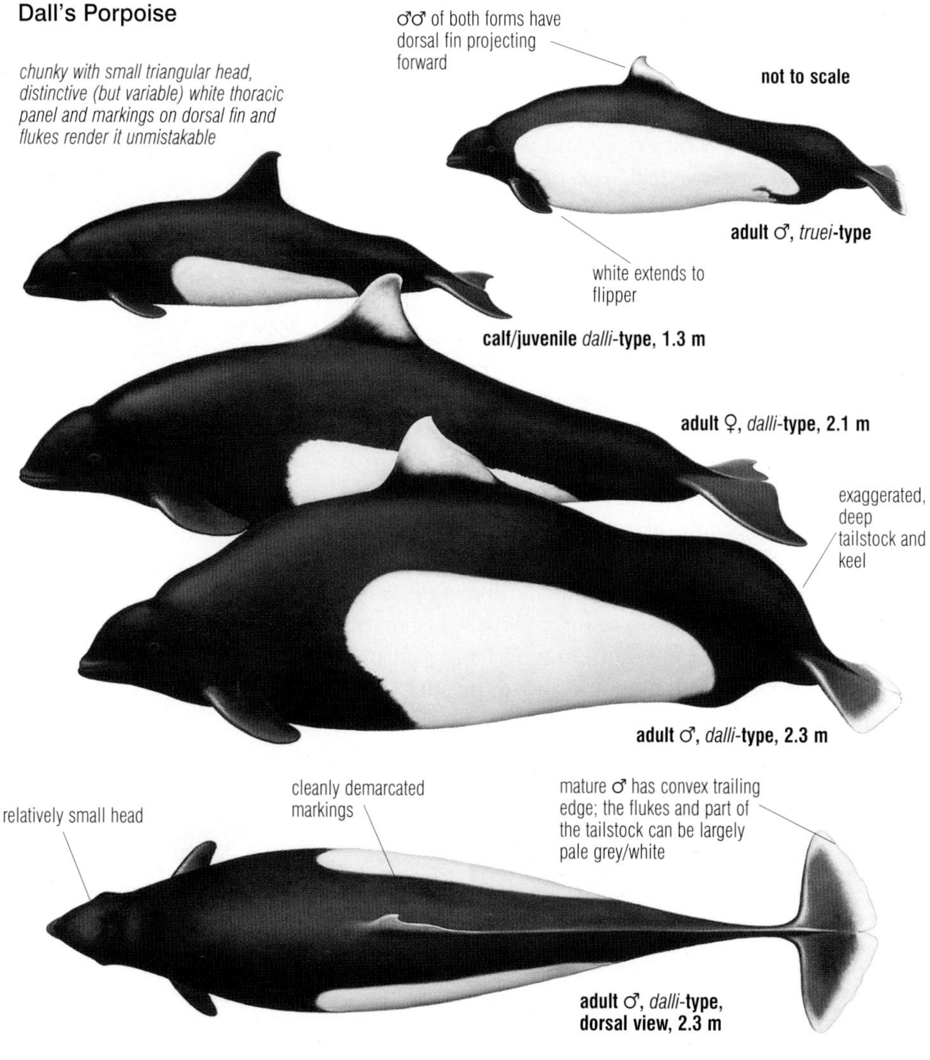

chunky with small triangular head, distinctive (but variable) white thoracic panel and markings on dorsal fin and flukes render it unmistakable

♂♂ of both forms have dorsal fin projecting forward

not to scale

adult ♂, *truei*-type

white extends to flipper

calf/juvenile *dalli*-type, 1.3 m

adult ♀, *dalli*-type, 2.1 m

exaggerated, deep tailstock and keel

adult ♂, *dalli*-type, 2.3 m

relatively small head

cleanly demarcated markings

mature ♂ has convex trailing edge; the flukes and part of the tailstock can be largely pale grey/white

adult ♂, *dalli*-type, dorsal view, 2.3 m

Sirenians (sea cows)

The Sirenia are the only herbivorous marine mammals and are distantly related to several other mammalian orders, namely elephants (Proboscidea), hyraxes (Hyracoidea) and aardvarks (Tubulidentata). Collectively, they are known as subungulates, which share internal and dental characteristics, and all lack a clavicle, nails and hooves. In fact, the only thing that sirenians possess in common with other marine mammals, like cetaceans, is that they are wholly aquatic, mostly in fresh and brackish water in the case of the manatees. This unique group, represented by 4 living species in 2 families, Dugongidae (with a single genus *Dugong*, the Dugong of the Indian and SW Pacific Oceans) and Trichechidae (3 species of manatees *Trichechus* in tropical coastal regions of the Atlantic and S American and W African rivers). The extinct Steller's Sea Cow, of the N Pacific, was placed in a separate genus, *Hydrodamalis*. Living Sirenians are tropical-water species, which have been extensively hunted in recent years, but despite their sluggish appearance, these animals can show a remarkable turn of speed when threatened. All have fatty, rounded bodies with a torpedo-like appearance, huge head (almost hippo-like with broad snout and thick 'lips'), chin and whisker-pad covered with short stiff dense bristles, and small eyes and nostrils on top of the snout. None has a dorsal fin but all have characteristic paddle-like forelimbs, whilst Dugong has whale-like flukes with a median notch, and the manatees a round fat tail, somewhat like a beaver. They are unlikely to be confused with other marine mammals (if seen well), but Dugong has cetacean-like flukes which often appear above the surface prior to diving.

Dugongs are herbivorous (this individual is feeding on sea grasses) and principally diurnal, but where heavily disturbed by man may largely feed at night.

Dugong showing typical surfacing profile: note large, round back and nostrils on top of snout.

Dugongs raise their whale-like flukes rather high prior to deep dives.

Sirenians (sea cows)

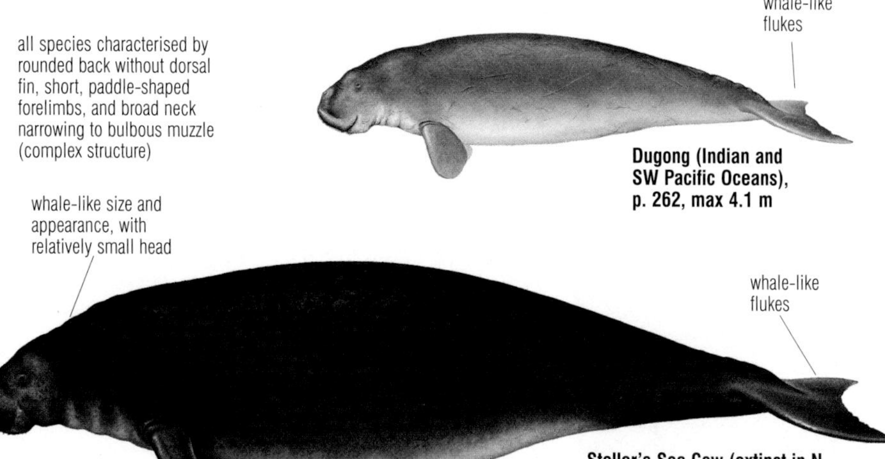

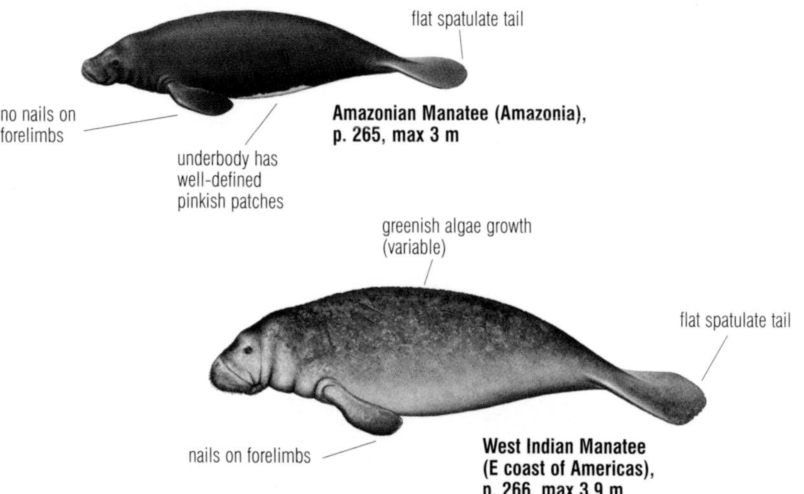

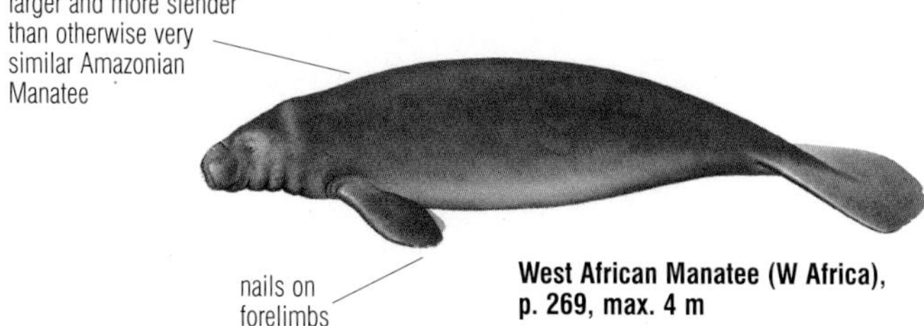

Dugong

Dugong dugon

Tropical Indo-Pacific coasts. Max 4.1 m.

Priority characters on surfacing

- *Large sea cow* with huge hippo-like head. Overall size as large dolphin.
- *Whale-like flukes* with median notch (unique among living sirenians).
- Head/muzzle slightly downcurved, widest and bulbous at tip; whisker-pad and chin covered with short, dense bristles. Nostrils (semi-circular) on top of snout; broad 'lips' almost conceal angled mouthline.
- Eyes small, but noticeable, dark with pale ring.
- Paddle-shaped forelimbs; flexible, but when swimming fast held close to body.
- Generally *slate grey to grey-brown*, slightly lighter on belly and smooth skin is sprinkled with short hairs and variable pale scars.
- Poorly developed sexual dimorphism and indistinct age differentiation. Colour contrast varies individually.

Typical behaviour at surface

- *Inshore waters, bays and channels*. Usually solitary or in small groups.
- *Just top of head and very rounded back exposed*, but often just nostrils break surface. When moving quickly, especially prior to deep dive, *flukes may be raised rather high*.
- Activity in inshore waters varies tidally and, often, according to human activities, but usually closest to shore in late afternoon and night.

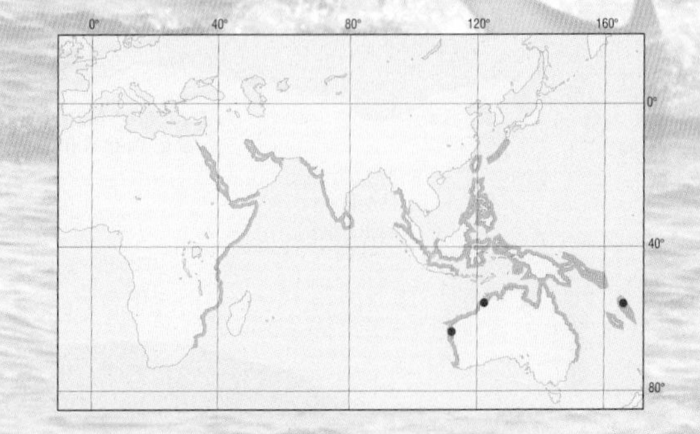

SIMILAR SPECIES

The only sirenian in range. However, can look slimmer and, if not seen well, could be confused with ***Finless Porpoise*** or ***Irrawaddy Dolphin***, but head/muzzle shape (double nostrils), among many other characters, permit separation.

Dugongs in dorsal view, showing typical head/muzzle shape and double nostrils.

VARIATION

Age/sex Sexual differences inconspicuous (♀ can be recognised when lactating by swollen mammary glands); overall size and dental features vary with age, and young generally paler and more uniform, lacking or have fewer scars. Calf generally pale cream, darker with age. **Physical notes** Ads reach *c.*4.1 m, mostly 2.5–3 m, and 250–420 kg (♀ perhaps marginally larger). Newborn *c.*1–1.5 m and 20–35 kg. **Taxonomy** Polytypic: *D. d. hemprichii* (Red Sea) is smaller and differs in some other respects from nominate *dugon* (rest of range). Australian animals have been separated as *D. d. australis*.

Dugongs usually feed on sea grasses in shallow waters, but may exploit deeper food sources at low-tide periods.

DISTRIBUTION & POPULATION

Discontinuously from S Africa and Madagascar north to Persian Gulf, thence east

Dugong

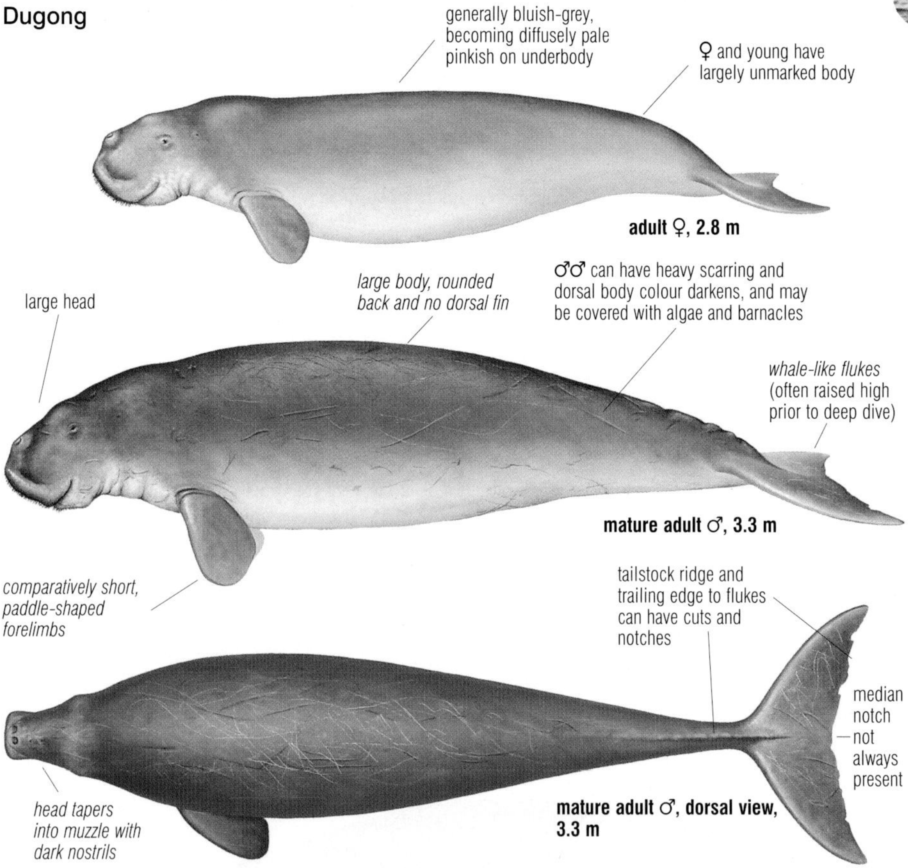

generally bluish-grey, becoming diffusely pale pinkish on underbody

♀ and young have largely unmarked body

adult ♀, 2.8 m

large head

large body, rounded back and no dorsal fin

♂♂ can have heavy scarring and dorsal body colour darkens, and may be covered with algae and barnacles

whale-like flukes (often raised high prior to deep dive)

mature adult ♂, 3.3 m

comparatively short, paddle-shaped forelimbs

tailstock ridge and trailing edge to flukes can have cuts and notches

median notch not always present

head tapers into muzzle with dark nostrils

mature adult ♂, dorsal view, 3.3 m

to New Guinea, including related islands, Vanuatu and Australia (south to Sydney), and north to S Japan. Movements largely unknown, but recorded as a vagrant on Mediterranean coast of Israel and in Fiji, and moves to deeper waters in winter. *Population* No overall estimate, but largest numbers perhaps in Australia, where currently thought to number 85,000.

ECOLOGY

Usually small groups of up to 6, occasionally 10s together. *Diving* Usually 1–4 min (up to 8 min). *Diet* Principally sea grasses. *Reproduction* Sexually mature at 9–10 yrs. Several ♂♂ usually compete for 1 ♀. Gestation 12–14 months. Calves year-round (peak Aug–Jan in Australia) and lactation c.18 months, though calves may remain with cows several yrs. Inter-calving interval 2.5–7 yrs. *Lifespan* Up to 73 yrs.

The mother/calf bond in Dugongs may persist for several years.

Steller's Sea Cow

Hydrodamalis gigas

Commander Islands, NW Pacific. Max 7.9 m.

Priority characters on surfacing

- *Huge, whale-like* sirenian. *Extinct* – description based on specimens and notes.
- Massive, *rotund body tapering sharply to very slender head.*
- Possibly rough or wrinkled skin *generally very dark or black*, perhaps with whitish patches, especially below.
- Head/muzzle typical of sirenians, with complex fleshy pads covered with short, dense bristles and nostrils on top of snout.
- *Forelimbs proportionately very short* with angled tips.
- Whale-like flukes.
- Eyes very small.

Typical behaviour at surface

- Almost unknown, described as placid, slow-moving animals of very shallow shores.

SIMILAR SPECIES

Extinct. Its huge size and dark skin were suggestive of some whales, but odd shape and coastal habitat distinctive.

VARIATION

Age/sex Largely unknown. **Physical notes** Ads reached 7.9 m and 4,500–5,900 kg, but fossil records suggest it may have reached up to 10 m.

DISTRIBUTION & POPULATION

Extinct since *c.*1766. Historically known only from the Commander Is (NW Pacific), but occurred throughout the N Pacific rim, from N Japan to Baja California (Mexico) until the late Pleistocene. Discovered in 1741 by Steller, when estimated to number 1,500–2,000 individuals, but by 1763 fur hunters had exterminated it.

ECOLOGY

Was often recorded in family groups and larger aggregations, with calves being protected within the centre of such groupings. Fed in shallow waters, grazing on marine algae, especially at river mouths, and never completely submerging.

Steller's Sea Cow

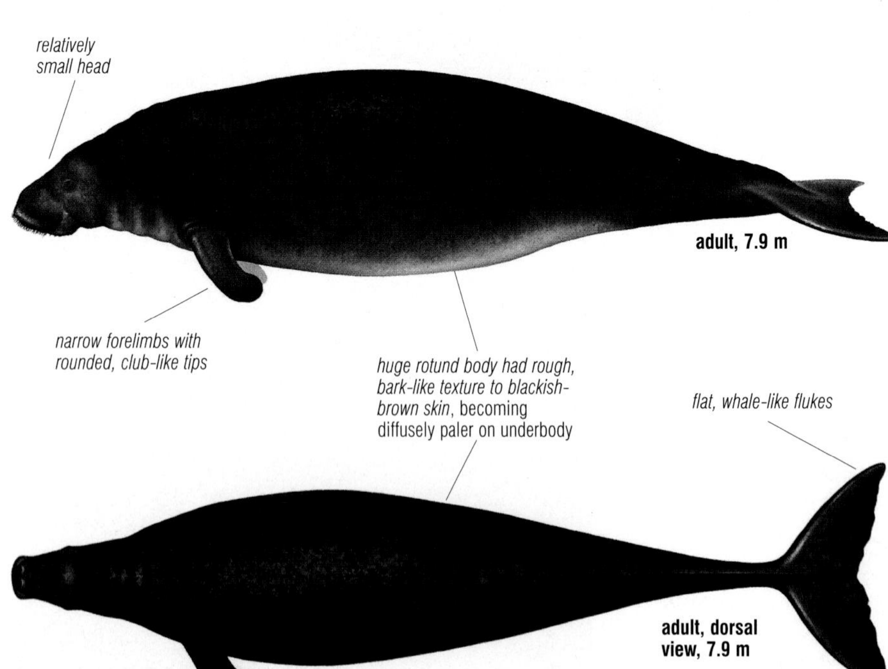

Amazonian Manatee

Trichechus inunguis

Amazonia. Max 3 m.

Priority characters on surfacing

- The *smallest and slimmest manatee*, but still robust and chunky.
- *Rounded tail* characteristic of genus.
- *Very broad head* with bulbous muzzle and complex 'lips' and whisker pads covered by short, dense thick bristles. Nostrils on top of snout. Eyes small and dark.
- *Smooth skin* (only sparsely covered by fine hairs) *dark to blackish-grey* with variable and irregular white or pinkish patches below (sometimes lacking). Poorly developed sex and age differences.
- Large paddle- and square-shaped forelimbs (flexible).

Typical behaviour at surface

- *Inhabits the Amazon and other large rivers*, precise range strongly influenced by seasonal floods.
- Usually solitary or in small feeding groups.
- *Very discreet and elusive, especially difficult to follow given poor visibility in water.*

SIMILAR SPECIES

Perhaps only occasionally overlaps with West Indian Manatee at mouth of Amazon R, but they differ sufficiently in size, shape and coloration. Two other marine mammals inhabit the Amazon – Amazon River Dolphin and Tucuxi – but given reasonable views should be easily separated.

Amazonian Manatee, mother and calf, feeding on aquatic grasses and herbs; usually bottom-feeders, but they occasionally float.

VARIATION

Age/sex Indistinct differentiation (lactating ♀ has swollen mammary glands); calf generally paler with less white on belly and somewhat wrinkled skin (replaced in first weeks of life). **Physical notes** Ads reach *c.*3 m and at least 450 kg. Newborn 75–105 cm and 10–15 kg.

Amazonian Manatee often only shows top of snout (and nostrils) when emerging to breathe.

DISTRIBUTION & POPULATION

Restricted to the Amazon drainage, including associated lakes, in Brazil, SE Colombia, E Ecuador and E Peru, with a disjunct population in Guyana. Inhabits deeper waters during periods of low water (principally Nov–Dec), but more widespread at other times. *Population* No overall estimates.

ECOLOGY

Usually <10 (strongest bond between cow and calf); larger aggregations formerly more frequent. *Diving* Few data. *Diet* Principally aquatic grasses and herbs; may fast for up to 7 months p.a. *Reproduction* Most births in Dec–Jul (peak Feb–Mar), with mating commencing same period. *Lifespan* Up to 60–70 yrs.

Amazonian Manatee

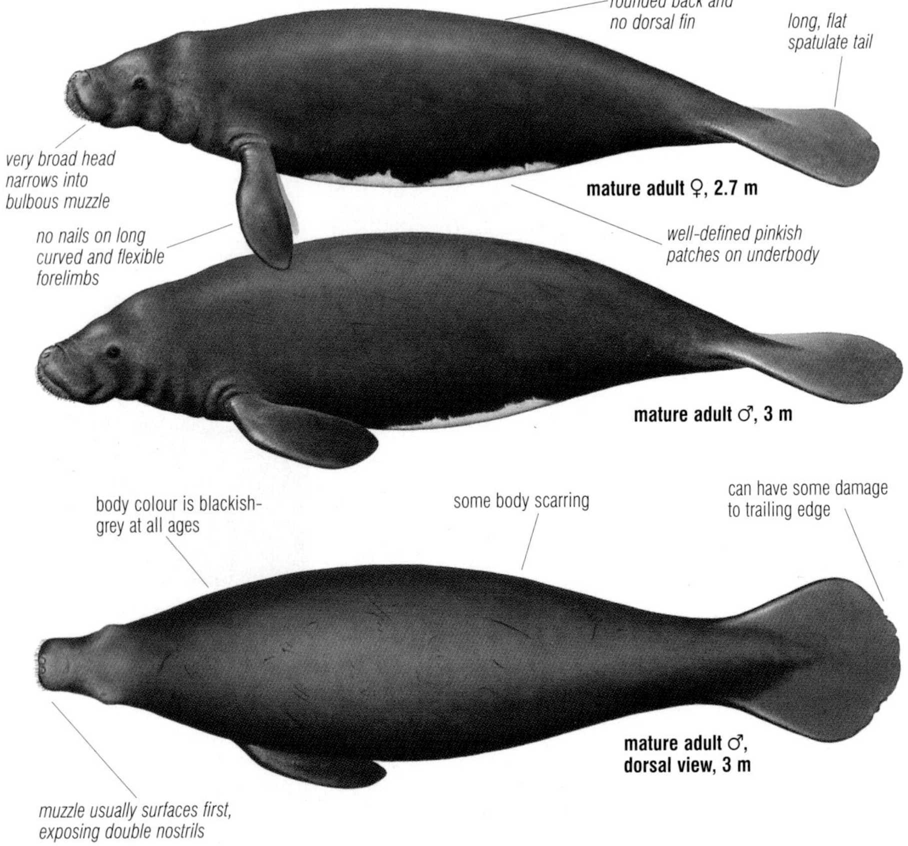

large body, rounded back and no dorsal fin

long, flat spatulate tail

very broad head narrows into bulbous muzzle

mature adult ♀, 2.7 m

no nails on long curved and flexible forelimbs

well-defined pinkish patches on underbody

mature adult ♂, 3 m

body colour is blackish-grey at all ages

some body scarring

can have some damage to trailing edge

mature adult ♂, dorsal view, 3 m

muzzle usually surfaces first, exposing double nostrils

West Indian Manatees, their muzzles just breaking the surface, whilst their rotund bodies and long, spatulate tails are visible below the surface.

West Indian Manatee

Trichechus manatus

E coast of the Americas. Max 3.9 m.

Priority characters on surfacing

- *Quite plump and rotund.*
- Paddle-shaped forelimbs (flexible).
- *Tail long, broad and round (spatulate).*
- Broad neck but rather small hippo-like head, with long thick, slightly downcurved muzzle, and fleshy whisker-pads and 'lips'.
- Frontal disk covered with short, stiff bristles and head-on lips appear to hang below mouthline.
- Two semi-circular nostrils on top of snout. Eyes small and dark.
- *Rough grey-brown skin with folds and wrinkles*, sometimes blotched paler or tinged greenish (algal growth), and has short hairs.
- No major differences between sexes. Young often darker, some black. Mainly varies individually.

Typical surfacing behaviour

- *Brackish and freshwater areas, within a few 100s of metres of the coast.*
- Slow and generally lethargic, often almost motionless at surface. Short, shallow diver.
- *Often surfaces with top of head/ muzzle, and when nostrils fully*

open, round head is like a bowling ball.

• Usually solitary, in mother–calf 'pairs' or small groups.

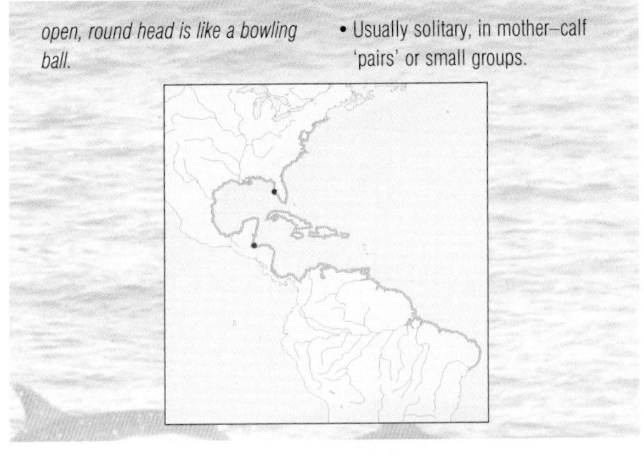

SIMILAR SPECIES

The only sirenian in its range but ***Amazonian Manatees*** could occasionally occur at Amazon R mouth. Latter smaller and slimmer, with smoother skin, (usually) pale belly and chest patches, and lacks nails on flippers. Beware stray Walrus (young without tusks), which superficially resemble manatees, but on close inspection West Indian Manatee unmistakable.

VARIATION

Age/sex Sexual differences inconspicuous (lactating ♀ accompanied by calf and has swollen mammary glands). Overall size and dental features vary with age. Calf generally darker, almost black, becoming paler with age. **Physical notes** Ads reach 3.9 m and 1,590 kg (♀ perhaps averages larger). Newborn up to *c*.1.6 m and *c*.30 kg. **Taxonomy** Polytypic: *T. m. latirostris* 'Florida Manatee' (Louisiana to Virginia in N Gulf of Mexico and SE USA, and *T. m. manatus* 'Antillean Manatee' (N Mexico to C Brazil and the Caribbean).

Mother and calf of West Indian Manatees moving along ocean floor using their forelimbs; note greenish algae growth on back.

West Indian Manatees can appear almost to frolic playfully during social and mating behaviour.

DISTRIBUTION & POPULATION

From SE USA through the Greater Antilles and Caribbean coast of C America south along Atlantic seaboard of S America to Espírito Santo (Brazil). Penetrates lower and middle reaches of Orinoco R (Venezuela) and disperses north to Virginia (USA) in summer. Occasionally wanders into

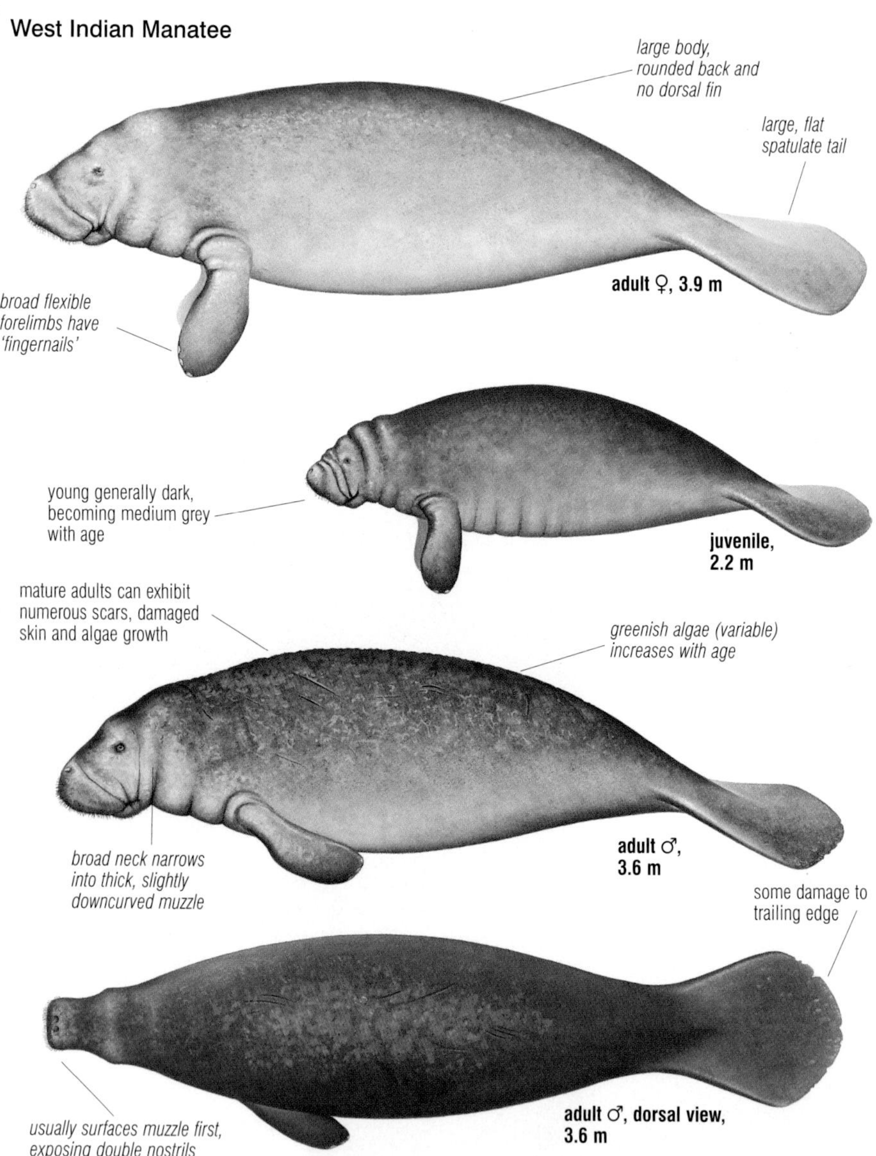

Panama Canal and Pacific coast of Panama. *Population* Florida Manatee estimated at 3,300, stable in mid-1990s. Antillean Manatee numbers are unknown, although it is generally rather uncommon, with peak numbers thought to occur in S Mexico/Belize.

ECOLOGY

Ephemeral groups of up to 200+ but usually fewer than 15. Strongest bond between cow and calf. *Diving* Mostly *c.*4 min (max 24 min recorded). *Diet* Chiefly aquatic and semi-aquatic vegetation. *Reproduction* ♀♀ sexually mature at 3–4 yrs. Several ♂♂ attempt to mate with 1 ♀ (peak Feb–Jul in Florida Manatee). Gestation 11–14 months. Most Florida Manatees give birth Mar–Sep. Twins occasional. Calves weaned at *c.*18 months. Inter-calving interval *c.*2.5 yrs. *Lifespan* 60+ yrs.

West African Manatee

Trichechus senegalensis

W Africa. Max. 4 m.

Priority characters on surfacing

- *Typical manatee, but comparatively slim* and small-headed. Restricted to W Africa.
- Paddle-shaped forelimbs (flexible).
- *Spatulate tail.*
- *Brown-grey or grey, with skin folds on neck.* No major sex or age differences.
- Stiff bristles on upper 'lip'; skin slightly wrinkled, with only sparse short hairs.
- Thick neck *narrows into head and slightly downcurved, bulbous snout*; fleshy whisker-pads and 'lips' very similar to West Indian Manatee.
- Two semi-circular nostrils on top of snout. Eyes small and dark, but clearly visible.

Typical surfacing behaviour

- *Coasts, rivers and estuaries, but rarely enters deeper water.*
- Slow and sedate, may float lethargically at surface; generally short, shallow dives. *Often surfaces with top of head/muzzle*, opening nostrils to breathe like West Indian Manatee.
- Usually solitary, mother–calf 'pair' or small aggregations.

and 30 kg. **Taxonomy** Monotypic. Freshwater populations have been listed as *T. s. vogelii.*

DISTRIBUTION & POPULATION

Coastal W Africa, from Senegambia (recently also listed for S Mauritania) to Angola, penetrating lower and middle reaches of most major rivers, and reaching up to 2,000 km inland (Mali). Formerly slightly more widespread. Seasonal movements along rivers. *Population* No overall estimates, but perhaps most numerous in Cameroon, Gabon, Guinea-Bissau, Côte d'Ivoire and Senegal.

ECOLOGY

Mostly as Amazonian Manatee; diet also like latter but no data for diving. *Reproduction* Mates principally in rainy season with several ♂♂ competing for 1 cow; gestation and calving each *c.*12 months. *Lifespan* Up to 60 yrs.

SIMILAR SPECIES

Easily identified as it is the only sirenian in its range.

VARIATION

Age/sex No significant size differences between sexes (lactating ♀ accompanied by calf and has swollen mammary glands). Overall size and dental features vary with age. Calf generally darker, almost black, becoming paler with age. **Physical notes** Ads reach 4 m (usually 2.5–3.3 m) and 750 kg (usually 400–500 kg). Newborn to *c.*1.5 m

A highly endangered West African Manatee feeding on sea lettuce.

West African Manatee principally feeds on emergent and floating vegetation, especially grasses.

West African Manatee

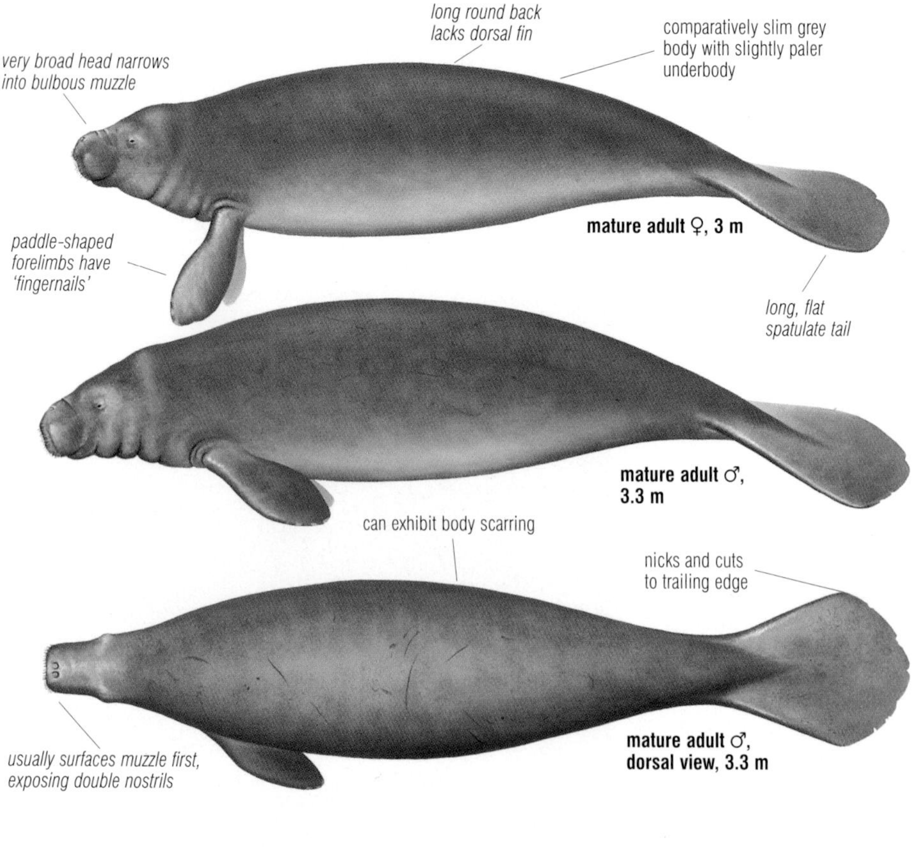

long round back lacks dorsal fin

comparatively slim grey body with slightly paler underbody

very broad head narrows into bulbous muzzle

mature adult ♀, 3 m

paddle-shaped forelimbs have 'fingernails'

long, flat spatulate tail

mature adult ♂, 3.3 m

can exhibit body scarring

nicks and cuts to trailing edge

mature adult ♂, dorsal view, 3.3 m

usually surfaces muzzle first, exposing double nostrils

Fur seals of northern/ mid-latitudes

The fur seals (Arctocephalinae), together with the sea lions (Otariinae), are placed in the family Otariidae, and are collectively known as **eared seals**, in reference to their external ear-flaps. These seals evolved 11–12 MYA in the N Pacific, and dispersed to the S Hemisphere (with sea lions diverging from fur seals *c.*3 MYA), but only to a limited degree to the S Atlantic. Fur seals and sea lions, due to their structure and unlike true seals, can walk or run with their limbs tucked below the body, with the foreflippers long and bent when walking and the hindflippers capable of being pointed forwards or rotated beneath the body. Both have limbs that can be splayed sideways to support the raised body; some digits have nails, usually set well back from the trailing edges. Compared to sea lions, fur seals generally are less heavily built and smaller/slimmer. Sea lions have a single thick pelage, whereas fur seals possess double layers and have more pointed, longer otter-like faces and muzzles (rounded and more compressed in sea lions, which are more dog-like with a broader, blunter nose). In fur seals, females tend to have darker or greyer, less sandy coats and bulls are much less heavy with less-dense manes than in corresponding sexes of sea lions. Also, the ear-flaps of fur seals are longer and lie lower on the head than in sea lions. Additionally, in areas where fur seals and sea lions coexist, sea lions often select open beaches sheltered from heavy surf, and forage closer to the coast.

Cow Juan Fernández Fur Seal: cows of all fur seals are noticeably smaller and lack the heavy mane of bulls. They are also virtually identical (with some individual variation in each species) and outside their normal ranges they (and immatures) are practically indistinguishable.

Separation, especially on land, of eared from true seals is easy, except in areas where more than one species of fur seal or, to some extent, where both a sea lion and fur seal coexist. Among northern and mid-latitude fur seals, the main issue is the separation of Northern and Guadalupe Fur Seals, which partially overlap in the NE Pacific and, especially, young animals could be confused with California and Northern Sea Lions. Further south the situation is slightly more complicated, as the wider-ranging South American Fur Seal could be confused with the near-identical Galápagos and Juan Fernández Fur Seals (very limited contact). South American Fur Seal broadly overlaps with South American Sea

Fur seals of northern/mid-latitudes and some overlapping sea lions

small head with short, conical face; long vibrissae
buff crest
adult ♂, max 2.1 m
distinct convex profile to face
adult ♀, max 1.5 m
no hair below wrist joint

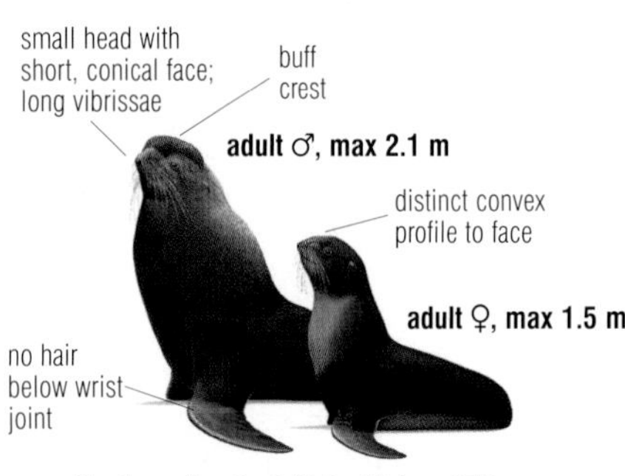

Northern Fur Seal (N Pacific), p. 273

adult ♂, max 3.3 m
for comparison with sympatric Northern Fur Seal
adult ♀, max 2.9 m

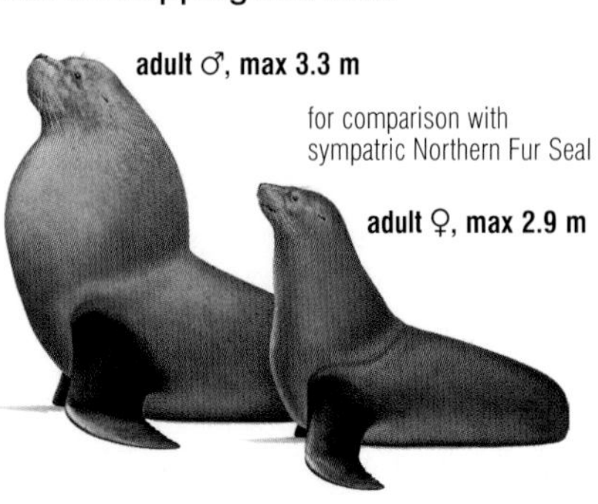

Northern (Steller's) Sea Lion (N Pacific), p. 305

pale, grizzled mane contrasts with dark body
adult ♂, max 2.4 m
longer, pointed muzzle and rather short vibrissae
rather pointed face
adult ♀, max 1.9 m
foreflippers fur-covered well below 'wrist'

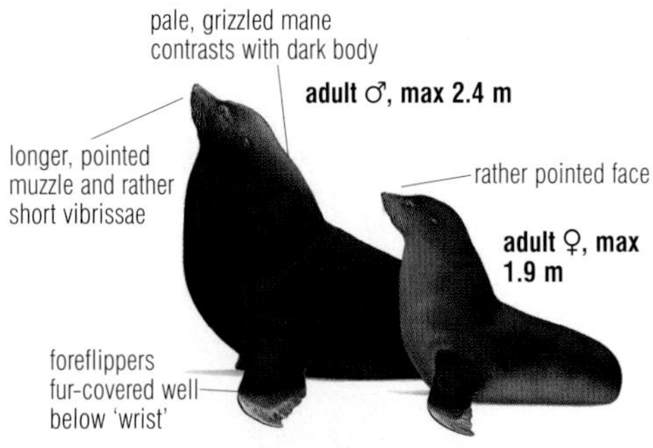

Guadalupe Fur Seal (Guadalupe Island, Mexico), p. 275

adult ♂, max 2.4 m
for comparison with partially sympatric Northern and Guadalupe Fur Seals
adult ♀, max 1.8 m

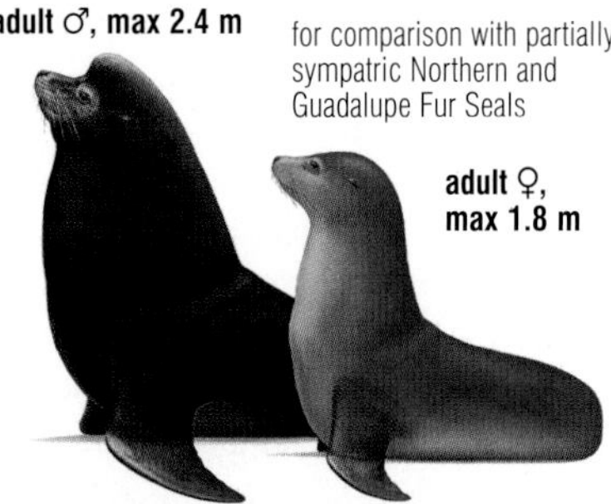

Californian and Galápagos Sea Lions (Galápagos & E Pacific), p. 296

contrasting paler crown and nape
adult ♂, max 2.1 m
robust ♀ has conical face
long, pointed muzzle (with bulbous nose)
adult ♀, max 1.5 m

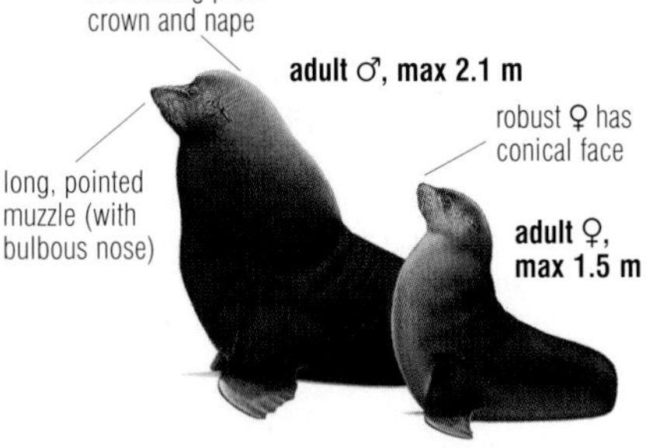

Juan Fernández Fur Seal (Juan Fernández Islands), p. 281

adult ♂, max 2.8 m
for comparison with sympatric South American Fur Seal
adult ♀, max 2.2 m

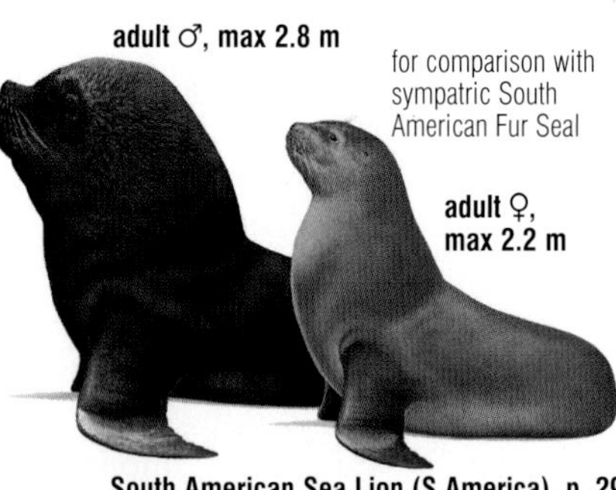

South American Sea Lion (S America), p. 299

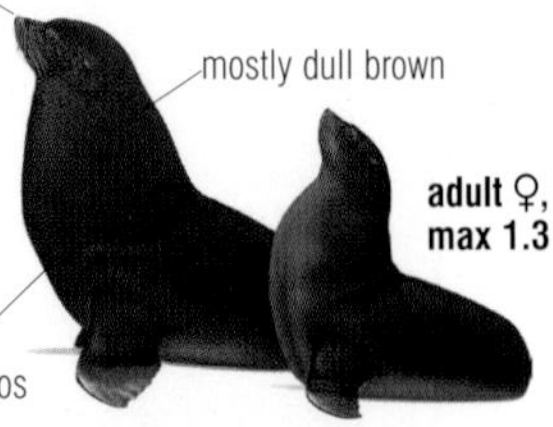

rather compact and short-faced
adult ♂, max 1.6 m
mostly dull brown
adult ♀, max 1.3 m
readily distinguished from much larger Galápagos Sea Lion

Galápagos Fur Seal (Galápagos archipelago), p. 279

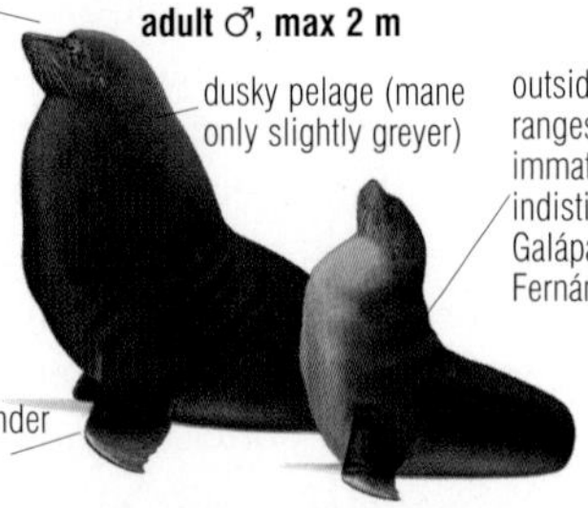

pointed, flat-topped muzzle
adult ♂, max 2 m
dusky pelage (mane only slightly greyer)
outside normal ranges ♀♀ (and immatures) practically indistinguishable from Galápagos and Juan Fernández Fur Seals
adult ♀, max 1.5 m
rather slender forelimbs

South American Fur Seal (S America), p. 277

Lion, and Galápagos Fur Seal with Galápagos Sea Lion, whilst vagrant South American Fur Seals could potentially come into contact with several southern congeners. Especially for observers without previous field experience and when dealing with animals away from breeding areas, identification may be impractical under many circumstances. Furthermore, identification at sea of fur seals and sea lions (both intra-group and even between them) is little known, very difficult and has been largely ignored in previous publications. When attempting separation of the various fur seals, it is best to use several features in combination, particularly overall size and proportions, head profile, in particular muzzle structure, flipper size/structure and, in some, fur coloration. Behaviour and movements can also be useful. Above all, however, it is important to remember that all display much individual variation in size, shape and coat colour, reflecting age development, the degree of sexual dimorphism, and marked seasonal changes in overall bulk. Fur condition can substantially vary according to wear (bleaching paler/browner), discoloration caused by local soil conditions, whilst texture and colour markedly differ when wet (much darker and less patterned). Moreover, shape and coloration are completely different on land, in surface water and in deeper water. The identification boxes describe animals with dry pelage, and identification to species level concentrates on bulls, not females or young, which are poorly known in most instances.

Newborn Juan Fernández Fur Seal. Newborn of most fur seals have a velvet-black, short-curled coat which moults to duskier and greyer at 3–4 months and is replaced after several months by more adult-like pelage.

Northern Fur Seal

Callorhinus ursinus

N Pacific. Max 2.1 m.

Priority characters on land (dry pelage)

- *Large-bodied fur seal (bull)*, small head and short snout characteristic.
- Bull: prominent mane of long guard hairs, medium dark brown to black, with hint of reddish, buff or silver-grey, particularly dense on neck, chest and upper back, and clearly defined across wrist (when fresh or in early breeding season). *Head looks small owing to very short downcurved muzzle, small nose and clump of hair on top of head.*
- Cow: noticeably smaller than ♂ with shorter, finer guard hairs, mostly medium to dark brownish-grey on head and belly, and paler buff or greyish chest, often as collar or on snout. *Particularly small head with convex crown and compressed muzzle.*
- Imm: sexing and ageing difficult until 4–5 yrs old, but advanced ♂ usually larger than all ages of ♀.
- *External ear-flaps (pinnae) conspicuous* (tips bare when older);

SIMILAR SPECIES

Only fur seal overlapping in range is ***Guadalupe*** (qv). Northern also overlaps and could be confused with ***California*** and ***Northern Sea Lions*** (note, Northern Fur Seal has somewhat similar clump of hair on top of head to Californian Sea Lion), but these, if seen well, are noticeably larger and heavier, and can be identified by the smaller head with shorter pointed muzzle and relatively longer, but lower ear-flaps of the fur seal. Sea lions possess shorter and uneven-length digit tips to the hindflippers (outer toe longer; toes more even-length in present species) and much broader, longer foreflippers with diagnostic hairy bases extending further below 'wrist'. They also differ in pelage, especially the denser mane of bulls, and both sexes of Northern Sea Lion are far paler. Identification of young/♀ otariids, especially out of range, is never easy and often impractical, and many features cannot be appreciated when animals are wet.

VARIATION

Age/sex Bull considerably larger and heavier, with prominent mane and is overall darker; ♀/young similar; newborn black to blackish-brown, but moults at 3–4 months and thereafter resembles ♀/imm. **Physical notes** Full-grown ♂ 1.9–2.1 m and 175–275 kg, ♀ 1.2–1.5 m and 30–60 kg. Pup at birth 60–65 cm and 4–6 kg. **Other data** *Moult* Post-natal, occupies 4–5 months.

DISTRIBUTION & POPULATION

Breeds on islands in N Pacific, Bering Sea and Sea of Okhotsk, principally on the Pribilofs and Commanders, and occurs as non-breeder to S California, where partially resident. Other populations migrate (from Oct) to C & E Pacific

whiskers moderately long and whiter in ads.

- *Foreflippers very broad and naked below 'wrist'*; elongated hindflippers (longest of any otariid) *with extremely long, cartilaginous terminal flaps* (digit tips).

Typical behaviour

- Polygynous, forms large rookeries, otherwise normally alone, in twos or small groups.
- Rafts buoyantly at surface (feeds mainly at night), raising flippers in air; fast porpoising.

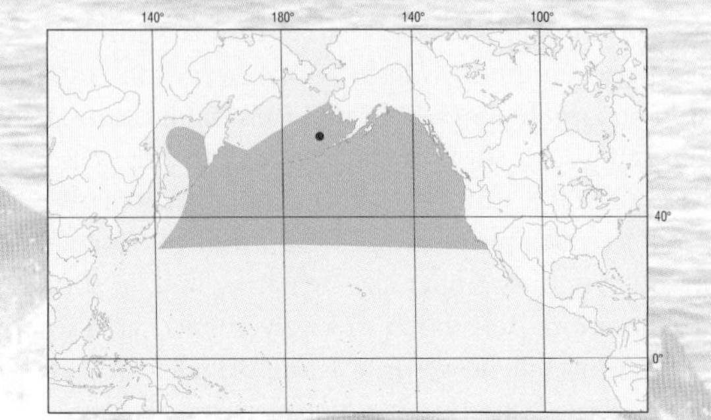

relatively small round head with short, conical face

clump of crown hair can appear prominent when dry

Northern Fur Seal

usually very long vibrissae

distinct convex profile to face

neck/upper chest often contrast with darker lower chest and throat

no hair below wrist joint

adult ♂, 2 m

very long fore- and hindflippers

adult ♀, 1.4 m

Bull, cow and newborn Northern Fur Seal: the bull's small round head, buff crest and highly compressed, pointed snout are characteristic; compressed muzzle and partial collar are features of the smaller cow.

in non-breeding season, returning north in Mar–Apr, with ♂♂ remaining at higher latitudes. *Population* c.1.2 million, with vast majority on the Pribilofs (74%). Previously 2.5 million in 1950s but declined 1956–83, stable until 1990 and has decreased since at 2% p.a.

ECOLOGY

Largely solitary at sea, but gregarious on land (45 days per annum in ♂♂, 35 days in ♀♀; extremely philopatric). Some do not return to colonies for several yrs. *Diving* Shallow diver, but can reach 400 m. *Diet* Fish, cephalopods, crustaceans and, occasionally, seabirds. *Reproduction* Bulls arrive first ½ of May and mate with up to 115 cows, ♀♀ c.1 month later and 1 day prior to giving birth; they mate with up to 2 ♂♂. Cows give birth late May–late Jun. Ads mate 5–8 days later, and cows spend 2–10 days at sea and 1–2 days ashore. Pups migrate south after cows have left. *Lifespan* Up to 26 yrs.

Guadalupe Fur Seal

Arctocephalus townsendi

Guadalupe Island, Mexico. Max 2.4 m.

Priority characters on land (dry pelage)

- Breeds only on Guadalupe and San Benito, off Baja California. Smaller than Northern and has distinctly *long, flat-topped and pointed muzzle*, and relatively large, round head.
- Bull: head and mane have very thick pelage, especially behind eyes, on neck and chest. *Crown and nape broad and convex, often distinctly grizzled paler*. Otherwise, dark greyish-brown to greyish-black.
- Cow: smaller and paler, but has *characteristic conical face, long pointed snout and sloping forehead*, and dense fur on neck and chest. Medium to pale grey-brown, variably tinged buff or sandy.
- Imm: sexing (if genitals concealed) and ageing difficult until well advanced, when ♂ clearly heavier than any ♀.
- Pinnae relatively long and prominent; whiskers whitish-cream and rather short.
- *Foreflippers quite long and upper surface fur-covered well below*

Convex crown, flat-topped, pointed muzzle, grizzled greyish pelage and short whiskers are characteristics of Guadalupe Fur Seal bull.

'wrist'; hindflippers and *terminal flaps relatively short* (*cf.* Northern Fur Seal).

Typical behaviour

- Polygynous, forms large rookeries, but normally solitary or in small parties at sea.
- Rafts on surface, often raising flippers in air; porpoises when travelling at speed.

SIMILAR SPECIES

Respective sexes/ages of ***Northern Fur Seal*** (slight overlap) have smaller head with compressed snout and broad foreflippers (fur *not* reaching beyond 'wrist'), and extremely long hindflippers and terminal flaps; Northern appears heavier and bull has hump on crown but lacks Guadalupe's greyish nape patch, and ♀/young have blunter, shorter downcurved muzzle and pronounced paler chest. Larger and heavier ***California*** and ***Northern Sea Lions*** possess more rounded, dog-like faces (pointed and otter-like in fur seals), with shorter ear-flaps; they also differ in structure and coloration of pelage, and structure and relative size of flippers. Identification of all 4 species in ♀♀/young sometimes almost impossible and, especially at sea, requires experience because size, shape and behaviour assume greater importance, as other characters obscured on wet fur.

VARIATION

Age/sex Bull considerably larger and heavier, with thick mane and is overall darker; ♀/young more alike; newborn black to blackish-brown, moults at 3–4 months when coloration approaches ♀/imm, albeit with paler elements. **Physical notes** Full-grown ♂ 1.9–2.4 m and 150–220 kg and ♀ 1.4–1.9 m and 40–55 kg. Newborn *c.*60

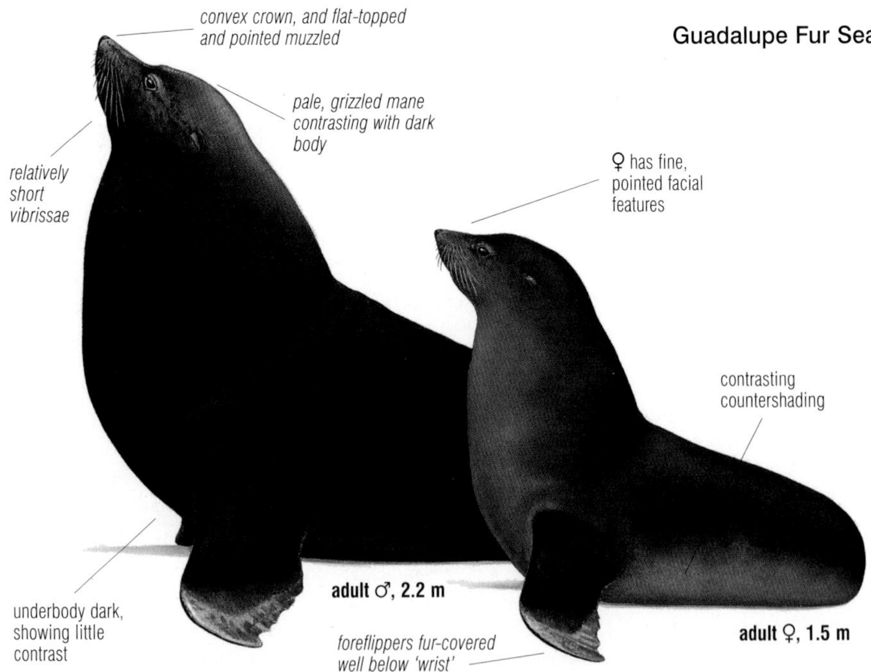

cm and 2–4 kg. **Other data** *Moult* Post-natal.

DISTRIBUTION & POPULATION

Almost entirely restricted as a breeder to Guadalupe Is, off Mexico, with small numbers on Islas Benito, Baja California, since 1997 and 1 pup born on San Miguel Is, off S California (USA), in 1997. Ranges north in autumn to C California, and south to the Gulf of California, but whereabouts at other times unknown. *Population* 10,000 in late 1990s.

Cow and pup Guadalupe Fur Seal: note foreflippers are fur-covered well below 'wrist' (cf. Northern Fur Seal).

ECOLOGY

Almost entirely unknown. Perhaps less social than other fur seals. *Diving* Shallow diver. *Diet* Pelagic squid, lanternfish and mackerel, mostly at night. *Reproduction* Bulls arrive first, and mate with up to 12 cows, ♀♀ 3–6 days prior to giving birth. ♀♀ give birth early Jun–Jul (peak mid to late Jun). Ads mate *c.*7 days after births, and ♀♀ spend 2–6 days at sea and 4–6 days nursing pups, which congregate ashore. Pups weaned at 9 months. *Lifespan* Up to 23 yrs (♀).

South American Fur Seal

Arctocephalus australis

S American coasts. Max 2 m.

Priority characters on land (dry pelage)

- Rather large and stocky, but size, structure and pelage vary with age and sex.
- Bull: *dark brownish-grey to dark olive-brown*, with prominent mane of longer and greyer guard hairs (especially on neck and shoulders); lower body variably tinged yellowish, and flippers dark reddish-brown. *Clearly pointed, flat-topped muzzle* (of mid length), pronounced due to steep, short forehead and rounded crown.
- Cow: uniform grey-brown or dusky above and on sides, paler tan ventrally, often to neck, head darker; most have variable dusky eye mask and paler muzzle and ears.
- Imm: sexing (if gentials concealed) and ageing difficult until well advanced, when ♂ larger but still lacks heavy mane.
- Pinnae long and prominent; *whiskers creamy-white, rather short* to moderate length.
- Fore and hindflippers relatively long and slender, and well covered in fur.

Typical behaviour

- Polygynous, forms large rookeries, but feeds in smaller groups at sea.
- Rafts buoyantly at surface with head down and flippers 'waving' in air.

SIMILAR SPECIES

Juan Fernández, ***Galápagos***, ***Antarctic*** and ***Subantarctic Fur Seals***, and ***South American*** and ***Galápagos Sea Lions*** all overlap to some degree with present species. Separation from Juan Fernández and Galápagos discussed under those species, whilst Subantarctic is distinctive and probably very rarely comes into contact. Antarctic, however, is very similar, but averages smaller with shorter muzzle, overall paler, and bull has more grizzled coat and longer whitish vibrissae. In practice, especially if dealing with ♀♀/young, they cannot be reliably separated outside their normal ranges. Separation from sea lions, if seen reasonably well, usually straightforward as latter larger, with more rounded head and blunter muzzle, relatively shorter ears, far more extensive manes in bulls, sandier coats in ♀♀, and different size and structure to flippers.

VARIATION

Age/sex Bull considerably larger with well-developed mane and is overall darker; ♀/young more alike. Newborn has velvet-black, short-curled coat, moulted to blackish-grey at 3–4 months; replaced after several months by olive-grey. **Physical notes** Full-grown ♂ 1.8–2 m and 150–200 kg, ♀ 1.4–1.5 m and 30–58 kg; newborn 60–65 cm (♂), 57–60 cm (♀) and 3.5–5.5 kg (♀). **Other data** *Moult* Post-natal. **Taxonomy** Previously considered polytypic, with nominate *australis* (Falklands), *A. a. gracilis* (S Brazil, Uruguay, Argentina and Chile, occasionally Peru) and *A. a. galapagoensis* (Galápagos). Latter smallest and now accorded species status, whilst Falklands animals largest; however, *A. a. gracilis* might not warrant recognition, and species perhaps best considered monotypic.

DISTRIBUTION & POPULATION

S South America, north to C Peru (at 6°S) and Uruguay (reaching S Brazil in winter), south to 45°S in Argentina and 54°S in Chile, and the Falklands. Vagrant to Colombia and Juan Fernández, but non-breeding period very poorly known, as spends most time at sea (up to 600 km from land). *Population* Recently 275,000–325,000 with perhaps 250,000 in Uruguay and overall numbers fluctuating due to El Niño events.

South American Fur Seal

slightly convex crown

not long but flat-topped muzzle with short vibrissae

dusky pelage and pronounced mane (with slightly greyer nape)

face generally appears short and compact

outside normal ranges, ♀♀ (and immatures) not reliably separated from several congeners

rather more slender forelimbs

adult ♂, 2 m

much smaller than bull; paler facial and ventral areas enhanced with wear

adult ♀, 1.4 m

Bull, cow and newborn South American Fur Seal: note bull's dark olive-brown pelage (slightly greyer at back of mane), not long but pointed and flat-topped muzzle, and slender forelimbs; some cows are paler, especially prior to moult.

ECOLOGY

Groups of up to 20 at sea. Often sympatric with South American Sea Lion, but prefers different beaches. *Diving* Up to 170 m and 7 min recorded. *Diet* Fish, sea snails, cephalopods and crustaceans. *Reproduction* Bulls arrive in Nov. Harems of 2–3. Cows give birth late Oct–mid Dec and mate 6–10 days later. ♀♀ alternate between 1–2 days ashore and 3–6 days at sea. Rookeries abandoned late Jan. *Lifespan* At least 21 yrs.

Galápagos Fur Seal

Arctocephalus galapagoensis

Galápagos archipelago. Max 1.6 m.

Priority characters on land (dry pelage)

- *Small and compact*, with somewhat less-pronounced sexual dimorphism than other otariids; *short, pointed muzzle, almost conical, ending in small nose*.
- Bull: large and heavy (though differs less radically from ♀ than in congeners), with *mane on neck to shoulders relatively less thick than other fur seals*. Largely dull and dark brown with fewer buff or grey tones, but slightly grizzled on mane.
- Cow: noticeably smaller and paler, even lighter on chest and foreneck, and belly often slightly rusty tan. Muzzle, face and forehead above eyes often paler in cows.
- Imm: closer to ♀, but advanced ♂ comparatively larger with decidedly thicker neck.
- Pinnae relatively long and prominent; whiskers creamy-white, fairly long in ads.
- Foreflippers long and broad; *hindflippers relatively short with shorter terminal flaps*.

Typical behaviour

- Polygynous, forms relatively small rookeries; at sea normally in small parties or alone.
- May raise flippers in air when rafting or resting at surface.

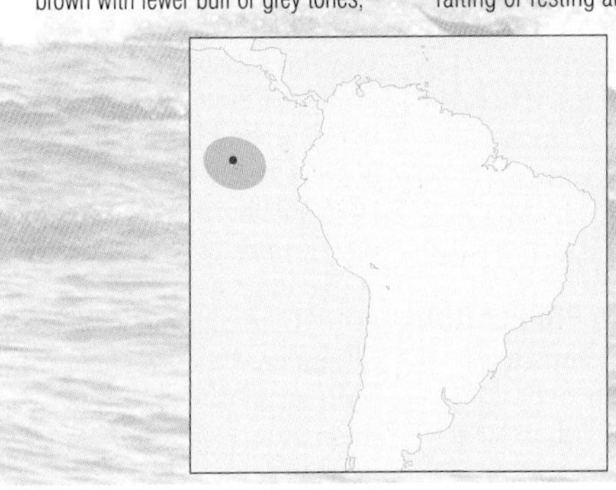

Bull Galápagos Fur Seals are relatively small and compact, with a compressed muzzle.

SIMILAR SPECIES

Ashore, in Galápagos archipelago, far more numerous ***Galápagos Sea Lion*** is chief confusion risk (note, South American Sea Lion could occur as a vagrant). However, on land respective sexes and ages of sea lions noticeably larger and heavier, and possess rounded, more dog-like, faces with blunter muzzles. Ear-flaps relatively shorter and pelage differs, altogether being much

Galápagos Fur Seal

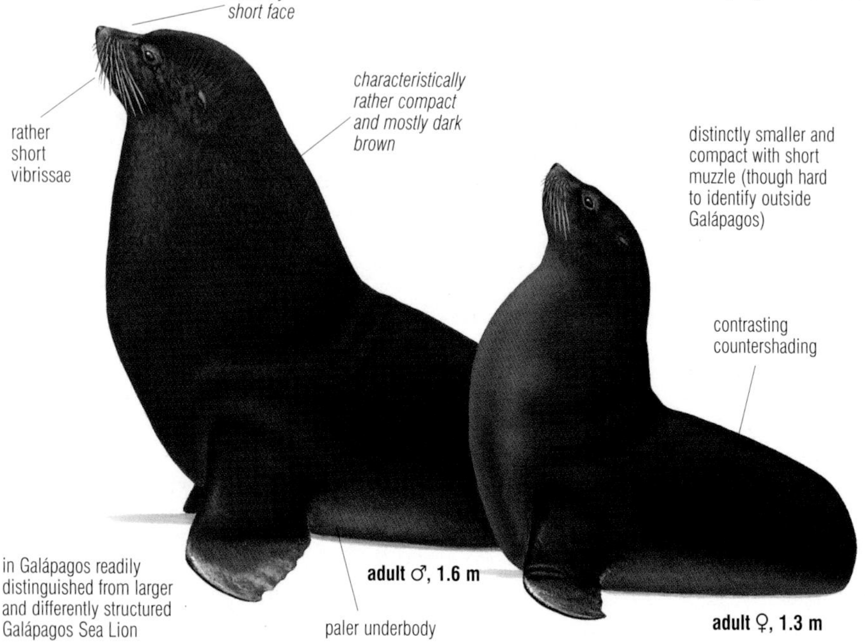

relatively short face

characteristically rather compact and mostly dark brown

rather short vibrissae

distinctly smaller and compact with short muzzle (though hard to identify outside Galápagos)

contrasting countershading

in Galápagos readily distinguished from larger and differently structured Galápagos Sea Lion

adult ♂, 1.6 m

paler underbody

adult ♀, 1.3 m

heavier and denser on head and shoulders in bulls, which have prominent sagittal crest, and sandier in ♀♀; hindflippers relatively shorter. Fur seal rookeries are on rocky shores, more open sandy beaches in sea lions, and they also differ considerably in calls. At sea, however, identification may be far from straightforward, especially of young.

Cow and newly born pup.

VARIATION

Age/sex Bull larger and heavier, with prominent mane and is overall darker; ♀/young paler but not readily separated from each other; newborn black to blackish-brown, moults at 3–4 months, thereafter much as ♀/imm. **Physical notes** Full-grown ♂ 1.6 m (max.) and 60–70 kg and ♀ 1.1–1.3 m and 21.5–40 kg; newborn 3–4 kg. **Other data** *Moult* Post-natal. **Taxonomy** Sometimes considered a race of South American Fur Seal.

DISTRIBUTION & POPULATION

Breeds on 15 islands in Galápagos, with over 33% on Isabela and other large colonies on Fernandina. Most colonies on west-facing coasts in areas of pronounced upwelling. Apparently resident. Foraging range unknown. *Population c.*40,000 in 1988, but El Niño events in 1982–3 and 1997–8 certainly affected numbers.

ECOLOGY

Usually in small numbers and undisturbed rocky areas. *Diving* Up to 169 m and *c.*8 min recorded. *Diet* Lanternfish and squid. *Reproduction* Bulls establish territories for up to 27 days. Cows arrive 2–3 days before giving birth (chiefly Sep–Oct) and mate *c.*8 days later. ♀♀ alternate between 1 day nursing pups and 1–3 days at sea. Pups weaned at 2–3 yrs old (among the longest of pinnipeds); cows that give birth again during this period frequently abandon the newborn.

Juan Fernández Fur Seal

Arctocephalus philippii

Juan Fernández archipelago and San Felix. Max 2.1 m.

Priority characters on land (dry pelage)

- Small but robust-bodied; *very long, pointed muzzle* (sharply demarcated from forehead and slightly convex crown); characteristic *large, bulbous nose*, especially in ♂.
- Bull: dark blackish-brown with conspicuous *buff-grey or golden-yellow crown to nape*, well-developed mane (slightly silver-tipped), and foreneck, *chest and belly intense black*.
- Cow: distinctly smaller, with small conical face, but muzzle long and pointed. Dusky to blackish grey-brown with variably paler buff hindcrown, collar and chest.
- Imm: sexing and ageing difficult except with well-advanced ♂.
- Pinnae relatively long and prominent; *short whitish-cream whiskers in ads*.
- *Fore- and hindflippers rather short and stubby*.

Typical behaviour

- Polygynous, forms medium to large rookeries; at sea normally in singles or small groups.
- Often rafts buoyantly at surface and raises flippers in air.

SIMILAR SPECIES

South American and ***Antarctic Fur Seals***, and ***South American Sea Lion*** all potentially come into contact with Juan Fernández Fur Seal as vagrants. It might, however, prove impossible to reliably identify vagrants of any of these fur seals, unless typical bull from Juan Fernández involved. South American Sea Lion distinguished from present species by same features that separate it from South American Fur Seal.

VARIATION

Age/sex Bull noticeably larger and heavier, with extensive mane and is overall darker; smaller ♀/young more alike; newborn mainly black, moults at 3–4 months becoming more like ♀/imm. **Physical notes** Full-grown ♂ 1.5–2.1 m and 140–159 kg, ♀ 1.4–1.5 m and *c*.50 kg; newborn 65–68 cm and 6.2–6.9 kg. **Other data** *Moult* Post-natal.

Bull Juan Fernández Fur Seal: note long, pointed muzzle with bulbous nose, and conspicuous buff-grey crown to nape.

DISTRIBUTION & POPULATION
Restricted as a breeder to rocky coastlines of the Juan Fernández and San Félix groups (hauling out on all islands in these archipelagos), off Chile. In autumn and winter has wandered to the Chilean coast, as far south as Punta San Juan, and north to Peru, but at-sea distribution poorly known. *Population* *c.*12,000 in late 1990s.

ECOLOGY
Generally solitary at sea. Gregarious but less social than some fur seals on land. *Diving* Increases nocturnally, usually reaching 10–90 m. *Diet* Lactating ♀♀ principally take lanternfish and squid, and mainly feed at night. *Reproduction* Cows give birth (chiefly late Nov–early Dec) and ads mate 7–9 days later. ♀♀ alternate *c.*5 day ashore and up to 25 days at sea. Pups weaned at *c.*10 months.

Cow Juan Fernández Fur Seal with newly born pup: note cow's small conical face and quite long muzzle.

Juan Fernández Fur Seal

long, pointed muzzle (with bulbous nose) and convex crown

crown and nape can contrast strongly against dark body

short vibrissae

robust ♀ has conical face

chest and belly intese black

adult ♂, 2.1 m

adult ♀, 1.4 m

Fur seals of the Southern Ocean

The fur seals described here are those that colonised the subantarctic islands and across the Southern Ocean to the Subtropical Convergence. On some islands more than one species occurs, often as a result of dispersal or recent colonisation. Graceful swimmers, they can porpoise rapidly, like penguins, and sometimes perform a forward somersault during such manoeuvres. Coincident with population recovery after overhunting of virtually all these fur seals, most species' populations are now robust and some islands might even be considered overpopulated, the animals having clear impacts on local plant and seabird communities at these sites. In places such as South Georgia, Antarctic Fur Seals may even cause disturbance to nesting birds the size of Wandering Albatrosses!

Bull Australian Fur Seal, showing characteristic thick dark mane, affording somewhat sea lion-like appearance, but still has long pointed muzzle.

Fur seals and sea lions on land

Both fur seals and sea lions should be treated with great respect, as they possess a somewhat aggressive reputation, have very sharp teeth and can run much faster than humans over most terrain. Aggressiveness varies with location, age/sex and stage in breeding cycle, but some species are generally more defensive of their territories whilst others more readily retreat from humans. It is best to stay at least 10–20 metres from these animals, depending on the number of individuals, the nature of the rookery and stage of the breeding season. Bear in mind that you are an uninvited visitor to their territorial rookeries. In some species, bulls, in particular, appear to regard the upright posture of humans as a threat, and move menacingly toward the observer. In such cases you should move away or continue your path whilst maintaining eye contact with the animal (do not run away!), and always attempt to keep a wide berth as they are capable of swift movements despite their ponderous appearance. In some areas it is best to have a walking stick to frighten aggressive animals. It is usually wise to follow the advice of local guides, who can suggest a good location for observations and photography that does not disturb the animals.

South African Fur Seal rookery. In many respects, all eared seals share the same ecology, social organisation, reproductive behaviour and seasonal cycles. All are, to some extent, polygynous, breed in large rookeries and are often strongly philopatric. Cows organise themselves based on a size-related dominance system, but gather in large, closely packed groups when ashore to moult or breed. Most ♂♂ do not choose a mate, but select only a breeding site (sometimes occupied for many years) and mate with any nearby ♀ at oestrus. Offspring are precocial and remain with the cows, although young ♂♂ may be excluded from the breeding areas.

Southern Ocean fur seals and some overlapping sea lions

Australian Sea Lion (S Australia), p. 301

South African and Australian Fur Seals (S Africa and Australia), p. 285

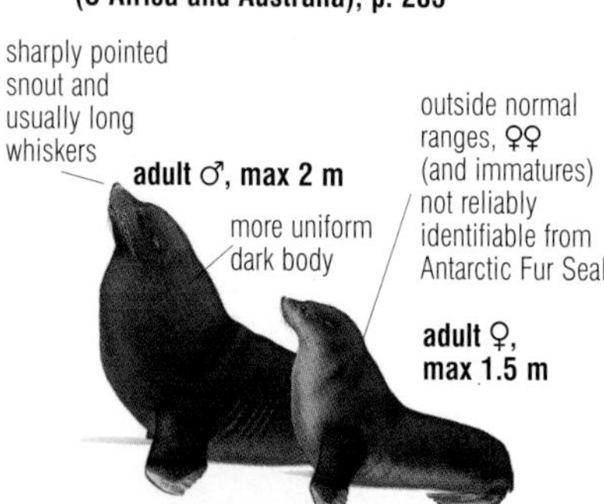

New Zealand Sea Lion (subantarctic New Zealand), p. 303

New Zealand Fur Seal (Australia and New Zealand), p. 287

Antarctic Fur Seal (Antarctic waters), p. 290

Subantarctic Fur Seal (subantarctic waters), p. 292

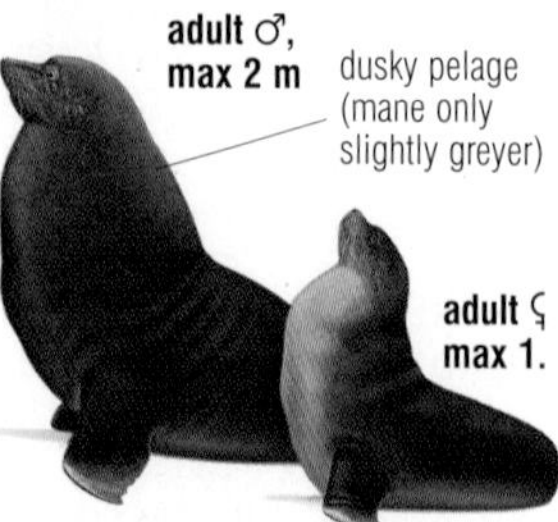

South American Fur Seal (S America), p. 277

South American Sea Lion (S America), p. 299

South African and Australian Fur Seals

Arctocephalus pusillus

S Africa and Australia.
Max 2.2 m.

Priority characters on land (dry pelage)

- A large fur seal and somewhat *more like a sea lion* than congeners. Size, structure and appearance vary strongly according to sex and age.
- Bull: typically very heavy chested and has thick dark mane; *head large with rather robust muzzle, but still pointed and somewhat upturned*, and typically has bulbous nose. Slightly greyish-tinged guard hairs give grizzled appearance, otherwise dark greyish-black to greyish-brown, flippers darker still, and slightly paler below.
- Cow: distinctly smaller and mainly brownish silver-grey above, paler brown ventrally, some lighter grey or yellowish on side of muzzle, face, throat and chest.
- Imm: sexing (if genitals concealed) and ageing difficult; younger ♂ smaller and lacks heavy mane (closer to ad ♀); near-mature ♂ has larger and heavier foreparts.
- Pinnae quite long and prominent; whiskers moderately long in ads, brownish to cream.
- *Foreflippers, covered by thin fur over at least ¾ of length*, and somewhat more curved and paddle-like; *hindflippers relatively very short* with shorter terminal flaps.

Typical behaviour

- Polygynous, forms large rookeries, but normally alone or in parties of up to 15 at sea. Several behavioural characters resemble sea lions.
- Rafts at surface, raising flippers in air. Apparently mainly a diurnal feeder. Often very active and social in water; porpoises when travelling fast.

0° 40° 80° 120°
0° 40° 80°
pusillus
doriferus

SIMILAR SPECIES

South African Fur Seal is unlikely to come into contact with other otariids (except perhaps vagrant ***Antarctic*** and ***Subantarctic Fur Seals***). Australian Fur Seal might be confused with overlapping ***New Zealand Fur Seal***, and to some extent (mainly young or at sea) with ***Australian Sea Lion***, especially owing to its relatively large size and somewhat sea lion character. Separation from Antarctic and New Zealand Fur Seals and Australian Sea Lion discussed under those species.

Cow Australian Fur Seal: note somewhat sea lion-like profile, the pale coloration adding to this impression.

VARIATION

Age/sex Bull notably larger and heavier, with extensive mane and is overall darker; ♀/young more alike. Bulls initially darken with age, but mane paler and more conspicuous, whilst older ♀ may be paler than younger individuals. Newborn mainly velvet-black, becomes more olive-grey or pale yellow after first moult at 3–5 months; replaced after 1 yr by silvery-grey coat, closer in colour to ♀/imm. **Physical**

Porpoising South African Fur Seals.

South African and Australian Fur Seals

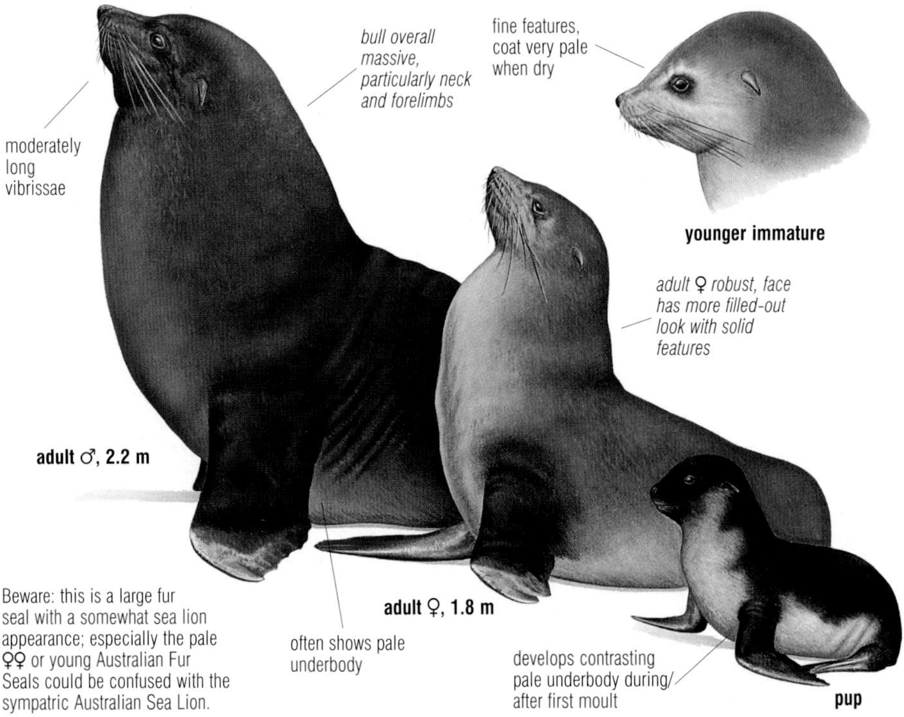

moderately long vibrissae

bull overall massive, particularly neck and forelimbs

fine features, coat very pale when dry

younger immature

adult ♀ robust, face has more filled-out look with solid features

adult ♂, 2.2 m

adult ♀, 1.8 m

pup

Beware: this is a large fur seal with a somewhat sea lion appearance; especially the pale ♀♀ or young Australian Fur Seals could be confused with the sympatric Australian Sea Lion.

often shows pale underbody

develops contrasting pale underbody during/after first moult

notes *pusillus*: full-grown ♂ reaches 2.2 m and 247–350 kg, ♀ 1.5–1.8 m and 57–120 kg; newborn 70 cm and 6.4 kg (♂) and 4.5 kg (♀); *doriferus*: full-grown ♂ 2.2 m and 279–360 kg, ♀ 1.7 m and 76–110 kg; newborn 80 cm and 8.1 kg (♂) and 7.1 kg (♀). **Other data** *Moult* Post-natal, commencing Jan in ads. **Taxonomy** Polytypic: nominate *pusillus* (***South African Fur Seal***) and *A. p. doriferus* (***Australian Fur Seal***), but debate as to whether they are specifically distinct, based mainly on slight cranial differences, or should be considered subspecies. S African seals generally darker than those in Australia, but no other external differences known.

Bull and cow South African Fur Seals: note cow's characteristic pale greyish and sandy pigments.

Bull Australian Fur Seal, showing characteristic heavy dark mane and broad, yet long and pointed (typically slightly upturned) muzzle.

DISTRIBUTION & POPULATION
Coastal South Africa, from Algoa Bay, to N Namibia, with movements of up to 1,500 km recorded, having reached Angola and Marion Is (nominate *pusillus*); and SE Australia, primarily off Victoria and Tasmania, where occurs on 9 islands in Bass Strait, and small numbers reach New South Wales in non-breeding season (*doriferus*). Both prefer inshore waters. *Population* Currently, 1.7 million in S Africa (increasing) and 60,000–80,000 in Australia (stable or increasing locally since 1945).

ECOLOGY
Highly gregarious. *Diving* Up to 204 m and 7.5 min recorded. *Diet* Small shoaling fish, cephalopods and (in Australia) crustaceans. *Reproduction* ♂♂ sexually mature at age 4–5 yrs (though may not breed until 8–13 yrs old); 3–4 yrs in ♀♀. Ads arrive mid to late Oct, bulls first. Cows give birth late Nov–early Dec. Mating occurs 6–10 days later. For first 3 months ♀ spends 2–3 days ashore and 3–4 days at sea. Pups weaned at 4–6 months, but some suckled for 1–2 yrs. *Lifespan* Up to 21 yrs.

New Zealand Fur Seal
Arctocephalus forsteri
Australia and New Zealand. Max 2 m.

Priority characters on land (dry pelage)
- Large and thick-bodied, generally approaching Antarctic Fur Seal, especially characteristic is the *more otter-like head with long, sharply pointed snout*. Size, structure and appearance strongly vary with sex and age.
- Bull: larger and heavier; mane moderate and chest rather heavy. Generally dark greyish olive-brown, including flippers; paler grey-brown ventrally, but compared to congeners more *evenly dusky-olive, with greyish grizzling on mane and neck less obvious*; fore snout often distinctly cream-coloured. *Nose large and bulbous* (protrudes slightly beyond mouth, nostrils pointed slightly downwards).
- Cow: smaller and paler greyish olive-brown above, variably paler ventrally, but in some cream colour covers entire underparts.
- Imm: sexing difficult but advanced young ♂ larger and heavier than any ♀; younger ♂ still distinctly smaller and lacks heavy mane of mature ♂.
- Pinnae relatively long and prominent; both sexes have *cream to white whiskers, especially luxuriant and long in bulls*.
- *Fore and hindflippers mid length, the former typically more triangular in shape and relatively rather short*; claws relatively small.

Typical behaviour
- Polygynous, forms large rookeries; at sea, various group sizes, larger rafts near colonies.
- Rafts buoyantly at surface in variety of postures (when resting; feeds mainly at night), typically raising flippers in air.

Bull New Zealand Fur Seal: uniform dark body, rufous around muzzle, sharply pointed snout and luxuriant, long white whiskers are all characteristic.

SIMILAR SPECIES
Shares range with ***Australian Fur Seal***, but only in few remote areas meets ***Antarctic*** and ***Subantarctic Fur Seals***. New Zealand Fur Seal may also be confused with partially overlapping ***New Zealand*** and ***Australian***

Sea Lions, mainly at sea and ♀♀/young. Previous experience required to eliminate Australian Fur Seal, which in corresponding ages/sexes is larger with a more sea lion appearance, especially bulls which are noticeably heavier chested and large-headed with robust muzzle, and darker/browner with less olive-tinged fur; both sexes usually have a more extensive and contrasting pale underbody and more curved, paddle-like foreflippers (rather than triangular), and bulls have, on average, shorter whiskers. Very similar to Antarctic Fur Seal, and outside main ranges might only be separated if typical bull of latter involved, which has well-developed, silver-streaked mane, longer vibrissae, shorter snout and round, inconspicuous nose (rather

New Zealand Fur Seal, like all eared seals, typically fans its flippers when rafting at the surface.

New Zealand Fur Seal

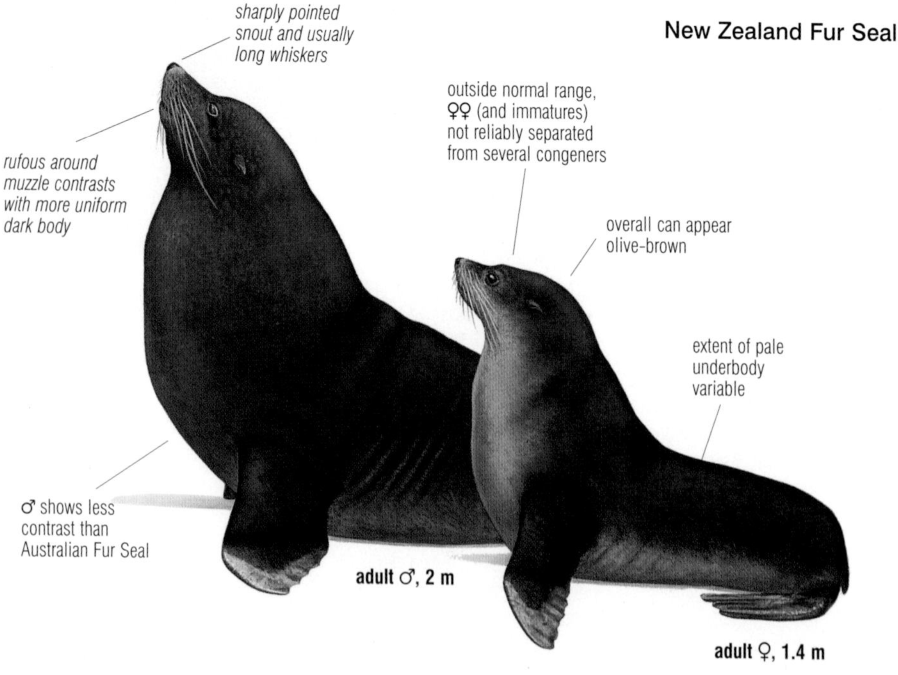

sharply pointed snout and usually long whiskers

rufous around muzzle contrasts with more uniform dark body

outside normal range, ♀♀ (and immatures) not reliably separated from several congeners

overall can appear olive-brown

extent of pale underbody variable

♂ shows less contrast than Australian Fur Seal

adult ♂, 2 m

adult ♀, 1.4 m

New Zealand Fur Seal in typical underwater pose.

than inflated and bulbous), and relatively shorter flippers. For comparison with Subantarctic Fur Seal see latter: bulls should be easily separable, but ♀♀/young might prove impossible to distinguish. Australian and New Zealand Sea Lions, especially on land, larger, with more rounded, dog-like heads and blunter muzzles, shorter ear-flaps, pelage far more extensive on foreparts in bulls, whilst ♀♀ generally sandier (both sea lions are uniquely coloured), and differ in proportionate length and structure of flippers.

VARIATION

Age/sex Bull considerably larger with very thick mane and is overall darker; ♀/young more alike. Newborn has velvet-black, short-curled coat, moults to olive-grey at 2–3 months; replaced several months later by more ♀-like pelage. **Physical notes** Full-grown ♂ 2 m and 180–200 kg, ♀ seldom exceeds 1.5 m and 50 kg; newborn 40–55 cm and up to 3.9 kg (♂) and 3.3 kg (♀). **Other data** *Moult* Post-natal. **Taxonomy** Monotypic, but significant genetic differences between New Zealand and Australian populations, and between subpopulations in former.

DISTRIBUTION & POPULATION

Islands and coasts of New Zealand (reaching Chatham, Campbell, Antipodes, Bounty and Auckland in non-breeding season), W & S Australia and off Tasmania. Non-breeders also move north, reaching as far as Queensland and New Caledonia, and subads and juvs appear on Macquarie in large numbers in Feb–May. *Population c.*85,000–135,000 in 1990s and increasing, with 20,000–22,000 at Westland and Fiordland (New Zealand) alone in 1989 and 35,000 in Australia.

ECOLOGY

Like other fur seals. *Diving* Up to 274 m and 11 min recorded. *Diet* Principally squid and octopus, with some fish, lampreys, rock lobster, crabs and penguins. *Reproduction* ♂♂ defend territories when *c.*10 yrs old but presumably reach sexual maturity earlier, whilst ♀♀ can breed at 5 yrs. Bulls arrive mid Oct–Nov, cows *c.*2–4 weeks later and give birth late Nov to mid Jan (most mid Dec); mate again 8–10 days later. ♀♀ then spend 1–7 days ashore and 1–5 days at sea. Pups weaned at 4–6 months, but some suckled for *c.*1 yr.

New Zealand Fur Seal feeding on octopus.

A bull New Zealand Fur Seal dominating its harem.

Antarctic Fur Seal

Arctocephalus gazella

Antarctic waters. Max 2 m.

Priority characters on land (dry pelage)

- Large and thick-bodied, with relatively long neck, *small head, short, strongly pointed muzzle and small nose*. Size, structure and appearance strongly vary with sex/age; *c*.1% of population is honey-blond morph (all ages/sexes).
- Bull: noticeably larger and heavier; generally dark brown, but *grizzled silver-white hair on convex crown, heavy mane, shoulders and breast* (face darker), and has broad dusky yoke, flippers and back, but belly and rear sides paler, often tinged ginger.
- Cow: smaller and more delicate, generally paler, being medium grey (even paler with age), darker above, and paler on foreneck, chest, underside and flanks; darkest are flippers, and around eye, whilst muzzle and face usually paler (contrasting with dark throat and crown).
- Imm: sexing (if genitals concealed) and ageing difficult but older imm ♂ larger and heavier than any ♀, especially on foreparts; younger ♂ still distinctly smaller and lacks heavy mane.
- Pinnae relatively long, prominent and bare at tip; *very long cream to white whiskers, particularly in bulls*, which have the longest of any pinniped (up to *c*.50 cm).
- Flippers rather short.

Typical behaviour

- Polygynous, forms huge rookeries; large rafts near colonies, but at sea smaller groups, usually of less than 5.
- Typically porpoises, often leaping clear of water, and often fans hindflippers when rafting at surface.

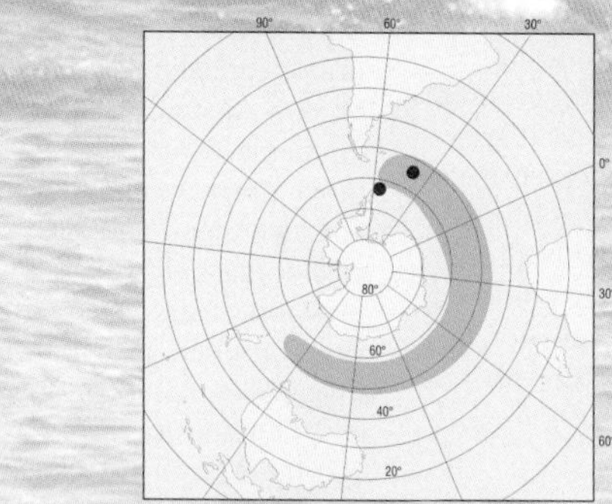

SIMILAR SPECIES

Especially away from breeding grounds could be overlooked as any other southern fur seal, but known to meet only ***Subantarctic Fur Seal*** on several subantarctic islands, especially in Indian Ocean, and ***New Zealand*** and perhaps ***South American Fur Seals***. Also reported from breeding grounds of Juan Fernández and South African Fur Seals.

Antarctic Fur Seal, honey-blond morph pup: unique among fur seals but only found in c*.1% of population (all ages/sexes).*

Subantarctic Fur Seal is very distinctive and, at least bulls and ad ♀♀, should be rather easily eliminated, especially on land. Others very similar to Antarctic and might not be certainly separated, unless typical bulls involved. Note overall size, structure, especially muzzle and nose, pigmentation, including amount of grizzled hair on head, mane and shoulders, and relative length of flippers and whiskers (latter may be broken). In wet conditions, especially in water, all appear very dark or black and almost unpatterned; identification then usually impossible.

Cow with her pup (right); nearby are two well grown pups (all pups are post-first moult).

Antarctic Fur Seal

VARIATION

Age/sex Bull considerably larger with broad mane and is overall darker; ♀♀/young smaller and paler. Newborn velvet-black, soon moulting to olive-grey, several months later replaced by more ♀-like pelage. **Physical notes** Full-grown ♂ reaches 2 m and ♀ 1.4 m; mean weights 188 kg, range 110–230 kg (♂) and 40 kg, range 22–51 kg (♀); newborn up to 67 cm (both sexes), 5.2 kg (♂) and 5.9 kg (♀). **Other data** *Moult* Post-natal, from Feb. **Hybrids** Hybridises with Subantarctic and New Zealand Fur Seals.

DISTRIBUTION & POPULATION

Breeds from 61°S to Antarctic Convergence, with 95% on S Georgia. Other colonies on S Orkney, S Shetland, S Sandwich, Bouvetøya, Marion, Kerguelen, Heard, McDonald and Macquarie. Non-breeders reach Weddell Sea, Argentina, the Juan Fernández Is and Antarctic Peninsula. *Population c.*1.6 million (perhaps 4 million), and increasing until 1970s.

ECOLOGY

Relatively sociable all year. *Diving* Up to 181 m and 10 min recorded. *Diet* Largely krill, but also fish, squid and penguins. *Reproduction* Sexually mature at 3–4 yrs (♂ do not usually get chance to breed before 7 yrs old). Breeds mid-Nov–late Dec on rocky coasts. Harems of 5–20. Cows give birth *c.*2 days after arriving and mate 7–10 days later. Pups nursed 5–8 days and ♀♀ then feed at sea for 3–6 days and visit pup for 1–2-day periods for first 4 months of life. *Lifespan* Up to 23 yrs.

Bull Antarctic Fur Seal: note short, well-pointed muzzle and small nose, but very long pale whiskers; grizzled silver-white hair on heavy mane, shoulders and breast, and the broad dusky band around body to flippers.

Subantarctic Fur Seal

Arctocephalus tropicalis

Subantarctic waters. Max 2 m.

Priority characters on land (dry pelage)

- Rather large and thick-bodied, and coat conspicuously patterned with orange-buff facial mask to chest. Prominent crest in bull diagnostic. *Muzzle short and rather compressed*, but quite pointed with small, slightly forward-pointing nose. Strong sex/-age-related variation, mainly in size and fur appearance.
- Bull: noticeably larger and heavier; mane moderate but still noticeably very thick on neck; *unlike congeners often appears to have tufted crest*, especially if excited, due to pale-tipped hair on forecrown. *Contrasting yellowish-orange lower face (to just above eyes but slightly below ears), muzzle and chest.* Otherwise dark olive-brown including flippers, with darker ginger belly (sometimes a blacker band between flippers). Generally few white hairs, but some increasingly grizzled with age.
- Cow: noticeably smaller (with blunter muzzle) and generally paler/greyer, but has *essentially paler fore face and underparts*; lacks mane and long hair on crown.
- Imm: sexing (if genitals concealed) and ageing difficult but near-mature ♂ larger and heavier on foreparts; younger ♂ distinctly smaller than ads with more uniform dark olive-brown fur, but to varying extent has characteristic paler face/underparts; young ♀♀ even less distinct.
- Pinnae quite long and prominent (close to centre of head, with bare dark tips); very long whitish whiskers.
- Flippers relatively short and broad.

Typical behaviour

- Polygynous, forms large rookeries; usually also gregarious at sea, with especially large rafts near colonies, otherwise small groups and singles.
- Rafts at surface in variety of postures, often with raised flippers.

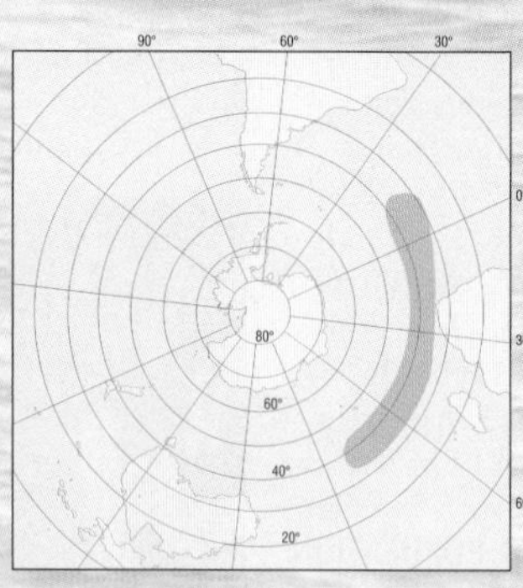

SIMILAR SPECIES

Disperses widely and may reach areas occupied or visited by congeners, principally ***Antarctic*** and perhaps also ***South African***, ***Australian***, ***New Zealand*** and ***South American Fur Seals***. However, given close views of well-marked animals, with yellowish and ginger pigments to face/chest and diagnostic crest (bulls), Subantarctic is safely identified. Other features, including overall size and shape, especially of muzzle and nose, and relative lengths of flippers and whiskers, are of less use due to extensive individual variation, and without comparative views or field experience, and it is doubtful whether many imms can be identified.

VARIATION

Age/sex Bull considerably larger with very thick neck and more strikingly patterned; ♀/young rather alike. Newborn has velvet-black or blackish-brown, short-curled coat, moulted to olive-grey after 3–4 months; replaced several months later by more ♀-like pelage. **Physical notes** Full-grown ♂ reaches 2 m and 88–165 kg, ♀ 1.4 m and 25–55 kg; newborn *c.*60 cm and 4.4 kg (♂) and 4 kg (♀). **Other data** *Moult* Post-natal. **Hybrids** Interbreeds with New Zealand and Antarctic Fur Seals, with latter on Macquarie, Marion and Prince Edward (where 0.1% of animals present in 1982 were hybrids), and lone bulls have established themselves in colonies on S Georgia.

Bull Subantarctic Fur Seal, showing diagnostic tufted crest and contrasting buff face and chest.

DISTRIBUTION & POPULATION Breeds on Tristan da Cunha and Gough, Prince Edward, Marion, Crozet, Amsterdam, St Paul and, recently, Macquarie. Vagrants have reached S Africa, S Georgia, Brazil, Madagascar, the Comoros, Australia and New Zealand, the Snares and Antipodes. *Population* 280,000–350,000, with 200,000 of these on Gough in 1970s and 50,000 on Amsterdam in early 1990s.

Cow and c.1 month-old pup Subantarctic Fur Seal: ♀ is distinctly smaller than bull with blunter muzzle and greyer body, but retains diagnostic (albeit less contrasting) paler foreface and underbody.

ECOLOGY
Relatively gregarious year-round. *Diving* Up to 208 m and 6.5 min recorded. *Diet* Squid, fish and krill, and some penguins. *Reproduction* Sexually mature at 4–8 yrs but ♂ rarely breed before latter age. Cows give birth mostly Nov/Dec. Harems of 5–15. Ads mate *c.*1 week after pups born and ♀♀ then alternate between nursing pups for 1–3 days and feeding for 5–12 days. *Lifespan* Up to 25 yrs.

Subantarctic Fur Seal

often-conspicuous tuft of raised hair

very long vibrissae in both sexes

clear demarcation compared to Antarctic Fur Seal

distinct contrast in both sexes (can be difficult to detect on wet/swimming animals)

adult ♂, 2 m

short flippers

adult ♀, 1.4 m

Sea lions

The sea lions (Otariidae, **eared seals**) are a highly variable group of five species, each placed in its own genus, with a stronghold in the Pacific and Southern Hemisphere. The general ecology, social organisation and reproductive behaviour of sea lions are very similar to those of fur seals. Sea lions are largely restricted to temperate and tropical latitudes, unlike fur seals which penetrate polar regions, although both originated in the North Pacific and share a common ancestor. A recent molecular study suggested that some sea lions are closely related to a number of the fur seals, with the exception of Northern Fur Seal. Clearly, much remains to be learned about their evolutionary relationships.

Hauled-out Northern Sea Lions: almost 60 ♀♀ and 2 bulls (note the ♂ on right has pale dry pelage whilst the other ♂ looks darker and slicker).

For identification, it is initially important to appreciate the differences between sea lions and fur seals as there is much greater overlap between the various sea lions and fur seals than between the different sea lions. Separation of young and females from the local fur seal is often not easy, and even with near-mature males and bulls the differences are not always clear-cut, especially to inexperienced observers. For example, Australian and Northern Fur Seals are relatively larger and can bear a somewhat stronger resemblance to sea lions. Overall, sea lions are more heavily built and larger. They have more rounded, dog-like faces and muzzles (rather than pointed and otter-like), sandier coats in females and much denser/complex manes and shoulders in bulls. Both sexes, especially males, appear to have smaller eyes and, unlike fur seals, the snout appears shorter, the nose generally broader and blunter, and the relatively shorter ear-flaps and are held closer to the centre of the head. In addition, ashore the two groups tend to favour different breeding terrain.

Bull California Sea Lion showing characteristic high-peaked crown with pale sagittal crest, and upturned muzzle.

Separation of the various sea lions is rather straightforward in bulls, but in females and young of most species, especially where some overlap occurs, is very difficult and unreliable, whilst identification at sea is largely unknown, very difficult or impossible (even from fur seals). Remember that all species display much individual variation in size, shape and pelage coloration, and there are

Sea lions

Northern (Steller's) Sea Lion (N Pacific), p. 305

Californian and Galápagos Sea Lions (Galápagos & E Pacific), p. 296

South American Sea Lion (S America), p. 299

Australian Sea Lion (S Australia), p. 301

New Zealand Sea Lion (subantarctic New Zealand), p. 303

often marked seasonal changes in overall bulk, whilst pelage texture and colour become much darker and less patterned when wet. Thus shape, coloration and general appearance are completely different on land, in surface water and in deeper water. It is best to rely on a combination of several characters, particularly overall size and structure, head profile, especially the muzzle and nose structure, flipper size/structure and, in some cases, fur coloration. Behaviour and vocalisations can also be useful aids. The identification boxes describe animals with dry pelage and typical animals of both sexes, but separation to species level of females or young is usually very difficult or impossible on current knowledge.

Californian Sea Lions: each animal is rather different, but all are ♂♂ of varying ages.

Porpoising California Sea Lion.

California and Galápagos Sea Lions

Zalophus californianus

NE & CE Pacific. Max 2.4 m.

Priority characters on land (dry pelage)

- Strongly built otariid (bull), considerably larger than any fur seal. *Dog-like muzzle quite long and not so blunt, with characteristic upturned profile* and round nose (especially bulls). Size, structure and appearance strongly vary with sex/age.
- Bull: larger and darker; *mane and head less enormous than other sea lions. High peaked crown with pale sagittal crest* (at sexual maturity). Face around muzzle, to eyes and ear pinnae, paler (with age), otherwise dark brown with sandy-brown sides, belly and rear body. Some distinctly paler.
- Cow: distinctly smaller and paler, *almost uniform tan (more greyish when fresh); lacks pronounced crest and has narrower head sloping rather gently into muzzle.*
- Imm: difficult to distinguish from ♀; sexing (if genitals concealed) and ageing difficult but near-mature ♂ larger and heavier; younger ♂ still distinctly smaller and lacks crest or heavy mane.
- Pinnae relatively short, close on head; short or mid-length cream to white whiskers.
- *Foreflippers short and broad, darker with hair on upper surface to beyond 'wrist', and tiny claws;* hindflippers and cartilaginous terminal flaps and claws short.

Typical behaviour

- Polygynous, forms large rookeries on open beaches; at sea in variety of group sizes, with larger concentrations near colonies.
- Rafts buoyantly at surface in variety of postures and frequently raises flippers above water. Young, especially, perform high vertical leaps; inquisitive around vessels, well adapted to modified environments and often associates with cetaceans.

SIMILAR SPECIES

California and Galápagos Sea Lions may coexist with ***Northern*** (qv) and ***South American Sea Lions***, respectively. However, they differ in overall size and shape, and that of muzzle and head/mane, and to some extent by pigmentation and features requiring close views, such as the flippers, although generally bulls are easily differentiated and young/♀♀ are not. California Sea Lion also comes into contact with ***Northern*** and ***Guadalupe Fur Seals***, whilst Galápagos Sea Lion shares the islands with Galápagos Fur Seal. All fur seals are distinctly smaller and differ in relative size and shape of head, muzzle and ear pinnae, the pelage and flippers.

VARIATION

Age/sex Bull considerably larger with thick mane;

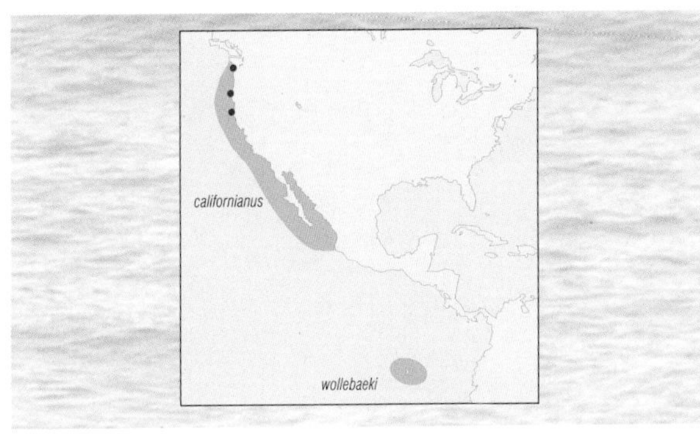

from Sep, bulls from Nov, following northward migration. **Taxonomy** Three subspecies (differ mainly in skull size and dentally): nominate *californianus* of NE Pacific (C Mexico north to British Columbia, including Gulf of California), *Z. c. wollebaeki* (Galápagos) and *Z. c. japonicus* (Japan and Korea but extinct).

distinctly paler ♀/young rather alike. Newborn has brownish-black (thick-curled) coat, moulted at end of first month of life; replaced 4–6 months later by ♀-like pelage. **Physical notes** Full-grown ♂ *Z. c. californianus* reaches 2.4 m and 390 kg, ♀ 1.8 m and 100 kg; *Z. c. wollebaeki* ♂ *c.*200 kg, ♀ 50–80 kg; newborn *c.*80 cm and 6–9 kg. **Other data** *Moult* Post-natal, ♀♀/juvs

Gathering of non-breeding immature ♂♂ Galápagos Sea Lions: note individual variation in colour (the darkest animals came ashore last, still having wet pelage).

California and Galápagos Sea Lions

DISTRIBUTION & POPULATION

Breeds on Channel Is off S California (USA), off Baja California, including Guadalupe Is, and islands in the southern part of the Gulf of California (Mexico), with large numbers reaching the northern Gulf and along the Pacific coast to British Columbia (Canada) in the non-breeding season, but others remaining close or at the rookeries year-round (*californianus*). Recently recorded south to the Guatemala border. *Z. c. wollebaeki* is restricted

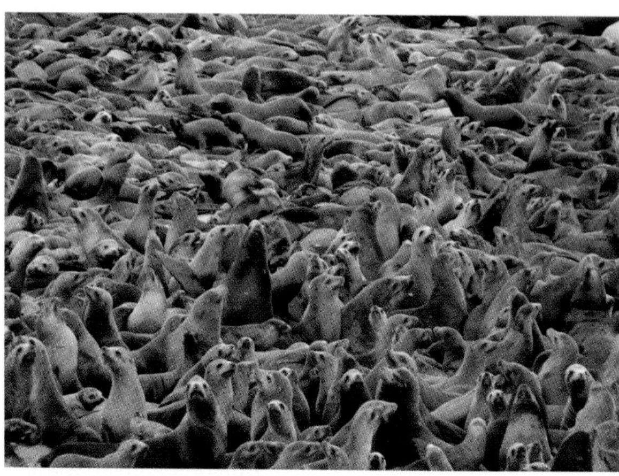

A dense rookery of California Sea Lions; a few bulls dominating their very large harems.

A California Sea Lion foraging for baitfish in kelp forest.

to the Galápagos, with a small colony recently established on La Plata Is (Ecuador), and vagrants reported north to Colombia and Costa Rica (Islas del Coco). *Population* 175,000 Californian Sea Lions in 2001, with 14,000 Galápagos Sea Lions in 1998 (20,000–50,000 in 1963). No reliable sightings of *japonicus* since 1950s (formerly 30,000–50,000).

ECOLOGY

Gregarious year-round. *Diving* Max. 536 m and 12 min. *Diet* Primarily fish, some squid. *Reproduction* Ads arrive May. Cows give birth late May–Jul (until Jan in Galápagos), 4–5 days after arrival. Mating occurs *c.*3–4 weeks later and ♀♀ thereafter alternate between 1–3 days at sea and 1 day ashore. Pups weaned at 4–8 months, but may be nursed for up to 1 yr (or even 3 yrs in Galápagos). *Lifespan* Up to *c.*30 yrs.

Bull, cow and pup Galápagos Sea Lions.

South American Sea Lion

Otaria byronia

S America. Max 2.8 m.

Priority characters on land (dry pelage)

- Powerful. In both sexes *muzzle compressed and relatively very short, broad and blunt-tipped*. Strong sex-/age-related variation in size, structure and appearance.
- Bull: far larger and heavier than ♀; *especially old bulls develop huge, lion-like shaggy rusty-brown mane extending to flipper level*, creating smaller body appearance; typically short muzzle somewhat curiously upturned at tip. Overall dark brown, duller tan-brown in summer. Mane often tinged paler.
- Cow: smaller and slimmer but still heavier than other southern sea lions, with denser coat; *mainly greyish-brown dorsally and dull yellowish-buff ventrally*, but can have paler head and neck, or be patchily patterned, with extensive pale oval marks all over (variation depends on stage of moult).
- Imm: at 9–18 months young ♂ resembles ♀; subsequently acquires darker, denser coat and partial mane, being smaller and lacking heavy mane but clearly larger than ♀.
- Ear pinnae relatively small and closer to face, particularly inconspicuous in bulls; longish whitish whiskers.
- *Foreflippers proportionately very large and broad*; hindflippers relatively short.

Typical behaviour

- Polygynous, forms huge dense rookeries; at sea occurs in variety of group sizes, with larger concentrations close to colonies.
- Rafts at surface and often feeds in association with cetaceans and seabirds.

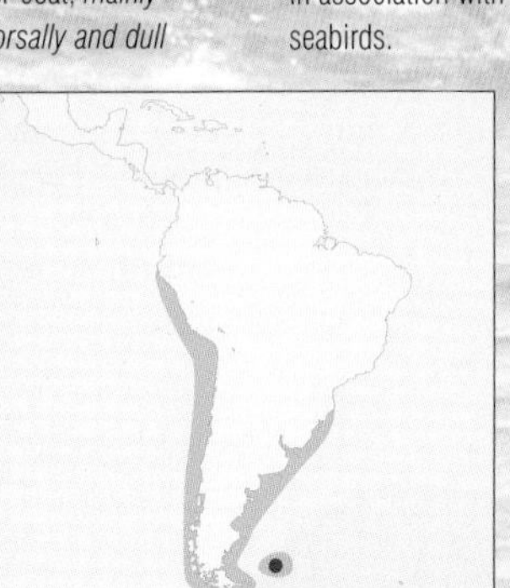

SIMILAR SPECIES

Ashore, separation from much smaller ***South American Fur Seal*** rather easy despite virtually identical ranges, although identification of young/♀♀ not always straightforward. Readily separated from vagrant fur seals, namely Galápagos, Juan Fernández, Antarctic and Subantarctic. ***Galápagos Sea Lion*** and South American Sea Lion may disperse over same area, but bulls highly distinctive: latter has head and mane far larger, broader and squarer, a shorter muzzle with less upturned tip, and no sagittal crest on crown. However, it is doubtful whether young/♀♀ can be reliably separated, unless very close comparison of head/muzzle shape (more compressed in present species), overall browner (less sandy) coloration and other differences, such as the flippers, is possible.

VARIATION

Age/sex Bull considerably larger with enormous head/mane and is overall darker; ♀/young rather alike. Newborn black or black-brown above, often some greyish-buff below, moults to dark brown at *c.*1 month, after few months to overall pale grey-brown, and yearlings become reddish-brown, more ♀-like, fading to paler brown or tan, with even paler face. **Physical notes** Full-grown ♂ reaches over 2.8 m and up to 350 kg, ♀ 2.2 m and 144 kg; newborn ♂ 75–86 cm and 12–15 kg, ♀ 73–82 cm and 10–14 kg. **Other data** *Moult* Post-natal,

Bull South American Sea Lions must continually fight to defend their territories and harems. Note the huge, lion-like and shaggy, rusty-brown mane.

Mating South American Sea Lions, the cow nursing her pup (which was born c.6 days ago).

late summer and autumn, ♀♀/juvs first. **Taxonomy** Debate over whether the name *flavescens* or *byronia* should be applied to this taxon but latter may have priority, as the holotype of (*Phoca*) *flavescens* is unidentifiable.

DISTRIBUTION & POPULATION

S South America, from S Brazil (vagrant north to Bahia) and Peru (vagrant to Galápagos, Colombia and Panama) south to Tierra del Fuego and islands south of Cape Horn, and the Falklands. Exceptionally has wandered as far as Tahiti. *Population c.*275,000 individuals in early 1980s but decreasing.

ECOLOGY

Gregarious ashore. *Diving* Max 175 m (up to 8 min). *Diet* Squid and crustaceans, small fish, penguins and young/♀ fur seals; may forage up to 150 km from colony. *Reproduction* Sexually mature at 4–6 yrs. Ads arrive in first ½ of Dec. Harems of 8–10. Cows give birth Sep–Mar, 2–3 days after arrival. Mating occurs *c.*6 days later and ♀♀ alternate between *c.*3 days at sea and 2 days ashore. Pups dependent 8–12 months. *Lifespan c.*20 yrs.

South American Sea Lion

Australian Sea Lion

Neophoca cinerea

S Australia. Max 2.5 m.

Priority characters on land (dry pelage)

- Bulky, typically silver grey, cream and fawn. Size, structure and appearance vary with sex/age, especially in bulls.
- Bull: larger and heavier with muzzle rather long and narrower at tip. Coal chocolate-brown with moderate mane and *striking yellowish-cream hairs on top of head and nape*, muzzle usually darker; whitish-cream crown patch and slightly paler throat accentuate *dark mask*. Greyer dorsally with duskier abdomen and flippers.
- Cow: smaller and paler, *with characteristic demarcation between darker dorsal area and top of head, and paler, creamy yellow underbody and head-sides. Whitish eye-ring and snout accentuate black nose, and many have dusky mouthline giving moustache effect when head upturned* (contrast variable).
- Imm: ♂ resembles ♀ for first 2 yrs, thereafter larger and bulkier with incomplete mane, also slightly spotted on chest, with whitish eye-ring and dark muzzle which gradually darken, and some white hairs on crown/nape. ♀ exhibits indistinct age-related variation.
- Pinnae relatively small and close up to face (very indistinct in bulls); moderately long whitish whiskers.
- Flippers proportionately short and slender, their claws short and poorly developed.

Typical behaviour

- Polygynous, forms rookeries that breed at different seasons; at sea occurs in smaller groups, with larger rafts near colonies.
- Rafts at surface in variety of postures; porpoises and surfs beach waves.

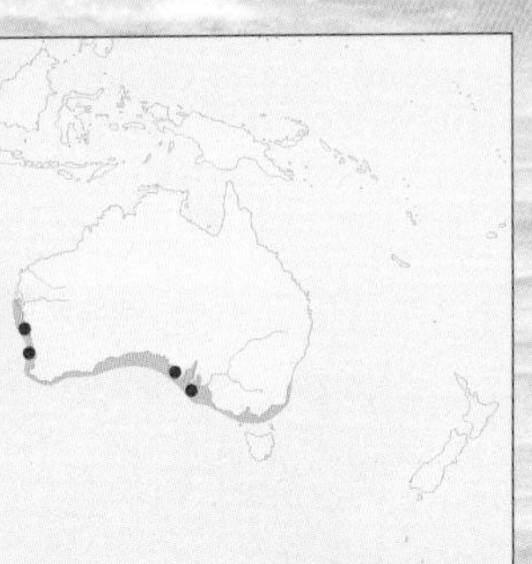

Cow Australian Sea Lion: darker dorsally and paler ventrally and on head-sides, with characteristic whitish eye-ring.

SIMILAR SPECIES

Only very rarely comes into contact with ***New Zealand Sea Lion***, and separation of bulls easy. The only sea lion restricted to Australian waters, and ashore unlikely to be confused with overlapping fur seals, namely ***Australian*** and ***New Zealand Fur Seals*** (qv), especially if seen well. Latter can be primarily eliminated by their smaller size, more pointed faces/muzzles and lower, longer ears. Coloration and structure of pelage also differ: bull Australian Sea Lion has massive head/mane with striking whitish crown patch and dusky face mask, unlike fur seals. ♀/young also distinctive, being tinged silver and yellowish (rather than dark grey and brown) and unlike fur seals have striking facial marks.

VARIATION

Age/sex Bull considerably larger with very thick mane and is overall darker; ♀/young more alike. Newborn has short-curled, chocolate-brown coat, paler crown and dark facial mask, becoming greyer prior to moult, then

Cow Australian Sea Lion, showing typically contrasting paler underbody and lower face, encircling eye.

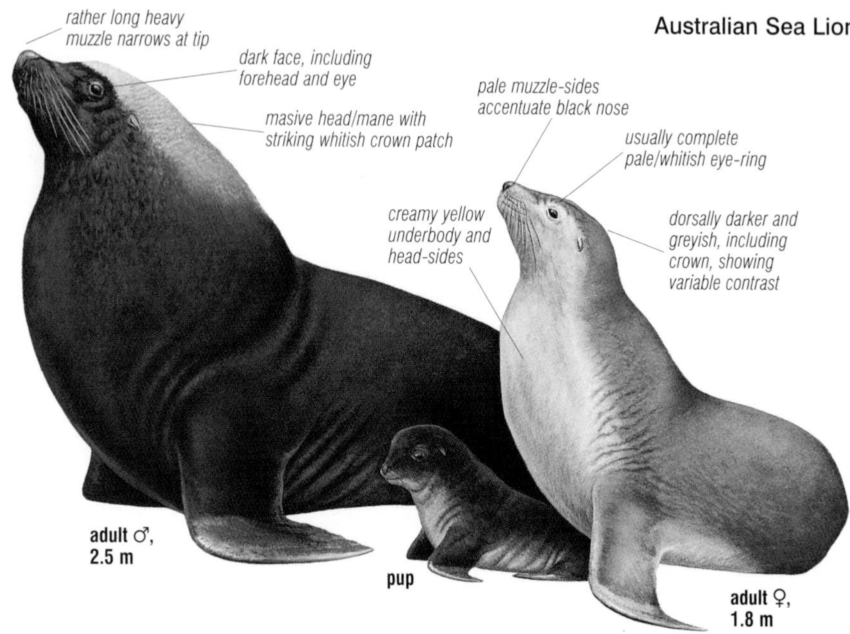

dusky creamy brown at 2 months; replaced after several months by more ♀-like coat (silvery grey to fawn dorsally and yellowish or light tan ventrally). **Physical notes** Full-grown ♂ 2–2.5 m and 300 kg, ♀ 1.3–1.8 m and 110 kg; newborn 62–68 cm and 6–8 kg (♂ larger from birth). **Other data** *Moult* Post-natal, but variable, imms first during breeding season, followed by cows 4 months after giving birth, and bulls 9 months after. **Taxonomy** Monotypic.

DISTRIBUTION & POPULATION

Offshore islands and 3 mainland sites, from W Australia to S Australia. Formerly perhaps in N Tasmania and occasionally reaches New South Wales and further north in W Australia. *Population* Stable but only 9,300–11,700, most in S Australia.

ECOLOGY

Larger aggregations near rookeries. *Diving* Max 150 m and 8 min. *Diet* Fish and squid, but also penguins. *Reproduction* Season varies. ♀♀ arrive 1–2 days before giving birth, in early Jan–Oct (peak Jun), and mating occurs 7–10 days after birth, but ♀ remains with pup almost constantly for 3 months (regular feeding forays of 2 days) and suckling continues 15–18 months.

Bull Australian Sea Lion; note rather long heavy muzzle, dark face with paler and rusty mane, and striking whitish-cream crown patch.

New Zealand Sea Lion

Phocarctos hookeri

S New Zealand & subantarctic islands. Max 3.5 m.

Priority characters on land (dry pelage)

- Very large, with fairly broad, short muzzle (almost flat profile). Marked sex-/age-related variation in size, structure and fur development, especially in bulls.
- Bull: larger and heavier; *predominantly dark brown to blackish-brown, with heavy mane, mainly on nape, neck and shoulders*, leaving small round face; older bulls have even denser and more richly coloured fur.
- Cow: smaller with narrower head and muzzle, and overall much paler, *generally dull yellowish-buff on face and underbody, and variably darker and/or more silvery grey to brownish dorsally including crown/nape;* variable brownish hue to sides of muzzle and *usually less obvious and incomplete pale eye-ring and inconspicuous dark mouthline*.
- Imm: ♂ at 9–18 months resembles ♀, and sexing and ageing difficult until becomes clearly larger and heavier on foreparts. Gradually acquires darker thicker fur; mane varies. ♀ exhibits indistinct age-related variation.
- Pinnae relatively small (very indistinct in bulls) set close to head; moderately long, whitish to pale brown whiskers.
- Flippers proportionately short and slender, as are claws.

Typical behaviour

- Polygynous, forms small to moderate rookeries on soft sandy beaches; at sea in small groups or alone, usually close to shore.
- Porpoises across surface, and also surfs beach waves or rafts at surface.

individuals. ***Australian Sea Lion*** apparently only rarely comes into contact with New Zealand Sea Lion, and differentiation, at least of bulls, easy. Latter distinctly larger, and differs in face/muzzle and mane, which are uniform (striking whitish crown patch and dusky face mask in Australian). ♀/young, however, very similar or inseparable, but New Zealand Sea Lion perhaps larger and more silver grey above (rather than brownish), with less-striking and incomplete whitish eye-ring, and usually has dark smudge on sides of muzzle (usually paler/whitish in Australian).

♀ New Zealand Sea Lion: note greyish sides to muzzle and incomplete pale eye-ring.

SIMILAR SPECIES

The only sea lion restricted to S New Zealand waters and, at least ashore, unlikely to be confused with overlapping ***New Zealand Fur Seal*** (or other fur seals which less frequently occur in or near range, e.g. Antarctic and Subantarctic). Note rounded dog-like face and muzzle, sandy coat of ♀ and much denser mane of bull; other features, such as size and shape of flippers and shape of outer toes on hindflippers, require very close views. See Australian Sea Lion for other differences from ♀ and young. All are much darker and appear unpatterned when wet, making separation difficult, even of classic

VARIATION

Age/sex Bull considerably larger with very thick mane and is overall darker; much paler ♀/young more alike. Newborn sexually dimorphic, with ♂ pale chocolate-brown, paler on nose to crown/nape, whilst ♀ predominantly pale, darker on head and nape; both sexes acquire more

New Zealand Sea Lion

well-developed thick mane, and small round face with short muzzle

in some, muzzle-sides as the rest of face and underbody but others have *diagnostic brownish hue* (*cf.* Australian Sea Lion)

usually indistinct and incomplete pale eye-ring (*cf.* Australian Sea Lion)

largely dark blackish-brown pelage

smaller cow typically dull yellowish-buff

variably darker and/or silver grey hue to brownish dorsal areas

adult ♂, 3.5 m

pup

adult ♀, 2 m

in older bulls pelage, and especially mane, even denser and richer/rustier coloured

♀-like pelage at 2 months. **Physical notes** Full-grown ♂ 2.4–3.5 m and 320–450 kg, ♀ 1.6–2 m and 90–230 kg; newborn 0.6–1 m and 7.2–7.9 kg, with ♂ larger at birth. **Other data** *Moult* Post-natal, commencing in Feb (juvs first), mostly Mar–Apr.

Mating New Zealand Sea Lions: the bull has largely dark blackish-brown pelage, and a small round face and heavy mane, whilst the smaller cow overall much paler, dull yellowish-buff.

DISTRIBUTION & POPULATION

Breeds on Auckland and Campbell, with very small numbers on Snares. Regular on New Zealand coast (breeds on Otago Peninsula), Macquarie and Stewart (formerly bred). Some non-breeders spend long periods up to 1 km inland on Enderby Is. *Population* Stable at 11,100–14,000 of which over ¾ occur on Auckland.

ECOLOGY

Prefers sandy beaches. *Diving* Max 500 m and 11 min (ave. 4–6 min). *Diet* Small fish, squid, crustaceans and, occasionally, penguins, fur and elephant seal pups. *Reproduction* Sexually mature at 4–5 yrs. Bulls arrive Nov and ♀♀ late Nov–early Dec. Harems of 12–25. Pups mainly born mid-Dec and ads mate 7–10 days later. ♀♀ spend 1–3 days foraging at sea and 1–2 days ashore. Lactation lasts 8–10 months and pup may be suckled for up to 1 yr. *Lifespan* Up to 23 yrs.

Northern Sea Lion

(Steller's Sea Lion)

Eumetopias jubatus

N Pacific. Max 3.3 m.

Priority characters on land (dry pelage)

- Huge, *distinctly pallid and heavier than other northern otariids. Both sexes robust in all ages, notably head/muzzle and neck.*
- Bull: larger and heavier; *head massive with rounded crown* (indistinct or no sagittal crest), *highly compressed, blunt muzzle* affording dog-like appearance. Very thick mane. Pale *yellow (blond) to very light brown* dorsally, darker and browner with some rust colour below. *Flippers always black.*
- Cow: smaller, with less heavy head/muzzle and neck. Differences not always clear at different ages.
- Imm: sexing (if genitals concealed) and ageing difficult; younger ♂ smaller and lacks heavy mane (closer to adult ♀); near-mature ♂ has larger and heavier foreparts.
- Pinnae relatively inconspicuous; rather long cream to white whiskers.
- *Foreflippers very long and broad and covered up to ¾ of length with thin fur;* hindflippers proportionately short and stubby, with longer cartilaginous terminal flaps.
- Long foreflippers, combined with long and broad neck, accentuate heavy forebody.
- *Unlike many pinnipeds, when wet, body still shows very pale pigmentation.*

Typical behaviour

- Polygynous, forms huge rookeries; at sea frequents coast to outer continental shelf, and usually in small groups or singles, but larger rafts near colonies.
- Rafts buoyantly at surface in variety of postures but mainly feeds at night. May be inquisitive of boats.

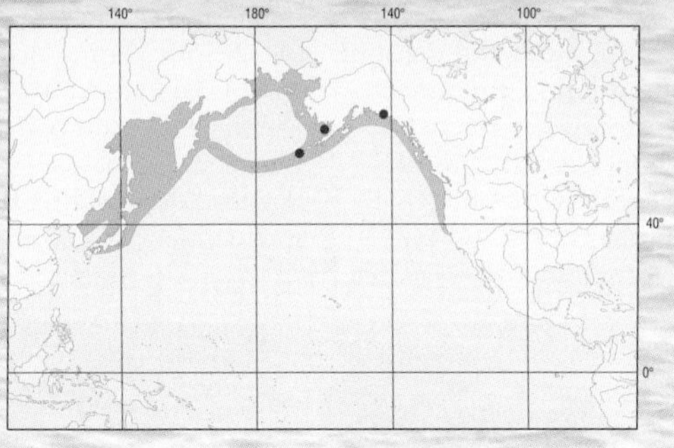

SIMILAR SPECIES

Most likely to be confused with ***California Sea Lion***, but Northern is larger, with longer/broader neck, broader head with compressed muzzle, and much flatter crown in bulls (no sagittal crest), as well as generally much paler pelage and perhaps longer foreflippers. Northern gives very loud 'roar', rather than 'bark' of California (in which only ♂♂ vocalise). Beware that ♀♀ and, especially, young are more similar in overall shape and coloration, but usually separable if using several characters in combination; the foreflipper and vocal characters are very useful. Distinctly larger and paler than overlapping ***Northern*** and ***Guadalupe Fur Seals***.

Bull Northern Sea Lion, showing massive head (note misleading effect of still dry, whitish crown contrasting with dark wet parts).

VARIATION

Age/sex Bull clearly larger with thicker neck and mane; ♀/young more alike. Newborn blackish-brown, moulting to a thinner and paler coat at *c.*4 months; pelage becomes paler with each consecutive moult. **Physical notes** Full-grown ♂ reaches *c.*3.3 m (mean 2.8 m) and 1,120 kg (mean 566–1,000 kg), max length for ad ♀ *c.*2.9 m (mean

Northern Sea Lions often form large aggregations near colonies.

Northern Sea Lion

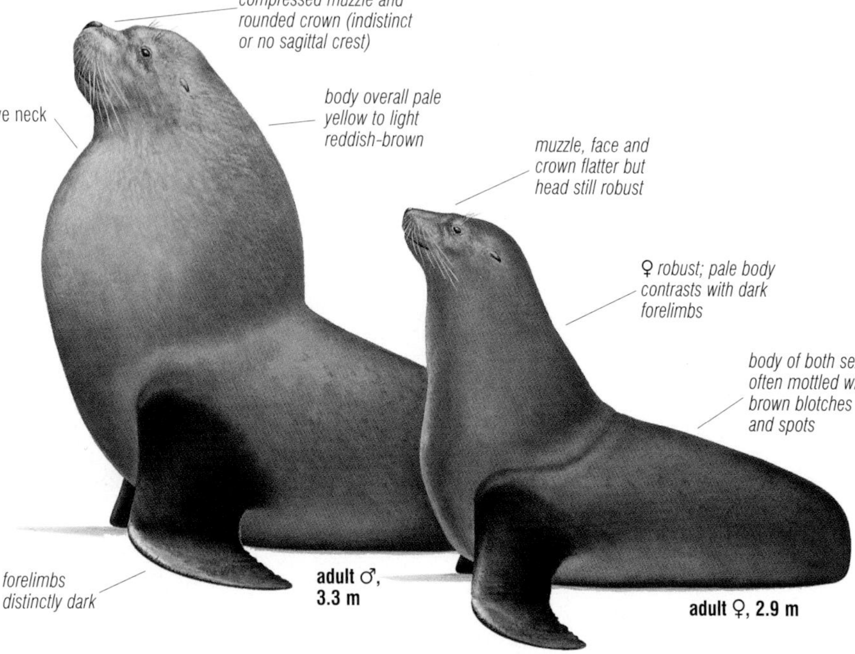

massive head with compressed muzzle and rounded crown (indistinct or no sagittal crest)

massive neck

body overall pale yellow to light reddish-brown

muzzle, face and crown flatter but head still robust

♀ robust; pale body contrasts with dark forelimbs

body of both sexes often mottled with brown blotches and spots

forelimbs distinctly dark

adult ♂, 3.3 m

adult ♀, 2.9 m

2.3 m) and 350 kg (mean 263 kg); newborn *c*.1 m and 16–23 kg. **Other data** *Moult* Post-natal, lasting from late summer to early winter (varies according to age/sex).

DISTRIBUTION & POPULATION

Breeds in N Pacific and S Bering Sea, ranging from Hokkaido (Japan) to the Aleutians and Pribilofs, and south to C California (USA). Most abundant in Alaska and British Columbia (Canada). Until 1980s bred on Channel Is, off California. Possibly ranges widely in non-breeding season. *Population* 60,000–70,000 by late 1990s (as many as 290,000 in 1985) declining presumably as a result of long-term environmental changes in N Pacific, increased commercial fishing in its range and high levels of contaminants.

ECOLOGY

Aggregates at breeding sites and when moulting. *Diving* Can reach 277 m. *Diet* Fish, squid and octopus all important. Sometimes visits freshwater rivers to fish. Occasionally predates other seals. Cows may make round trips of 2,200 km when foraging. *Reproduction* Sexually mature 3–8 yrs. Bulls arrive early–mid May, cows late May–Jun, giving birth *c*.3 days later. Harems of 12–150. Mating occurs 11–14 days after birth and ♀♀ thereafter alternate between 1–3 days at sea and 1–2 days ashore. Pups independent at 12 months. *Lifespan* Up to 25 yrs.

Bull (behind) and cow Northern Sea Lions: both sexes are pale (with contrasting black forelimbs) and heavier than other northern eared seals.

True seals

True seals (Phocidae) spend much of their life in the water and are excellent swimmers and divers, with some capable of remaining submerged for up to two hours and reaching significant depths. Despite this, none is totally independent of land. Generally they rely on their back-pointed hindlimbs for locomotion but, unlike eared seals, on land these trail and cannot be rotated forward to support the body. But, if they appear very ungainly and ungraceful on land, in the water they are supremely agile creatures capable of surprising manoeuvres. The phocids are further diagnosed by their lack of ear-flaps (pinnae), having only a small ear canal. Elephant seals differ in some respects from other phocid seals, in particular sexual differences being much more pronounced. Pups of some species are born with a soft, downy coat that is moulted after 2–4 weeks and shortly afterwards the new coat is shed, whereas other species moult into juvenile coat at foetal stage; others forgo the juvenile coat and moult directly to an adult-like coat.

Harbour Seal (widespread in Northern Hemisphere). True seals are accomplished divers, taking fish, crustaceans, cephalopods and other molluscs, often in deep water.

Phocidae are grouped into two subfamilies, the Phocinae, the true seals of the Northern Hemisphere, and Monachinae, monk seals and 'southern' seals, which are chiefly distributed in the Southern Hemisphere and represented in the Northern Hemisphere only by the monk seals. However, the latter grouping may actually consist of three groups, the Antarctic true seals (Lobodontini), the elephant seals (*Mirounga*) and the monk seals (*Monachus*).

Separation, especially on land, from eared seals is straightforward. Major risks of confusion occur in areas where more than one species of northern true seals overlap. Harbour Seal is the most widespread and familiarity with its variation is required for accurate separation from Largha (Spotted) and Grey Seals; Ringed Seal must be separated from all these, but coat pattern is wholly distinctive in close views; Grey (plainer animals) and Bearded Seals, and Grey (female/blotchy young) and female Hooded Seals sometimes require careful identification; whilst Northern Elephant, Hooded, Harp and Ribbon Seals are generally rather distinctive. Especially for observers without previous field experience, or when

Immature ♀ Hooded Seal: less specifically distinct with more rounded/compressed and less dark face than ♂, and with smaller, dark body patches than adult ♀.

Northern true seals

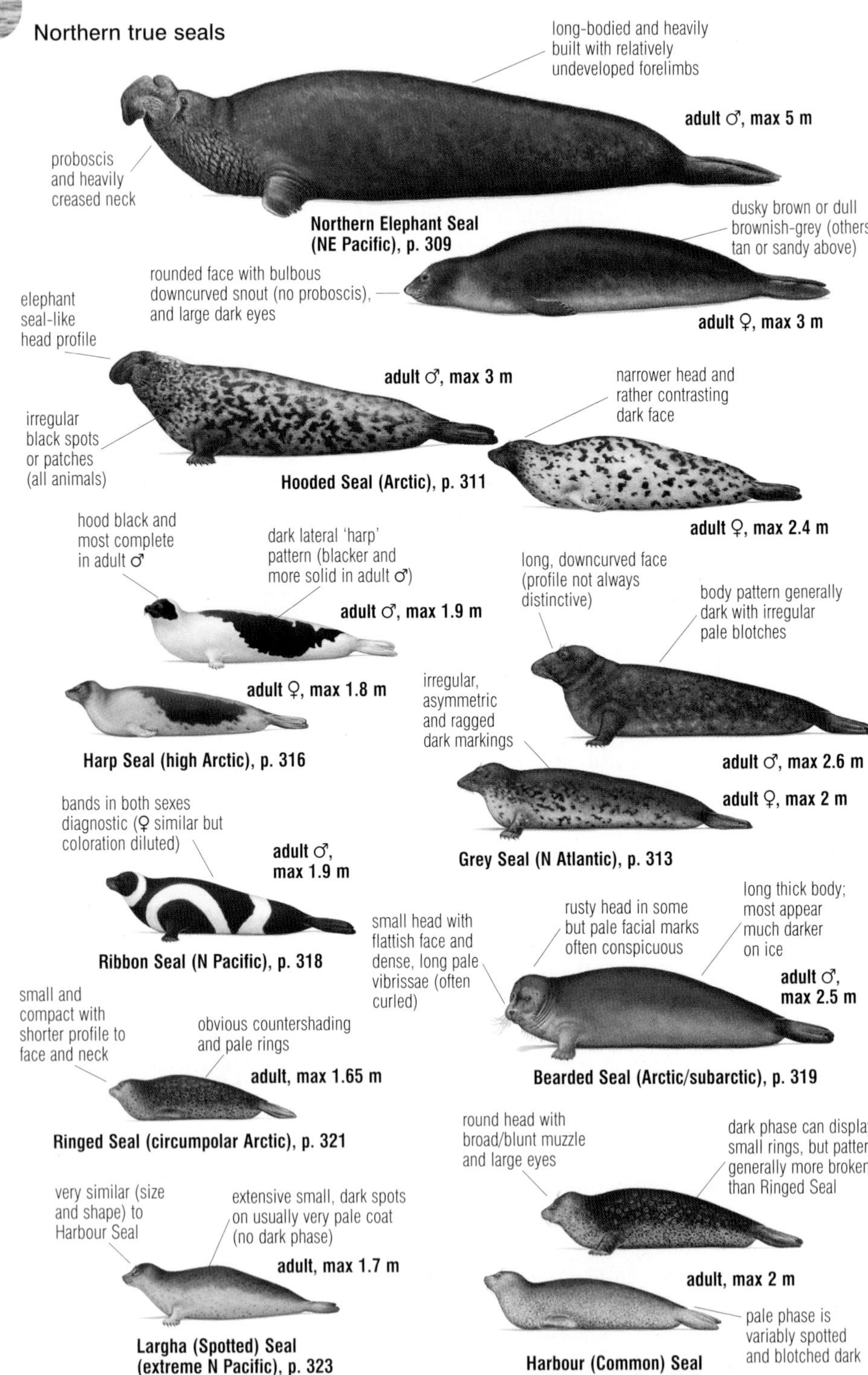

dealing with animals away from their main ranges, identification can be taxing. Separation of females, young and poorly marked animals can be very difficult and might require longer and closer views. In addition, identification at sea is often unknown even with adults, mainly because coat colour appears darker and less patterned when wet. Identifying seals in the water is further complicated because only parts of the animal are usually seen and for rather brief periods. It is best to use several features in combination, particularly overall size and structure, head and muzzle profile/shape and facial appearance, fur coloration and pattern, and, in some, flipper size/shape, whilst general behaviour and movements are sometimes useful.

Pup Harp Seal with soft, downy coat. In general, the world's Phocidae give birth to a single pup, and mate in the water, both within a short timeframe. The pups gain weight rapidly and swiftly become independent.

Northern true seals

Northern true seals comprise nine species: Northern Elephant (NE Pacific), Hooded (Arctic), Grey (N Atlantic, temperate/subarctic), Harp (high Arctic), Ribbon (N Pacific), Bearded (Arctic/subarctic), Ringed (circumpolar Arctic), Largha (extreme N Pacific) and Harbour Seals (widespread in N Hemisphere).

Northern Elephant Seal

Mirounga angustirostris

NE Pacific. Max 5 m.

Priority characters on land (dry pelage)

- *Huge long-bodied seal.* Heavily built, but overall size, facial structure and appearance vary with age and sex. *Dark eyes large and round.*
- Bull: larger with *square-shaped head. Elongated proboscis* (normally limp, overhanging mouth) acts as a resonating chamber when roaring at each other. *Skin folds completely encircle neck*, heavily scarred and deeply creased, and bleed in combat. Head, face and proboscis paler with age. Foreneck tinged pinker and overall darker/browner than ♀.
- Cow: *smaller with more rounded face and no proboscis (bulbous and downcurved snout).* Coat varies from dusky brown to tan or sandy.
- Imm: sexing difficult but near-mature ♂ clearly larger and possesses ad-like head characters. Growth in ♂ accelerates at puberty, at 5–6 yrs but mostly from 7 yrs, when the larger/squarer head, thicker neck and proboscis become apparent.
- Coat of short stiff hair mainly greyish or brown (when newly moulted, duller brown or rustier and tan, being discoloured by sun, mud and excrement), and usually darker dorsally and paler ventrally.
- *When moulting, coat typically has patchy appearance due to bleached old hair.*
- Short black whiskers, and 1–2 nasal whiskers; prominent vibrissae above eyes.

Bull Northern Elephant Seals; note proboscis, which acts as a resonating chamber when they roar at each other; pinker skin folds are heavily scarred and creased, and often bloody through combat.

SIMILAR SPECIES

Adult ♂ unmistakable due to huge size and large, fleshy proboscis. Also, at least on land, ♀ and young readily separated from any phocid, including Harbour Seal, which is usually much smaller than elephant seals and has a spotted coat, whilst all eared seals have distinctive structure and appearance.

VARIATION

Age/sex Considerable age-/sex-related variation in overall size, proportions, facial structure and appearance. Newborn has black coat, replaced after 5–6 weeks by bright silver (gradually becoming browner/darker) fur, darker above and paler below, and already has heavy body shape, round face and disproportionately large eyes. **Physical notes** Full-grown ♂ up to *c*.5 m and 2,200 kg, ♀ 3 m and 800 kg. Newborn to *c*.1.25 m and 35 kg. **Other data** *Moult* ♀ and young preceding bulls, generally Apr–Aug.

DISTRIBUTION & POPULATION

Breeds in *c*.15 colonies

- Foreflippers quite broad, with longer outer digits and large blackish-brown claws; hindflippers and cartilaginous terminal flaps short, but broad when fanned.

Typical behaviour

- Very clumsy on land, using body for propulsion in caterpillar-like fashion (so-called 'humping' gait).
- Polygynous, forms large colonies on open beaches. ♂ *combats and vocalising occur in mating season*.
- Mainly underwater, thus only occasionally recorded at sea.
- Near colonies, floats with head and hindflippers above surface, submerges tail first, head drawn down vertically. Rest intervals at surface very short, usually only a few min, when at sea.

140°
180°
140°
100°
40°
0°
female range
male migration route
breeding and moulting range

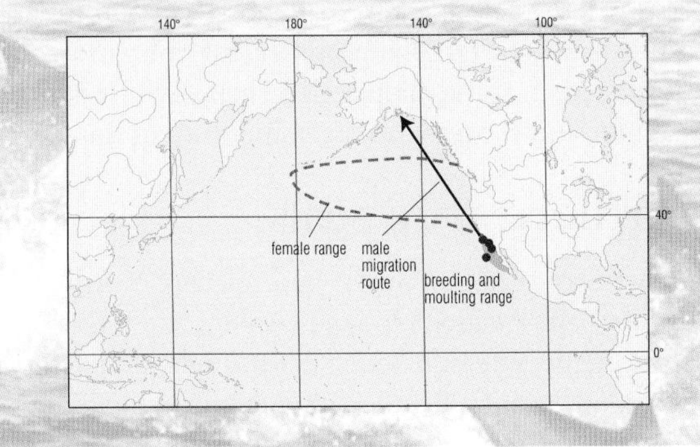

Northern Elephant Seal

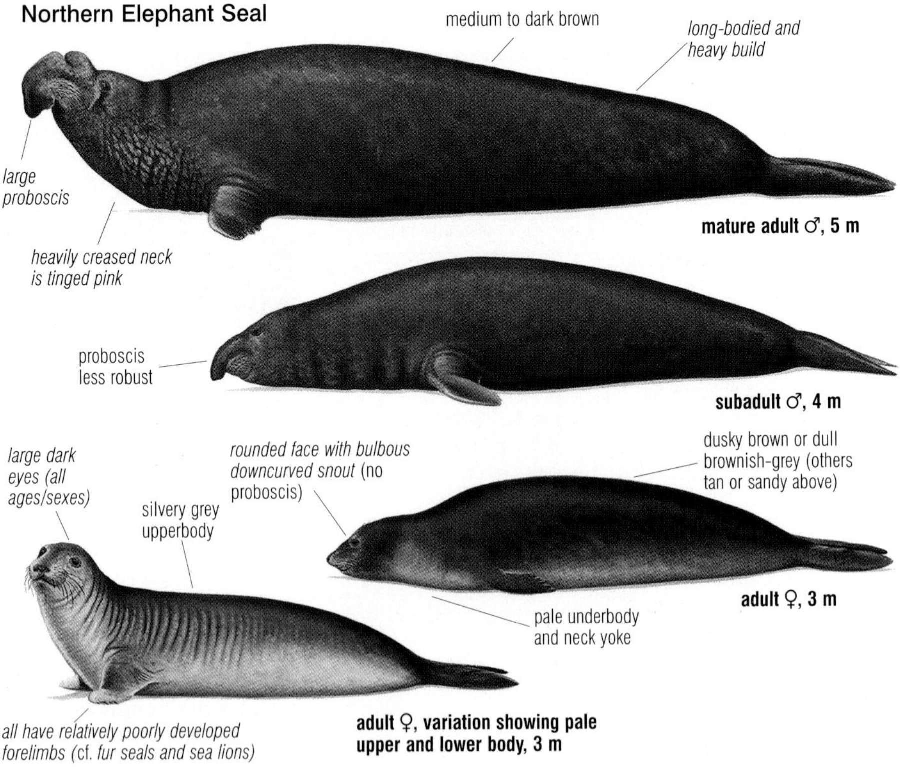

medium to dark brown
long-bodied and heavy build
large proboscis
heavily creased neck is tinged pink
mature adult ♂, 5 m
proboscis less robust
subadult ♂, 4 m
large dark eyes (all ages/sexes)
silvery grey upperbody
rounded face with bulbous downcurved snout (no proboscis)
dusky brown or dull brownish-grey (others tan or sandy above)
adult ♀, 3 m
pale underbody and neck yoke
all have relatively poorly developed forelimbs (cf. fur seals and sea lions)
adult ♀, variation showing pale upper and lower body, 3 m

Bull, cow and newborn Northern Elephant Seal. Inflated proboscis is used to hold cow during mating. Black coat of pup is shed when 5–6 weeks old.

Population Increasing and expanding since early 1900s.

ECOLOGY

Prefers sandy beaches. *Diving* Max 1,567 m and for 2 hrs. *Diet* Principally mesopelagic fish and squid. *Reproduction* Bulls arrive in Dec, ♀♀ up to 1 month later and 6–8 days prior to giving birth. Dominant bulls mate with up to 100 cows. Ads mate 3 weeks after births (peak in Feb), and pups swiftly weaned (at *c.*27 days). Cows depart from Feb; pups leave 4–6 weeks later. *Lifespan* Up to 25 yrs.

in eastern N Pacific, in California (USA) and islands off Baja California (Mexico), with more than ⅔ on the Channel Is (C California). Smaller numbers breed in mainland California. Some moult as far north as British Columbia (Canada). Non-breeders and foraging animals range north and west into the Pacific as far north as Alaska and the Aleutians, and vagrants (juvs) have reached Midway (Hawaii) and Japan.

Young Northern Elephant Seals: the pups are swiftly weaned and later in season form large post-breeding gatherings to fast and moult.

Hooded Seal

Cystophora cristata

Arctic. Max 3 m.

Priority characters on land (dry pelage)

- Robust, strikingly shaped and patterned seal. Ads unlikely to be confused.
- *Whitish to pale silver grey coat with irregular (partially coalescing) black spots or patches.* Wet coat appears more greyish and less patterned.
- Head large, broad and relatively compressed with very broad, fleshy muzzle overhanging mouth. Muzzle varies with sex and age, black in ads.
- Bull: larger with *thicker head and elongated proboscis*, which can, when inflated, double apparent size of head (like 2 separate dark balls, above and below), and is used in display. By closing 1 nostril, *can extrude huge reddish-brown membrane,* in form of crescent-shaped balloon, from other nostril.
- Cow: smaller with narrower head and muzzle with, at most, indistinct proboscis (blunt slightly downcurved snout); tends to have

Older immature ♂ Hooded Seals already have a broad, fleshy muzzle, slightly overhanging mouth, and extensively dark head that appears triangular in profile.

SIMILAR SPECIES

Only small juvs could be confused with other phocids in arctic waters, namely ***Grey***, ***Ringed***, ***Harbour***, ***Harp*** and ***Bearded Seals*** (which see), but differences in head shape and coat colour should identify it. Imm and even ads, in distant views, might be confused with Bearded Seal, especially on the ice, and in water with Harp Seal.

VARIATION

Age/sex Bull averages larger and differs in structure of head and muzzle; newborn as juv. **Physical notes** Full-grown ♂ up to 3 m long and 400 kg, ♀ 2.4 m and 300 kg; newborn 87–115 cm and 11–30 kg. **Other data** *Moult* Jun–Aug.

more contrasting dark head and paler body.

- Imm: juvs ('bluebacks') blue-grey on back with whitish lower sides and belly, and dark foreflippers, face/muzzle (especially behind eyes) until first or second annual moult. Sexing difficult but near-mature ♂ larger and has advanced head characters.
- Flippers relatively short, slightly pointed and angular with longer first digit.
- Whiskers short; dark in young and pale in ads.

Typical behaviour

- Hauls-out on ice floe; clumsy, 'humping' gait. Breeds on pack-ice, away from edges.
- Loose groups in mating period, often of a ♂ and 2 ♀♀, but otherwise usually solitary.
- ♂ aggressively patrols territory, and ♀ fiercely defends pup. ♂ simultaneously emits a high ringing sound when extruding nasal membrane.
- Generally elusive at sea and shy of boats.

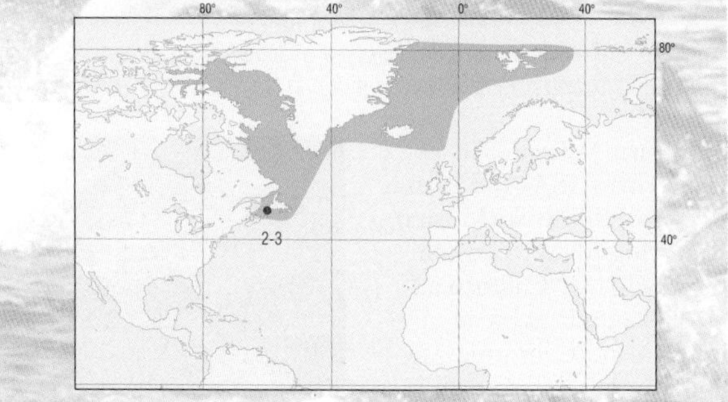

DISTRIBUTION & POPULATION

N Atlantic from Jan Mayen to Beaufort Sea (Canada), with principal breeding sites in Davis Strait off W Greenland, E Newfoundland (Canada) and the West Ice off Jan Mayen. Most appear to moult on pack-ice in Denmark Strait (Greenland) and stays close to pack-ice year-round. Vagrants have reached Portugal and Florida. *Population* Perhaps 0.5 million, with 250,000 near Jan Mayen and 300,000 off Newfoundland in early 1990s.

ECOLOGY

Solitary, except when breeding or moulting. *Diving* Max 1,000 m and for 52 min. *Diet* Mainly fish, also crustaceans and octopus. *Reproduction* Polygynous or serial monogamy: loosely aggregates on pack-ice (up to 10 bulls may compete for a single cow) mid-Mar to early Apr, with births peaking late Mar; following copulation (*c.*5–7 days after birth), bull searches for next cow; pups weaned in just 4 days, the shortest period for any mammal. *Lifespan* Up to 35 yrs.

Displaying bull Hooded Seal, with inflated reddish membrane; the cow is nursing her pup.

Hooded Seal

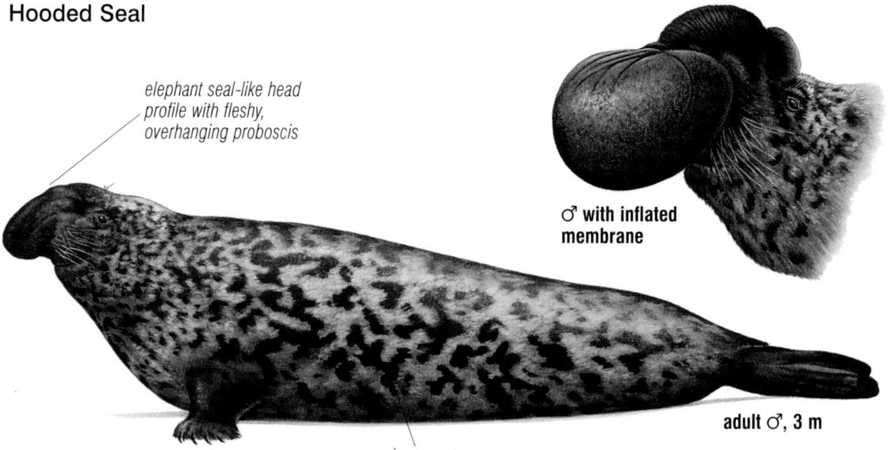

elephant seal-like head profile with fleshy, overhanging proboscis

♂ **with inflated membrane**

adult ♂, 3 m

narrower head and fleshy muzzle with rather contrasting dark face

irregular black spots or patches (all animals)

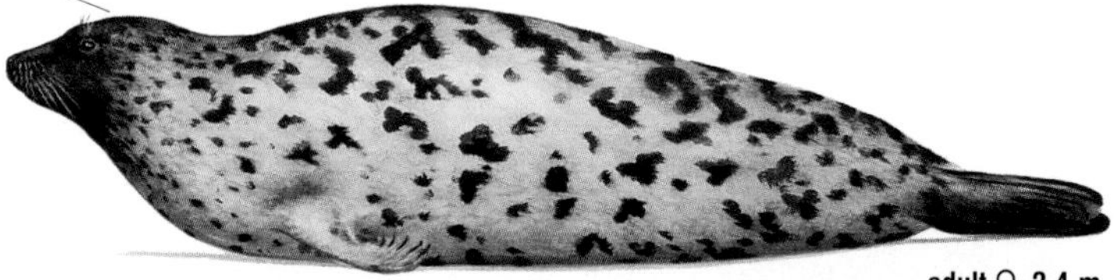

adult ♀, 2.4 m

Grey Seal

Halichoerus grypus

N Atlantic, temperate to subarctic. Max 2.6 m.

Priority characters on land (dry pelage)

- Medium-sized, robust phocid with broad elongated body, tapering backwards and has *relatively short/ broad and forward-set foreflippers.*
- Bull has, *rectangular, large horse-like head. ♀/young, however, confusingly smaller and round-headed without typical long flat muzzle.*
- Chiefly dark grey on back and paler grey below, with irregular spots or blotches. *Colour varies, both individually and with age and sex.* Some altogether uniform, others *distinctly paler, especially just prior to moult* (pale tan or even whitish, with dark markings obscure). Often tinged orange to reddish on neck and below.
- Bull: noticeably larger and heavier with very thick neck (scarred, heavily folded and wrinkled). Muzzle broadens into convex fleshy snout. Overall darker, some almost blackish, or has *dark smudges on sides less broken and thus more uniform.*
- Cow: smaller with narrower head and slightly convex muzzle. Overall paler, especially on belly and flanks where *dark smudges broken to form striking spots or blotches.*
- Imm: sexing difficult but near-mature ♂ larger and has advanced head characters. Generally paler with few, if any, blotches.
- *Broad open nostrils widely separated and parallel. Eyes close-set, further back from nostrils and realtively closer to ears.*

Cow (in foreground) and bull Grey Seals have bleached uniform coats when moulting (late winter in UK, as here); note strong sexual differences in head profile.

SIMILAR SPECIES

Bear in mind that ♀♀ are less strikingly shaped than bulls and often have strongly blotched flanks which can lead to confusion with ***Harbour*** and even ***Hooded Seals***. Head shape, the relatively long muzzle and almost parallel nostrils, different structure and position of eyes and nostrils/ears are useful characters. Hooded can also be differentiated by pelage markings. See also ***Ringed*** and ***Bearded Seals***.

Typical behaviour
- Hauls-out on sandy or rocky banks and offshore islands; clumsy, 'humping' gait. *Shares haul-out sites with Harbour Seal in areas of overlap.*
- Loosely gregarious, *sometimes in large aggregations on sandy beaches*. Usually solitary in water. Disperses widely in non-breeding season.
- Polygynous, but ♂♂ do not usually defend territories or harems.
- May adopt vertical 'bottling posture' with head and upperbody out of the water.

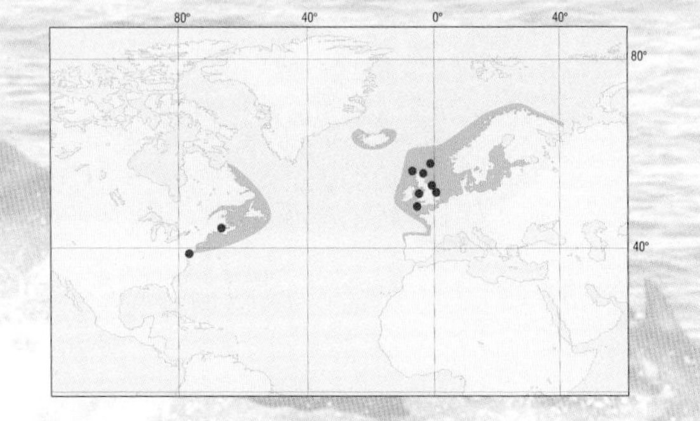

VARIATION

Age/sex Bull considerably larger with different head/muzzle and is overall darker than ♀ and young, which appear to have pale skin and dark makings (rather than mostly dark skin broken by pale makings). Newborn typically has silky, creamy-white coat, occasionally with greyish tinge, replaced over 2–4 weeks by a pale ♀-like coat that is even more subtly marked. Some pups assume a melanistic pelage, mostly ♂♂. **Physical notes** Full-grown ♂ up to 2.6 m and 400 kg, ♀ to 2 m and 250 kg; newborn 90–110 cm and 10–12 kg (♂ larger from birth). **Other data** *Moult* Mar–Jun (but ♀♀ in UK moult Jan–Mar); partial/complete pre-natal. **Taxonomy** Polytypic. Two races and 3 geographic populations differ mainly in size, e.g. Canadian seals almost 20% larger than British animals, and cranium: N Baltic (*H. g. macrorhynchus*), NE Atlantic and northeastern N America (nominate).

Cow Grey Seal with her pup: the latter's white coat will be replaced after 2–4 weeks.

Juvenile Grey Seal: following first moult, juveniles are closer to adult ♀♀ in coat colour and pattern.

DISTRIBUTION & POPULATION

N Atlantic, with major populations in Baltic Sea (mainly Gulf of Finland), Iceland, the Faeroes, Norway and Britain, and NE Canada

Grey Seal

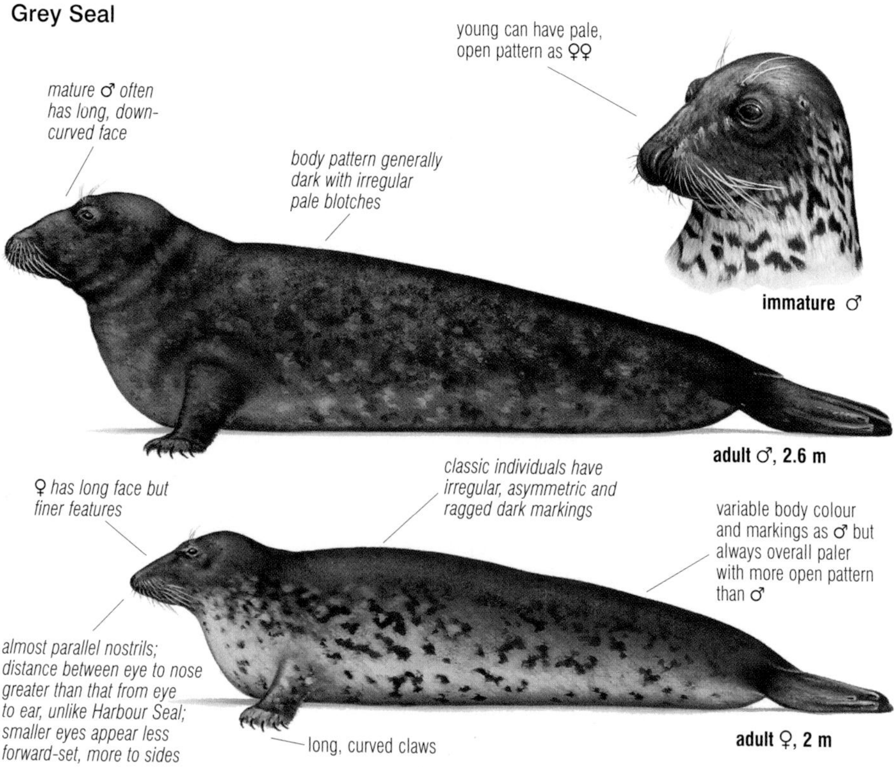

young can have pale, open pattern as ♀♀

mature ♂ often has long, down-curved face

body pattern generally dark with irregular pale blotches

immature ♂

adult ♂, 2.6 m

♀ has long face but finer features

classic individuals have irregular, asymmetric and ragged dark markings

variable body colour and markings as ♂ but always overall paler with more open pattern than ♂

almost parallel nostrils; distance between eye to nose greater than that from eye to ear, unlike Harbour Seal; smaller eyes appear less forward-set, more to sides

long, curved claws

adult ♀, 2 m

(in the Gulf of St Lawrence, Labrador and Nova Scotia). Some wander in non-breeding season, especially juvs, and vagrants recorded south to Portugal. *Population* Increasing in Atlantic, where *c.*160,000 in the northwest in late 1980s, and *c.*121,000 in northeast (mainly Britain) in early 1990s, but in substantial decline in Baltic, where currently just 2,000–3,000 (100,000 in early 1990s).

ECOLOGY

Breeding or moulting concentrations may number 100s, but more solitary at sea. *Diving* Occasionally reaching >300 m (max 30 min). *Diet* Varies regionally, but essentially fish and cephalopods; also seabirds. *Reproduction* Bulls may mate with up to 10 cows. Both sexes loosely aggregate on beaches, islands or pack-ice in Sep–Mar (season varies regionally). Pups weaned at 2.5–4 weeks, when ads mate. *Lifespan* Up to 40 yrs.

Cow (bottom) and bull Grey Seal: adult ♀ generally has paler coat with striking dark markings, rather than a mostly dark coat smudged paler, as in ♂ (although there is much individual and age-related variation); note differences in head profile between the sexes.

Harp Seal

Pagophilus groenlandicus

High arctic. Max 1.9 m.

Priority characters on land (dry pelage)

- *Medium-sized, compact seal of high-arctic regions*. Head rather round and broad with slightly flat crown, short, pointed face/muzzle and close-set eyes.
- *Greyish/white and black*. Size, structure and pelage change with age. Sexual dimorphism indistinct.
- Ads have *black hood and saddle* ('harp', formed by *2 lateral bands of variable width that join on shoulders*), and rest whitish to creamy. Hood and harp perhaps often muted, with ragged edges, and body variably spotted in ♀, but much variation.
- Juvs darker and greyer, spotted black. Imm ('spotted harp') has extensive dark spots and blotches, but hood and harp at most partial; others, described as 'sooty harps', have dusky-grey rather than white ground colour, may be near-ad, especially ♂♂, but wet coats always appear greyer or darker.
- Flippers relatively small, fore ones slightly pointed and angular, with a short row of digit endings, and claws strong and dark. Rather long, cream to white whiskers.

Typical behaviour

- Chiefly on pack-ice, but also occurs away from it in summer. May adopt vertical 'bottling posture' with head and upperbody emerging from water.
- Huge concentrations on pack-ice, where they pup. During mating very active in water and sometimes travels in tight noisy groups; often surface upturned, on its back.

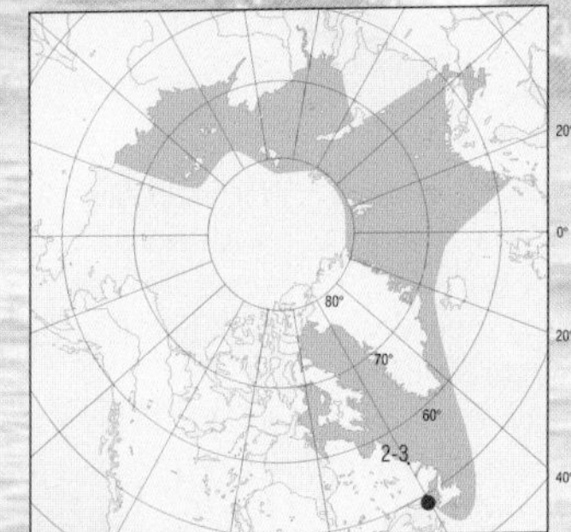

SIMILAR SPECIES

Ads with conspicuous black harp pattern and hood unlikely to be confused with other seals in range (***Hooded***, ***Bearded***, ***Grey***, ***Harbour*** and ***Ringed Seals***). However, young and other darker animals could pose some difficulties in distant or poor views, and travelling groups might even be mistaken for small cetaceans.

VARIATION

Age/sex Indistinct sexual variation, but ♀ slightly smaller and has more ill-defined, less intense hood and harp. Newborn ('whitecoats') possess lanugo coat for 12 days (initially discoloured yellowish by amniotic fluid), after which grey pelt develops, this being shed patchily after 21 days, producing advanced pup ('ragged-jackets'), giving way to medium grey juv coat with black blotches ('beaters'). At 13–14 months moult again to greyish and blotchy black imm pelage (still lacking harp or hood), retained for several moults until ad coat develops. **Physical notes** Full-grown ad 1.6–1.9 m and up to 140 kg (♂ only slightly larger than ♀ which reaches 1.8 m and 130 kg); newborn *c.*90 cm and *c.*10 kg. **Other data** *Moult* Commences Apr; ad ♂♂ and juvs first, followed by cows. **Taxonomy** Polytypic. Three geographic populations, in the White Sea, near Jan Mayen, and in W Atlantic, are treated as 2 races (differing in size, cranial features and pelage coloration): *P. g. oceanicus* of White Sea, and nominate elsewhere.

Cow Harp Seal nursing her pup; ♀ has variable but incomplete, more ill-defined and less intense dark hood.

DISTRIBUTION & POPULATION

NW Atlantic and Arctic Oceans, principally breeding in White Sea, off Jan Mayen, the Gulf of St Lawrence and S Labrador (Canada). Ranges extensively at sea, principally moving north (following the ice) in summer and south in winter, up to 1,600 km. Vagrants have reached NW Europe and Virginia (USA). *Population* At least 6 million, with 4.5 million in NW Atlantic, 1.5–2 million in White Sea and 300,000 off Jan Mayen.

Breeding Harp Seals give birth and nurse their pups on ice in early spring; the 2 nearest adults in profile illustrate the strong sexual dimorphism (bull at right), but not all are so well differentiated.

Harp Seal

Immature Harp Seals, extensively blotched, lack dark hood and 'harp' and are often greyer.

ECOLOGY

Breeds or moults in 1,000s and gregarious at sea. *Diving* Usually to 90 m, occasionally 250 m. *Diet* Principally fish, but also krill. *Reproduction* Both sexes loosely aggregate on pack-ice Feb–Mar, with cows giving birth mid-Feb to early Mar. Ads mate late Mar–early Apr, and pups weaned in 12 days. *Lifespan* Up to 30 yrs.

Often when travelling at sea, they accelerate vertically above the surface in a 'bottling posture'.

SIMILAR SPECIES

Distribution closely matches that of ***Largha Seal***, but ***Harbour***, ***Ringed*** and ***Bearded Seals*** also overlap to some extent. Ads, even ♀♀, wholly unmistakable if seen well. Presence of dark spots, blotches and rings in above-mentioned species readily eliminate them, and structure and pelage coloration of Bearded Seal conclusive. Problem of identifying juvs without visible bands unevaluated, as extent to which they might mix with juvs of other seals unknown.

VARIATION

Age/sex Clear sexual dimorphism in pelage coloration and young easily identifiable. Newborn has woolly, whitish lanugo, shed at *c*.5 weeks to grey pelage. **Physical notes** Full-grown ads reach max of *c*.1.9 m and 72–148 kg; newborn pup *c*.70–100 cm and 6–10 kg. **Other data** *Moult* Juvs Apr–May, ads May–Jul.

DISTRIBUTION & POPULATION

Confined to pack-ice in Bering Sea, S Chukchi Sea and Sea of Okhotsk (principal breeding areas in the first and last of these) in Jan–May, but may wander more widely in non-breeding season, being more pelagic and ranging south to Aleutians, Hokkaido (Japan) and C Pacific. Exceptionally recorded south to California (USA). Some move north in summer following ice edge. *Population* Total population estimated at 240,000 in late 1970s. Numbers in Bering Sea 120,000–140,000 in 1987 and fluctuate widely in Sea of Okhotsk, between

Ribbon Seal

Histriophoca fasciata

N Pacific. Max 1.9 m.

Priority characters on land (dry pelage)

- Medium-sized, slender and *strikingly banded seal*. Small head with round face, flat crown and indistinct forehead, somewhat cat-like in profile. Muzzle blunt, tapers slightly and ends in thicker nose with broad nostrils; large, close-set eyes.
- Bull: reddish black-brown with broad whitish bands encircling foreflippers and shoulders, the neck, and flanks/abdomen. *In head-on view black hood and chest and white collar distinctive*. Bands vary greatly (on some very wide and partially coalesce).
- Cow: *also banded, but basal pelage dull buff-brown* and bands creamier and contrast between them obscure, thus rendering boldness of bands less obvious, and paler, and mainly tan to pale brown.
- Juv: fairly plain, darker above and paler greyish on lower flanks and belly, *at most has only hint of bands of ad ♀*.
- Imm: *approaches ♀, but advanced young ♂ variable*, with browner back, crown and upper foreflippers, becoming silver grey on flanks and below, and mixed facial pattern, mainly pale but with dark muzzle to chin.
- Short or moderate and fairly prominent whitish whiskers.
- Foreflippers short, pointed and have *different digit lengths (outer longer)* with long, narrow, hooked claws; hindflippers long and broad when fanned.

Typical behaviour

- Solitary. Approachable by boat, but escapes rapidly on ice despite 'humping' gait.
- Frequents southern edge of pack-ice in winter to early summer; bulls mostly unseen during nursing period. Pelagic in Bering Sea during summer.

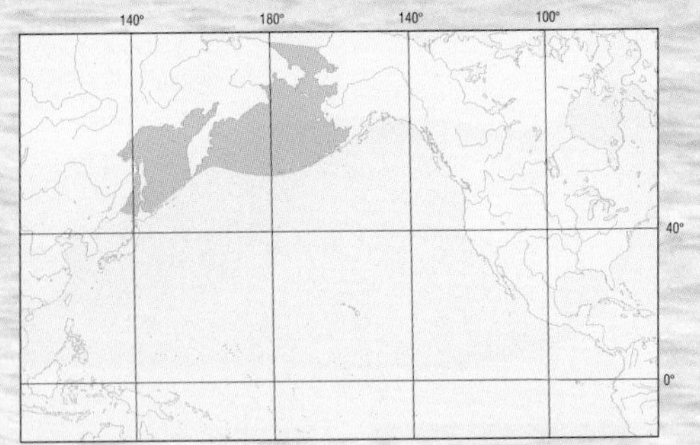

Adult ♂ Ribbon Seal is one of the most attractive marine mammals, and unlikely to be confused with any other species; note banding varies individually to a large extent.

Ribbon Seal

200,000 (1968–74) and 630,000 (1988–90).

ECOLOGY

Scattered groups or pairs on ice (moulting concentrations much denser). *Diving* Can reach 600 m. *Diet* Principally fish and cephalopods. *Reproduction* Monogamous. Gives birth on sea-ice in Mar–May (some seasonal variation). Ads mate May, with pups weaned at 3–4 weeks. *Lifespan* Up to 30 yrs.

Adult ♀ Ribbon Seal mirrors the ♂ pattern, but is far less contrasting.

Bearded Seal

Erignathus barbatus

Arctic/subarctic. Max 2.5 m.

Priority characters on land (dry pelage)

- *Large heavy-bodied seal with comparatively small head* and short foreflippers. Small close-set eyes; *elongated muzzle, broad and fleshy, with wide-spaced nostrils*.
- *Conspicuously long and pale whiskers (often as dense patch) with at least some curling inwards at tips* (when wet they tend to be straighter).
- Ads generally darker on back than below and vary from *pale or dark grey to brown or tawny-brown*, and often faintly mottled (variably blotched), especially in young. Face and flippers sometimes discoloured rusty.
- Facial pattern often distinctive, *paler cheeks, muzzle-sides, area above eye, around ears and nape*.

Bearded Seal in typical low surfacing profile.

SIMILAR SPECIES

Long thick body, proportionately small head with unique facial structure, very long whiskers and squared-off flippers make ad easily separable from smaller ***Harbour***, ***Largha*** and ***Ringed Seals***, which are clearly more compact, spotted, blotched or ringed, whilst ***Ribbon*** is smaller and altogether distinctive in pattern and shape. ***Grey Seal***, in distant view, especially imms prior to moult can appear equally uniform and may be similarly elongated and heavy, with same facial expression, but closer inspection will reveal its shorter whiskers, pointed flippers and different muzzle/nostril structure and facial markings, as well as 2 (instead of 4) nipples. On ice, might be mistaken for young ***Hooded Seal*** and, in water, confusion with young ***Harp Seal*** possible.

- *Foreflippers short, broad and square-shaped,* unique in that digits are of even length, with relatively broad, strong claws; hindflippers proportionately short.

Typical behaviour

- Usually on pack-ice in shallow seas. Solitary, rarely several together.
- Hauls-out on ice and maintains breathing holes with its powerful claws. Pups born on open ice.
- Shy and wary, and tends to swim with head close to surface, so that, if disturbed, it can easily escape. However, often performs vertical 'bottling posture'.

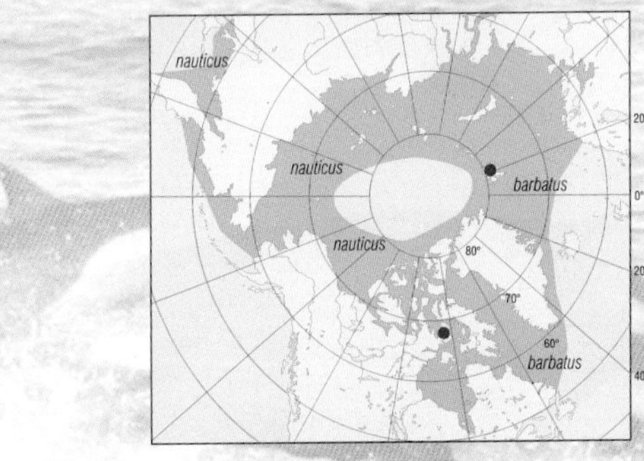

Bearded Seal has a proportionately long thick body but small flippers, and a unique pale patch of long whiskers (usually at least some of which have curled tips); some animals are tinged noticeably rusty on head.

DISTRIBUTION & POPULATION

Circumpolar but patchy in N Hemisphere, in arctic and subarctic waters of N Canada, Greenland, Barents Sea, across Russian Arctic to Bering Sea and Sea of Okhotsk. Prefers drifting pack-ice. Range poorly known outside the breeding and moulting seasons, but has wandered to W Europe, Newfoundland and Japan. *Population* Estimated at over 500,000, of which more than 50% in Bering Sea.

ECOLOGY

Solitary, except if breeding

VARIATION

Age/sex Minor age-related variation and indistinct sexual dimorphism; ♀ larger. Newborn has long, dark, wavy juv coat (white lanugo shed prior to birth), with up to 4 paler, transverse bands from back to crown, and black cape usually continues between eyes and over top of muzzle, with dark eye-patches affording spectacled effect. **Physical notes** Full-grown ads up to 2.5 m and 425 kg, but most 2.1–2.4 m and 200–250 kg. Newborn *c.*1.3 m and *c.*35 kg. **Other data** *Moult* Juvs Apr–Aug. **Taxonomy** Polytypic: nominate *barbatus* in N Atlantic and NE Canada, and *E. b. nauticus* in rest of range.

Bearded Seal: some essentially dark and uniform, but still have distinctive pale facial markings.

Bearded Seal

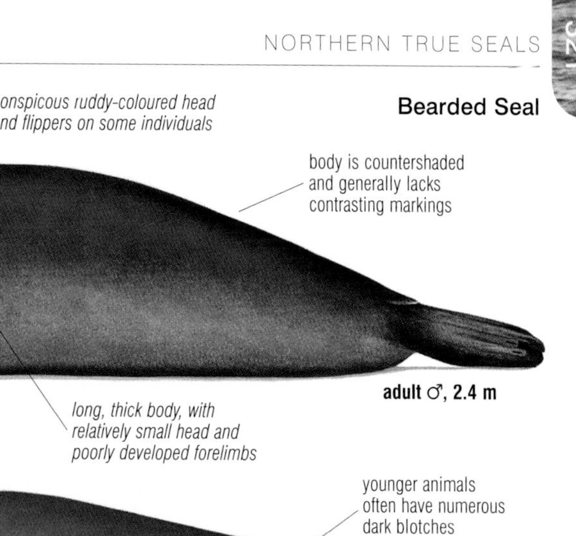

Characteristics of Bearded Seal's pup and juvenile poorly documented: note here pup's black cape to top of muzzle, and dark eye-patches.

or moulting. *Diving* Max 288 m and 19 min, but usually above 100 m and <10 min. *Diet* Cod, flatfish, crabs, shrimp, molluscs, octopus, even marine algae. *Reproduction* Sexually mature at 5–7 yrs. Cow gives birth on pack-ice late Mar–early May. Ads mate after pups weaned at 15–24 days. *Lifespan* Up to 31 yrs.

Immature Bearded Seal: young especially often faintly mottled and blotched, with stronger facial markings.

Ringed Seal

Pusa hispida

Circumpolar Arctic.
Max 1.65 m.

Priority characters on land (dry pelage)

- *Small, stocky compact seal*; girth measures up to 80% of the animal's length.
- Proportionately *short neck and small rounded head* with compressed muzzle and large forward-facing eyes. *Somewhat cat-like facial expression.*
- *Diagnostic pale ring-like marks on medium to dark grey back and sides.*
- Underparts paler cream-grey and almost unspotted.
- Sexes alike. Rings develop with age and may partially coalesce on older ads, which overall appear exceedingly pale.

A Ringed Seal in its breathing hole: note paler, almost unspotted underbody, neckless, small rounded head with short muzzle and large forward-facing eyes.

SIMILAR SPECIES

Most likely to be confused with ***Harbour*** and ***Largha Seals***, but these are less plump and thickset than Ringed Seal which, despite variation, is usually profusely covered with distinct rings above and on sides, and lacks or has very few spots below. Harbour and especially Largha Seals are more evenly spotted. Five other phocids overlap with Ringed Seal, but confusion is unlikely: ***Bearded***, ***Harp***, ***Ribbon Hooded*** and ***Grey Seals***. Care may be required, however, with distant juvs of Ringed, Harp and Grey Seals.

VARIATION

Age/sex Indistinct sexual dimorphism, but young differ. Newborn has woolly whitish lanugo shed after 2–3 weeks; by 6–8 weeks

- Juv almost unmarked, dark grey on back and silver below, with scattered dark spots and only limited, if any, rings, which mainly develop after first annual moult (when 1 yr).
- Foreflippers small with pointed tips that are strongly 'fingered'; hindflippers proportionately short and dumpy.
- Pale-coloured short whiskers.

Typical behaviour

- *Births and lactation occur in special hollows, or lairs, on fast-ice. Most frequent are oblong, or multi-chambered lairs; searching for them often helps locate the species.*
- Often performs vertical 'bottling posture'. Rather wary and elusive toward Polar Bears and humans. Encountered either singly or in small groups.

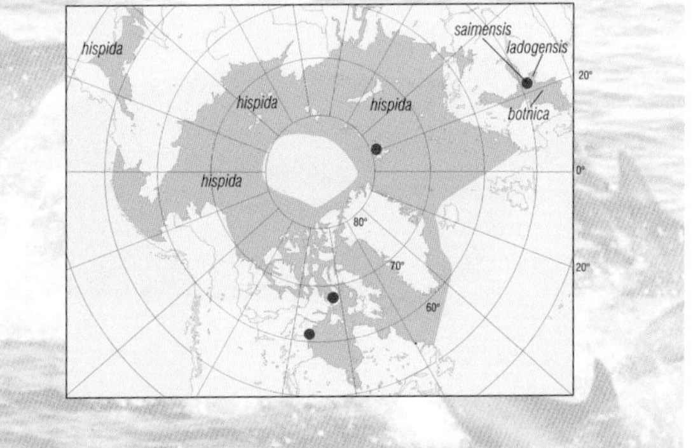

Ringed Seal

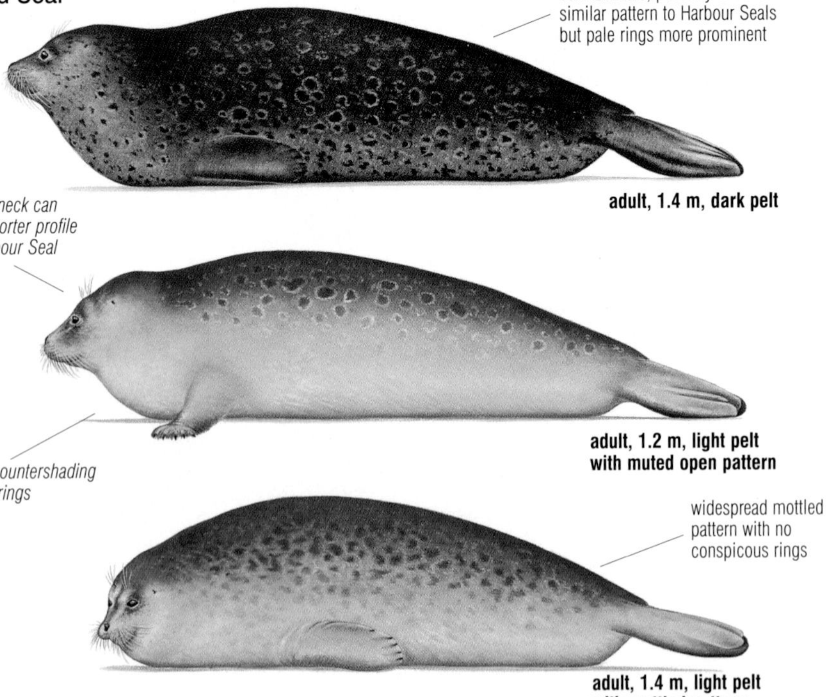

dark animals, possibly ♂ have similar pattern to Harbour Seals but pale rings more prominent

adult, 1.4 m, dark pelt

face and neck can exhibit shorter profile than Harbour Seal

obvious countershading and pale rings

adult, 1.2 m, light pelt with muted open pattern

widespread mottled pattern with no conspicous rings

adult, 1.4 m, light pelt with mottled pattern

Ringed Seals have a slow surfacing motion and keep low in the water: note the very broad body with pale ring-like marks.

fully moulted to coat with finer and slightly longer fur than ads, almost unmarked dark grey above, grading to silver below. **Physical notes** Full-grown ad up to *c.*1.65 m (mostly 1.1–1.5 m; ♂ averages slightly larger) and 110 kg (mostly 50–70 kg); newborn 60–65 cm and 4–5 kg. **Other data** *Moult* Jun–Jul, on ice or land (*saimensis*). **Taxonomy** Five races (differ mainly in size and cranial measurements): nominate *hispida* (Arctic basin), *P. h. ochotensis* (Seas of Okhotsk and Japan), *P. h. botnica* (Baltic), *P. h. saimensis* (Lake Saimaa, E Finland) and *P. h. ladogensis* (Lake Ladoga, NW Russia).

DISTRIBUTION & POPULATION

Throughout Arctic Ocean, south into Hudson Bay (Canada), the Baltic and Bering Seas, and freshwater populations in Finland and NW Russia. In spring, moves north in response to receding ice cover. Vagrant south to California (USA), Portugal and Japan. *Population* A minimum 2.5 million, and perhaps 4 million, but Lakes Saimaa (2,000–5,000 in 1950s) and Ladoga populations (5,000–10,000 in 1950s) rather small.

ECOLOGY

Solitary, but family triads in breeding season. *Diving* Mostly to 45 m, max 145 m (usually <8 min, max 23 min). *Diet* Principally cod in summer, but other small fish, amphipods and euphausiids too. *Reproduction* Sexually mature *c.*5 years. Young born in lairs on pack-ice (or snow-drifts at Lake Saimaa), mid Mar–Apr. Ads mate after pups weaned, Apr–May (peak mid Apr). *Lifespan* Up to 45 yrs.

Largha Seal

(Spotted Seal)

Phoca largha

Extreme N Pacific. Max. 1.7 m.

Priority characters on land (dry pelage)

- Rather small but chunky, with structure *like familiar Harbour Seal*.
- Smaller headed, but blunt muzzle appears narrow with slightly forward-pointing nostrils.
- Sexes alike and no clear-cut age differences in pelage. Pelage as light-phase Harbour Seal. Characters below differ from latter.
- Generally *pale, silver grey, rather evenly marked with irregular dark spots and blotches. Lacks pale rings.*
- Conspicuous *dark head and back*: markings usually denser on back

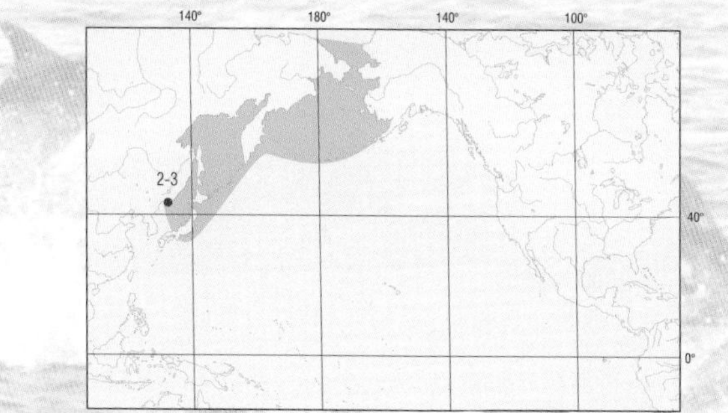

SIMILAR SPECIES

Harbour Seal very similar and often difficult or impossible to distinguish from present species. However, Largha is decidedly smaller and more compact, rather more evenly spotted and blotched, may have contrastingly darker face and back, and lacks rings of mainly dark-phase Harbour Seal. Additionally, Largha does not possess a dark phase, and is more restricted to icy seas, unlike Harbour. Two other phocids overlap with Largha, the Ringed and Ribbon Seals, but both are wholly distinctive.

VARIATION

Age/sex Indistinct sexual dimorphism; young apparently are less dark on face and back. Newborn has woolly, whitish lanugo, shed after 2–4 weeks (unlike Harbour Seal); moulted juv coat similar to ad but more evenly spotted/bleached, without or less apparent dark face and back. **Physical** and tend to merge, density and contrast vary and seem to be enhanced with age.

- Face and muzzle often darker too.

Typical behaviour

- *Pack-ice inhabitant, unlike Harbour Seal*, but may haul-out on beaches and sandbars. Often found along fractures in larger floes. Moves slowly on ice.
- Usually solitary or in small groups. Rather wary and elusive.

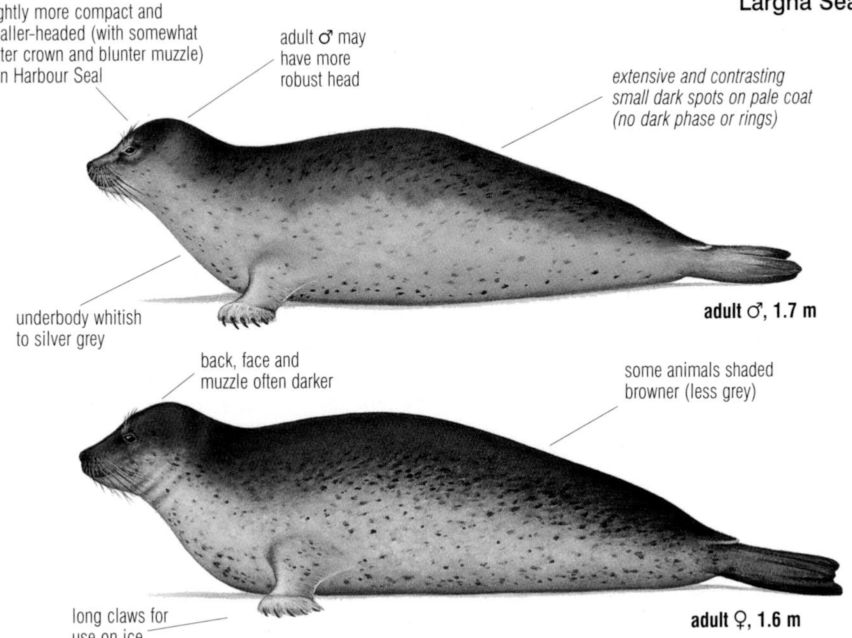

notes Full-grown ♂ reaches 1.7 m and ♀ 1.6 m; both sexes 82–123 kg. Newborn 77–92 cm and 7–12 kg. **Other data** *Moult* Late spring (mostly May–Jun), post-natal. **Taxonomy** Monotypic, but some morphological differences between eastern and western populations. Until recently considered a subspecies of Harbour Seal, but morphological, biochemical and behavioural differences support specific status.

DISTRIBUTION & POPULATION

N Pacific, from Japan and Sea of Okhotsk and Alaska north into Bering and W Beaufort Seas. Reaches south to N Yellow Sea in non-breeding season. Breeds on pack-ice and follows ice edge during course of year. *Population* Estimated at 350,000–400,000, with *c.*50% in Bering and Chukchi Seas.

Cow Largha Seal (and pup), showing classic dense, contrasting spotting on pale silver grey coat of adults.

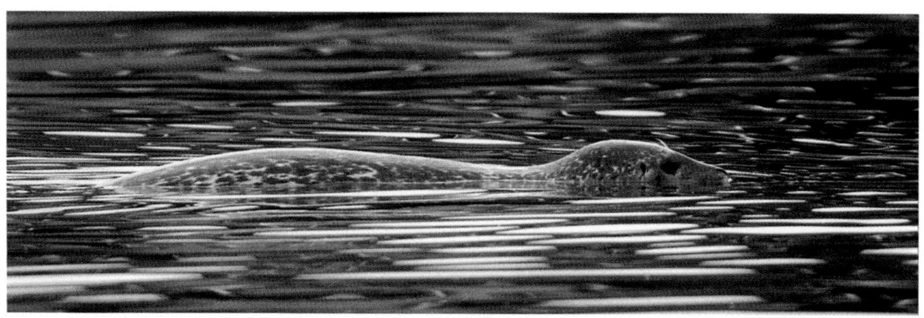

Adult Largha is more evenly spotted, with darker face and back, and lacks rings of dark-phase Harbour Seals.

ECOLOGY

Solitary, but forms well-spaced family triads in breeding season and small herds in summer, sometimes larger concentrations in favoured areas in early autumn. *Diving* To 300 m. *Diet* Schooling fish, crabs and octopus. *Reproduction* Sexually mature at 3–5 yrs. Seasonally monogamous. Cows give birth on pack-ice Jan–Apr (peak latter half of Mar). Ads mate after pups weaned at 2–4 weeks. *Lifespan* Up to 35 yrs.

A young Largha Seal (at right) within a group of Harbour Seals (race stejnegeri, W Pacific): note the former's dark-spotted but otherwise very pale coat, flatter crown, blunter muzzle and darker face.

Harbour Seal

(Common Seal)

Phoca vitulina

N Hemisphere. Max. 2 m.

Priority characters on land (dry pelage)

- *Small- to medium-sized and typically spotted seal.* Chunky, *rather plump* and short-necked with rounded head and wide/blunt muzzle with slightly upturned nose. *Elderly dog-like facial expression.*
- Sexes alike and indistinct age differences. 2 colour phases.
- **Pale phase** *Pale, creamy or buff-white to pale or medium silver grey, liberally spotted and blotched dark.* Some more spotted than others.
- **Dark phase** *Very dark, metallic black and faintly, but conspicuously, marked with irregular pale spots, blotches and broken rings.* Some streakier than others.
- Some intermediates paler below with fewer scattered markings, but many uniform. May have rusty discoloration, primarily on head and upperbody.
- Foreflippers small with pointed tips and long, hooked claws; hindflippers proportionately small and somewhat square-ended.
- Pale-coloured short whiskers. *Nostrils small and form V (almost converge) when seen head-on.* Large eyes, equidistant between ears and nose. Ears prominent.

Harbour Seal in typical surfacing profile.

SIMILAR SPECIES

Might be confused with several similar-sized phocids, e.g. ***Largha*** and spotty/young ***Grey Seals***, but separated by colour pattern, head shape/muzzle and position of the nostrils (qv for details).

VARIATION

Age/sex Indistinct differences. Newborn has flecked and finely spotted silver grey lanugo which they usually shed *in utero*, but may be retained for *c*.2 weeks after birth. Subsequent juv very much like ad, but smaller. **Physical notes** Full-grown ad 1.2–2 m and 65–170 kg (♂ slightly larger; max ♀ 1.7 m and 130 kg); newborn 65–100 cm and 8–12 kg. **Other data** *Moult* Jun–Oct (varies across range). **Taxonomy** At least 5 races: nominate *vitulina* (E Atlantic from Portugal to Arctic), *P. v. concolor* (W Atlantic, USA to Canadian Arctic, Iceland and Greenland), *P. v. richardii* (E Pacific from Baja California, Mexico, to E Aleutians, includes *P. v. geronimensis*), *P. v. stejnegeri* (W Pacific, Japan to Kamchatka Peninsula east to W Aleutians) and *P. v. mellonae* (freshwater lakes in NE Canada). At least *P. v. stejnegeri* is distinctly larger and darker than *P. v. richardii*. However, generally northern animals, especially in Pacific, are larger/heavier; light phase and intermediates predominate in north of range, whilst dark phase more frequent in central and southern areas, but discrete populations/variants occur.

Typical behaviour

- Usually small groups but up to 100s on rocky beaches and sandbars, especially at low tide.
- Ashore wary and shy. Characteristic *resting posture 'banana-like'* (with head and tail raised) observed on land and in water.
- Shares haul-out sites with other true seals, e.g. Grey Seal, and also California Sea Lion.
- In water, only head visible above surface.

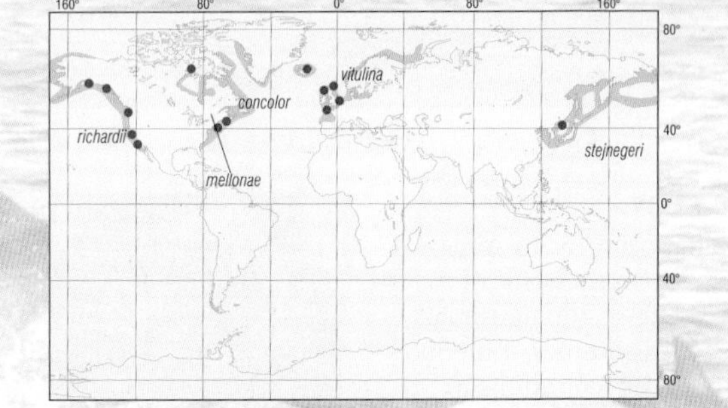

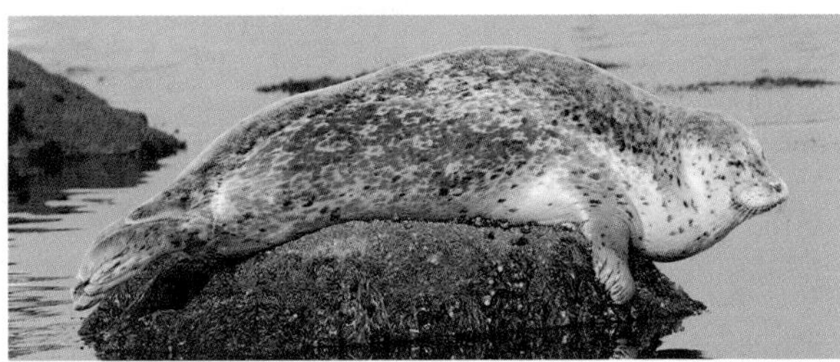

Pale-phase Harbour Seal (race richardii*, E Pacific) is liberally spotted and blotched dark.*

Race vitulina (E Atlantic): some Harbour Seals are streakier than others.

DISTRIBUTION & POPULATION

Widespread on coasts of N America south to Baja California and New Jersey, S Greenland, Iceland, NW Europe (south to Portugal), Svalbard and, in N Pacific, from Kamchatka south to Japan and east to Alaska. Vagrant to Guadalupe

Dark-phase Harbour Seal (race richardii*, E Pacific) is metallic black, variably spotted and blotched, and has some broken rings.*

Dark- and pale-phase Harbour Seals (race richardii*, E Pacific): note degree of individual variation.*

Harbour Seal

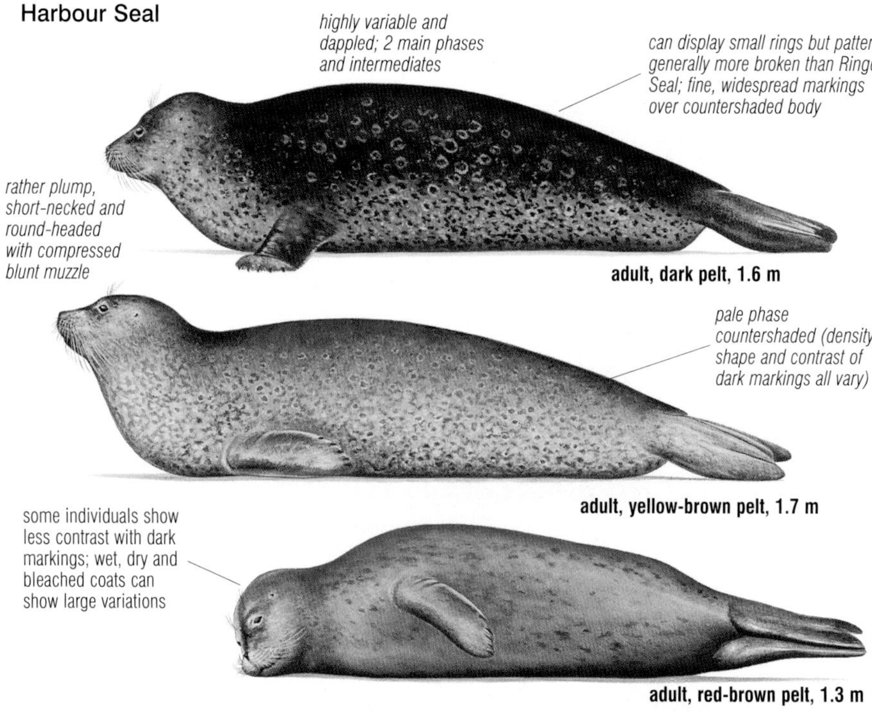

highly variable and dappled; 2 main phases and intermediates

can display small rings but pattern generally more broken than Ringed Seal; fine, widespread markings over countershaded body

rather plump, short-necked and round-headed with compressed blunt muzzle

adult, dark pelt, 1.6 m

pale phase countershaded (density, shape and contrast of dark markings all vary)

adult, yellow-brown pelt, 1.7 m

some individuals show less contrast with dark markings; wet, dry and bleached coats can show large variations

adult, red-brown pelt, 1.3 m

Is (Mexico) and Florida (USA). Has reached 79°N (Ellesmere Is, Canadian Arctic). Principally marine but occasionally enters freshwater rivers and lakes connected to sea. Largely resident or performs short-distance movements in response to prey availability, but some longer-range migrations noted. *Population* Perhaps 500,000, but some subpopulations (e.g. in Baltic) now rather rare.

ECOLOGY

Gregarious during moulting period, but generally solitary at sea. *Diving* Recorded to 450 m, but generally 10–150 m (max 31 min, mostly <10 min). *Diet* Pelagic fish, octopus and squid. *Reproduction* Cows give birth on rocky and sandy beaches, and ice, in spring and summer (Jan–Oct across range, generally earlier further south). Ads mate after pups weaned at 2–6 weeks. *Lifespan* Up to 35 yrs.

The larger race stejnegeri *(W Pacific): Harbour Seals often adopt a 'banana-like' posture.*

Mid-latitude true seals

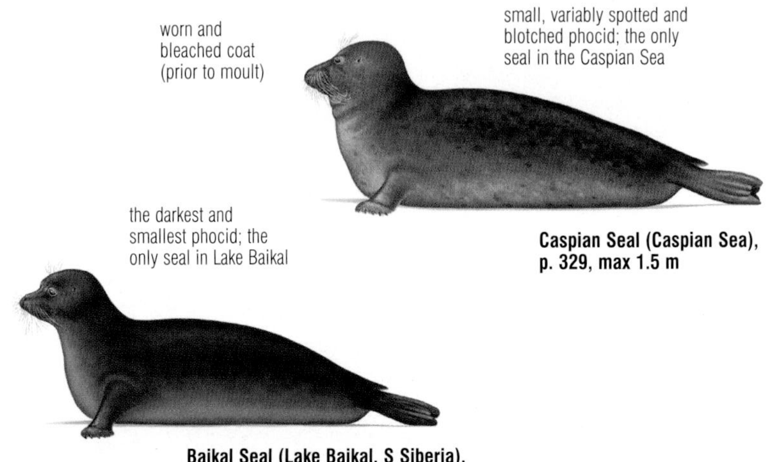

Caspian Seal (Caspian Sea), p. 329, max 1.5 m

Baikal Seal (Lake Baikal, S Siberia), p. 331, max 1.4 m

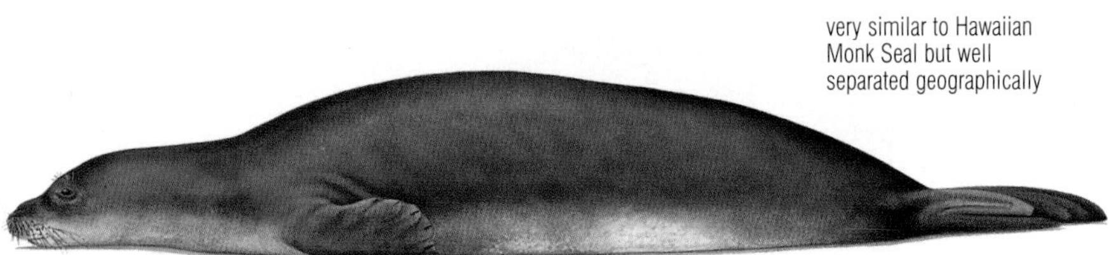

Mediterranean Monk Seal (Mediterranean & NW Africa), p. 332, max 2.8 m

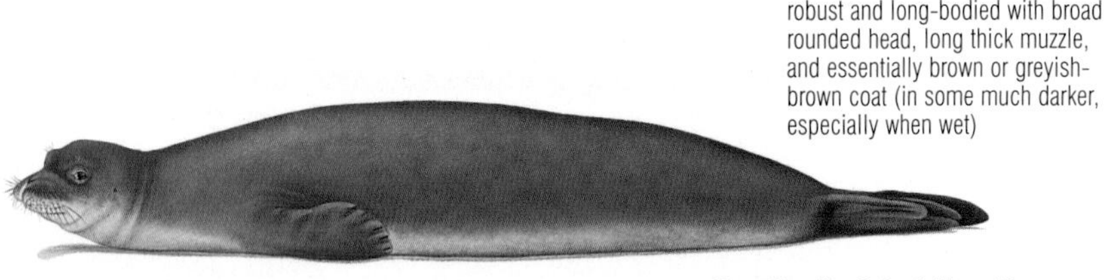

Hawaiian Monk Seal (Hawaii), p. 334, max 2.4 m

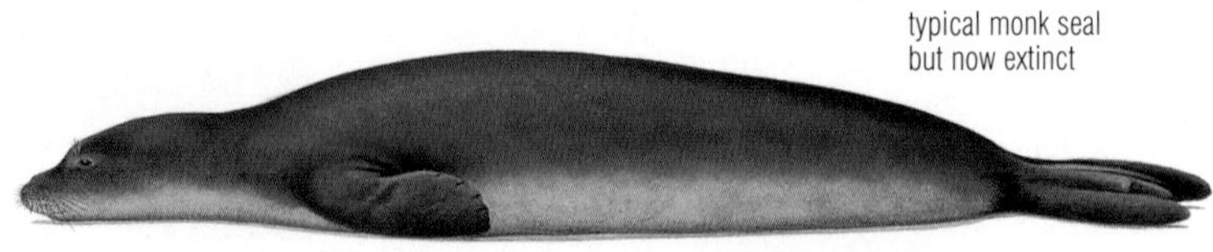

West Indian Monk Seal (Caribbean Sea), p. 336, max 2.4 m

Mid-latitude true seals

These include some of the rarest and most isolated marine mammals, with single species inhabiting the Caspian Sea (Caspian Seal) and Lake Baikal (Baikal Seal). One is already extinct (West Indian or Caribbean Monk Seal) and two others are highly endangered (Mediterranean and Hawaiian Monk Seals). Although most phocids occur in temperate or cold seas, monk seals inhabit tropical and subtropical waters. Caspian and Baikal Seals are most closely related to the northern true seals (and part of the subfamily Phocinae), especially the Ringed Seal of arctic regions. On the other hand, monk seals are usually considered to be closer to 'southern' seals (subfamily Monachinae), but only occur in the Northern Hemisphere.

Caspian Seal

Pusa caspica

Caspian Sea. Max 1.5 m.

Priority characters on land (dry pelage)

- *Small, lightly blotched phocid. The only seal in the Caspian Sea.*
- Limited sexual dimorphism and age differentiation.
- Chunky, thick-bodied, with somewhat longer neck, large rounded head and long, blunt muzzle tapering to forward-pointing nostrils.
- Greyish-yellow to dark grey above, grading to paler below.
- Irregularly spotted/blotched brown to black, especially above, often heavier in ♂, which is usually also marked laterally and ventrally.
- Foreflippers short but broad, round with 'fingered' tips and moderately hooked claws; hindflippers proportionately small and somewhat square-ended.
- Pale-coloured, moderately long whiskers. Relatively large eyes set forward.

Typical behaviour

- *Confined to saline waters of the Caspian Sea and its main rivers.* Hauls-out on quiet, undisturbed open beaches. Ashore wary and shy. Pups on open ice in winter.
- Usually in small groups but larger gatherings, especially when moulting.
- *In the water, only the head and part of back show above the surface.*

Caspian Seal in typical surfacing profile; probably ♂ given extensive spotting.

SIMILAR SPECIES

No other pinniped occurs in the Caspian Sea.

VARIATION

Age/sex Indistinct sexual dimorphism. Newborn has woolly, whitish lanugo, replaced at *c.*3 weeks by short dark juv pelage, similar to ad, but back perhaps more sparsely spotted. **Physical notes** Ad ♂ reaches 1.5 m and ♀ 1.4 m; both sexes weigh *c.*86 kg. Newborn 64–79 cm and *c.*5 kg. **Other data** *Moult* At end of breeding season (spring). **Taxonomy** Thought to be an early offshoot from, or relict population of, Ringed Seal.

Caspian Seal

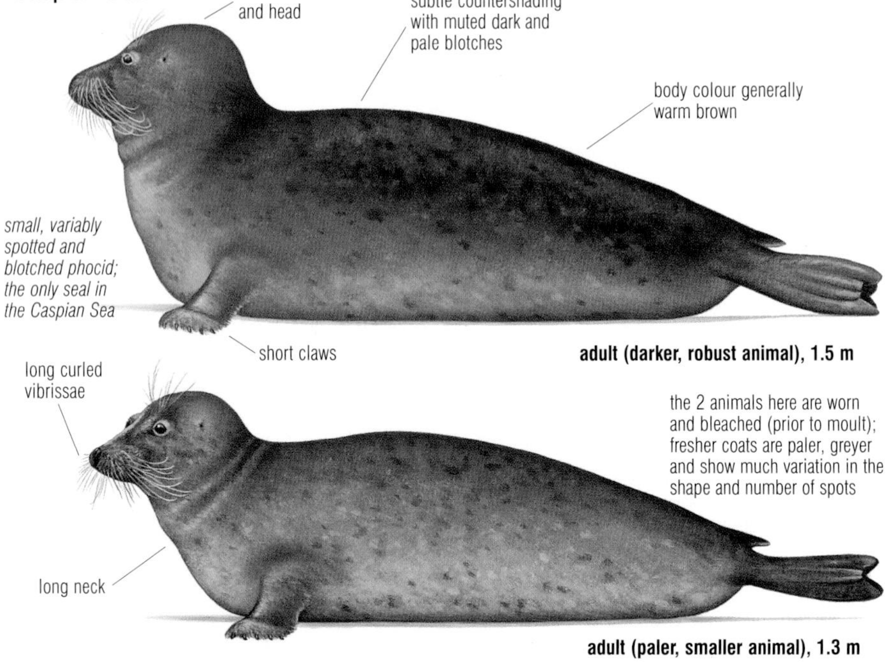

rounded muzzle and head

subtle countershading with muted dark and pale blotches

body colour generally warm brown

small, variably spotted and blotched phocid; the only seal in the Caspian Sea

short claws

adult (darker, robust animal), 1.5 m

long curled vibrissae

the 2 animals here are worn and bleached (prior to moult); fresher coats are paler, greyer and show much variation in the shape and number of spots

long neck

adult (paler, smaller animal), 1.3 m

DISTRIBUTION & POPULATION

Confined to the Caspian, where principally breeds in north, but also on islands off Turkmenistan coast. Although some migrate south and others remain in the north during the ice-free period, the whereabouts of the vast majority of seals at this season is unknown. *Population* Considered stable at *c*.400,000 in early 1990s, but several large mortalities have since occurred.

ECOLOGY

Large groups gather to moult, but generally asocial. *Diving* Can reach 200 m (3+ min). *Diet* Fish and crustaceans. *Reproduction* Sexually mature at 4–6 yrs. Polygynous. Cows give birth on sea-ice mid Jan–late Feb (mostly in northern Caspian). Ads mate after pups weaned at 4–5 weeks. *Lifespan* Up to 43.5 yrs.

Hauled-out Caspian Seals showing much age/sex and individual variation: among the adults, the heavier spotted animal is probably a ♂, whilst the smaller, sparsely spotted and dark-backed individuals are juveniles.

Baikal Seal

Pusa sibirica

Lake Baikal. Max 1.4 m.

Priority characters on land (dry pelage)

- *Small, dark phocid, endemic to, and the only seal in, Lake Baikal.*
- Dumpy, with long neck, small rounded head, high steep forehead and long, blunt-tipped muzzle.
- No clear sexual dimorphism and indistinct age differentiation.
- Essentially dusky grey-brown (almost black when wet), except variable paler throat and abdomen; some are overall paler/greyer.
- Essentially unspotted but some appear slightly marbled and less uniform.
- Foreflippers short, but broad and round, with well-fingered tips and well-developed hooked claws; hindflippers proportionately small.
- Whiskers rather long and pale. Relatively large eyes set forward.

Typical behaviour

- *In winter maintains breathing holes in ice and uses snow-covered lairs (where pups born) on lake ice.* Ashore shy, hauling-out on only undisturbed open beaches.
- Solitary or small groups but larger gatherings especially when moulting.
- *In the water, only head and part of back visible above surface.*

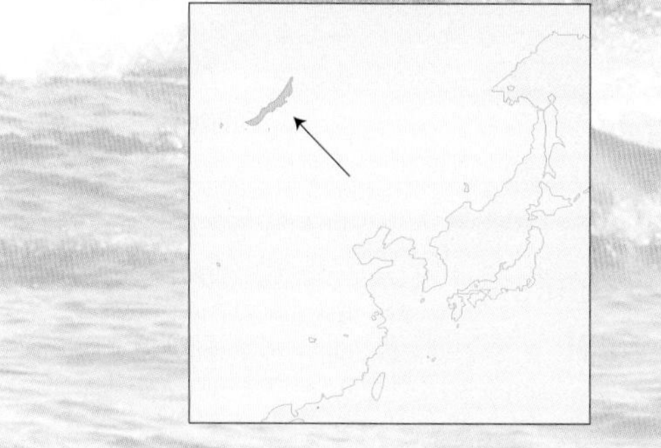

Baikal Seal, a small, dark phocid, endemic to Lake Baikal, showing its broad foreflippers with well-fingered tips and well-developed hooked claws.

SIMILAR SPECIES

No other pinniped occurs in Lake Baikal.

VARIATION

Age/sex Indistinct sexual and age-related variations. Newborn has woolly, whitish lanugo, replaced at 4–6 weeks by short dark juv pelage, similar to ad. **Physical notes** Ads reach up 1.4 m and 80–90 kg (♂ larger); newborn 64–66 cm and 4–4.2 kg. **Other data** *Moult* At end of breeding season (spring). **Taxonomy** MtDNA evidence suggests close relationship to Ringed Seal.

DISTRIBUTION & POPULATION

Lake Baikal, SW Siberia, with most in north and some movement south in autumn and winter. Occasionally penetrates some of the lake's feeder rivers, including the lower Angara R. *Population* Perhaps 100,000 in 1994, but apparently declining with only *c.*85,000 in 2000.

ECOLOGY

Solitary, but small groups gather to moult. *Diving* Max depth 300 m (occasionally up to 40+ min) but usually to 50 m and for 2–6 min. *Diet* Wide variety of fish. *Reproduction* Sexually mature at 6–7 yrs. Cows give birth on ice (in lairs or pressure ridges), mid-Feb–Mar (peak mid Mar), with pups emerging in Apr and weaned at 2–3 months, sometimes earlier in south. *Lifespan* Up to 56 yrs.

Baikal Seal: this isolated species is seriously declining due to high levels of pollution, poaching, commercial harvesting and fishery bycatch.

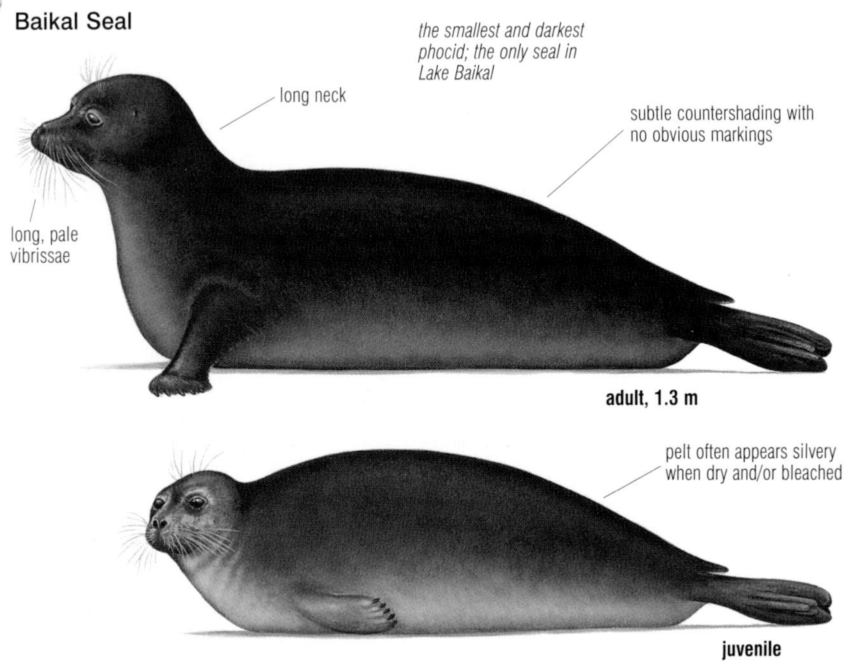

Hauled-out Mediterranean Monk Seal: note paler/whiter underbody and characteristic head shape with thick whisker pads and long, smooth (not coarse) whiskers.

SIMILAR SPECIES

No other pinniped overlaps with this species. Northern species, namely ***Harbour***, ***Grey*** and ***Hooded Seals***, could reach south to areas where monk seals have wandered, but are readily distinguished by their conspicuous spots/blotches, head/muzzle shape, coarse whiskers and only 2 mammary teats.

Mediterranean Monk Seal

Monachus monachus

Mediterranean and NW Africa. Max 2.8 m.

Priority characters on land (dry pelage)

- *Large, robust phocid with highly restricted range in Mediterranean and NW Africa*. Now very rare.
- Elongated, with *long neck, broad round head* (flattish crown) and long, thick round-lipped muzzle.
- *Essentially brown above and paler below*, either sharply or poorly demarcated. Short coat. No clear sexual dimorphism; indistinct age differentiation.
- *Some are predominantly darker grey (almost black when wet, probably ♂♂)*. Other extreme (mostly ♀♀, which are also extensively paler below) is very dull silvery grey-brown.
- In strongly marked animals, white belly patch enhanced and some may develop variable faint white or darker blotching, although still essentially uniform.
- *Foreflippers very short* with correspondingly small claws; hindflippers long and slim.
- *Whiskers pale, rather long and smooth* (not coarse). *Relatively large eyes* positioned slightly to the side and widely spaced. *Whisker pads rather thick and fleshy*, and *slightly extended nostrils that open upwards* (not forwards, as on most phocids).

Typical behaviour

- Usually solitary or 2–3, ashore and in water. Rather wary and shy, *tends to haul-out on inaccessible rocky beaches* or very secluded sites with sea caves, but in W Africa on open beaches.
- When swimming, only head and part of back show above surface.

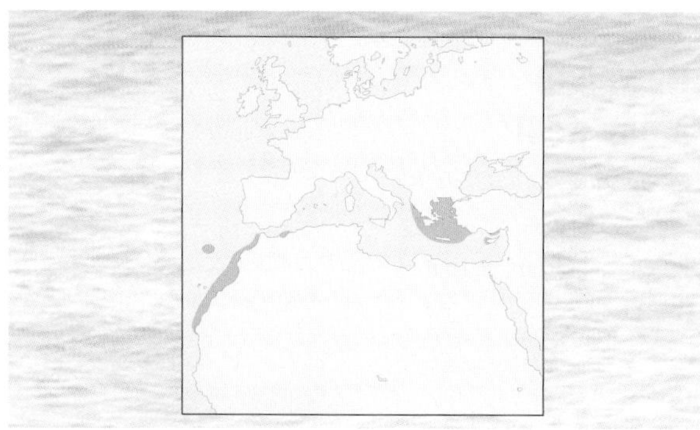

Head-on posture; note large eyes.

VARIATION

Age/sex No obvious sexual variation and few age differences. Newborn has woolly blackish coat, often irregularly spotted or blotched white and tinged yellowish-white below, replaced at 4–7 weeks by a short juv coat of silver grey, paler below, which is similar to ad but has fewer scars. ♂♂ may become very dark at age 4. **Physical notes** Ads reach 2.8 m and 240–320 kg. Newborn 80–120 cm and 15–26 kg. **Other data** *Teats* All monk seals have 4 (instead of 2) retractable nipples. *Moult* Post-natal. Has rapid epidermal moult of hair and skin, which detaches patchily (as in elephant seals).

DISTRIBUTION & POPULATION

Restricted to Mediterranean and coastal NW Africa, with largest colony at Cabo Blanco (S Morocco), ranging from Turkey and the former Yugoslavia west to Madeira. Core range now Aegean and Ionian Seas (Greece/Turkey). Vagrants recorded south to Senegambia and north to Atlantic coast of France. *Population* Perhaps just 450 in mid-1990s and in serious decline, with local extinctions in the Azores, Black Sea and Italy (still occurs as a vagrant).

ECOLOGY

Cow and pup have only important bond, though loose groups gather to moult. *Diving* Up to *c.*70 m. *Diet* Fish, octopus and squid. *Reproduction* Sexually mature at 2–3 yrs. Cows give birth all yr, peak Oct–Nov, in isolated sea caves. *Lifespan* To 44 yrs.

Mediterranean Monk Seals often stay underwater for 5+ minutes.

Mediterranean Monk Seal

a true seal of highly restricted range; generally robust and long-bodied, with broad round head, large eyes, and essentially darker above and paler below

much like Hawaiian Monk Seal

diffuse pale or more distinct pale patches on belly, variable in size and shape

adult ♂, 2.4 m

adult ♀, 2.2 m

♀ has much paler underbody

those illustrated have dry pelage (much darker when wet)

SIMILAR SPECIES

No other pinnipeds regularly visit the range of Hawaiian Monk Seal. Northern Elephant Seal has occurred on Midway, but is much larger and has completely different head and face/muzzle shapes, and only 2 teats.

Monk seals have a striking epidermal moult of hair and skin, which detaches patchily.

VARIATION

Age/sex No well-defined sexual variation and few age differences. Newborn has woolly blackish coat, replaced at *c.*6 weeks by short juv coat, mainly greyish-brown with paler cream underparts, rather similar to ♀. **Physical notes** Ads reach 2.4 m and *c.*270 kg (♀ slightly larger and often heavier than ♂). Newborn *c.*1 m and 16–18 kg. **Other data** *Teats* All monk seals have 4 (instead of 2) retractable nipples. *Moult* May–Sep; cows only after weaning competed. Like elephant seals has striking epidermal moult of hair and skin, which detaches patchily.

Hawaiian Monk Seal

Monachus schauinslandi

Hawaiian Islands. Max 2.4 m.

Priority characters on land (dry pelage)

- Large, robust phocid, *endemic to the main and Northwest Hawaiian Islands*.
- *Long body with characteristic long neck, broad rounded head* (proportionately small flat crown) and a long, thick round-lipped muzzle.
- *Brown above and paler below*, with some sexual dimorphism but only indistinct age differentiation. Pelage very short.
- Fresh ♂♂ and presumably older ♀♀ dusky-brown, but when wet all generally very dark or blackish, and sometimes with contrasting whitish mouthline on both lips.
- Fresh ♀♀ and young rather uniform silvery to slate grey dorsally, becoming cream or pale silver grey below. With age, darker and browner above and hence more like ♂♂.
- All *bleach to dull or tan brown*. Moult patchy. Some possess irregular pale blotching and older animals, chiefly ♂♂, variable deep body scars. May be discoloured reddish or greenish by algal growth.
- *Foreflippers proportionately very short and broad* with small claws; hindflippers long and slim.
- *Whiskers dark with pale tips, short to moderately long and smooth (not coarse). Relatively large eyes* positioned on sides of head and widely spaced.
- *Whisker pads rather large and fleshy; nostrils extend slightly forward with somewhat upward opening (not forward as on most phocids).*

Typical behaviour

- Polygynous, not gregarious, sometimes in small dispersed groups, but *usually solitary or ♀♀ with pups*. Up to 3x more mature ♂♂ than ♀♀ occur in some rookeries.
- Hauls-out on sandy or rocky/coral beaches. Ashore often reacts to presence of intruder, another seal or human, by rolling back to expose underside, and flipper may be waved up or mouth opened.
- *In water, only head and sometimes part of back, visible above surface.*

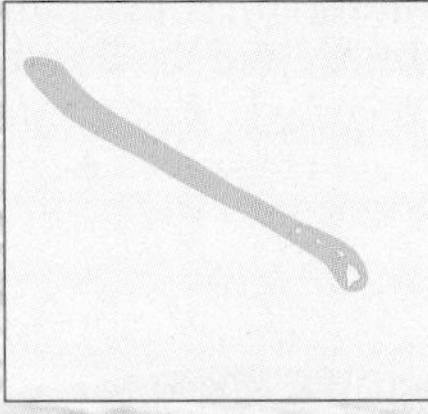

Hawaiian Monk Seal forages for reef fish, cephalopods and invertebrates.

DISTRIBUTION & POPULATION

Principally confined to 6 islands and atolls in the Northwest Hawaiian islands with increasing numbers appearing on the main islands in recent yrs. Strongly philopatric, although movements between colonies recorded, but rarely wanders to non-breeding atolls. *Population* Estimated at 1,400 in 2000.

ECOLOGY

Only important bond between cow and pup, though loose groups gather to moult. *Diving* Usually 60 m (or 4 min) or less below surface. Occasionally reaches 250 m (or max *c.*30 min). *Diet* Principally reef fish and cephalopods. *Reproduction* Sexually mature *c.*5 yrs. Mates Mar–Aug. Cows give birth to single pup Mar–Jun (peak late Mar–early Apr) and pups weaned at 4–6 weeks. *Lifespan* Up to 30 yrs.

Cow Hawaiian Monk Seal with newborn black-coloured pup (which will shed at c.6 weeks of age).

Hawaiian Monk Seal

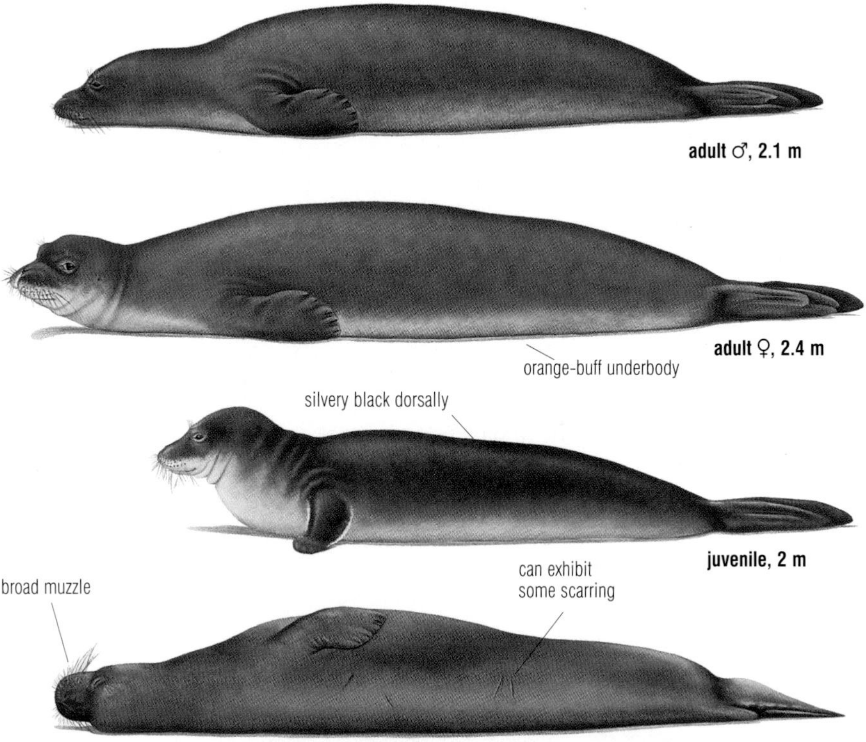

a robust, long-bodied seal, with broad round head, long thick muzzle, and essentially brown or greyish-brown coat (much darker when wet)

adult ♂, 2.1 m

adult ♀, 2.4 m

orange-buff underbody

silvery black dorsally

juvenile, 2 m

broad muzzle

can exhibit some scarring

adult ♂, 2.2 m (dorsal head profile)

Hawaiian Monk Seal in typical low surfacing profile; in some lights and when wet they can look blackish.

West Indian Monk Seal

Monachus tropicalis

Caribbean Sea. Max 2.4 m.

Priority characters on land (dry pelage)

- Rather large, robust phocid, formerly endemic to the Caribbean.
- Structure and coloration typical of genus.
- *Elongated body, with long neck, broad rounded head and flattish crown, and long thick muzzle.*
- *Pale to dark brown*, tinged grey above, grading paler below. Short coat.
- No data on sexual dimorphism or ageing, but presumably like other monk seals.
- *Foreflippers proportionately very short* with small claws; hindflippers slim.
- *Whiskers long, whitish and smooth (not coarse)*, relatively *large, well-spaced eyes*, and *rather large whisker pads with extended nostrils that opened upwards*, like congeners.

Typical behaviour

- Unknown, as the species is principally known from specimens.

SIMILAR SPECIES

Extinct, but no similar pinnipeds were known to overlap with this species.

VARIATION

Age/sex No reliable information. Newborn reportedly had a soft, glossy black coat. **Physical notes** Ads reached at least 2.4 m (♂ slightly larger than ♀); newborn probably *c.*1 m. **Other data** *Teats* All monk seals have 4 (instead of 2) retractable nipples. *Moult* Unknown.

DISTRIBUTION & POPULATION

Extinct since 1952, when a small colony was observed between Jamaica and Honduras. Range formerly encompassed the tropical W Atlantic as far north as Georgia (USA), throughout the Greater and Lesser Antilles, and western, southern and north-east Gulf of Mexico, and the S Caribbean Sea along the north coast of C & S America as far east as Guyana. Breeding grounds known from Arrecife Triangulos (Yucatán, Mexico) and the Bahamas. Movements, if any, unknown.

ECOLOGY

Based on historical records, occurred in large groups (up to 100) when abundant, young and ads may have formed different age groups when hauled out. Mainly on remote islands and atolls, and only rarely on mainland or in deep waters. *Diving* Unknown. *Diet* Probably fish and crustaceans. *Reproduction* Early Dec was peak breeding season, at least in Mexico. Records indicate long pupping season.

West Indian Monk Seal

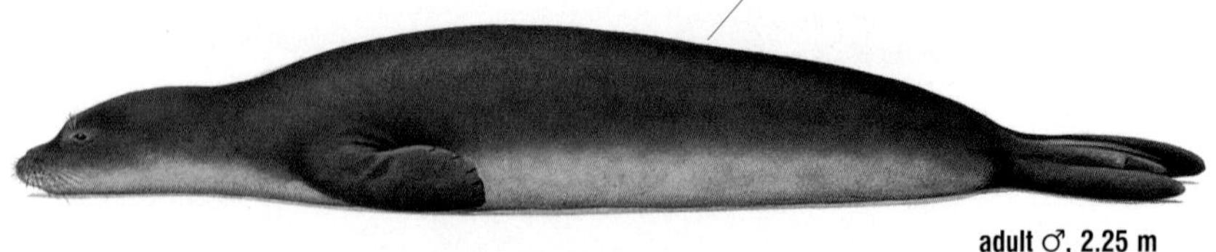

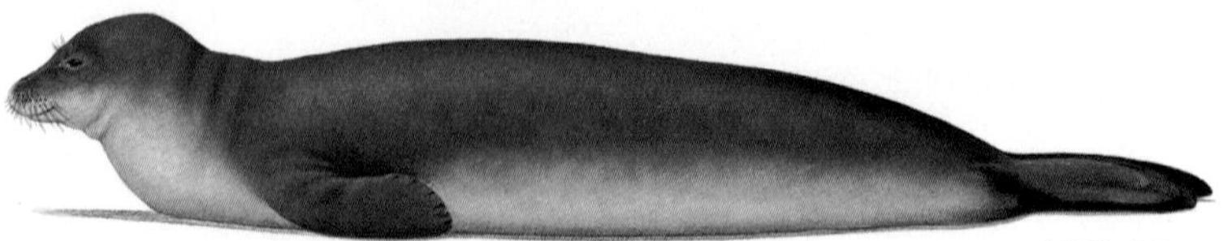

Subantarctic and Antarctic true seals

Amongst the most interesting pinnipeds – even a brief visit to the environs of the Antarctic Peninsula will ensure that you see 3–4 of the following species, although Ross Seal is most widespread in the dense consolidated pack-ice of East Antarctica and is the least known and most rarely seen of the group. Aside from Southern Elephant Seal, which primarily breeds on subantarctic islands, populations are largely restricted to the pack-ice zone around the continent, and the animals only periodically disperse to subantarctic waters, although they can reach well north of the Antarctic Convergence. All are very distinctive, sufficiently so for each to be placed in different genera, and all are usually placed, together with the monk seals, in the subfamily Monachinae. Being true seals, they are very closely related to their northern counterparts of the subfamily Phocinae, and wholly distinctive from the eared seals (Otariidae).

Pup Southern Elephant Seals have rounded and compressed faces with big black eyes.

All should be rather easily identified, especially if seen well, but even experienced observers need to remember that Leopard, Crabeater and Weddell Seals can be very variable, in their seasonal weight (amount of body fat), degree of bleaching and moult, and even according to age and sex, thus their markings can overlap to some degree. Close, prolonged observations may sometimes be required to reach a positive identification, especially if faced with an intermediate or abnormal animal.

Cows of Southern Elephant Seal, showing huge individual variation due to discoloration and various stages of epidermal moult, during their annual gathering in Dec/Jan.

Subantarctic and Antarctic true seals

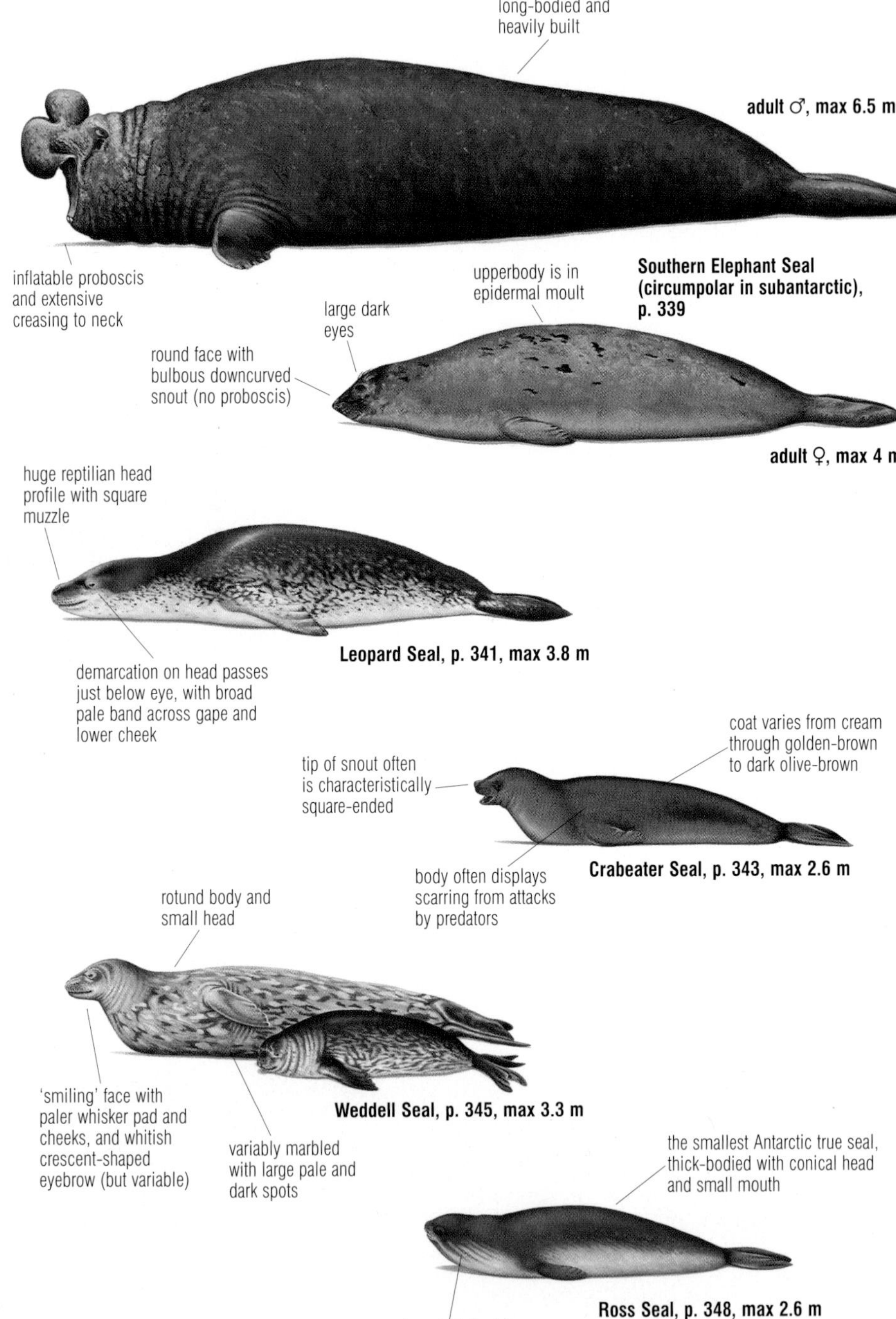

Southern Elephant Seal

Mirounga leonina

S Hemisphere. Max 6.5 m.

Priority characters on land (dry pelage)

- *Huge and impressive*. Robust but elongated, with proportionately small flippers and skin folds behind head. *Dark eyes large and round*.
- Bull: noticeably larger with *square-shaped head and conspicuous proboscis* (normally limp and overhangs mouth), but if inflated acts as a resonating chamber when bulls roar at rivals. *Skin folds well developed, and neck/chest heavily scarred through combat*. Overall darker brown than ♀♀, though some paler with age, especially on face.
- Cow: distinctly smaller with *rounder face and no proboscis (blunt or slightly bulbous downcurved nose)*, and often has paler neck 'yoke' due to bites when mating. *Coat dusky brown to tan or sandy*.
- Imm: sexing difficult but 3–4-yr-old ♂ larger with thicker neck, larger/squarer head and partially developed proboscis (still short and flat).
- Coat of short, stiff greyish or brown hair when newly moulted, but duller, browner or rustier and tan-coloured owing to discoloration by sand, mud and excrement.
- *Moults ashore, skin peeling rather distinctively*.
- Short black whiskers and 1–2 nasal whiskers; prominent vibrissae above eyes.
- Foreflippers broad with longer outer digits and blackish-brown claws; hindflippers and cartilaginous terminal flaps short but broad if fanned.

Typical behaviour

- *Hauls out on open sandy and stony beaches, where moves in caterpillar-like fashion*. Frequently cools off in mud wallows.
- Many breeding/moulting areas *close to penguin colonies especially of King Penguins*; displays and vocalisations obvious during mating season.
- At sea elusive and shy of boats. Rest intervals at surface very short.
- Close to breeding sites, floats with head and hindflippers clear of water, submerges tail first, head up and withdrawn vertically.

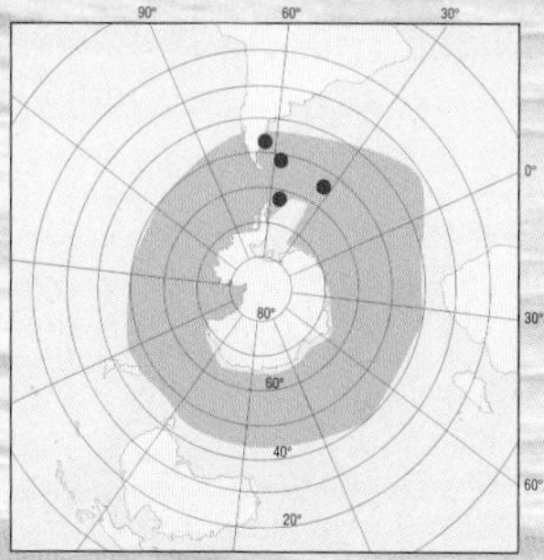

SIMILAR SPECIES

Very similar Northern Elephant Seal (NE Pacific) not known to come into contact with this species. Bulls unmistakable because of their size and large, fleshy proboscis. At least on land, cows and young readily separated from Weddell, Ross, Crabeater and Leopard Seals, as latter usually much smaller with mottled coats, whilst all eared seals have distinctive structure and appearance. Inexperienced observers may confuse pups with other seals at times.

VARIATION

Age/sex Significant age-/sex-related variation in size, proportions, facial structure and appearance. Newborn has blackish-brown coat, replaced after 3 weeks by shorter greyer coat, slightly paler below, and already has typical body shape, rounded face and large eyes. **Physical notes** Full-grown ♂ 4.5–6.5 m and *c.*3,700 kg; ♀ 2.5–4 m and 359–800 kg. Newborn *c.*1.3 m and 36–50 kg. **Other data** *Moult* Mainly Dec–Apr, ♀♀ and young preceding bulls. Epidermal moult usually starts in axilla region (coat typically has patchy appearance and becomes browner due to bleaching of old hair, dark brown-grey when fresh). **Taxonomy** Monotypic but low gene-flow between S Atlantic, S Indian Ocean, S Pacific and Argentina. Three subspecies proposed late 19th century – *M. l. falclandicus* (Falklands and dependencies), *M. l. macquariensis* (Macquarie, possibly Chatham) and *M. l. crosetensis* (Crozet, perhaps Kerguelen and Heard) – and up to 5 by some early-20th century authors.

Young ♂ in typical surfacing pose.

Southern Elephant Seal

extensive creasing to neck

long-bodied and heavily built

inflatable proboscis

mature adult ♂, 6 m

large dark eyes (all ages/sexes)

proboscis less developed

subadult ♂, 4.5 m

uniform coat, and rounded and flattened face with large black eyes, are useful distinctions from other Antarctic phocids

all have poorly developed forelimbs

juvenile, 3 m

orange-brown to pale tan when moulting

bluish-black upperbody with pale silvery grey underbody

rounded face with bulbous downcurved snout (no proboscis)

adult ♀ in moult, 4 m

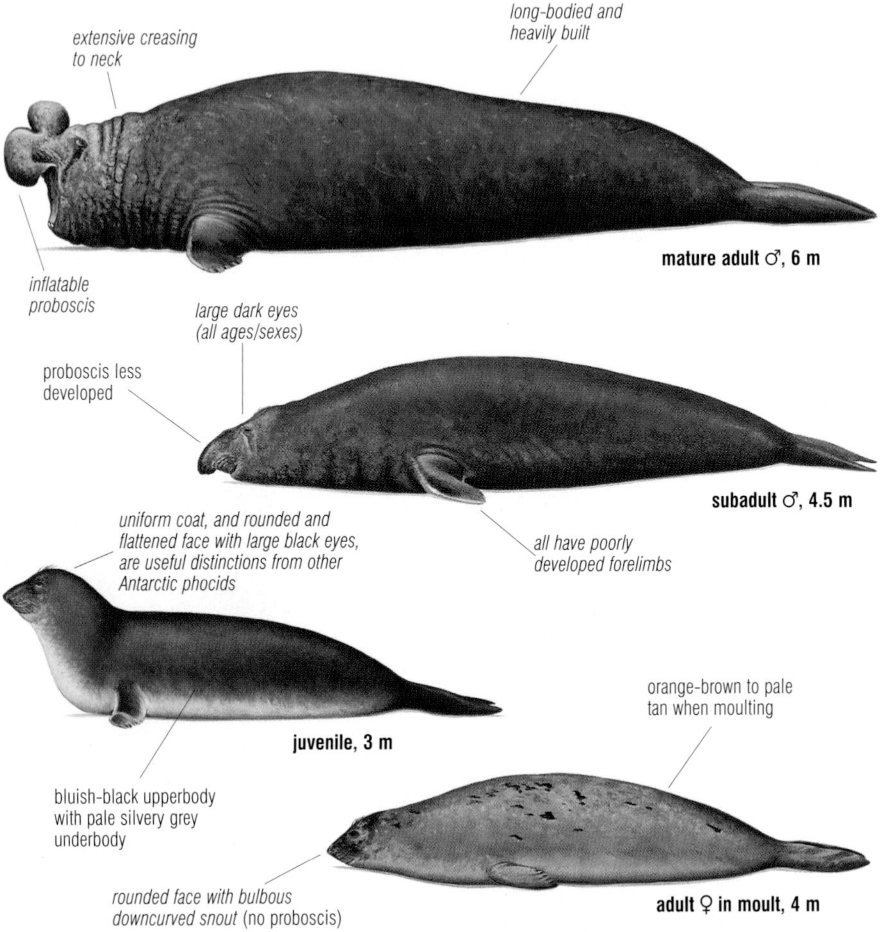

DISTRIBUTION & POPULATION

Both sides of Antarctic Convergence (sometimes even to 78°S), in S Argentina and most subantarctic islands, normally on sandy or shingle coasts. Occasionally far from breeding grounds (north to Angola and Oman), but movements poorly known and dispersal perhaps random. Imms move south to Antarctica (to 77°S in Weddell Sea) and north to Uruguay, S Africa (occasionally breeds), Australia and New Zealand.

Cow Southern Elephant Seal cooling using her foreflippers to flick sand and stones over her body during a warm sunny subantarctic day.

During mating the bull holds the cow with foreflipper and proboscis.

Population 640,000 in 1990s, but declining in S Pacific and S Indian Oceans.

ECOLOGY

Highly social on land. *Diving* To 1,444 m (max *c.* 2 hrs), but most dives reach 400–600 m and last 20–27 minutes. *Diet* Mainly deep-water fish and cephalopods. *Reproduction* Polygynous, bulls arrive from late Aug and may control up to 100 cows (ave. *c.*30), which arrive late Sep–Oct. Pups weaned 3–3.5 weeks. Ads mate 18–19 days after births. Ads fast during much of breeding season. Rookeries decline from Oct/Nov but reoccupied by moulting gatherings of different age/sex class; by mid-Mar/Apr, most gone and very few seen in winter. Sexually mature at c.4 (♂) or 2–6 yrs (♀) Due to high mortality and intense mate competition, most ♂♂ never breed. Few breed in 1+ season (and not before age 10). *Lifespan* 15–23 yrs.

Southern Elephant Seals: bull, cow and her fast-growing pup.

Leopard Seal

Hydrurga leptonyx

Antarctic/subantarctic. Max 3.8 m.

Priority characters on land (dry pelage)

- *Long sleek Antarctic seal* with near-serpentine appearance, comparatively long neck and *large, flat reptilian head*.
- Head broadest at eyes, which are dark, relatively small and set well apart; long/broad muzzle (nostrils on top), *powerful jaws and broad gape*, all of which are distinctive.
- Poorly developed sexual dimorphism and indistinct age differences. Colour and spotted pattern mainly varies individually.
- *Silver to dark blue-grey*, can appear almost blackish-grey, but usually dark above and on sides, and paler ventrally. Dark area variably spotted darker grey and black, with some paler marks. *Basal foreflippers, lower flanks and belly almost silver with contrasting dark spots*.
- In most, demarcation between dark/pale areas on head is just below eye, with paler, *broad silver grey band across gape and lower cheek*.
- *Foreflippers long and broad (somewhat otariid-like), near centre of body* and each digit has short terminal claw; hindflippers proportionately small.
- Pale whiskers rather short and inconspicuous.

Typical behaviour

- *Usually solitary*. May haul-out on ice and land, where mostly inactive or asleep.
- In water often cranes neck to

Leopard Seal (together with Killer Whale) is the top predator in the Antarctic food chain, taking other seals and penguins, enjoying a (somewhat undeserved) fierce reputation as a result.

SIMILAR SPECIES

Mainly due to superficially similar, slim body appearance and elongated head profile, on ice ***Crabeater***, especially young or distant animals, is most likely confusion risk.

However, Leopard Seal's characteristic massive head and reptilian face permit identification. Young/slimmer ***Weddell Seal*** could be confused, but only temporarily if seen poorly or distantly, and only by inexperienced observers, as latter has much heavier body and smaller rounded head, as well as different coloration. See also ***Ross Seal***, but latter has very different structure, although, to some extent, confusingly similar coloration, mainly in young animals.

VARIATION

Age/sex ♀♀ slightly longer and heavier, but not useful

view objects of interest and characteristically reveals back when submerging (head first, sometimes tail first); characteristic head shape permits immediate identification.

- *Patrols penguin colonies*; best known for predating penguins.
- On ice responds to human presence with slithering, deliberate movements.
- Swims with long, powerful, coordinated sweeps of foreflippers (not side-to-side strokes of hind-flippers typical of most phocids).

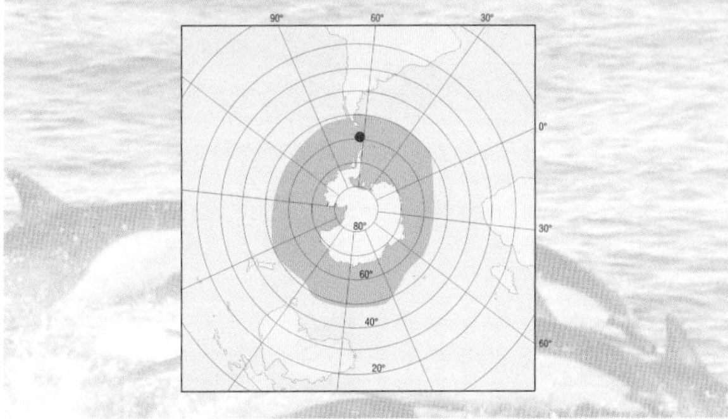

Leopard Seal

huge elongated head

square muzzle

adult ♀, 3.8 m

juvenile, 1.7 m

clearly demarcated pelt with inconspicuous spotting

wide gape

adult ♂, 3.3 m

large foreflippers

body pattern generally more demarcated with irregular markings compared to Weddell Seal

demarcation on head passes just below eye, with broad pale band across gape and lower cheeks

adult ♂, 3.3 m

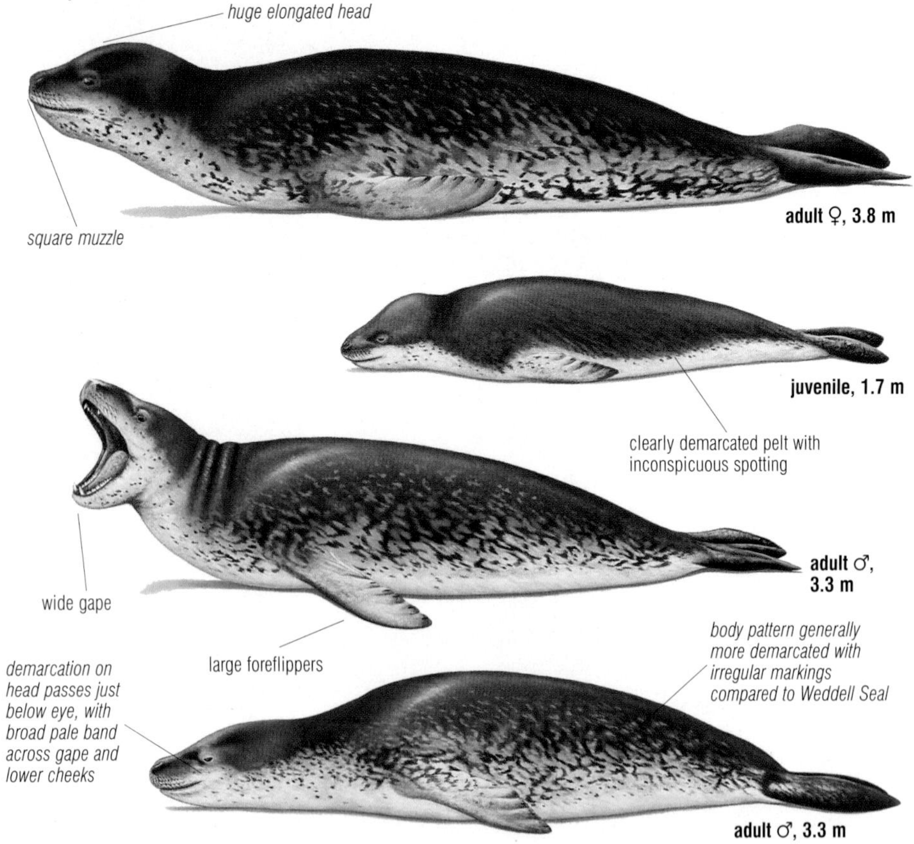

Leopard Seal skinning penguin by banging it against water.

for field separation. First-/second-yrs also distinctly smaller, sometimes slightly browner than ads, otherwise coloration at all ages similar. Pup similar but has denser, softer fur. **Physical notes** ♀ reaches 3.8 m and 500 kg, but records above that require verification; ♂ 2.8–3.3 m (300 kg). Newborn *c.*1–1.2 m and 30 kg. **Other data** *Moult* Ads Jan–Feb (occasionally until Jun). Coat generally fades only slightly prior to moult.

DISTRIBUTION & POPULATION

Widespread but uncommon in Antarctic and subantarctic zones south to 78°S. Breeding confined to pack-ice. Uncommon winter visitor to subantarctic islands (numbers peak at several 100s in this region every 4–5 yrs, most frequent on Heard in Jul–Sep), and not infrequently to New Zealand, Australia, S America and S Africa, exceptionally Tristan da Cunha, Lord Howe, Cook and Juan Fernández Is. *Population* At least 100,000 and perhaps 220,000–450,000 in 1980s.

ECOLOGY

Solitary. *Diving* Presumably close to surface. *Diet* Principally krill, fish, seabirds, especially penguins, and young of other seals. *Reproduction* ♂♂ highly vocal prior to and during breeding season, early Nov–Jan (perhaps to Mar). Cows give birth on pack-ice Sep–Jan (peak Nov–Dec) and lactation lasts *c.*1 month. *Lifespan* Unknown.

Leopard Seal: note reptilian head profile, dark demarcation on head, passing just below eye, and broad pale band on gape and lower cheeks.

Crabeater Seal

Lobodon carcinophaga

Antarctic. Max 2.6 m.

Priority characters on land (dry pelage)

- Medium-sized Antarctic seal, *comparatively slim and lithe*.
- Long neck and *square head with protruding dog-like muzzle* (nostrils on top) and *long mouth. Slight forehead and upturned snout*, and small dark eyes set well apart.
- Marked seasonal and individual variation in colour; ages vary mainly in size.
- Ads grey-brown dorsally, paler ventrally; *variable chocolate-brown patches on silver grey body-sides, largest near head/neck-sides, smaller behind foreflippers and at rear*.
- Coat gradually becomes uniformly paler, especially when bleached prior to moult. Thus, many *in summer easily identified by uniform appearance lacking any blotching*.
- Many diagnostically *deeply scarred*

SIMILAR SPECIES

Given slim body and elongated head, an inexperienced observer faced with a distant, especially, young animal, might confuse present species with ***Leopard*** and, to some degree, ***Weddell Seals***. Former eliminated by massive reptilian head with strong jaws, longer foreflippers, different spotting and whitish lips/cheeks, whilst latter has proportionately small head, short neck and more rotund body, and is usually more profusely blotched, and both never routinely occur in large groups like Crabeater. To lesser extent confusion can occur with ***Ross Seal***.

The fore parts of mature Crabeater Seal are often heavily bleached and scarred (as a result of breeding season disputes).

VARIATION

Age/sex Indistinct age/sex differences. Newborn usually has soft, woolly,

on back and body-sides due to attacks by Leopard Seals and sometimes Killer Whales.

- Face, neck and foreflippers often heavily bleached and scarred (inflicted in breeding season).
- *Foreflippers long, somewhat otariid-like, larger than Weddell*, and pointed (with only slightly elongated outer digit); hindflippers proportionately rather long/slender.
- Pale whiskers short and inconspicuous.

Typical behaviour

- *Almost confined to Antarctic pack-ice. In small or large groups.*
- Hauls-out on ice to sleep, but capable of moving rapidly with sinuous motions of back, aided by flippers and with raised neck and head. When approached, raises head as if 'pointing' and often moves quickly to water.
- Very seldom seen at sea. Head visible, submerges revealing back. Herds travelling together breathe and dive almost synchronously.

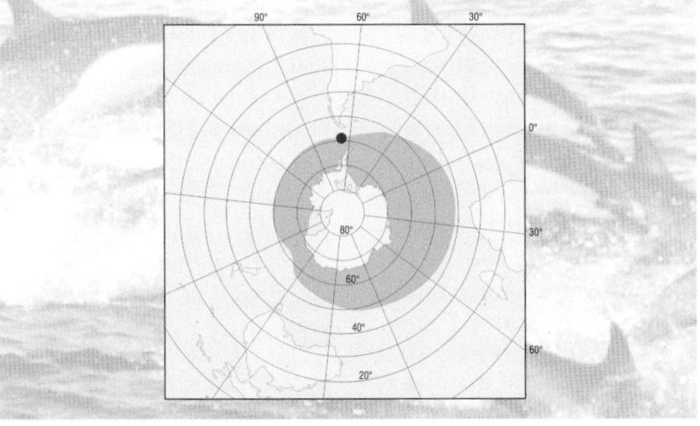

Crabeater Seal

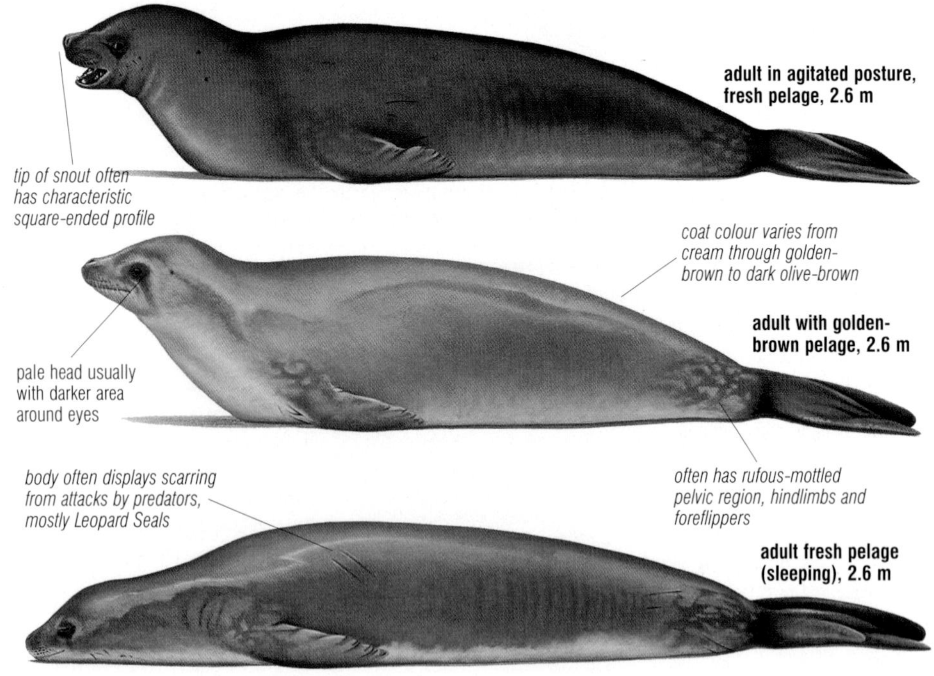

adult in agitated posture, fresh pelage, 2.6 m

tip of snout often has characteristic square-ended profile

coat colour varies from cream through golden-brown to dark olive-brown

adult with golden-brown pelage, 2.6 m

pale head usually with darker area around eyes

body often displays scarring from attacks by predators, mostly Leopard Seals

often has rufous-mottled pelvic region, hindlimbs and foreflippers

adult fresh pelage (sleeping), 2.6 m

Crabeater Seals; note diagnostic, deeply scarred body-sides owing to attacks by Leopard Seals and, sometimes, Killer Whales.

milky coffee-brown fur with darker hindflippers, moulted at *c*.2–3 weeks to ad-like juv pelage. First-/second-yr noticeably smaller than ad; non-breeders best aged by tooth condition, but 5–8 yr-olds apparently still smaller than older animals. **Physical notes** Ads reach 2–2.6 m and 180–410 kg (♀ averages slightly larger); newborn *c*.1.1 m and 36 kg.

DISTRIBUTION & POPULATION
Confined when breeding to Antarctic pack-ice, south to 79°S, but occasionally visits subantarctic islands, New Zealand, Australia, S Africa, the Falklands and S America north to SE Brazil. Other movements unknown. Recorded 113 km from open water. *Population* Estimated 50–75 million in early 1980s (but perhaps 'just' 10–15 million).

ECOLOGY
Singly or in groups of <10, but occasionally 1,000. *Diving* To 530 m, but mostly 20–30 m and for 4–5 min. *Diet* Mainly krill, also fish and squid. *Reproduction* Polygynous (or serially monogamous), usually in family pairs, but after copulation bulls may seek another cow. Gives birth Sep–Oct, lactation lasts 2–5 weeks, and mates 1–2 weeks after pup weaned. *Lifespan* Up to 25–30 yrs.

Hauled-out Crabeater Seals.

Weddell Seal

Leptonychotes weddellii

Coastal Antarctica. Max 3.3 m.

Priority characters on land (dry pelage)

- Among the largest, plumpest seals, with proportionately *rotund body*, small flippers and head.
- *Somewhat cat-like face with blunt, only slightly protruding muzzle and close-set, large dark eyes.*
- Short dense coat characteristically patterned at all ages; no obvious sexual differences and ages vary mainly in size.
- Bluish-black to dark silvery grey (fresh), *irregularly streaked and blotched greyish-white, with patches gradually increasing, chiefly between sides and paler abdomen*.
- May be browner and buffer prior to moult, and blotching perhaps yellowish.
- *Mouthline short and slightly upturned, affording slight 'smiling' appearance*; facial pattern consists of *paler whisker pad, muzzle-sides and cheeks, and whitish crescent-shaped markings above eyes*.
- *Foreflippers shortest of any Antarctic phocid*, relatively angular and pointed; hindflippers proportionately small.

SIMILAR SPECIES
Crabeater, which can have blotchy coat and somewhat rounded head, is most significant confusion risk. With experience, however, Crabeater usually

Weddell Seal, a deep diver, is seen here eating an Antarctic toothfish.

clearly slimmer with more elongated and square-shaped head (though beware extensive weight loss during breeding season which makes Weddell slightly less thick-bodied in comparison, and less distinctly small-headed). Crabeater has different behaviour, being more active and fast-moving. If present, blotches usually rather limited, and very often deeply scarred on body-sides, unlike Weddell. Conversely, some Weddell may be confusingly pale and more uniform, but never like most Crabeater, and

- Whiskers pale, short and sparse, generally inconspicuous.

Typical behaviour

- Hauls out on ice and land, moves very slowly with 'humping' gait. Asocial.
- Maintains breathing holes.
- *Very placid and almost docile, ignores humans (often remains asleep or may roll on side with head and flipper raised in 'salute').*

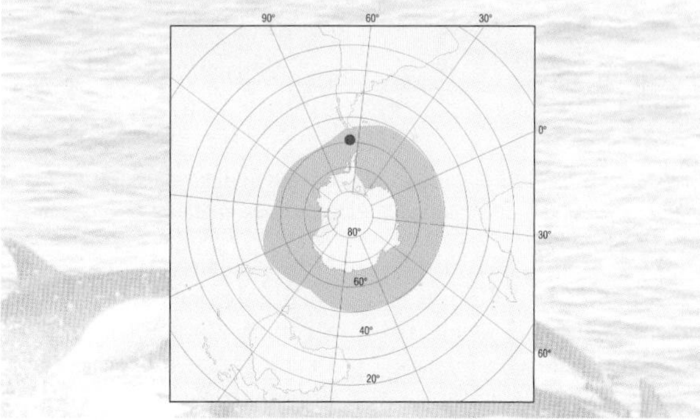

Weddell Seal

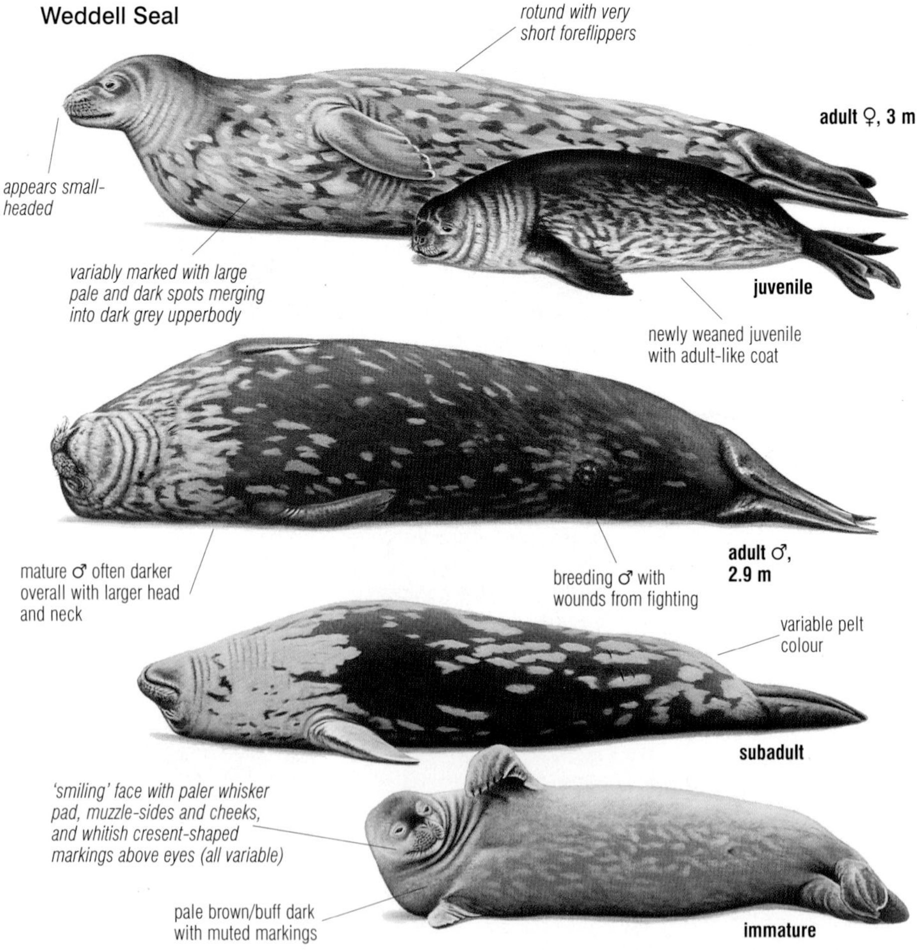

rotund with very short foreflippers

adult ♀, 3 m

appears small-headed

variably marked with large pale and dark spots merging into dark grey upperbody

juvenile

newly weaned juvenile with adult-like coat

mature ♂ often darker overall with larger head and neck

breeding ♂ with wounds from fighting

adult ♂, 2.9 m

variable pelt colour

subadult

'smiling' face with paler whisker pad, muzzle-sides and cheeks, and whitish cresent-shaped markings above eyes (all variable)

pale brown/buff dark with muted markings

immature

Mother and pup Weddell Seal: for every kg gained by the pup, the mother loses 2 kg; immediately after giving birth the cow weighs 450 kg, but after weaning the pup for c.7 weeks is only 300 kg.

coat never wears as pale as extreme, whitish-bleached Crabeater. See also ***Leopard*** and ***Ross Seals***.

VARIATION

Age/sex Indistinct sexual dimorphism; ♀ only slightly larger and ♂ has thicker neck, broader head and muzzle. Latter often darker on upper surface and hindflippers usually broader and shredded from fighting. Newborn has silver grey, grey-brown or golden, woolly coat, with dark stripe on back, shed after 4 weeks; juv coat similar to ad. First-/second-yr noticeably smaller than ads; age of non-breeders best estimated by tooth condition. **Physical notes** ♂ reaches 2.5–3 m, ♀ 2.6–3.3 m, and both sexes 400–600 kg. Newborn *c.*1.2–1.5 m and 22–29 kg. **Other data** *Moult* Dec–Mar.

DISTRIBUTION & POPULATION

The most southerly breeding seal, circumpolar in distribution, being most abundant near Antarctic coast, inhabiting both pack and fast-ice south to 78°S, and also reaches S Orkney, S Shetland, S Georgia and S Sandwich. Occasional sightings on Auckland, Campbell, Macquarie and other subantarctic islands, and vagrant to New Zealand, S Australia and S America (north to Uruguay and to Juan Fernández Is). Moves north with expansion of pack-ice in winter and other more complex, seasonal movements also reported. *Population* 250,000–400,000 in 1980s, but recently suggested perhaps 500,000 to 1 million would be a more accurate estimate.

ECOLOGY

Asocial when not breeding but may congregate at breathing holes in ice. *Diving* Up to 750 m, but mostly 50–500 m (15–20 min). *Diet* Mainly fish, also cephalopods, crustaceans and penguins. *Reproduction* First breeding *c.*6–8 yrs; may be significantly earlier in cows. Sometimes breeds in loose assemblages of several

Weddell Seal: note proportionately rotund body, small flippers and head; coat bluish or dark silvery grey with greyish-white streaks and blotches.

100s. Gives birth mainly on ice late Sep–mid Nov. Occasionally 2 pups, weaned at 50–55 days. ♀♀ largely spends days 1–12 on ice with pup, thereafter 30–40% in water. Mates Nov–Dec. (♂♂ may mate with any ♀ in territory). *Lifespan c.*30 yrs.

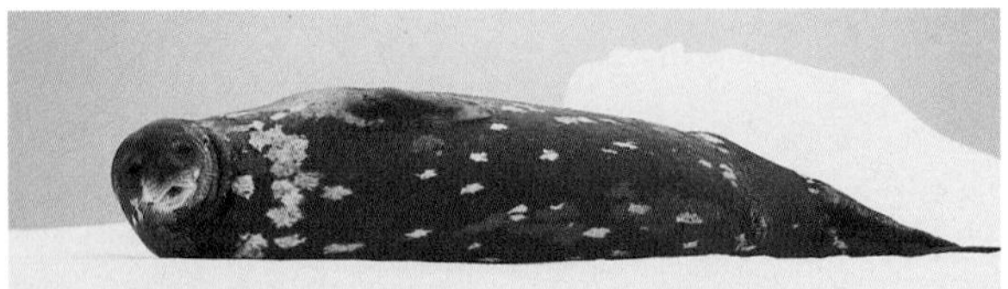

Weddell Seal, showing typical facial appearance head-on; note individual variation in pale markings.

SIMILAR SPECIES

All other Antarctic species, especially younger animals, when asleep on ice or if seen distantly, can appear superficially similar to the scarcer Ross. For instance, younger Weddell with superficially more striped body-sides and due to its rather rounded head and heavy appearance, could be mistaken for Ross, whilst Leopard and some very blotchy, darker Crabeater are paler ventrally and can appear to have striped body-sides. However, some Ross have confusingly reduced throat/neck stripes. Close views are needed to confirm identification. Ross usually smaller and has relatively thicker, uniquely striped throat/neck, with characteristic head and body profile, and different behaviour. As always, once characteristics are known the species is readily recognised.

VARIATION

Age/sex Some sex-/age-related variation, mainly in size (♀ slightly larger), and tone and contrast of streaks and spots varies, mainly individually. Newborn has dense, mainly dark brown lanugo, paler yellowish/silvery ventrally, perhaps with similar throat striping to ad. **Physical notes** ♂

Ross Seal

Ommatophoca rossii

Antarctica. Max 2.6 m.

Priority characters on land (dry pelage)

- The *smallest Antarctic seal*. Graceful.
- *Appears neckless*; body very thick around head/chest, tapering abruptly at rear.
- *Head small but broad and round, with short, blunt muzzle and small mouth*; dark eyes relatively large and set wide apart.
- Short, velvety coat, *back and flippers mainly dark grey* (few streak-shaped spots), sharply demarcated from silver or buff ventral surface. No obvious sexual differences and ages vary mainly in size.
- *Characteristic dark (tinged chestnut or chocolate) longitudinal stripes or patches on throat-sides, head/neck and sometimes flanks* (individually variable).
- Dusky eye-mask can be apparent, and narrower, *variable spots and streaks on flanks*, especially rear. Most ads have pale scars on neck/'shoulders'.
- *Foreflippers rather long, situated quite far forward on body*; hindflippers proportionately long and slim. Claws very short.
- Whiskers short and few in number, pale and very thin.

Typical behaviour

- Chiefly on dense consolidated pack-ice, and generally rather poorly known and rarely seen. Usually solitary or in small groups.
- Hauls-out on ice in summer, mainly from midday.
- Rather slow, *typically raises head and foreparts almost vertically, with back arched and chest enlarged*, and often with open mouth.
- Close to may be heard to utter trilling, cooing and siren-like sounds.

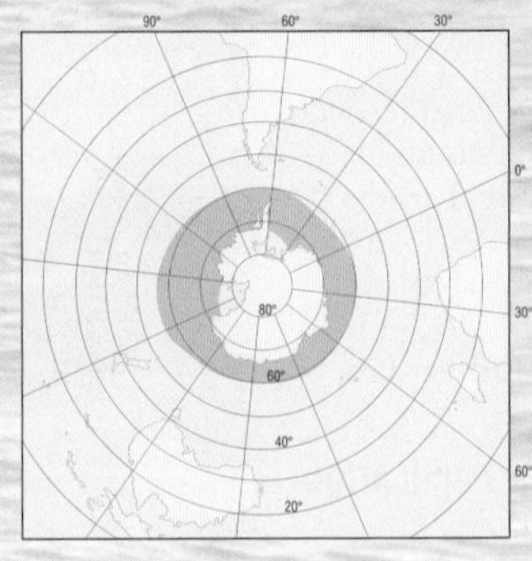

Ross Seal

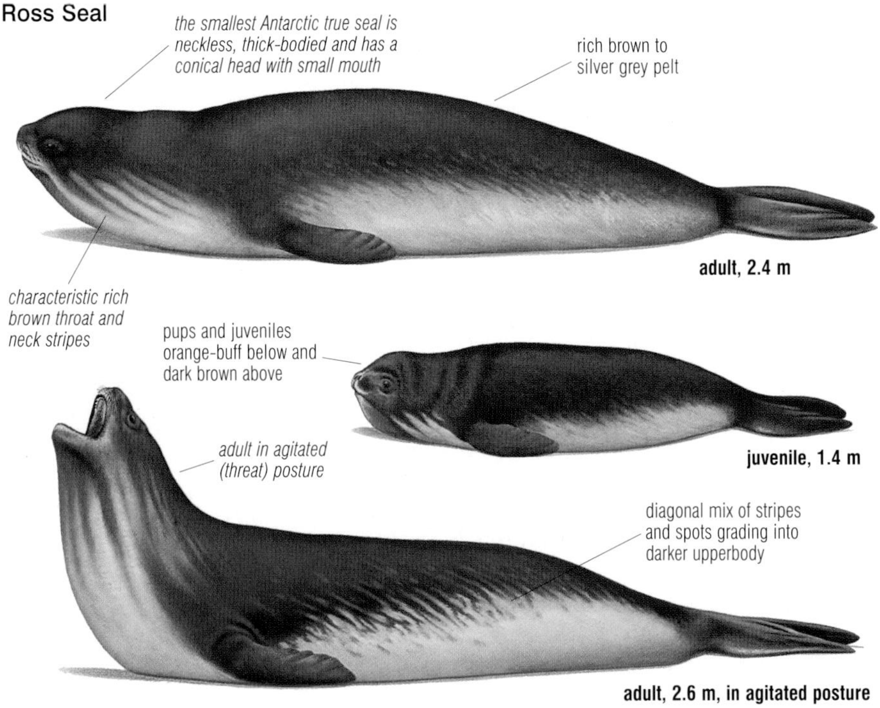

the smallest Antarctic true seal is neckless, thick-bodied and has a conical head with small mouth

rich brown to silver grey pelt

characteristic rich brown throat and neck stripes

adult, 2.4 m

pups and juveniles orange-buff below and dark brown above

juvenile, 1.4 m

adult in agitated (threat) posture

diagonal mix of stripes and spots grading into darker upperbody

adult, 2.6 m, in agitated posture

1.65–2.08 m, ♀ 1.96–2.6 m. Mean estimated weights 173 kg (♂; range 129–216 kg) and 186 kg (♀; range 159–201 kg), but reaches 225 kg. Newborn up to 1.2 m and 27 kg. **Other data** *Moult* Jan–Feb (varies according to age and sex); reportedly has epidermal moult that involves shedding small pieces of skin.

DISTRIBUTION & POPULATION
Amongst the least-known of pinnipeds. Circumpolar in pack-ice of Antarctic Ocean, south to 78°S but recorded north to the Falklands, S Australia, Kerguelen and Heard Is. *Population* Perhaps *c.*220,000 in early 1970s, but also estimated to number between 100,000 and 650,000.

ECOLOGY
Largely solitary, especially in summer, but loose clusters occasionally noted and perhaps more social than is known. *Diving* Up to 212 m and 10 min; most dives reach depths above 110 m and <6 min. *Diet* Krill, migrating squid and mid-water fishes. *Reproduction* Probably serially monogamous. Cows give birth on pack-ice in Nov–Dec (peak first half of Nov) and mate late Dec–early Jan. Pups weaned at 3–4 weeks. *Lifespan* 21+ yrs.

Ross Seal is thick-bodied with a conical head and small mouth. This individual lacks the dark longitudinal stripes on the throat-sides, thus, for some animals, small size and head shape take priority.

Arctic animals

Walrus and Polar Bear are some of the most sought-after animals of the Arctic wilderness and among the principal reasons to purchase a cruise there. To observe these animals in the wild must rate among the most exciting experiences. Although grouped here, their classification is very different with Walrus belonging to the suborder Pinnipedia, where it is the sole member of the family Odobenidae, and thus most closely related to seals, whereas Polar Bear belongs to the suborder Fissipedia and is the only marine member of the family Ursidae. Polar Bear represents a comparatively recent divergence from the Brown Bear, probably less than one million years ago.

Another member of the order Carnivora is sometimes considered to be a marine mammal. Arctic Fox *Vulpes lagopus* is widespread through northern North America and northern Eurasia including islands in the Arctic Ocean. Two colour phases occur: white (brownish-grey in summer) and blue (uniform year-round), of which the former is primarily a mainland animal and the other principally coastal. Coastal individuals may make prolonged sorties onto sea-ice (having been sighted within 100 km of the North Pole) where they scavenge Polar Bear kills and seize Ringed Seal pups in their lairs. However, it is not known to be aquatic, or to swim long distances, unlike Polar Bear and the otters treated here.

Immature Walruses (note rather short tusks) are often very playful and demonstrative.

Adult ♀ Walrus.

SIMILAR SPECIES
Unmistakable.

Walrus

Odobenus rosmarus

Arctic coasts. Max 3.6 m.

Priority characters

- Bulky Arctic endemic. Up to *c.*1-m *pale curved tusks make imm or ad unmistakable*.
- ♂ larger and heavier and has longer tusks (juv lacks tusks). Coloration generally varies with age, wear and activity.
- Very thick skin covered with fine hair is *wrinkled, heavily creased and folded, mostly greyish dull brown, tinged buff or chestnut, sometimes reddish*.
- Neck, chest and shoulders massive, and older ♂ may have lumps on neck/chest.
- *Square-shaped head* very broad, with *frontal whisker pad of many sensory, stiff vibrissae*.
- Eyes small, set well apart and somewhat protruding; nostrils atop muzzle.
- *Foreflippers otariid-like*, relatively broad and square, adapted to smooth surfaces; claws very small.
- *Hindflippers phocid-like*, with rather broad webs between digits, each with a small claw.

Typical behaviour

- Hauls out on sandy or rocky

shores, and ice floes, to rest and moult; at sea in small groups.

- In summer, mostly in shallow water and coastal areas, but in winter generally follows pack-ice.
- Has above-surface and underwater vocalisations, ♂ roars, barks, knocks, clicks, grunts, also a bell-like sound and 'rutting whistle'; young give underwater 'twittering'. Loud whistles when swimming.
- Tusks used as tools, for hauling out and in social interactions.

Mature Walruses flush rosy-red on land according to blood circulation and in response to temperature changes.

VARIATION

Age/sex ♂ has sparser hair, especially with age (when also paler), and protuberances on neck; some old bulls almost whitish-buff; tusks larger and sturdier than ♀, and ♂ generally 20% longer and 50% heavier than equivalent-age ♀. Ads, especially ♂♂, in water even paler, but flush rosy-red on land (blood circulation in response to temperature). Calf and juv duskier. **Physical notes** ♂ reaches *c.*3.6 m and 1,900 kg, ♀ *c.*3 m and 1,200 kg. Newborn 1–1.4 m and 45–85 kg.

Other data *Moult* Jun–Aug, rather protracted. *Teeth* Upper canines (tusks) less curved and diverge further in bulls, but often partially or wholly broken off in both sexes. **Taxonomy** Polytypic: *O. r. rosmarus*, E Canadian Arctic and Greenland east to Novaya Zemlya; *O. r. divergens*, in Bering Sea and adjacent Arctic Ocean (apparently somewhat larger); and *O. r. laptevi*, principally Laptev Sea, north of Siberia. Latter dubiously distinct, but mtDNA evidence confirms separation of other populations.

DISTRIBUTION & POPULATION

In Bering and Chukchi Seas, NE Canada and Greenland, Svalbard and Franz Josef Land, Barents and Kara Seas, and Laptev Sea of N Siberia. Follows pack-ice movements. Vagrants have reached Kamchatka, N Japan, the Beaufort Sea, Iceland and NW Europe south to Bay of Biscay. *Population* Estimated at *c.*220,000; most in extreme N Pacific region.

ECOLOGY

Sexes and age classes remain separate but congregate on

Near-mature bull Walrus with Ivory Gulls Pagophila eburnea *in pristine Arctic environment.*

Walrus

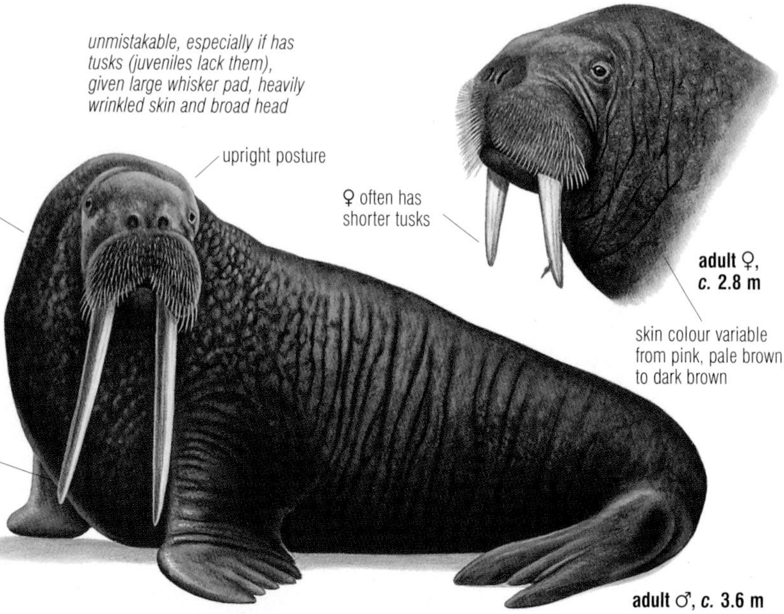

unmistakable, especially if has tusks (juveniles lack them), given large whisker pad, heavily wrinkled skin and broad head

upright posture

skin very rough and wrinkled

♀ often has shorter tusks

adult ♀, *c.* 2.8 m

skin colour variable from pink, pale brown, to dark brown

tusks often broken

adult ♂, *c.* 3.6 m

Mature ♂ Walruses have long, less curved and closer canines: different sexes and age classes remain separate for much of the year.

land, lying on top of each other to conserve heat. Sexes only mix in breeding season. *Diving* To 130 m, usually for *c.*5 min, but can spend up to 24 min underwater. *Diet* Takes benthic invertebrates, principally bivalve molluscs, on ocean floor, using sensory whiskers to identify prey. Less commonly takes seabirds, scavenges at carcasses, or takes live seals and cetaceans. *Reproduction* Sexually mature at 5–7 (♀) or 7–10 yrs (♂). Polygynous. Bulls attempt to mate (with receptive cows in their aquatic territories) Jan–Apr at small number of particular sites. Gestation *c.*15 months. Gives birth on ice floes Apr–early Jun, and calf weaned at *c.*1–3 yrs, but calves remain among groups of cows for several yrs. Inter-calving interval *c.*3 yrs. *Lifespan* 30–40 yrs.

Cow and calf Walrus; the former has mid-length tusks, the latter none.

Polar Bear

Ursus maritimus

Arctic. Max 2.5 m.

Priority characters

- *Typical bear*, with large, powerful body, broad rectangular head, small ears and tail, strong thick legs and, above all, *white coat*; unmistakable.
- *No other bear has white coat and no other similar-shaped animal exists in Arctic range.*
- Almost pure white to whitish-cream with slight yellowish tinge; black eyes, nose, lips and footpads.
- Sexes and ages mainly differ in size. Coloration slightly varies seasonally and with light.

Typical behaviour

- *Associated with sea-ice.*
- Normally singly, in pairs or ♀♀ with cubs, but large corpses may attract more. Sometimes visits habitation in search for food.
- Active year-round, but in severe weather may excavate dens.
- *Strong swimmer*, even crossing open seas. Large, oar-like front paws.

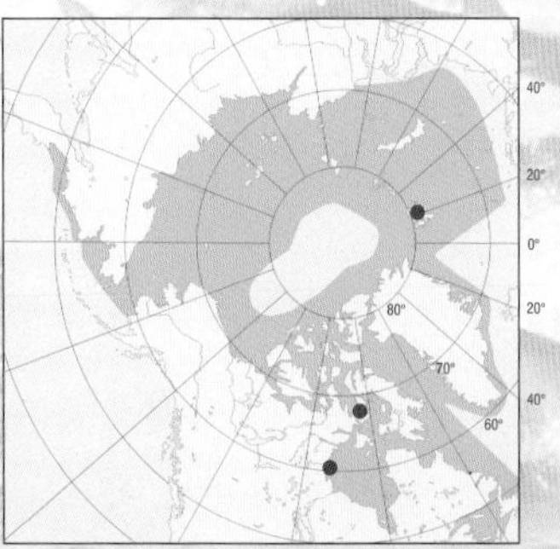

SIMILAR SPECIES

In some areas, Grizzly, Brown or American Black Bears may overlap with Polar Bear, but are readily separated by colour. Depending on light conditions and/or pelage wear, Polar Bear can appear yellow-tinged or even pale brown and grey, and some are discoloured by dirt, but never to the extent that they could be confused with above-mentioned species. Even in poor weather conditions, unlikely to be confused with any pinniped.

VARIATION

Age/sex Sexual differences limited to size and structure (♂ can be as twice as large); ad ♀ often accompanied by cubs. **Physical notes** ♂ reaches 2–2.5 m and 400–800 kg, ♀ 1.8–2 m and 200–350 kg. Newborn *c.*1 kg. **Taxonomy** Some

Polar Bears are not only the Arctic's top predators but also scavengers: here ♀♀ and cubs gather at a Grey Whale carcass, surrounded by Glaucous Gulls Larus hyperboreus; *note pelage discoloured by dirt and blood.*

Polar Bear

mature ♂ has
huge, broad
muscular head
mature ♂, 2.5 m
characteristic
long neck
unmistakable large,
powerful bear, with white
(but often dirty) coat
cubs typically
have white face
mature ♀, 2 m
bluish-black lips,
nose and tongue;
eyes reddish-brown
cub/juvenile
develops long face
with slight curve
to nose
adult head
overall, fur colour is
often yellowish-ochre
adult head profile

geographic variation in size and 2 subspecies occasionally recognised: nominate in Atlantic and *U. m. marinus* in Russia and Bering Sea.

DISTRIBUTION & POPULATION
Circumpolar south to S Labrador, S Greenland and C Kamchatka (Russia). Vagrants have reached N Scandinavia, N Japan, the Pribilofs (USA), Quebec and Newfoundland (Canada), and to within 300 km of N Pole, but usually avoids areas of multi-year pack-ice. Prefers coastal areas and inter-island channels in autumn to spring. *Population* 22,000–27,000 in 1997.

Young Polar Bears are particularly playful.

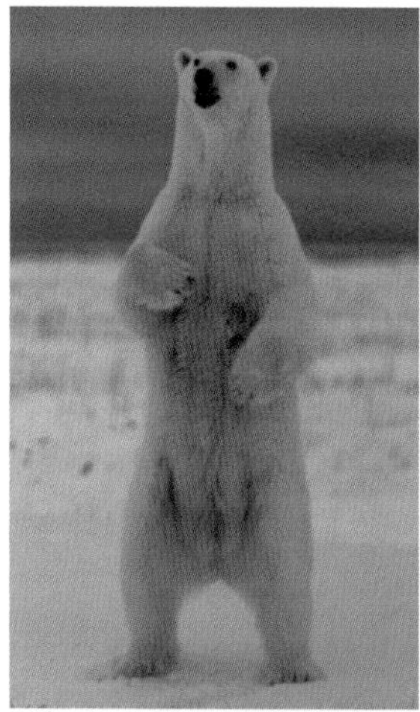
Like other bears, Polar Bears can easily stand on their hind legs.

Adult ♂ Polar Bear in typical swimming profile: a slow but excellent swimmer, the species is even capable of crossing open-sea areas.

A mother and her 2 recently born cubs.

ECOLOGY
Usually solitary or in mother/cub groups, occasional loose aggregations at food resources. *Diving* Only superficial dives. *Diet* Most commonly takes Ringed and Bearded Seals, occasionally Walruses, Belugas, Narwhals and seabirds. May feed all yr, but mostly spring/early summer. Most fast for *c.*4 months, mid-Jul to mid-Nov. Pregnant ♀♀ do not feed for up to 8 months. *Reproduction* Breeds every 3+ yrs. Sexually mature at 5 (♀) and 8 (♂) yrs. Mates Apr–May and gives birth to 1–3 cubs in dens within land snowdrifts (sometimes on sea-ice) mid-Nov–mid-Dec. Cubs nursed by ♀ until late Mar/early Apr, when leave den. Weaned at *c.*2.5 yrs. *Lifespan* Up to 30+ yrs.

Otters

Of the world's 9–14 otter species (all of which are placed in the Mustelidae, subfamily Lutrinae) only two are described here, namely the Sea Otter of the North Pacific and Marine Otter of western South America. The others are mainly associated with fresh water and therefore excluded here (including the familiar Eurasian and American River Otters which, in places, inhabit marine environments, chiefly in scattered rocky coastal habitats, where they are still much dependent on surrounding fresh water and land). Marine-dwelling otters occupy varied coastal habitats and present a comparatively recent radiation from terrestrial mammals, making it unsurprising that they bear a strong resemblance to their land-based cousins. These otters probably possess a strong sense of smell, but their mobility on land is rather reduced, in contrast to their powerful swimming and diving capabilities.

Adult Sea Otter: older individuals become almost white-headed.

SIMILAR SPECIES

Might only be confused with American River Otter (of which 3–4 races overlap in Alaska, Canada and W USA), but latter smaller, more slender and has longer tail, lacks flipper-like hindlimbs, and swims belly down at surface. Sea Otters surface on their backs.

VARIATION

Age/sex Sexual differences inconspicuous in field, but

Sea Otter

Enhydra lutris

N Pacific. Max 1.48 m.

Priority characters

- *Typical otter, elongated body with long slender tail* and limbs adapted to aquatic life. Only occasionally, and always briefly, hauls-out.
- *Large round head* with blunt snout; neck short and broad.
- *Eyes and nose relatively small, dark and close together*; vibrissae whitish, rather stiff and long.
- *Fore limbs short and used to hold food*; hindlimbs large and webbed, somewhat flipper-like and can be oriented backwards.
- Tail noticeably tapered, flattened horizontally into paddle-like structure.
- Very dense pelage (except nose pad, *inside of otariid-like ear-flaps*, and footpads), dark brown to reddish-brown, but appears blackish.
- *Older individuals grizzled, almost white around head*, neck, and shoulders.

Typical behaviour

- Truly marine, *occurs in shallow, near-shore waters with kelp beds.*
- Usually solitary, in pairs or family parties. Sometimes small groups, but periodically may form large rafts in Alaska.
- *Rafts buoyantly at surface face-up*, with forelimbs held close to face.

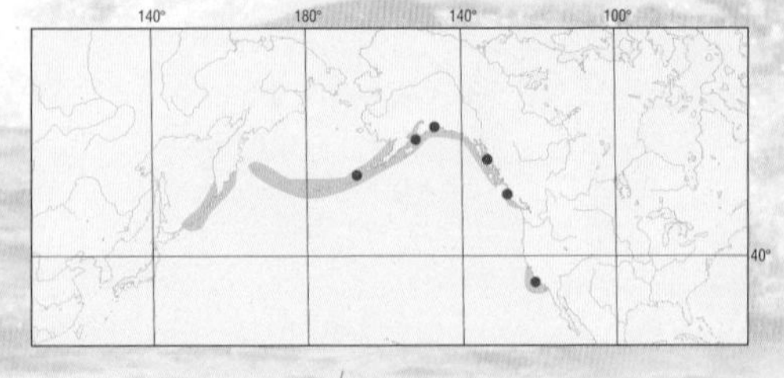

Sea Otters (race nereis*, California), showing typical rafting and feeding behaviour. The forelimbs are used like hands and the belly as a table.*

♂ usually more robust; pup more uniform and buffier, and lacks grizzled foreparts (first pelage replaced at 13 weeks); juv/imm have more guard hairs. **Physical notes** ♂ reaches 1.48 m and 45 kg, ♀ 1.4 m and 32.5 kg. Newborn *c.*60 cm and 1.8–2.3 kg. **Other data** *Moult* Continuous, mostly summer. **Taxonomy** Polytypic. Three races (differ mainly in size) representing 4 disjunct populations: Commander Is to SE Kamchatka and N Hokkaido, Japan (*E. l. lutris*); Aleutians and Pribilofs, Alaska, and south to Washington/Oregon, USA (*E. l. kenyoni*); and N California to Baja California, Mexico (*E. l. nereis*). Alaskan animals are larger/heavier than those in California.

DISTRIBUTION & POPULATION

From N Japan to Alaska, and thence south through British Columbia (Canada), Washington, Oregon and California (USA). Most west-coast N America populations reintroduced following extinction in 19th century. Currently a vagrant to Baja California. *Population* Overall numbers unknown, but just 1,700 in California in 2000 and *c.*3,500 in Asia (post-1990).

ECOLOGY

Social but ♂♂ usually segregated from ♀♀/pups. Dozens or more may gather

Sea Otters (probably nominate lutris*, NW Pacific); note large, webbed hindlimbs.*

Sea Otter

at favoured feeding areas. Outstanding loose aggregation of *c.*2,000 animals in Alaska. Very occasionally haul-out, and rather tame where undisturbed. *Diving* Mostly for 30–60 sec (max *c.*4.5 min); reaches 100 m. *Diet* Principally invertebrates such as lobsters, shellfish and clams, but also fish, cephalopods and even birds. May use rocks as tools to crush shells of shellfish. *Reproduction* Sexually mature at 4–6 yrs. Polygynous, but ♂♂ may mate with several ♀♀ per season. Gestation 8–10 months. Gives birth all yr, but mostly Dec–Feb in California and May–Jun in Alaska. Pup weaned at 6–12 months, but can forage alone at *c.*6 weeks. *Lifespan* 15–20 yrs.

Sea Otter (Alaska), probably race kenyoni.

SIMILAR SPECIES

On southwest coasts of S America the only truly marine otter, although American River Otter (subspecies *provocax*) overlaps in parts of Chile and S Argentina, and conversely Marine Otters do enter rivers. River otters generally larger and more robust, with longer, more slender tails, darker and more uniform, finer fur, and have spotted nose pads, throat and lips. They also segregate by habitat, with river otters preferring more sheltered areas than wave-exposed coastal regions favoured by present species.

VARIATION

Age/sex No sexual dimorphism known; juv and imm by size. **Physical notes** Ads reach 1.15 m and 4.5 kg. No data on pups. **Other data** *Moult* Unknown. **Taxonomy** Two races sometimes recognised: *L. f. peruviensis* in Peru to N Chile (perhaps paler) and

Marine Otter

Lutra felina

Western S America. Max 1.15 m.

Priority characters

- *Rather small, has freshwater otters' generally rodent-like appearance.* Compared to Sea Otter, limb and tail structure equipped for aquatic and nearby land habitats.
- Head flat and broad, with slight forehead and rather elongated, blunt snout; neck rather long.
- Dark nose pad naked and flattened; dark eyes set well apart; vibrissae whitish, rather stiff and long. *Ear-flaps comparatively well developed*, round and small but often erect.
- *Fore limbs strong and slightly webbed; hindlimbs large, flat and well webbed, somewhat flipper-like, and can be oriented backwards*, but not as broad and long as in Sea Otter.
- *Tail typical of freshwater otters*, sharply tapered but noticeably short.
- Dense pelage is medium to dark brown above, paler fawn below, including throat and lower cheeks. When wet coat silkier, patternless and sometimes even paler, almost shiny silvery-grey.

Typical behaviour

- Exposed *rocky shores* of southwest S America, *sometimes enters rivers*.
- Usually solitary, in pairs or small family parties.

Marine Otter

adult, 1.15 m

nominate *felina* throughout rest of range, but often considered monotypic. Sometimes placed in the genus *Lontra* with the American river otters.

When wet Marine Otter's coat is silkier, patternless, and paler and shinier.

DISTRIBUTION & POPULATION Southern S America from C Peru (around Chimbote) south to Chile and Argentina, in Tierra del Fuego and Cape Horn, and perhaps still Staten Is. May penetrate inland rivers, perhaps to 650 m asl. Absent from E Strait of Magellan. Prefers exposed, rocky coasts. *Population* No estimates.

ECOLOGY Very poorly known. Primarily diurnal. *Diving* Usually near rocky seaweed and may descend 30–50m (mostly to 15–30 sec). *Diet* Fish, crustaceans, molluscs, freshwater prawns, sea urchins and marine worms. Not observed using tools like other otters. *Reproduction* Sexually mature at 2–3 yrs. Mating system unknown, but ♂♂ apparently territorial (thus perhaps monogamous); mating occurs Dec–Jan. Gives birth to 2–4 (5) pups in caves or crevices in Jan–Mar after 60–120 days gestation (delayed implanting). Pups remain with both ads for up to 10 months. *Lifespan* Unknown.

Marine Otter in its undisturbed coastal habitat; most populations are currently declining as a result of habitat destruction, hunting and fishery bycatch.

Glossary

Technical terms for anatomical features of marine mammals are not listed here for reasons of space. See Topography drawings on inside front cover.

Amphipods Major food source of baleen whales; amphipods are a family of crustaceans.

Antarctic Convergence Dynamic boundary between cold, southern polar waters and temperate seas, situated at slightly higher or lower latitudes according to season and/or longitude.

Axilla The region around the posterior base of the flipper in a cetacean (plural axillae).

Balaenopterid A rorqual or baleen whale (i.e. family Balaenopteridae).

Baleen Series of comb-like plates, suspended from upper jaws of mysticete whales, on which fibres guide zooplankton and small fish into the mouth, functioning like a sieve.

Benthic Bottom-dwelling organisms.

Blackfish A descriptive name given to pilot whales and superficially similar species.

Blow Cloud of warm, moist air expelled from the blowhole of a cetacean on surfacing.

Bow-riding Some dolphins habitually use the pressure waves associated with the head of a moving vessel or large whale, or to some extent behind (wake-riding).

Breaching A leap clear, or virtually so, of the water by a cetacean.

Breathing hole Patch of open water in ice maintained by seals, using their teeth or foreflipper claws, to breath.

Bubble feeding Technique used by Humpback Whales to trap small fish using 'clouds' of bubbles, and usually performed cooperatively.

Bycatch That part of a fishery catch consisting of accidentally-taken animals, principally dolphins and seals.

Callosities Peculiar to right whales, callosities are raised and roughened patches of skin which appear white or greyish due to their being infested with whale lice. Their pattern varies individually.

Cephalopod A deep-water mollusc, e.g. squid and octopus, with large head and eyes, and tentacles around the mouth. May or may not have a shell.

Continental shelf The submerged part of a continental landmass (up to 180 m below the surface) which extends up to 800 km from land, beyond which the continental slope may reach huge depths.

Countershading Camouflaged skin coloration, darker dorsally and paler ventrally, which when viewed from above may lead to the animal appearing invisible, or at least harder to see.

CITES The Convention on International Trade in Endangered Species (CITES) of Wild Fauna and Flora was signed in Geneva in 1973, to regulate trade in threatened plants and animals.

Cookie-cutter Shark Small tropical-water shark (*Isistius brasiliensis*) that temporarily attaches itself to cetaceans using its teeth. The resulting wounds are round or oval-shaped.

Copepods Eaten by some baleen whales, these are tiny, shrimp-like crustaceans.

Delphinid Member of the dolphins (toothed whales), i.e. of the family Delphinidae.

Demersal Animals that occur close to the seabed.

Diatoms Tiny phytoplankton covering parts of the bodies of some cetaceans, and discolouring them.

Drift-net Fishery net suspended vertically to catch swimming or drifting animals.

El Niño El Niño Southern Oscillation (ENSO) events occur in the eastern Pacific comparatively regularly. They result in current changes, sea temperature increases and declines in upwelling, with resulting loss of food for birds and marine mammals. ENSO events may produce short-lived, 'knock-on' climatic and environmental changes almost worldwide.

Falcate Refers to the dorsal fin being back-curved or sickle-shaped.

Fast-ice Floating ice that is attached to a landmass.

Filter feeding A process, particularly characteristic of baleen whales, whereby water is strained through the baleen (or in Crabeater Seals the teeth) to ensnare prey.

Gill-net Type of drift-net in which fish (and other species) are entrapped by the mesh, entangling their gills or other body parts.

Genus A grouping containing one or more species which forms a subset of a family (plural genera).

Gulp feeding Process by which baleen whales intake huge volumes of seawater (distending the throat) and swallow the attendant prey, following expulsion of the water through the baleen.

Haul-out Site used by pinnipeds to rest (or moult) ashore, or the process by which they do so.

IUCN International Union for the Conservation of Nature and Natural Resources, founded in 1948, is best known for producing Red Lists of endangered species.

International Whaling Commission (IWC) Formed in 1946 to oversee the whaling industry and the animals' conservation. Membership is open to any state that wishes to adhere to the International Convention for the Regulation of Whaling.

Krill (also known as euphasiids) Small, shrimp-like crustaceans that form the bulk of zooplankton. Important food source for whales in Antarctica.

Lanugo White, woolly coat of hair around a foetus and occasionally retained post-birth in seals.

Lobtailing The habit of some whales and dolphins of slapping the water with the flukes.

Logging Period of rest whilst a cetacean floats virtually motionless at the surface.

Longline fishing Type of fishing that uses baited hooks for tuna, sharks etc., set on long lines over large expanses of ocean.

Lunge feeding Some baleen whales rush to the water surface, mouth wide open to ensnare prey, giving rise to this expression.

Mass-stranding An event whereby some numbers of cetaceans come ashore.

Mesopelagic Midwater organism, i.e. neither surface- nor bottom-dwelling.

Mesoplodonts Beaked whales of the genus *Mesoplodon*.

Mouthline Front tip of jaws to corners of mouth. Some dolphins have 'smiling' mouthlines.

Otariid One of the eared seals, i.e. fur seals and sea lions (the Otariidae).

Pack-ice Sea-ice which habitually shifts to some degree.

Pair bond Close relationship between ♂ and ♀, principally for the purpose of rearing young.

Phocid Species of true seal (of the family Phocidae).

Pinniped Any member of the Phocidae (phocids), Otariidae (otariids) and Odobenidae (Walrus).

Plankton Surface organisms that habitually drift or swim en masse. Animal forms are referred to as zooplankton and include krill. Plant forms are referred to as Phytoplankton.

Pod Socially affiliated group of cetaceans.

Porpoising Low, arcing leaps above the surface, made by some pinnipeds and many cetaceans.

Red tide Red to reddish-brown surface-water discoloration (also called toxic water bloom) caused by large concentrations of tiny organisms, especially toxic dinoflagellates.

Roll On surfacing to breathe, many marine mammals initially expose the nostrils before arching the back to submerge themselves, a movement known as 'rolling'.

Rooster tail Some porpoises and dolphins surface at speed, creating a spray of water (a 'rooster tail').

Rostrum The upper jaw of a cetacean, but also sometimes (although not in this work) used in reference to the entire beak, i.e. both jaws.

Sirenian A member of the order Sirenia (i.e. the Dugong and manatees).

Spermacetic organ A cavity filled with liquid wax located in the head of Sperm Whale (and a handful of other species), which is highly prized in the production of cosmetics.

Splashguard Protuberance immediately ahead of the blowholes in a baleen whale that prevents water entering via the breathing holes.

Spyhopping Habit of some cetaceans of raising the head to beyond eye level above the water and then rotating the body as if scanning the surroundings.

Tail-slapping See Lobtailing.

Taxon Any taxonomic unit; can refer to subspecies (the most frequent use in this guide), species, genus or even family (plural taxa).

Transient Non-permanent, often refers to a migrant.

Tubercle Knob-like protuberances, e.g. on the heads of Humpback Whales, but also on the flippers or dorsal fin of other cetaceans.

Upwelling Nutrient-rich waters forced to the surface by prevailing winds or currents.

Vestigial Refers to an organ or feature that is a mere vestige of a similar or the same, more-developed feature in an ancestral form of the animal.

Zooplankton Animal plankton.

Selected marine mammal sites

The following is a brief guide to many of the essential *and* easily accessed hotspot destinations for observing marine mammals, especially cetaceans. Opportunities for whale and dolphin watch activities are increasing in many areas and for this reason we have avoided recommending specific operations. The internet is an invaluable and constantly updated resource, whilst the summary of whale-watching sites by Carwardine *et al.* (1998), and the use of more detailed local guidebooks for certain areas, e.g. Gill & Burke (1999) for Australia and New Zealand, and Cresswell & Walker (2001) for Europe, is recommended. This section was written with help from Graeme Cresswell.

Europe

Europe might not spring to mind as a hotspot for marine mammals but there is a number of exciting destinations, and it now boasts two of the fastest-growing whale-watching areas on the planet, the Canaries and Iceland, and, due in large part to the relatively large number of observers, NW Europe has played host to a remarkable number of vagrants, including many of the northern true seals, and even Walrus.

Svalbard (Spitsbergen)

Species Walrus (best looked for late summer), Arctic Fox, Polar Bear, Bearded Seal, Ringed Seal (especially early season), Beluga (rather rare), Harp Seal (also uncommon, best looked for mid–late Jun), White-beaked Dolphin and Minke Whale.

Seasonality Best Jun–Aug, and would-be visitors are unlikely to find a suitable tour at other periods.

Main areas/activities Many cruise tour companies operate 3 to 10 days tours around, visiting a wider variety of areas in W, and NW of, Spitsbergen. Some shorter wildlife or whale-watch tours also operate.

Iceland

Species Blue Whale (late Jun–late Jul only, at least from land, and much rarer in recent years), Sei Whale, Fin Whale (scarce in shelf waters but relatively common offshore), Minke Whale, Humpback Whale, Sperm Whale, Killer Whale, Atlantic White-sided Dolphin, White-beaked Dolphin, Harbour Porpoise.

Seasonality Boreal summer, May–Sep, and best Jun–Aug.

Main areas/activities Principal ports are Húsavík (NE Iceland), where whales are sometimes even visible from town, Höfn (SE Iceland), Stykkishólmur, and Ólafsvík (Blue Whale). The latter is, arguably, the best site in Iceland. Whale-watch from land at W end of the Snaefellsnes Peninsula for Killer, Humpback and Minke Whales, and White-beaked Dolphin. Keflavík (SW Iceland) is just 30 min drive from Reykjavik and has White-beaked Dolphins and Minke Whales, with Killer and Humpback Whales occasional.

Further tips Whale-watching out of Húsavík is easily combined with birdwatching at Lake Myvatn.

Norway

Species Sperm Whale, Fin Whale, Minke Whale, Long-finned Pilot Whale, Killer Whale, Atlantic White-sided Dolphin, White-beaked Dolphin, Harbour Porpoise.

Seasonality Late May–Sep for most species but late Oct–Dec for Killer Whale (varies).

Main areas/activities Andenes (Andøy Island) for Sperm Whale and most other species, and Tysfjord in Oct–Dec for Killer Whale.

Further tips Sightings of the principal two species, Sperm and Killer Whales almost guaranteed in season.

Britain & Ireland

Species Minke Whale, Northern Bottlenose Whale (rare), Long-finned Pilot Whale, Risso's Dolphin, Killer Whale, Common Bottlenose Dolphin, White-beaked Dolphin, Atlantic White-sided Dolphin, Short-beaked Common Dolphin, Harbour Porpoise, Grey Seal, Harbour Seal. Small numbers of Fin and Humpback Whales currently annual off S Ireland, usually arriving spring and present until Dec, with peak numbers autumn. Often visible from prominent headlands such as Galley Head and Old Head of Kinsale, and Cape Clear I.

Seasonality Apr–Oct, but Jun–Sep best, especially in Northern and Western Isles, but some dolphins year-round.

Main areas/activities Hebrides, Orkney, Shetland and Moray Firth (Scotland), Cornwall (England), Cardigan Bay and Dyfed (Wales), and Co. Cork and Co. Kerry (Ireland). Many opportunities for land-based viewing, and whale-watching companies operate from several ports.
Further tips Many national and regional bird information services provide up-to-date information concerning cetacean sightings, including rare visitors.

Bay of Biscay

Species Blue Whale (rare), Sei Whale, Fin Whale, Humpback Whale (rare), Minke Whale, Sperm Whale, Northern Bottlenose Whale, Cuvier's Beaked Whale, Sowerby's Beaked Whale (very rare), True's Beaked Whale (very rare), Common Bottlenose Dolphin, Short-beaked Common Dolphin, White-beaked Dolphin (rare), Atlantic White-sided Dolphin (rare), Long-finned Pilot Whale, False Killer Whale (very rare), Killer Whale, Risso's Dolphin, Striped Dolphin and Harbour Porpoise.
Seasonality Interesting species seen year-round but summer to early autumn (Jun–Sep) probably best, especially for large whales.
Main areas/activities Ferries operate from two ports in SW England – Plymouth and Portsmouth, to Santander and Bilbao, in Spain.
Further tips As these are car ferries, it is possible to organise a trip to the Pyrenees or Picos de Europa for birdwatching in conjunction with a Biscay crossing or, alternatively, seek local boatmen willing to make day trips to deep continental shelf waters off Spain. Visit www.biscay-dolphin.org.uk for weekly reports and useful links.

Canaries, Madeira and Azores

Species Sperm Whale, Bryde's Whale, Short-finned Pilot Whale, Blainville's, Cuvier's and other beaked whales (including Sowerby's in the Azores), Common Bottlenose Dolphin, Risso's Dolphin, Short-beaked Common Dolphin, Striped Dolphin, Atlantic Spotted Dolphin. Many others possible, and Fin and Sei Whales are annual, albeit quite scarce. Rough-toothed Dolphin scarce but regular year-round off Gran Canaria and La Gomera. False Killer Whale is irregular.
Seasonality Year-round, but May–Oct is best in the Azores.
Main areas/activities Most islands in the Canaries offer tours, with Tenerife most popular but El Hierro, La Gomera and Lanzarote best for beaked whales. Gran Canaria is probably the best island in the Canaries for variety of dolphins. Pico and Faial are the main islands offering tours in the Azores, and both also have opportunities for land-based observations, e.g. at Vigia da Queimada.

Mediterranean

Species Fin Whale, Sperm Whale, Cuvier's Beaked Whale, Long-finned Pilot Whale, False Killer Whale (rare), Killer Whale (Strait of Gibraltar), Common Bottlenose Dolphin, Risso's Dolphin, Short-beaked Common Dolphin, Striped Dolphin.
Seasonality Year-round, but Jun–Sep best.
Main areas/activities Gibraltar (Spain) for dolphins, Toulon (France) and San Remo and Imperia (Italy) for Fin Whale, and Kalamar Is (Greece) for chance of Sperm and Cuvier's Beaked Whales. Half-day, full-day and some multi-day tours available; also Porto Sole (Italy); Almería or Barcelona (Spain); Kalamos Island (Greece); and Veli Losinj (Croatia).
Further tips Unfortunately, the animal that takes its name from this sea, the Mediterranean Monk Seal, is now extremely rare and (extremely) unlikely to be seen by the casual visitor. False Killer Whale is very local in the W Mediterranean.

Eastern North America

One of the most exciting parts of the world for cetaceans, this region boasts such renowned 'sites' as the Gulf of St Lawrence and NE Maritimes where the accent is on large whales, some high-arctic mammals, and difficult species such as Northern Bottlenose Whale. Several sites offer good land-based viewing options and, at the other end of the scale, there is the possibility to swim with Atlantic Spotted Dolphins in the Bahamas.

Greenland

Species Fin Whale, Sei Whale, Minke Whale, Humpback Whale, Bowhead Whale (rare), Northern Bottlenose Whale, Narwhal, Beluga, Killer Whale, Harbour Porpoise, many seals, Walrus, Polar Bear.

Seasonality Jun–Oct but weather can be poor after Aug, although some of the more exciting species, including Narwhal and Bowhead Whale, may be commoner later in the season. Best for Humpbacks is Jul–Sep.
Main areas/activities Paamiut (SW Greenland), Disko Bay (W Greenland) and Melville Bay (NW Greenland). Hooded and Harp Seals moult in large numbers on the ice S and SE of Greenland from late Jul.
Further tips Rather remote and expensive to visit, those in search of the high-arctic specialties will probably find a trip to Canada easier and more affordable.

Churchill (Canada)

Species Beluga, Polar Bear.
Seasonality Beluga from Jun, Polar Bear from early Jul, but Sep–Nov best for latter.
Main areas/activities Several tours can be booked in the town. Trips to the breeding grounds of Harp and Hooded Seals can be organised in Feb/Mar.
Further tips If you wish to see both key species, Aug is probably the best month.

Gulf of St Lawrence (Canada)

Species Blue Whale, Fin Whale, Minke Whale, Humpback Whale, Beluga, Killer Whale, Atlantic White-sided Dolphin, White-beaked Dolphin, Harbour Porpoise.
Seasonality Jun–Nov, with the greatest variety of species probably Aug onwards.
Main areas/activities Tadoussac (N shore) is the main centre, and Mingan (extreme northern gulf) is also well set-up for whale-watching tourists but there are many good watchpoints along the N and, to a lesser extent, the S shore. Half-day, full-day and multi-day tours available; also try Baie-Ste-Catherine, Grandes-Bergeronnes, Les Escoumins, Godbout, Baie-Comeau, Baie-Trinite or Pointes-des-Monts (St Lawrence River); Mingan or Havre-Saint-Pierre (Gulf of St Lawrence); Gaspé or Rivière-du-Renard (Gaspé Peninsula).
Further tips Off Mingan it is possible to observe cetacean research in action, but conditions can be quite rugged.

The Maritimes (Canada)

Species Blue Whale (rare), Fin Whale, Sei Whale, Minke Whale, North Atlantic Right Whale, Humpback Whale, Sperm Whale, Northern Bottlenose Whale, Long-finned Pilot Whale, Killer Whale, Atlantic White-sided Dolphin, White-beaked Dolphin, Common Bottlenose Dolphin.
Seasonality Jun–early Nov, with Aug onwards best for North Atlantic Right Whale, but dolphins year-round (best in summer).
Main areas/activities Grand Manan Is (New Brunswick), multi-day trips off Nova Scotia, and good land-based watching possible off St John's (Newfoundland). Half-day, full-day and multi-day tours available; also try Leonardville or Fredericton (New Brunswick); Halifax, Tiverton, Cheticamp or Capstick (Nova Scotia); Westport (Brier Is); St Johns's, Bay Bulls, Trinity or Twillingate (Newfoundland).
Further tips The 'Gully', *c.*160 km off Nova Scotia, is one of *the* places to see Northern Bottlenose Whale, but is difficult to access for casual visitors. A trip to the Maritimes might be considered as part of a two-centre holiday also including the Gulf of St Lawrence for those with more time.

New England (USA)

Species Fin Whale, Minke Whale, North Atlantic Right Whale, Humpback Whale, Long-finned Pilot Whale, Atlantic White-sided Dolphin, Harbour Porpoise, Harbour Seal, Grey Seal.
Seasonality Apr–Oct, but Jun onwards perhaps, and North Atlantic Right Whale occurs year-round in Gulf of Maine.
Main areas/activities The main area is the Stellwagen Bank between Cape Cod (Massachusetts) and Cape Ann (Boston), but for North Atlantic Right Whale, Lubec (Maine) may be the best bet Aug–Sep.
Further tips Seabirding also productive and several species of sea turtles are present year-round.

Florida (USA) and the Bahamas

Species Sperm Whale, Humpback Whale, Short-finned Pilot Whale, False Killer Whale, chance of beaked whales, Common Bottlenose Dolphin, Atlantic Spotted Dolphin, Rough-toothed Dolphin, West Indian Manatee.

Seasonality May–Sep best, but most dolphins occur year-round.
Main areas/activities Key West (Florida) and Grand Bahama and Great Abaco (Bahamas) for pelagic trips (up to 11 days long), and the Florida Keys and Sarasota, on the Gulf coast, for land-based viewing.
Further tips Bear in mind the hurricane season commences Sep.

Western North America

The Pacific coast of North America boasts as many exciting cetacean-watching opportunities as the Atlantic side, and also has quite a number of pinnipeds, some of them of rather restricted range. Whilst in the east the main focus is on the northern sites in the boreal summer, on this seaboard it is watching large whales (and a range of other marine mammals) on their wintering grounds in the southern North Pacific that has attracted most attention. Nonetheless, areas in British Columbia and, further north, in Alaska, offer some fine whale-watching possibilities in the boreal summer, even if they are somewhat overshadowed by localities at the same latitude on the east coast.

Alaska (USA)

Species Bowhead Whale (rare), Fin Whale, Minke Whale, Humpback Whale, Killer Whale, Pacific White-sided Dolphin, Dall's Porpoise, Harbour Porpoise, Harbour Seal, Steller's Sea Lion, Sea Otter.
Seasonality Jun–early Sep.
Main areas/activities Glacier Bay and Gustavus, but several other ports offer cruises and long-range trips operate from as far afield as California.
Further tips Dedicated whale-watch trips are highly recommended whilst cruise ships are the only means of access to some remote areas.

British Columbia (Canada)

Species Gray Whale, Humpback Whale, Killer Whale, Pacific White-sided Dolphin, Dall's Porpoise, Harbour Porpoise, Harbour Seal, California Sea Lion, Steller's Sea Lion, Sea Otter.
Seasonality Principally May–Sep for most species, but Mar–Apr for migrant Gray Whales.
Main areas/activities Vancouver Is, with many tours commencing Telegraph Cove, tours from Udulet and Tofino best for Gray Whale. Half-day, full-day and multi-day tours available; try Alert Bay, Telegraph Cove, Port McNeill, Sointula, Victoria or Nanaimo (British Columbia); Anacortes, Bellingham, Friday Harbour or Seattle (Puget Sound area)

California–Washington (USA)

Species Blue Whale, Gray Whale, Humpback Whale, Fin Whale, Minke Whale, Baird's and Cuvier's Beaked Whales, Pacific White-sided Dolphin, Risso's Dolphin, Northern Right Whale Dolphin, Dall's Porpoise, Harbour Porpoise, Northern Elephant Seal, California Sea Lion. Both Long-beaked and Short-beaked Common Dolphins are seen in numbers off S & C California. The former is more abundant in winter, the latter in summer and autumn.
Seasonality Year-round, but seasonal peaks: Aug–Oct best off California, Dec–Sep elsewhere, especially for Gray Whale.
Main areas/activities Many localities off California, including San Juan Is, but those in Monterey Bay, Bodega Bay (Cordell Bank) and Channel Is (Santa Barbara) usually best, with fewer ports in Oregon (e.g. Charleston) and Washington (Westport).
Further tips The key season off C California is also an excellent period for seabirds.

Baja California (Mexico)

Species Blue Whale, Sei Whale (rare), Bryde's Whale, Fin Whale, Minke Whale, Gray Whale, Humpback Whale, Sperm Whale, Short-finned Pilot Whale, Common Bottlenose Dolphin, Pacific White-sided Dolphin, Short-beaked Common Dolphin, Gulf of California Porpoise, Guadalupe Fur Seal.
Seasonality Some species present year-round, but Jan–Apr best when the large whales are present.
Main areas/activities 1–2-week tours from San Diego and La Paz arguably best, but land-based watching from Magdalen Bay productive. For Gulf of California Porpoise take a boat from Puerto Penasco.
Further tips Baja California is an increasingly popular destination for whale-watchers.

Hawaii (USA)

Species Fin Whale, Bryde's Whale (rare), Humpback Whale, Sperm Whale, Pgymy and Dwarf Sperm Whales, Blainville's Beaked Whale (one of the best places in the world to see this species), False Killer Whale, Melon-headed Whale, Pygmy Killer Whale, Short-finned Pilot Whale, Common Bottlenose Dolphin, Rough-toothed and Striped Dolphins (both rare), Hawaiian Spinner Dolphin, Pantropical Spotted Dolphin, Hawaiian Monk Seal.
Seasonality Year-round for most species, but late Dec–Apr (especially Feb–Mar) for Humpback Whales.
Main areas/activities Tours available from many islands, but those out of Maui best for Humpbacks.

Latin America

Whilst this region might not possess the high profile some of the other regions enjoy for cetacean watching, e.g. Australia and New Zealand, and North America, it boasts some fine areas for marine mammal viewing. Dedicated whale-watching trips are, however, still in their relative infancy in Latin America, although trips into Caribbean waters are being offered with increasing frequency, but in the extreme south, in Argentina, it is possible to combine land-based viewing of Southern Elephant Seals and Southern Sea Lions ashore with Southern Right and Killer Whales close inshore, whilst general ecotours to the Galápagos may also prove rewarding, if carefully chosen, for those interested in cetaceans and pinnipeds. Jungle tours to the Amazon, again if carefully selected, also offer the chance to see some of the remarkable freshwater 'marine' mammals.

Caribbean

Species Humpback Whale, Sperm Whale, Pygmy Sperm Whale, Dwarf Sperm Whale, Short-finned Pilot Whale, False Killer Whale, Melon-headed Whale, Killer Whale, Common Bottlenose Dolphin, Atlantic Spotted Dolphin, Risso's Dolphin, Spinner Dolphin, Clymene Dolphin, Fraser's Dolphin (especially off Dominica).
Seasonality Virtually year-round, but some differences between islands, Jan–Apr for Humpback Whale.
Main areas/activities Dominican Republic (Humpback Whale), Puerto Rico, Guadeloupe, Dominica (one of the widest varieties of species), Martinique, St Vincent, Grenada. Half-day, full-day and multi-day tours available; try Samaná, Puerto Plata, Santa Domingo (Dominican Republic); Rincon (Puerto Rico); Long Bay, St Thomas (US Virgin Is); Road Town, Tortola (British Virgin Is); Le Moule (Guadeloupe); Carbet (Martinique); Arnos Vale (St Vincent); and St George's or Carriacou (Grenada).
Further tips The N Caribbean is one of the best areas in the world for listening to 'singing' Humpback Whales.

Ecuador and the Galápagos

Species Bryde's Whale, Humpback Whale, Sperm Whale, False Killer Whale, Killer Whale, Common Bottlenose Dolphin, Spinner Dolphin, Striped Dolphin, Risso's Dolphin, Pantropical Spotted Dolphin, Galápagos Fur Seal, Galápagos Sea Lion.
Seasonality Year-round in Galápagos, but principally Mar–Aug, and Dec–May in mainland Ecuador, though Humpback Whale only present Jun–mid-Sep.
Main areas/activities Isla La Plata (Humpback Whale), Machalilla National Park and nearby areas, Guayaquil, Galápagos. Half-day, full-day and multi-day tours available; also try Puerto Lopez or Salango (mainland Ecuador).

Brazil

Species Southern Right Whale, Humpback Whale, Common Bottlenose Dolphin, Spinner Dolphin, Amazon River Dolphin, Tucuxi, Franciscana, Amazonian Manatee.
Seasonality Year-round in Amazonia, although best in dry season when animals more concentrated, and for dolphins on coast, but Jun–Dec for large whales.
Main areas/activities Manaus (Amazonas), Santa Catarina Is (Santa Catarina), Abrolhos National Marine Park (Bahia) and Fernando do Noronha (Pernambuco). Santa Catarina Is good for Tucuxi (year-round) and Southern Right Whale (Jun–Sep/Oct), whilst Abrolhos archipelago best visited Jun–Dec for Humpbacks.
Further tips Amazonian species can also be found in Colombia, Ecuador and Peru.

Argentina and Chile

Species Southern Right Whale, Killer Whale, Commerson's Dolphin, Dusky Dolphin, Peale's Dolphin, Burmeister's Porpoise, South American Sea Lion, Southern Elephant Seal.
Seasonality Mid Jul–Dec for Southern Right Whale, year-round for Killer Whale, southern dolphins best Dec–Mar.
Main areas/activities Peninsula Valdés, Puerto Deseado (Argentina) and Punto Delgado/Strait of Magellan (Argentina/Chile).
Further tips Boat trips available at Peninsula Valdés but excellent views of most species from shore. The area is also excellent for birdwatching.

Australia and New Zealand

These countries are rightly regarded amongst the premier destinations for marine mammal watching in the world. They possess several endemic cetaceans and pinnipeds, and between them offer the chance of seeing a remarkable range of more widespread temperate and subtropical species. Numerous dedicated cetacean (particularly whale) watching pelagic trips are offered, but landlubbers are well favoured too, with some fine possibilities for shore-based viewing, especially in Australia. If the range of options described below is insufficient, New Zealand also acts as a gateway to E Antarctica and several subantarctic islands. For those with real time (and money) at their disposal a visit to this part of the world really could offer the marine mammal trip of a lifetime, although it might be added that trips to the Antarctic Peninsula from southern South America are cheaper and, if fortuitously timed with productive (and calm) crossings of the Drake Passage, potentially even more productive for cetacean 'buffs'.

Western Australia

Species Blue Whale, Bryde's Whale, Minke Whale, Dwarf Minke Whale, Southern Right Whale, Humpback Whale, Common Bottlenose Dolphin, Indo-Pacific Humpback Dolphin, Irrawaddy Dolphin, Spinner Dolphin, Dugong, Australian Sea Lion, New Zealand Fur Seal (occasional).
Seasonality Varies slightly with locality but chiefly May–Oct for Southern Right Whale, and Jun–Jul /Sep–Nov for Humpback Whale. Year-round for other species.
Main areas/activities The best areas include the Augusta and Perth regions, the famous Monkey Mia, where you can wade in the shallows with Common Bottlenose Dolphins, and Broome, which perhaps attracts the widest range of species. Land-based whale watching and boat trips of various durations available from Perth, South Perth, Hillary's Harbour, Fremantle, Geraldton, Exmouth, Carnarvon, Albany and Denham. In Monkey Mia there is land-based watching only.

Southern Australia

Species Blue Whale, Fin Whale, Sei Whale, Bryde's Whale, Minke Whale, Southern Right Whale, Sperm Whale, Humpback Whale, Short-finned Pilot Whale, False Killer Whale, Killer Whale, Common Bottlenose Dolphin, Dusky Dolphin, Southern Right-whale Dolphin, Australian Fur Seal, Australian Sea Lion.
Seasonality Most species year-round but large whales seasonal, Southern Right Whale chiefly May–Oct and Humpback Whale May–Jul and Oct–Dec.
Main areas/activities Warrnambool (Victoria) is a shore-based watchpoint, arguably the best in the state, whilst Coles Bay and Bruny Is (Tasmania), and Adelaide and the Head of Bight (South Australia) are also good, with the latter sometimes billed as the best land-based whale-watch site in the world. Half- and full-day boat trips also available.

Eastern Australia

Species Blue Whale, Fin Whale, Minke Whale, Dwarf Minke Whale, Bryde's Whale, Southern Right Whale, Humpback Whale, Short-finned Pilot Whale, False Killer Whale, Killer Whale, Risso's Dolphin, beaked whales, Common Bottlenose Dolphin, Indo-Pacific Humpback Dolphin, Dugong, Australian Fur Seal.
Seasonality Year-round for most dolphins, but Jul–Sep best in Queensland when Humpback and Dwarf Minke Whales are present, and this period also best in New South Wales where Southern Right Whale is also present May–Oct.
Main areas/activities Cairns–Port Douglas (best for Dwarf Minke and Bryde's Whales), Hervey Bay

(Humpback Whale) and the Brisbane area (all Queensland), and Byron Bay (one of the best sites in Australia for seeing Humpbacks from land), Sydney (has the advantage of easy access), Wollongong (deep-water cruises available, also excellent for birds), and Eden (all New South Wales).
Further tips In Queensland tours available Airlie Beach, Bundaberg, Hervey Bay or Tangalooma; in New South Wales, from Byron Bay, Coff's Harbour, Eden, Fairy Meadow or Wollongong.

New Zealand

Species Bryde's Whale, Sperm Whale, Killer Whale, False Killer Whale (rare), Long-finned Pilot Whale, Common Bottlenose Dolphin, Short-beaked Common Dolphin, Dusky Dolphin, Hector's Dolphin, Southern Right-whale Dolphin (occasional), New Zealand Fur Seal.
Seasonality Year-round for dolphins and Sperm Whale off Kaikoura, but Apr–Jul best for latter species.
Main areas/activities Kaikoura (South Is) is arguably one of the best sites in the world for cetaceans (and seabirds), and those with limited time are advised to head there, but Hector's Dolphin also easily seen around the Banks Peninsula (South Is), and Paihia (North Is) can be worth a visit with boat tours year-round.

Indian Ocean and Asia

Only just developing as a region for cetacean watchers, the Maldives, in particular, has quickly become one of the ultimate destinations in the world to head for.

Maldives

Species *Common*: Spinner Dolphin, Common Bottlenose Dolphin, Risso's Dolphin, Spotted Dolphin, Short-finned Pilot Whale and Dwarf Sperm Whale. *Regular*: Striped Dolphin, Fraser's Dolphin, Melon-headed Whale, False Killer Whale, Cuvier's Beaked Whale, Tropical Bottlenose Whale and Bryde's Whale. *Less common*: Blue Whale, Humpback Whale, Sperm Whale, Pygmy Killer Whale, Killer Whale, Blainville's Beaked Whale, Ginkgo-toothed Beaked Whale and Rough-toothed Dolphin.
Seasonality Year-round for dolphins, but Blue Whale Nov–Apr. Calmest weather usually late Jan–Apr and Oct–Nov.
Main areas/activities Entire country, but Melon-headed Whale only common in S, not in N.
Further tips A specialised cetacean-watching live-aboard 'safari' cruise offers the best chance of many encounters with a number of different species. Alternatively, for those seeking just the odd encounter as part of a beach or diving holiday, some resorts offer evening boat trips to see Spinner Dolphins.

Sri Lanka

Species Sperm Whale, Blue Whale, Bryde's Whale, Humpback Whale, Spinner Dolphin, Spotted Dolphin, Striped Dolphin, Common Bottlenose Dolphin, Risso's Dolphin, Short-finned Pilot Whale, Fraser's Dolphin and False Killer Whale.
Seasonality Year-round for dolphins. Trincomalee (E coast): best for weather and large whales, Feb–Apr. S coast: best in Mar. W coast: best weather Dec–Mar.
Main areas/activities Day and half-day boat trips. E coast offers best chance of large whales, with facilities currently being developed and should be open for 2006 season. W coast has well-developed tourist infrastructure, but visitors need to arrange own boats.
Further tips Do not visit without taking some time to view the magnificent wildlife on land and spectacular historic monuments.

Japan

Species Bryde's Whale, Humpback Whale, Sperm Whale, Killer Whale, False Killer Whale, Pygmy Killer Whale, Melon-headed Whale, Short-finned Pilot Whale, Risso's Dolphin, Common Bottlenose Dolphin, Spinner Dolphin, Pacific White-sided Dolphin, Rough-toothed Dolphin, Striped Dolphin, Fraser's Dolphin (rare), Northern Right Whale Dolphin, Dall's Porpoise.
Seasonality Year-round for dolphins, but Feb–Apr best for Humpbacks off Ogasawara and Okinawa, May–Sep for Bryde's Whales off Kochi Prefecture, and Mar–Dec for Sperm Whales in same area.
Main areas/activities Ogasawara (Bonin) Is, Okinawa, Ogata (Kochi Prefecture).
Further tips Ogata, close to Tokyo, is arguably amongst the best places in the world for Bryde's Whale.

Conservation checklist

Although primarily a field guide, it is impossible to ignore the great damage that Man has had (and continues to have) on many species covered by this book. Thus, the objective of this list is to provide both the most widely recognised systematic order of the main groups and up-to-date taxonomic status for all species and selected subspecies, *and* their conservation status, together with a brief description of the main threats facing the various forms. We also recommend reading the overview chapter dealing with Conservation in the introduction (p. 15). For details of each species' range, see the individual species accounts.

Nomenclature and systematic order principally follows Rice (1998), with some additions and changes based on recent publications in the technical literature. Recently extinct taxa are denoted by an asterisk (*). As mentioned elsewhere, even mid-level relationships within some families are in considerable flux as molecular techniques throw new light on existing perceptions. It is obvious that the list of the world's marine mammals might be subject to considerable refinement: (a) in the number of species (which is likely to grow, both through the recognition of previously undescribed taxa and the reassessment of taxa currently considered subspecies), (b) in the number of recognised genera and families (both of which may decrease), and (c) by the reclassification of some species, genera and even families, which may lead to changes in the overall order in which different species or groupings appear in such a list.

Some of the current threats to marine mammals include continued hunting, e.g. almost 27,000 whales have been hunted by Norway, Iceland and Japan since the moratorium on whaling in 1986, and more than 300,000 cetaceans are estimated to die each year as a result of bycatch. Pollutants in the food chain reduce reproductive health. Vessel collisions are also an ongoing threat, but the numbers of animals struck is impossible to estimate. Ocean noise is becoming an increasing problem for all marine mammals, as is climate change, habitat degradation and prey competition. Human disturbance is also on the rise as a result of unregulated marine mammal viewing.

This list was prepared with the collaboration of William Perrin (Southwest Fisheries Science Center, NOAA, USA), Regina Asmutis-Silvia (WDCS) and Guy Kirwan.

Conservation status

Critically Endangered (CR): extremely high risk of extinction in the immediate future

Endangered (EN): very high risk of extinction in the near future

Vulnerable (VU): high risk of extinction in the medium-term future

Lower Risk (LR): species that qualify under one of the following categories:

Conservation Dependent (CD): the focus of species- or habitat-specific conservation, the cessation of which would result in it qualifying for one of the first three categories

Near Threatened (NT): species that does not qualify as Conservation Dependent, but close to Vulnerable

Least Concern (LC): species that does not qualify as Conservation Dependent or Near Threatened

Data Deficient (DD): insufficient data to make a direct, or indirect, assessment of its risk of extinction

Not Evaluated (NE): conservation status not assessed.

Conservation status follows the most recent (2004) listing by IUCN, but several taxa were not considered therein. In addition, all cetaceans, all sirenians and several marine carnivores (seals, otters, Walrus and Polar Bear) are protected under CITES (Convention on International Trade in Endangered Species).

Order Carnivora

Suborder Pinnipedia Pinnipeds – fur seals, Walrus, sea lions and true seals

Thirty-three to 36 modern species, with 1 recently extinct, in 3 modern families and 22 genera. Of these families, the Otariidae are referred to as eared seals because the ears possess external flaps, whilst the other large family within this suborder, the Phocidae, lacks such flaps. The Odobenidae, represented in the present only by the Walrus, is midway between the others, in that it lacks ear flaps, possesses foreflippers much like eared seals and hindflippers similar to those of phocids, although the latter are capable of being rotated.

Family Otariidae – fur seals and sea lions (eared seals)

South African Fur Seal *Arctocephalus pusillus* (includes *A. p. pusillus* **South African Fur Seal** and *A. p. doriferus* **Australian Fur Seal**) **LR/LC** South African increasing (numbers controlled by regulated sealing); Australian stable or locally increasing.

Antarctic Fur Seal *Arctocephalus gazella* **LR/LC** Still locally increasing or stable and protected in many areas. Most mortality is caused by entanglement in fishing nets and other debris.

Subantarctic Fur Seal *Arctocephalus tropicalis* **LR/LC** Numbers mostly increasing, except on Crozet, and now protected.

Guadalupe Fur Seal *Arctocephalus townsendi* **VU** 10,000. Formerly bred elsewhere off California, but commercial hunting decimated species almost to extinction. Poaching and disturbance continue on Guadalupe, which was designated a sanctuary in 1975, but protected in US waters.

Juan Fernández Fur Seal *Arctocephalus philippii* **VU** *c.*12,000. Harvested from 1687 and feared extinct by 1900, but rediscovered in 1965. Protected since 1978, but small-scale poaching by fisherman continues on Más Afuera Is.

New Zealand Fur Seal *Arctocephalus forsteri* **LR/LC** Currently increasing, though some licensed sealing is permitted and quite large numbers die in trawl fishery nets.

South American Fur Seal *Arctocephalus australis* **LR/LC** Numbers fluctuate as a result of El Niño events, and probably declining in some areas, e.g. Peru.

Galápagos Fur Seal *Arctocephalus galapagoensis* **VU** *c.*40,000 in 1988. Commercial exploitation commenced early 1800s and continued until 1934, by when virtually extinct. Well protected since 1959, when most islands included within a national park. A no-fishing zone, established around the archipelago in 1998, is subject to frequent violation.

Northern Fur Seal *Callorhinus ursinus* **VU** *c.*1.2 million, most on Pribilofs (74%). Previously 2.5 million in 1950s but declined 1956–83, and has decreased since 1990 at 2% p.a. Commercial harvesting continued until 1911 and subsistence harvests still permitted on Pribilofs. Most important threats are bycatch in derelict fishing nets and extraction of prey resources by commercial fishing operations.

California Sea Lion *Zalophus californianus* (includes *Z. c. californianus* **California Sea Lion**, *Z. c. wollebaeki* **Galápagos Sea Lion**, and *Z. c. japonicus* **Japanese Sea Lion**) 175,000 Californian Sea Lions in 2001, with 14,000 Galápagos Sea Lions in 1998, but no reliable sightings of *japonicus* since 1950s. Commercial harvesting commenced 1800s. Protected since 1970s in USA and Mexico. Galápagos form listed as **VU**, California form as **LR/LC** and Japanese form **Extinct**.

Northern (Steller's) Sea Lion *Eumetopias jubatus* **EN** 60,000–70,000 in late 1990s but declining, presumably due to long-term environmental changes in N Pacific, increased commercial fishing and high levels of contaminants. Subsistence hunting by indigenous peoples has continued for millennia, but substantial numbers taken early 1900s and at least 45,000 pups harvested in the Aleutians in 1959–73.

Australian Sea Lion *Neophoca cinerea* **LR/LC** Stable but only 9,300–11,700, most in S Australia. Protected, but fishermen continue to kill some and others trapped in monofilament nets.

New Zealand Sea Lion *Phocarctos hookeri* **VU** Stable population currently numbers 11,100–14,000, mostly on Auckland Is. Commercially harvested from early 19th century, but protected since 1946, and all of its breeding areas are nature reserves. Diseases may produce large mortalities.

South American Sea Lion *Otaria byronia* **LR/LC** Decreasing, in part due to El Niño events but principally because of hunting. Largest numbers in Chile, where licensed exploitation still practised.

Family Odobenidae – Walrus

Walrus *Odobenus rosmarus* (includes *O. r. rosmarus*, *O. r. laptevi* and *O. r. divergens*) **LR/LC** Population estimated at *c.*220,000, with most in extreme N Pacific, but perhaps declining. Subsistence hunting continues and some are taken as bycatch.

Family Phocidae – true seals

Bearded Seal *Erignathus barbatus* **LR/LC** Estimated population 500,000, but trend unknown, though subsistence harvests appear to be main threat in many areas.

Harbour (Common) Seal *Phoca vitulina* (includes *P. v. vitulina*, *P. v. concolor*, *P. v. richardii*, *P. v. stejnegeri* and *P. v. mellonae*) **LR/LC** Perhaps 500,000. Legal hunting continues in some countries. Diseases, oil spills and competition with fisheries are all threats, and some subpopulations (e.g. in Baltic) now rare.

Largha (Spotted) Seal *Phoca largha* **LR/LC** Estimated 350,000–400,000, with low-level subsistence hunting and fisheries bycatch the only known threats.

Ringed Seal *Pusa hispida* (includes *P. h. hispida, P. h. botnica, P. h. ochotensis, P. h. ladogensis* and *P. h. saimensis*) **LR/LC** Numbers at least 2.5–4 million. Heavy pollution jeopardises Baltic population, as do poaching and fisheries bycatch for those at Lake Saimaa, and elsewhere subsistence hunters take comparatively large numbers.

Caspian Seal *Pusa caspica* **VU** Stable population of *c.*400,000 in early 1990s, but several large mortalities since (possibly 1 million early 20th century). Hunted for several centuries, but since 1970 catches regulated at fewer than 25,000 pups p.a. However, over-fishing and increasing pollution are now significant threats.

Baikal Seal *Pusa sibirica* **VU** Declining (*c.*85,000 in 2000) due, in part, to high levels of pollution, poaching, commercial harvesting and fisheries bycatch.

Grey Seal *Halichoerus grypus* **LR/LC** Increasing in Atlantic, where *c.*160,000 in NW in late 1980s, and *c.*121,000 in NE in early 1990s, but substantial decline in Baltic. Large numbers taken in early 1900s in NE Atlantic and Baltic, where pollution also a major factor, along with poaching and bycatch.

Ribbon Seal *Histriophoca fasciata* **LR/LC** Estimated 240,000 in late 1970s, with subsequent max quota of 10,000 harvested annually, and fisheries bycatch may also be significant.

Harp Seal *Pagophilus groenlandicus* **LR/LC** At least 6 million, though subsistence hunting continues in Canada, Greenland, Russia and Norway, and bycatch in fisheries also responsible for substantial deaths.

Hooded Seal *Cystophora cristata* **LR/LC** Perhaps 0.5 million, with significant numbers perhaps taken as bycatch, though hunting appears to be greatest threat.

Mediterranean Monk Seal *Monachus monachus* **CR** Perhaps just 450 in mid 1990s and in serious decline, with some still taken as bycatch and is actively hunted by fishermen, especially in Greece. Recently extirpated in Black Sea and elsewhere.

Hawaiian Monk Seal *Monachus schauinslandi* **EN** *c.*1,400 in 2000. On brink of extinction by early 20th century due to indiscriminate hunting and commercial harvesting, whilst military activities had impact on certain islands. Largest colony declining, but most subpopulations stable or increasing. Net and plastic debris are hazards for young seals, and human disturbance and competition from fisheries are other threats.

★ **West Indian Monk Seal** *Monachus tropicalis* **Extinct** (since 1952). Regularly hunted throughout 17–18th centuries, and by 1880s was extremely rare. Specific surveys since the last recorded sighting have all drawn a blank.

Southern Elephant Seal *Mirounga leonina* **LR/LC** Overall numbers 640,000 in 1990s, but declining in S Pacific and S Indian Oceans. Hunted almost to extinction in 19th and early 20th centuries, but now protected almost everywhere.

Northern Elephant Seal *Mirounga angustirostris* **LR/LC** Increasing and expanding since early 1900s, and currently perhaps over 150,000.

Weddell Seal *Leptonychotes weddellii* **LR/LC** Population 250,000–400,000 in 1980s, but perhaps 500,000–1 million, and protected since 1961. Has been little hunted for research purposes.

Ross Seal *Ommatophoca rossii* **LR/LC** Perhaps *c.*220,000 in early 1970s, but considered the least-abundant Antarctic phocid. No data on population trends, but few threats known.

Crabeater Seal *Lobodon carcinophaga* **LR/LC** Estimated 50–75 million in early 1980s and protected since 1978. Declines noted recently, perhaps because due to over-fishing of krill.

Leopard Seal *Hydrurga leptonyx* **LR/LC** Perhaps 220,000–450,000 in 1980s. Protected and subject to very little commercial fishing or research hunting.

Suborder Fissipeda

Representatives of 2 families are 'true' marine mammals: Polar Bear is the only non-terrestrial member of the Ursidae, whilst the 2 marine otters belong to the largest family within the Carnivora. The Mustelidae have their long, thin bodies and short legs well adapted for swimming. Several other otters also regularly enter marine habitats, but none is exclusively tied to them like the Marine and Sea Otters.

Family Ursidae – bears

Polar Bear *Ursus maritimus* (includes *U. m. maritimus* and *U. m. marinus*) **LR/CD** Population 22,000–27,000 in 1997; no data on trends, but contaminant levels in food chain, climate warming and subsistence hunting all pose potential threats.

Family MUSTELIDAE – weasels, otters

Marine Otter *Lutra felina* **EN** No population estimates, though possibly declining. Protected but poached for its fur and due to perceived competition with shellfish industry; fisheries bycatch also perhaps significant.

Sea Otter *Enhydra lutris* **EN** Hunted almost to extinction by 1911, and pre-exploitation population perhaps 150,000–300,000. Has recovered substantially since, though subsistence harvests, fisheries bycatch and oil spills are significant threats.

Order CETACEA Cetaceans – dolphins, porpoises and whales

Suborder MYSTICETI

The Mysticeti or mysticetes are baleen whales, all of which lack teeth. Their taxonomy is in a state of considerable flux, with probably at least 14 modern species within the 4 families and 6 genera. The largest family, the Balaenopteridae, possesses sleek, streamlined bodies and long pleats on the lower jaw, giving rise to their common vernacular name, rorquals, a corruption of a Danish word meaning 'pleated' whale. In contrast, the much stockier whales of the Balaenidae lack such pleats and any dorsal fin, and their baleen plates are very long and narrow. The other 2 families both contain single modern-day species. The Neobalaenidae appears to represent a well-diagnosed family, clearly differentiated on molecular and anatomical grounds, but the 'jury is currently out' on the Eschrichtiidae, which appears to represent only a subfamily of the Balaenopteridae according to molecular research.

Family BALAENIDAE – right whales

North Atlantic Right Whale *Eubalaena glacialis* **EN** Population just *c.*300. Once abundant, but hunted almost to extinction and currently endangered by ship strikes and entanglement with fishing gear.

North Pacific Right Whale *Eubalaena japonica* **EN** Population *c.*100, making it the most endangered great whale. Despite cessation of hunting, apparently not recovering, mainly due to continued habitat loss/modification, human disturbance and marine pollution.

Southern Right Whale *Eubalaena australis* **LR/CD** Currently increasing at *c.*7–8% p.a. Protected since 1937 but hunted by Soviet whalers until 1960s, with current threats including human disturbance, entanglement in nets, habitat degradation and over-fishing of prey species.

Bowhead Whale *Balaena mysticetus* **LR/CD** Probably slowly increasing. Formerly widespread and quite common, but whaling (until at least 1960s) left stocks heavily depleted. Current threats include limited whaling and perhaps over-fishing of prey species.

Family NEOBALAENIDAE – Pygmy Right Whale

Pygmy Right Whale *Caperea marginata* **LR/LC** Probably not rare. Few data concerning threats or population trends, but some incidental mortality and deliberate inshore fishing. Other threats linked to environmental changes.

Family ESCHRICHTIIDAE – Grey Whale

Grey Whale *Eschrichtius robustus* **LR/CD** Population in western N Pacific listed as **CR** Most populations increasing but hunting, habitat loss, human disturbance, chemical pollution and entanglement in fishing nets are still threats.

Family BALAENOPTERIDAE – rorquals

Humpback Whale *Megaptera novaeangliae* **VU** Estimated 33,000–35,000; once abundant but extensively hunted from 1820s. Still threatened by hunting in certain areas and, due to coastal habits, vulnerable to collisions with vessels, habitat degradation, and pollution, whilst significant numbers are trapped in fishing gear.

Northern Minke Whale *Balaenoptera acutorostrata* (includes *B. a. acutorostrata* **Common Minke Whale**, and *B. a. scammoni* **Northern Pacific Minke Whale**) **LR/NT** Presently *c.*185,000 in Atlantic with unknown numbers elsewhere. An important commercial species, but 1985–6 moratorium banned further commercial fishing, though Iceland, Japan and Norway still take some annually.

Dwarf Minke Whale *B. [acutorostrata]* species/allospecies **NE** (often considered an undescribed race of *B. acutorostrata* but here afforded species/allospecies status; pending further study.) No population estimates, but considered relatively abundant by some sources. Presumably susceptible to same threats as other Minkes.

Antarctic Minke Whale *Balaenoptera bonaerensis* **LR/CD** Recently estimated at 510,000–1.4 million, though perhaps many fewer. Following decline of great whales, commercial fleets turned their attention to the species, but 1985–6 moratorium banned further commercial fishing. Japan takes 400+ from Antarctic waters annually for 'scientific' purposes.

Bryde's Whale *Balaenoptera edeni* (includes *B. (e.) edeni* **Eden's Whale** and *B. (e.) brydei* **Bryde's Whale**) **DD** Recently *c.*90,000, and stocks in some areas already recovering following moratorium on whaling in 1977. Japanese boats still take some annually.

Omura's Whale *Balaenoptera omurai* Recently described, but nomenclature uncertain. **DD**

Sei Whale *Balaenoptera borealis* (includes *B. b. borealis* **Northern Sei Whale**, and *B. b. schlegelli* **Southern Sei Whale**) **EN** Numbers just *c.*60,000, but in 1940s–60s formed major part of Antarctic whale catch, despite relatively low oil yields. Meat highly prized in Japan. Numbers may have increased recently.

Fin Whale *Balaenoptera physalus* (includes *B. p. physalus* **Northern Fin Whale**, and *B. p. quoyi* **Southern Fin Whale**) **EN** Roughly 119,000 (a fraction of former total; up to 750,000 taken 1904–79). Now threatened by environmental change (including underwater noise), chemical pollution and, in some areas, ship-strikes.

Blue Whale *Balaenoptera musculus* (includes *B. m. musculus* **Northern Blue Whale** and *B. m. intermedia* **Southern Blue Whale**; *B. m. indica* **Indian Ocean Blue Whale** and *B. m. brevicauda* **Pygmy Blue Whale** seem identical and warrant specific status as **Pygmy Blue Whale** *B. (m.) indica*). **EN** Perhaps fewer than 10,000: pre-exploitation population *c.*500,000, of which 350,000 hunted in first part of 20th century; still threatened by environmental change, including noise and chemical pollution; NE Pacific population shows steady recovery.

Suborder Odontoceti

This large grouping contains *c.*71 species, 34 genera and 10 families of toothed whales. Several families (and genera) might not appear well defined to the casual observer, but are chiefly characterised by their anatomical structure and molecular distinctiveness. The odontocetes contain the 2 largest families of cetaceans: beaked whales, characterised by a notable beak, just 2 teeth (erupt from mouth in ♂♂), pair of throat grooves, flipper 'pockets' and dorsal fin set far back, but no median flukes notch; and the oceanic dolphins (Delphinidae), which have numerous conical, undifferentiated teeth, a variable often well-defined beak, central placed dorsal fin and notched tail flukes.

Family Physteridae – Sperm Whale

Sperm Whale *Physeter macrocephalus* **VU** *c.*1.9 million in late 1970s, but has perhaps declined since. Commercially hunted for several centuries though numbers taken in recent years smaller; human disturbance, net entanglement, ship-strikes and chemical pollution probably most significant conservation problems.

Family Kogiidae – Pygmy sperm whales

Pygmy Sperm Whale *Kogia breviceps* **LR/LC** Population largely unknown. Entanglement in fishing gear, ship-strikes and ingestion of plastics are causes for concern.

Dwarf Sperm Whale *Kogia sima* **LR/LC** No overall population estimate. Never hunted commercially, but shore-based whalers have recently taken small numbers in some areas. Entanglement in fishing gear, ship-strikes and ingestion of plastics are causes for concern.

Family Ziphiidae – beaked whales

Cuvier's Beaked Whale *Ziphius cavirostris* **DD** No estimates or information concerning threats or population trends. Some bycatch and small-scale hunting known; also, susceptible to navy sonar and noise pollution, which may cause strandings.

Arnoux's Beaked Whale *Berardius arnuxii* **LR/CD** No estimates or data concerning threats or population trends. Not hunted.

Baird's Beaked Whale *Berardius bairdii* **LR/CD** Perhaps more than 10,000; hunted in Japanese waters since 17th century and smaller numbers formerly taken off N America.

Shepherd's (Tasman) Beaked Whale *Tasmacetus shepherdi* **LR/LC** No population estimates or data on threats or trends.

Longman's Beaked (Tropical Bottlenose) Whale *Indopacetus pacificus* [formerly *Mesoplodon pacificus*] **DD** No population estimates; occasionally taken by whalers in Philippines and some accidental mortality may occur in tropical fisheries.

Northern Bottlenose Whale *Hyperoodon ampullatus* **LR/CD** Exploited from 1850s with at least 80,000 taken in total, but unknown whether populations have recovered since protection. Oil and gas exploration, and exploitation, may cause ongoing disturbance locally.

Southern Bottlenose Whale *Hyperoodon planifrons* **LR/CD** No abundance estimates, and no threats known.

Hector's Beaked Whale *Mesoplodon hectori* **DD** No data concerning threats or trends. Not hunted and incidental mortality due to entanglement in fishing gear unknown.

True's Beaked Whale *Mesoplodon mirus* **DD** Perhaps naturally rare. Not commercially hunted and unrecorded as bycatch.

Gervais' Beaked Whale *Mesoplodon europaeus* **DD** Not hunted and only occasionally trapped in fishing gear, but some mortality as a result of military sonar reported.

Sowerby's Beaked Whale *Mesoplodon bidens* **DD** Low-level threat from entanglement in fishing gear.

Gray's Beaked Whale *Mesoplodon grayi* **DD** No data on threats or population trends. Long-term risk from commercial squid fisheries and entanglement in nets.

Pygmy Beaked Whale *Mesoplodon peruvianus* **DD** Some taken as bycatch off western S America.

Andrews' Beaked Whale *Mesoplodon bowdoini* **DD** No data on trends or potential threats. Not commercially hunted.

Spade-toothed Beaked Whale *Mesoplodon traversii* **DD** Nothing known as to its population or conservation.

Hubbs' Beaked Whale *Mesoplodon carlhubbsi* **DD** Occasionally hunted opportunistically by Japanese fishermen and formerly caught with some frequency in gillnets.

Ginkgo-toothed Beaked Whale *Mesoplodon ginkgodens* **DD** Probably uncommon. No data concerning threats or population trends. Hunted opportunistically, and may be taken as bycatch.

Stejneger's Beaked Whale *Mesoplodon stejnegeri* **DD** No data on trends, but small numbers taken as bycatch.

Strap-toothed Whale *Mesoplodon layardii* **DD** Appears widespread and is not hunted. No data on threats or trends, though entanglement in nets and commercial squid fisheries are potentially long-term threats.

Blainville's Beaked Whale *Mesoplodon densirostris* **DD** Probably not rare, but no data on threats or trends. Mortality from military sonar reported.

Perrin's Beaked Whale *Mesoplodon perrini* **DD** Population unknown and no threats yet identified.

Family Platanistidae – Indian river dolphins

Ganges River Dolphin *Platanista [gangetica] gangetica* **EN** Probably several 1,000s. Range has contracted considerably since 19th century, and threats include habitat modification through damming and dredging, entanglement in fishing gear, collision with vessels, hunting and pollution.

Indus River Dolphin *Platanista [gangetica] minor* **EN** Estimated at 1,000+ in 2001. Threatened by dam construction and associated developments, and still hunted, despite ban in 1974, with pollution also a significant threat.

Family Iniidae – Amazon River Dolphin

Amazon River Dolphin (Boto) *Inia geoffrensis* (includes *I. g. geoffrensis*, *I. g. humboldtiana* and *I. g. boliviensis*) **VU** No complete population estimates but probably not uncommon. Increasingly taken as bycatch, and dams isolate subpopulations and affect prey abundance, whilst chemical pollution and habitat degradation are other problems.

Family Lipotidae – Chinese River Dolphin

Chinese River Dolphin (Baiji) *Lipotes vexillifer* **CR** Just 13 in 1997 (400 in 1979–80) and continually declining due to collisions with vessels, severe habitat degradation through pollution and damming, and fisheries bycatch.

Family PONTOPORIIDAE – Franciscana

Franciscana *Pontoporia blainvillei* **DD** Considerable numbers taken as bycatch, and habitat degradation, due to pollutant run-off, boat traffic, tourism and industrial fishing are also threats.

Family MONODONTIDAE – Beluga and Narwhal

Beluga *Delphinapterus leucas* **VU** Currently 100,000+, but commercial whaling decimated original stocks and hunting, still the most significant threat, continues to place small, local populations at risk. Other threats include high contaminant levels, diseases and, locally, human disturbance from oil exploration, hydroelectric plants, vessel traffic and recreational sports.

Narwhal *Monodon monoceros* **DD** Probably 50,000+; whaling commenced 17th century, but rarely intensive. Inuit (native Canadians and Greenlanders) are most important hunters, and climatic change and contaminants may be significant threats.

Family DELPHINIDAE – dolphins

Commerson's Dolphin *Cephalorhynchus commersonii* **DD** No data on trends. Hunted in southern S America, but practice now illegal. Also taken as bycatch in other fisheries.

Chilean (Black) Dolphin *Cephalorhynchus eutropia* **DD** No detailed data on trends, but probably declining due to illegal hunting and bycatch.

Haviside's (Heaviside's) Dolphin *Cephalorhynchus heavisidii* **DD** Trends unknown, but some hunted for food and become entangled in fishing nets.

Hector's Dolphin *Cephalorhynchus hectori* **EN** Probably still declining due to bycatch (perhaps by 50% since 1970). Pollution levels of several contaminants are cause for concern, as is high-speed vessel traffic and port developments.

Rough-toothed Dolphin *Steno bredanensis* **DD** Threats few, principally low levels of bycatch and collisions with fishing gear.

Indo-Pacific Humpback Dolphin *Sousa chinensis* (includes *S. c. chinensis* **Pacific Humpback Dolphin** and *S. c. plumbea* **Indian Humpback Dolphin**) **DD** Threats include over-fishing, pollution, heavy vessel traffic, habitat degradation and deliberate hunting.

Atlantic Humpback Dolphin *Sousa teuszii* **DD** Threats as previous species.

Tucuxi *Sotalia fluviatilis* (includes *S. (f.) fluviatilis* **Freshwater Tucuxi** and *S. (f.) guianensis* **Marine Tucuxi**) **DD** Frequently recorded as bycatch and sometimes deliberately hunted for meat or shark bait. Under pressure from river damming, mining, habitat destruction and modification, and water and noise pollution.

Common Bottlenose Dolphin *Tursiops truncatus* **DD** Threats include habitat destruction and degradation, entanglement in nets, over-fishing of prey species and pollution – especially for the inshore form.

Indo-Pacific Bottlenose Dolphin *Tursiops aduncus* **DD** Threats include pollutants, environmental degradation, gillnet mortality and some deliberate hunting.

Pantropical Spotted Dolphin *Stenella attenuata* (includes *S. a. attenuate* **Pantropical Spotted Dolphin**, *S. a. graffmani* **Eastern Pacific Coastal Spotted Dolphin**, *S. a.* undescribed subspecies **Hawaiian Spotted Dolphin**, and *S. a.* undescribed subspecies **Eastern Pacific Offshore Spotted Dolphin**) **LR/CD** Probably at least 3 million worldwide, with large numbers killed in drive fisheries off the Solomons and Japan, and incidental catch in tuna fisheries may have reduced E Pacific population to only 25% of its former abundance.

Atlantic Spotted Dolphin *Stenella frontalis* **DD** Threats include opportunistic harpooning and bycatch.

Spinner Dolphin *Stenella longirostris* (includes *S. l. longirostris* **Gray's (Hawaiian) Spinner Dolphin**, *S. l. orientalis* **Eastern Spinner Dolphin**, *S. l. centroamericana* **Central American Spinner Dolphin**, and *S. l. roseiventris* **Dwarf Spinner Dolphin**) **LR/CD** At least 1.5 million in E Pacific, where large numbers taken as bycatch in tuna fisheries in 1950s to 1970s. Gillnets and purse seines still take some, and habitat degradation and deliberate harvesting are other threats.

Clymene Dolphin *Stenella clymene* **DD** Naturally uncommon, with small numbers harpooned in Lesser Antilles and others taken as bycatch or for bait in shark fisheries.

Striped Dolphin *Stenella coeruleoalba* **LR/CD** Large numbers killed by drift-net fishing and habitat degradation is a source of concern. Intensive drive fishing has substantially reduced some subpopulations in Japanese waters.

Short-beaked Common Dolphin *Delphinus delphis* **LR/CD** No data on trends, but local declines marked in some areas due to deliberate killing, capture in fishing gear and pollution.

Long-beaked Common Dolphin *Delphinus capensis* (includes *D. c. capensis* **Long-beaked Common Dolphin** and *D. c. tropicalis* **Indo-Pacific or Arabian Common Dolphin**) **LR/CD** Similar threats as previous species, with bycatch in gillnets significant and large numbers currently taken off Peru for shark bait or human consumption.

Fraser's Dolphin *Lagenodelphis hosei* **DD** Small numbers taken as bycatch and opportunistic harpooning occurs in diverse areas.

White-beaked Dolphin *Lagenorhynchus albirostris* **LR/LC** Notable decrease off NE USA since 1970s, matched by increase in same period off Europe. Occasionally hunted and some bycatch also reported.

Atlantic White-sided Dolphin *Lagenorhynchus acutus* **LR/LC** No threats other than that of bycatch.

Pacific White-sided Dolphin *Lagenorhynchus obliquidens* **LR/LC** Increasing in Alaska and Canada, but large numbers taken in some areas, particularly in Asian waters.

Dusky Dolphin *Lagenorhynchus obscurus* (includes *L. o. obscurus* **South African Dusky Dolphin**, *L. o. fitzroyi* **South American Dusky Dolphin**, and *L. o.* undescribed subspecies **New Zealand Dusky Dolphin**) **DD** Few data on threats or trends but relatively frequently taken in gillnets and some hunted for human consumption.

Peale's Dolphin *Lagenorhynchus australis* **DD** No estimates or information concerning trends, but was hunted for bait used in crab fisheries in late 1970s–1980s, especially in Chile, and is sometimes entangled in fishing nets. Pollution perhaps also a threat and acoustic seismic devices reported to have a negative effect.

Hourglass Dolphin *Lagenorhynchus cruciger* **LR/LC** No data on threats or trends but recent surveys demonstrated it to be commoner than previously considered.

Northern Right Whale Dolphin *Lissodelphis borealis* **LR/LC** Much reduced, but perhaps no longer declining. In late 1980s, 15,000–24,000 p.a. taken in pelagic drift-net fisheries in central N Pacific, but a 1993 moratorium has almost certainly reduced problem.

Southern Right Whale Dolphin *Lissodelphis peronii* **DD** Probably threatened by entanglement in nets, and increasing numbers taken as bycatch or deliberately off western S America.

Risso's Dolphin *Grampus griseus* **DD** Threats and trends poorly known, but deliberate fishing, bycatch and pollution may all pose threats.

Melon-headed Whale (Electra Dolphin) *Peponocephala electra* **LR/LC** Harpooned on an opportunistic basis, but no significant threats known.

Pygmy Killer Whale *Feresa attenuata* **DD** Small numbers hunted in various parts of world, usually opportunistically.

False Killer Whale *Pseudorca crassidens* **LR/LC** Longline bycatch may be unsustainable in some regions. No data on trends, but mass-strandings occasionally reported and known to ingest plastic and toxins.

Killer Whale *Orcinus orca* **LR/CD** Rarely hunted, but occasionally taken with other dolphins and deliberately hunted in Greenland, Japan, Indonesia and West Indies. Also taken alive for zoos, whilst oil spills and variety of other toxic pollutants, and impact of human fisheries on prey, are concerns elsewhere, as is habitat encroachment.

Long-finned Pilot Whale *Globicephala melas* (includes *G. m. melas* **Atlantic Long-finned Pilot Whale** and *G. m. edwardii* **Southern Long-finned Pilot Whale**) **LR/LC** Hunted since at least 16th century and recently significant numbers perhaps taken as bycatch. Oceanic heavy metal and organochlorine contaminations are of long-term concern.

Short-finned Pilot Whale *Globicephala macrorhynchus* **LR/CD** Hunted off Japan, Indonesia, Lesser Antilles and Sri Lanka, but few other known threats.

Irrawaddy Dolphin *Orcaella brevirostris* **DD** Despite widespread legal protection, hunted for oil, and bycatch also significant. Explosives used for fishing may be particularly damaging. Habitat degradation and pollution also concerns, and hydroelectric dams threaten freshwater Indochina population.

Australian Snubfin Dolphin *Orcaella heinsohni* **DD** Bycatch is perhaps main threat given its shallow-water range.

Family Phocoenidae – porpoises

Finless Porpoise *Neophocaena phocaenoides* (includes *N. p. phocaenoides* **Indo-Pacific Finless Porpoise**, *N. p. asiaorientalis* **Yangtse Finless Porpoise**, and *N. p. sunameri* **Chinese Finless Porpoise**) **DD** Numbers severely reduced due to bycatch, habitat degradation, vessel collisions, reduced prey availability and high levels of contaminants.

Harbour Porpoise *Phocoena phocoena* (includes *P. p. phocoena* **North Atlantic Harbour Porpoise**, *P. p. relicta* **Black Sea Harbour Porpoise**, *P. p.* undescribed subspecies **Western North Pacific Harbour Porpoise**, and *P. p. vomerina* **Eastern North Pacific Harbour Porpoise**) **VU** No overall estimate, but *c.*340,000 in NW European waters in 1994, despite substantial reductions in many subpopulations, especially in Black and Baltic Seas. Mortality in bottom-set gillnets is among the most significant threats throughout range.

Gulf of California Porpoise (Vaquita) *Phocoena sinus* **CR** Currently just 500–600, and much reduced due to habitat alteration and commercial fishing, and 39–84 p.a. still caught in illegal fisheries, despite creation of a biosphere reserve.

Spectacled Porpoise *Phocoena (Australophocaena) dioptrica* **DD** Apparently uncommon away from Patagonia, but no data concerning trends; probably at risk from some incidental and deliberate hunting, and entanglement in nearshore gillnets.

Burmeister's Porpoise *Phocoena spinipinnis* **DD** No data on threats or trends. Heavily exploited in Peru and Chile, where taken incidentally in gillnets and intentionally for bait.

Dall's Porpoise *Phocoenoides dalli* **LR/CD** Reasonably abundant, but large numbers hunted, directly or indirectly, making the species' conservation prospects of some concern, and environmental pollution and habitat degradation pose additional threats.

Order Sirenia – Sirenians

Two families and 3 genera, of which 1 recently extinct. Four species extant. This order is one of a number of subungulate orders, also including elephants, which share several anatomical characteristics. Dugongs and manatees are the only aquatic members of the subungulates and possess the following general characters: lack of a dorsal fin, paddle-like flippers, sparse body hair and long, heavy bodies.

Family Trichechidae – manatees

West Indian Manatee *Trichechus manatus* (includes *T. m. manatus* **Antillean Manatee** and *T. m. latirostris* **Florida Manatee**) **VU** Undoubtedly has declined. Protected, but illegal hunting continues in many areas, whilst water pollution, boat collisions, bycatch and drowning in locks are all significant threats.

West African Manatee *Trichechus senegalensis* **VU** Protected, but is hunted for meat and oil. Habitat destruction, such as rivers being dammed, bycatch and water pollution constitute additional threats.

Amazonian Manatee *Trichechus inunguis* **VU** Extensively hunted since 1600s, with 80,000–140,000 taken in Brazil in 1935–54 alone. Water pollution and human disturbance are increasing concerns. Dam construction may isolate subpopulations.

Family Dugongidae – Dugong and sea cow

Dugong *Dugong dugon* (includes *D. d. dugon* and *D. d. hemprichii*) **VU** Numbers and range historically larger, but hunted for several millennia, perhaps most determinedly in 17–19th centuries, and incidental fisheries bycatch and oil spills are also threats.

★ **Steller's Sea Cow** *Hydrodamalis gigas* **Extinct** since *c.*1766. Discovered in 1741, when estimated to number 1,500–2,000 individuals, but by 1763 fur hunters had exterminated it.

Selected bibliography

Balcomb, K. C. (2002) *The Whales of Hawaii and Other Marine Mammals*. Island Heritage Publishing, Hawaii.

Berta, A. & Sumich, J. L. (1999) *Marine Mammals: Evolutionary Biology*. Academic Press, London.

Bonner, N. (1993) *Whales of the World*. Blandford Press, London.

Bonner, N. (2004) *Seals and Sea Lions of the World*. Facts on File, London.

Carwardine, M. & Camm, M. (1995) *Whales, Dolphins and Porpoises*. Dorling Kindersley, London.

Carwardine, M., Hoyt, E., Fordyce, R. E. & Gill, P. (1998) *Whales and Dolphins: The Ultimate Guide to Marine Mammals*. HarperCollins, London.

Cresswell, G. & Walker, D. (2001) *Whales and Dolphins of the European Atlantic: The Bay of Biscay and the English Channel*. WILDGuides, Old Basing.

Evans, P. G. H. (1987) *The Natural History of Whales and Dolphins*. Christopher Helm, London.

Evans, P. G. H. (1995) *Guide to the Identification of Whales, Dolphins and Porpoises in European Seas*. Sea Watch Foundation, Sussex.

Evans, P. G. H. & Raga, J. A. (eds.) (2001) *Marine Mammal Science: Biology and Conservation*. Plenum Press/Kluwer Academic Press, London.

Gill, P. & Burke, C. (1999) *Whale Watching in Australian and New Zealand Waters*. New Holland, Sydney.

Hoelzel, A. R. (ed.) (2003) *Marine Mammal Biology: An Evolutionary Approach*. Blackwell, Oxford.

Jefferson, T. A., Webber, M. A. & Pitman, R. L. (in prep.) *Marine Mammals of the World: A Comprehensive Guide to Their Identification*. Academic Press/Elsevier, London.

Jefferson, T. A., Leatherwood, S. & Webber, M. (1993) *Marine Mammals of the World*. FAO, Rome.

Kinze, C. C. (2001) *Marine Mammals of the North Atlantic*. Princeton University Press, Princeton.

Laws, R. M. (ed.) (1993) *Antarctic Seals: Research Methods and Techniques*. Cambridge University Press, Cambridge.

Leatherwood, S., Reeves, R. R. & Foster, L. (1983) *Sierra Club Handbook of Whales and Dolphins*. Sierra Club, San Diego.

Perrin, W. F., Würsig, B. & Thewissen, J. G. E. (eds.) (2002) *Encyclopedia of Marine Mammals*. Academic Press, London.

Reeves, R. R., Smith, B. D., Crespo, E. A. & Notarbartolo di Sciara, G. (compilers) (2003) *Dolphins, Whales and Porpoises: 2002–2010 Conservation Action Plan for the World's Cetaceans*. IUCN/SSC Cetacean Specialist Group. IUCN, Gland & Cambridge.

Reeves, R. R., Stewart, B. S., Clapham, P. J. & Powell, J. A. (2002) *Sea Mammals of the World*. A & C Black, London.

Reeves, R., Stewart, B. S. & Leatherwood, S. (1992) *Sierra Club Handbook of Seals and Sirenians*. Sierra Club, San Diego.

Reid, J. R., Evans, P. G. H. & Northridge, S. P. (eds.) (2003) *Atlas of Cetacean Distribution in North-West European Waters*. Joint Nature Conservation Committee, Peterborough.

Rice, D. W. (1998) *Marine Mammals of the World: Systematics and Distribution*. Special Publication No. 4, Society for Marine Mammalogy.

Ridgway, S. H. & Harrison, R. J. (eds.) (1981–99) *Handbook of Marine Mammals*. Vols. 1–6. Academic Press, London.

Shirihai, H. (2002) *The Complete Guide to Antarctic Wildlife*. Alula Press, Degerby.

Swash, A. & Still, R. (2005) *Birds, Mammals and Reptiles of the Galápagos Islands*. 2nd edition. Christopher Helm, London.

Photographic credits

A&C Black would like to thank the following for providing photographs and for permission to reproduce copyright material. While every effort has been made to trace and acknowledge all copyright holders, we would like to apologise for any errors or omissions, and invite readers to inform us so that corrections can be made in any future editions of the book. The initials alongside the page numbers stand for top, middle, bottom, top left, top right, and so on.

1m Masa Ushioda/imagequestmarine.com
7b Michael S. Nolan/SeaPics.com
10t Troels Jacobsen
10b Hadoram Shirihai
11t Dennis Buurman
11b Morten Jörgensen
12b F. Lanting/Minden
13t Michael S. Nolan/SeaPics.com
13m Hadoram Shirihai
13b Doug Perrine/SeaPics.com
14t James D. Watt/SeaPics.com
15t Doug Perrine/SeaPics.com
15b Hadoram Shirihai
16t Hadoram Shirihai
16b F. Nicklen/Minden
21m Tony Wu/SeaPics.com
22m Yuri Artukhin
22b Michael S. Nolan/SeaPics.com
24t Lin Sutherland/SeaPics.com
24m Kim Westerskov
24b R. McLanaghan/IFAW/SeaPics.com
25t Dylan Walker
25m Morten Jörgensen
26t Morten Jörgensen
26m Morten Jörgensen
26b Kim Westerskov
28t James D. Watt/imagequest3d.com
28b Michael S. Nolan/SeaPics.com
29t Hiroya Minakuchi/SeaPics.com
29m Morten Jörgensen
29b Duncan Murrell/SeaPics.com
30t Kim Westerskov
30m Masa Ushioda/imagequestmarine.com
30b Doug Perrine/SeaPics.com
31m Bob Cranston/SeaPics.com
32b Michael S. Nolan/SeaPics.com
33t Todd Pusser/SeaPics.com
33m Michael S. Nolan/SeaPics.com
33b Phillip Colla/SeaPics.com
34m Cole Brandon/Still Pictures
34b Hadoram Shirihai
35b Hadoram Shirihai
36m Steven Morello/Still Pictures
36b Brett Jarrett
37t Hadoram Shirihai
37m Rob Dolton
37b Robert L. Pitman, SWFC/NOAA, US
38t Kim Westerskov
38m F. Nicklin/Minden
38b Armin Maywald/SeaPics.com
40t F. Nicklin/Minden
40b Martin Hale
42t F. Nicklin/Minden
42m F. Nicklin/Minden
42b F. Nicklin/Minden
45t Robert L. Pitman/SeaPics.com
45m Kenji Tuda
45bl Kenji Tuda
45br Kenji Tuda
46t Francisco Luiz Vicentini Neto
46m Benjamin Kahn/APEX Environmental
46b Benjamin Kahn/APEX Environmental
48t Doc White/SeaPics.com
48m Phillip Colla/SeaPics.com
49t Phillip Colla/SeaPics.com
49m Phillip Colla/SeaPics.com
49b Doc White/SeaPics.com
50b Hadoram Shirihai
51t Morten Jörgensen
51ml Morten Jörgensen
51mr Hadoram Shirihai
51b Michael F. Richlen SWFC/NOAA, US
52t Hadoram Shirihai
52m Chas Anderson
52b Phillip Colla/SeaPics.com
53t Michael S. Nolan/SeaPics.com
53m Bruce Mactavish
53b T. De Roy/Minden
55t Michael S. Nolan/SeaPics.com
55m Michael F. Richlen SWFC/NOAA, US
55b Graeme Cresswell
56b Doug Perrine/SeaPics.com
57t Stephen Wong
58t Hadoram Shirihai
58m Marc Guyt
59m Graeme Cresswell
59b Hadoram Shirihai
61tl Hadoram Shirihai
61tm Hadoram Shirihai
61tr Michael F. Richlen SWFC/NOAA, US
61b Hadoram Shirihai
62t Brett Jarrett
62b Hadoram Shirihai
64t Graeme Cresswell
64m Yuri Artukhin
64b F. Nicklin/Minden
65b Kike Calvo/V & W/SeaPics.com
66m Saul Gonor/SeaPics.com
67t Morten Jörgensen
67b Morten Jörgensen
68b Kim Westerskov
69t Robert L. Pitman/SeaPics.com
69b Morten Jörgensen
72t Morten Jörgensen
72m Michael F. Richlen SWFC/NOAA, US
72b Michael F. Richlen SWFC/NOAA, US
73t Michael F. Richlen SWFC/NOAA, US
73m Michael F. Richlen SWFC/NOAA, US
73b Chris Huss/SeaPics.com
74t Debra Shearwater, Shearwater Journeys
74m Crozet Base Collection, TAAF
74b Jasmine Rossi/SeaPics.com
75t Hiroya Minakuchi/SeaPics.com
75m Lori Mazzuca/SeaPics.com
75b Jasmine Rossi/SeaPics.com
76t Amos Nachoum/SeaPics.com
76m H. Kersten
76b Kim Westerskov
77b Masa Ushioda/SeaPics.com
79m Hadoram Shirihai
81t M. Parry/Minden
81m Masa Ushioda/SeaPics.com
81b Graeme Cresswell
82b Robin W. Baird/SeaPics.com
84t Robin W. Baird/SeaPics.com
84m Robin W. Baird/SeaPics.com
84b Barbara Todd
85t Benjamin Kahn/APEX Environmental
85m Chas Anderson
85b Robert L. Pitman/SeaPics.com
87b James D. Watt/imagequest3d.com
89t H. Minakuchi/Miden
89m James D. Watt/SeaPics.com
91t Colin D. MacLeod
91m Colin D. MacLeod
91b Doug Perrine/SeaPics.com
92b Robin W. Baird/SeaPics.com (taken under NMFS permit #731)
94t Morten Jörgensen
94m Robert L. Pitman/SeaPics.com
94b Janet Baxter
96t Graeme Cresswell
96m Graeme Cresswell

96b Danny Frank/SeaPics.com
97m Goran Ehlme/SeaPics.com
99t Armin Maywald/SeaPics.com
99m F. Nicklin/Minden
99b F. Nicklin/Minden
100b F. Nicklin/Minden
101t John K.B. Ford/Ursus/SeaPics.com
101m Doc White/SeaPics.com
101b Saul Gonor/SeaPics.com
103t Todd Pusser
103m Paula A. Olsen
103b Masa Ushioda/SeaPics.com
107m Todd Pusser
108t Colin D. MacLeod
108tl Matt Hobbs
108ml Graeme Cresswell
108b Graeme Cresswell
110t Todd Pusser
111b Rich W. Pagen
112t Sylvia Stevens
112m Brett Jarrett
112b Brett Jarrett
114t Brett Jarrett
114m Brett Jarrett
114b Yuri Artukhin
117b Chas Anderson
118t Chas Anderson
119m Sascha Hooker/SeaPics.com
119b Robin W. Baird/SeaPics.com
121t Sascha Hooker/SeaPics.com
121m Joao Quaresma/SeaPics.com
121bl F. Nicklin/Minden
121br Graeme Cresswell
122b Robert L. Pitman/SeaPics.com
123bl Morten Jörgensen
123br Paula A. Olsen
124t Dylan Walker
125b Nick Gales
126m Dylan Walker
126b Dylan Walker
129b Dylan Walker
130t Matthew Hobbs
131t Matthew Hobbs
133t Nick Gales
133ml Paula A. Olsen
133mr Andy Black
134bl Michael F. Richlen SWFC/NOAA, US
134br Michael F. Richlen SWFC/NOAA, US
135bl Annie B. Douglas
135br Annie B. Douglas
143b John Hewitt
144t Colin D. MacLeod
144m Colin D. MacLeod
144b Todd Pusser
145b Chas Anderson
146tl Robin W. Baird
146tr Hadoram Shirihai
146ml Graeme Cresswell
146mr Graeme Cresswell
148t Robert Pitman SWFC/NOAA, US
148m Michel Newcomer
150t Gary Friedrichsen
152t Michael S. Nolan/SeaPics.com
152ml Barbara Taylor
152mr Robert L. Pitman/SeaPics.com
152bl L. Hickmott
152br Robin W. Baird
153t Doug Perrine/SeaPics.com
153b Thomas Jefferson/SeaPics.com
155t Dennis Buurman
155b Cole Brandon/Still Pictures
156t Dennis Buurman
156b Michael S. Nolan/SeaPics.com
158t Doug Perrine/SeaPics.com
158b Armin Maywald/SeaPics.com
159b Ingrid Visser/SeaPics.com
160b Claire Garrigue
161t Hadoram Shirihai
161m Thomas Jefferson/SeaPics.com
163t Thomas Jefferson/SeaPics.com
163m Thomas Jefferson/SeaPics.com
163b Thomas Jefferson/SeaPics.com
164b Martin Nicoll/Still Pictures
165t Martin Nicoll/Still Pictures
165b Dylan Walker
167t Graeme Cresswell
167b James D. Watt/imagequest3d.com
170t Doug Perrine/SeaPics.com
170m Benjamin Kahn/APEX Environmental
170b Benjamin Kahn/APEX Environmental
171t Michael F. Richlen SWFC/NOAA, US
171m Janet Baxter
172t Brett Jarrett
172b Kim Westerskov
174t Michael F. Richlen SWFC/NOAA, US
174m Brett Jarrett
176t Michael S. Nolan/SeaPics.com
176b Michael F. Richlen SWFC/NOAA, US
177t Masa Ushioda/SeaPics.com
177b James D. Watt/SeaPics.com
181tl Michael S. Nolan/SeaPics.com
181tr Hadoram Shirihai
18m Brett Jarrett
181b Michael F. Richlen SWFC/NOAA, US
182t Michael F. Richlen SWFC/NOAA, US
182m Michael F. Richlen SWFC/NOAA, US
182b Michael F. Richlen SWFC/NOAA, US
183t Michael F. Richlen SWFC/NOAA, US
183m Michael F. Richlen SWFC/NOAA, US
183b Michael F. Richlen SWFC/NOAA, US
184t Brett Jarrett
184m Todd Pusser
185b Robert L. Pitman/SeaPics.com
186m Michael F. Richlen SWFC/NOAA, US
187t Hugh Harrop
188t Michael F. Richlen SWFC/NOAA, US
188b Michael F. Richlen SWFC/NOAA, US
189t Michael F. Richlen SWFC/NOAA, US
189b Brett Jarrett
191t Brett Jarrett
191m Michael F. Richlen SWFC/NOAA, US
191b Michael F. Richlen SWFC/NOAA, US
192b Graeme Cresswell
193b Doug Perrine/SeaPics.com
194t James D. Watt/SeaPics.com
194b Graeme Cresswell
195m Troels Jacobsen
197b Michael F. Richlen SWFC/NOAA, US
198b Michael F. Richlen SWFC/NOAA, US
199b Troels Jacobsen
200b Morten Joergenson
201b Mark Carwardine/Still Pictures
203b James D. Watt/SeaPics.com
204b Michael F. Richlen SWFC/NOAA, US
205t Randy Morse/SeaPics.com
205m Todd Pusser
206b Morten Jörgensen
208t Robert L. Pitman/SeaPics.com
209b Hadoram Shirihai
210b Dennis Buurman
211t Dennis Buurman
211m Michael F. Richlen SWFC/NOAA, US
213m Morten Jörgensen
214m Olivier Durier
214b Paul A. Sutherland/SeaPics.com
216t Todd Pusser
216b Todd Pusser
218t Morten Jörgensen
218b Todd Pusser
219b Todd Pusser
220b Ingrid Visser/SeaPics.com
222t Kim Westerskov
222m Kim Westerskov
222b Ingrid Visser/SeaPics.com
223t Hadoram Shirihai
223b Don Doolittle
224m James D. Watt/SeaPics.com
224b Todd Pusser/SeaPics.com
226m Dennis Buurman
226b Dennis Buurman
227b Dennis Buurman
228t Fernando Trujillo/Fundación Omacha
228m Marcos Santos/Projeto Atlantis
228b Gabriel Franciscana

230t Fernando Trujillo/Fundación Omacha
230m Fernando Trujillo/Fundación Omacha
230b Marcos Santos/Projeto Atlantis
231b Marcos Santos/Projeto Atlantis
232t Paulo Flores/SeaPics.com
232b Simon Cook
234m F. Nicklin/Minden
235b Fernando Trujillo/SeaPics.com
236t Gregory Ochocki/SeaPics.com
236m Fernando Trujillo/SeaPics.com
237m Roland Seitre
237b Roland Seitre
239b Dr. Najam Khurshid
240b Jean-Pierre Sylvestre/Still Pictures
242t Hadoram Shirihai
243t Guido J. Parra
243b Guido J. Parra
244b Hadoram Shirihai
245m Roland Seitre/Still Pictures
245b Hadoram Shirihai
246t Morten Jörgensen
246m Roland Seitre
246b Hadoram Shirihai
248b Jean-Pierre Sylvestre/Still Pictures
250m Thomas Jefferson/SeaPics.com
250b Keiko Sekiguchi
252t Keiko Sekiguchi
252m W. J. Strietman
254m Graeme Cresswell
256m Sonja Heinrich
256b Sonja Heinrich
258b Earthviews
259t Yuri Artukhin
260m Ingrid Visser/SeaPics.com
260bl Claire Garrigue
260br Claire Garrigue
262t Doug Perrine/SeaPics.com
262b Doug Perrine/SeaPics.com
263b Doug Perrine/SeaPics.com
265t Doug Perrine/SeaPics.com
265b Doug Perrine/SeaPics.com
266b Phillip Colla/SeaPics.com
267m Doug Perrine/SeaPics.com
267b Phillip Colla/SeaPics.com
269b Masa Ushioda/SeaPics.com
270t Masa Ushioda/SeaPics.com
271m Fred Bruemmer/Still Pictures
273m Fred Bruemmer/Still Pictures
275t Tom Vezo/DanitaDelimont.com
275b Robert L. Pitman/SeaPics.com
277t Phillip Colla/SeaPics.com
279t Rene Pop
279m T. De Roy/Minden
280b T. De Roy/Minden
281b Fred Bruemmer/Still Pictures
282t Fred Bruemmer/Still Pictures
283t Brett Jarrett
283m Morten Jörgensen
285t Brett Jarrett
285b Ralf Kiefner/SeaPics.com
286b Claudia Adams/DanitaDelimont.com
287t Brett Jarrett
287m Kim Westerskov
288m Kim Westerskov
289t Kim Westerskov
289m Dennis Buurman
289b Hadoram Shirihai
290m Hadoram Shirihai
290b Hadoram Shirihai
291b Hadoram Shirihai
292b Hadoram Shirihai
293t Hadoram Shirihai
294t Yuri Artukhin
294m Hadoram Shirihai
296t Hadoram Shirihai
296m Michael S. Nolan/SeaPics.com
297m Kevin Schafer/SeaPics.com
298t F. Lanting/Minden
298m Randy Morse/SeaPics.com
298b T. De Roy/Minden
299b Hadoram Shirihai
300t Jasmine Rossi/SeaPics.com
301t Takaji Ochi/V&W/imagequestmarine.com
301b David B. Fleetham/SeaPics.com
302b Fred Bruemmer/Still Pictures
303m Kim Westerskov
304m K. Wothe/Minden
305m Yuri Artukhin
305b Yuri Artukhin
306b Yuri Artukhin
307t Steve Drogin/SeaPics.com
307b Morten Jörgensen
309t Hugh Harrop
309b T. Fitzharris/Minden
311t Todd Gustafson/DanitaDelimont.com
311m F. Lanting/Minden
311b Morten Jörgensen
312b Roy Tanami/Ursus/SeaPics.com
313m Graeme Cresswell
314m Graeme Cresswell
314b Graeme Cresswell
315b Graeme Cresswell
316b Kevin Schafer/SeaPics.com
317t G. Lacz
317bl Morten Jörgensen
317br Hadoram Shirihai
318b Carleton Ray/Science Photo Library
319m Kathy Frost
319b F. Nicklin/Minden
320m F. Nicklin/Minden
320b Morten Jörgensen
321ml Steven Kazlowski/SeaPics.com
321mr Hadoram Shirihai
321b F. Nicklin/Minden
323t Doc White/SeaPics.com
324b Steven Kazlowski/SeaPics.com
325t Yuri Artukhin
325m Yuri Artukhin
325b Michael F. Richlen SWFC/NOAA, US
326t Hadoram Shirihai
326m Graeme Cresswell
326b Hadoram Shirihai
327t Toshio Minami/e-photography/SeaPics
327b Yuri Artukhin
329m Thomas Tennhardt
330b Thomas Tennhardt
331t K. Wothe/Minden
331b Charles McRae/Visuals Unlimited
332m Panda Photo
333tl Luis Quinta/SeaPics.com
332mr Panda Photo
334t Dave Homcy/SeaPics.com
334b James D. Watt/imagequest3d.com
335t Mimi Olry
335b Brett Jarrett
337m Hadoram Shirihai
337b Hadoram Shirihai
339m Hadoram Shirihai
340b Hadoram Shirihai
341t Hadoram Shirihai
341m Hadoram Shirihai
341b Franco Banfi/SeaPics.com
343t Morten Jörgensen
343m Morten Jörgensen
344t Morten Jörgensen
345t Morten Jörgensen
345m Morten Jörgensen
345b Kim Westerskov
347t Kim Westerskov
347b Morten Jörgensen
348t Morten Jörgensen
349b Mark Jones/SeaPics.com
350t Hadoram Shirihai
350b Kevin Schafer/SeaPics.com
351t Kevin Schafer/SeaPics.com
351b Morten Jörgensen
352m M. Hoshino/Minden
352b Foto Natura/Minden
353b Howie Garber/DanitaDelimont.com
355t Thomas Mangelsen / DanitaDelimont.com
355ml Thomas Mangelsen / DanitaDelimont.com
355mr Hadoram Shirihai
355b Dennis Fast/V&W/imagequestmarine.com
356m Michael Sewell/Still Pictures
357t James D. Watt/SeaPics.com
357m Yuri Artukhin
358t Daisy Gilardini/DanitaDelimont.com
359m Jeffrey Mangel
359b Carlos Olavarria Barrera

Index